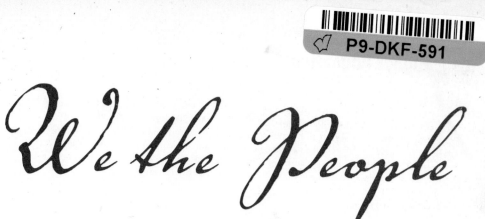

We the People

A CONCISE INTRODUCTION TO AMERICAN POLITICS

EIGHTH EDITION

Thomas E. Patterson

Bradlee Professor of Government and the Press
John F. Kennedy School of Government
Harvard University

Boston   Burr Ridge, IL   Dubuque, IA   New York   San Francisco   St. Louis
Bangkok   Bogotá   Caracas   Kuala Lumpur   Lisbon   London   Madrid   Mexico City
Milan   Montreal   New Delhi   Santiago   Seoul   Singapore   Sydney   Taipei   Toronto

P9-DKF-591

ISBN: 978-0-07-337896-1
MHID: 0-07-337896-8

Editor in Chief: *Michael Ryan*
Director, Editorial: *Beth Mejia*
Sponsoring Editor: *Mark Georgiev*
Marketing Manager: *Bill Minick*
Director of Development: *Nancy Crochiere*
Developmental Editor: *Erin K. Grelak*
Production Editor: *David Blatty*
Manuscript Editor: *Thomas L. Briggs*
Design Manager: *Ashley Bedell*
Cover Designer: *Stacy Anthony*
Lead Photo Editor: *Alexandra Ambrose*
Photo Research: *Toni Michaels/PhotoFind*
Production Supervisor: *Rich DeVitto*
Composition: *10/12 Palatino by Aptara®, Inc.*
Printing: *45# New Era Matte Plus, R.R. Donnelley*

Cover Photo: © J. Emilio Flores/Corbis

Credits: The credits section for this book begins on page 716 and is considered an extension of the copyright page

Library of Congress Cataloging-in-Publication Data

Patterson, Thomas E.
  We the people / Thomas Patterson. — 8th ed.
    p. cm.
  Includes index.
  ISBN-13: 978-0-07-337896-1 (alk. paper)
  ISBN-10: 0-07-337896-8 (alk. paper)
  1. United States—Politics and government. I. Title.
JK274.P36 2009
320.473—dc22   2008045655

www.mhhe.com

To
Alex and Leigh

About the Author

Thomas E. Patterson is Bradlee Professor of Government and the Press in the John F. Kennedy School of Government at Harvard University. He was previously Distinguished Professor of Political Science in the Maxwell School of Citizenship at Syracuse University. Raised in a small Minnesota town near the Iowa and South Dakota borders, he attended South Dakota State University as an undergraduate and served in the military in Vietnam before enrolling at the University of Minnesota, where he received his Ph.D. in 1971.

He is the author of numerous books and articles, which focus mainly on elections and the media. His book *The Vanishing Voter* (2002) describes and explains the long-term decline in Americans' electoral participation. An earlier book, *Out of Order* (1994), received national attention when President Clinton said every politician and journalist should be required to read it. In 2002, *Out of Order* received the American Political Science Association's Graber Award for the best book of the past decade in political communication. Another of Patterson's books, *The Mass Media Election* (1980), received a *Choice* award as Outstanding Academic Book, 1980–1981. Patterson's first book, *The Unseeing Eye* (1976), was selected by the American Association for Public Opinion Research as one of the fifty most influential books of the past half century in the field of public opinion.

His research has been funded by major grants from the National Science Foundation, the Markle Foundation, the Smith-Richardson Foundation, the Ford Foundation, the Knight Foundation, The Carnegie Corporation, and the Pew Charitable Trusts.

CONTENTS

CHAPTER FIVE

CHAPTER SIX

CHAPTER SEVEN

POLITICAL PARTICIPATION AND VOTING: EXPRESSING THE POPULAR WILL   225

CHAPTER EIGHT

POLITICAL PARTIES, CANDIDATES, AND CAMPAIGNS: DEFINING THE VOTER'S CHOICE   253

CHAPTER THIRTEEN

THE FEDERAL BUREAUCRACY: ADMINISTERING THE GOVERNMENT

CHAPTER FOURTEEN

THE FEDERAL JUDICIAL SYSTEM: APPLYING THE LAW

CHAPTER FIFTEEN

ECONOMIC AND ENVIRONMENTAL POLICY: CONTRIBUTING TO PROSPERITY

CHAPTER SIXTEEN

CHAPTER SEVENTEEN

PREFACE

I have tried to write a text that expands students' horizons as well as informs their thinking, a text that they will *want* to read as opposed to one they are simply required to read. Three features of the text support this aim:

Narrative Style

This is a narrative-based text. Unlike a text that piles fact upon fact and in the process squeezes the life out of its subject, the narrative style brings the subject to life. Studies have shown that students read more attentively and for a longer period of time when a text is narrative in form. The narrative draws students into the material, rousing their interest. Of all the social sciences, political science is the liveliest subject. Politics has all the elements of high drama while affecting the lives of real people.

Critical Thinking

A key goal of this text is to help students think critically. Students cannot learn to think critically by engaging in rote memorization; they develop the capacity for critical thinking by reflecting on what they have read, resolving challenges to their assumptions, and confronting inconvenient truths. In the first chapter, for example, I discuss the inexact meanings and unfinished promise of Americans' most cherished ideals, including liberty and equality. The discussion includes the "Chinese Exclusion," a grotesque and not widely known chapter in our history that forces students to consider what it means to be an American.

In addition, two of the book's boxed features, "How the United States Compares" and "States in the Nation," are designed to promote critical thinking; these features help students gain a better understanding of their nation or state through an increased awareness of how it differs from others.

Politics as Discipline and Practice

I have presented American government through the analytical lens of political science but in a way that captures the vivid world of real-life politics. In writing this text, I regularly reminded myself that only a tiny percentage of introductory students intend to pursue an academic political science career. Most students take the course because they are required to do so or because they like politics. I have sought to write a book that will kindle political interest in the first type of student and deepen it in the second type.

Political Culture and Other Dimensions of American Politics

Political scientists have identified several tendencies that are critical to a systematic understanding of the U.S. political system. These tendencies are introduced in Chapter 1 and developed in subsequent chapters. Even if students forget many of the points made in this book, they may at least retain an understanding of these regularities of American politics:

- Enduring ideals that are the basis of Americans' political identity and culture and a source of many of their beliefs, aspirations, and conflicts.
- Extreme fragmentation of governing authority based on an elaborate system of checks and balances. These checks and balances protect against abuses of political power but also make it difficult for political majorities to assert power when confronting an entrenched or intense political minority.
- Many competing groups—the result of the nation's great size, population diversity, and economic complexity—that exercise considerable influence on public policy, sometimes to society's benefit and sometimes to its detriment.
- Strong emphasis on individual rights, which results in substantial benefits to the individual and places substantial restrictions on majorities.
- Preference for the marketplace as a means of allocating resources, which has the effect of placing many economic issues beyond the reach of political majorities.

All these regularities figure prominently in this book, but the first one on the list has a special place. As Tocqueville, Bryce, Hartz, Rossiter, and other observers have stressed, Americans' deep-rooted political beliefs are the basis of their national identity.

Americans are a diverse people with origins in many lands. Their nation was founded on a set of principles—including liberty, self-government, equality, and individualism—that became the people's unifying bond. When an American confronts an everyday situation and responds by saying "It's my right," he or she is acting in a way that is distinctly if not uniquely American. And when all such patterned behaviors are taken into account, they constitute a unique political perspective—an American political perspective.

Although this text's primary focus is the workings of political institutions and processes, these occur within the context of the nation's political culture.

Why, for example, is the United States the only affluent democracy without government-provided medical care for all? Or why do Americans, though deeply divided over America's involvement in Iraq, universally believe the Iraqi people would be better off if they lived in a democracy? Why are issues such as stem-cell research and biological evolution larger controversies in the United States than in other Western democracies? Why do lobbying groups have more political clout in the United States than elsewhere?

No analysis of American institutions or processes can fully answer such questions. Americans' cultural beliefs must also be taken into account. Government-provided health care for all, as an example, is at odds with American individualism, which emphasizes self-reliance. Presidents Roosevelt and Johnson both backed away from proposing universal health care, and Presidents Truman and Clinton failed when they attempted it. Americans govern themselves differently than do other people because they have different beliefs about the purposes of government. Indeed, each of the other regularities on the previous list is a prominent feature of U.S. politics because it stems from Americans' cultural beliefs. The prominence in American politics of the marketplace, of interest groups, of individual rights, and of checks and balances is owed in significant part to Americans' deep-seated ideas about the proper way to govern.

The significance of political culture in this text is apparent in the "Political Culture" boxes, which challenge students to think about the encompassing nature of America's political culture. The box in the opening chapter, for example, explores the connection between Americans' political ideals and their religious traditions.

NEW TO THIS EDITION

The chapters have been thoroughly updated to include recent scholarship and the latest developments at home and abroad. The largest changes were occasioned by the 2008 presidential election, which in both its candidates and its consequences has altered American politics far more than anyone would have predicted two years ago, when the previous edition was published. A key change to this edition is the complete revision and reorganization of Chapter 10 on the news media. This front to back revision addresses the extraordinary changes taking place in the media, not only in regard to Internet-based communication but also in regard to traditional news media (for example, the decline in the newspaper). The chapter reflects the mix of messages—informational, critical, and partisan—that Americans encounter through the media. New to the chapter is a section on how Americans use the media—exposure to different amounts and kinds of information as well as increased interactivity. A main point in the revised version of the chapter is how today's media system fosters political polarization and a widening information gap between America's best informed and least informed citizens.

Other Important Changes

Chapter 1, American Political Culture: The discussion of the limits and power of America's cultural ideals and of the theoretical underpinnings of the U.S. political system have been tightened and sharpened to help students see more clearly their connection to American politics.

Chapter 3, Federalism: No Child Left Behind (NCLB) and policies relating to the war on terrorism are explored for their effect on federalism.

Chapter 4, Civil Liberties: This chapter includes the most important cases from the 2006–2008 Supreme Court terms.

Chapter 5, Equal Rights: The sections on Native Americans and Hispanics have been expanded, as has the discussion of the immigration issue. The Louisville and Seattle school busing decisions are discussed at length. They are important symbolically and substantively, as well as for what they say about the Supreme Court's positioning. The justices' sharp division over the application of the equal-protection clause—and the legal reasoning of the two sides—is a topic that will engage students.

Chapter 6, Public Opinion: The section on "Problems with Polls" has been expanded. Telephone-based polling is becoming increasingly problematic as a result of rising refusal rates and the spread of cell phone usage. As well, the emergence of Barack Obama as a top presidential candidate resurrected an earlier survey issue that is discussed in the chapter—namely, whether respondents are truthful when it comes to expressing opinions that relate to race and similar subjects. The section on ideology has been reworked to reflect the latest research and to frame the section in the context of how ordinary citizens understand and apply ideological labels.

Chapter 7, Political Participation: The turnout increase in the 2008 election is discussed. The Internet as a medium of political participation is given additional attention, including its role in the 2008 primaries. A new topic is the move by several state legislatures to impose a photo ID requirement on registration and voting.

Chapter 8, Political Parties, Candidates, and Campaigns: This chapter has been substantially reworked to include, wherever sensible, material on the 2008 presidential campaign. The section on third parties has been reworked to sharpen the argument about their role in the American party system. Campaign finance receives additional attention, as does the Internet's role in the modern campaign. The chapter includes an expanded discussion of candidate-centered campaigns, including, as an example, the political history of Barack Obama.

Chapter 11, Congress: The revised chapter more fully separates the discussion of the party and committee systems within Congress so that students can see more clearly the contribution of each system to the functioning of the institution. Results of the 2008 congressional elections have been included.

Chapter 12, Presidency: The 2008 Democratic and Republican presidential nominating races and the 2008 general election campaign receive considerable attention in the new edition, as does the final phase of the Bush presidency.

Chapter 14, Judiciary: In addition to picking up the significance of Alito's appointment to the Court, the revised chapter includes an expanded discussion of the judiciary's role in a democracy. In addition to a discussion of judicial review and judicial activism, this chapter includes a discussion of the difference between and implications of the originalism school of thought represented by, for example, Justice Scalia and the "living Constitution" school reflected in the opinions of, for example, Justice Breyer.

Chapter 15, Economic and Environmental Policy: The section on environmental policy has been expanded, and oil and gas policy have been added. The country's current economic woes are addressed in the context of fiscal and monetary policy.

Chapter 16, Welfare and Education Policy: The No Child Left Behind Act and the controversy surrounding it get more attention in this edition, as do the pending problems of out-year expenditures on social security, Medicare, and Medicaid. The health care issue as it played out in the 2008 presidential campaign is also addressed.

Chapter 17, Foreign and Defense Policy: The chapter's revisions include, among other things, the evolving situation in Iraq and in the Afghanistan-Pakistan theater, the rising tide of trade protectionism, and the implications for America's place in the world of the weakening dollar.

FEATURES

The eighth edition of the text retains the following popular features:

- **States in the Nation,** included in each chapter, illustrate differences and similarities among states. Each box includes a color-coded U.S.

map that enables readers to see at a glance how their state compares
with other states on specific topics.

- **How the United States Compares** features, also found in each chapter, indicate how the U.S. system differs from other democracies on key dimensions such as political party systems.
- **Leaders** boxes highlight the contributions of exemplary Americans.
- **Historical background icons** highlight the inclusion of important historical discussions that are seamlessly woven throughout the narrative.

Finally, in response to suggestions from instructors who have found that many of today's students are less than voracious readers, I have shortened this edition, not by cutting content but by tightening the discussion and eliminating a few frills. In doing this, I acquired a deeper appreciation of what Thomas Jefferson wrote in a letter to John Adams: "I didn't have time to write a short letter, so I wrote a long one instead." Streamlining does take more time, but the resulting prose is clearer and more vigorous.

YOUR SUGGESTIONS ARE INVITED

We the People has been in use in college classrooms for nearly twenty years. During that time, the text (including its full-length edition, *The American Democracy*) has been adopted at roughly a thousand colleges and universities. I am extremely grateful to all who have used it. I am particularly indebted to the many instructors and students who have sent me corrections or recommendations. Professor Paul David in the University of Nevada system, for example, pointed out a mistaken entry on Nevada state politics. Joe Sheeler, a student at the University of Maryland, caught an error in a date in one of the chapters. You can contact me at the John F. Kennedy School, Harvard University, Cambridge, MA 02138, or by email: thomas_patterson@ harvard.edu.

Thomas E. Patterson

SUPPLEMENTS PACKAGE

This text is accompanied by supplementary materials. Please contact your local McGraw-Hill representative or McGraw-Hill Customer Service (800-338-3987) for details concerning policies, prices, and availability, as some restrictions may apply.

FOR STUDENTS AND INSTRUCTORS

Online Learning Center

www.mhhe.com/pattersonwtp8e
The book's website includes separate instructor and student areas. The instructor area contains the instructor's manual, test bank, and PowerPoints, while the student area hosts a wealth of study materials such as chapter outlines, chapter objectives, multiple choice and essay quizzes, flashcards, and weblinks. All chapter-by-chapter material has been updated for the new edition.

FOR INSTRUCTORS

Instructor's Manual/Test Bank/PowerPoints

Available online, the instructor's manual includes the following for each chapter: learning objectives, focus points and main points, a chapter summary, a list of major concepts, and suggestions for complementary lecture topics. The test bank consists of approximately fifty multiple-choice questions and five suggested essay topics per chapter, with page references given alongside the answers.

PowerPoints and CPS questions are also available to instructors via the book's website.

CourseSmart

CourseSmart is a new way for faculty to find and review eTextbooks. It's also a great option for students who are interested in accessing their course materials digitally and saving money. CourseSmart offers thousands of the most commonly adopted textbooks across hundreds of courses from a wide variety of higher education publishers. It is the only place for faculty to review and compare the full text of a textbook online, providing immediate access without the environmental impact of requesting a print exam copy. At CourseSmart, students can save up to 50% off the cost of a print book, reduce their impact on the environment, and gain access to powerful web tools for learning including full text search, notes and highlighting, and e-mail tools for sharing notes between classmates.

PRIMIS Online

Instructors can use this text as a whole, or they can select specific chapters and customize the text to suit their specific classroom needs. The customized text can be created as a hardcopy or as an e-book. Also available in this format are custom chapters on "California Government" and "Texas Government."

FOR STUDENTS

Study Material

Through the book's Online Learning Center, students have free access to the following materials: chapter outlines, chapter objectives, multiple choice and essay quizzes, flashcards, and weblinks. In addition, the site offers a Presidential Timeline, a Spanish-English Glossary, and guidelines for avoiding plagiarism.

ACKNOWLEDGMENTS

For this new, eighth edition of *We the People*, I received an enormous amount of sound advice. Reviewers are the lifeblood of a text, and I was fortunate to have the assistance of a skilled group of scholars. I am deeply grateful to each of them for their help:

P. Faye Collins, *Northern Kentucky University*
Sean D. Foreman, *Barry University*
Madhavi McCall, *San Diego State University*
Anthony C. Petty, *Wake Technical Community College*
Shari B. Sowards, *Salt Lake Community College*
Christopher Sprecher, *Texas A&M University*
Joe Sutter, *Tarrant County College*
Phillip S. Warf, *Mendocino College*

I also want to thank those at McGraw-Hill who contributed to the eighth edition. Mark Georgiev, my editor, assumed that position shortly before we began the revision process and provided a seamless transition to the new edition. Nancy Crochiere, director of development, was, as always, superb in guiding the revision process. Erin Grelak, the development editor, was my everyday contact on the revisions and was enormously helpful in keeping the revision process moving along smoothly and constructively. Briana Porco, editorial assistant, helped with a thousand administrative details.

I would also like to thank the book's production editor, David Blatty. He carefully oversaw the book's production and schedule. Thomas Briggs was the copyeditor, and he had a deft touch that strengthened the prose. Toni Michaels was again involved in the photo research, providing a marvelous set of choices.

At Harvard, I had the diligent and cheerful support of my extraordinary faculty assistant, Alyssa Barrett, who helped update the text and copied endless drafts of it. Alex Patterson served as my photo adviser and photo researcher; his keen eye is behind each of the photo selections in this edition. I owe both of them a deep thank you.

Thomas Patterson

CHAPTER 1

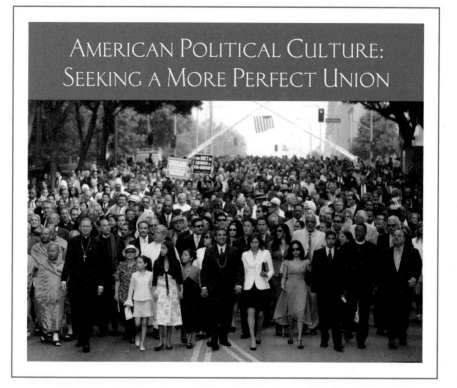

AMERICAN POLITICAL CULTURE: SEEKING A MORE PERFECT UNION

❝ One hears people say that it is inherent in the habits and nature of democracies to change feelings and thoughts at every moment. . . . But I have never seen anything like that happening in the great democracy on the other side of the ocean. What struck me most in the United States was the difficulty experienced in getting an idea, once conceived, out of the head of the majority. **❞**

ALEXIS DE TOCQUEVILLE[1]

On the night of November 4, 2008, Barack Obama gave his first speech as president-elect of the United States. Earlier that day, more than 100 million Americans had cast their ballots, choosing Obama over his Republican challenger, John McCain. In his victory speech, Obama spoke of renewing the American dream. He called upon Americans to reclaim their sense of citizenship, to move forward in common purpose, and to put aside the divisions that had kept them apart. He said that, as president, he would listen to the American people, using their voices as his guide. He pledged to use his office to reinvigorate the nation's values and to restore Americans' trust in their government.

The ideals that guided Obama's speech would have been familiar to any generation of Americans. These ideals have been invoked when Americans have gone to war, declared peace, celebrated national holidays, launched major policy initiatives, and asserted new rights.[2] The ideals contained in Obama's speech were the same ones that had punctuated the speeches of George Washington and Abraham Lincoln, Susan B. Anthony and Franklin D. Roosevelt, Martin Luther King and Ronald Reagan.

The ideals were also there at the nation's beginning, when they were put into words in the Declaration of Independence and the Constitution. Of course, the practical meaning of these words has changed greatly during the more than two centuries the United States has been a sovereign nation. When the writers of the Constitution began the document with the words "We the People," they did not have all Americans equally in mind. Black slaves, women, and white men without property did not have the same rights as white men with property.

Nevertheless, America's ideals have been remarkably enduring. Throughout their history, Americans have embraced the same set of core values. They have quarreled over the meaning and practice of these ideals, but they have never seriously questioned the principles themselves. As historian Clinton Rossiter concluded, "There has been in a doctrinal sense, only one America."[3]

This book is about contemporary American politics, not U.S. history or culture. Yet American politics today cannot be understood apart from the nation's heritage. Government does not begin anew with each generation; it builds on the past. In the case of the United States, the main link between past and present lies in the nation's founding ideals. The Frenchman Alexis de Tocqueville was among the first to see that major tendencies in American politics cannot be understood without taking into account the country's core beliefs. "Habits of the heart" was Tocqueville's description of Americans' ingrained ideals.[4]

This chapter briefly examines the principles that have helped shape American politics since the nation's earliest years. The chapter also explains basic concepts—such as power, pluralism, and constitutionalism—that are important in the study of American politics. The main points made in this chapter are these:

* ★ *The American political culture centers on a set of core ideals—liberty, equality, and self-government—that serve as the people's common bond.* These mythic principles have a substantial influence on what Americans will regard as reasonable and acceptable and on what they will try to achieve.

* ★ *Politics is the process that determines whose values will prevail in society.* The play of politics in the United States takes place in the context of

democratic procedures, constitutionalism, and capitalism and involves elements of majority, pluralist, bureaucratic, and elitist rule.

★ *Politics in the United States is characterized by a number of major patterns.* These include a division of governing authority, a high degree of pluralism, an extraordinary emphasis on individual rights, and a substantial separation of the political and economic spheres.

POLITICAL CULTURE: THE CORE PRINCIPLES OF AMERICAN GOVERNMENT

The people of every nation have a few central ideals that characterize their political life, but, as James Bryce observed, Americans are a special case.[5] Their ideals are the basis of their national identity. Other people take their identity from the common ancestry that led them gradually to gather under

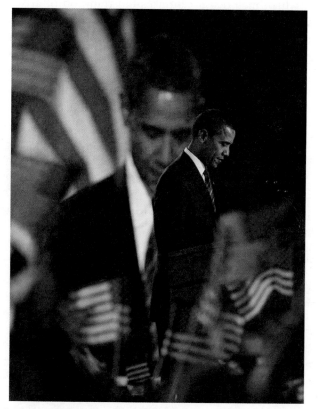

In accepting victory on election night, Barack Obama, as America's leaders have done throughout the nation's history, invoked America's founding ideals. In the background, Obama appears on one of the giant television screens set up to project his image to the large crowd that had gathered in Chicago for his acceptance speech.

one flag. Thus, long before there was a France or a Japan, there were French and Japanese people, each a kinship group united through ancestry. Even today, it is kinship that links them. There is no way to become fully Japanese except to be born of Japanese parents. Not so for Americans. They are a multitude of people from different lands—England, Germany, Ireland, Africa, Italy, Poland, Mexico, and China, to name just a few. Americans are linked not by a shared ancestry but by allegiance to a common set of ideals.

These ideals are habits of mind, a customary way of thinking about the world. They are part of what social scientists call **political culture,** a term that refers to the characteristic and deep-seated beliefs of a particular people about government and politics.[6]

America's core ideals are rooted in the European heritage of the first white settlers. They arrived during the Enlightenment period, when people were awakening to the idea of human progress. These settlers were not trying to invent a wholly new way of life.[7] Their goals were shaped by their European experiences, which included a centuries-old tradition of aristocratic rule. However, their vision of society changed as they discovered the possibilities that America offered. There was in America no hereditary nobility that controlled nearly all the power and land. The opportunities provided by the New World's vast territory and its great distance from European rulers gave ordinary people a level of freedom and opportunity unimaginable in the Old World. In the end, the colonists rejected the European way of governing.

U.S. politics is remarkable for its historical continuity, which is celebrated here in a ceremony at the Capitol in Washington, D.C.

The American Revolution was the first successful large-scale rebellion in human history driven largely by an image of an entirely different form of government.[8] In the words of the Declaration of Independence:

> We hold these truths to be self-evident, that all men are created equal; that they are endowed by their Creator with certain unalienable rights; that among these, are life, liberty, and the pursuit of happiness. That, to secure these rights, governments are instituted among men, deriving their just powers from the consent of the governed; that, whenever any form of government becomes destructive of these ends, it is the right of the people to alter or to abolish it, and to institute a new government, laying its foundation on such principles, and organizing its powers in such form, as to them shall seem most likely to effect their safety and happiness.

AMERICA'S CORE VALUES

An understanding of America's ideals begins with the recognition that they are based on the notion that government exists to serve the people. The cornerstone of society is the individual rather than the government.

Liberty, Equality, and Self-Government

Liberty, equality, and self-government are widely regarded as America's core political ideals (see Table 1-1). **Liberty** is the principle that individuals should be free to act and think as they choose, provided they do not infringe unreasonably on the freedom and well-being of others. The United States, as political scientist Louis Hartz said, was "born free."[9] The Declaration of Independence rings with the proclamation that people are entitled to "life, liberty, and the pursuit of happiness." The preamble to the Constitution declares that the U.S. government was founded to secure "the Blessings of Liberty to ourselves and our Posterity." The Statue of Liberty stands in New York harbor as the symbol of the American people, and the "Star-Spangled Banner" rings out with the words "land of the free."

For early Americans, liberty was nearly a birthright. Ordinary people did not have to accept the European system of absolute government and aristocratic privilege when greater personal liberty was as close as the next area of unsettled land. Not surprisingly, these early Americans were determined, when forming their own government, to protect their liberty. The First Amendment of the Constitution prohibits laws that restrict personal freedom: "Congress shall make no law respecting the establishment of religion, or prohibiting the free exercise thereof; or abridging the freedom of speech, or of the press; or the right of the people to peaceably assemble, and to petition the Government for a redress of grievances."

| table | 1-1 | AMERICA'S CORE POLITICAL IDEALS |

The United States was founded on a set of political ideals that have served as its people's common bond. Foremost among these ideals are liberty, equality, and self-government.

Ideal	Description	Origin (In Part)
Liberty	The principle that individuals should be free to act and think as they choose, provided they do not infringe unreasonably on the rights and freedoms of others.	Colonial America's vast open lands offered a degree of liberty unattainable in Europe; the American Revolution was fought over liberty.
Equality	The notion that all individuals are equal in their moral worth, in their treatment under the law, and in their political voice.	Colonial America's openness made Europe's aristocratic system unenforceable; greater personal opportunity in America fostered a sense of social equality.
Self-government	The idea that the people are the ultimate source and proper beneficiary of governing authority and must have a voice in how they are governed.	Colonial America had a degree of self-government; Americans' sense of personal freedom and equality led them to want self-determination in public affairs as well.

Liberty for early Americans meant economic opportunity as well as political freedom. Property ownership was widespread, as was a commitment to self-reliance. Frontier America was marked by a "rugged individualism" that became a key cultural value. **Individualism** is a commitment to personal initiative and self-sufficiency; it rests on the belief that people should be free of undue government restraints as they seek to advance themselves economically.

Americans' demand for political and economic liberty has persisted. Observers from Tocqueville onward have seen fit to note that liberty in America, as in no other country, is ingrained in people's thinking. Americans' chief aim, wrote Tocqueville, "is to remain their own masters."

A second American political ideal is **equality**—the notion that all individuals are equal in their moral worth and thereby entitled to equal treatment under the law. America provided its white settlers a new level of equality. Europe's rigid aristocratic system based on land ownership was unenforceable in frontier America. Almost any free citizen who wanted to own land could obtain it. It was this natural sense of personal equality that Thomas Jefferson expressed so forcefully in the Declaration of Independence: "We hold these truths to be self-evident, that all men are created equal."

Equality, however, has always been a less clearly defined concept than liberty. Even Jefferson professed not to know its exact meaning. A slave owner, Jefferson distinguished between free citizens, who were entitled to equal rights, and slaves, who were not. After slavery was abolished, Americans continued to argue over the meaning of equality, and the debate continues today. Does equality require that wealth and opportunity be widely shared? Or does it merely require that artificial barriers to advancement be removed? Despite differing opinions about such questions, an insistence on equality is a distinctive feature of the American experience. Americans, said Bryce, reject "the very notion" that some people might be "better" than others merely because of birth or position.[10]

America's third great political ideal is **self-government**—the principle that the people are the ultimate source of governing authority and should have a voice in their governing. "Governments," the Declaration of Independence proclaims, "deriv[e] their just powers from the consent of the governed." In his Gettysburg Address, Lincoln extolled a government "of the people, by the people, for the people." Etched in a corridor of the nation's Capitol building are the words Alexander Hamilton spoke when asked about the foundation of the nation's government: "Here, sir, the people govern."

Americans' belief in self-government formed in colonial America. The Old World was an ocean away, and European governments had no option but to allow the American colonies a degree of self-determination. Out of this experience came the vision of a self-governing nation. It was an ideal that led tens of thousands of ordinary farmers, merchants, and tradesmen to risk their lives in the cause of self-government during the American Revolution. The ensuing federal and state constitutions were based on the idea that government is properly founded on the will of the people. The Constitution of the United States opens with the words "We the People."

America's principles hold out the promise of a government of high purpose, in which power is widely shared and used for the common good. The principles are not, however, wholly compatible with each other. They derive from somewhat different experiences and philosophical traditions, and there are points at which they conflict. Self-government, for example, emphasizes majority rule, whereas liberty emphasizes personal freedom and security. Conflict between the two is inevitable at times—for example, the

POLITICAL CULTURE

Liberty, Equality, and Self-Government: Religion and American Ideals

The United States is a nation established in 1776 on a set of principles—liberty, equality, and self-government. These ideals derived in part from broad lessons of history, the direct experiences of the colonists, and treatises such as those of Locke and Rousseau. Religious beliefs also played a major part.

Many of the early colonists came to America in order to practice their religions freely. Church and state in Europe were joined. Government there sided with a particular religion—Roman Catholicism in France and Spain, Anglicanism in England. Rhode Island's founder, the Reverend Roger Williams, was a Calvinist who left his native England for reasons of religious freedom. Williams was the first to assert that church and state in America ought to be separate. Williams argued that salvation required an acceptance of God, which is meaningful only if it is an act of free will—and this is impossible if religion is imposed on the individual by the state. To Williams and others, religious liberty and political liberty were inseparable. The prevalence of this view is apparent in the First Amendment to the Constitution, which at once provides for freedom of political expression *and* for religious freedom.

Liberty is not the only American ideal with a religious basis. Equality was considered God's work: "all men are created equal." Every individual was a child of God and thus equal in his eyes. (This belief posed a dilemma for slaveholders, who finessed it by claiming that slaves either were soulless or were secondary beings in God's "natural order.") Self-government, too, had a religious foundation, though a Protestant one. Unlike the Catholic Church, which was hierarchical in its organization, with the pope and bishops at its head, many Protestant sects had self-governing congregations. This feature affected their members' views on the proper form of government.

America, said the British writer G. K. Chesterton, is "a nation with the soul of a church" and "the only country founded on a creed." He could have added that America is also a nation that emulated a religious model in its governing document. The first colonists formed religious communities governed by written covenant, a model for the written Constitution drafted and ratified by Americans more than a century later.

ideal of self-government asserts that the view of the many should prevail over the opinion of the few, whereas the principle of liberty asserts that individuals have inviolate rights. How far should the majority be permitted to go in imposing its will on the individual? To what extent should the individual be allowed to act in ways objectionable to the majority? These are everyday questions of American politics, affecting issues as diverse as taxes, gay marriage, capital punishment, affirmative action, property use, abortion, and national security.

Moreover, America's core ideals are general principles, not fixed rules of conduct. During the writing of the Declaration of Independence, Thomas Jefferson and John Adams argued over the meaning of liberty, with Jefferson contending that its basis was in individual freedom and Adams countering that it rested on the nation's freedom. This debate has been restaged many times in U.S. history. After the terrorist attacks on New York and Washington on September 11, 2001, President George W. Bush secretly ordered the monitoring of Americans' telephone and email communication. When the policy was exposed, Bush claimed he was protecting Americans' liberty from the terrorist threat. Bush said, "Given that choice, I will defend America every time." Critics said Bush's policy was an assault on Americans' liberty. Senator Patrick Leahy (D-Vt) said the "rights of American citizens are being arrogantly abridged at almost every turn in the name of national security."

The Power and Limits of Americans' Ideals

Cultural beliefs originate in a country's political and social practices, but they are not perfect representations of these practices. They are mythic ideas—symbolic positions taken by a people to justify and give meaning to their way of life.[11] Myths contain elements of truth, but they are not the full truth.

Ideals affect people's aspirations, but they exist alongside other impulses. For some people and at some times, politics is purely an issue of self-interest. In *Federalist* No. 10, James Madison deplored the readiness of people "to oppress each other [rather] than to cooperate for their common good." The clearest proof of this tendency in the American case is the human tragedy that began nearly four centuries ago and continues today. In 1619 the first black slaves were brought in chains to America. Slavery lasted 250 years. Slaves worked in the fields from dawn to dark (from "can see, 'til can't"), in both the heat of summer and the cold of winter. The Civil War brought an end to slavery but not to racial oppression. Slavery was followed by the Jim Crow era of legal segregation: black people in the South were

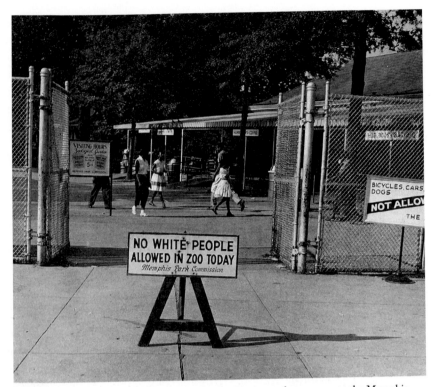

During the era of racial segregation in the South, this sign at the entrance to the Memphis public zoo meant that it was Tuesday—the only day black people were allowed to go to the zoo. On the other six days of the week, the sign excluded black people from entering. The Memphis zoo was typical of life in the South during the so-called Jim Crow era that followed the Civil War. Such policies were pursued despite Americans' professed commitment to equality and were upheld by federal courts despite prohibitions against discrimination set forth in the U.S. Constitution.

forbidden by law to use the same schools, hospitals, restaurants, and restrooms as white people. Those who spoke out against this system were subjected to beatings, firebombings, castrations, rapes, and murder—hundreds of African Americans were lynched in the early 1900s by white vigilantes. Today African Americans have equal rights under the law, but in fact they are far from equal. Compared with whites, blacks are twice as likely to live in poverty, twice as likely to be unable to find a job, and twice as likely to die in infancy.[12] There have always been two Americas, one for whites and one for blacks.

Historical Background

Despite the lofty claim that "all men are created equal," equality has never been an American birthright. In 1882, Congress suspended Chinese immigration on the assumption

figure   1-1   THE CHANGING FACE OF IMMIGRATION

Until 1965, immigration laws were biased in favor of European immigrants. The laws enacted in 1965 increased the proportion of immigrants from Asia and Latin America. *Source: U.S. Immigration and Naturalization Service, 2008. Percentages are totals for each decade, for example, the 2000 figures are for the 1991–2000 period.*

that the Chinese were an inferior people. Calvin Coolidge in 1923 asked Congress for a permanent ban on Chinese immigration, saying that people "who do not want to be partakers of the American spirit ought not to set-tle in America."[13] Not until 1965 was discrimination against the Chinese and other Asians eliminated from U.S. immigration laws. Tight limits on Hispanic immigration were also lifted at this time, and since then, most im-migrants have come from Latin America and Asia (see Figure 1-1).

The claim that the United States is a gigantic melting pot is a blend of fact and fiction. On the one hand, no other nation has so fully opened its doors to groups from around the world. Even today, Americans are sub-stantially more likely than Europeans to say that recent immigrant groups are having a positive influence on the society. Nevertheless, established groups in America have never fully embraced new arrivals. When Catholics and Jews from Ireland, Italy, and eastern Europe came to this country in large numbers in the nineteenth and early twentieth centuries, many Americans, including some members of Congress, sought to bar them from entry because of their religious beliefs. After the September 11, 2001, ter-rorist attacks on the World Trade Center and the Pentagon, polls indicated that most Americans wanted Middle East immigration sharply reduced or halted entirely.

America's callous treatment of some groups is not among the stories that the American people like to tell about themselves. A University of Virginia survey found that American adults are far more likely to want children to be taught about the nation's achievements than its shortcomings (see Table 1-2). Selective memory can be found among all peoples, but the tendency

| table | 1-2 | TELLING THE STORY TO CHILDREN |

Americans' values and myths are reflected in their preferences in teaching children about the nation's history.

In Teaching the American Story to Children, How Important Is the Following Theme?	Essential/ Very Important	Somewhat Important	Somewhat Unimportant/ Very Unimportant Leave It Out of the Story
With hard work and perseverance, anyone can succeed in America.	83%	14%	4%
Our founders limited the power of government so government would not intrude too much into the lives of its citizens.	74	19	8
America is the world's greatest melting pot in which people from different countries are united into one nation.	73	21	5
America's contribution is one of expanding freedom for more and more people.	71	22	6
Our nation betrayed its founding principles by cruel mistreatment of blacks and American Indians.	59	24	17
Our founders were part of a male-dominated culture that gave important roles to men while keeping women in the background.	38	28	35

Source: Used by permission of the Survey of American Political Culture, James Davison Hunter and Carol Bowman, directors, Institute for Advanced Studies in Culture, University of Virginia.

to recast history is perhaps exaggerated in the American case because Americans' beliefs are so idealistic. How could a nation that claims to be the model of human equality have barred the Chinese, enslaved the blacks, massacred the Indians, and subordinated women?

Although ideals do not determine exactly what people will do, they do affect their hopes and desires. If racial, gender, ethnic, and other forms of intolerance constitute the nation's sorriest legacy, the centuries-old struggle of Americans to build a more equal society is among its finest. Few nations have battled so relentlessly against the insidious discrimination that stems from superficial human differences such as the color of one's skin. The abolition and suffrage movements of the 1800s and the more recent civil rights movements of black Americans, women, Hispanics, and gays testify to Americans' persistent effort to build a more equal society. At the height of the Civil War, which was the bloodiest conflict to date in the whole of world history, Abraham Lincoln emancipated the slaves, saying "I never, in my life, felt more certain that I was doing right."[14]

The power of Americans' commitment to equality is today evident in the country's elaborate system of higher education, which includes nearly three thousand two-year and four-year institutions. In many countries, access to a college education is sharply restricted and widely available only to the children of wealthy families. America's higher education system has a different foundation: it is designed to promote equality of opportunity. Although some young Americans do not have a realistic prospect of attending college, the nation's higher education system is an open one compared with those elsewhere. About a fourth of America's adult citizens have a college degree, the world's highest rate. Even West Virginia, the American state with the lowest proportion of college graduates (see "States in the Nation"), has a higher percentage than do most European countries.

The principles of liberty and self-government have also shaped American society. No country holds as many elections or has as many publicly elected officials as does the United States, which is also nearly the only country to allow voters through primary elections to decide which candidates will be the party nominees in the general election. And few people have as many legally protected individual rights—ranging from free-expression rights to fair-trial protections—as do Americans.

The power of American ideals is perhaps nowhere more evident, however, than in their continuing influence. Their fulfillment is an ongoing quest, not a settled issue. The Great Depression of the 1930s, for example, forced Americans to reconsider the meaning of personal liberty. Until then, freedom had been a matter of freedom *from* government. But this type of freedom was an empty promise for the tens of millions who were jobless, homeless,

★ STATES IN THE NATION

A College Education

Reflecting their cultural beliefs of individualism and equality, Americans have developed the world's largest college system. Every state has at least eight colleges within its boundaries. No European democracy has as many colleges as either California or New York—each of which has more than 300 institutions of higher education. The extensive U.S. college system has enabled large numbers of Americans to earn a college degree. Among adults twenty-five years of age and older, roughly one in four is a college graduate. Even the states that rank low on this indicator have a higher percentage of college graduates than do most European countries.

Q: Why do the northeastern and western coastal states have a higher percentage of adults with college degrees?

A: The northeastern and western coastal states are more affluent and urbanized than most states. Accordingly, young people in these states can better afford the costs of college and are more likely to require a college degree for the careers they pursue.

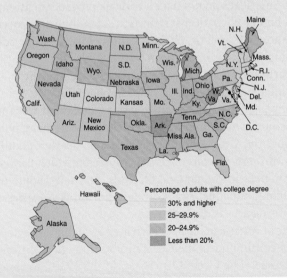

Source: U.S. Bureau of the Census, 2008. Based on percentage of adults twenty-five years of age or older with a college degree.

and hungry as a result of the depression. A fourth of American laborers were unemployed, and another fourth could find only part-time work. Americans turned *to* government for help. In his 1941 State of the Union Address, President Franklin D. Roosevelt spoke to people's hopes when he declared that "freedom from want" was among Americans' fundamental liberties.

Like the Great Depression generation, every generation of Americans has embraced the nation's founding principles and sought ways to update and strengthen them. The writer Theodore H. White aptly described America as a nation relentlessly "in search of itself."[15] *A defining feature of the U.S. political system is Americans' ongoing pursuit of the political ideals upon which the nation was founded.*

POLITICS: THE RESOLUTION OF CONFLICT

Although cultural values affect what people seek through politics, politics is more than shared ideals. It is also a struggle for power and advantage. Commenting on the competitive nature of politics, political scientist Harold Lasswell described politics as the struggle over "who gets what, when, and how."[16] **Politics** is the process through which a society settles its conflicts and decides the policies by which it will be governed.

Political conflict has two primary sources. One is *scarcity*. Even the richest societies do not have enough wealth to satisfy everyone's desires, and conflict over the distribution of resources is the predictable result. Consider, for example, the issue of school quality. Affluent suburban districts have better schools than do poor inner-city districts. Lacking a strong local tax base, inner-city residents have pressured state governments to provide equal funding to all schools. Residents of suburban communities have fought this arrangement, fearing that it would increase their taxes and weaken their local schools.

Differences in values are the other main source of political conflict. People see issues differently as a result of differences in their backgrounds and interests. Abortion is an issue of freedom of choice for some and an issue of murder for others. People bring to politics a wide range of conflicting standards—about abortion, the environment, crime and punishment, the poor, the economy, and countless other issues.

The Social Contract

Politics operates by "rules" that determine whose voice will prevail when conflict arises over resources and values. Without such rules, people would be constantly at each other's throats, and society would dissolve into anarchy.

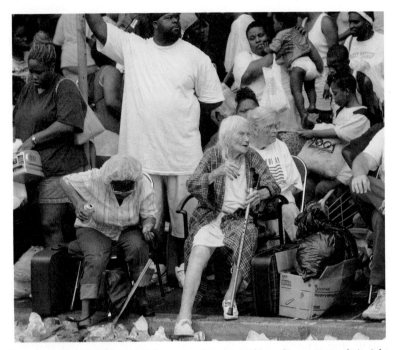

Social contract theory holds that people agree to be governed in order to protect their rights and interests. Neither the government nor the people always hold up their side of the bargain. Shown here are some of the thousands of New Orleans residents who were abandoned by government as Hurricane Katrina roared in from the Gulf Coast. A much smaller number of New Orleans residents took advantage of the chaos to loot homes and businesses.

For a long period of world history, the rules of politics were stacked against ordinary people. They had no say in their governing and were at the mercy of those in authority. Government was controlled by absolute monarchs, whose word was law. Many of them were tyrants, and others levied onerous taxes in order to build lavish palaces.

Roughly four centuries ago, ideas about the proper form of government began to change. Ironically, one of the theorists who contributed to this development was an advocate of absolute rule. In *Leviathan* (published in 1651), the English philosopher Thomas Hobbes argued that government rests on a **social contract** in which ordinary people surrender the freedom they would have in a state of nature in return for the protection that a sovereign ruler can provide. People give up their freedom, Hobbes said, because life in its natural state is "nasty, brutish, and short"—the strong prey on the weak. For this reason, people seek the protection of rulers whom they are obliged to obey, even if some rulers turn out to be cruel or inept. The alternative—a never-ending "war of all against all"—is far worse.

Four decades later, the English philosopher John Locke used Hobbes's concept of a social contract to argue *against* absolutism. In his *Second Treatise on Civil Government* (1690), Locke claimed that all individuals have certain natural (or inalienable) rights, including those of life, liberty, and property. When people form governments for the purpose of securing their physical safety, they retain these individual rights. The social contract—their agreement to submit to governing authority—is based on the premise that government will protect these rights. If it fails to do so, said Locke, the people can overthrow it and form a new government.

Three-quarters of a century later, the French philosopher Jean-Jacques Rousseau extended the idea of a social contract to include popular sovereignty. Like Locke, Rousseau despised absolute government. "Man was born free, but everywhere he is in chains" are the opening words of Rousseau's *Social Contract* (1762). Rousseau claimed that people in their natural state are innocent and happy. Accordingly, the only legitimate government is one that promotes their interests and governs with their consent. As Rousseau saw it, government is simply the instrument for carrying out the people's will. Sovereignty rests with them, not the government. Rousseau worried, however, that the people would act selfishly and claimed that popular rule also had proper limits. It would be legitimate only if the people acted in the interests of all—what Rousseau called "the general will."

These ideas—that people have individual rights and should have a say in their governing—sparked the American Revolution in 1776. A decade later, the writing of the Constitution formalized the basic principle of social contract theory—that the power of leaders is limited by a prescribed set of rules.

The Rules of American Politics

The major rules of American politics—democracy, constitutionalism, and capitalism—establish a political process that is intended to promote self-government, uphold equality, and defend political and economic rights. The U.S. political system is, at once, a democratic system, a constitutional system, and a capitalist (free-market) system.

Democracy   Democracy is a set of rules intended to give ordinary people a significant voice in government. The word *democracy* comes from the Greek words *demos*, meaning "the people," and *kratis*, meaning "to rule." In simple terms, **democracy** is a form of government in which the people govern, either directly or through elected representatives (see Chapter 2). A democracy thus is different from an **oligarchy** (in which control rests with a small group, such as top-ranking military officers or a few wealthy families) and from an **autocracy** (in which control rests with a single individual, such as a king or dictator).

A *democratic system* reflects the Rousseauist idea that legitimate authority stems from the consent of the governed, which in practice has meant majority rule through voting in elections. More direct forms of democracy exist, such as the town meeting in which citizens vote directly on issues affecting them, but the impracticality of such an arrangement in a large society has made majority rule through elections the basic form of self-government in modern democracies, including the United States.

Unlike some countries, the United States has an unbroken history of free elections as the means of acquiring governmental power. At no time has power been obtained through a military coup or mass uprising. However, America's voters do not control their government as directly as voters in some democracies. The U.S. electoral system was established in a period when the power of government—whether it rested with a monarch or the majority—was greatly feared. To protect against abuses of power, the writers of the U.S. Constitution devised an elaborate system of checks and balances. Authority was divided among the executive, legislative, and judicial branches so that each branch could act as a check on the power of the others (see Chapter 2). Indeed, *a substantial division of governing authority is a defining characteristic of the American political system.* One result of this constitutional arrangement is that majority rule is less direct in the United States than in many democracies. In most European countries, a majority has the power through its vote in a single election to give full executive and legislative power to the victorious political party. In the United States, however, there are separate elections for the president, U.S. senators, and U.S. representatives, and their terms of office differ in length. Thus, a voting majority in the United States must have the lasting power to dominate a series of elections in order to assert its full influence (see Chapter 2).

Constitutionalism   The concept of democracy implies that the will of the majority should prevail over the wishes of the minority. If unrestrained, this principle would allow a majority to ride roughshod over the minority. The majority would have the power to deprive the minority even of its liberty, a clearly unacceptable outcome. Individuals have rights and freedoms that cannot lawfully be denied by the majority.

Constitutionalism holds that there are limits on the rightful power of government over its citizens. In a *constitutional system*, officials govern according to law, and citizens have basic rights that government cannot deny or abridge.[17] Free speech is an example. The U.S. government is prohibited by the First Amendment from infringing on free speech. No right is absolute, which means that some restrictions are allowed. No student, for example, has a First Amendment right to shout loudly and disrupt a classroom. Nevertheless, free speech is broadly protected by the courts.

During the buildup to war with Iraq in 2003, tens of thousands of antiwar demonstrators took to the streets. Those who vocally opposed the government's war policy did so without risk of fine or imprisonment.

The constitutional tradition in the United States is as strong as the democratic tradition.[18] *A defining characteristic of the American political system is its extraordinary emphasis on individual rights.* Americans have a broad set of individual rights, ranging from those surrounding free expression to those guaranteeing due process of law. Moreover, issues that in other democracies would be resolved through elections and in legislative bodies are, in the United States, decided in courts of law as well. Abortion rights, nuclear power, busing, toxic waste disposal, and welfare services are among the scores of issues that in recent years have played out in part as questions of rights to be settled through the courts.

Constitutionalism is not practiced by all governments. Although every country has a constitution that supposedly restricts government's lawful powers, these constitutional guarantees are sometimes not worth the paper on which they are written. **Authoritarian governments** openly repress their political opponents as a means of staying in power, although they do so in varying degrees. Some of these regimes are **totalitarian governments,** meaning they assert complete dominance over individuals and the institutions of society. They control the media, direct the economy, dictate

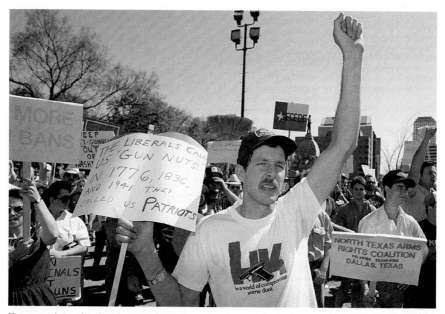

Free speech is a familiar feature of constitutionalism. This anti–gun control rally took place in Austin, Texas.

what can and cannot be taught in schools, define family relations, and decide which religions—if any—can be practiced openly. In fact, virtually no area of life is beyond their sphere of control, which results in brutal one-party rule. Millions of individuals in Adolf Hitler's Nazi Germany and in Josef Stalin's Soviet Union were imprisoned or murdered by the state. Other authoritarian regimes—including most of those that have taken power in Latin America, Africa, and Asia in recent decades as a result of military coups—are less repressive because those nations have other powerful institutions, such as religious organizations or large corporations, that might actively oppose them if they go too far.

Capitalism   Just as democracy and constitutionalism are sets of rules for allocating power in American society, so too is capitalism. **Capitalism** holds that the government should interfere with the economy as little as possible. In a capitalist system, firms are allowed to operate in a free marketplace, and individuals are expected to rely on their own initiative to establish their economic security. Firms decide what they will produce and how much they will charge for their goods, while consumers decide what they will buy and at what price. Meanwhile, following a Lockean principle, private property rights are vigorously protected through government action.

Alternatives to capitalism include **socialism,** which assigns government a large role in the ownership of the means of production, in economic decision making, and in providing for the economic security of the individual. Under the form of socialism practiced in Sweden and some other democracies, the government does not attempt to manage the overall economy. Under **communism,** which characterized the former Soviet Union and is practiced today in North Korea and a few other countries, the government owns most or all major industries and also takes responsibility for overall management of the economy, including production quotas, supply points, and pricing.

The United States has a largely capitalist (free-market) system. The government does play an economic role through its tax, regulatory, monetary, and spending policies, but the bulk of economic decisions are made by private firms and consumers (see Chapter 15). Like the rules of democracy and constitutionalism, the rules of capitalism are not neutral. Whereas democracy responds to numbers and constitutionalism responds to individual rights, capitalism responds to wealth. "Money talks" in a capitalist system, which means, among other things, that wealthier interests have disproportionate political influence, as well as the lion's share of economic power (see Chapters 7 and 9).

Capitalist systems characterize most Western countries, but the United States relies more heavily on the free market than do the others (see "How the United States Compares"). Health care is an example. In Europe

Tax Rates

The United States was labeled "the country of individualism par excellence" by William Watts and Lloyd Free in their book *State of the Nation*. They were referring to the emphasis that Americans place on economic self-reliance and free markets.

In European democracies, such views also prevail but are moderated by a greater acceptance of tax and social policies that redistribute wealth. The differences between the American and European culture reflect their differing political traditions. America was an open country ruled by a foreign power, and its revolution was fought largely over the issue of personal liberty. In European revolutions, economic and social equality was also at issue, because wealth was held by hereditary aristocracies. Europeans' concern with equality was gradually translated into a willingness to use government as a means of economic redistribution. An example is government-paid medical care for all citizens, which is provided throughout nearly the whole of Europe and Canada, but not in the United States. More than forty million Americans are without health insurance.

Such differences affect tax rates. Although many Americans complain that their taxes are too high, the tax rate in the United States is lower than in Canada and Europe, reflecting the degree to which the various countries seek through taxes to provide economic security to the less-well-off. According to figures obtained in 2008 from the Organization for Economic Cooperation and Development (OECD), the tax rates—the total amount of individual taxes relative to a country's Gross Domestic Product (GDP)—in the following countries are:

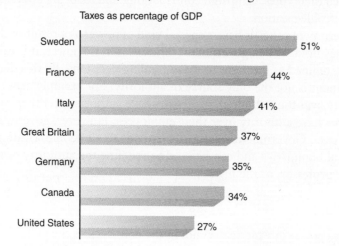

Taxes as percentage of GDP

- Sweden: 51%
- France: 44%
- Italy: 41%
- Great Britain: 37%
- Germany: 35%
- Canada: 34%
- United States: 27%

and Canada, health care is paid for by the government and is universal—every citizen has access to medical care at government expense. In contrast, health care in the United States is delivered largely through the private sector, and access to it depends in part on the individual's ability to pay. In effect, many of the economic benefits and costs that are allocated through the political process in other countries are allocated through the economic system in the United States. *A major characteristic of the American system is a relatively sharp distinction between what is political, and therefore to be decided in the public realm, and what is economic, and therefore to be settled in the private realm.*

POLITICAL POWER AND AUTHORITY: THE CONTROL OF POLICY

Rules are necessary in politics because the stakes are so high. Politics is a struggle for control of **public policy**—a decision by government to pursue a particular course of action. **Power** refers to the ability of persons, interests, or institutions to control public policy.[19] Americans who have enough power can levy or cut taxes, permit or prohibit abortions, protect or take away private property, provide or refuse health benefits, impose or relax trade barriers, and make war or declare peace. With so much at stake, it is not surprising that Americans, like people elsewhere, seek political power.

Political power resides with private individuals and organizations as well as in the hands of those who occupy government positions. A case in point is the power exercised by the National Rifle Association (NRA) over gun control policy. NRA members oppose restrictions on gun ownership and have used their votes, campaign contributions, and lobbying efforts to block gun control legislation.

Government officials have a special kind of power as a result of the positions they hold. When government officials exercise power, it is called **authority**, defined as the right to make binding decisions. By this definition, government is not the only source of authority. For example, parents have authority over their children, professors have authority over their students, and firms have authority over their employees. However, government is a special case. Government's authority extends to all people within its geographical boundaries and can be used to redefine the authority of the parent, the professor, or the firm.

Theories of Power

Who has power in America? Who, in the end, decides the policies that the U.S. government pursues? Do the people themselves hold this power, or

| table | 1-3 | THEORIES OF POWER: WHO GOVERNS AMERICA? |

There are four theories of power in America, each of which must be taken into account in any full explanation of the nation's policies.

Theory	Description
Majoritarianism	Holds that numerical majorities determine issues of policy
Pluralism	Holds that policies are effectively decided through power wielded by special interests that dominate particular policy areas
Elitism	Holds that policy is controlled by a small number of well-positioned, highly influential individuals
Bureaucratic rule	Holds that policy is controlled by well-placed administrators within the government bureaucracy

does it reside in the hands of a relatively small group of influential individuals, either within or outside of government?

This issue is compelling because the ultimate question of any political system is the question of who governs. Is power widely shared and used for the benefit of the many, or is it narrowly held and used to the advantage of the few? The issue is compelling for a second reason: power is easy to define but hard to pinpoint. Consider, for example, the votes that a member of Congress casts. Are these votes an expression of the member's power, or are they an expression of the power of groups on whom the member depends for reelection?

The pattern of political power in America has been shown to differ substantially across individuals, institutions, and policy areas. There are four broad theories of who holds power in America (see Table 1-3). None of them describes every aspect of American politics, but each applies in some situations.

Majoritarianism: Government by the People   A basic principle of democracy is the idea of majority rule. **Majoritarianism** is the notion that the majority should prevail not only in the counting of votes but also in the determination of public policy.

At times, a majority of the American public in effect decides policy issues. When Congress in 1996 passed a welfare reform bill that required welfare recipients to accept a job or job training after a two-year period or face the loss of their welfare benefits, it was acting in accord with the thinking of most Americans. They had come to believe that too many able-bodied individuals were taking advantage of the welfare system. A fuller assessment of majority power is provided by Benjamin Page and Robert Shapiro's study of the relationship between majority opinions and more than three hundred policy issues. On major issues particularly, Page and Shapiro found that when majority opinion shifted, public policy tended to shift in the same direction.[20]

Nevertheless, most policy decisions are not determined by majority opinion. Government makes thousands of policy decisions each year, and the general public is neither aware of nor interested in most of them (see Chapter 6). Other theories of power are required to explain these cases.

Pluralism: Government by Groups   One such theory is **pluralism,** which focuses on group activity and holds that many policies are effectively decided through power wielded by diverse (plural) interests. Farm subsidies, for example, are ordinarily determined more by pressure from agricultural groups than by pressure from the general public.

From a pluralist perspective, society's general interest is served if a diverse range of interests have a voice in government policy. Pluralists see society largely as a collection of separate interests. Farmers, broadcasters, truck drivers, and multinational corporations have different needs and, according to the pluralist view, should have the major voice in policies directly affecting them. Thus, as long as numerous groups have influence in their policy area, government is responding to the interests of most Americans. Pluralists such as Robert Dahl have argued that this is in fact the way the American political system operates most of the time.[21]

Critics argue that pluralists wrongly assume that the public interest is somehow represented in a system that allows special interests, each in its own sphere, to set public policy (see Chapter 9). Any such outcome, they say, represents the triumph of minority over majority rule. Critics also say that society's wealthier interests have undue advantage because they have the organization and money to lobby government effectively.

Elitism: Government by a Few   Elite theory offers a largely pessimistic view of power in America. **Elitism** holds that power is held by a small number of well-positioned, highly influential individuals. A leading proponent of elite theory was sociologist C. Wright Mills, who argued that key policies are decided by an overlapping coalition of select leaders, including corporate executives, top military officers, and centrally placed public officials.[22] Other proponents of elite theory have defined the core group somewhat differently, but their contention is the same: America is governed not by

★ LEADERS

Thomas Jefferson
(1743–1836)

Thomas Jefferson was the principal author of the Declaration of Independence. It was Jefferson who at age thirty-three coined the renowned words "Life, Liberty, and the Pursuit of Happiness." A man of contradictions, Jefferson owned slaves while arguing for human equality and liberty. Elected to the presidency in 1800, Jefferson was a proponent of states' rights and of a strict interpretation of the national government's constitutional powers. Yet he overlooked the Constitution, which had no authorization for such an act, in purchasing the Louisiana Territory from the French emperor Napoleon in 1803, doubling the area of the United States. A quiet man who was a better writer than public speaker, Jefferson dedicated much of his energy to strengthening his home state of Virginia. He drafted the state's Bill of Rights, which included a provision for religious freedom—a right not guaranteed in all states at the time. After retiring to his Monticello estate following his two terms as president, Jefferson designed and founded the University of Virginia, calling it one of his greatest achievements. To Jefferson, the success of the American experiment in self-government rested ultimately on an educated citizenry.

majorities or by a plurality of groups but by a small number of well-placed, privileged individuals.

Proponents of elite theory differ, however, in the extent to which they believe elites control policy for their own purposes. Some observers claim that elites operate behind the scenes in order to manipulate government for largely selfish purposes.[23] Other observers claim that elites, in part to protect their privileged positions and in part from a sense of public duty, pursue policies that serve society's interest as well as their own. One such view holds that competing elites appeal to voters for support and, in the process, adopt policy positions favored by large blocs of voters.[24]

Unquestionably, certain policies are basically decided by a small circle of influential people. When the U.S. financial system went into a tailspin in 2008, for example, the federal government provided billions of dollars in subsidies and loans to troubled banks. Some of the decisions were made in near secrecy by the Federal Reserve Board chairman, the Treasury secretary, and a few others. In announcing the decisions, they claimed to be acting in the public's interest. The most immediate beneficiaries, however, were a select number of America's most powerful financial institutions.

Bureaucratic Rule: Government by Administrators   A fourth theory holds that power resides in the hands of career government bureaucrats. The leading proponent of the theory of **bureaucratic rule** was the German sociologist Max Weber, who argued that all large organizations tend toward the bureaucratic form, with the result that decision-making power devolves to career administrators whose experience and knowledge of policy issues exceed those of elected officials.[25] Another sociologist, Roberto Michels, propounded the "iron law of oligarchy," concluding that power inevitably gravitates toward experienced administrators at the top of large-scale organizations, even in the case of organizations that aim to be governed democratically.[26]

Bureaucratic politics raises the possibility of a large, permanent government run by unaccountable administrators. Elections come and go, but the bureaucrats who staff executive agencies stay on. As public policy issues have become increasingly complex, bureaucrats often are the most knowledgeable on these issues and also are well positioned to influence their resolution. Modern government could not function without career bureaucrats, but in most cases, they are not instruments of the majority. They tend instead to act in ways that will promote their own agency and its programs (see Chapter 13).

Who Governs?

The perspective of this book is that each of these theories—majoritarianism, pluralism, elitism, and bureaucratic rule—must be taken into account in any full explanation of politics and power in America. As subsequent chapters will demonstrate, some policies are decided by majority influence, while others reflect the influence of special interests, bureaucrats, or elites.

One thing is certain. Few countries in the world have more competing interests than does the United States. The nation's settlement by people of different lands and religions, its great size and geographical variation, and its economic complexity have made the United States a diverse nation. *Competition for power among a great many interests of all kinds is a major characteristic of*

American politics. Indeed, America's great diversity helps explain why its political life is not a life-and-death struggle. In *Federalist* No. 10, James Madison argued that government is most dangerous when a single group is powerful enough to gain full political control. In such cases, the group will use government to further its interests at the expense of all others in society. Because the United States is so diverse, however, interests normally must work together to exercise power, a process that requires them to accommodate the interests of others.

THE CONCEPT OF A POLITICAL SYSTEM AND THIS BOOK'S ORGANIZATION

As the foregoing discussion suggests, American government consists of a great many related parts. It is instructive to view these components as constituting a **political system.** The parts are separate, but they connect with one another, affecting how each performs. Political scientist David Easton, who was a pioneer in this conception of politics, said that it makes little sense to study political relations piecemeal when they are, in reality, "interrelated."[27]

The political-system concept is the basis for this book's organization (see Figure 1-2). The political system operates against the backdrop of a constitutional framework that defines how power is to be obtained and exercised. This structure is the focus of the opening chapters, which examine how the

figure 1-2   THE AMERICAN POLITICAL SYSTEM

This book's chapters are organized within a political-system framework.

Constitution defines, in theory and practice, the institutions of government and the rights of individuals. Another part of the political system is *inputs:* the demands people and organizations place on government and the support they provide for institutions, leaders, and policies. These inputs are explored in chapters on public opinion, political participation, political parties, interest groups, and the news media. The functioning of governing officials is addressed in chapters on the nation's *political institutions*—Congress, the presidency, the federal bureaucracy, and the federal courts. Some of the discussion in these chapters is devoted simply to describing these institutions, but much of the discussion explores their interrelationships and the way their actions are affected by inputs and by the constitutional system in which they operate. Throughout the book, but particularly in the closing chapters, attention is given to the political system's *outputs*—policy decisions that are binding on society. These decisions, which are made by political institutions in response to inputs, affect American life in many areas, including the economy, the environment, social welfare, education, foreign affairs, and national defense.

The chapters are collectively designed to convey a reliable body of knowledge that will enable the reader to think systematically about the nature of the American political system. This body of knowledge derives from the full range of methodological approaches that political scientists have applied to the study of politics. Political science, unlike some academic disciplines, has been defined more by its subjects of inquiry than by a particular methodology. Normative theory, historical reasoning, legal analysis, and cultural analysis are among the strains, along with political psychology, political sociology, and political economy. Rational choice theory, organizational theory, and institutional analysis are other strains. Each approach can illuminate certain aspects of politics. For example, rational choice theory is based on the assumption that actors pursue their interests rationally and has proved to be a powerful model to describe, for instance, the behavior of elected officials as they seek to position themselves for reelection. As another example, cultural analysis is a powerful lens through which to view the values that motivate political action.

Political scientists have uncovered numerous tendencies in American political behavior, institutions, and processes. Five of these tendencies have been identified in this opening chapter as deserving special attention:

- Enduring cultural ideals that are Americans' common bond and a source of their political goals
- A substantial division of governing authority that is based on an elaborate system of checks and balances
- Many competing interests that are the result of the nation's great size, population diversity, and economic complexity

- A strong emphasis on individual rights, which is a consequence of the nation's political traditions
- A relatively sharp separation of the political and economic spheres that has the effect of placing many economic issues outside the reach of political majorities

As subsequent chapters will reveal, these tendencies are a key to understanding how the American political system operates. They are not the full story, however, nor could they be. The fact is, America's democracy is an unfinished story, one that will be decided in turn by each new generation. The political scientist E. E. Schattschneider said it best: "In the course of centuries, there has come a great deal of agreement about what democracy is, but nobody has a monopoly on it and the last word has not been spoken."[28]

SUMMARY Self-Test www.mhhe.com/pattersonwtp8e

The United States is a nation that was formed on a set of ideals. Liberty, equality, and self-government are foremost among these ideals, which also include the principles of individualism, diversity, and unity. These ideals became Americans' common bond and today are the basis of their political culture. Although they are mythic, inexact, and conflicting, these ideals have had a powerful effect on what generation after generation of Americans has tried to achieve politically, for themselves and others.

Politics in the United States plays out through rules of the game that include democracy, constitutionalism, and capitalism. Democracy is rule by the people, which in practice refers to a representative system of government in which the people rule through their elected officials. Constitutionalism refers to rules that limit the rightful power of government over citizens. Capitalism is an economic system based on a free-market principle that allows the government only a limited role in determining how economic costs and benefits will be allocated.

Politics is the process by which it is determined whose values will prevail in society. The basis of politics is conflict over scarce resources and competing values. Those who have power win out in this conflict and are able to control governing authority and policy choices. In the United States, no one faction controls all power and policy. Majorities govern on some issues, while groups, elites, and bureaucrats each govern on other issues.

KEY TERMS

authoritarian government (*p. 19*)
authority (*p. 22*)
autocracy (*p. 17*)
bureaucratic rule (*p. 26*)
capitalism (*p. 20*)
communism (*p. 20*)

constitutionalism (*p. 18*)
democracy (*p. 17*)
elitism (*p. 24*)
equality (*p. 6*)
individualism (*p. 6*)
liberty (*p. 5*)

majoritarianism (*p. 23*)

oligarchy (*p. 17*)

pluralism (*p. 24*)

political culture (*p. 4*)

political system (*p. 27*)

politics (*p. 15*)

power (*p. 22*)

public policy (*p. 22*)

self-government (*p. 7*)

social contract (*p. 16*)

socialism (*p. 20*)

totalitarian government (*p. 19*)

SUGGESTED READINGS

Dahl, Robert, *On Democracy*. New Haven, Conn.: Yale University Press, 1998. A handbook on democracy by a leading advocate of pluralism.

Domhoff, G. William. *Who Rules America? Power and Politics*, 5th ed. New York: McGraw-Hill, 2005. A critical assessment of American government by a leading proponent of elite theory.

Ferguson, Robert A. *Reading the Early Republic*. Cambridge, Mass.: Harvard University Press, 2004. Claims that Americans have always been a people striving to live up to their ideals.

Foley, Michael. *American Credo: The Place of Ideas in American Politics*. New York: Oxford University Press, 2007. An analysis of the political influence of Americans' core beliefs.

Katz, Michael B., and Mark J. Stern. *One Nation Divisible: What America Was and What It's Becoming*. New York: Russell Sage Foundation, 2006. A penetrating look at the transformation of American society during the twentieth century.

Lipset, Seymour Martin. *American Exceptionalism: A Double-Edged Sword*. New York: Norton, 1996. Argues that Americans' tendency to view society in idealized terms is a source of both alienation and progress.

Schuck, Peter H. *Diversity in America: Keeping Government at a Safe Distance*. Cambridge, Mass.: Belknap Press of Harvard, 2003. A far-reaching analysis of when diversity does and does not serve America's interests.

Stout, Jeffrey. *Democracy and Tradition*. Princeton, N.J.: Princeton University Press, 2004. An analysis of the moral claims associated with democracy.

White, John Kenneth. *The Values Divide*. Washington, D.C.: CQ Press, 2002. A look at Americans' values in a time of change.

LIST OF WEBSITES

http://www.conginst.org/ A site that provides up-to-date survey data on the American political culture.

http://www.loc.gov/ The Library of Congress website; provides access to over 70 million historical and contemporary U.S. documents.

http://www.stateline.org/ A University of Richmond/Pew Charitable Trusts site dedicated to providing citizens with information on major policy issues.

http://www.tocqueville.org/ Includes biographical and other references to Alexis de Tocqueville and his writings.

POLITICS IN THEORY AND PRACTICE

Thinking: How are Americans' beliefs about liberty, equality, and self-government related to their preference for constitutionalism? For capitalism? For democracy?

Participating: The American political culture includes a belief in liberty, equality, and self-government. As a prelude to getting involved in public affairs, reflect on what these ideals mean to you. What types of political activity are associated with each of these ideals? Thinking of your own experiences, what have you done to promote these ideals? What might you consider doing in the future to promote them?

Extra Credit

For up-to-the-minute *New York Times* articles, interactive simulations, graphics, study tools, and more links and quizzes, visit the text's Online Learning Center at www.mhhe.com/pattersonwtp8e.

What We Love About America

By James Carroll

A defining feature of American politics is the nation's founding ideals. For more than two centuries, they have served as Americans' common bond and their vision of a more perfect union. These ideals are invoked particularly during times of national crisis or triumph and also—as in the case of this essay by Boston Globe *columnist James Carroll—on national holidays.*

It is better to be a half-formed and rough idea than a brilliant cliché. Such preference for the imperfect new defines America. As we celebrate the birth of our nation, can we put words on the reason we love it? Let me try.

Because Europeans measured what they found here against what they had left behind, newness was the main note of the settled land. In the beginning, religiously inflamed politics had made life intolerable in the old country, a story that achieved its master form with the coming to Virginia and Massachusetts of the English dissidents. But even the mythic 1492 had carried an implication of the New World's liberating significance, for in addition to sponsoring Christopher Columbus, monarchs Ferdinand and Isabella chose that year to expel Jews and Muslims from Spain, establishing the totalitarian principle in Europe. Even as Spaniards then wreaked purposeful and accidental havoc in the New World, they opened an unforeseen escape route from the old.

America, for all of its nascent idealism, began as an instance of brutal European imperialism, with the exterminating of indigenous peoples and the enslavement of Africans as essential elements. But because that nascent idealism found articulation in the solemn compacts of the early generations—culminating first in the Declaration of Independence that we commemorate tomorrow, then in the US Constitution, then in the Bill of Rights—American imperialism contained principles of its own self-criticism. Slavery came to be seen as an abomination less in contrast to the practice of other nations than to the establishing theory of this one. America began, that is, as a half-formed and rough idea, but that idea became the meaning against which all life in this country has been measured ever since. That idea has been a perpetual source of newness, even as it has become more fully formed and clearly articulated.

And what is that idea? It comes to us by now as the brilliant cliché of the Fourth of July, but with stark simplicity it still defines the ground of our being: "All men are created equal." That the idea is dynamic, propelling a permanent social transformation, is evident even in the way that word "men" strikes the ear as anachronistic now. That Jefferson and the others were not thinking of women matters less than the fact that they established a principle that made the full inclusion of women inevitable. And so with those who owned no property, and those who were *themselves* owned property.

How new is this idea today? Its transforming work continues all around us. Last week, the US Supreme Court faulted the

Bush administration for its treatment of detainees in Guantanamo, implicitly affirming that one need not be a citizen of this nation to claim basic rights. The foundational principle extends to enemy combatants. They, too, are created equal. And so in other areas. US politics is obsessed with the question of the place of immigrants, legal and illegal. The mainstream argument takes for granted that even here liberalizing change is underway. Confronted with an "illegal" person, the law must still give primacy to personhood. And, on another front, is it an accident that American Episcopalians are the ones challenging the world Anglican body on the question of equality for gays and lesbians?

America is by definition unfinished, because it forever falls short of itself. Not that this nation is more moral than others, but its half-formed foundational ideal required a moral purpose at the start—and a moral purpose to the end. That is both creative and creatively undermining. Born in a challenge to authority, American authority continually inhibits its own exercise (what the Supreme Court did last week in challenging the executive and legislative branches over Guantanamo). Recognitions of personal alienation inevitably open into demands for the reform of alienating systems—and in America that is the work of politics. It never stops.

Contention is essential to such a social dynamic. Much as the polarized character of national life is bemoaned, the red state/blue state acrimony reveals the genius of what the founders began, for the structures of this public order evolve within a framework that continually transforms conflict into energy for change. The irony, of course, is that those who declare their loyalty to the brilliant cliché of an unchanging past are themselves at the service of the imperfect new. After all, to be an American traditionalist—and isn't this what we universally celebrate tomorrow?—is to affirm the revolution.

What's Your Opinion?

Do you think that America's founding principles are still the glue that holds Americans together and defines their aspirations? Or, as some suggest, are today's Americans bound together and driven largely by a shared culture of consumerism?

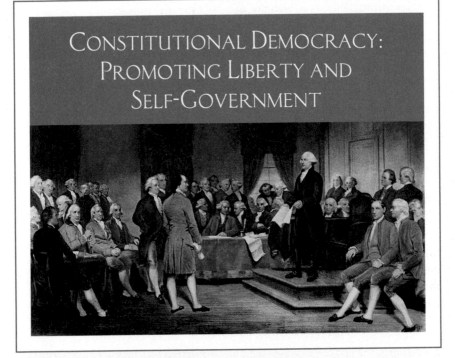

CHAPTER 2

CONSTITUTIONAL DEMOCRACY:
PROMOTING LIBERTY AND
SELF-GOVERNMENT

❝ The people must be governed by a majority, with whom all power resides. But how is the sense of this majority to be obtained? **❞**

FISHER AMES (1788)[1]

On the night of June 17, 1972, a security guard at the Watergate apartment–office complex in Washington, D.C., noticed that the latch on the door to the Democratic Party's national headquarters had been taped open. He called the police, who captured the five burglars inside. As it turned out, the men had links to Republican President Richard Nixon's Committee to Re-elect the President. Nixon called the incident "bizarre" and denied that anyone on his staff had a part in the break-in.

The reality was that the Watergate break-in was part of an orchestrated campaign of "dirty tricks" designed to ensure Nixon's reelection. The dirty-tricks campaign included wiretaps, tax audits, and burglaries of Nixon's political opponents (the "enemies list"), who included journalists and antiwar activists in addition to Democrats. Although the Nixon White House managed for a time to hide the truth, the facts of the dirty-tricks campaign gradually became known. During Senate investigative hearings, a White House assistant revealed that Nixon had tape-recorded all his telephone calls and personal conversations in the Oval Office. Nixon at first refused to release the tapes but then made public what he claimed were "all the relevant" ones. Congress demanded additional tapes, as did the special prosecutor who had been appointed to investigate criminal aspects of the Watergate affair. In late July, the U.S. Supreme Court, which included four justices appointed by Nixon, unanimously ordered the president to supply sixty-four additional tapes. The tapes were incriminating, and two weeks later, on August 9, 1974, Richard Nixon resigned from office, becoming the first president in U.S. history to do so.

Nixon's downfall was owed in no small measure to the handiwork two centuries earlier of the writers of the Constitution. They were well aware that power could never be entrusted to the goodwill of leaders. "If angels were to govern men," James Madison wrote in *Federalist* No. 51, "neither external nor internal controls on government would be necessary." Madison's point, of course, was that leaders are not angels and can harbor a lust for power—hence the Framers' insistence on constitutional checks on power, as when they gave Congress the authority to impeach and remove the president from office.

The writers of the Constitution were determined through their system of checks and balances to protect liberty from the threat of a too-powerful government. The Framers sought a **limited government:** one that is subject to strict limits on its lawful uses of power. They also had a second and partly conflicting objective. They wanted **self-government:** a government based on the people and subject to their control. Self-government requires that the majority through its representatives have the power to rule. However, limited government requires that majority rule stop at the point where it infringes on the legitimate rights and interests of the minority. This consideration led the Framers to forge a Constitution that provides for majority rule but has built-in restrictions on the majority's power.

This chapter describes how the principles of self-government and limited government are embodied in the Constitution and explains the tension between them. The chapter also indicates how these principles have been modified in practice in the course of American history. The main points of this chapter are these:

★ *America during the colonial period developed traditions of limited government and self-government.* These traditions were rooted in governing practices, philosophy, and cultural values.

★ *The Constitution provides for limited government mainly by defining lawful powers and by dividing those powers among competing institutions.* The Constitution, with its Bill of Rights, also prohibits government from

infringing on individual rights. Judicial review is an additional safeguard of limited government.

★ *The Constitution in its original form provided for self-government mainly through
indirect systems of popular election of representatives.* The Framers' theory of
self-government was based on the notion that political power must be separated from immediate popular influences if sound policies are to result.

★ *The idea of popular government—in which the majority's desires have a more
direct and immediate impact on governing officials—has gained strength since
the nation's beginning.* Originally, the House of Representatives was the
only institution subject to direct vote of the people. This mechanism
has been extended to other institutions and, through primary elections,
even to the nomination of candidates for public office.

BEFORE THE CONSTITUTION: THE COLONIAL AND REVOLUTIONARY EXPERIENCES

Early Americans' admiration for limited government was based partly on
their British heritage. Unlike other European governments of the time,
Britain did not have an absolute monarchy. Parliament was an independent
body with lawmaking powers, and British subjects had certain rights, including that of jury trial. This tradition carried over to the American colonies.
In each colony, there was a right to trial by jury. There was also freedom of
expression, although of a limited kind. Not all colonies, for example, granted
freedom to all religions. The colonies also had a degree of self-government.
Each had an elected representative assembly, which was subject to British
oversight but nonetheless had substantial legislative powers.

The colonists also had the example of Native American governments, particularly that of the Iroquois Confederacy. This confederacy was a union of
the Mohawk, Oneida, Onondaga, Cayuga, and Seneca tribes, governed by a
fifty-member council made up of representatives of the five tribes. To protect
each tribe's separate interests, the confederacy's constitution included a system of checks and balances—a feature that would become a hallmark of the
U.S. Constitution. Historians disagree over the extent of the influence of the
Iroquois Confederacy on colonial thought, but Benjamin Franklin and Thomas
Jefferson were among those who admired the confederacy's governing system.

"The Rights of Englishmen"

The Revolutionary War was partly a rebellion against Britain's failure to
respect its own tradition of limited government in the colonies. Many of the
colonial charters had conferred upon Americans "the rights of Englishmen,"

Historical
Background

but Britain showed progressively less respect for these rights over time. During the French and Indian War (1756–1763), the colonists fought alongside British soldiers to drive the French out of the western territories. At the end of the war, however, Britain for the first time imposed heavy taxes on the colonies. The war with France, which was also waged in Europe, had created a budget crisis in Britain. Taxing the colonies was a way to reduce the debt, so Parliament levied a stamp tax on colonial newspapers and business documents. The colonists were not represented in Parliament, and they responded angrily. "No taxation without representation" became the rallying cry.

Although Parliament backed down and repealed the Stamp Act, it then passed the Townshend Act, which imposed taxes on all glass, paper, tea, and lead. The colonists again objected, and Parliament again backed down, except for the tax on tea, which was kept to demonstrate that Britain was still in charge of colonial affairs. The tea tax sparked an act of defiance that became known as the "Boston Tea Party." In December 1773, under the cover of darkness, a small band of patriots disguised as Native Americans boarded an English ship in Boston Harbor and dumped its cargo of tea overboard.

In 1774, the colonists met in Philadelphia at the First Continental Congress to decide what they would demand from Britain. They asked for their own councils for the imposition of taxes, an end to the British military occupation, and a guarantee of trial by local juries. (British authorities had resorted to shipping "troublemakers" to London for trial.) King George III rejected their demands, and British troops and colonial minutemen clashed at Lexington and Concord on April 19, 1775. Eight colonists died on the Lexington green in what became known as "the shot heard 'round the world." The American Revolution had begun.

The Declaration of Independence

Although grievances against Britain were the immediate cause of the American Revolution, ideas about the proper form of government were also on the colonists' minds.[2] The century-old theory of John Locke was particularly influential. Locke held that people have **inalienable rights** (or **natural rights**)—including those of life, liberty, and property—and can rebel against a ruler who tramples on these rights (see Chapter 1).

Thomas Jefferson declared that Locke "was one of the three greatest men that ever lived, without exception," and Jefferson paraphrased Locke's ideas in passages of the Declaration of Independence, including

Drafting the Declaration of Independence, a painting by J. L. Ferris. Benjamin Franklin, John Adams (seated, center), and Thomas Jefferson (standing) drafted the historic document. Jefferson was the principal author; he inserted the inspirational words about liberty, equality, and self-government. Jealous of the attention that Jefferson received, Adams declared that there wasn't anything in Jefferson's words that others hadn't already said. Later, they became bitter political rivals, with Jefferson defeating Adams in the presidential election of 1800. Still later, they reconciled and corresponded frequently. They died on the same day, July 4, 1826, the fiftieth anniversary of the writing of the Declaration of Independence.

those asserting that "all men are created equal," that governments derive "their just powers from the consent of the governed," and that "it is the right of the people to alter or abolish" a tyrannical government. The Declaration was a call to revolution rather than a framework for a new form of government, but the ideas it contained—liberty, equality, individual rights, self-government, lawful powers—became the basis, eleven years later, for the Constitution of the United States. (The Declaration of Independence and the Constitution are reprinted in their entirety in the book's appendixes.)

The Articles of Confederation

The first government of the United States was based not on the Constitution but on the Articles of Confederation. The Articles, which were adopted during the Revolutionary War, created a very weak national government that was subordinate to the states. The colonies had always been governed separately, and their people considered themselves Virginians, New Yorkers, Pennsylvanians, and so on as much as they thought of themselves as Americans. Moreover, they were wary of a powerful central government. The American Revolution was sparked by grievances against the arbitrary policies of King George III, and Americans were in no mood to replace him with a strong national authority of their own making.

Historical Background

Under the Articles of Confederation, each state retained its "sovereignty, freedom and independence." There was a national Congress, but its members were appointed and paid by their respective state governments. Each of the thirteen states had one vote in Congress, and the agreement of nine states was required to pass legislation. Moreover, any state could block constitutional change: the Articles of Confederation could be amended only by unanimous approval of the states.

The American union held together out of necessity during the Revolutionary War. If the states had not stayed together, they would have had no choice but to surrender to the British. But once the war ended, the states felt free to go their separate ways. Several states sent representatives abroad to negotiate their own trade agreements with foreign nations. New Hampshire, with its eighteen-mile coastline, even established its own navy. In a melancholy letter to Thomas Jefferson, George Washington wondered whether the United States deserved to be called "a nation."

Congress was expected to provide for the nation's defense and establish the basis for a general economy, but the Articles of Confederation did not give it the powers necessary to achieve these goals. The Articles prohibited Congress from interfering in the states' commerce policies, and the states were soon engaged in ruinous trade wars. The Articles also denied to Congress the power to tax, and as a result, it had no money with which to build a navy or hire an army.

Shays's Rebellion: A Nation Dissolving

By 1784, the new nation was unraveling. Congress was so weak that its members often did not bother to attend its sessions.[3] Then, in late 1786, a revolt in western Massachusetts prompted leading Americans to seek a change in the country's form of government. A ragtag army of two thousand farmers armed with pitchforks marched on county courthouses to prevent foreclosures on their land. Many of the farmers were veterans of the Revolutionary War; their leader, Daniel Shays, had been a captain in the American army. They had been given assurances during the Revolution that their land, which sat unploughed because they were away at war, would not be confiscated for unpaid debts and taxes. They were also promised the back pay owed to them for their military service. (Congress had run out of money during the Revolution.) Instead, they received no back pay, and heavy new taxes were levied on their farms. Many farmers faced not only losing their property but being sent to prison for unpaid debts.

Shays's Rebellion frightened wealthy interests, who called on the governor of Massachusetts to put down the revolt. He in turn asked Congress for help, but it had no army to send. The governor finally raised enough money to hire a militia that put down the uprising, but Shays's Rebellion made it clear that Congress and the army were weak and that civil unrest was spreading. The crisis could not be ignored. Five states held an emergency meeting in Annapolis and sent a plea to Congress to authorize a constitutional convention of all the states in Philadelphia. Congress authorized the convention but placed a restriction on it: the delegates were to meet for "the sole and express purpose of revising the Articles of Confederation."

NEGOTIATING TOWARD A CONSTITUTION

The delegates to the Philadelphia constitutional convention ignored the instructions of Congress, instead drafting a plan for an entirely new form of government. Prominent delegates (among them George Washington, Benjamin Franklin, and James Madison) were determined from the outset to establish an American nation built on a strong central government.

The Great Compromise: A Two-Chamber Congress

Debate at the constitutional convention of 1787 began over a plan put forward by the Virginia delegation, which was dominated by strong nationalists. The **Virginia Plan** (also called the **large-state plan**) called for a two-chamber Congress that would have supreme authority in all areas "in which the separate states are incompetent," particularly defense and interstate trade. The Virginia Plan also provided that representation in both chambers would be based on size. Small states such as Delaware and Rhode Island would be allowed only one representative in the lower chamber, while large states such as Massachusetts and Virginia would have more than a dozen.

The Virginia Plan was sharply attacked by delegates from the smaller states. They rallied around a counterproposal made by New Jersey's William Paterson. The **New Jersey Plan** (also called the **small-state plan**) called for a stronger national government with the power to tax and to regulate commerce among the states; in most other respects, however, the Articles would remain in effect. Congress would have a single chamber in which each state, large or small, would have a single vote.

The debate over the two plans dragged on for weeks before the delegates reached what is now known as the **Great Compromise.** It provided for a bicameral (two-chamber) Congress. One chamber, the House of Representatives, would be apportioned among the states on the basis of population. The other chamber, the Senate, would be apportioned on the basis of an equal number of votes (two) for each state. This compromise was critical. The small states would not have agreed to join a union in which their vote was always weaker than that of large states, a fact reflected in Article V of the Constitution: "No state, without its consent, shall be deprived of its equal suffrage in the Senate."

The North-South Compromise: The Issue of Slavery

The separate interests of the states were also the basis for a second major agreement: the **North-South Compromise** on economic issues. The southern states feared that the states of the North, which were more numerous and had a larger population, would use their numerical majority in Congress to tax them unfairly. If Congress imposed high tariffs on manufactured goods imported from Europe in order to protect domestic manufacturers, the South would be disadvantaged, since U.S. manufacturing was largely based in the North. Then, if Congress also imposed high tariffs on agricultural exports, the South would again be disadvantaged because it was the prime source of agricultural exports, which, if taxed, would be more expensive and therefore of less interest to European buyers. The South's delegates were also concerned that northern representatives in Congress would tax or even bar the importation of slaves.

After extended debate, a compromise was reached. Congress would have the authority to tax imports but would be prohibited from taxing exports. Congress also would be prohibited until 1808 from passing laws to end the slave trade. However, the most controversial trade-off was the so-called Three-Fifths Compromise. For purposes of apportionment of taxes and seats in the U.S. House of Representatives, each slave was to count as less than a full person. Northern delegates had argued against the counting of slaves because they did not have legal rights. Southern delegates wanted to

The photo shows a Civil War–era building in Atlanta that was a site of slave auctions.

count them as full persons for purposes of apportioning House seats (which would have the effect of increasing the number of southern representatives) and to count them as nonpersons for purposes of apportioning taxes (which would have the effect of decreasing the amount of federal taxes levied on the southern states). The delegates finally settled on a compromise that included both taxation and apportionment but counted each slave as three-fifths of a person. Although the southern states did not get all that they wanted, they got the better end of the bargain. If slaves had not been counted at all, the southern states would have had only slightly more than 35 percent of House seats. With the compromise, they held nearly 45 percent of the seats, giving them considerable power over national policy.

These compromises have led critics to claim that the Framers of the Constitution had no objections to slavery. In fact, most of the delegates were deeply troubled by it, recognizing the stark inconsistency between the practice of slavery and a professed belief in liberty and equality. "It is inconsistent with the principles of the Revolution," Maryland's Luther Martin stated. George Mason, a Virginian and a slaveholder, said: "[Slaveholders] bring the judgment of heaven on a country."[4] Benjamin Franklin and Alexander Hamilton were among the delegates who were involved in antislavery organizations.

Yet the southern states' dependence on slavery was a reality that the delegates had to confront if there was to be a union of the states. The

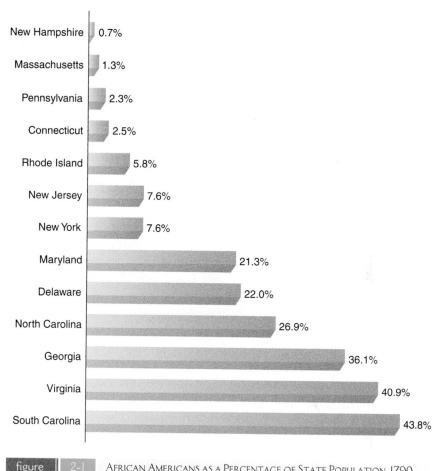

New Hampshire	0.7%
Massachusetts	1.3%
Pennsylvania	2.3%
Connecticut	2.5%
Rhode Island	5.8%
New Jersey	7.6%
New York	7.6%
Maryland	21.3%
Delaware	22.0%
North Carolina	26.9%
Georgia	36.1%
Virginia	40.9%
South Carolina	43.8%

figure 2-1 AFRICAN AMERICANS AS A PERCENTAGE OF STATE POPULATION, 1790

At the time of the writing of the Constitution, African Americans (most of whom were slaves) were concentrated in the southern states. *Source: U.S. Bureau of the Census.*

northern states had few slaves, whereas the southern economies were based on slavery (see Figure 2-1). John Rutledge of South Carolina asked during the convention debate whether the North regarded southerners as "fools." Southern delegates declared that they would form their own union rather than join one that banned slavery.

A Strategy for Ratification

The compromises over slavery and the structure of the Congress took up most of the four months that the convention was in session. Some of the other issues, such as the structure and powers of the federal judiciary, were the subject of surprisingly little debate.

There remained a final issue, however: would those Americans not attending the convention support the proposed Constitution? The delegates realized that ratification was not a sure thing. Congress had not authorized a wholesale restructuring of the federal government. In fact, in authorizing the Philadelphia convention, Congress had stated that any proposed change in the Articles of Confederation would have to be "agreed to in Congress" and then "confirmed by [all of] the states." The delegates recognized that if unanimous consent were required, the Constitution would have no chance of ratification. Rhode Island had refused even to send a delegation to the convention. In a bold move, the delegates established their own ratification process. They instructed Congress to submit the document directly to the states, where it would become law after having been approved by at least nine states in special ratifying conventions of popularly elected delegates. It was a masterful strategy. There was little hope that all thirteen state legislatures would approve the Constitution, but nine states through conventions might be persuaded to ratify it. Indeed, North Carolina and Rhode Island were steadfastly opposed to the new union and did not ratify the Constitution until the other eleven states had ratified it and begun the process of establishing the new government.

The Ratification Debate

The debate over ratification was contentious. The **Anti-Federalists** (as opponents of the Constitution were labeled) raised arguments that still echo in American politics. They claimed that the national government would be too powerful and would threaten self-government in the separate states and the liberty of the people. Many Americans had an innate distrust of centralized power and worried that the people's liberty could be eclipsed as easily by a distant American government as it had been by the British king. The fact that the Constitution contained no bill of rights heightened this concern. Did its absence indicate that the central government would be free to define for itself what the people's rights would be?

The presidency was another source of contention. No such office had existed under the Articles of Confederation, and some worried that it would lead to the creation of an American monarchy. The fact that the president would be chosen by electors appointed by the states (the Electoral College) lessened but did not eliminate this concern.

Even the motives of the men who wrote the Constitution came under attack. They were men of wealth and education who had acted in response to debtors' riots. Would the Constitution become a tool by which the wealthy ruled over those with little or no money? And who would bear the burden of additional taxation? For Americans struggling with local and state tax payments, the thought of paying national taxes as well was not appealing.

Most Anti-Federalists acknowledged a need to strengthen national commerce and defense. What they opposed was the creation of a powerful national government as the mechanism. They favored a revision of the Articles of Confederation, which in their opinion could accomplish these goals without the risk of establishing a government that could threaten their liberties, their livelihoods, and their local interests. (The Anti-Federalist argument is discussed further in Chapter 3.)

The **Federalists** (as the Constitution's supporters called themselves) responded with a persuasive case of their own. Their strongest arguments were set forth by James Madison and Alexander Hamilton, who along with John Jay wrote a series of essays that were published in a New York City newspaper under the pen name Publius. (The essays, collectively referred to as *The Federalist Papers*, are widely acknowledged as a brilliant political treatise.) Madison and Hamilton argued that the government of the Constitution would correct the defects of the Articles; it would have the power necessary to forge a secure and prosperous union. At the same time, because of restrictions on its powers, the new government would endanger neither the states nor personal liberty. In *Federalist* Nos. 47, 48, 49, 50, and 51, for example, Madison explained how the separation of national institutions was designed both to empower and to restrict the federal government. (The Federalist argument is discussed further in Chapter 3.)

Whether the ratification debate changed many minds is unclear. Historical evidence suggests, however, that a majority of ordinary Americans opposed the Constitution's ratification. But their voice in the state ratifying conventions was smaller than that of wealthier interests, which in the main supported the change. The pro-ratification forces were also bolstered by the assumption that George Washington, the country's most trusted and popular leader, would become the first president. In the view of historians, this assumption, and the fact that Washington had presided over the Philadelphia convention, tipped the balance in favor of ratification.

Delaware was the first state to ratify the Constitution, and Connecticut, Georgia, and New Jersey followed, an indication that the Great Compromise had satisfied several of the small states. In the early summer of 1788, New Hampshire became the ninth state to ratify. The Constitution was law. But neither Virginia nor New York had ratified it, and a stable union without these major states was almost unthinkable. As large in area as many European countries, they conceivably could have survived as independent nations. In fact, they nearly did choose a separate course. In both states, the Constitution barely passed, and then only after the Federalists promised to support a bill of rights designed to protect individual liberty from the power of the central government.

The Framers' Goals

The Englishman James Bryce ranked America's Constitution as its greatest contribution to the practice of government. The Constitution offered the world a new model of government in which a written document defining the government's lawful powers would represent a higher authority than the actions of any political leader or institution.

A **constitution** is the fundamental law that defines how a government will legitimately operate—the method for choosing its leaders, the institutions through which these leaders will work, the procedures they must follow in making policy, and the powers they can lawfully exercise. The U.S. Constitution is exactly such a law; it is the highest law of the land. Its provisions define how power is to be acquired and how it can be used.

The Constitution embodied the Framers' vision of a proper government for the American people (see Table 2-1). One of the Framers' goals was the creation of a national government strong enough to meet the nation's needs, particularly in the areas of defense and commerce. Another goal was to preserve the states as governing entities. Accordingly, the Framers established a system of government (federalism) in which power is divided between the national government and the states. Federalism is discussed at length in Chapter 3, which also explains how the Constitution laid the foundation for a strong national government.

The Framers' other goals were to establish a national government that was restricted in its lawful uses of power (limited government) and that gave the people a voice in their governance (self-government). These two goals and the story of how they were written into the Constitution are the focus of the rest of this chapter.

table 2-1 MAJOR GOALS OF THE FRAMERS OF THE CONSTITUTION

1. To establish a government strong enough to meet the nation's needs—an objective sought through substantial grants of power to the federal government in areas such as defense and commerce (see Chapter 3)
2. To establish a government that would not threaten the existence of the separate states—an objective sought through federalism (see Chapter 3) and through a Congress connected to the states through elections
3. To establish a government that would not threaten liberty—an objective sought through an elaborate system of checks and balances
4. To establish a government based on popular consent—an objective sought through provisions for the direct and indirect election of public officials

PROTECTING LIBERTY: LIMITED GOVERNMENT

A challenge facing the Framers of the Constitution was how to control the coercive force of government. Government's unique characteristic is that it alone can legally arrest, imprison, and even kill people who break its rules. Force is not the only basis of effective government, but government must be able to use force to prevent lawless elements from brutalizing innocent people. The dilemma is that government itself can use its force to abuse its opponents. "It is a melancholy reflection," James Madison wrote to Thomas Jefferson shortly after the Constitution's ratification, "that liberty should be equally exposed to danger whether the government has too much or too little power."[5]

The men who wrote the Constitution sought to establish a government strong enough to enforce national interests, including defense and commerce among the states (see Chapter 3), but not so strong as to destroy liberty. Limited government is built into the Constitution through both grants of political power and restrictions on that power (see Table 2-2).

Grants and Denials of Power

The Framers chose to limit the national government in part by confining its scope to constitutional **grants of power.** Congress's lawmaking powers are specifically listed in Article I, Section 8 of the Constitution. Seventeen in number, these listed powers include, for example, the powers to tax, to establish an army and navy, to declare war, to regulate commerce among the states, to create a national currency, and to borrow money. Powers *not* granted to the government by the Constitution are in theory denied to it. In a period when other governments had unrestricted powers, this limitation was remarkable.

The Framers also used **denials of power** as a means to limit government, prohibiting certain practices that European rulers had routinely used to intimidate political opponents. The French king, for example, could imprison a subject indefinitely without charge. The U.S. Constitution prohibits such action: citizens have the right to be brought before a court under a writ of habeas corpus for a judgment as to the legality of their confinement. The Constitution also forbids Congress and the states from passing ex post facto laws, under which citizens can be prosecuted for acts that were legal at the time they were committed.

As a further denial of power, the Framers made the Constitution difficult to amend, thereby making it hard for those in power to increase their lawful authority by changing the Constitution. An amendment could be proposed

| table | 2-2 | CONSTITUTIONAL PROVISIONS FOR LIMITED GOVERNMENT |

The U.S. Constitution creates an elaborate governing structure designed to protect against the abusive exercise of power—in short, to create a limited government.

Mechanism	Purpose
Grants of power	Powers granted to the national government; accordingly, powers not granted it are denied it unless they are necessary and proper to the carrying out of the granted powers.
Separated institutions	The division of the national government's power among three power-sharing branches, each of which is to act as a check on the powers of the other two.
Federalism	The division of political authority between national government and the states, enabling the people to appeal to one authority if their rights and interests are not respected by the other authority.
Denials of power	Powers expressly denied to the national and state governments by the Constitution.
Bill of Rights	The first ten amendments to the Constitution, which specify rights of citizens that the national government must respect.
Judicial review	The power of the courts to declare governmental action null and void when it is found to violate the Constitution.
Elections	The power of the voters to remove officials from office.

only by a two-thirds majority in both chambers of Congress or by a national constitutional convention called by two-thirds of the state legislatures. Such a proposal would then become law only if ratified by three-fourths of state legislatures or state conventions. In all but one case (the Twenty-first Amendment), state legislatures have done the ratifying. The national constitutional convention as a means of proposing amendments has never been used.

Using Power to Offset Power

Although the Framers believed that grants and denials of power could act as controls on government, they had no illusion that written words alone would suffice. As a consequence, they sought to control government by dividing its powers among separate institutions.[6]

The idea of a **separation of powers** had been proposed decades earlier by the French theorist Montesquieu. His reasoning was widely accepted in America, and when the states drafted new constitutions after the start of the Revolutionary War, they built their governments around this concept. Pennsylvania was an exception, and its experience only seemed to prove the necessity of separated powers. Unrestrained by an independent judiciary or executive, Pennsylvania's all-powerful legislature ignored basic rights and freedoms: Quakers were disenfranchised for their religious beliefs, conscientious objectors to the Revolutionary War were prosecuted, and the right of trial by jury was eliminated.

In *Federalist* No. 10, Madison asked why governments often act according to the interests of overbearing majorities rather than according to principles of justice. He attributed the problem to "the mischiefs of faction." People, he argued, are divided into opposing religious, geographical, ethnic, economic, and other factions. These divisions are natural and desirable in that free people have a right to their personal opinions and interests. Yet factions can themselves be a source of oppressive government. If a faction gains full power, it will use government to advance itself at the expense of all others. (*Federalist* No. 10 is widely regarded as the finest political essay ever written by an American. It is reprinted as the reading at the end of this chapter.)

Out of this concern came the Framers' special contribution to the doctrine of the separation of powers. They did not believe that it would be enough, as Montesquieu had suggested, to divide the government's authority strictly along institutional lines, granting all legislative power to the legislature, all judicial power to the courts, and all executive power to the presidency. This total separation would make it too easy for a single faction to exploit a particular area of political power. A faction that controlled the legislature, for example, could enact laws ruinous to other interests. A better system of divided government would be one in which political power could be applied forcibly only when institutions agreed on its use. This system would require separate but overlapping powers. Because no one faction could easily gain control over all institutions, factions would have to work together, a process that would require each of them to respect the interests of the others.[7]

Separated Institutions Sharing Power: Checks and Balances

The Framers' concept of divided powers has been described by political scientist Richard Neustadt as the principle of **separated institutions sharing power.**[8] The separate branches are interlocked in such a way that an elaborate system of **checks and balances** is created (see Figure 2-2). No institution can act decisively without the support or acquiescence of the other institutions. Legislative, executive, and judicial powers in the

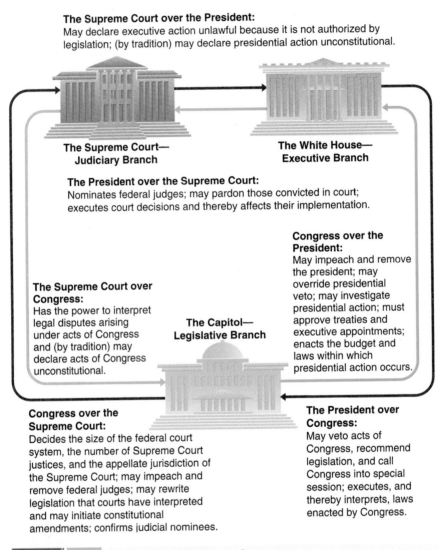

The Supreme Court over the President:
May declare executive action unlawful because it is not authorized by legislation; (by tradition) may declare presidential action unconstitutional.

The Supreme Court—
Judiciary Branch

The White House—
Executive Branch

The President over the Supreme Court:
Nominates federal judges; may pardon those convicted in court; executes court decisions and thereby affects their implementation.

Congress over the President:
May impeach and remove the president; may override presidential veto; may investigate presidential action; must approve treaties and executive appointments; enacts the budget and laws within which presidential action occurs.

The Supreme Court over Congress:
Has the power to interpret legal disputes arising under acts of Congress and (by tradition) may declare acts of Congress unconstitutional.

The Capitol—
Legislative Branch

Congress over the Supreme Court:
Decides the size of the federal court system, the number of Supreme Court justices, and the appellate jurisdiction of the Supreme Court; may impeach and remove federal judges; may rewrite legislation that courts have interpreted and may initiate constitutional amendments; confirms judicial nominees.

The President over Congress:
May veto acts of Congress, recommend legislation, and call Congress into special session; executes, and thereby interprets, laws enacted by Congress.

figure   2-2   THE SYSTEM OF CHECKS AND BALANCES

This elaborate system of divided spheres of authority was provided by the U.S. Constitution as a means of controlling the power of government. The separation of powers among the branches of the national government, federalism, and the different methods of selecting national officers are all part of this system.

American system are divided in such a way that they overlap: each of the three branches of government checks the others' powers and balances those powers with powers of its own.

As natural as this system now might seem to Americans, most democracies are of the parliamentary type, with executive and legislative power combined in a single institution rather than vested in separate ones. In a parliamentary system, the majority in the legislature selects the prime minister, who then serves as both the legislative leader and the chief executive (see "How the United States Compares").

Shared Legislative Powers   Under the Constitution, Congress has legislative authority, but that power is partly shared with the other branches and thus checked by them. The president can veto acts of Congress, recommend legislation, and call special sessions of Congress. The president also has the power to execute—and thereby interpret—the laws Congress makes.

The Supreme Court has the power to interpret acts of Congress that are disputed in legal cases. The Court also has the power of judicial review: it can declare laws of Congress void when it finds that they are not in accord with the Constitution.

Within Congress, there is a further check on legislative power: for legislation to be passed, a majority in each chamber of Congress is required. Thus, the Senate and the House of Representatives can block each other from acting.

Shared Executive Powers   Executive power is vested in the president but is constrained by legislative and judicial checks. The president's power to make treaties and appoint high-ranking officials, for example, is subject to Senate approval. Congress also has the power to impeach and remove the president from office. In practical terms, Congress's greatest checks on executive action are its lawmaking and appropriations powers. The executive branch cannot act without laws that authorize its activities or without the money that pays for these activities.

The judiciary's major check on the presidency is its power to declare an action unlawful because it is not authorized by the legislation that the executive claims to be implementing.

Shared Judicial Powers   Judicial power rests with the Supreme Court and with lower federal courts, which are subject to checks by the other branches of the federal government. Congress is empowered to establish the size of the federal court system, to restrict the Supreme Court's appellate jurisdiction in some circumstances, and to impeach and remove federal judges from office. More importantly, Congress can rewrite legislation that the courts have misinterpreted and can initiate amendments when it disagrees with the courts' rulings on constitutional issues.

The president has the power to appoint federal judges with the consent of the Senate and to pardon persons convicted in the courts. The president also is responsible for executing court decisions, a function that provides opportunities to influence the way rulings are carried out.

⊕ HOW THE UNITED STATES COMPARES

Checks and Balances

All democracies place constitutional limits on the power of government. The concept of rule by law, for example, is characteristic of democratic governments but not of authoritarian regimes. Democracies differ, however, in the extent to which political power is restrained through constitutional mechanisms. The United States is an extreme case in that its government rests on an elaborate system of constitutional checks and balances. The system employs a separation of powers among the executive, legislative, and judicial branches. It also includes judicial review, the power of the courts to invalidate actions of the legislative or executive branch. These constitutional restrictions on power are not part of the governing structure of all democracies.

Most democracies have parliamentary systems, which invest both executive and legislative leadership in the office of prime minister. Britain is an example of this type of system. Parliament under the leadership of the prime minister is the supreme authority in Britain. Its laws are not subject to override by Britain's high court, which has no power to review the constitutionality of parliamentary acts.

In parliamentary systems, moreover, either there is only one legislative chamber or, if there are two, power resides primarily in one chamber. The British House of Lords, for example, has only a limited ability to check the actions of the British House of Commons, which the prime minister heads. In the United States, the two legislative chambers—the House and the Senate—are coequal bodies. Because legislation can be enacted only with the approval of both houses, each serves as a check on the other.

Country	Separation of Executive & Legislative Powers?	Judicial Review?
Belgium	No	Yes
Canada	No	Yes
France	Yes	No
Germany	No	Yes
Great Britain	No	No
Italy	No	Yes
Japan	No	Yes
Mexico	Yes	Yes
United States	Yes	Yes

The Bill of Rights

Although the delegates to the Philadelphia convention discussed the possibility of placing a list of individual rights (such as freedom of speech and the right to a fair trial) in the Constitution, they ultimately decided that such a list was unnecessary because of the doctrine of expressed powers: government could not lawfully engage in actions, such as the suppression of speech, that were not authorized by the Constitution. Moreover, the delegates argued that a bill of rights was undesirable because government might feel free to disregard any right that was inadvertently left off the list or that might emerge in the future.

These arguments did not persuade leading Americans who believed that no possible safeguard of liberty should be omitted. "A bill of rights," Jefferson argued, "is what the people are entitled to against every government on earth, general or particular, and what no just government should refuse or rest on inference." Jefferson had included a bill of rights in the constitution he wrote for Virginia at the outbreak of the Revolutionary War, and all but four states had followed Virginia's example.

Ultimately, the demand for a bill of rights led to its addition to the Constitution. Madison himself introduced a series of amendments during the First Congress, ten of which were soon ratified by the states. These amendments, traditionally called the **Bill of Rights,** include rights such as freedom of speech and religion and due process protections (such as jury trial and legal counsel) for persons accused of crimes. (These rights, termed *civil liberties*, are discussed in Chapter 4.)

The Bill of Rights is a precise expression of the concept of limited government. In consenting to be governed, the people agree to accept the authority of government in certain areas but not in others; the people's constitutional rights cannot lawfully be denied by government officials.

Judicial Review

The writers of the Constitution both empowered and limited government. But who was to decide whether officials were operating within the limits of their constitutionally authorized powers? The Framers did not specifically entrust this power to a particular branch of government, although they did grant the Supreme Court the authority to decide on "all cases arising under

Historical
Background

this Constitution." Moreover, at the ratifying conventions of at least eight of the thirteen states, it was claimed that the judiciary would have the power to nullify actions that violated the Constitution.[9]

Nevertheless, because the Constitution did not explicitly grant the judiciary this authority, the principle had to be established in practice. The opportunity arose with an incident that occurred after the election of 1800, in which John Adams lost his bid for a second presidential term after a bitter campaign against Jefferson. Between November 1800, when Jefferson was elected, and March 1801, when he was inaugurated, the Federalist-controlled Congress created fifty-nine additional lower-court judgeships, enabling Adams to appoint loyal Federalists to those positions before he left office. However, Adams's term expired before his secretary of state could deliver the judicial commissions to all the appointees. Without this authorization, an appointee could not take office. Knowing this, Jefferson told his secretary of state, James Madison, not to deliver the commissions. William Marbury was one of those who did not receive his commission, and he asked the Supreme Court to issue a writ of mandamus (a court order directing an official to perform a specific act) that would force Madison to deliver it.

Marbury v. Madison (1803) became the foundation for judicial review by the federal courts. Chief Justice John Marshall wrote the *Marbury* opinion, which declared that Marbury had a legal right to his commission. The opinion also said, however, that the Supreme Court could not issue him a writ of mandamus because it lacked the constitutional authority to do so. Congress had passed legislation in 1789 that gave the Court this power, but Marshall noted that the Constitution prohibits Congress from expanding the Supreme Court's authority except through a constitutional amendment. That being the case, Marshall argued, the legislation that provided the authorization was constitutionally invalid.[10] In striking down this act of Congress on constitutional grounds, the Court asserted its power of **judicial review**—that is, the power of the judiciary to decide whether a government official or institution has acted within the limits of the Constitution and, if not, to declare its action null and void.

Marshall's decision was ingenious because it asserted the power of judicial review without creating the possibility of its rejection by either the executive or the legislative branch. In declaring that Marbury had a right to his commission, the Court in effect said that President Jefferson had failed in his constitutional duty to execute the laws faithfully. However, because it did not order Jefferson to deliver the commission, he was deprived of the opportunity to disregard the Court's ruling. At the same time, the Court reprimanded Congress for passing legislation that exceeded its constitutional authority. But Congress also had no way to retaliate. It could not force the Court to accept the power to issue writs of mandamus if the Court itself refused to do so.

★ LEADERS

Alexander Hamilton
(1757–1804)

Born an illegitimate child, Alexander Hamilton left his native West Indies in his teens for New York. A brilliant student and essayist, Hamilton joined the Revolutionary Army, distinguishing himself in early fighting around New York, and became aide to General George Washington—the beginning of a relationship that would serve both men well. After the war, Hamilton pursued a career in law and politics and went to the 1787 Philadelphia convention as a New York delegate. A firm believer in a strong national government, Hamilton contributed to the Constitution's ratification through his *Federalist Papers* essays. Appointed the nation's first secretary of the treasury by President Washington, he fought with Secretary of State Thomas Jefferson over the direction of national policy. In a brilliant political move, Hamilton agreed to locate the nation's capital at the tip of Virginia in exchange for Jefferson's support of the consolidation of state debts at the federal level. This financial system, along with the creation of the First Bank of the United States, enabled Hamilton to establish a national fiscal policy. Creditors at home and abroad henceforth would place their trust in the federal government. His dispute with Jefferson led to the creation of America's first political parties—the Republicans, founded by Jefferson, and the Federalists, founded by Hamilton. When John Adams replaced Washington as president, Hamilton stayed on as secretary of the treasury, a situation that became uncomfortable when several members of Adams's cabinet showed more loyalty to Hamilton than to Adams. In 1804, Hamilton was fatally wounded in a pistol duel with Aaron Burr, a political and personal foe.

PROVIDING FOR SELF-GOVERNMENT

"We the People" is the opening phrase of the Constitution. It expresses the idea that in the United States the people will have the power to govern themselves. In a sense, there is no contradiction between this idea and the Constitution's provisions for limited government, because individual *liberty* is an essential element of *self-government*. If people cannot express themselves freely, they cannot be self-governing. In another sense, however, the contradiction is clear: restrictions on the power of the majority are a denial of its right to govern society as it sees fit.

The Framers believed that the people deserved and required a voice in their government, but they worried that the people would become inflamed by a passionate issue or fiery demagogue and act rashly. To the Framers, the great risk of popular government was **tyranny of the majority:** the people acting as an irrational mob that tramples on the rights of the minority. Their fear was not without foundation. The history of democracies was filled with examples of majority tyranny, and there were even examples from the nation's brief history. In 1786, for instance, debtors had gained control of Rhode Island's legislature and made paper money a legal means of paying debts, even though existing contracts called for payment in gold. Creditors were then hunted down and held captive in public places so that debtors could come and pay them in full with worthless paper money. A Boston newspaper wrote that Rhode Island should be renamed Rogue Island.

Democracy Versus Republic

No form of self-government could eliminate completely the threat to liberty of majority tyranny, but the Framers believed that the danger would be greatly diminished by creating a republican government as opposed

Rhode Island was nicknamed "Rogue Island" for its disregard of property rights. Shown here is the Rhode Island three-dollar bank note, which came to be worth no more than the paper on which it was written and yet was used to pay off gold debts.

to a democratic government.[11] Today, the terms **democracy**, **republic**, and **representative government** are often used interchangeably to refer to a system of government in which political power rests with the people through their ability to choose representatives in free and fair elections. To the writers of the Constitution, however, a democracy and a republic were different forms of government.

By the term *democracy*, the Framers meant a government in which the power of the majority is unlimited, whether exercised directly (as in the case of town meetings open to all citizens) or through a representative body. The majority's rule is absolute. Should it decide to act tyrannically—to run roughshod over the minority—there is nothing in the law to stop it. By the term *republic*, the Framers meant a government that is based on majority rule but that protects the minority through a guarantee of individual rights and other checks on majority power. The purpose of republican government is to limit the power of the majority, not as a means of preventing the people from governing themselves but as a means of safeguarding minority rights and interests. The majority rules, but it does so within prescribed limits.[12]

The Framers believed that a republican government is superior to a democratic one. They also believed that a republic, to work well in practice, requires virtuous representatives—lawmakers who have an enlightened sense of the public interest. In this respect, their outlook was similar to that of the English theorist Edmund Burke (1729–97). In his *Letter to the Sheriffs of Bristol*, Burke argued that representatives should act as the public's **trustees;** representatives are obliged to serve the interest of those who elect them, but the nature of this interest is for the representatives, not the voters, to decide. Burke was concerned with the ease with which a majority can think like a mob, and he claimed that representatives should not surrender their judgment to irrational majorities.

Limited Popular Rule

The Constitution provided that all power would be exercised through representative institutions. There was no provision for any form of direct popular participation in the making of policy decisions. In view of the fact that the United States was much too large to be governed directly by the people in popular assemblies, a representative system was necessary. The Framers went beyond what was necessary, however, and placed officials at a considerable distance from the people they represented (see Table 2-3).

The House of Representatives was the only institution that would be based on direct popular election—its members would be elected to serve for two years by a vote of the people. Frequent and direct election of House

| table | 2-3 | METHODS OF CHOOSING NATIONAL LEADERS |

Fearing the concentration of political power, the Framers devised alternative methods of selection and terms of service for national officials.

Office	Method of Selection	Term of Service
President	Electoral College	4 years
U.S. senator	State legislature	6 years (one-third of senators' terms expire every 2 years)
U.S. representative	Popular election	2 years
Federal judge	Nominated by president, approved by Senate	Indefinite (subject to "good behavior")

members was intended to make government sensitive to the concerns of popular majorities.

U.S. senators would be appointed by the legislatures of the states they represented. Because state legislators were popularly elected, the people would be choosing their senators indirectly. Every two years, a third of the senators would be appointed to six-year terms. The Senate was expected to check and balance the House. The Senate, by virtue of the less frequent and indirect election of its members, presumably would be less responsive to popular whim.

Presidential selection was an issue of considerable debate at the Philadelphia convention. Direct election of the president was twice proposed and twice rejected because it would link executive power directly to popular majorities. The Framers finally chose to have the president selected by the votes of electors (the so-called **Electoral College**). Each state would have the same number of **electoral votes** as it had members in Congress and could select its electors by a method of its choosing. The president would serve four years and be eligible for reelection.

The Framers decided that federal judges and justices would be appointed rather than elected. They would be nominated by the president and confirmed through approval by the Senate. Once confirmed, they would "hold their offices during good behavior." In effect, they would be allowed to hold office for life unless they committed a crime. The judiciary was an unelected institution that would uphold the rule of law and serve as a check on the elected branches of government.[13]

These differing methods of selecting national officeholders would not prevent a determined majority from achieving unchecked power, but control could not be attained quickly. Unlike the House of Representatives, institutions such as the Senate, presidency, and judiciary would not yield to an impassioned majority in a single election. The delay would reduce the likelihood that government would degenerate into mob rule driven by momentary passions.

Altering the Constitution: More Power to the People

The Framers' conception of self-government was at odds with what the average American in 1787 had come to expect. Every state but South Carolina held annual legislative elections, and several states also chose their governors through direct annual election. Not long after ratification of the Constitution, Americans began to challenge the Constitution's restrictions on majority rule (see Table 2-4).

Jeffersonian Democracy: A Revolution of the Spirit   Thomas Jefferson, who otherwise admired the Constitution, was among the prominent Americans who questioned its provisions for self-government—and it was Jefferson who may have spared the nation a bloody civil conflict over the issue of popular sovereignty. Under John Adams, the second president, the national government increasingly favored the nation's wealthy interests. Adams publicly indicated that the Constitution was designed for a governing

table 2-4 MEASURES TAKEN TO MAKE GOVERNMENT MORE RESPONSIVE TO POPULAR MAJORITIES

The U.S. Constitution created barriers designed to limit direct popular influence on government. Subsequent changes were designed to lower these barriers and increase the power of voting majorities.

Earlier Situation	Subsequent Development
Separation of powers, as a means of dividing authority and blunting passionate majorities	Political parties, as a means of uniting authorities and linking them with popular majorities
Indirect election of all national officials except House members, as a means of buffering officials from popular influence	Direct election of U.S. senators and popular voting for president (linked to electoral votes), as a means of increasing popular control of officials
Nomination of candidates for public office through political party organizations	Primary elections, as a direct means of selecting party nominees

Historical
Background

elite and hinted that he might use force to suppress dissent.[14] Jefferson asked whether Adams, with the aid of a strong army, intended to deprive ordinary people of their rights. Jefferson challenged Adams in the next presidential election and, upon defeating him, hailed his victory as the "Revolution of 1800."

Although Jefferson was a champion of the common people, he had no clear vision of how a popular government might work in practice. He saw Congress, not the presidency, as the institution better suited to representing majority opinion.[15] He also had no illusions about a largely uneducated population's ability to play a substantial governing role and feared the consequences of inciting the masses to rise against the rich. Jeffersonian democracy was mostly a revolution of the spirit. Jefferson taught Americans to look on national government institutions as belonging to all, not just to the privileged few.[16]

Jacksonian Democracy: Linking the People and the Presidency   Not until the election of Andrew Jackson in 1828 did the nation have a powerful president who was willing and able to involve the public more fully in government. Jackson carried out the constitutional revolution that Jeffersonian democracy had foreshadowed.

Jackson recognized that the president was the only official who could legitimately claim to represent the people as a whole. Unlike the president, members of Congress were elected from separate states and districts rather than from the entire country. Yet the president's claim to popular leadership was weakened by the fact that the president was chosen by electors rather than by the voters. Jackson's ingenious solution was to have each state give its electoral votes to whichever candidate got the most popular votes in the state. This arrangement, still in effect, places the selection of the president in the voters' hands in most elections. The candidate who gets the most popular votes nationally is also likely to finish first in enough states to win a majority of the electoral votes. Since Jackson's time, only three candidates— Rutherford B. Hayes in 1876, Benjamin Harrison in 1888, and George W. Bush in 2000—have won the presidency after losing the popular vote. (The Electoral College is discussed further in Chapter 12.)

The Progressives: Senate and Primary Elections   The Progressive Era of the early 1900s brought another wave of democratic reforms. The Progressives rejected the Burkean idea of representatives as trustees, instead embracing the idea of representatives as **delegates**—officeholders who are obligated to respond directly to the expressed opinions of the people they represent.

The Progressives sought to place power more directly in the hands of the people.[17] They succeeded in changing the way some state and local governments operate. Progressive reforms at state and local levels included the initiative and the referendum, which enable citizens to vote directly on legislative issues (see "States in the Nation"). Another Progressive reform was the recall election, which enables citizens through petition to force an officeholder to submit to reelection before the regular expiration of his or her term. (In 2003, a recall election in California resulted in the election of actor Arnold Schwarzenegger as the state's new governor.)

The Progressives also instigated two changes in federal elections. One was the direct election of U.S. senators, who before the Seventeenth Amendment was ratified in 1913 had been chosen by state legislatures and were widely perceived as agents of big business (the Senate was nicknamed the "Millionaires' Club"). Senators who stood to lose their seats in a direct popular vote had blocked earlier attempts to change the Constitution. However, the Senate was persuaded to support an amendment following pressure from the Progressives and revelations that corporate bribes had influenced the selection of several senators. The second change was the **primary election,** which gives rank-and-file voters the power to select party nominees. In the early 1900s, nearly all states adopted the primary election as a means of choosing nominees for at least some federal and state offices. Prior to this change, nominees were selected by party leaders.

The Progressive Era spawned attacks on the Framers. A prominent criticism was laid out in historian Charles S. Beard's *An Economic Interpretation of the Constitution.*[18] Arguing that the Constitution grew out of wealthy Americans' fears of the debtor rebellions, and noting that many of the Framers were themselves wealthy men, Beard claimed that the Constitution's elaborate systems of power and representation were devices for keeping power in the hands of the rich. Beard's thesis was challenged by other historians, and he later acknowledged that he had not taken the Framers' full array of motives into account. Their conception of separation of powers, for example, was a governing principle that had earlier been incorporated into state constitutions. Although the Framers did not have great trust in popular rule, to conclude that they were foes of democracy would be inaccurate. They were intent on balancing the demand for self-government with the requirement for limited government, believing that unchecked majority rule would lead to oppressive government.

Since the Progressive Era, no major structural changes have taken place in the process by which Americans elect their leaders. Nevertheless, the question of how best to achieve self-government in practice continues to engage Americans. During the 1960s, for example, public demands led to fairer voter registration laws, including the elimination of literacy tests and poll taxes, which

★ | STATES IN THE NATION

Direct Democracy: The Initiative and Popular Referendum

In some states, by gathering enough signatures on a petition, citizens can directly enact or defeat legislation through their votes in an election. This action can occur through either an *initiative* (where citizens place a legislative proposal of their own choosing on the ballot) or a *popular referendum* (where citizens place an act of the state legislature on the ballot, which the voters can then accept or reject). A popular referendum is different from a *legislative referendum,* where the state legislature itself places a proposal on the ballot for the voters to accept or reject. All states have a form of the legislative referendum, but only some states, as indicated in the map below, have the initiative and the popular referendum.

Q: Why are southern and northeastern states less likely to have the initiative and popular referendum than states in other areas?

A: The initiative and popular referendum were introduced in the early 1900s by the Progressives, who sought to weaken the power of political bosses and give voters a larger voice in their governance. In the Northeast, party machines had enough strength in state legislatures to block their enactment. In the South, these devices were blocked by the white establishment, which feared that blacks and poor whites would make use of them.

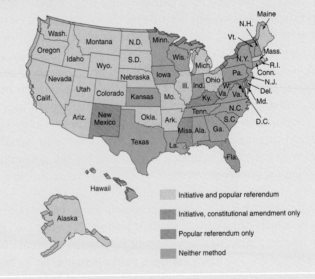

Initiative and popular referendum

Initiative, constitutional amendment only

Popular referendum only

Neither method

Source: Initiative and Referendum Institute at the University of Southern California.

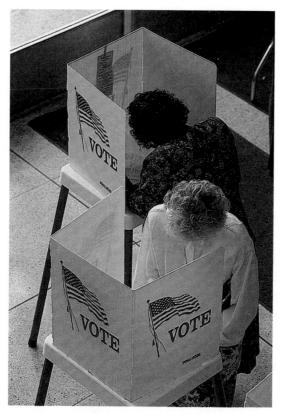

The Constitution originally provided for direct popular election only in the case of the House of Representatives. Not until the 1830s was popular voting for the office of president pervasive, even though then, as today, the choice of a president rested with electors. In 1914, for the first time in all states holding congressional elections, U.S. senators were chosen by popular vote. At roughly the same time, primary elections were widely adopted as a means of nominating candidates for public office. Today, the United States holds elections more often and for more offices than virtually any other nation—a development that is contrary to what the writers of the Constitution believed was proper.

were devices designed to keep minorities and poor people from voting. More recent efforts include campaign finance laws that place limits on how much wealthy donors can contribute to individual candidates for public office.

CONSTITUTIONAL DEMOCRACY TODAY

The type of government created in the United States in 1787 is today called a **constitutional democracy.** It is *democratic* in its provisions for majority influence through elections and *constitutional* in its requirement that power gained through elections be exercised in accordance with law and with due respect for individual rights.

By some standards, the American system of today is a model of *self-government*.[19] The United States schedules the election of its larger legislative chamber (the House of Representatives) and its chief executive more frequently than does any other democracy. In addition, it is the only major democracy to rely extensively on primary elections rather than party organizations for the selection of party nominees. The principle of popular election to office, which the writers of the Constitution regarded as a prerequisite of popular sovereignty but a method to be used sparingly, has been extended further in the United States than anywhere else.

By other standards, however, the U.S. system is less democratic than some. Popular majorities must work against the barriers to influence devised by the Framers—divided powers, staggered terms of office, and separate constituencies. In fact, the link between an electoral majority and a governing majority is less direct in the American system than in nearly all other democratic systems. In the European parliamentary democracies, for example, legislative and executive power is not divided, is not subject to close check by the judiciary, and is acquired through the winning of a legislative majority in a single national election. The Framers' vision was a different one, dominated by a concern with liberty and therefore with controls on political power. It was a response to the experiences they brought with them to Philadelphia in the summer of 1787.

SUMMARY   Self-Test www.mhhe.com/pattersonwtp8e

The Constitution of the United States is a reflection of the colonial and revolutionary experiences of the early Americans. Freedom from abusive government was a reason for the colonies' revolt against British rule, but the English tradition also provided ideas about government, power, and freedom that were expressed in the Constitution and, earlier, in the Declaration of Independence.

The Constitution was designed in part to provide for a limited government in which political power would be confined to proper uses. The Framers wanted to ensure that the government they were creating would not itself be a threat to freedom. To this end, they confined the national government to expressly granted powers and also denied it certain specific powers. Other prohibitions on government were later added to the Constitution in the form of stated guarantees of individual liberties in the Bill of Rights. The most significant constitutional provision for limited government, however, was a separation of powers among the three branches. The powers given to each branch enable it to act as a check on the exercise of power by the other two, an arrangement that during the nation's history has in fact served as a barrier to abuses of power.

The Constitution, however, made no mention of how the powers and limits of government were to be judged in practice. In its historic ruling in *Marbury v. Madison*, the Supreme Court assumed the authority to review the constitutionality of legislative and executive actions and to declare them unconstitutional and thus invalid.

The Framers of the Constitution, respecting the idea of self-government but distrusting popular majorities, devised a system of government that they felt would temper popular opinion and slow its momentum so that the public's "true interest" (which includes a regard for the rights and interests of the minority) would guide public policy. Different methods were advanced for selecting the president, the members of the House and Senate, and federal judges as a means of insulating political power against momentary majorities.

Since the adoption of the Constitution, the public gradually has assumed more direct control of its representatives, particularly through measures that affect the way officeholders are chosen. Presidential popular voting (linked to the Electoral College), direct election of senators, and primary elections are among the devices aimed at strengthening the majority's influence. These developments are rooted in the idea, deeply held by ordinary Americans, that the people must have substantial direct influence over their representatives if government is to serve their interests.

KEY TERMS

Anti-Federalists (*p. 44*)
Bill of Rights (*p. 53*)
checks and balances (*p. 49*)
constitution (*p. 46*)
constitutional democracy (*p. 63*)
delegates (*p. 60*)
democracy (*p. 57*)
denials of power (*p. 47*)
Electoral College (*p. 58*)
electoral votes (*p. 58*)
Federalists (*p. 45*)
grants of power (*p. 47*)
Great Compromise (*p. 41*)
inalienable (natural) rights (*p. 37*)

judicial review (*p. 54*)
limited government (*p. 35*)
New Jersey (small-state) Plan (*p. 41*)
North-South Compromise (*p. 41*)
primary election (*p. 61*)
representative government (*p. 57*)
republic (*p. 57*)
self-government (*p. 35*)
separated institutions
    sharing power (*p. 49*)
separation of powers (*p. 49*)
trustees (*p. 57*)
tyranny of the majority (*p. 56*)
Virginia (large-state) Plan (*p. 40*)

SUGGESTED READINGS

Beard, Charles S. *An Economic Interpretation of the Constitution.* New York: Macmillan, 1941. Argues that the Framers had selfish economic interests uppermost in their minds when they wrote the Constitution.

Edling, Max M. *A Revolution in Favor of Government.* New York: Oxford University Press, 2003. Argues that the Framers intended the Constitution to create a strong government.

Ellis, Joseph J. *Founding Brothers: The Revolutionary Generation.* New York: Vintage, 2002. A riveting account of the lives of America's leading Founders.

Federalist Papers. Many editions, including a one-volume paperback version edited by Isaac Kramnick (New York: Penguin, 1987). A series of essays written by Alexander Hamilton, James Madison, and John Jay under the pseudonym

Publius; the essays, published in a New York newspaper in 1787–88, explain the Constitution and support its ratification.

Hardin, Russell. *Liberalism, Constitutionalism, and Democracy.* New York: Oxford University Press, 1999. Analysis of the great ideas that underlie the Constitution.

McGerr, Michael. *A Fierce Discontent: The Rise and Fall of the Progressive Movement in America, 1870–1920.* New York: Free Press, 2005. Assessment of the Progressive movement's contribution to American democracy.

Ostrom, Vincent. *The Political Theory of a Compound Republic: Designing the American Experiment.* Lanham, Md.: Lexington Books, 2007. An analysis of the logic of the Constitution as its writers envisioned it.

Tocqueville, Alexis de. *Democracy in America*, vols. 1 and 2, ed. J. P. Mayer. New York: Doubleday/Anchor, 1969. A classic analysis (originally published 1835–40) of American democracy by an insightful French observer.

Wilentz, Sean. *The Rise of American Democracy: Jefferson to Lincoln.* New York: Norton, 2005. An account of how democratic ideas triumphed over aristocratic ones.

LIST OF WEBSITES

http://www.nara.gov/ The National Archives site; includes an in-depth look at the history of the Declaration of Independence.

http://odur.let.rug.nl/~usa/P/aj7/about/bio/jackxx.htm A site that focuses on Andrew Jackson and his role in shaping U.S. politics.

http://www.yale.edu/lawweb/avalon/constpap.htm Includes documents on the Constitution, the American Revolution, and the constitutional convention.

http://www.yale.edu/lawweb/avalon/presiden/jeffpap.htm A site that includes the papers of Thomas Jefferson, as well as his autobiography.

POLITICS IN THEORY AND PRACTICE

Thinking: How does the division of power in the U.S. political system contribute to limited government? How do the provisions for representative government (the various methods of choosing national officials) contribute to limited government?

Participating: The classroom provides an everyday opportunity to develop a skill that is basic to effective citizenship—the ability to speak clearly and persuasively. To the Greek philosopher Aristotle, rhetoric was the defining skill of citizenship. Aristotle did not define rhetoric as it is often used today, as a derisive term for speech that is long on wind and short on reason. Rather, he saw rhetoric as a tool in the search for truth, a form of persuasion that flourishes when people exchange ideas. The college classroom is a place to develop rhetorical skills. Speak up in the classroom when you have a point to make and can support it.

Rhetorical skills are honed only through practice, and few settings offer more opportunities for practice than the classroom.

Extra Credit

For up-to-the-minute *New York Times* articles, interactive simulations, graphics, study tools, and more links and quizzes, visit the text's Online Learning Center at www.mhhe.com/pattersonwtp8e.

The Mischiefs of Faction

By James Madison

James Madison wrote Federalist *No. 10 during the debate over ratification of the Constitution. It has been described as the finest political essay ever written by an American. In it, Madison argues that a "republican" form of government is the surest protection against abuse of political power. He argues that people naturally and passionately pursue their self-interest and, therefore, that power placed directly in the hands of a popular majority is likely to be directed against minority interests. Madison's solution, as described in this chapter, is a constitutional system in which popular influence works through, and is moderated by, representative institutions.*

Among the numerous advantages promised by a well-constructed Union, none deserves to be more accurately developed than its tendency to break and control the violence of faction. . . .

By a faction I understand a number of citizens, whether amounting to a majority or minority of the whole, who are united and actuated by some common impulse of passion, or of interest, adverse to the rights of other citizens, or to the permanent and aggregate interests of the community.

There are two methods of curing the mischiefs of faction: the one, by removing its causes; the other, by controlling its effects.

There are again two methods of removing the causes of faction: the one, by destroying the liberty which is essential to its existence; the other, by giving to every citizen the same opinions, the same passions, and the same interests.

It could never be more truly said than of the first remedy that it was worse than the disease. Liberty is to faction what air is to fire, an ailment without which it instantly expires. But it could not be a less folly to abolish liberty, which is essential to political life, because it nourishes faction than it would be to wish the annihilation of air, which is essential to animal life, because it imparts to fire its destructive agency.

The second expedient is as impracticable as the first would be unwise. As long as the reason of man continues fallible, and he is at liberty to exercise it, different opinions will be formed. As long as the connection subsists between his reason and his self-love, his opinions and his passions will have a reciprocal influence on each other; and the former will be objects to which the latter will attach themselves. The diversity in the faculties of men, from which the rights of property originate, is not less an insuperable obstacle to a uniformity of interest. The protection of these faculties is the first object of government. From the protection of different and unequal faculties of acquiring property, the possession of different degrees and kinds of property immediately results; and from the influence of these on the sentiments and views of the respective proprietors ensues a division of the society into different interests and parties.

The latent causes of faction are thus sown in the nature of man; and we see them everywhere brought into different degrees of activity, according to the different circumstances of civil society. A zeal for different opinions concerning religion, concerning government, and many other points, as well of speculation as of practice; an attachment to different leaders ambitiously contending for pre-eminence and power; or to persons of other descriptions whose fortunes have been interesting to the human passions, have, in turn, divided mankind into parties, inflamed them with mutual animosity, and rendered them much more disposed to vex and oppress each other than to cooperate for their common good. So strong is this propensity of mankind to fall into mutual animosities that where no substantial occasion presents itself the most frivolous and fanciful distinctions have been sufficient to kindle their unfriendly passions and excite their most violent conflicts. But the most common and durable source of factions has been the various and unequal distribution of property. Those who hold and those who are without property have ever formed distinct interests in society. . . .

The inference to which we are brought is that the causes of faction cannot be removed and that relief is only to be sought in the means of controlling its *effects*.

If a faction consists of less than a majority, relief is supplied by the republican principle, which enables the majority to defeat its sinister views by regular vote. . . . When a majority is included in a faction, the form of popular government, on the other hand, enables it to sacrifice to its ruling passion or interest both the public good and the rights of other citizens. To secure the public good and private rights against the danger of such a faction, and at the same time to preserve the spirit and the form of popular government, is then the great object to which our inquiries are directed.

By what means is this object attainable? Evidently by one of two only. Either the existence of the same passion or interest in a majority at the same time must be prevented, or the majority, having such coexistent passion or interest, must be rendered, by their number and local situation, unable to concert and carry into effect schemes of oppression. If the impulse and the opportunity be suffered to coincide, we well know that neither moral nor religious motives can be relied on as an adequate control. They are not found to be such on the injustice and violence of individuals, and lose their efficacy in proportion to the number combined together, that is, in proportion as their efficacy becomes needful.

From this view of the subject it may be concluded that a pure democracy, by which I mean a society consisting of a small number of citizens, who assemble and administer the government in person, can admit of no cure for the mischiefs of faction. A common passion or interest will, in almost every case, be felt by a majority of the whole, a communication and concert results from the form of government itself; and there is nothing to check the inducements to sacrifice the weaker party or an obnoxious individual. Hence it is that such democracies have ever been spectacles of turbulence and contention; have ever been found incompatible with personal security or the rights of property; and have in general been as short in their lives as they have been violent in their deaths. . . .

A republic, by which I mean a government in which the scheme of representation takes place, opens a different prospect and promises the cure for which we are seeking. Let us examine the points in which it varies from pure democracy, and we shall comprehend both the nature of the cure and the efficacy which it must derive from the Union.

The two great points of difference between a democracy and a republic are: first, the delegation of the government, in the latter, to a small number of citizens elected by the rest; secondly, the greater number of citizens and greater sphere of country over which the latter may be extended.

The effect of the first difference is, on the one hand, to refine and enlarge the public views by passing them through the medium of a chosen body of citizens, whose wisdom may best discern the true interest of their country and whose patriotism and love of justice will be least likely to sacrifice it to temporary or partial considerations. Under such a regulation it may well happen that the public voice, pronounced by the representatives of the people, will be more consonant to the public good than if pronounced by the people themselves, convened for the purpose. . . .

The other point of difference is the greater number of citizens and extent of territory which may be brought within the compass of republican than of democratic government; and it is this circumstance principally which renders factious combinations less to be dreaded in the former than in the latter. The smaller the society, the fewer probably will be the distinct parties and interests composing it; the fewer the distinct parties and interests,

the more frequently will a majority be found of the same party; and the smaller the number of individuals composing a majority, and the smaller the compass within which they are placed, the more easily will they concert and execute their plans of oppression. Extend the sphere and you take in a greater variety of parties and interests; you make it less probable that a majority of the whole will have a common motive to invade the rights of other citizens; or if such a common motive exists, it will be more difficult for all who feel it to discover their own strength and to act in unison with each other. . . .

Hence, it clearly appears that the same advantage which a republic has over a democracy in controlling the effects of faction is enjoyed by a large over a small republic—is enjoyed by the Union over the States composing it.

What's Your Opinion?

Do you agree with Madison's assumption and argument? If given a chance, will society's factions use the power of government to promote their selfish interests at the expense of those of society as a whole? Has the American system of checks and balances served to reduce the ability of powerful factions to exploit other interests?

CHAPTER 3

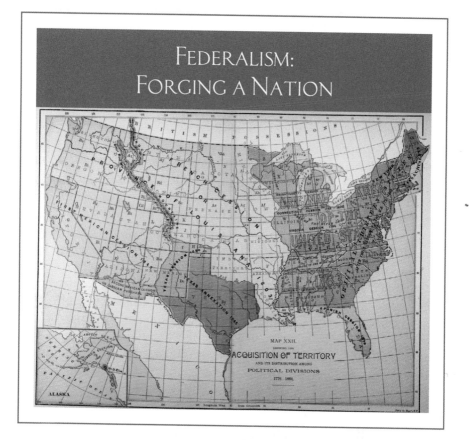

FEDERALISM:
FORGING A NATION

MAP XXII.
SHOWING THE
ACQUISITION OF TERRITORY
AND ITS DISTRIBUTION AMONG
POLITICAL DIVISIONS
1776-1884.

ALASKA

> ❝ The question of the relation of the states to the federal government is the cardinal question of our Constitutional system. It cannot be settled by the opinion of one generation, because it is a question of growth, and each successive stage of our political and economic development gives it a new aspect, makes it a new question. ❞
>
> WOODROW WILSON[1]

As the reauthorization of the No Child Left Behind (NCLB) Act remained unresolved as Congress headed into 2008, it was unclear whether either side could muster the support necessary to get their way. The legislation had been in effect since 2002 when its most prominent supporter, President George W. Bush, signed it into law. NCLB had required states to test their primary and secondary school students annually and to show improvement in test scores or face a reduction in federal funding.

NCLB was arguably the most intrusive federal initiative yet on how local schools operate. Education has traditionally been the domain of state and local governments. More than 90 percent of the education funding is provided by states and localities, which also set most of the education standards, from teachers' qualifications to the length of the school day. NCLB was a sharp break from that tradition, and opponents said it was destructive of the schools' mission. They claimed that teachers were being forced "to teach to the test," administrators were being swamped with test-related paperwork, and schools were receiving insufficient federal funding to administer the program. Supporters of NCLB did not dismiss these complaints entirely but held to their belief that strict federal testing standards were necessary if America's schools were to be improved.

As the formal deadline for NCLB's reauthorization came and went, the U.S. secretary of education, Margaret Spellings, said: "If Congress doesn't produce a strong bill quickly, I will move forward," adding "we must stay true" to NCLB's goals. Earlier, a bipartisan commission formed by the National Conference of State Legislators had issued a critical assessment of NCLB, saying it had "questionable constitutional underpinnings." Calling the program "overly rigid" and "thinly funded," the commission noted that the Tenth Amendment reserves education policy to the states and that the federal government cannot impose a testing program unless it provides adequate funding and does not "coerce" states into participating.[2] Utah and several other states said they would not comply with any NCLB provision that was not properly funded.

The controversy surrounding the No Child Left Behind Act is one of thousands of disagreements over the course of American history that have hinged on whether national or state authority should prevail. Americans possess what amounts to dual citizenship: they are citizens both of the United States and of the state where they reside. The American political system is a *federal system*, in which constitutional authority is divided between a national government and state governments: each government is assumed to derive its powers directly from the people and therefore to have sovereignty (final authority) over the policy responsibilities assigned to it. The federal system consists of nation *and* states, indivisible yet separate.[3]

The relationship between the nation and the states was the most pressing issue when the Constitution was written in 1787. This chapter describes how that issue helped shape the Constitution. The chapter's closing sections discuss how federalism has changed throughout the nation's history and conclude with a brief overview of contemporary federalism. The main points presented in the chapter are these:

★ *The power of government must be equal to its responsibilities.* The Constitution was needed because the nation's preceding system (under the Articles of

Confederation) was too weak to accomplish its expected goals, particularly those of a strong defense and an integrated economy.

⋆ *Federalism—the Constitution's division of governing authority between two levels, nation and states—was the result of political bargaining.* Federalism was not a theoretical principle, but a compromise made necessary in 1787 by the prior existence of the states.

⋆ *Federalism is not a fixed principle for allocating power between the national and state governments, but a principle that has changed over time in response to new political needs.* Federalism has passed through several distinct stages in the course of the nation's history.

⋆ *Contemporary federalism tilts toward national authority, reflecting the increased interdependence of American society.* However, there are also efforts to reduce the scope of federal authority.

FEDERALISM: NATIONAL AND STATE SOVEREIGNTY

At the time of the writing of the Constitution, some of America's top leaders were dead set against the creation of a strong national government. When rumors circulated that the delegates to the constitutional convention were planning to devise such a government, Patrick Henry, an ardent believer in state-centered government, said that he "smelt a rat." After the convention had adjourned, he realized that his fears were justified. "Who authorized them," he asked, "to speak the language of 'We, the People,' instead of 'We, the States'?"

The question of "people versus states" was precipitated by the failure of the Articles of Confederation. The government under the Articles (see Chapter 2) was a union of states rather than also a union of people. The government had no direct control over citizens. It could not, for example, require them to pay taxes. Congress could pass laws affecting the states, which they were obliged in principle to obey. However, they often ignored national laws that they deemed disagreeable or inconvenient. Georgia and North Carolina, for example, contributed no money at all to the national treasury between 1781 and 1786. The national government could do little more than beg them to pay their allotted share of the costs of defense and other national policies.

The only realistic solution to this problem—if the United States was to be a nation in more than name only—was a government that had direct power over the people. If individuals were ordered to pay taxes, for example, they would ordinarily do so. The alternatives to not paying—imprisonment or confiscation of their property—were too onerous.

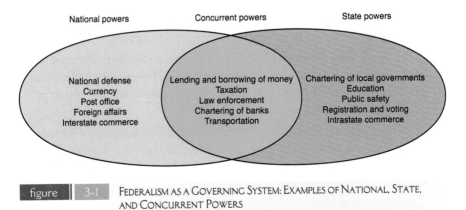

figure   **3-1**   FEDERALISM AS A GOVERNING SYSTEM: EXAMPLES OF NATIONAL, STATE, AND CONCURRENT POWERS

The American federal system divides sovereignty between a national government and the state governments. Each is constitutionally protected in its existence and authority, although their powers overlap somewhat even in areas granted to one level (for example, the federal government has a role in education policy).

Although the writers of the Constitution sought a national government based directly on the people, they also aimed to preserve the states as governing bodies. The states already existed, had their own constitutions, and enjoyed popular support. When Virginia's George Mason said that he would never agree to a union that abolished the states, he was speaking for virtually all the delegates. The Philadelphia convention therefore devised a system of government that came to be known as **federalism.** Federalism is the division of **sovereignty,** or ultimate governing authority, between a national government and regional (that is, state) governments. Each directly governs the people and derives its authority from them.

American federalism is basically a system of divided powers (see Figure 3-1). The system gives states the power to address local issues in ways of their choosing. At the same time, federalism gives the national government the power to decide matters of national scope. Although state authority and national authority overlap in some areas, there is also a division of responsibilities. The national government is in charge of national defense and the currency, among other things, while the states have primary responsibility for policy areas such as public education and police protection. The national and state governments also have some concurrent powers (that is, powers exercised over the same policy areas)—for example, the power to raise taxes and borrow money.

A federal system is different from a **confederacy,** the type of government established by the Articles. In a confederacy, the states alone are sovereign. The authority of the central government is derived from them, and they have the power to redefine its authority. Federalism is also different from a **unitary**

system, in which sovereignty is vested solely in the national government. Under a unitary system, the people are citizens or subjects only of the national government. Other governments in such a system have only as much authority as it permits. The national government can even abolish them as governing bodies. In contrast, a federal system invests sovereignty—final authority—in both the national and state governments. Each level of government has a permanent existence and authority that is independent of that of the other level.

Federalism was invented in America in 1787. It was different not only from a confederate or a unitary system but also from any other form of government previously known. The ancient Greek city-states and the medieval Hanseatic League were confederacies. The governments of Europe were unitary in form. The United States of America would be the first nation to be governed through federalism.

The Argument for Federalism

Unlike many decisions made at the Philadelphia convention, the choice of federalism had no clear basis in political theory. Federalism was a practical necessity: there was a need for a stronger national government, and yet the states existed and were determined to retain their sovereignty. Nevertheless, the Framers developed arguments for the superiority of federalism. They claimed it would protect liberty, moderate the power of government, and provide the basis for an effective national government.

Protecting Liberty   Although theorists such as John Locke and Montesquieu had not proposed a division of power between national and local authorities as a means of protecting liberty, the Framers came to view federalism as part of the Constitution's system of checks and balances (see Chapter 2). Alexander Hamilton argued in *Federalist* No. 28 that the American people could shift their loyalties back and forth between the national and state governments in order to keep each under control. "If [the people's] rights are invaded by either," Hamilton wrote, "they can make use of the other as the instrument of redress."

Moderating the Power of Government   To the Anti-Federalists (opponents of the Constitution), the sacrifice of the states' power to the nation was as unwise as it was unnecessary. They claimed that a distant national government could never serve the people's interests as well as the states could. Liberty *and* self-government, they argued, were enhanced by state-centered government. In support of their contention, the Anti-Federalists turned to Montesquieu, who had concluded that a small republic is more likely than a large one to serve the people. When government encompasses a small area, he argued, its leaders are in closer touch with the people and have more concern for their welfare.

In *Federalist* No. 10, James Madison took issue with this claim. He argued that whether a government serves the common good is a function not of its size but of the range of interests that share political power. The problem with a smaller republic, Madison claimed, is that it is likely to have a dominant faction—whether it be landholders, financiers, an impoverished majority, or some other group—that is strong enough to seize control of government and use it for selfish purposes. A large republic is less likely to have such an all-powerful faction. If financiers are strong in one area of a large republic, they are likely to be weaker elsewhere. The same will be true of farmers, merchants, laborers, and other groups. A large republic, Madison concluded, would make it hard for any single group to gain control and would force groups to work together. "Extend the sphere," said Madison, "and you take in a greater variety of parties and interests; you make it less probable that a majority of the whole will have a common motive to invade the rights of other citizens."

Strengthening the Union   The most telling argument in 1787 for a federal system was that it would overcome the deficiencies of the Articles.

Historical
Background

The Articles had numerous flaws (including a very weak executive and a judiciary subservient to the state courts), and two of them were fatal: the government had neither the power to tax nor the power to regulate commerce.

Under the Articles, Congress was given responsibility for national defense but was not granted the power to tax, so it depended on the states for the money to maintain an army and a navy. During the first six years under the Articles, Congress asked the states for $12 million but received only $3 million—not even enough to pay the interest on Revolutionary War debts. By 1786, the national government had become so desperate for money that it sold the navy's ships and reduced the army to fewer than a thousand soldiers—this at a time when England had an army in Canada and when Spain occupied Florida.

Congress also was expected to shape a national economy, yet it was powerless to do so because the Articles prohibited it from interfering with the states' commerce policies. States, free to do whatever they wanted, exploited the situation by trying to cripple their competitors. Connecticut, for example, placed a higher tariff on manufactured goods from its trading rival Massachusetts than it placed on the same goods shipped from England.

The Articles of Confederation showed the fallacy of the adage "That government is best which governs least." The consequences of an overly weak authority were abundantly clear: public disorder, economic chaos, and inadequate defense.

Patrick Henry was a leading figure in the American Revolution ("Give me liberty or give me death!"). He later opposed ratification of the Constitution on grounds that the national government should be a union of states and not also of people.

The Powers of the Nation

The Philadelphia convention met to decide the national government's structure. The delegates had not been sent to determine the form of the state governments. Accordingly, the U.S. Constitution addresses the lawful authority of the national government, which is provided through *enumerated and implied powers.* Authority that is not granted to the national government is left—or "reserved"—to the states. Thus, the states have *reserved powers.*

Enumerated Powers   Article I of the Constitution grants to Congress seventeen **enumerated (expressed) powers.** The Framers intended these powers to be the basis for a government strong enough to forge a union that was secure in its defense and stable in its commerce. Congress's powers to regulate commerce among the states, to create a national currency, and to borrow money, for example, would provide a foundation for a sound national economy. Its power to tax, combined with its authority to establish an army and a navy and to declare war, would enable it to provide for the common defense. In addition, the Constitution prohibits the states from actions that would undermine the national government's lawful pow

Article I, Section 10 prohibits the states from making treaties with other nations, raising armies, waging war, printing money, or entering into commercial agreements with other states without the approval of Congress.

The writers of the Constitution recognized that the lawful exercise of national authority would at times conflict with the actions of the states. In such instances, national law was intended to prevail. Article VI of the Constitution grants this dominance in the so-called **supremacy clause,** which provides that "the laws of the United States . . . shall be the supreme law of the land."

Implied Powers   The Framers of the Constitution worried that a narrow definition of national authority could result in a government incapable of adapting to change. Under the Articles of Confederation, Congress was strictly confined to those powers expressly granted to it, which limited its ability to respond effectively to the country's changing needs after the Revolutionary War. Concerned that the enumerated powers by themselves would be too restrictive of national authority, the Framers added the **"necessary and proper" clause** or, as it later came to be known, the **elastic clause.** Article I, Section 8 gives Congress the power "to make all laws which shall be necessary and proper for carrying into execution the foregoing [enumerated] powers." This grant gave the national government **implied powers:** the authority to take action that is not expressly authorized by the Constitution but that supports actions that are so authorized.

The Powers of the States

The Framers' goal of a sovereign national government was not shared in 1787 by all Americans. Although Anti-Federalists recognized a need to strengthen defense and boost interstate commerce, they feared the consequences of a strong central government. The interests of the people of New Hampshire were not identical to those of Georgians or Pennsylvanians, and the Anti-Federalists argued that only state-centered government would protect the differences. Self-government, they claimed, would be weakened if power resided with a distant national government.

The Federalists responded by saying that the national government would have no interest in depriving the states of their liberty or of their right to decide local matters.[4] The national government would take responsibility for establishing a strong defense and for promoting a sound economy, while the states would retain nearly all other governing functions, including public education and safety.

This argument did not persuade the Anti-Federalists that their fear of an overly powerful national government was baseless. The supremacy and "necessary and proper" clauses were particularly worrisome, because they provided a constitutional basis for expansion of national authority. Such concerns led to demands for a constitutional amendment that would protect states' rights and interests. Ratified in 1791 as the Tenth Amendment to the Constitution, it reads: "The powers not delegated to the United States by the Constitution, nor prohibited by it to the States, are reserved to the States." The states' powers under the U.S. Constitution are thus called **reserved powers.**

⊕ HOW THE UNITED STATES COMPARES

Federal Versus Unitary Governments

Federalism involves the division of sovereignty between a national government and subnational (such as state) governments. It was invented in 1787 in order to maintain the pre-existing American states while establishing an effective central government. Since then, other countries have established a *federal* government, but most countries continue to have a *unitary* government, in which all sovereignty is vested in the national government.

Even within these alternative political systems, differences exist. In Germany's federal system, for example, the states have limited lawmaking powers but exercise broad authority in determining how national laws will be implemented. By comparison, the U.S. federal system grants substantial lawmaking powers to the states except in specified areas such as national defense and currency.

Unitary systems also differ. In Britain, the national government has delegated substantial authority to regions; Scotland, for example, has its own parliament, which exercises lawmaking powers. In France's unitary government, on the other hand, political authority is highly centralized.

In nearly all federal systems, the national legislature has two chambers—one apportioned by population (as in the case of the U.S. House of Representatives) and one apportioned by geographical area (as in the case of the U.S. Senate). The U.S. Senate is a pure federal institution in the sense that each state has the same number of senators. In some federal systems, such as Germany's, the states are not equally represented even in the legislative chamber that is apportioned on the basis of geography rather than population.

Unitary systems typically have but a single national legislative chamber, which is apportioned by population—there is no constitutional justification for a second chamber based on geography.

(continued)

Country	Form of Government
Canada	Federal
France	Unitary
Germany	Federal
Great Britain	Modified unitary
Italy	Modified unitary
Japan	Unitary
Mexico	Modified federal
Sweden	Unitary
United States	Federal

FEDERALISM IN HISTORICAL PERSPECTIVE

Since ratification of the Constitution over two centuries ago, no aspect of it has provoked more frequent or bitter conflict than federalism. By establishing two levels of sovereign authority, the Constitution created competing centers of power and ambition, each of which was sure to claim disputed areas as belonging to it.

Conflict between national and state authority was also ensured by the brevity of the Constitution. The Framers deliberately avoided detailed provisions, recognizing that brief phrasing would lend flexibility to the government they were creating. The document does not define, for example, the difference between *inter*state commerce (which the national government is empowered to regulate) and *intra*state commerce (which is reserved for regulation by the states).

Not surprisingly, federalism has been a contentious and dynamic system, its development determined less by constitutional language than by the strength of contending interests and by the country's changing needs. Federalism can be viewed as having progressed through three historical eras, each of which has involved a different relationship between the nation and the states.

An Indestructible Union (1789–1865)

The issue during the first era, which lasted from the Constitution's beginnings in 1789 through the end of the Civil War in 1865, was the Union's survival. Given the state-centered history of America before the Constitution, it was inevitable that the states would dispute national policies that threatened their interests.

The Nationalist View: McCulloch v. Maryland   A first dispute over federalism arose when President George Washington's secretary of the treasury, Alexander Hamilton, proposed that Congress establish a national bank. Thomas Jefferson, Washington's secretary of state, opposed the bank on the grounds that its activities would benefit the rich at the expense of ordinary people. Jefferson said the bank was unlawful because the Constitution did not expressly authorize it. Hamilton and his supporters claimed that because the federal government had constitutional authority to regulate currency, it had the "implied power" to establish a national bank.

Historical
Background

Hamilton's view prevailed when Congress in 1791 established the First Bank of the United States, granting it a twenty-year charter. Although Congress did not renew the bank's charter when it expired in 1811, Congress decided in 1816 to establish the Second Bank of the United States. State and local banks did not want competition from a national bank and sought help from their state legislatures. Several states, including Maryland, levied taxes on the national bank's operations within their borders, hoping to drive it out of existence by making it unprofitable. Edwin McCulloch, who was in charge of the Maryland branch of the national bank, refused to pay the Maryland tax and the resulting dispute was heard by the Supreme Court.

The chief justice of the Supreme Court, John Marshall, was a strong nationalist, and in *McCulloch v. Maryland* (1819) the Court ruled decisively in favor of national authority. It was reasonable, Marshall concluded, to infer that a government with powers to tax, borrow money, and regulate commerce could establish a bank in order to exercise those powers effectively. Marshall's argument was a clear statement of *implied powers*—the idea that through the "necessary and proper" clause the national government's powers extend beyond a narrow reading of its enumerated powers.

Marshall's ruling also addressed the meaning of the Constitution's supremacy clause. The state of Maryland had argued that, even if the national bank was a legal entity, a state had the sovereign authority to tax it. The Supreme Court rejected Maryland's position, concluding that valid national law prevailed over conflicting state law. Because the national government had the power to create the bank, it also could protect the bank from actions by the states, such as taxation, that might destroy it.[5]

A first dispute over federalism was whether the Constitution allowed the creation of a Bank of the United States (shown here in an early-nineteenth-century painting). The Constitution had a clause authorizing the printing of currency but not the establishment of a bank itself.

The *McCulloch* decision served as precedent for later rulings in support of national power. In *Gibbons v. Ogden* (1824), for example, the Marshall-led Court rejected a New York law granting a monopoly on a ferry that operated between New York and New Jersey, concluding that New York had encroached on Congress's power to regulate commerce among the states. The Court also ruled that Congress's commerce power extended *into* a state when commerce between two or more states was at issue.[6]

Marshall's opinions asserted that legitimate uses of national power took precedence over state authority and that the "necessary and proper" clause and the commerce clause were broad grants of national power. As a nationalist, Marshall provided the U.S. government with the legal justification for expanding its power in ways that fostered the development of the United States as a nation rather than as a collection of states. This constitutional vision was of utmost significance. As Justice Oliver Wendell Holmes Jr. noted a century later, the Union could not have survived if each state had been allowed to determine for itself the extent to which it would accept national authority.[7]

The States'-Rights View: The Dred Scott *Decision*   Although John Marshall's rulings helped strengthen national authority, the issue of slavery posed a growing threat to the Union's survival. Fearing that northern members of Congress might move to abolish slavery, southern leaders did what others have done throughout American history: they devised a constitutional argument to fit their political desires. John C. Calhoun of South Carolina argued that the Constitution had created "a government of states . . . not a government of individuals."[8] This line of reasoning led Calhoun to his famed "doctrine of nullification," which declared that any state had the constitutional right to nullify a national law.

In 1832, South Carolina invoked this doctrine, declaring "null and void" a tariff law that favored northern interests. President Andrew Jackson called South Carolina's action "incompatible with the existence of the Union," a position that was strengthened when Congress authorized Jackson to use military force if necessary against South Carolina. The state backed down when Congress amended the tariff act to soften its impact on the South.

The clash foreshadowed the Civil War, a confrontation of far greater consequence. Although war would not break out for another three decades, conflict over states' rights was intensifying. Westward expansion and immigration into the northern states were tilting power in Congress toward the free states, which increasingly signaled their determination to outlaw slavery in the United States at some future time. Attempts to find a compromise acceptable to both the North and the South were fruitless.

The Supreme Court's infamous *Dred Scott* decision (1857), written by Chief Justice Roger Taney, an ardent states'-rights advocate, exacerbated the conflict. Dred Scott, a slave who had lived in the North for four years, applied for his freedom when his master died, citing a federal law—the Missouri Compromise of 1820—that made slavery illegal in a free state or territory. The Supreme Court ruled against Scott, claiming that persons of African descent were barred from citizenship and thereby could not sue for their freedom in federal courts. The Court also invalidated the Missouri Compromise. The Court ruled that slaves were property, not people, and as such could be taken into any state or territory. Accordingly, Congress did not have the power to outlaw slavery in any part of the United States.[9]

The Taney Court's decision provoked outrage in the North and contributed to a sectional split in the nation's majority party, the Democrats. In 1860, the Democratic Party's northern and southern wings nominated separate candidates for the presidency, which split the Democratic vote, enabling the Republican candidate, Abraham Lincoln, to win the presidency with only 40 percent of the popular vote. Lincoln had campaigned on a platform that called, not for an immediate end to slavery, but for its gradual abolition through payments to slaveholders. Nevertheless, southern states saw Lincoln's election as a grave threat to their sovereignty. By

The American Civil War was the bloodiest conflict the world had yet known. Ten percent of fighting-age males died in the four-year war, and uncounted others were wounded. The death toll—618,000 (360,000 from the North, 258,000 from the South)—exceeded that of the American war dead in World War I, World War II, the Korean War, and the Vietnam War combined. This death toll was in a nation with a population only one-tenth the size it is today. Shown here, in one of the earliest war photos ever taken, are the bodies of soldiers killed at the battle of Antietam.

the time Lincoln assumed office, seven southern states, led by South Carolina, had left the Union. Four more states were to follow. In justifying his decision to wage war on the secessionists, Lincoln said, "The Union is older than the states." In 1865, the superior strength of the Union army settled by force the question of whether national authority is binding on the states.

Dual Federalism and Laissez-Faire Capitalism (1865–1937)

Although the Civil War preserved the Union, new challenges to federalism were surfacing. Constitutional doctrine held that certain policy areas, such as interstate commerce and defense, belonged exclusively to the national government, whereas other policy areas, such as public health and intrastate commerce, belonged exclusively to the states. This doctrine, known as **dual federalism,** was based on the idea that a precise separation of national and state authority was both possible and desirable. "The power which one possesses," said the Supreme Court, "the other does not."[10]

Frederick Douglass
(1818–95)

Born a slave, Frederick Douglass never knew his father and rarely saw his mother, who died when he was seven. He spent part of his early childhood in Baltimore, where he was treated decently and learned to read. In his early teens, Douglass was sent to work on a Maryland farm owned by a brutal slave-holder, who whipped Douglass mercilessly. It took Douglass more than two years to escape north to Massachusetts, where he joined the antislavery movement and discovered that he had unusual oratorical skill. As his speaking fame grew, Douglass toured the northern states and Europe, seeking support for abolition. He argued that the Constitution guaranteed freedom for all, not just those of the white race. As much as Douglass despised the slave states, he was dedicated to saving the Union, arguing that abandoning it would mean abandoning those enslaved in the South. After the Civil War ended, Douglass sought constitutional amendments that would give equal rights to former slaves.

American society, however, was in the midst of changes that raised questions about the suitability of dual federalism as a governing concept. The Industrial Revolution had given rise to large business firms, which were using their economic power to dominate markets and exploit workers. Government was the logical counterforce to this economic power. Which level of government—state or national—would regulate business?

There was also the issue of the former slaves. The white South had lost the war but was hardly of a mind to share power with newly freed slaves. Would the federal government be allowed to intervene in state affairs to ensure the fair treatment of African Americans?

Dual federalism became a barrier to an effective response to these issues. From the 1860s through the 1930s, the Supreme Court held firm to the idea that there was a sharp line between national and state authority and, in both areas, a high wall of separation between government and the economy. The era of dual federalism was characterized by state supremacy in racial policy and business supremacy in commerce policy.

The Fourteenth Amendment and State Discretion   Ratified after the Civil War, the Fourteenth Amendment was intended to protect the newly freed slaves from discriminatory action by state governments. A state was prohibited from depriving "any person of life, liberty, or property without due process of law," from denying "any person within its jurisdiction the equal protection of the laws," and from abridging "the privileges or immunities of citizens of the United States."

Historical Background

Supreme Court rulings in subsequent decades, however, helped to undermine the Fourteenth Amendment's promise of liberty and equality for all. The Court held, for example, that the Fourteenth Amendment did not substantially limit the power of the states to determine the rights to which their residents were entitled.[11] Then, in *Plessy v. Ferguson* (1896), the Court issued its infamous "separate but equal" ruling. A black man, Homer Adolph Plessy, had been convicted of violating a Louisiana law that required white and black citizens to ride in separate railroad cars. The Supreme Court upheld his conviction, concluding that state governments could require blacks to use separate railroad cars and other accommodations as long as those facilities were "equal" in quality to those reserved for use by whites. "If one race be inferior to the other socially," the Court concluded, "the Constitution of the United States cannot put them on the same plane." The lone dissenting justice in the case, John Marshall Harlan, had harsh words for his colleagues: "Our Constitution is color-blind and neither knows nor tolerates classes among citizens. . . . The thin disguise of 'equal' accommodations . . . will not mislead anyone nor atone for the wrong this day done."[12]

With its *Plessy* decision, the Court undercut the Fourteenth Amendment and allowed southern states to segregate the races. Black children were forced into separate schools that seldom had libraries and usually had few teachers. Hospitals for blacks had few doctors and nurses and almost no medical supplies and equipment. Legal challenges to these discriminatory practices were generally unsuccessful. The *Plessy* ruling had become a justification for the separate and *unequal* treatment of black Americans.

Judicial Protection of Business   Through its rulings after the Civil War, the Supreme Court also provided a constitutional basis for unrestricted economic power. Most of the Court's justices believed in laissez-faire capitalism (which holds that business should be "allowed to act" without interference), and they interpreted the Constitution in ways that restricted government's attempts to regulate business activity. In 1886, for example, the Court decided that corporations were "persons" within the meaning of the Fourteenth Amendment, and thereby were protected from substantial regulation by the states.[13] The irony was inescapable. A constitutional amendment that had been enacted to protect the liberty of newly freed slaves was ignored for this purpose but used instead to protect fictitious persons—business corporations.

The Court also weakened the national government's regulatory power by narrowly interpreting its commerce power. The Constitution's **commerce clause** says that Congress shall have the power "to regulate commerce" among the states. However, the clause does not spell out the economic activities included in the grant of power. When the federal government invoked the Sherman Antitrust Act (1890) in an attempt to break up a monopoly on the manufacture of sugar, the Supreme Court blocked the action, claiming that interstate commerce covered only the "transportation" of goods, not their "manufacture."[14] Manufacturing was deemed part of intrastate commerce and thus, according to the dual federalism doctrine, subject to state regulation only. However, because the Court had previously decided that the states' regulatory powers were limited by the Fourteenth Amendment, the states for the most part were also denied the authority to regulate manufacturing activity in a significant way.

Although some business regulation was allowed, the Supreme Court remained an obstacle to efforts to curb abusive business practices. An example is the case of *Hammer v. Dagenhart* (1918), which arose from a 1916 federal act that prohibited the interstate shipment of goods produced by child labor. The act was popular because factory owners were exploiting children, working them for long hours at low pay. Citing the Tenth Amendment, the Court invalidated the law, ruling that factory practices could be regulated only by the states.[15] However, in an earlier case, *Lochner v. New York* (1905), the Court had prevented a state from regulating labor practices, concluding that such action violated firms' property rights.[16]

In effect, the Court had negated the principle of self-government. Neither the people's representatives in Congress nor their representatives in the state legislatures were allowed to regulate business activity. America's corporations, with the Supreme Court as their protector, were in command.[17]

National Authority Prevails   Judicial supremacy in the economic sphere ended abruptly in 1937. For nearly a decade, the United States had been mired in the Great Depression, which President Franklin D. Roosevelt's New Deal sought to alleviate. However, the Supreme Court had ruled that much

of the New Deal's economic recovery legislation was unconstitutional. A constitutional crisis of historic proportions seemed unavoidable until the Court suddenly reversed its position. In the process, American federalism was fundamentally changed.

Historical
Background

During the Great Depression, millions of Americans lost their jobs and homes. State and local governments could not cope with the enormous problems created by the Great Depression, so the federal government stepped in with its New Deal programs, greatly changing the nature of federal-state relations.

The Great Depression revealed that Americans had become a national community with national economic needs. More than half the population lived in cities (compared to one-fifth in 1860), and more than 10 million workers were employed by industry (compared to one million in 1860). Urban workers typically were dependent on landlords for their housing, on farmers and grocers for their food, and on corporations for their jobs. Farmers were more independent, but they too were increasingly a part of a larger economic network. Farmers' income depended on market prices and shipping and equipment costs.[18] This economic interdependence meant that, when the depression hit in 1929, its effects could not be contained. At the depths of the Great Depression, one-fourth of the nation's workforce was unemployed and another fourth could find only part-time work.

The states by tradition had responsibility for helping the unemployed, but they were nearly penniless because of declining tax revenues and the huge demand for welfare assistance. Roosevelt's New Deal programs were designed to ease the hardship. The 1933 National Industry Recovery Act (NIRA), for example, established a federal jobs program and enabled major industries to coordinate their production decisions. Economic conservatives strenuously opposed such programs, accusing Roosevelt of leading the country into communism. They found an ally in the Supreme Court. In *Schecter v. United States* (1935), just as it had done in previous New Deal cases, the Supreme Court in a 5-4 ruling declared the NIRA to be unconstitutional.[19]

Frustrated by the Court's opposition, Roosevelt in 1937 proposed that Congress expand the Supreme Court by passing legislation that would allow an additional justice to be appointed whenever a seated member passed the age of seventy. If enacted, the legislation would have enabled Roosevelt to appoint enough new justices to swing the Court to his side. Congress rejected Roosevelt's plan, but the controversy ended with "the switch in time that saved nine." For reasons that have never been fully clear, Justice Owen Roberts switched sides on New Deal cases, giving the president a 5-4 majority on the Court.

Within months, the Court upheld the 1935 National Labor Relations Act, which gave employees the right to organize and bargain collectively.[20] In passing the legislation, Congress claimed that labor–management disputes disrupted the nation's economy and therefore could be regulated through the commerce clause. In upholding the act, the Supreme Court in effect granted Congress the authority to broadly apply its commerce powers.[21] During this same period, the Court also loosened its restrictions on Congress's power to tax and spend.[22] These decisions removed the constitutional barrier to increased federal authority, a change the Court later acknowledged when it said that Congress's commerce power is "as broad as the needs of the nation."[23]

The Supreme Court had finally acknowledged the obvious: that an industrial economy is not confined by state boundaries and must be subject to national regulation. It was a principle that business itself increasingly accepted. The nation's banking industry, for example, was saved in the 1930s from almost complete collapse by the creation of a federal regulatory agency, the Federal Deposit Insurance Corporation (FDIC). By insuring depositors' savings against loss, the FDIC stopped the panic withdrawals that had bankrupted many of the nation's banks.

Toward National Citizenship

The fundamental change in the constitutional doctrine of federalism as applied to economic issues that took place in the 1930s was paralleled by subsequent changes in other areas, including civil rights. In *Brown v. Board of Education* (1954), for example, the Supreme Court held that states could not force black children to attend public schools separate from those for white children (see Chapter 5).[24] National citizenship—the notion that Americans should be equal in their rights and opportunities regardless of the state in which they reside—became a more encompassing idea than it had previously been.

FEDERALISM TODAY

Since the 1930s, the relation of the nation to the states has changed so fundamentally that dual federalism is no longer even a roughly accurate description of the American situation. An understanding of today's federalism requires a recognition of two countervailing trends. The first trend is a long-term *expansion* of national authority that began in the 1930s and continued for the next half-century. The national government now operates in many policy areas that were once almost exclusively within the control of states and localities. The national government does not dominate in these policy areas, but it does play a significant role. Much of this national influence stems from social welfare policies enacted in the 1960s as part of President Lyndon Johnson's Great Society program, which included initiatives in health care, public housing, nutrition, welfare, urban development, and other areas previously reserved to states and localities.

The second, more recent trend involves a partial contraction of national authority. Known as *devolution*, this trend involves the "passing down" of authority from the national government to the state and local levels in selected areas. Devolution has reversed the decades-long increase in federal authority, but only to a moderate degree.

In short, the national government's policy authority has expanded greatly since the 1930s, even though that authority has been reduced somewhat in recent years. We will explain each trend in more detail.

Interdependency and Intergovernmental Relations

Interdependency is a reason that national authority increased dramatically in the twentieth century. Modern systems of transportation, commerce, and communication transcend local and state boundaries. These systems are national—and even international—in scope, which means that problems affecting Americans living in one part of the country are likely to affect Americans living elsewhere. This situation has required Washington to assume a larger policy role. National problems typically require national solutions.

Interdependency has also encouraged national, state, and local policymakers to work together to solve policy problems. This collaborative effort has been described as **cooperative federalism**.[25] The difference between cooperative federalism and the older dual federalism has been likened to the difference between a marble cake, whose levels flow together, and a layer cake, whose levels are separate.[26]

Cooperative federalism is based on shared policy responsibilities rather than sharply divided ones. An example is the Medicaid program, which was created in 1965 as part of President Johnson's Great Society

Since the 1930s, the relationship between the federal and state governments has best been described by the term *cooperative federalism*. The two levels, along with the local government level, cooperate in addressing problems of joint concern, such as the wild fires that have erupted with increasing frequency in recent years because of droughts and other factors.

initiative and provides health care for the poor. The Medicaid program is jointly funded by the national and state governments, operates within eligibility standards set by the national government, and gives states some latitude in determining recipients' benefits. The Medicaid program is not an isolated example. Literally hundreds of policy programs today are run jointly by the national and state governments. In many cases, local governments are also involved. These programs have the following characteristics:

- Jointly funded by the national and state governments (and sometimes by local governments)
- Jointly administered, with the states and localities providing most of the direct service to recipients and a national agency providing general administration
- Jointly determined, with both the state and national governments (and sometimes the local governments) having a say in eligibility and benefit levels and with federal regulations, such as those prohibiting discrimination, providing an element of uniformity to the various state and local efforts

Cooperative federalism should not be interpreted to mean that the states are powerless and dependent. States have retained most of their traditional authority in areas such as education, health, public safety, and roadways. Nevertheless, the federal government's involvement in policy areas traditionally reserved for the states has increased its policy influence and diminished state-to-state policy differences. Before the enactment of the federal Medicaid program in 1965, for example, poor people in many states were not entitled to government-paid health care. Now most poor people are eligible for health benefits regardless of where they reside.

Government Revenues and Intergovernmental Relations

The interdependency of American society—the fact that developments in one area affect what happens elsewhere—is one of two major reasons the federal government's policy role has expanded greatly since the early twentieth century. The other reason is the federal government's superior taxing capacity. States and localities are in a competitive situation with regard to taxation. A state with high taxes will lose firms and people to states with lower taxes. Firms and people are less likely to move to another country in search of lower taxes. The result is that the federal government raises more tax revenues than do all fifty states and the thousands of local governments combined (see Figure 3-2).

Fiscal Federalism   The federal government's revenue-raising advantage has made money a basis for relations between the national government and the states and localities. **Fiscal federalism** refers to the expenditure of federal funds on programs run in part through state and local governments.[27] The

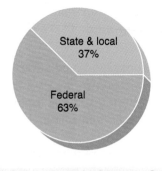

figure | 3-2   FEDERAL, STATE, AND LOCAL SHARES OF GOVERNMENT TAX REVENUE

The federal government raises more tax revenues than all state and local governments combined. *Source: U.S. Department of Commerce, 2008.*

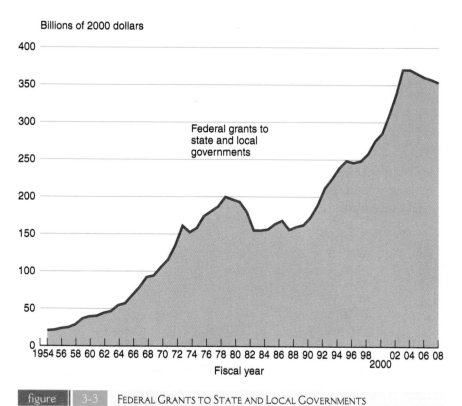

Billions of 2000 dollars

Federal grants to
state and local
governments

Fiscal year

| figure | 3-3 | FEDERAL GRANTS TO STATE AND LOCAL GOVERNMENTS |

Federal aid to states and localities has increased dramatically since the 1950s. *Source: Office of Management and Budget, 2008. Figure is based on constant (2000) dollars in order to control for the effects of inflation.*

federal government provides some or all of the money through **grants-in-aid** (cash payments) to states and localities, which then administer the programs. The pattern of federal assistance to states and localities is shown in Figure 3-3. Federal grants-in-aid have increased dramatically during the past half-century. Roughly one in every five dollars spent by local and state governments in recent decades has been raised not by them, but by the federal government in Washington (see "States in the Nation").

Cash grants to states and localities have increased Washington's policy influence. State and local governments can reject a grant-in-aid, but if they accept it they must spend it in the way specified by Congress. Also, because most grants require states to contribute matching funds, the federal programs in effect determine how states will allocate some of their own tax dollars. Further, federal grants have pressured state and local officials to adopt national goals, such as the elimination of racial and other forms of

★ STATES IN THE NATION

Federal Grants-in-Aid to the States

Federal assistance accounts for a significant share of state revenue, but the variation is considerable. New Mexico (with a third of its total revenue coming from federal grants-in-aid) is at one extreme. Nevada (a seventh of its revenue) is at the other.

Q: Why do states in the South, where anti-Washington sentiment is relatively high, get more of their revenue from the federal government than most other states?

A: Many federal grant programs are designed to assist low-income people, and poverty is more widespread in the South. Moreover, southern states traditionally have provided fewer government services, and federal grants accordingly constitute a larger proportion of their budgets.

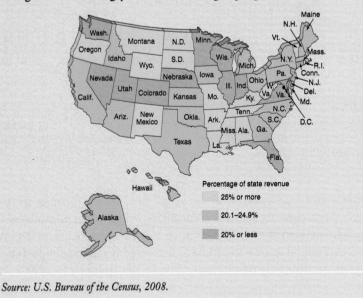

Percentage of state revenue

25% or more

20.1–24.9%

20% or less

Source: U.S. Bureau of the Census, 2008.

discrimination. A building constructed with the help of federal funds, for example, must be accessible to persons with disabilities. Nevertheless, federal grants-in-aid also serve the policy interests of state and local officials. While these officials often complain that federal grants contain too many restrictions and infringe too much on their authority, they are eager to obtain the money because it permits them to offer services they could not otherwise afford.

Categorical and Block Grants   State and local governments receive two major types of assistance—categorical grants and block grants—which differ in the extent to which Washington defines the conditions of their use. **Categorical grants,** the more restrictive type, can be used only for a designated activity. An example is funds directed for use in school lunch programs. These funds cannot be diverted to other school purposes, such as the purchase of textbooks or the hiring of teachers. **Block grants** are less restrictive. The federal government specifies the general area in which the funds must be used, but state and local officials select the specific projects. A block grant targeted for the health area, for example, might give state and local officials the authority to decide whether to use the money for hospital construction, medical equipment, the training of nurses, or some other health care activity.

State and local officials prefer federal money that comes with fewer strings attached and thus favor block grants. In contrast, members of Congress have at times preferred categorical grants, because this type of assistance gives them greater control over how state and local officials spend federal funds. Recently, however, officials at all levels have looked to block grants as the key to a more workable form of federalism. This tendency is part of a broader trend—devolution.

Devolution

Devolution embodies the idea that American federalism can be strengthened by a partial shift in power from the federal government to the state and local governments.[28] Devolution rests on a belief—held more strongly by Republicans than Democrats—that federal authority has extended too far into areas traditionally governed through state and local governments.

Although lawmakers of both parties had voted for expansions of federal authority, Democrats, led by Presidents Roosevelt and Johnson, had been the strongest advocates of a larger role for the national government, with strong backing from the public. After the 1960s, however, public support for federal domestic spending declined. Some of the programs, particularly those providing welfare benefits to the poor, were widely seen as too costly, too bureaucratic, and too lax—there was a widespread perception that many welfare recipients were getting benefits they neither needed nor deserved. Republican leaders increasingly questioned the effectiveness of the programs. Republican Presidents Richard Nixon and Ronald Reagan proposed versions of a "new federalism" in which some areas of public policy for which the federal government had assumed responsibility would be returned to states and localities.

The Republican Revolution   When the Republican Party scored a decisive victory in the 1994 congressional elections, Speaker of the House Newt Gingrich declared that "1960s-style federalism is dead." Republican lawmakers proposed to cut some federal programs, but, even more, they sought to increase state and local control. Congressional Republicans passed legislation to reduce *unfunded mandates*—federal programs that require action by states or localities but provide no or insufficient funds to pay for it. For example, states and localities are required by federal law to make their buildings accessible to the physically handicapped, but Washington pays only part of the cost of these accommodations. In the Unfunded Mandates Reform Act of 1995, Congress eliminated some of these mandates, although under threat of a veto by Democratic President Bill Clinton, those relating to civil rights were retained. The GOP-controlled Congress also took action to lump additional categorical grants into block grants, thereby giving states more control over how federal money would be spent.

The most significant change occurred in 1996, when Congress enacted the sweeping Welfare Reform Act. Opinion polls at the time revealed that a majority of Americans felt that government was spending too much on welfare and that too many welfare recipients were taking advantage of the system. The Welfare Reform Act tightened spending and eligibility. The legislation's key element, the Temporary Assistance for Needy Families (TANF) block grant, ended the decades-old program that granted cash assistance to every poor family with children. TANF restricts a family's eligibility for federal assistance to five years, and after two years, a family head normally has to go to work for the benefits to continue. Moreover, TANF gives states wide latitude in setting benefit levels, eligibility criteria, and other regulations affecting aid to poor families. TANF also places states in charge of developing training and education programs that will move people off of welfare and into jobs. (TANF and other aspects of the 1996 welfare reform legislation are discussed further in later chapters.)

After passage of the 1996 Welfare Reform Act, congressional efforts to reduce federal authority declined sharply. Welfare had been the main target of Republican lawmakers, and other broad initiatives were politically more difficult to achieve. Devolution had succeeded in rolling back only a small proportion of the federal programs enacted since the 1930s, but it was a significant development nonetheless.

However, the political impulse did not last. One of the first major initiatives of Republican President George W. Bush was the No Child Left Behind Act, which thrust federal authority deeper into local and state education policy. The terrorist attacks of September 11, 2001, led to a further expansion of federal authority when Congress and President Bush established the Department of Homeland Security, a cabinet-level federal agency with policing and emergency-response functions that traditionally have been the responsibility of state and local governments.

As these examples suggest, there are substantial limits on the amount of power that can reasonably be returned to the states. Because of the increased interdependency of American society, the states will never again enjoy the autonomy they had prior to the 1930s.

Devolution, Judicial Style   In the five decades after the 1930s, the Supreme Court granted Congress broad authority in the enactment of policies affecting state and local governments. In *Garcia v. San Antonio Authority* (1985), the Court held that federal minimum wage standards apply even to state and local governments' own employees.[29] The idea that these governments cannot decide fully the wage scale for the people they hire would have been unthinkable in an earlier era.

In recent years, however, the Court has restricted to a degree Congress's power to enact laws binding on the states. Newly appointed justices to the Supreme Court since the 1970s have been mainly Republican-appointed conservatives, most of whom believe that Congress has overstepped its constitutional authority in some areas.[30] In *United States v. Lopez* (1995), for example, the Court cited the Tenth Amendment in striking down a federal law that prohibited the possession of guns within 1,000 feet of a school. Congress had invoked the commerce power in passing the bill, but the Court ruled that the ban had "nothing to do with commerce, or any sort of economic activity."[31] Two years later, in *Printz v. United States* (1997), the Court struck down a provision of the federal Handgun Violence Prevention Act (the so-called Brady bill) that required local law enforcement officers to conduct background checks on prospective handgun buyers. The Court said the provision violated the Tenth Amendment because it required state officials—in this case, police officers—to "enforce a federal regulatory program."[32] Congress can require federal officials to take such action, but it cannot order state officials to do so.

The Eleventh Amendment has also been used to trim Congress's authority over state governments. The Eleventh Amendment protects a state from being sued without its consent in federal court by a private citizen. In *Kimel v. Florida Board of Regents* (2000)[33] and *Board of Trustees of the University of Alabama v. Garrett* (2002),[34] the Supreme Court held that states cannot be sued by their own employees for violations of federal age and disability discrimination laws. The Court said that, unlike race or gender, age and disability are not protected from state action by the Fourteenth Amendment, and so states and localities are free to decide the age and disability policies that will apply to their own workers.

POLITICAL CULTURE
Liberty, Equality, and Self-Government

Federalism
During the debate over ratification of the Constitution, Americans argued over whether liberty, equality, and self-government would be better protected by the states or by the nation. The Anti-Federalists argued that a small republic was closer to the people and therefore would do more to uphold individuals' rights. James Madison, arguing on behalf of the Federalists, countered by saying that a large republic was preferable because its wide diversity of interests would lead groups to find compromise solutions.

Which view—that of the Anti-Federalists or that of the Federalists—is better supported by history? Have America's founding ideals been better nurtured through state governments or through the national government? For a long period in U.S. history, the answer was clear. As political scientist William Riker noted, state-centered government before and after the Civil War was the tool by which white Americans dominated black Americans, first through slavery and later through institutionalized racism (for example, the separation by law of black and white schoolchildren). As Madison prophesied, a smaller republic makes it easier for a dominant faction to run roughshod over others.

Legal racial discrimination is now a thing of the past, and state governments are less likely to side with one faction against others. How would you judge today's situation? In your view, which level of government—federal or state—is more likely to protect and enhance the ideals of liberty, equality, and self-government? Which level of government is more likely to promote the interests of a particular group at the expense of other groups? In what areas of public policy—taxation, education, public safety, and so on—do you think your opinion is most supported?

These rulings are significant, but not earthshattering, in that they are limited to state and local government employees and do not apply to other people residing in a state or locality. These individuals are protected by the federal laws in question. Moreover, the Supreme Court in other recent rulings has endorsed congressional authority. In *Gonzales v. Raich* (2005), for example, the Supreme Court upheld Congress's power to regulate marijuana use. Nearly a dozen states, including California, had passed laws enabling patients, with a physician's prescription, to grow and use marijuana.

Although the marijuana in question was not shipped across state lines, the Supreme Court held that the commerce clause allows Congress to ban marijuana even for medical purposes.[35]

Most importantly, the Supreme Court has not retreated from the principle established in the 1930s that Congress's taxing, spending, and commerce powers are broad and substantial. This principle has enabled the federal government, through grants-in-aid and regulatory policies, to exercise authority in policy areas once reserved for the states. Even when recent Supreme Court decisions are taken into account, American federalism is a far different governing system today than it was prior to the 1930s.[36] The states remain powerful governing bodies, but they operate within a system of expanded federal authority.

THE PUBLIC'S INFLUENCE: SETTING THE BOUNDARIES OF FEDERAL–STATE POWER

Public opinion has had a decisive influence on the ebb and flow of federal power during the past century. As Americans' attitudes toward the federal government and the states changed, the balance of power between these two levels of government also shifted.

During the Great Depression, when it was clear that the states would be unable to help, Americans turned to Washington for relief. For people without jobs, the fine points of the Constitution were of little consequence. President Roosevelt's programs, though a radical departure from the past, quickly gained public favor. A 1936 Gallup poll indicated, for example, that 61 percent of Americans supported Roosevelt's social security program, whereas only 27 percent opposed it. This support reflected a new public attitude: the federal government, not the states, was expected to take the lead in protecting Americans from economic hardship.[37]

The second great wave of federal social programs—Lyndon Johnson's Great Society—was also driven by public demands. Income and education levels had risen dramatically after the Second World War, and Americans wanted more and better services from government.[38] When the states were slow to respond, Americans pressured federal officials to act. The Medicare and Medicaid programs, which provide health care for the elderly and the poor, respectively, are examples of the Johnson administration's response.

Public opinion was also behind the rollback of federal authority in the 1990s. Americans' dissatisfaction with federal programs provided the springboard for the Republican takeover of Congress in the 1994 midterm election, which led to policies aimed at devolving power to the states, including the widely popular 1996 Welfare Reform Act.[39]

The public's role in determing the boundaries between federal and state power would come as no surprise to the Framers of the Constitution. For them, federalism was a pragmatic issue, one to be decided by the nation's needs rather than by inflexible rules. James Madison predicted as much when he said that Americans would look to whichever level of government was more responsive to their interests. Indeed, each succeeding generation of Americans has seen fit to devise a balance of federal and state power suited to its needs.

SUMMARY   Self-Test www.mhhe.com/pattersonwtp8e.

A foremost characteristic of the American political system is its division of authority between a national government and state governments. The first U.S. government, established by the Articles of Confederation, was essentially a union of the states.

In establishing the basis for a stronger national government, the U.S. Constitution also made provision for safeguarding state interests. The result was the creation of a federal system in which sovereignty was vested in both national and state governments. The Constitution enumerates the general powers of the national government and grants it implied powers through the "necessary and proper" clause. Other powers are reserved to the states by the Tenth Amendment.

From 1789 to 1865, the nation's survival was at issue. The states found it convenient at times to argue that their sovereignty took precedence over national authority. In the end, it took the Civil War to cement the idea that the United States was a union of people, not of states. From 1865 to 1937, federalism reflected the doctrine that certain policy areas were the exclusive responsibility of the national government, whereas responsibility in other policy areas belonged exclusively to the states. This constitutional position validated the laissez-faire doctrine that big business was largely beyond governmental control. It also allowed the states to discriminate against African Americans in their public policies. Federalism in a form recognizable today began to emerge in the 1930s.

In the areas of commerce, taxation, spending, civil rights, and civil liberties, among others, the federal government now plays an important role, one that is the inevitable consequence of the increasing complexity of American society and the interdependence of its people. National, state, and local officials now work closely together to solve the nation's problems, a situation known as cooperative federalism. Grants-in-aid from Washington to the states and localities have been the chief instrument of national influence. States and localities have received billions in federal assistance; in accepting federal money, they also have accepted both federal restrictions on its use and the national policy priorities that underlie the granting of the money.

The issue of the relationship between the nation and the states has changed somewhat as a result of devolution—a shift of power downward to the states. This change, like changes throughout U.S. history, sprang from the demands of the American people.

KEY TERMS

block grants (*p. 95*)

categorical grants (*p. 95*)

commerce clause (*p. 87*)

confederacy (*p. 74*)

cooperative federalism (*p. 90*)

devolution (*p. 95*)

dual federalism (*p. 84*)

enumerated (expressed) powers (*p. 77*)

federalism (*p. 74*)

fiscal federalism (*p. 92*)

grants-in-aid (*p. 93*)

implied powers (*p. 78*)

"necessary and proper" (elastic) clause (*p. 78*)

reserved powers (*p. 79*)

sovereignty (*p. 74*)

supremacy clause (*p. 78*)

unitary system (*p. 74*)

SUGGESTED READINGS

Beer, Samuel H. *To Make a Nation: The Rediscovery of American Federalism*. Cambridge, Mass.: Belknap Press of Harvard University, 1993. An innovative interpretive framework for understanding the impact of federalism and nationalism on the nation's development.

Chopra, Pran. *Supreme Court Versus the Constitution: A Challenge to Federalism*. Thousand Oaks, Calif.: Sage Publications, 2006. A look at the Supreme Court's view of federalism.

Cornell, Saul. *The Other Founders: Anti-Federalism and the Dissenting Tradition in America*. Chapel Hill: University of North Carolina Press, 1999. An analysis of Anti-Federalist thought, its origins, and its legacy.

Elkins, Stanley, and Eric McKitrick. *The Age of Federalism: The Early American Republic, 1788–1800*. New York: Oxford University Press, 1993. An award-winning book on the earliest period of American federalism.

Garry, Patrick M. *An Entrenched Legacy: How the New Deal Constitutional Revolution Continues to Shape the Role of the Supreme Court*. State College: Pennsylvania State University Press, 2008. An analysis showing the durability of the constitutional changes in federalism established in the 1930s.

Ross, William G. *A Muted Fury: Populists, Progressives, and Labor Unions Confront the Courts, 1890–1937*. Princeton, N.J.: Princeton University Press, 1993. A valuable study of the political conflict surrounding the judiciary's laissez-faire doctrine in the period 1890–1937.

Teaford, John. *The Rise of the States: Evolution of American State Government*. Baltimore, Md.: Johns Hopkins University Press, 2002. A historical assessment of state government that spans the past century.

Walker, David B. *The Rebirth of Federalism*, 2d ed. Chatham, N. J.: Chatham House, 2000. An optimistic assessment of the state of today's federalism.

LIST OF WEBSITES

http://lcweb2.loc.gov/ammem/amlaw/lawhome.html A site containing congressional documents and debates from 1774 to 1873.

http://www.csg.org/ The site of the Council of State Governments; includes current news from each of the states and basic information about their governments.

http://www.temple.edu/federalism/ The site of the Center for the Study of Federalism, located at Temple University; offers information and publications on the federal system of government.

http://www.yale.edu/lawweb/avalon/federal/fed.htm A documentary record of the *Federalist Papers*, the Annapolis convention, the Articles of Confederation, the Madison debates, and the U.S. Constitution.

POLITICS IN THEORY AND PRACTICE

Thinking: How have interdependency and the federal government's superior taxing power contributed to a larger policy role for the national government? Do you think these factors will increase or decrease in importance in the future? What will this trend mean for the future of American federalism? (You might find it helpful to think about these questions in the context of a specific policy area, such as the terrorist threat facing the country.)

Participating: The U.S. federal system of government offers an array of channels for political participation. Vital governing decisions are made at the national, state, and local levels, all of which provide opportunities for citizens to make a difference and also to build skills, such as public speaking and working with others, that will prove valuable in other areas of life. You have a participatory arena close at hand: the college campus. Most colleges and universities support a variety of activities in which students can engage. Student government is one such opportunity; another is the student newspaper. Most colleges and universities offer a wide range of groups and sponsored programs, from debate clubs to fraternal organizations. If you are not now active in campus groups, consider joining one. If you join—or if you already belong to such a group—take full advantage of the participatory opportunities it provides.

Extra Credit

For up-to-the-minute *New York Times* articles, interactive simulations, graphics, study tools, and more links and quizzes, visit the text's Online Learning Center at www.mhhe.com/pattersonwtp8e.

The National Idea in American Politics

By Samuel H. Beer

In his essay, retired Harvard professor Samuel Beer discusses the "national idea" as a prevailing theme of American politics. He focuses on two aspects of federalism that were discussed in Chapter 3: the distribution of power between the two levels of government and the use of power at each level. By contrasting Hamilton with Jefferson and Johnson with Reagan, he shows the persistent nature of the conflict between those Americans who favor activist national government and those who oppose what they regard as excessive centralization. Beer's accounting is a capsule summary of federalism—a system of government in which sovereign power is simultaneously invested in two levels of government, resulting in a dynamic system in which competing visions of America are played out.

The national idea is a way of looking at American government and American society. It embraces a view of where the authority of government comes from and a view of what it should be used for. As a concept of authority, it identifies the whole people of the nation as the source of the legitimate powers of any and all governments. As a concept of purpose, it tells us that we are one people and guides us toward what we should make of ourselves as a people. The national idea envisions one people, at once sovereign and subject, source of authority and substance of history, affirming, through conflict and in diversity, our unity of being and becoming.

Because the national idea is also a democratic idea, these concepts of authority and purpose are interdependent. Self-government is reflexive. The people who govern are also the object of government. A government of the people, therefore, gets its legitimacy both from being a government by the people and from being a government for the people.

This theory of legitimacy is national and democratic. It is also federal. In the national perspective, although we are one people who enjoy a common life as one nation, we have set up not a unitary but a dual system of government. In establishing this system, the American people authorized and empowered two sets of governments: a general government for the whole, and state governments for the parts. The constitutional authority for the two sets of government is therefore coordinate. Neither created the other, and both are subject to the same ultimate legitimating power, the sovereign people. And periodically the people in this constituent capacity amend these institutions, by which in their governing capacity they direct the day-to-day affairs of the nation.

From our revolutionary beginnings the national idea has been widely accepted as a description of historical fact and a theory of legitimacy of American federalism. The American political tradition, however, has also sustained another view. In this opposing view, one of these levels of government, the federal government, was brought into existence not by the act of a sovereign people but by a compact among sovereign states. From this compact theory inferences follow that radically contradict the conclusions of the national theory. While the national theory has, on balance, had much the greater influence on thought and action, the compact theory has survived and continues even today to show itself in the feelings of citizens, the rhetoric of politicians, and the actions of governments.

When President Reagan took office in 1981, for instance, he proclaimed a "new federalism." Its central thrust was to cut back on the activities of the federal government by reducing or eliminating a vast number of programs, the principal cuts falling on federal aid to state and local governments. The President wished to do this because he judged these activities to be inefficient, unnecessary, and sometimes positively harmful. He also claimed that they were improper under the Constitution. . . .

In his first inaugural address on January 20, 1981, accordingly, President Reagan promised to "restore the balance between levels of government." And while he did not elaborate his political philosophy, he made clear in a phrase or two his reliance upon the compact theory of the Constitution to justify his new federalism. "The Federal government," he declared at one point in his address, "did not create the states; the states created the Federal government."

This allegation did not pass without comment. In response to President Reagan's use of the compact theory, eminent academic critics counterattacked in terms of the national theory. Richard P. Morris of Columbia University called the President's view of the historical facts "a hoary myth about the origins of the Union" and went on to summarize the evidence showing that "the United States was created by the people in collectivity, not by the individual states."

No less bluntly, Henry Steele Commager of Amherst College said President Reagan did not understand the Constitution, which in its own words asserts that it was ordained by "We, the People of the United States," not by the states severally. . . .

The argument between the President and the professors was not simply about history. Nor was it mainly about the constitutional authority of the federal and state governments. Their primary disagreement was over public policy, specifically, the use of federal authority in recent years to expand the social and economic programs of the welfare state, especially those dating from the "new federalism" of Lyndon Johnson. President Reagan had taken office as the champion of conservative attitudes that had been gathering force around the country for a generation. He articulated these attitudes in a distinctive vision of American society at home and abroad and in a set of strategies for realizing that vision. Expressing in a new public philosophy the old and familiar values of rugged individualism, he sought to cut back the welfare state and to restore the free market—or in the language of political economy, to shift social choice from public choice toward market choice. Declaring in his first inaugural address that the excessive growth of the public sector in recent years meant that "government is not the solution to our problem; government is the problem," he proposed to "reverse" that growth. Intrinsic to this goal was his promise of another "new federalism" which would "restore the balance between levels of government." The reduction of federal grant programs would at once help restore the federal-state balance and promote the free market.

Some critics called him insincere, claiming that when he said he wanted to restore the federal-state balance, what he really wanted to do was to cut federal spending on social and economic programs. No doubt he was mainly interested in the impact of his policies on American society. But that is no reason for saying that he was not also interested in reducing what he thought was excessive centralization of power in the federal system. In American politics, thinking about federalism has usually had those two aspects: a concern with both the pattern of authority and the pattern of purpose, with the balance of power between levels of government and with the policies for which that power is used. When President Reagan called in the compact theory to lend support to his views on public policy, he was doing what its adherents before him had often done. In their way the nationalists had done the same, right from the days when Alexander Hamilton, as Secretary of the Treasury, set the course of the first administration of George Washington. . . .

Hamilton's nationalism was expressed not only in his belief that Americans were "one people" rather than thirteen separate peoples but even more emphatically in his commitment to governmental activism. This concern that the American people must make vigorous use of their central government for the tasks of nation-building separated him

sharply from Thomas Jefferson, Washington's Secretary of State, who leaned toward the compact theory. . . .

Hamilton is renowned for his statecraft—for his methods of using the powers of government for economic, political, and social ends. But that emphasis obscures his originality, which consisted in his conceptualization of those ends. . . . [E]arlier craftsmen of the modern state in Bourbon France or Hohenzollern Prussia or Whig Britain could take for granted the established authority of a monarchic and aristocratic regime. They too had their techniques for enhancing the attachment of the people to the prince. But in America the people *were* the prince. To enhance their attachment to the ultimate governing power, therefore, meant fortifying the bonds that united them as a people. If the authority of this first nation-state was to suffice for its governance, the purpose of the state would have to become the development of the nation. This was the essential Hamiltonian end: to make the nation more of a nation.

What's Your Opinion?

Which interpretation of the Constitution do you find more convincing, that of Alexander Hamilton or that of Ronald Reagan? If you had a choice of a nation of states or a nation of people, which would you choose? Explain in terms of the impact on how Americans would be governed.

CHAPTER 4

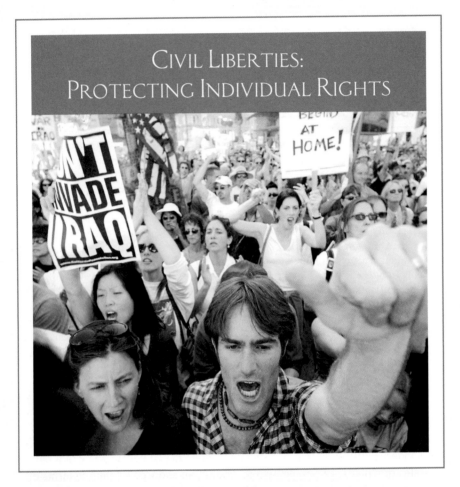

CIVIL LIBERTIES:
PROTECTING INDIVIDUAL RIGHTS

66 A bill of rights is what the people are entitled to against every government on earth, general or particular, and what no just government should refuse, or rest on inference. 99

THOMAS JEFFERSON[1]

Robert and Sarisse Creighton and their three children were asleep when FBI agents and local police broke into their home in the middle of the night. Brandishing guns, the officers searched the house for a relative of the Creightons who was suspected of bank robbery. When asked to show a search warrant, the officers said, "You watch too much TV." The suspect was not there, and the agents and officers left as abruptly as they had entered.

The Creightons sued the FBI agent in charge, Russell Anderson, for violating their Fourth Amendment right against unlawful search.

The Creightons won a temporary victory when the U.S. Circuit Court of Appeals for the Eighth Circuit—noting that individuals are constitutionally protected against warrantless searches unless officers have good reason ("probable cause") for a search and unless they have good reason ("exigent circumstances") for conducting that search without a warrant—concluded that Anderson had been derelict in his duty. In the judgment of the appellate court, Anderson should have sought a warrant from a judge, who would have decided whether a search of the Creightons' home was justified.

The Supreme Court of the United States overturned the lower court's ruling. The Court's majority opinion stated: "We have recognized that it is inevitable that law enforcement officials will in some cases reasonably but mistakenly conclude that probable cause is present, and we have indicated that in such cases those officials . . . should not be held personally liable." Justice John Paul Stevens and two other justices sharply dissented. Stevens accused the Court's majority of showing "remarkably little fidelity" to the Fourth Amendment.[2] Civil liberties groups claimed that the Court's decision gave police an open invitation to invade people's homes on the slightest pretext. For their part, law enforcement officials praised the decision, saying that a ruling in the Creightons' favor would have made them hesitant to pursue suspects for fear of a lawsuit whenever the search failed to produce the culprit.

As this case illustrates, issues of individual rights are complex and political. No right is absolute. For example, the Fourth Amendment protects Americans not from *all* searches but from *unreasonable* searches. The public would be unsafe if law officials could never pursue a suspect into a home. Yet the public would also be unsafe if police could invade homes anytime they wanted. The challenge for a civil society is to establish a level of police authority that balances the demands of public safety with those of personal freedom. The balance point, however, is always subject to dispute. Did Agent Anderson have sufficient cause for a warrantless search of the Creightons' home? Or was his evidence so weak that his forcible entry constituted an unreasonable search? Not even the justices of the Supreme Court could agree on these questions. Six justices sided with Anderson, and three backed the Creightons' position.

This chapter examines issues of **civil liberties**—specific individual rights, such as freedom of speech and protection against self-incrimination, that are constitutionally protected against infringement by government. As seen in Chapter 2, the Constitution's failure to enumerate individual freedoms led to demands for the **Bill of Rights** (see Table 4-1). Enacted in 1791, these first ten amendments to the Constitution specify certain rights of life, liberty, and

table **4-1** THE BILL OF RIGHTS: A SELECTED LIST OF CONSTITUTIONAL PROTECTIONS

The Bill of Rights refers to the first ten amendments to the Constitution, which include protections of individual rights.

First Amendment

Speech: You are free to say almost anything except that which is obscene, slanders another person, or has a high probability of inciting others to take imminent lawless action.

Assembly: You are free to assemble, although government may regulate the time and place for reasons of public convenience and safety, provided such regulations are applied evenhandedly to all groups.

Religion: You are protected from having the religious beliefs of others imposed on you, and you are free to believe what you like.

Fourth Amendment

Search and seizure: You are protected from unreasonable searches and seizures, although you forfeit that right if you knowingly waive it.

Arrest: You are protected from arrest unless authorities have probable cause to believe that you have committed a crime.

Fifth Amendment

Self-incrimination: You are protected against self-incrimination, which means that you have the right to remain silent and to be protected against coercion by law enforcement officials.

Double jeopardy: You cannot be tried twice for the same crime if the first trial results in a verdict of innocence.

Due process: You cannot be deprived of life, liberty, or property without proper legal proceedings.

Sixth Amendment

Counsel: You have a right to be represented by an attorney and can demand to speak first with an attorney before responding to questions from law enforcement officials.

Prompt and reasonable proceedings: You have a right to be arraigned promptly, to be informed of the charges, to confront witnesses, and to have a speedy and open trial by an impartial jury.

Eighth Amendment

Bail: You are protected against excessive bail or fines.

Cruel and unusual punishment: You are protected from cruel and unusual punishment, although this provision does not protect you from the death penalty or from a long prison term for a minor offense.

property that the national government is obliged to respect. A later amendment, the Fourteenth, became the basis for protecting these rights from infringment by state and local governments.

Rights have full meaning only as they are protected in law. A constitutional guarantee is not worth the paper on which it is written if authorities can violate it at will. The primary responsibility for seeing that authorities uphold people's rights rests with courts of law. For the most part, they determine what people's rights mean in practice. In some areas, the judiciary devises a specific test to determine whether government action is lawful. A test applied in the area of free speech, for example, is whether general rules (such as restrictions on the time and place of a political rally) are applied fairly. Government officials do not meet this test if they apply one set of rules for groups that they like and a harsher set of rules for those they dislike.

Issues of individual rights have become increasingly complex. The Framers of the Constitution could not possibly have foreseen the United States of the early twenty-first century, with its huge national government, enormous corporations, pervasive mass media, urban crowding, and vulnerability to terrorist acts. These developments are potential threats to personal liberty, and the judiciary in recent decades has seen fit to expand the rights to which individuals are entitled. However, these rights are constantly being balanced against competing rights and society's collective interests. The Bill of Rights operates in an untidy world where people's highest aspirations collide with their worst passions, and it is at this juncture that issues of civil liberties arise. Should an admitted murderer be entitled to recant a confession? Should the press be allowed to print military secrets whose publication might jeopardize national security? Should extremist groups be allowed to publicize their messages of prejudice and hate? Such questions are among the subjects of this chapter, which focuses on these points:

★ *Freedom of expression is the most basic of democratic rights, but like all rights, it is not unlimited.* In recent decades, free expression has been strongly supported by the Supreme Court.

★ *"Due process of law" refers to legal protections (primarily procedural safeguards) designed to ensure that individual rights are respected by government.*

★ *During the last half-century particularly, the civil liberties of individual Americans have been substantially broadened in law and given greater judicial protection from action by all levels of government.* Of special significance has been the Supreme Court's use of the Fourteenth Amendment to protect individual rights from action by state and local governments.

★ *Individual rights are constantly being weighed against the demands of majorities and the collective needs of society.* All political institutions are involved in this process, as is public opinion, but the judiciary plays a central role and is the institution that is most protective of civil liberties.

FREEDOM OF EXPRESSION

Freedom of political expression is the most basic of democratic rights. Unless citizens can openly express their political opinions, they cannot properly influence their government or act to protect their other rights. As Justice Harlan Fiske Stone argued in 1938, the right of free expression is the foundation for all other rights. If government can control what people will hear, it can control their thoughts and thereby deprive them of their right to freely decide how they will be governed.[3]

The First Amendment provides the foundation for **freedom of expression**—the right of individual Americans to hold and communicate views of their choosing. For many reasons, such as a desire to conform to social pressure or a fear of harassment, Americans do not always choose to express themselves freely. Moreover, freedom of expression, like other rights, is not absolute. It does not entitle individuals to say or do whatever they want, to whomever they want, whenever they want. Free expression can be denied, for example, if it endangers national security, wrongly damages the reputation of others, or deprives others of their basic rights. Nevertheless, the First Amendment provides for freedom of expression by prohibiting laws that would unreasonably abridge the freedoms of conscience, speech, press, assembly, and petition.

Free expression is vigorously protected by the courts. Today, under most circumstances, Americans can freely express their political views without fear of governmental interference or retribution. In earlier times, however, Americans were less free to express their opinions.

The Early Period: The Uncertain Status of the Right of Free Expression

The first attempt by the U.S. government to restrict free expression was the Sedition Act of 1798, which made it a crime to print harshly critical newspaper stories about the president or other national officials. Thomas Jefferson called the Sedition Act an "alarming infraction" of the Constitution and, upon replacing John Adams as president in 1801, pardoned those who had been convicted under it. Because the Supreme Court did not review the sedition cases, however, the judiciary's position on free expression was an

**Historical
Background**

open question. The Court also did not rule on free speech during the Civil War era, when the government severely restricted individual rights.

In 1919, the Court finally ruled on a free-expression case. The defendant had been convicted under the 1917 Espionage Act, which prohibited forms of dissent, including the distribution of anti-war leaflets, that could harm the nation's effort in World War I. In *Schenck v. United States* (1919), the Court unanimously upheld the constitutionality of the Espionage Act. In the opinion written by Justice Oliver Wendell Holmes, the Court said that Congress could restrict speech that was "of such a nature as to create a clear and present danger" to the nation's security. In a famous passage, Holmes argued that not even the First Amendment would permit a person to falsely yell "Fire!" in a crowded theater and create a panic that could kill or injure innocent people.[4]

Although the *Schenck* decision upheld a law that limited free expression, it also established a constitutional standard—the **clear-and-present-danger test**—for determining when government could legally do so. Government could ban speech that posed a clear and present danger, but it could *not* ban speech that posed no such danger. (The clear-and-present-danger test was later replaced by the *imminent lawless action test*, which is discussed later in the chapter.)

The Modern Period: Protecting Free Expression

Until the twentieth century, the tension between national security interests and free expression was not a pressing issue in the United States. The country's great size and ocean barriers provided protection from potential enemies, minimizing concerns about internal subversion. World War I, however, intruded on America's isolation, and World War II brought it to an abrupt end. Since then, Americans' rights of free expression have been defined largely in the context of national security concerns.

Free Speech   In the period after World War II, many Americans believed that the Soviet Union was bent on destroying the United States, and the Supreme Court allowed government to limit certain types of expression. In 1951, for example, the Court upheld the convictions of eleven members of the U.S. Communist Party who had been prosecuted under a law that made it illegal to voice support for the forceful overthrow of the U.S. government.[5]

By the late 1950s, however, fear of internal communist subversion was subsiding, and the Supreme Court permenently changed its stance.[6] For the past half-century, it has held that national security must be *directly and*

The Supreme Court has ruled that flag burning is a constitutionally protected form of free expression. Shown here is a scene outside California's San Quentin Prison in 2005. The crowd is burning the American flag to protest the execution of convicted murderer Stanley Williams, whose case attracted national attention.

substantially imperiled before government can lawfully prohibit citizens from speaking out. During this period, which includes the Vietnam and Iraq wars, not a single individual has been convicted solely for criticizing the government's war policies. (Some dissenters have been found guilty on other grounds, such as inciting a riot or assaulting a police officer.)

The Supreme Court's protection of **symbolic speech** has been less substantial than its protection of verbal speech. For example, the Court in 1968 upheld the conviction of a Vietnam protester who had burned his draft registration card. The Court concluded that the federal law prohibiting the destruction of draft cards was intended primarily to protect the military's need for soldiers, not to prevent people from criticizing government policy.[7] Nevertheless, the Supreme Court has been broadly protective of symbolic speech. In 1989, for example, the Court ruled that the symbolic burning of the American flag is a lawful form of expression. The ruling came in the case of Gregory Lee Johnson, who had set fire to a flag outside the hall in Dallas where the 1984 Republican National Convention was being held. The Supreme Court rejected the state of Texas's argument that flag burning is, in every instance, an imminent danger to public safety. "If there is a bedrock principle underlying the First Amendment," the Court ruled in the *Johnson* case, "it is that the Government may not prohibit the expression of an idea simply because society finds the idea itself offensive or disagreeable."[8]

Press Freedom and Prior Restraint   Freedom of the press also receives strong judicial protection. In *New York Times Co. v. United States* (1971), the Court ruled that the *Times*'s publication of the "Pentagon Papers" (secret government documents revealing that officials had deceived the public about aspects of the Vietnam War) could not be blocked by the government, which claimed that publication would hurt the war effort. The documents had been illegally obtained by antiwar activists, who then gave them to the *Times*. The Court ruled that "any system of prior restraints" on the press is unconstitutional unless the government can clearly justify the restriction.[9]

The unacceptability of **prior restraint**—government prohibition of speech or publication before the fact—is basic to the current doctrine of free expression. The Supreme Court has said that any attempt by government to prevent expression carries "a 'heavy presumption' against its constitutionality."[10] News organizations are legally responsible after the fact for what they report or say (for example, they can be sued by an individual whose reputation is wrongly damaged by their words), but government generally cannot stop the media in advance from reporting their views. One exception is the reporting on U.S. military operations during wartime. The courts have allowed the government to censor reports filed by journalists who are granted access to the battlefront. The courts have also upheld the government's authority to ban uncensored publications by certain past and present government employees, such as CIA agents, who have knowledge of classified information and programs.

Free Expression and State Governments

In 1790, Congress rejected a proposed constitutional amendment that would have applied the Bill of Rights to the states. Thus, the freedoms provided in the Bill of Rights initially were protected only from action by the national government.[11] The effect was that the Bill of Rights had limited meaning to the lives of ordinary Americans because state and local governments carry out most of the activities, such as law enforcement, in which people's rights are at issue.

Historical
Background

Not until the twentieth century did the Supreme Court begin to protect individual rights from infringement by state and local governments. The instrument for this change was the **due process clause of the Fourteenth Amendment** to the Constitution.

The Fourteenth Amendment and Selective Incorporation   The Fourteenth Amendment, ratified in 1868, includes a clause that forbids a state from depriving any person of life, liberty, or property without due process of law (due process refers to the legal procedures, such as the right to a lawyer, that have been established as a means of protecting individuals' rights).

Although Congress, in passing the Fourteenth Amendment, did not say that it was intended to protect First Amendment rights from infringement by the states, the Supreme Court, six decades later, interpreted it as doing so. In *Gitlow v. New York* (1925), the Supreme Court upheld Benjamin Gitlow's conviction for violating a New York law making it illegal to advocate the violent overthrow of the U.S. government but held that states are not completely free to limit expression. The Court said: "For present purposes we may and do assume that freedom of speech and of the press—which are protected by the First Amendment from abridgement by Congress—are among the fundamental personal rights and 'liberties' protected by the due process clause of the Fourteenth Amendment from impairment by the states."[12]

The Supreme Court justified this new interpretation of the Fourteenth Amendment by referring to **selective incorporation**—the process by which certain of the rights contained in the Bill of Rights become applicable through the Fourteenth Amendment to actions by the state governments. The process is selective in the sense that only particular Bill of Rights guarantees, as opposed to all of them, are applied to the states. The process is significant because it enables federal courts to determine whether state governments have acted properly in upholding civil liberties. In the *Gitlow* case, the Court reasoned that the Fourteenth Amendment's due process clause, which says in part that states cannot deprive residents of their personal liberty, would be meaningless if states were allowed to prevent their residents from speaking freely. Thus, through *Gitlow*, the Court selectively incorporated the First Amendment guarantee of free speech into the Fourteenth Amendment, enabling citizens who believe that their free speech rights have been violated by a state to bring suit against the state in federal court.

This interpretation of the Fourteenth Amendment provided the Court with a legal basis for striking down state laws that infringed unreasonably on other forms of free expression. Within a dozen years (see Table 4-2), the Court had issued four rulings that invalidated state laws restricting expression in the areas of speech (*Fiske v. Kansas*), press (*Near v. Minnesota*),

table 4-2	SELECTIVE INCORPORATION OF RIGHTS OF FREE EXPRESSION	

In the 1920s and 1930s, the Supreme Court selectively incorporated the free-expression provisions of the First Amendment into the Fourteenth Amendment so that these rights would be protected from infringement by the states.

Supreme Court Case	Year	Constitutional Right at Issue
Gitlow v. New York	1925	Fourteenth Amendment protection of free expression
Fiske v. Kansas	1927	Free speech
Near v. Minnesota	1931	Free press
Hamilton v. Regents, U. of California	1934	Religious freedom
DeJonge v. Oregon	1937	Freedom of assembly and of petition

religion (*Hamilton v. Regents, University of California*), and assembly and petition (*DeJonge v. Oregon*).[13] The *Near* decision is the best known of these rulings. Jay Near was the publisher of a Minneapolis weekly newspaper that regularly made defamatory statements about blacks, Jews, Catholics, and labor union leaders. His paper was closed down on authority of a state law banning "malicious, scandalous, or defamatory" publications. Near appealed the shutdown on the grounds that it infringed on freedom of the press, and the Supreme Court ruled in his favor, saying that the Minnesota law was "the essence of censorship."[14]

Limiting the Authority of the States to Restrict Expression   Since the 1930s, the Supreme Court has broadly protected freedom of expression from action by the states and by local governments, which derive their authority from the states. The Court has held that the states cannot restrict free expression except when it is almost certain to provoke immediate lawless action such as a rampage or riot. A leading free speech case was *Brandenburg v. Ohio* (1969). Clarence Brandenburg was a Ku Klux Klan member who, in a speech delivered at a Klan rally, said that "revenge" might have to be taken if the national government "continues to suppress the white Caucasian race." He was convicted under an Ohio law, but the Supreme Court reversed the conviction, saying a state cannot prohibit speech that advocates the unlawful use of force "except where such advocacy is directed to inciting or producing imminent lawless action, and is likely to produce such action."[15]

This test—the likelihood of **imminent lawless action**—is a severe limit on the government's power to restrict expression. It is rare for words alone

Exercising their right of free speech and assembly, antiabortion protesters gather outside a government building. Individuals do not have a constitutional right to demonstrate in any place at any time, but government is required to accommodate requests for marches and other displays of free expression.

to incite others to immediately take unlawful action. In effect, Americans are free to say almost anything they want on political issues. This protection includes hate speech. In a unanimous 1992 opinion, the Court struck down a St. Paul, Minnesota, ordinance making it a crime to engage in speech likely to arouse "anger or alarm" on the basis of "race, color, creed, religion or gender." The Court said that the First Amendment prohibits government from "silencing speech on the basis of its content."[16] This protection of hate *speech* does not, however, extend to hate *crimes*, such as assault, motivated by racial or other prejudice. A Wisconsin law that provided for increased sentences for hate crimes was challenged as a violation of the First Amendment. In a unanimous 1993 opinion, the Court said that the law was aimed at "conduct unprotected by the First Amendment" rather than the defendant's speech.[17]

In a key case involving freedom of assembly, the U.S. Supreme Court in 1977 upheld a lower-court ruling against local ordinances of Skokie, Illinois, that had been invoked to prevent a parade there by the American Nazi Party.[18] Skokie had a large Jewish population, including many survivors of Nazi Germany's oncentration camps. The Supreme Court held that the right of free expression takes precedence over the mere *possibility* that the exercise of that right might have undesirable consequences. Before government can lawfully prevent a speech or rally, it must demonstrate that the event will cause harm and also must demonstrate the lack of alternative ways (such as assigning police officers to control the crowd) to prevent the harm from happening.

The Supreme Court has recognized that freedom of speech and assembly may conflict with the routines of daily life. Accordingly, individuals do not have the right to hold a public rally at a busy intersection during rush hour, nor do they have the right to immediate access to a public auditorium or the right to turn up the volume on loudspeakers to the point where they can be heard miles away. The Court has held that public officials can regulate the time, place, and conditions of public assembly, provided that these regulations are reasonable and are applied evenhandedly to all groups, including those that hold unpopular views.[19]

In general, the Supreme Court's position is that the First Amendment makes any government effort to regulate the *content* of a message highly suspect. In the flag-burning case, Texas was regulating the content of the message—contempt for the flag and the principles it represents. Texas could not have been regulating the act itself, for the Texas government's own method of disposing of worn-out flags is to burn them. But a content-neutral regulation (no public rally can be held at a busy intersection during rush hour) is acceptable as long as it is reasonable and does not discriminate against certain groups or ideas.

Libel and Slander

The constitutional right of free expression is not a legal license to avoid responsibility for the consequences of what is said or written. If false information that greatly harms a person's reputation is published (**libel**) or spoken (**slander**), the injured party can sue for damages. If it were easy for public officials to claim defamation and win large amounts of money, individuals and organizations would be reluctant to criticize those in power. As it happens, slander and libel laws in the United States are based on the assumption that society has an interest in encouraging citizens and news organizations to express themselves freely. Accordingly, public officials can be criticized nearly at will without fear that the writer or speaker will have to pay them damages for slander or libel. (The courts are less protective of the writer or speaker when allegations are made about a private citizen. What is said about private individuals is considered to be less basic to the democratic process than what is said about public officials.)

The Supreme Court has held that true statements disseminated by the media have "full constitutional protection."[20] In other words, factually accurate statements, no matter how damaging they might be to a public official's career or reputation, are a protected form of expression. Even false or conjectural statements enjoy considerable legal protection. In *New York Times Co. v. Sullivan* (1964), the Supreme Court overruled an Alabama state court that had found the *New York Times* guilty of libel for printing an advertisement that criticized Alabama officials for mistreating student civil rights activists. Even though some of what was alleged was false, the Supreme Court ruled in favor of the *Times*, saying that libel of a public official requires proof of actual malice, which was defined as a knowing or reckless disregard for the truth.[21] It is very difficult to prove that a publication has acted with reckless or deliberate disregard for the truth. In fact, no federal official has won a libel judgment against a news organization in the four decades since the *Sullivan* ruling.

Obscenity

Obscenity is a form of expression that is not protected by the First Amendment and thus can be prohibited by law. However, the Supreme Court has found it difficult to define with precision the criteria by which material is to be judged obscene. The Court set forth the first explicit test for obscenity in *Roth v. United States* (1957) by saying that material is obscene if "taken as a whole" it appeals to "prurient interest" and has no "redeeming social value." This assessment was to be made from the standpoint of "the average person, applying contemporary community standards."[22] However, the test proved unworkable in practice. Even the justices of the Supreme Court, when they personally examined allegedly obscene material, argued over whether it appealed to prurient interest and was without redeeming social value. In the end, they usually concluded that the material at issue had at least some social significance.

In *Miller v. California* (1973), the Court narrowed "contemporary community standards" to the local level. The Court said that what might offend residents of "Mississippi might be found tolerable in Las Vegas."[23] But even this test proved too restrictive. The Court subsequently ruled that material cannot be judged obscene simply because the "average" local resident might object to it. "Community standards" were to be judged in the context of a "reasonable person"—someone whose outlook is broad enough to evaluate the material on its overall merit rather than its most objectionable feature. The Court later also modified its content standard, saying that the material must be of a "particularly offensive type."[24] These efforts illustrate the difficulty in defining obscenity and, even more, in establishing a clear legal standard that judges can apply consistently when obscenity cases arise. A basic legal principle is that a person's guilt or innocence should not depend on a judge's uncertainty about the meaning of the law in question.

The Supreme Court has distinguished between obscene materials in public places and those in the home. A unanimous ruling in 1969 held that what adults read and watch in the privacy of their homes cannot be made a crime.[25] The Court created an exception to this rule in 1990 by upholding an Ohio law making it a crime to possess pornographic photographs of children.[26] The Court reasoned that the purchase of such material encourages producers to use children in the making of pornographic materials, which is a crime. In a 2008 decision, the Court extended the ban by upholding a 2003 federal statute that makes it a crime to offer or solicit child pornography, even if the material is based on computer-generated or digitally altered images that merely appear to be those of children. Writing for the majority in the Court's 7-2 decision, Justice Antonin Scalia said: "Offers to provide or requests to obtain child pornography are categorically excluded from the First Amendment."[27]

Children have also been a consideration in court cases involving material transmitted on cable television or over the Internet. On several occasions, Congress has passed legislation (for example, the 1998 Child Online Protection Act) that would restrict the transmission of sexually explicit material that children can access. The Supreme Court has held that the restrictions, though well intentioned, have been so broad that they would ban material adults have a constitutional right to view if they so choose.[28] The Court has directed officials to find less restrictive ways to keep such material from being seen by children. An example is the federal requirement that cable operators must scramble the signal of channels that convey sexually explicit material if a subscriber requests it.

FREEDOM OF RELIGION

Free religious expression is the precursor of free political expression, at least within the English tradition of limited government. England's Glorious, or Bloodless, Revolution of 1689 centered on the issue of religion and resulted in the Act of Toleration, which gave members of all Protestant sects the right to worship freely and publicly. The English philosopher John Locke (1632–1704) extended this principle, arguing that legitimate government could not inhibit free expression, religious or otherwise. The

Historical
Background

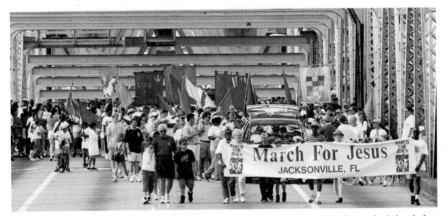

The First Amendment's protection of free expression includes religious freedom, which has led the courts to hold that government cannot in most instances promote or interfere with religious practices.

First Amendment reflects this tradition, providing for freedom of religion along with freedom of speech, press, assembly, and petition.

In regard to religion, the First Amendment reads: "Congress shall make no law respecting an establishment of religion, or prohibiting the free exercise thereof." The prohibition on laws aimed at "establishment of religion" (the establishment clause) and its "free exercise" (the free-exercise clause) applies to states and localities through the Fourteenth Amendment.

The Establishment Clause

The **establishment clause** has been interpreted by the courts to mean that government may not favor one religion over another or support religion over no religion. (This position contrasts with that of a country such as England, where Anglicanism is the official, or "established," state religion, though no religion is prohibited.) The Supreme Court's interpretation of the establishment clause has been described as maintaining a "wall of separation" between church and state. The Court held in *Engel v. Vitale* (1962) that the establishment clause prohibits the reciting of prayers in public schools.[29] A year later, the Court struck down Bible readings in public schools.[30]

Religion is a powerful force in American life, and the Supreme Court's ban on religious teaching in public school classrooms has evoked strong opposition. An Alabama law attempted to circumvent the prayer ruling by permitting public schools to set aside one minute each day for silent prayer or meditation. In 1985, the Court declared the law unconstitutional, ruling that "government must pursue a course of complete neutrality toward religion."[31] The Court in 2000 reaffirmed the ban by extending it to include organized student-led prayer at public school football games.[32]

The Supreme Court also has banned religious displays on public property when the purpose of such a display is overtly religious and lacks a historical context. Because of the prominence of religion in American life, many public buildings sport religious symbolism. For instance, a statue of Moses holding the Ten Commandments stands in the rotunda of the Library of Congress building, which opened in 1897. Legal challenges to such displays are unlikely to succeed. In *Van Orden v. Perry* (2005), for example, the Supreme Court rejected a suit asking for the dismantling of a display of the Ten Commandments on a monument on the grounds of the Texas State Capitol. The Court noted that the display had been installed nearly a half-century earlier, had been paid for by a nonreligious group, and had not previously been the subject of dispute.[33] On the other hand, in *McCreary County v. American Civil Liberties Union* (2005), the Supreme Court struck down displays of the Ten Commandments on the walls of two Kentucky courthouses. The displays were recent and had initially hung by themselves on the courtroom walls. Only after county officials were sued did they mount a few historical displays alongside the religious ones. The Supreme Court concluded that the officials had religious purposes in mind when they erected the displays and thus had to remove them.[34]

The Supreme Court generally has taken a pragmatic approach to religious controversies, permitting some establishment activities while disallowing others. For instance, the Court has allowed states to pay for secular textbooks used in church-affiliated schools[35] but has not allowed them to pay part of the salaries of the teachers in such schools.[36] Such distinctions are based on the Court's standard for judging such issues: whether government action involves "*excessive* entanglement with religion."[37] In allowing public funds to be used by religious schools for secular textbooks but not for teachers' salaries, the courts have indicated that, whereas a math or science text would have little if any religion in it, some teachers might use the classroom as an opportunity to promote religious teachings.[38] Accordingly, public funding of church-affiliated schoolteachers' salaries would involve excessive entanglement with religion whereas public funding of secular textbooks would not.

In a key 2002 decision, however, the Supreme Court upheld an Ohio law that allows students in Cleveland's failing public schools to receive a tax-supported voucher to attend private or parochial school. The Court's majority argued in *Zelman v. Simmons-Harris* that the program did not violate the establishment clause because students had a choice between secular and religious education. Four members of the Court dissented sharply with the majority's reasoning. Justice John Paul Stevens said the ruling had removed a "brick from the wall that was once designed to separate religion from government."[39] A piece of the brick was restored in 2004 when the Court in *Locke v. Davey* held that publicly funded scholarships can be denied to students pursuing religious careers. At issue was a state of Washington scholarship program that excluded otherwise eligible students who were studying for the ministry. The state justified the exclusion on grounds that the use of public funds to educate ministers would involve it in the establishment of religion.[40]

The establishment clause is also at issue in the use of faith-based organizations to provide federally funded services, such as drug treatment programs. This use increased with the election of President George W. Bush, who created the White House Office of Faith-Based and Community Initiatives. Although religious organizations are prohibited from promoting their beliefs in the process of providing federally funded services, critics say the prohibition is meaningless because many of these services are provided by religious officials at religious sites, which inevitably serves to promote religion. In *Hein v. Freedom from Religion* (2007), the Supreme Court in a 5-4 ruling held that taxpayers could not sue to stop expenditures by the Office of Faith-Based and Community Initiatives. The Court's majority held that, if money appropriated by Congress is improperly used by the White House for religious purposes, it is up to Congress, not the courts, to fix the problem. In his dissenting opinion, Justice David Souter cited the establishment clause, saying that citizens should have the right to sue in situations where their tax dollars are being used in ways that support religion.[41]

The Free-Exercise Clause

The First and Fourteenth Amendments also prohibit government interference with the free exercise of religion. The idea underlying the **free-exercise clause** is clear: Americans are free to believe what they want. However, they are not always free to act on their beliefs. The courts have allowed government interference in the exercise of religious beliefs when such interference is the secondary result of an overriding social goal. An example is the legal protection of children with life-threatening illnesses whose parents deny them medical treatment on religious grounds. A court may order that such children be given medical assistance because the social good of saving their lives overrides their parents' free-exercise rights.

In a few circumstances, the free-exercise clause has been the basis for allowing certain individuals to disobey otherwise valid laws. The Supreme Court ruled in 1972 that Amish families did not have to abide by a state law requiring children to attend school until they were sixteen years of age because the law conflicted with the age-old Amish religious practice of having children leave school and begin work at an early age.[42] In up-holding free exercise in such cases, the Court may be said to have violated the establishment clause by granting preferred treatment to people who hold a particular religious belief. The Court has recognized the potential conflict between the free-exercise and establishment clauses and, in such situations, tries to strike a reasonable balance between them.

When the free-exercise and establishment clauses cannot be balanced, the Supreme Court has been forced to choose. In 1987, the Court overturned a Louisiana law requiring that creationism (the Bible's account of how the world was created) be taught along with the theory of evolution in public school science courses. The Court concluded that creationism is a religious doctrine, not a scientific theory, and that its inclusion in public school curricula violates the establishment clause by promoting a religious belief.[43] In 2005, a federal judge barred a Pennsylvania public school district from requiring that intelligent design (the belief that God has guided evolution) be taught in science classes along with evolution. The judge concluded that the theory of intelligent design is a disguised version of creationism, has no basis in science, and violates the First Amendment's establishment clause. Some religious groups argue that such decisions trample on the free exercise of religion because children are required to study the theory of evolution even though it conflicts with their beliefs about creation.

THE RIGHT TO BEAR ARMS

The Second Amendment to the Constitution says: "A well regulated Militia, being necessary to the security of a free State, the right of the people to keep and bear Arms, shall not be infringed." Remarkably, more than two centuries passed before the Supreme Court issued a clear-cut ruling on how the amendment was to be interpreted. It was widely accepted that the amendment blocked the federal government from abolishing state militias, which would have the effect of placing all military power under its full control. What was unclear was whether the amendment also gave individuals the right to possess weapons outside their use in military service. Although some Supreme Court decisions had made reference to the Second Amendment, they had done so only in passing or in an ambiguous way.

In 2008, a sharply divided Supreme Court issued the first ruling to address squarely the meaning of the Second Amendment. In *District of Columbia v. Heller*, the Court ruled that "the Second Amendment protects an individual right to possess a firearm unconnected with service in a militia, and to use that arm for traditionally lawful purposes, such as self-defense within the home." The ruling struck down a District of Columbia law that had banned the possession of handguns but not rifles or shotguns within the district's boundaries. Writing for the 5-4 majority, Justice Antonin Scalia said that the justices were "aware of the problem of handgun violence in this country." But Scalia concluded: "The enshrinement of constitutional rights necessarily takes certain policy choices off the table. These include the absolute prohibition of handguns held and used for self-defense in the home."[44]

In a dissenting opinion, Justice John Paul Stevens said the majority had devised a ruling that fit its partisan aims rather than what the Framers intended when they wrote the Second Amendment. Stevens declared: "When each word in the text is given full effect, the Amendment is most naturally read to secure to the people a right to use and possess arms in conjunction with service in a well-regulated militia. So far as it appears, no more than that was contemplated by its drafters or is encompassed within its terms."

Although the *Heller* decision was a victory for advocates of gun rights, the scope of the ruling was unclear. The District of Columbia is federal territory, and the question remains whether the Supreme Court through selective interpretation will impose the same limitation on the gun laws of state and local governments. The *Heller* decision also leaves open the question of how far government can lawfully go in regulating firearms. The Court's majority was careful to say that some gun restrictions are allowable, such as bans on ownership by former felons. Nevertheless, the Court did not provide strict guidelines on which restrictions are constitutionally permissible and which are not, leaving the issue to be decided by future court cases. Within days of the *Heller* decision, opponents of gun control had filed suit against restrictive gun laws in Chicago, San Francisco, and other cities.

THE RIGHT OF PRIVACY

Until the 1960s, Americans' constitutional rights were confined largely to those listed in the Bill of Rights. This situation prevailed despite the Ninth Amendment, which reads, "The enumeration in the Constitution, of certain rights, shall not be construed to deny or disparage others retained by the people." In 1965, however, the Supreme Court added to the list of individual rights, declaring that Americans have "a right of privacy." This judgment arose from the case of *Griswold v. Connecticut*, which challenged a state law prohibiting the use of birth control devices, even by married couples. The Supreme Court struck down the statute, concluding that a state had no business interfering with a married couple's decision regarding contraception. The Court did not invoke the Ninth Amendment but reasoned instead that the freedoms in the Bill of Rights imply an underlying **right of privacy**. The Court held that individuals have a "zone of [personal] privacy" that government cannot lawfully infringe upon.[45]

The right to privacy has not been broadly applied by the courts. For example, the Supreme Court chose not to apply it in a challenge to a state of Washington law that prohibits physician-assisted suicide for terminally ill patients who voluntary choose it. In denying the petitioner's claim, the Court said that the right of privacy embedded in the U.S. Constitution does not extend to physician-assisted suicide, which has left the issue for each state to decide on its own.[46] In 2008, Washington residents voted to legalize physician-assisted suicide. Such examples notwithstanding, the Supreme Court has invoked a constitutional right to privacy in two major areas—a woman's right to choose an abortion and consensual relations among same-sex adults.

Abortion

The right of privacy was the basis for the Supreme Court's ruling in *Roe v. Wade* (1973), which gave women full freedom to choose abortion during the first three months of pregnancy. In overturning a Texas law banning abortion except to save the life of the mother, the Court said that the right to privacy is "broad enough to encompass a woman's decision whether or not to terminate her pregnancy."[47]

The *Roe* decision was met with praise by some Americans and condemnation by others, provoking a long-lasting debate. Americans are sharply divided over the abortion issue and have been throughout the more than three decades that abortion has been legal. The dispute has included violent confrontations at abortion clinics. In 1994, Congress passed a law that makes it illegal to obstruct the entrance to abortion clinics or otherwise prevent people from entering. (The Supreme Court upheld the law, concluding that it regulated abortion protesters' actions as opposed to their words and thus did not violate their right to free speech.[48])

Since *Roe*, antiabortion activists have pursued a variety of strategies in an effort to reverse or limit the scope of the Court's ruling. Attempts at a constitutional amendment that would ban abortions have been unsuccessful, which has prompted abortion foes to seek other ways to restrict the practice. They campaigned successfully to prohibit the use of government funds to pay for abortions for poor women. Then, in *Webster v. Reproductive Health Services* (1989), the Supreme Court upheld a Missouri law that prohibits abortions from being performed in Missouri's public hospitals and by its public employees.[49]

The *Webster* decision was followed in 1992 by the Pennsylvania abortion case *Planned Parenthood v. Casey*, which antiabortion advocates had hoped would reverse the *Roe* precedent. Instead, by a 5-4 margin, the Supreme Court upheld the principle that a woman has a right to abortion in the earliest months of pregnancy. The Court said that "the essential holding of *Roe v. Wade* should be retained and once again reaffirmed."[50] At the same time, however, the Court also said that a state can impose regulations that do not place an "undue burden" on women seeking an abortion. In this vein, the Court upheld a provision of the Pennsylvania law that requires a minor to have parental or judicial consent before obtaining an abortion, saying that it did not constitute an "undue burden." On the other hand, the Court in 2006 struck down by unanimous vote a

Abortion rights activists demonstrate outside the Supreme Court while the justices inside hear arguments on Pennsylvania's controversial abortion law. By a 5-4 vote, the Court narrowly reaffirmed the principle that a woman has the right to choose abortion during the early months of pregnancy.

New Hampshire law that had no medical emergency exception to its parental-consent requirement, concluding that this ommission constituted an "undue burden."[51]

In *Gonzales v. Carhart* (2007), the Supreme Court for the first time upheld a ban on the use of a particular method of abortion. At issue was the federal Partial-Birth Abortion Ban Act, passed by Congress in 2003. The law prohibits a form of abortion in which the fetus's life is terminated during delivery even if the mother's life or health is in danger. Any physician who performs such an abortion is subject to a fine and prison term. The Supreme Court in an earlier case, *Stenberg v. Carhart* (2000), had invalidated a Nebraska law that prohibited partial-birth abortion on the grounds that the procedure is sometimes the most appropriate way to protect the mother's health.[52] However, the Nebraska case was decided by a narrow 5-4 margin, with Justice Sandra Day O'Connor providing the swing vote, By the time the 2007 case reached the Supreme Court, she had retired, and her replacement, the more conservative Samuel Alito, voted the opposite way, resulting in a 5-4 vote upholding the congressional ban on partial-birth abortion. Writing for the majority, Justice Anthony Kennedy said that the federal act did not place an "undue burden" on women. In her dissenting opinion, Justice Ruth Bader Ginsburg, the lone woman on the Court, called the decision "alarming," arguing that it ignored established legal precedent.[53]

Sexual Relations Among Consenting Adults

Although it was widely said at the time that the Supreme Court's 1965 *Griswold* ruling on contraceptive use took "government out of people's bedrooms," a clear exception remained. All states prohibited sexual relations between consenting adults of the same sex. A number of states eliminated this prohibition over the next two decades, and others stopped enforcing it. Nevertheless, in a 1986 Georgia case, *Bowers v. Hardwick*, the Supreme Court held that the right of privacy did not extend to homosexual acts among consenting adults.[54]

In 2003, however, the Court reversed itself and in the process struck down the sodomy laws of the thirteen states that still had them. The ruling came in response to a Texas law prohibiting consensual sex between adults of the same sex. In *Lawrence v. Texas*, the Court in a 6-3 vote concluded that the Texas sodomy law violated privacy rights protected by the due process clause of the Fourteenth Amendment. The Court said: "The petitioners are entitled to respect for their private lives. The State cannot demean their existence or control their destiny by making their private sexual conduct a crime."[55] The decision was hailed by gay and lesbian rights groups but condemned by some religious leaders, who said it opened the door to same-sex marriage (see Chapter 5).

RIGHTS OF PERSONS ACCUSED OF CRIMES

Due process refers to legal protections that have been established to preserve the rights of individuals. The most significant form of these protections is **procedural due process;** the term refers primarily to procedures that authorities must follow before a person can legitimately be punished for an offense. No system of justice is foolproof. Even in the most careful systems, innocent people have been wrongly accused, convicted, and punished with imprisonment or death. But the scrupulous application of procedural safeguards, such as a defendant's right to legal counsel, greatly increases the likelihood that justice will prevail. "The history of liberty has largely been the history of the observance of procedural guarantees," said Justice Felix Frankfurter in *McNabb v. United States* (1943).[56]

The U.S. Constitution provides for several procedures designed to protect a person from wrongful arrest, conviction, and punishment. According to Article I, Section 9, any person taken into police custody is entitled to seek a writ of habeas corpus, which requires law enforcement officials to bring the suspect into court and to specify the legal reason for the detention. The Fifth and Fourteenth Amendments provide generally that no person can be deprived of life, liberty, or property without due process of law. Specific procedural protections for the accused are spelled out in the Fourth, Fifth, Sixth, and Eighth Amendments:

- The Fourth Amendment forbids the police to conduct searches and seizures unless they have probable cause to believe that a crime has been committed.
- The Fifth Amendment protects against double jeopardy (being prosecuted twice for the same offense); self-incrimination (being compelled to testify against oneself); indictment for a crime except through grand jury proceedings; and loss of life, liberty, and property without due process of law.
- The Sixth Amendment provides the right to have legal counsel, to confront witnesses, to receive a speedy trial, and to have a trial by jury in criminal proceedings.
- The Eighth Amendment protects against excessive bail or fines and prohibits the infliction of cruel and unusual punishment on those convicted of crimes.

These protections have been subject to interpretation. The Sixth Amendment, for example, provides the right to have legal counsel. But what if a person cannot afford a lawyer? For most of the nation's history, poor people had virtually no choice but to act as their own attorney. Even though they had a constitutional right to a lawyer, they could not afford to hire one. Today, if a person is accused of a serious crime and cannot afford a lawyer, the government must provide one. This change came about not through a constitutional amendment but through Supreme Court rulings that expanded the protection provided by the Sixth Amendment.

Selective Incorporation of Procedural Rights

Early in the nation's history, the procedural protections in the Bill of Rights applied only to the actions of the national government. States in their criminal proceedings were not bound by them. There were limited exceptions, such as a 1932 Supreme Court ruling that a defendant charged in a state court with a crime carrying the death penalty had to be provided with an attorney.[57] Nevertheless, even as the Court was moving to protect free-expression rights from state action in the 1930s, it held back on doing the same for the rights of the accused. The Court claimed that free-expression rights were more deserving of federal protection because they are "the indispensable condition of nearly every other form of freedom."[58]

This view changed abruptly in the 1960s when the Supreme Court required states also to safeguard a broad set of procedural rights. Changes in public education and communication had made Americans more aware of their rights, and the civil rights movement dramatized the fact that rights were administered unequally: the poor and minority group members had many fewer rights in practice than did other Americans. In response, the Supreme Court in the 1960s "incorporated" Bill of Rights protections for the accused by ruling that these rights are protected from state infringment by the Fourteenth Amendment's guarantee of due process of law (see Table 4-3).

The selective incorporation process began with *Mapp v. Ohio* (1961). Police forcibly entered the home of Dollree Mapp, a black woman, saying they had a tip she was harboring a fugitive. After discovering that the fugitive was not there, they handcuffed her and began rummaging through her closets. In the basement, they found a chest that contained obscene photographs. Mapp was arrested and convicted of violating an Ohio law that prohibited the possession of pornography. The Supreme Court overturned her conviction, ruling that police had acted unconstitutionally, citing the Fourth Amendment, which reads, "The right of the people to be secure in their persons, houses, papers, and effects, against unreasonable searches and seizures, shall not be violated . . ." Evidence acquired through table | 4-3 | SELECTIVE INCORPORATION OF RIGHTS OF THE ACCUSED

In the 1960s, the Supreme Court selectively incorporated the fair-trial provisions of the Fourth through Eighth Amendments into the Fourteenth Amendment so that these rights would be protected from infringement by the states.

Supreme Court Case	Year	Constitutional Right (Amendment) at Issue
Mapp v. Ohio	1961	Protection against unreasonable search and seizure (Fourth)
Robinson v. California	1962	Protection against cruel and unusual punishment (Eighth)
Gideon v. Wainwright	1963	Right to counsel (Sixth)
Malloy v. Hogan	1964	Protection against self-incrimination (Fifth)
Pointer v. Texas	1965	Right to confront witnesses (Sixth)
Miranda v. Arizona	1966	Protection against self-incrimination and right to counsel (Fifth and Sixth)
Klopfer v. North Carolina	1967	Speedy trial (Sixth)
Duncan v. Louisiana	1968	Jury trial in criminal cases (Sixth)
Benton v. Maryland	1969	Protection against double jeopardy (Fifth)

such a search, the Court said, cannot be used to obtain a conviction in state courts.[59]

Two years later, the Court's decision in *Gideon v. Wainwright* (1963) required the states to furnish attorneys for poor defendants in all felony cases. Clarence Gideon, an indigent drifter, had been convicted and sentenced to prison in Florida for breaking into a poolroom. The judge had denied his request for counsel, and he was forced to act as his own lawyer. He successfully appealed his conviction on the grounds that he had been denied due process because he did not have proper legal counsel during his trial.[60]

During the 1960s, the Court also ruled that defendants in state criminal proceedings cannot be compelled to testify against themselves,[61] have the right to remain silent and to have legal counsel at the time of arrest,[62] have the right to confront witnesses who testify against them,[63] must be granted a speedy trial,[64] have the right to a jury trial,[65] and cannot be subjected to double jeopardy.[66] The best known of these cases is *Miranda v. Arizona* (1966), which arose when Ernesto Miranda confessed during police interrogation to kidnap and rape. The Supreme Court overturned his conviction on the grounds that he had not been informed of his rights to remain silent and to have legal assistance. This ruling led to the development of the "Miranda warning" that police are now required to read to suspects: "You have the right to remain silent. . . . Anything you say can and will be used against you in a court of law. . . . You have the right to an attorney." (Miranda was subsequently retried and convicted on the basis of evidence other than his confession.)

In a 2000 case, *Dickerson v. United States*, the Supreme Court reaffirmed the *Miranda* decision, saying that it was an established "constitutional rule" that Congress could not abolish by ordinary legislation.[67] The Court further strengthened the Miranda precedent in *Missouri v. Siebert* (2004). This ruling came in response to a police strategy of questioning suspects first and then reading them their Miranda rights, followed by a second round of questioning. In such instances, suspects who admitted wrongdoing in the first round of questioning tended also to do so in the second round. The Court concluded that the strategy was intended "to undermine the Miranda warnings" and was therefore unconstitutional.[68]

Limits on Defendants' Rights

In the courtroom, the rights to have counsel, to confront witnesses, and to remain silent are of paramount importance. Before the courtroom phase in a criminal proceeding, the main protection is the Fourth Amendment's restriction on illegal search and seizure. This restriction holds that police must have suspicion of wrongdoing (and, sometimes, a judge's permission) before they can search your person, your car, or your residence, although involvement in an offense (such as driving faster than the speed limit) can lead to a permissible search that uncovers wrongdoing of another kind (such as drug possession). Without search-and-seizure protection, individuals would be subject to arbitrary police harassment and intimidation, characteristics of a totalitarian state, not a free society.

However, the Fourth Amendment does not provide blanket protection against searches. In 1990, for example, the Supreme Court held that police roadblocks to check drivers for signs of intoxication are legal as long as the action is systematic and not arbitrary (for example, stopping only young drivers would be unconstitutional, whereas stopping all drivers is acceptable). The Court justified its decision by saying that roadblocks serve a public safety purpose.[69] However, the Court does not allow the same types

Most of the controversies surrounding procedural due process involve the conduct of police officers. They operate under constitutional restraints in terms of apprehending, searching, and questioning suspects. If they ignore these restraints, evidence they obtain is not admissable in court in some instances.

of roadblocks to check for drugs. In *Indianapolis v. Edmund* (2001), the Court held that narcotics roadblocks, because they serve a general law enforcement purpose rather than one specific to highway safety, violate the Fourth Amendment's requirement that police have suspicion of wrongdoing before they can search an individual's auto.[70] The Supreme Court has also held that police cannot use a thermal-imaging device to scan homes to detect the presence of heat sources that might be related to the production of illegal drugs. Police cannot enter a home without a warrant issued by a judge who has reviewed the evidence for the suspicion of criminal activity and found it compelling enough to justify the entry; the Court has ruled that searches based on modern technology must meet the same standard.[71]

The Fourth Amendment protects individuals in their persons as well as in their homes and vehicles. In *Ferguson v. Charleston* (2001), for example, the Court held that patients in public hospitals cannot be forced to take a test for illegal drugs if the purpose is to turn over to the police those patients who test positive. Such action, said the Court, constitutes an illegal search of the person.[72] Authorities have more leeway when it comes to students in public schools. The Court in *Board of Education of Independent School District No. 92 of Pottawatomie County v. Earls* (2002) held that random drug testing of high school students involved in extracurricular activities does not violate the ban on unreasonable searches.[73]

The Exclusionary Rule　In recent decades, the Supreme Court has reduced but not eliminated the protections afforded to the accused by *Mapp* and other 1960s rulings. The 1960s Court was dominated by liberal justices who saw fit to expand individual rights. Turnover in the Court's membership moved it in a conservative direction and toward positions that give law enforcement officials more leeway. The change can be seen in the application of the **exclusionary rule,** which bars the use in trials of evidence obtained in violation of a person's constitutional rights. The rule was formulated in a 1914 Supreme Court decision,[74] and its application was expanded in federal cases. The *Mapp* decision extended the exclusionary rule to state trial proceedings. Subsequent decisions of the Supreme Court broadened its application to the point where almost any type of illegally obtained evidence was considered inadmissible in a criminal trial. In the 1980s, however, the Court reversed the trend by placing restrictions on the rule's application, holding that illegally obtained evidence can sometimes be admitted in trial if the procedural errors are inadvertent or if the prosecution can show that it would have discovered the evidence anyway.[75]

Recent decisions have also lowered the standard that must be met for police to lawfully search someone. In the 1960s, the Court developed the principle that police had to have a solid basis ("probable cause") for believing that an individual was involved in a specific crime before they could stop a person and engage in search-and-seizure activity. This principle has been modified, as illustrated by *Whren v. United States* (1996), which upheld the conviction of an individual who had been found with drugs in the front seat of his car. The police had no evidence (no "probable cause") indicating that drugs were in the car, but they had a hunch that the driver was involved in drug dealing and used a minor traffic infraction as a pretext to stop and check him. The Supreme Court accepted defense arguments that the police had no concrete evidence to back their suspicion, that the traffic infraction was not the real reason the individual was stopped, and that police usually do not stop a person for the infraction in question (turning a corner without signaling). However, the Court concluded that the officers' motive was irrelevant, as long as an officer in some situations might reasonably stop a car for the infraction that occurred. Thus, the stop-and-search action was deemed to meet the Fourth Amendment's reasonableness standard.[76]

In general, the Court has sought to weaken the exclusionary rule without going so far as to allow police to act as they please. However, some observers believe that the Court has narrowed the exclusionary rule nearly to the point where it applies only to the most outrageous instances of police misconduct. In *Hudson v. Michigan* (2006), the Court overthrew the "knock-and-announce" rule, which originated in thirteenth-century England. Under this rule, police with a search warrant are required to knock on the door and announce their presence before entering a suspect's house. Detroit police did not do so when they entered the home of Booker Hudson, and he sought to have his conviction for drug possession tossed out on the grounds that the evidence was obtained illegally. In rejecting his position in a 5-4 ruling, the Court's majority argued that the knock-and-announce rule is no longer necessary because the police today are more professional and because individuals whose homes or persons are illegally searched can sue the police for monetary damages. In a dissenting opinion, Justice Stephen Breyer ridiculed this reasoning, saying that the Court's majority could not "cite a single reported case" in which someone whose home had wrongly been invaded by police officers had been awarded an amount of money worth the effort required to get it.[77]

Habeas Corpus Appeals   The Supreme Court has also restricted habeas corpus appeals to federal courts by individuals who have been convicted of crimes in state courts. (Habeas corpus gives defendants access to federal courts in order to argue that their rights under the Constitution of the United States were violated when they were convicted in a state court.) A 1960s Supreme Court precedent had given prisoners the right to have their appeal heard in federal court unless they had "deliberately bypassed" the opportunity to first make their appeal in state courts.[78] This precedent was overturned in 1992 when the Court held that inmates can lose the right to a federal hearing even if a lawyer's mistake is the reason they failed to first present their appeal properly in state courts.[79] In *Bowles v. Russell* (2007), the Court in a 5-4 decision even went so far as to deny an appeal in a case where the deadline for filing the appeal was missed because a federal judge had given the inmate's lawyer the wrong date.[80]

The greatest restriction on habeas corpus appeals is a federal law, upheld by the Supreme Court in *Felker v. Turpin* (1996), that in most cases prohibits a federal habeas corpus appeal by a state prison inmate who has already filed one such appeal.[81] This legislation was designed to prevent frivolous and multiple federal court appeals. State prisoners had used habeas corpus appeals to contest even small issues, and some inmates—particularly those on death row—had filed appeal after appeal. An effect was the clogging of

★ | LEADERS

Martin Luther King Jr.
(1929–68)

Martin Luther King Jr. is the only American of the twentieth century to be honored with a national holiday. The civil rights leader was the pivotal figure in the movement to gain legal and political rights for black Americans. The son of a Baptist minister, King attended a segregated public school in Georgia before going to Morehouse College, a traditional African American institution. He later earned a doctorate from Boston University before taking a pastorate in Montgomery, Alabama.

Already active on civil rights issues, King used rhetorical skills and nonviolent tactics to galvanize the black community and sweep aside a century of governmental discrimination. High points were a protest march in Selma, Alabama, that exposed white brutality and a triumphal gathering of a quarter million supporters on the Washington Mall. Among King's concerns was the unequal treatment of African Americans by police and courts. He spoke of a community "staggered by the winds of police brutality." The recipient of the Nobel Peace Prize in 1964 (the youngest person ever to receive that honor), King was assassinated in Memphis in 1968 as he was preparing to lead a protest march on behalf of the city's sanitation workers.

the federal courts and a delay in hearing other cases. The Supreme Court has ruled that, except in unusual cases,[82] it is fair to ask inmates to first pursue their options in state courts and then to confine themselves to a single federal appeal. At the same time, though, the Court has taken steps to ensure that meritorious appeals are heard. In two 2003 cases, for example, the Court expressed concern that lower federal courts in some instances were not being sufficiently careful in identifying legitimate appeals.[83]

Despite modifications of the appeal process and the exclusionary rule, there has not been a return to the lower procedural standards that prevailed prior to the 1960s. Many of the vital precedents established in that decade remain in effect, including the most important one of all: the principle that procedural protections guaranteed to the accused by the Bill of Rights must be observed by the states as well as by the federal government.

Crime, Punishment, and Police Practices

The theory and practice of procedural guarantees are often two quite different things, as Adrienne Cureton discovered on January 2, 1995. She was a plainclothes police officer who, with a uniformed partner, was called to the scene of a domestic dispute. A struggle ensued, and her partner radioed for help. When the officers arrived, Cureton and her partner had already handcuffed the homeowner. The officers barged in and mistook Cureton, an African American, for the other person involved in the dispute. They grabbed her by the collar, dragged her by the hair onto the porch, and clubbed her repeatedly with flashlights, despite her screams that she was a police officer.[84]

There is no reliable estimate of how often Americans' rights are violated in practice, but infringements of one sort or another are commonplace. Minorities and the poor are the more likely victims. *Racial profiling* (the assumption that certain groups are more likely to commit particular crimes) is a common police practice and results in the unequal treatment of minorities.[85] An American Civil Liberties Union study found, for example, that 80 percent of the motorists stopped and searched by Maryland State Police on Interstate 95 were minorities and only 20 percent were white, despite the fact that white motorists constituted 75 percent of all drivers and were just as likely as minority motorists to violate the traffic laws. African Americans refer mockingly to a traffic infraction they call DWB—"driving while black."

Another issue of justice in America is whether adherence to proper legal procedures produces reasonable outcomes. The Eighth Amendment prohibits "cruel and unusual punishment" of those convicted of crime, but judgments in this area are subjective. Although the Supreme Court in a few instances has ordered officials to relieve inmate overcrowding and to improve prison facilities, it has held that inmates cannot sue over inadequate prison conditions unless prison officials show "deliberate indifference" to the situation.[86] The severity of a sentence also can be an Eighth Amendment issue. The Supreme Court in 1991 upheld a conviction under a Michigan law that mandated life imprisonment without parole for a nonviolent first offense involving 1.5 pounds of cocaine.[87] More recently, the Court upheld a conviction under California's "three strikes and you're out" law that sent a twice previously convicted felon to prison for life without parole for shoplifting videotapes worth $100.[88] Although many people would regard such penalties as too severe, the Supreme Court has seldom invoked the Eighth Amendment's prohibition on cruel and unusual punishment. The Court has allowed Congress and the state legislatures to decide the appropriate penalties for crime, believing that it lacks the capacity to devise consistent rules that would differentiate between cruel and acceptable levels of punishment.

★ STATES IN THE NATION

The Death Penalty

Most crimes and punishments in the United States are defined by state law. Nowhere is this more obvious than in the application of the death penalty. Some states prohibit it, and others apply it liberally. Texas, Florida, and Virginia are far and away the leaders in its application. Roughly a third of all executions in the past quarter-century have taken place in Texas alone.

Q: What do many of the states that prohibit capital punishment have in common?

A: States without the death penalty are concentrated in the North. Most of these states are relatively affluent, rank high on indicators of educational attainment, and have a small minority-group population.

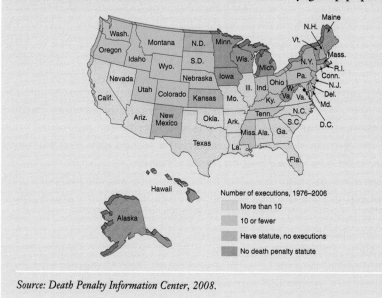

Number of executions, 1976–2006
- More than 10
- 10 or fewer
- Have statute, no executions
- No death penalty statute

Source: Death Penalty Information Center, 2008.

In an exception to this tendency, the Supreme Court has recently employed the Eighth Amendment to narrow the use of the death penalty. In *Atkins v. Virginia* (2002) and again in *Panetti v. Quarterman* (2007), the Court outlawed the death penalty for the mentally retarded on grounds it constitutes "cruel and unusual punishment."[89] The Court has also recently invoked the Eighth Amendment to ban the death penalty in cases involving juveniles and for crimes where the victim was not killed.[90] The second of these rulings overturned the death sentence of a Louisiana man who had been convicted of child rape. The Court recently addressed an Eighth Amendment challenge to how states carry out executions. At issue was the mix of chemicals used in lethal injections. Studies indicated that some of the chemicals used by states can cause excruciating pain before death occurs. In 2008, the Court rejected a challenge to Kentucky's three-drug mix (a combination also used in several other states), concluding that it did not violate the Eighth Amendment while holding open the question of whether certain drug mixes constitute cruel and unusual punishment.[91]

Although the Eighth Amendment has been at the center of sentencing issues, the Sixth Amendment's guarantee of trial by jury recently came into play. Traditionally, the right to a jury trial has applied only to the question of the defendant's guilt or innocence, and not also to the sentence the defendant receives if convicted. That decision could be made by a judge. However, in *Ring v. Arizona* (2002), the Supreme Court held that the right of jury trial prohibits a judge from deciding in a capital case whether the death penalty will be imposed. The Court ruled that a jury has to make that determination.[92] This principle was expanded in *Blakley v. Washington* (2004) to include sentences that are longer than the law prescribes. The Supreme Court held that the Sixth Amendment requires that a jury decide whether aggravating factors, such as the cruelty of a crime, justify a stiffer sentence.[93] The *Blakley* ruling was widely criticized on grounds that it would overburden the courts by requiring a second jury trial whenever the prosecution seeks an extra-long prison sentence.

As these Sixth and Eighth Amendment cases indicate, the judiciary plays a part in deciding the rules to be applied in punishing those convicted of crime. The primary role, however, rests with elected officials, who enact the laws that specify the punishments for various crimes. Not surprisingly, perhaps, they often prefer laws that are harsh rather than lenient. Being "tough on crime" is popular with some voters, and Congress and most state legislatures during the past two decades have enacted stiffer penalties for crimes while also limiting the ability of judges to reduce sentences, even in cases of nonviolent crime where the perpetrator has no prior criminal record. As a result, the number of federal and state prisoners has more than doubled since 1990. In fact, on a per capita basis, the United States has the largest prison population in the world (see "How the United States Compares"). Russia is the only country that is even close to the United States in terms of the percentage of its citizens who are behind bars. The United States imprisons five times as many people per capita as Great Britain does.

⊕ HOW THE UNITED STATES COMPARES

Law and Order

Individual rights are a cornerstone of the American governing system and receive strong protection from the courts. The government's ability to restrict free expression is severely limited, and the individual's right to a fair trial is protected through elaborate due process guarantees.

According to Amnesty International, a watchdog group that monitors human rights achievements and violations around the world, the United States has a commendable record in terms of its constitutional protection of civil liberties. A number of countries in Asia, Africa, eastern Europe, the Middle East, and Latin America are accused by Amnesty International of "appalling human rights catastrophes" that include the torture, rape, and execution of persons accused of crime or regarded as opponents of the government. However, Amnesty International does not rank the United States as high as the countries of northern Europe in terms of respect for human rights. Among other problems, Amnesty International faults police in the United States for "excessive force" in their treatment of prisoners and faults U.S. immigration officials for the forcible return of asylum seekers to their country of origin without granting them a hearing.

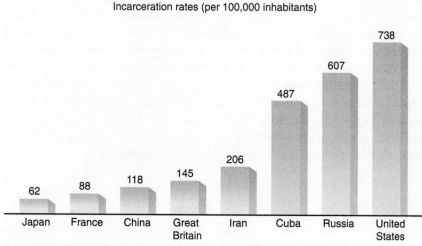

Incarceration rates (per 100,000 inhabitants)

Japan	France	China	Great Britain	Iran	Cuba	Russia	United States
62	88	118	145	206	487	607	738

Source: National Council on Crime and Delinquency data, 2006.

(continued)

Although human rights groups admire America's elaborate procedural protections for those accused of crime, they are critical of its sentencing and incarceration policies. The United States is the world leader in the number of people it places behind bars and in the length of sentences for various categories of crime. Defenders of U.S. policy say that although overall crime rates are about the same here as elsewhere, there is more violent crime in America. Critics reply that although the murder rate is high in the United States, it is also true that more than half of the people in prison were convicted of nonviolent offenses, such as drug use or a crime against property. Whatever the exact reasons, the United States is rivaled only by Russia in the proportion of its people who are in prison.

As the human and financial costs of keeping so many people in prison have risen, debate over America's criminal justice system has intensified. The incarceration of nonviolent drug offenders is one of the issues. U.S. policy in this area is at odds with that of other Western countries, which rely more heavily on treatment programs than on prisons in dealing with drug offenders. Critics also cite studies showing that minorities and the poor receive harsher sentences than middle-class white persons convicted of comparable crimes. An example is the disparity in sentences for those convicted of powder- and crack-cocaine offenses. The federal courts handle more than 10,000 cocaine-related cases each year, which divide almost equally between crack- and powder-cocaine offenses. The defendants in these cases differ, however. African Americans make up roughly three-fourths of the crack-cocaine defendants but only one-fourth of the powder-cocaine defendants. Federal laws call for nearly twice as much prison time for a crack-cocaine conviction as for a powder-cocaine conviction involving a comparable amount of cocaine.[94] In a 2007 decision, the Supreme Court held that judges have the authority to reduce crack-cocaine sentences below the federal guidelines to bring them closer into line with powder-cocaine sentences.[95]

RIGHTS AND THE WAR ON TERRORISM

In time of war, the courts have upheld government policies that would not be permitted in peacetime. After the Japanese attack on Pearl Harbor in 1941, for example, President Franklin D. Roosevelt ordered the forced relocation of tens of thousands of Japanese Americans living on the West

Coast to detention camps in Arizona, Utah, and other inland locations. Congress endorsed the policy, and the Supreme Court upheld it.[96] Another Supreme Court ruling during World War II denied a U.S. citizen arrested as a Nazi collaborator a court trial after the government decided to try him before a military tribunal.[97]

After the terrorist attacks of September 11, 2001, the Bush administration invoked precedents such as these in declaring that customary legal protections had to be altered if the war on terrorism was to be waged successfully. "[There is] the necessity for certain types of action . . . when we are in danger," said Solicitor General Theodore Olson.

Detention of Enemy Combatants

The Bush administration soon announced its policy for handling "enemy combatants"—individuals judged to be engaged in terrorism directed at the United States. They were to be detained without access to lawyers or family members until the president chose to release them. The Administration also claimed the authority to round up and hold in secret any individual living in the United States who is suspected of having terrorist ties. Hundreds of individuals, nearly all of Middle Eastern descent, were taken into custody. Although nearly all of them were eventually cleared of wrongdoing by the FBI, some were held for months and others were deported for immigration violations.

As the war on terrorism shifted into military operations in Afghanistan and then Iraq, the United States began to detain and interrogate the enemy fighters it captured. Some prisoners were sent to a detention facility created at the U.S. Naval Base at Guantanamo Bay on the tip of Cuba. Others were imprisoned in Afghanistan, Iraq, and elsewhere. Requests by lawyers and international agencies like the Red Cross to see the detainees were denied or strictly limited. President Bush claimed that the detainees were enemy combatants rather than prisoners of war and accordingly did not have the legal protections provided by U.S. law or by the Geneva Conventions. President Bush did not publicly announce that the prisoners would be subject to harsh interrogation, but such treatment was practiced at Abu Ghraib prison in Iraq and at Guantanamo Bay and presumably took place at secret CIA prisons in undisclosed locations.

In 2004, the Supreme Court issued its first ruling on these various practices, holding that the Guantanamo Bay detainees had the right to challenge their detention in court. The Court reasoned that the naval base, though in Cuba, is on land leased to the United States and therefore under the jurisdiction of U.S. courts.[98] In a second 2004 case (*Hamdi v. Rumsfeld*), the Court ruled that one of the Guantanamo Bay detainees, who was a U.S. citizen by virtue of having been born in the United States though he was raised in Saudi Arabia, had the right to be heard in U.S. courts. The Court said that a citizen was entitled to a "fair opportunity to rebut the government's factual assertions before a neutral [judge]" and that "essential constitutional promises may not be eroded" because of the security situation. The Court went on to say, "As critical as the government's interest may be in detaining those who actually pose an immediate threat to the national security of the United States during ongoing international conflict, history and common sense teach us that an unchecked system of detention carries the potential to become a means of oppression and abuse of others who do not present that sort of threat."[99]

Two years later, the Court issued its sharpest rebuke yet of the Bush administration's detention policies. In a ruling nearly unprecedented in its challenge to a president's wartime authority, the Court held that the detainees were protected both by the U.S. Uniform Code of Military Justice and by the Geneva Conventions. At issue was the Bush administration's use of secret military tribunals to try detainees. In these trials, detainees were to have no right to see the evidence against them and would not necessarily be allowed to gather evidence or call witnesses that might exonerate them. The Court held in *Hamdan v. Rumsfeld* (2006) that the tribunals were unlawful, saying "the Executive is bound to comply with the Rule of Law. . . ."[100] In essence, the Court said that a wartime president does not have blanket authority to ignore U.S. and international law. In response to the ruling, President Bush negotiated legislation, which Congress enacted in 2006, that grants legal protections to detainees held by the U.S. military. However, at Bush's insistence, the legislation excluded CIA interrogations conducted overseas, an exception that the Supreme Court could conceivably rule upon in the future.

The 2006 law, also at the Bush administration's insistence, denied federal courts the authority to hear habeas corpus petitions from prisoners who seek to challenge their detention. In 2008, the Supreme Court struck down the provision. Writing for the majority in a 5-4 decision, Justice Anthony Kennedy said: "The laws and Constitution are designed to survive, and remain in force, in extraordinary times." In a dissenting opinion, Justice Antonin Scalia said the ruling "will almost certainly cause more Americans to be killed. The nation will live to regret what the court has done today."[101]

Surveillance of Suspected Terrorists

After the September 11 terrorist attacks and in response to the Bush administration's request for expanded surveillance powers, Congress passed the USA Patriot Act, which lowered the standard for judicial approval of wiretapping when terrorist activity was at issue. The law also allowed information from intelligence surveillance to be shared with criminal investigators when evidence was found of criminal activity unrelated to terrorism. Previously, such information could be shared only if it was obtained by the stricter standards that officials must follow in criminal investigations. The new law also gave government increased authority to examine medical, financial, and student records and allowed the government in some situations to secretly search homes and offices.

Critics claimed that the USA Patriot Act was at odds with America's constitutional tradition. "No one is questioning the government's authority to prosecute spies and terrorists," said Ann Beeson of the American Civil Liberties Union, "but we do not need to waive the Constitution to do so."[102] For their part, officials said that the September 11 attacks had forced a change in the rules. "The danger that darkened the United States and the civilized world on September 11 did not pass with the atrocities committed that day," said Attorney General John Ashcroft.

The Bush administration promised to act with restraint in its exercise of the new powers, and congressional oversight committees were generally satisfied with its actions until the *New York Times* revealed in late 2005 that without judicial approval President Bush had secretly authorized the National Security Agency (NSA) to wiretap international phone calls and e-mail messages originating in the United States. Such wiretaps are expressly prohibited by the Foreign Intelligence Surveillance Act (FISA) of 1978. Bush rejected allegations that he had broken the law, saying that he had acted legally under his wartime powers as commander-in-chief and under authority implicitly granted him by the Patriot Act.

The question of governing authority—whether the Bush administration's NSA surveillance activities are within or outside the law—is only now being heard in lower courts. The first such ruling occurred in August of 2006; the district judge in that case held that President Bush had exceeded his statutory and constitutional authority in ordering wiretaps without a judicial warrant. Most analysts believe, however, that a definitive judgment on this issue will not come until the Supreme Court itself decides the issue or unless the White House persuades Congress to change the laws governing intelligence-gathering wiretaps.

THE COURTS AND A FREE SOCIETY

The United States was founded on the idea that individuals have an innate right to liberty—to speak their minds, to worship freely, to be secure in their homes and persons, to be assured of a fair trial. Americans embrace these freedoms in the abstract. In particular situations, however, many Americans would prefer policies that diminish the freedom of those who hold minority views or have a different physical appearance than most Americans. After the September 11 terrorist attacks, for example, a third of Americans in polls said that Arab Americans should be placed under special surveillance and half said that Arab Americans should be required to carry special identification cards. Two-fifths said they would ban college lectures by speakers who argue that aspects of U.S. foreign policy have contributed to terrorist activity.

The judiciary is not isolated from the public mood. Judges inevitably must balance society's need for security and public order against the rights of the individual. Nevertheless, judges can ordinarily be expected to be more protective of individual rights than either elected officials or the general public. How far the courts will go in protecting a person's rights depends on the facts of the case, the existing status of the law, prevailing social needs, and the personal views of the judges. Nevertheless, most judges and justices regard the protection of individual rights as a constitutional imperative, which is the way the Framers saw it. The Bill of Rights was created in order to transform the abstract idea that individuals have inalienable rights to life, liberty, and happiness into a set of specified constitutional rights, thereby bringing them under the protection of courts of law.[103]

SUMMARY   Self-Test www.mhhe.com/pattersonwtp8e

The Bill of Rights was added to the Constitution shortly after its ratification. These amendments guarantee certain political, procedural, and property rights against infringement by the national government.

Freedom of expression is the most basic of democratic rights. People are not free unless they can freely express their views. Nevertheless, free expression may conflict with the nation's security needs during times of war and insurrection. The courts at times have allowed government to limit expression substantially for purposes of national security. In recent decades, however, the courts have protected a wide range of free expression in the areas of speech, press, and religion. They have also established a right of privacy, which in some areas, such as abortion, remains a source of controversy and judicial action.

The guarantees embodied in the Bill of Rights originally applied only to the national government. Under the principle of selective incorporation of these guarantees into the Fourteenth Amendment, the courts extended them to state governments, though the process was slow and uneven. In the 1920s and 1930s, First Amendment guarantees of freedom of expression were given protection from infringement by the states. The states continued to have wide discretion in criminal proceedings until the early 1960s, when most of the fair-trial rights in the Bill of Rights were given federal protection.

Due process of law refers to legal protections that have been established to preserve individual rights. The most significant form of these protections consists of procedures or methods (for example, the right of an accused person to have an attorney present during police interrogation) designed to ensure that an individual's rights are upheld. A major controversy in this area is the breadth of the exclusionary rule, which bars the use in trials of illegally obtained evidence. The Supreme Court in recent decades has narrowed the rule's application, granting police wider discretion in the search and seizure of suspects.

The war on terrorism that began after the attacks on September 11, 2001, has raised new issues of civil liberties, including the detention of enemy combatants, the use of harsh interrogation techniques, and warrantless surveillance. The Supreme Court has not ruled on all such issues but has generally held that the president's war-making power does not include the authority to disregard provisions of statutory law, treaties (the Geneva Conventions), and the Constitution.

Civil liberties are not absolute but must be balanced against other considerations (such as national security or public safety) and against one another when different rights conflict. The judicial branch of government, particularly the Supreme Court, has taken on much of the responsibility for protecting and interpreting individual rights. The Court's positions have changed with time and conditions, but the Court is usually more protective of civil liberties than elected officials or popular majorities are.

KEY TERMS

Bill of Rights (p. 107)
civil liberties (p. 107)
clear-and-present-danger test (p. 111)
due process clause (of the Fourteenth
   Amendment) (p. 114)
establishment clause (p. 20)
exclusionary rule (p. 133)
freedom of expression (p. 110)
free-exercise clause (p. 122)

imminent lawless action test (p. 115)
libel (p. 117)
prior restraint (p. 113)
procedural due process (p. 128)
right of privacy (p. 125)
selective incorporation (p. 114)
slander (p. 117)
symbolic speech (p. 112)

SUGGESTED READINGS

Abraham, Henry J. *Freedom and the Court.* New York: Oxford University Press, 2003. A comprehensive analysis of the Supreme Court's work on civil rights and civil liberties.

Ackerman, Bruce. *Before the Next Attack: Preserving Civil Liberties in an Age of Terrorism.* New Haven, Conn.: Yale University Press, 2007. A thoughtful analysis of how Western democracies should treat civil liberties in the era of global terrorism.

Gup, Ted. *Nation of Secrets: The Threat to Democracy and the American Way of Life*. New York: Doubleday, 2007. An award-winning book that documents government's effort to hide from public view an ever-increasing amount of information on its activities.

Hull, N. E. H., and Peter Charles Hoffer. *Roe v. Wade: The Abortion Rights Controversy in American History*. Lawrence: University Press of Kansas, 2001. A thorough assessment of both sides of the abortion conflict, beginning with the *Roe v. Wade* decision.

Perry, Michael J. *Religion in Politics: Constitutional and Moral Perspectives*. New York: Oxford University Press, 1997. A legal and philosophical analysis of the role of religion in politics.

Schwarz, John E. *Freedom Reclaimed: Rediscovering the American Vision*. Baltimore, Md.: Johns Hopkins University Press, 2005. An impassioned argument for an expansive view of liberty, both from and through government action.

Stone, Geoffrey. *War and Liberty: An American Dilemma: 1790 to the Present*. New York: Norton, 2007. A historical assessment of the tension between civil liberties and national security.

LIST OF WEBSITES

http://www.fepproject.org/ Includes information and opinions on a wide range of free-expression policy issues.

http://www.aclu.org/ The American Civil Liberties Union site; provides information on current civil liberties and civil rights issues, including information on recent and pending Supreme Court cases.

http://www.findlaw.com/casecode/supreme.html An excellent source of information on Supreme Court and lower court rulings.

http://www.ncjrs.org/ The site of the National Criminal Justice Reference Service, a federally funded organization that compiles information on a wide range of criminal-justice issues.

POLITICS IN THEORY AND PRACTICE

Thinking: What is the process of selective incorporation, and why is it important to the rights you have today?

Participating: Although their right of free expression is protected by law, Americans often choose not to exercise this right for fear of social pressure or official reprisal. Yet constitutional rights tend to wither when people fail to exercise them. The failure of citizens to speak their mind, Alexis de Tocqueville said, reduces them "to being nothing more than a herd of timid and industrious animals of which government is the shepherd." Think of an issue that you care about but that is unpopular on your campus or in your community. Consider writing a letter expressing your opinion to the editor of your college or local newspaper. (Practical advice: Keep the letter short and to the point; write a lead sentence that will get readers' attention; provide a convincing and courteous argument for your position; be sure to sign the letter and provide a return address so the editor can contact you if there are questions.)

Extra Credit

For up-to-the-minute *New York Times* articles, interactive simulations, graphics, study tools, and more links and quizzes, visit the text's Online Learning Center at www.mhhe.com/pattersonwtp8e.

A Constitutional Amendment to Ban Flag Burning

By Sam Brownback/Russell Feingold

The Supreme Court has held that free expression is the most fundamental of civil liberties, a position that has led it to strike down most laws that would restrict expression. The Court has even ruled that the burning of the American flag is protected speech. This ruling has prompted several attempts by Congress to pass a constitutional amendment that would ban flag burning. In 2006 Congress came within a single Senate vote of obtaining the two-thirds majority required in each chamber. The Senate debate was marked by thoughtful statements from both advocates and opponents of the amendment. The statements of two of the senators who participated in that debate are given here. Senator Sam Brownback argued for the amendment, and Senator Russell Feingold argued against it.

Senator Sam Brownback (R-Kans.): I was preparing for this debate and thinking about the Lincoln Memorial. What if somebody today, yesterday, or some other time had taken spray paint and sprayed on the Lincoln Memorial: "We want freedom" or "Death to tyrants" or "Down with the flag"? Let's say they wrote that in big spray paint on the Lincoln Memorial and defaced the memorial and then [were] caught and brought to trial and claimed: Wait a minute, I have a first amendment right to say what I want to say, and I believe it is important that I say it anywhere, and I want to say it on the Lincoln Memorial. I want to make my message known, and I am going to spray-paint it all over here; this is free speech, and I ought to be able to do that and this is the place to do it, and Lincoln would approve of that; he believed in free speech, so he wouldn't mind that the memorial was sprayed upon, that it was defaced.

We would all recognize that as being something wrong, violating the law, and something there should be a law against. We don't have a problem with a person standing on the Lincoln Memorial and shouting at the top of his lungs for as long as he wants whatever he wants to say—if it is about the war in Iraq, if it is about the President, if it is about somebody in the Senate, if it is about myself, if it is about the Chair, if it is about anything he wants. We don't have any problem with that. But if he defaces the memorial, we do.

It is interesting, that was the dissent Justice Stevens used in the *Texas v. Johnson* case. He made that same point. We have no problem with a person speaking on the Lincoln Memorial. We have a problem with him defacing the Lincoln Memorial. We have no problem with people speaking against the flag. We have a problem with them defacing the flag. Justice Stevens in his dissent—which I think was rightly said—said: "Had he chosen to spray-paint or perhaps convey with a motion picture projector his message of dissatisfaction on the facade of the Lincoln Memorial, there would be no question about the power of Government to prohibit this means of expression. The prohibition will be supported by the legitimate interests in preserving the quality of an important national asset."

That is what we are talking about today: preserving the quality of an important national asset that people follow into battle, that we have had and honored for years and years, and until recently the court has held up as saying: Yes, this is something that should be protected and is protected by the laws of the land, and these laws are appropriate and are not limitations on free speech.

I think if you follow this court ruling, where does it end? If you say actions are speech, wouldn't you have a legitimate objective in defacing the Lincoln Memorial, particularly if it was some form of political free speech that you wanted to express and put forward? . . . . This is not a complicated issue. It is about whether we are going to have some authority and ability to be able to limit and to be able to honor and to uphold something so precious as our American flag. I think we should do that. I think because of the people who follow this flag and because we are a nation of symbols, and symbols are what unite us, and because of the words and thought that are conveyed by this flag, we should be able to uphold this mighty national asset.

Senator Russell Feingold (D-Wisc.): Let me make one thing clear at the outset. Not a single Senator who opposes the proposed constitutional amendment, as I do, supports burning or otherwise showing disrespect to the flag. Not a single one. None of us think it is "OK" to burn the flag. None of us view the flag as "just a piece of cloth." On those rare occasions when some malcontent defiles or burns our flag, I join everyone in this Chamber in condemning that action.

But we must also defend the right of all Americans to express their views about their Government, however hateful or spiteful or disrespectful those views may be, without fear of their Government putting them in jail for those views. America is not simply a Nation of symbols, it is a Nation of principles. And the most important principle of all, the principle that has made this country a beacon of hope and inspiration for oppressed peoples throughout the world, is the right of free expression. This amendment threatens that right, so I must oppose it.

We have heard at various times over the years that this amendment has been debated that permitting protestors to burn the American flag sends the wrong message to our children about patriotism and respect for our country. I couldn't disagree more with that argument. We can send no better, no stronger, no more meaningful message to our children about the principles and the values of this country than if we oppose efforts to undermine freedom of expression, even expression that is undeniably offensive. When we uphold first amendment freedoms despite the efforts of misguided and despicable people who want to provoke our wrath, we explain what America is really about. Our country and our people are far too strong to be threatened by those who burn the flag. That is a lesson we should proudly teach our children. . . .

It has been almost exactly 17 years since the Supreme Court ruled that flag burning is a form of political speech protected by the first amendment. Proposals to amend the Constitution arose almost immediately and have continued unabated. But while the interest of politicians in this course of action seems as strong as ever, public interest in it seems to be waning. Opinion polls show support for the amendment has fallen. Amending the Constitution to prohibit flag desecration is just not the foremost thing on the minds of the American people. Perhaps that is because it is long since clear that our Republic can survive quite well without this amendment. Nearly a generation has passed since the *Texas v. Johnson* decision, and our Nation is still standing strong. . . .

Indeed, outward displays of patriotism are greater today than they were in 2000. We all know why that is. Our country was viciously attacked on September 11, 2001, and America responded. We didn't need a constitutional amendment to teach Americans how to love their country. They showed us how to do it by entering burning buildings to save their fellow citizens who were in danger, by standing in line for hours to give blood, by driving hundreds of miles to search through the rubble for survivors and to help in cleanup efforts, by praying in their houses of worship for the victims of the attacks and their families.

September 11 inspired our citizens to perform some of the most selfless acts of bravery and patriotism we have seen in our entire history. No constitutional amendment could ever match those acts as a demonstration of patriotism, or create similar acts in the future. We do not need a constitutional amendment to teach Americans how to love their country or how to defend it from our enemies.

What's Your Opinion?

Which argument—Brownback's or Feingold's—do you find more persuasive? What additional claims might you make to support your position on the constitutional issue of flag burning?

CHAPTER 5

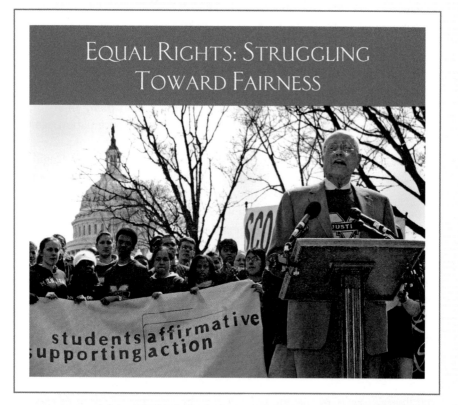

EQUAL RIGHTS: STRUGGLING TOWARD FAIRNESS

students affirmative
supporting action

SCO
JUSTI

> **"** I have a dream that one day this nation will rise up and live out the true meaning
> of its creed: 'We hold these truths to be self-evident: that all men are created
> equal.' **"**
>
> MARTIN LUTHER KING JR.[1]

The producers of ABC television's *Primetime Live* put hidden cameras on two young men, equally well dressed and groomed, and then sent them on different routes to do the same things—search for an apartment, shop for a car, look at albums in a record store. The cameras recorded people's reactions to the two men. One was usually greeted with smiles and quick service, while the other was more often greeted with suspicious looks and was sometimes made to wait. Why the difference? The explanation was straightforward: the young man who was routinely well received was white; the young man who was sometimes treated poorly was black.

The Urban Institute conducted a more substantial experiment. It included pairs of specially trained white and black male college students who were comparable in all respects—education, work experience, speech patterns,

physical builds—except for their race. The students responded individually
to nearly five hundred classified job advertisements in Chicago and
Washington, D.C. The black applicants got fewer interviews and received
fewer job offers than did the white applicants. An Urban Institute spokes-
person said, "The level of reverse discrimination [favoring blacks over whites]
that we found was limited, was certainly far lower than many might have
been led to fear, and was swamped by the extent of discrimination against
black job applicants."[2]

These two experiments suggest why some Americans are still struggling
to achieve equal rights. In theory Americans have equal rights, but in reality
they are not now equal nor have they ever been. African Americans, women,
Hispanic Americans, the disabled, Jews, Native Americans, Catholics, Asian
Americans, gays and lesbians, and members of other minority groups have
been victims of discrimination in fact and in law. The nation's creed—"all men
are created equal"—has encouraged minorities to demand equal treatment.
But inequality is built into almost every aspect of U.S. society. For example,
compared with whites, African Americans with correctable health problems
are significantly less likely to receive coronary artery bypass surgery, to receive
a kidney transplant, or to undergo surgery for early-stage lung cancer.[3]

This chapter focuses on **equal rights,** or **civil rights**—terms that refer
to the right of every person to equal protection under the laws and equal access to society's opportunities and public facilities. As Chapter 4 explained,
civil liberties refer to specific *individual* rights, such as freedom of speech,
that are protected from infringement by government. Equal rights, or civil
rights, have to do with whether individual members of differing *groups*—
racial, sexual, and the like—are treated equally by government and, in some
areas, by private parties.

Although the law refers to the rights of individuals first and to those
of groups in a secondary and derivative way, this chapter concentrates on
groups because the history of civil rights has been largely one of group
claims to equality. The chapter emphasizes these points:

★ *Disadvantaged groups have had to struggle for equal rights.* African
  Americans, women, Native Americans, Hispanic Americans, Asian
  Americans, and others have all had to fight for their rights in order
  to come closer to equality with white males.

★ *Americans have attained substantial equality under the law.* They have, in
  legal terms, equal protection under the laws, equal access to accommodations and housing, and an equal right to vote. Discrimination by
  law against persons because of race, sex, religion, or ethnicity has been
  virtually eliminated.

★ *Legal equality for all Americans has not resulted in de facto equality.* African Americans, women, Hispanic Americans, and other traditionally disadvantaged groups have a disproportionately small share of America's opportunities and benefits. Existing inequalities, discrimination, and political pressures still are major barriers to their full equality. Affirmative action is a policy designed to help the disadvantaged achieve a fuller degree of equality.

THE STRUGGLE FOR EQUALITY

Equality has always been the least fully developed of America's founding concepts. Not even Thomas Jefferson, who had a deep admiration for the "common man," believed that a precise meaning could be given to the claim of the Declaration of Independence that "all men are created equal."[4]

The history of America shows that disadvantaged groups have rarely achieved a greater measure of justice without a struggle.[5] Their gains have nearly always followed intense and sustained political action, such as the civil rights movement of the 1960s, that forced entrenched interests to relinquish or share their privileged status (see Chapter 7). Although disadvantaged groups have a shared history of political exclusion, each has a distinctive history as well, as is evident in a brief review of the equal rights efforts of African Americans, women, Native Americans, Hispanic Americans, Asian Americans, and other groups.

African Americans

No Americans have faced greater hardship than have black Americans. Their ancestors came to this country as slaves after having been captured in

 Africa, shipped in chains across the Atlantic, and sold in open markets in Charleston, Boston, and other seaports.

Historical   The Civil War ended slavery—but not racism. When fed-
Background   eral troops withdrew from the South in 1877, the region's
white majority took over the state governments, passing laws that kept blacks from voting. They were also forbidden to use the same public facilities as whites.[6] In *Plessy v. Ferguson* (1896), the Supreme Court endorsed these laws, ruling that "separate" public facilities for the two races did not violate the Constitution as long as the facilities were "equal."[7] The *Plessy* decision became a justification for the separate and *unequal* treatment of African Americans. For example, black children were forced into separate schools that rarely had libraries and had few teachers.

Black Americans challenged these discriminatory practices through legal action, but not until the late 1930s did the Supreme Court begin to respond.

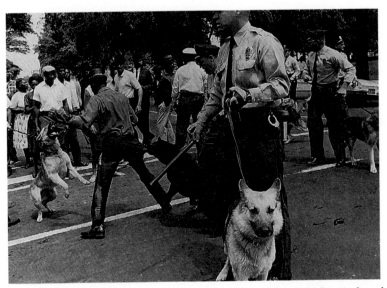

Two police dogs attack a black civil rights activist (*center left*) during the 1963 Birmingham demonstrations. Such images of hatred and violence shook many white Americans out of their complacency about the plight of African Americans.

The Court began modestly by ruling that where no separate public facilities existed for African Americans, they must be allowed to use those reserved for whites. When Oklahoma, which had no law school for blacks, was ordered to admit Ada Sipuel as a law student in 1949, it created a separate law school for her—she sat alone in a roped-off corridor of the state capitol building. The white students, meanwhile, continued to meet at the University of Oklahoma's law school in Norman, twenty miles away. The Supreme Court then ordered the law school to admit her to regular classes. The law school did so but roped off her seat from the rest of the class and stenciled the word "colored" on it. She was also forced to eat alone in a roped-off area of the law school's cafeteria.[8]

The Brown *Decision*   Substantial judicial intervention on behalf of African Americans finally occurred in 1954 with *Brown v. Board of Education of Topeka*. The case began when Linda Carol Brown, a black child in Topeka, Kansas, was denied admission to an all-white elementary school that she passed every day on her way to her all-black school, which was twelve blocks farther away. In its decision, the Court reversed its *Plessy* doctrine by declaring that racial segregation of public schools "generates [among black children] a feeling of inferiority as to their status in the community that may affect their hearts and minds in a way unlikely ever to be undone. . . .

Separate educational facilities are inherently unequal."[9] A 1954 Gallup poll indicated that a substantial majority of southern whites opposed the *Brown* decision. The same poll found that only a narrow majority of whites outside the South agreed with the decision.

The Black Civil Rights Movement   After *Brown*, the struggle of African Americans for their rights became a political movement. Perhaps no single event turned national public opinion so dramatically against segregation as a 1963 march led by Dr. Martin Luther King Jr. in Birmingham, Alabama. As the nation watched on television in disbelief, police officers led by Birmingham's sheriff, Eugene "Bull" Connor, attacked King and his followers with dogs, cattle prods, and fire hoses.

The modern civil rights movement peaked with the triumphant March on Washington for Jobs and Freedom of August 28, 1963. It attracted 250,000 marchers, one of the largest gatherings in the history of the nation's capital. "I have a dream," the Reverend King told the gathering, "that my four little children will one day live in a nation where they will not be judged by the color of their skin but by the content of their character." A year later, after a months-long fight in Congress marked by every parliamentary obstacle that opponents could muster, the Civil Rights Act of 1964 was enacted. The legislation provided African Americans and other minorities with equal access to public facilities and prohibited job discrimination. President Lyndon Johnson, who had been a decisive force in the battle to pass the Civil Rights Act, called for new legislation that would also end racial barriers to voting. Congress answered with the 1965 Voting Rights Act.

The Aftermath of the Civil Rights Movement   Although the most significant progress in history toward the legal equality of all Americans occurred during the 1960s, Dr. King's dream of a color-blind society has remained elusive.[10] Even the legal rights of African Americans do not, in practice, match the promise of the civil rights movement. Studies have found that African Americans accused of crime are more likely to be convicted and to receive stiff sentences than are white Americans on trial for comparable offenses. The U.S. Department of Justice found, for example, that among persons convicted of drug felonies in state courts, half of black defendants received prison sentences compared with a third of white defendants.[11] It should come as no surprise that many African Americans believe that the nation has two standards of justice.

One area in which African Americans have made substantial progress since the 1960s is elective office (see "States in the Nation"). Although the percentage of black elected officials is still far below the proportion

★ | STATES IN THE NATION

Black and Latino Representation in State Legislatures

For a long period in U.S. history, there were almost no minorities among the ranks of state legislators. Minorities are still underrepresented relative to their numbers in the population. Although one in every three Americans is a minority-group member, only one in eight state legislators comes from a minority group; of these, about two-thirds are African American.

Q: What accounts for differences between the states in the percentage of minority-group members in their legislatures?

A: States with large populations of minorities tend to have a larger percentage of legislators from minority groups. Alabama and Mississippi have large black populations and have the highest proportion of African American legislators. New Mexico, with its large Hispanic population, has the highest proportion of Latino lawmakers.

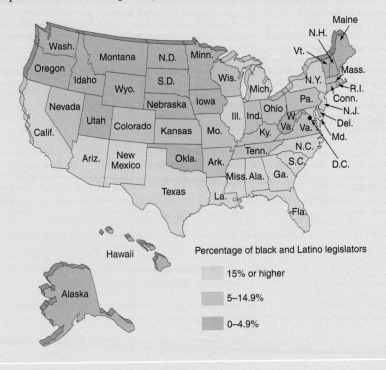

Source: National Conference of State Legislatures, 2008.

of African Americans in the population, it has risen sharply in recent decades.[12] There are now roughly five hundred black mayors and more than forty black members of Congress. The most stunning advance, of course, was the election of Barack Obama in 2008 as the first African American president.

Women

The United States carried over from English common law a political disregard for women, forbidding them to vote, hold public office, or serve on juries.[13] Upon marriage, a woman essentially lost her identity as an individual and could not own and dispose of property without her husband's consent. Even a wife's body was not fully hers. A wife's adultery was declared by the Supreme Court in 1904 to be a violation of the husband's property rights![14]

Historical Background

The first women's rights convention in America was held in 1848 in Seneca Falls, New York, after Lucretia Mott and Elizabeth Cady Stanton had been barred from the main floor of an antislavery convention. Thereafter, the struggle for women's rights became closely aligned with the abolitionist movement. However, when the Fifteenth Amendment was ratified after the Civil War, women were not included; the amendment declared that the right to vote could not be abridged on account of race or color but said nothing about sex. Not until passage of the Nineteenth Amendment in 1920 did women gain the right to vote.

Women's Legal and Political Gains   Ratification of the Nineteenth Amendment encouraged leaders of the women's movement to propose in 1923 a constitutional amendment that would guarantee equal rights for women. Congress rejected that proposal but sixty years later approved the Equal Rights Amendment (ERA) and submitted it to the states for their consideration. The ERA failed by three states to receive the three-fourths majority required for ratification.[15] Other efforts were more successful, however. Among the congressional initiatives were the Equal Pay Act of 1963, which prohibits sex discrimination in salary and wages by some categories of employers; Title IX of the Education Amendment of 1972, which prohibits sex discrimination in education; and the Equal Credit Act of 1974, which prohibits sex discrimination in the granting of financial credit.

Women are also protected by Title VII of the Civil Rights Act of 1964, which bans gender discrimination in employment. This protection extends to sexual harassment. Lewd comments and unwelcome advances are part of the workplace reality for many American women. However, the courts have held, and with increasing firmness, that companies and government agencies can be sued if they do not try hard to prevent this type of behavior.[16] In a 2006 decision, for example, the Supreme Court made it easier for employees to sue an organization that retaliates against them for filing a sexual harassment complaint. The case involved a woman who, after filing such a complaint, was removed from her position as a forklift operator and assigned a less desirable job in the company.[17]

Women have made substantial gains in the area of appointive and elective offices. In 1981, President Ronald Reagan appointed the first woman to serve on the Supreme Court, Sandra Day O'Connor. When the Democratic Party in 1984 chose Geraldine Ferraro as its vice presidential nominee, she became the first woman to run on the national ticket of a major political party. The selection of Sarah Palin as Republican vice-presidential nominee in 2008 marked only the second time a woman has run on a major party's national ticket. In 2008, Hillary Clinton nearly won the Democratic presidential nomination, which would have been the first time that a woman headed the national ticket of a major American political party. Despite such signs of progress, women are still a long way from attaining political equality with men.[18] Women occupy roughly one in six congressional seats and one in five statewide and city council offices (see "How the United States Compares").

Although women are underrepresented in political office, their vote is increasingly powerful. Until the 1970s, the political behavior of women and men was nearly identical. Today, there is a substantial **gender gap:** women and men differ in their opinions and their votes.[19] Women are more supportive than men of government programs for the poor, minorities, children, and the elderly. They also have a greater tendency to cast their votes for Democratic candidates (see Figure 5-1). The gender gap is discussed further in Chapter 6.

Job-Related Issues: Family Leave, Comparable Worth, and Sexual Harassment In recent decades, increasing numbers of women have sought employment outside the home. Government statistics indicate that employment-age women are six times more likely to work outside the home compared with a half-century ago. Women have made gains in many traditionally male-dominated fields. For example, women now make up nearly half of the new lawyers and physicians who graduate each year. The change in women's work status is also reflected in education statistics. A few decades ago, more white, black, and Hispanic men than women were enrolled in college. Today, the reverse is true, with more women than men of each group enrolled. A U.S. Education Department report issued in 2006 showed that women are ahead of men in more than just college enrollment.

🌐 HOW THE UNITED STATES COMPARES

Women's Representation in National Legislatures

For a long period in world history, women were largely barred from holding positions of political power. The situation has changed dramatically in recent decades, and women now hold more seats in national legislatures than at any time in history. Yet there are less than a handful of countries where they have nearly reached parity with men. The Scandinavian countries rank highest in terms of the percentage of female lawmakers. Other northern European countries have lower levels, but their levels are higher than in the United States, as the figure below indicates.

The reason the United States ranks relatively low in comparison with other Western democracies has only partly to do with social biases. In general, women hold more legislative seats in democracies that use a proportional system of election. In such countries, the parties get seats in proportion to the votes they receive in the election, and the parties themselves decide which party members will occupy the seats. In America's system, candidates compete directly for the vote, and the candidate who gets the most votes in a district wins the seat. Further, U.S. incumbents have a very high reelection rate, one that far exceeds the rate in European parliaments. U.S. incumbents are difficult to dislodge, which works against the entry of new members, regardless of sex (see Chapter 11).

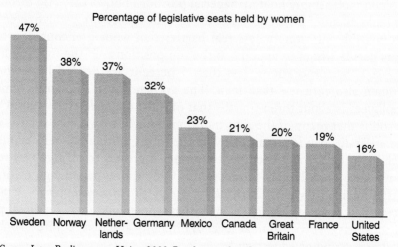

Percentage of legislative seats held by women

Sweden	Norway	Netherlands	Germany	Mexico	Canada	Great Britain	France	United States
47%	38%	37%	32%	23%	21%	20%	19%	16%

Source: Inter-Parliamentary Union, 2008. Based on number of women in the single or lower legislative chamber. In the case of the United States, that chamber is the U.S. House of Representatives.

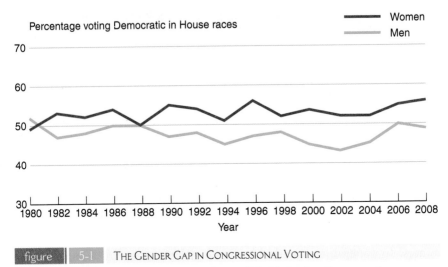

Percentage voting Democratic in House races

Source: National Election Studies (1988–1998); exit polls (2000–2006); 2008 figure based on preliminary data.

figure 5-1   THE GENDER GAP IN CONGRESSIONAL VOTING

Women and men differ, on average, in their political behavior. For example, women are more likely than men to vote Democratic, as shown by the difference between the women's vote and the men's vote for Democratic candidates in U.S. House races.

Compared with men, they are also more likely to complete their degree, to do it in a shorter period, and to get better grades.[20]

Nevertheless, women have not achieved equality when it comes to jobs. Women increasingly hold managerial positions but, as they rise through the ranks, many of them encounter the so-called *glass ceiling*, which refers to the invisible but nonetheless real barrier that women encounter when firms decide whom to appoint to the top positions. Of the five hundred largest U.S. corporations, less than 5 percent are headed by women. Women also earn less than men. The average pay for full-time female employees is about three-fourths that of full-time male employees. One reason is that many of the jobs traditionally held by women, such as office assistant, pay less than many of the jobs traditionally held by men, such as truck driver. Attempts by women's groups to change this tendency have been largely unsuccessful. Only a tiny percentage of firms and municipalities have instituted a policy of *comparable worth*. Under this policy, wage scales are set such that women and men get equal pay for jobs that involve a similar level of difficulty and that require a similar level of training or education.[21]

Women gained a major victory in the workplace when Congress passed the Family and Medical Leave Act in 1993. It provides for up to twelve

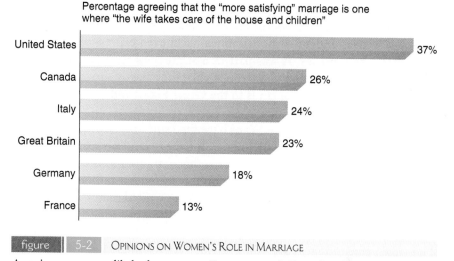

Percentage agreeing that the "more satisfying" marriage is one where "the wife takes care of the house and children"

- United States 37%
- Canada 26%
- Italy 24%
- Great Britain 23%
- Germany 18%
- France 13%

figure 5-2 OPINIONS ON WOMEN'S ROLE IN MARRIAGE
Americans are more likely than western Europeans to believe that the "more satisfying" marriage is one where "the wife takes care of the house and children" rather than one where "the husband and wife both have jobs." *Source: Global Attitudes Survey (2002) by the Pew Research Center for the People and the Press.*

weeks of unpaid leave for employees to care for a new baby or a seriously ill family member. Upon return from leave, the employee ordinarily must be given the original or an equivalent job position with equivalent pay, benefits, and other employment terms. These provisions apply to men as well as women, but women were the instigating force behind the legislation and are its primary beneficiaries because they still bear the larger share of responsibility for sick and young family members.

Traditional practices are reflected in Americans' attitudes toward the role of women in society. Roughly two in five adults believe the ideal marriage is one where the wife stays home to take care of the house. This opinion is more prevalent in the United States than in Europe (see Figure 5-2), even though women's legal and employment gains in the United States have been at least as impressive as those in Europe.

Native Americans

When white settlers began arriving in America in large numbers during the seventeenth century, roughly 10 million Native Americans were living in the territory that would become the United States. By 1900, the Native American population had plummeted to less than one million. No people in human history suffered a steeper loss. Diseases brought by white

Historical
Background

settlers took the largest toll on the various Indian tribes, but wars and massacres contributed. "The only good Indian is a dead Indian" is not simply a hackneyed expression from cowboy movies. It was part of a strategy of westward expansion, as settlers and U.S. troops alike mercilessly drove the eastern Indians from their ancestral lands to the Great Plains and later seized most of these lands as well.

In recent years, Native Americans have filed suit to reclaim lost ancestral lands and have won a few settlements. But they stand no realistic chance of getting back even those lands that had been granted to them by federal treaty but later were sold off or seized forcibly by federal authorities. Native Americans were not even official citizens of the United States until passage of an act of Congress in 1924. Their citizenship status came too late to be of much help; their traditional way of life had already largely disappeared. The tragic consequences are still evident. Native Americans are less than half as likely to have completed college as other Americans, their life expectancy is more than ten years lower than the national average, their poverty rate is twice that of the national average, and their infant mortality rate is more than three times higher than that of white Americans.[22]

Today, full-blooded Native Americans, including Alaska Natives, number more than 2 million, about half of whom live on or close to reservations set aside for them by the federal government. Reservations are governed by treaties signed when they were established. State governments have no direct authority over federal reservations, and the federal government's authority is limited by the terms of a particular treaty. Although U.S. policy toward the reservations has varied over time, the current policy is to promote self-government and economic self-sufficiency.[23] Preservation of Native American cultures is also a policy goal. For example, Native American children can now be taught in their own languages; at an earlier time in schools run by the Bureau of Indian Affairs, children were required to use English. Nevertheless, Native American languages have declined sharply in use. Of the larger tribes, the Navajo and Pueblo are the only ones where a majority of the people still speak the native language at home. Ninety percent or more of the Cherokee, Chippewa, Creek, Iroquois, and Lumbee speak only English.

The civil rights movement of the 1960s at first did not include Native Americans. Then, in the early 1970s, militant Native Americans occupied the Bureau of Indian Affairs in Washington, D.C., and later seized control of the village of Wounded Knee on a Sioux reservation in southwestern South Dakota, exchanging gunfire with U.S. marshals. These episodes highlighted the grievances of Native Americans and may have contributed to legislation that in 1974 granted Native Americans living on reservations greater control over federal programs that affect them. Native Americans had already benefited from the legislative climate created by the 1960s civil rights movement: in 1968, Congress enacted the Indian Bill of Rights, which gives Native Americans on reservations constitutional guarantees similar to those given to other Americans.

In recent years, some tribes have erected gaming casinos on reservation land. The world's largest casino, Foxwoods, is operated by the Mashantunket Pequots in Connecticut. Casinos have brought opportunities to the Native Americans living on or near the affected reservations. Their employment in these areas has increased by a fourth, and their population has grown by more than 10 percent.[24] However, the casinos have also brought controversy—traditionalists argue that the casinos are creating a gaming culture that, whatever its economic benefits, has a perverse effect on the traditional culture. Ben Nighthorse Campbell, a Native American who served two terms before retiring from the U.S. Senate in 2003, worried that casinos were pitting "tribe against tribe," creating disputes over which tribes would be allowed to have casinos and at what price to tribal traditions. "It becomes much more difficult to find a solution when nobody wants to give," said Campbell.[25]

Hispanic Americans

The fastest-growing minority in the United States is Hispanic Americans, that is, people of Spanish-speaking background. Hispanics recently surpassed African Americans as the nation's largest racial or ethnic minority group. More than 35 million Hispanics live in the United States, an increase of 40 percent over the 1990 census. They have emigrated to the United States primarily from Mexico and the Caribbean islands, mainly Cuba and Puerto Rico. About half of all Hispanics in the United States were born in Mexico or claim a Mexican ancestry. Hispanics are concentrated in their states of entry; thus Florida, New York, and New Jersey have large numbers of Caribbean Hispanics, while California, Texas, Arizona, and New Mexico have many immigrants from Mexico. More than half the population of Los Angeles is of Hispanic—mostly Mexican—descent.

Legal and Political Action   Hispanic Americans have benefited from laws and court rulings aimed primarily at protecting other groups. Although the Civil Rights Act of 1964 was largely a response to the condition of black people, its provisions against discrimination apply broadly to other groups.

Nevertheless, Hispanics had their own civil rights movement. Its hallmark was the farmworkers' strikes of the late 1960s and the 1970s, which

LEADERS

Cesar Estrada Chavez
(1927–93)

Cesar Chavez led the first successful farm-workers' strike in U.S. history. Founder of the United Farm Workers of America, Chavez was called "one of the heroic figures of our time" by Robert F. Kennedy and is widely regarded as the most influential Latino leader in modern U.S. history. A migrant worker as a child, Chavez knew firsthand the deprivations suffered by farm laborers. Like Martin Luther King Jr., Chavez was an advocate of nonviolent protest, and he organized food boycotts that eventually caused agricultural firms to improve wages and working conditions for farmworkers. In 1994, Chavez was posthumously awarded the Presidential Medal of Freedom, the highest civilian honor an American can receive.

sought basic labor rights for migrant workers. Migrants were working long hours for low pay, were living in shacks without electricity or plumbing, and were unwelcome in many local schools as well as in some local hospitals. Farm owners at first refused to bargain with the workers, but a well-organized national boycott of California grapes and lettuce forced that state to pass a law giving migrant workers the right to bargain collectively. The strikes were led in California by Cesar Chavez, who himself grew up in a Mexican American migrant family. Chavez's tactics were copied with less success in other states, including Texas.

The Hispanic civil rights movement also pursued social and political goals. Hispanics had some success, for example, in pressuring federal, state, and local governments to expand bilingual education programs. They also persuaded Congress to require states to provide bilingual ballots in local areas with a sizable number of non-English-speaking residents.

Hispanics are one of the nation's oldest ethnic groups. Some Hispanics are the descendants of people who helped colonize California, Texas, Florida, New Mexico, and Arizona before those areas were annexed by the United States. However, most Hispanics are recent immigrants or their descendants. A significant number—more than 10 million by some estimates—are in the United States illegally. In past eras, immigration officials could more easily control newcomers because most of them arrived by ship through a port of entry, such as Ellis Island. But most Hispanics have arrived by land, many of them crossing illegally from Mexico. U.S. authorities have had only limited success in stopping this influx. Most of the illegal aliens have come to America seeking jobs, and they now make up an estimated 5 percent of the U.S. workforce. They have had broad support in the Hispanic community, which has sought to ease immigration restrictions and to expand the rights and privileges of illegal aliens—positions that are unpopular with some other Americans.

In 2005, Republican lawmakers pushed a bill through the House of Representatives that would have cracked down sharply on illegal immigrants. The Hispanic community responded with huge protest rallies—ones reminiscent of the 1960s civil rights movement. The rally in Los Angeles drew an estimated half million marchers, reputedly the largest such gathering in the city's history. The scale of the rallies caught even seasoned political observers by surprise. It was by far the largest demonstration ever of Hispanic political solidarity and helped prompt the Senate to kill the legislation.

In 2007, President George W. Bush and a bipartisan congressional coalition, including most of the Senate and House leadership, developed a comprehensive immigration reform bill that contained a provision for guest workers. Under the plan, workers who are in the United States illegally could enroll in the program, which would allow them to work in the country for up to six years. Other noncitizens could enter the United States as guest workers if they had a job waiting for them. The proposal was intended to address the nation's labor needs while simultaneously reducing illegal immigration by increasing border surveillance and by raising penalties on employers who hire undocumented aliens. The plan had support from the business community and was backed by most congressional Democrats. However, the plan failed to get the support of most congressional Republicans and was defeated. Opponents insisted, as preconditions for considering any type of guest worker program, that U.S. borders first be secured against illegal entry, that current laws against hiring illegal aliens be enforced rigorously, and that illegal residents be identified and deported.

The split within Congress reflects public opinion on the issue. Polls indicate that most Americans believe stricter restrictions should be placed on immigration, including tightening the borders and penalizing employers who hire illegal immigrants. However, there is no consensus on how to handle the illegal immigrants already in the country. Most Americans favor some path to citizenship for these individuals, provided they meet certain conditions, including holding a job and having no criminal record. A substantial minority, however, want to deport all illegal immigrants and

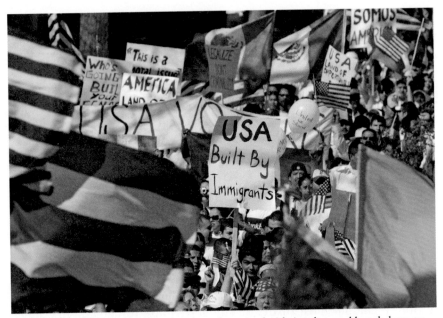

When Congress in 2006 seemed on the verge of enacting legislation that would crack down on illegal immigrants, most of whom are from Mexico, pro-immigrant rallies were held in nearly every American city with a sizable Hispanic population. The rally in Los Angeles was the largest in the city's history. Even in locations more distant from Mexico, the rallies were large and enthusiastic. The scene here is of the rally in Lincoln, Nebraska, where the flags of the United States and Mexico were readily visible.

are dead set against any policy that would place them near the front of the line for citizenship. These divisions of opinion have made it difficult to build a congressional majority in support of a specific immigration policy. One thing is certain: the immigration issue is not going away. Each year, an estimated half million illegal immigrants enter the United States, adding to the pressure on government to act.

Growing Political Power   More than four thousand Hispanic Americans nationwide hold public office. Hispanics have been elected to statewide office in several states, including New Mexico and Arizona. About twenty Hispanic Americans currently serve in the House of Representatives.

Hispanic Americans are a growing political force. By the middle of the century, Hispanics are projected to become the largest racial or ethnic group in California. Their political involvement, like that of other immigrant groups, will increase as they become more firmly rooted in society. At present, about half of all Hispanics are not registered to vote, and only about a third actually vote, limiting the group's political power. Nevertheless, the

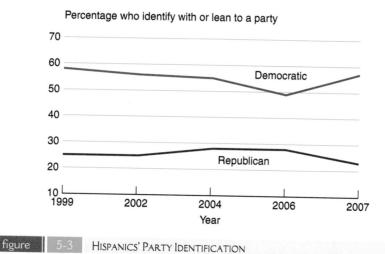

Percentage who identify with or lean to a party

figure | 5-3 | HISPANICS' PARTY IDENTIFICATION

Hispanics' party loyalties lean heavily toward the Democratic Party. This tendency increased in 2007 after congressional Republicans attempted to enact tough legislation for dealing with illegal immigrants, most of whom are Hispanic. *Source: Pew Hispanic Center, 2002, 2006, 2007; National Survey of Latinos, 2004; Washington Post/Kaiser Family Foundation/Harvard University survey, 1999.*

sheer size of the Hispanic population in states such as Texas and California makes the group a potent force, as was evident in the 2008 election when both the Republicans and the Democrats mounted massive efforts to woo Hispanic voters.

With the exception of the conservative Republican-leaning Cuban Americans of southern Florida, Hispanics lean toward the Democratic Party. This tendency has intensified since congressional Republicans attempted to tighten immigration laws. Hispanics who regard themselves as Democrats outnumber those who consider themselves as Republicans by more than two to one (see Figure 5-3). Polls indicated that nearly 70 percent of Hispanics voted Democratic in the 2006 congressional races, a 10 percent increase from the 2004 level. Democrats also carried the Hispanic vote by a wide margin in the 2008 election. However, compared with African Americans, Hispanics are a less cohesive voting bloc. Whereas blacks of all income levels are solidly Democratic, lower-income Hispanics vote Democratic at substantially higher rates than upper-income Hispanics. Opinion surveys show that Hispanics tend to be relatively liberal on economic issues and relatively conservative on social issues. These tendencies suggest that Hispanics will lean Democratic in the near future but divide more evenly between the parties as their income rises.[26]

Asian Americans

Chinese and Japanese laborers were brought to the western states during the late 1800s to work in mines and to build railroads. When the need for this labor declined, Congress in 1892 ordered a temporary halt to Asian immigration. Over the next three decades, informal agreements kept all but a few Asians from entering the country. In 1930, Congress completely blocked the entry of Japanese. Japan had protested a California law that prohibited persons of Japanese descent from buying property in the state. Rather than trying to finesse what was called "the California problem," Congress bluntly told Japan that its people were not wanted in the United States.[27]

Discrimination against Asians did not ease substantially until 1965, when Congress enacted legislation that adjusted the immigration quotas to favor those who had previously been assigned very small numbers. This change in the law was a product of the 1960s civil rights movement, which increased public awareness of all forms of discrimination. Asian Americans now number about 12 million, or roughly 4 percent of the total U.S. population. Most Asian Americans live on the West Coast, particularly in California. China, Japan, Korea, India, Vietnam, and the Philippines are the ancestral homes of most Asian Americans.

The rights of Asian Americans have been expanded primarily by court rulings and legislation, such as the Civil Rights Act of 1964, that were initiated in response to pressure from other minority groups. Howevere, in *Lau v. Nichols* (1974), a case initiated by a Chinese American family, the Supreme Court ruled unanimously that placing public school children for whom English is a second language in regular classrooms without special assistance is a violation of the Fourteenth Amendment's equal-protection clause, because it denies them an equal educational opportunity.[28] The Court did not mandate bilingual instruction, but the *Lau* decision prompted many schools to establish bilingual instruction. Since then, some states have restricted its use. For example, California's Proposition 227, enacted in 1998, requires most children for whom English is a second language to take their courses in English after their first year in school.

Asian Americans are an upwardly mobile group. Most Asian cultures emphasize family-based self-reliance, which, in the American context, includes an emphasis on academic achievement. For example, Asians make up a disproportionate share of the students at California's leading public universities, which base admission primarily on high school grades and standardized test scores. However, Asian Americans are still underrepresented in certain areas of the workplace. According to U.S. government figures, Asian Americans account for about 5 percent of professionals and technicians, slightly more than their

Chinese workers were brought to the United States in the late 1800s to work on the railroads and in the mines, but when the need for their labor diminished, they were discouraged from staying in America. Immigration policies that discriminated against Asians lasted until the 1960s.

percentage of the total population. Yet past and present discrimination has kept them from obtaining a proportionate share of top business positions—they hold less than 2 percent of managerial jobs. They are also underrepresented politically, even by comparison with Hispanics and blacks.[29] Not until 1996 was an Asian American elected governor of a state other than Hawaii, and not until 2000 did an Asian American hold a presidential cabinet position.

Other Groups and Their Rights

The 1964 Civil Rights Act (discussed further later in the chapter) prohibits discrimination by sex, race, or national origin. This act classified women and racial and ethnic minorities as legally protected groups, enabling them to pursue their rights in court. As these minority groups gained success, other disadvantaged groups began to press their claims.

Older Americans Older Americans are one such group. The Age Discrimination Act of 1975 and the Age Discrimination in Employment Act of 1967 prohibit discrimination against older workers in hiring for jobs in which age is not clearly a crucial factor in job performance. More recently, mandatory retirement ages for most jobs have been eliminated by law.

However, forced retirement for reasons of age is permissible if it is justified by the nature of a particular job or by the performance of a particular
employee. Commercial airline pilots, for example, are required by law to
retire at sixty-five years of age and must pass a rigorous physical examination
to continue flying after they reach sixty years of age. As the example suggests,
older Americans are not as fully protected by law as women and minority-
group members are. Age discrimination is not among the forms of discrimination prohibited by the U.S. Constitution, and the courts have given government and employers leeway in setting their age-based policies.[30]

Disabled Americans   Roughly 40 million Americans have a physical or
mental disability, such as difficulty in seeing, hearing, or walking. In an effort to give them greater access to society's opportunities, Congress passed
the Americans with Disabilities Act in 1990. The legislation grants employment and other protections to the disabled. Earlier, through the Education
for All Handicapped Children Act of 1975, Congress required that schools
provide all children, however severe their disability, with a free, appropriate education. Before the legislation, 4 million children with disabilities
were getting either no education or an inappropriate one (as in the case of a
blind child who is not taught Braille). The Supreme Court has also granted
protection to the disabled, ruling, for example, that state governments must
take reasonable steps, such as adding access ramps to government buildings, to make public services and facilities available to the disabled.[31]
    Although the disabled have substantial legal protections, they, like the
elderly, are not a constitutionally protected group. Accordingly, actions
that have the effect of discriminating against the disabled are in some cases
legal. For example, a business is not required to provide free home delivery
when a buyer is disabled and unable to transport a purchased item.

Gays and Lesbians   Gays and lesbians have historically been the object
of hostility and discrimination. Until recently, they usually responded by
hiding their sexual orientation. Some still do so, but many gays and lesbians
now openly pursue a claim to equal protection under the law.[32]
    Gays and lesbians gained a significant legal victory when the Supreme
Court in *Romer v. Evans* (1996) struck down a Colorado constitutional
amendment that nullified all existing and any new legal protections for
homosexuals. In a 6-3 ruling, the Court said that the Colorado law violated
the Constitution's guarantee of equal protection because it subjected individuals to employment and other discrimination simply because of their sexual
preference. The Court concluded that the law had no reasonable purpose but
was instead motivated by hostility toward homosexuals.[33] In *Lawrence v. Texas*
(2003), the Court handed gays and lesbians another victory by invalidating

state laws that prohibited sexual relations between consenting adults of the same sex (see Chapter 4).[34]

These gains have been partially offset by setbacks. In 2000, for example, the Supreme Court held that the Boy Scouts, as a private organization that has a right to free association, can ban gays because the Scout creed forbids homosexuality.[35] Gays and lesbians who are open about their sexual preference are also barred from serving in the military. However, they can serve under the military's "don't ask, don't tell" (sometimes called the "don't harass, don't pursue") policy. As long as they do not by words or actions reveal their sexual preference, they are allowed to enlist and stay in the service. In turn, soldiers are instructed not to inquire about other soldiers' sexual orientation, nor are they to try to entrap those they suspect of being gay or lesbian. The courts have upheld the military's ban, citing the unusually close physical proximity with minimal privacy that occurs in the military.

Gay and lesbian couples are currently seeking the same legal status that the law extends to opposite-sex married couples. During the past decade, same-sex couples have succeeded in getting some states, cities, and firms to extend employee benefits, such as health insurance, to their employees' same-sex partners. These arrangements, however, do not extend to things such as inheritance and hospital visitation rights, which are reserved by state law for married couples and their families. In 2000, Vermont became the first state to legalize the civil union of same-sex couples, thereby granting them the same legal rights as those held by opposite-sex married couples. In 2004, upon order of the state's high court, Massachusetts gave same-sex couples the right to marry, becoming the first state to do so. In 2008, California's Supreme Court overturned that state's ban on same-sex marriage, a decision that was challenged by a ballot initiative to amend the state's constitution to prohibit such unions. California voters approved the ban, which led same-sex marriage proponents to file a lawsuit challenging the ballot initiative.

The claim that gay and lesbian couples should have the same legal rights as opposite-sex married couples has been hotly contested. Even before Vermont authorized same-sex unions, Congress passed the Defense of Marriage Act, which defines marriage as "a legal union of one man and one woman as husband and wife." This 1996 law authorizes states to deny marital rights to a same-sex couple that has been granted these rights by another state. Under the U.S. Constitution's "full faith and credit clause," states are required to recognize the laws and contracts of other states, although Congress can create exceptions, as it did with the Defense of Marriage Act.

Social conservatives have sponsored ballot initiatives like the one in California to ban same-sex marriage. In the two dozen or so states where the issue has been on the ballot, the voters in nearly every case have enacted

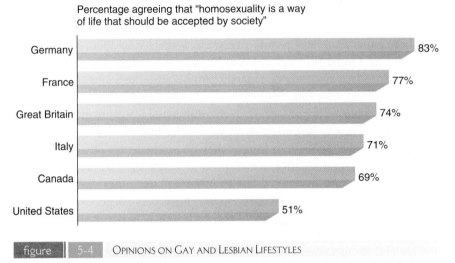

Percentage agreeing that "homosexuality is a way of life that should be accepted by society"

Germany	83%
France	77%
Great Britain	74%
Italy	71%
Canada	69%
United States	51%

figure 5-4   OPINIONS ON GAY AND LESBIAN LIFESTYLES

Americans are less likely than western Europeans to believe that society should accept gay and lesbian lifestyles. *Source: Global Attitudes Survey (2002) by the Pew Research Center for the People and the Press.*

the ban, usually by a wide margin. Americans, perhaps because of their deeper religious beliefs (see Chapter 6), are less supportive of gay and lesbian lifestyles than are Europeans (see Figure 5-4).

Nevertheless, Americans have become more accepting of gay and lesbian relationships. Connecticut and a half dozen other states have recently extended substantial legal rights to same-sex couples, and support for civil unions has increased to the point where a near majority now say they favor them. A 2008 ABC/Washington Post poll, for example, found that Americans were almost evenly split on support for and opposition to civil unions, with only 3 percent undecided about the policy. For its part, Congress has not taken the issue of same-sex unions beyond the Defense of Marriage Act. An attempt by congressional conservatives in 2006 to initiate a constitutional amendment to ban same-sex marriage fell far short of the requisite two-thirds vote in the House and Senate. One thing is sure: issues of gay and lesbian rights, including same-sex marriage and civil union, will be sources of political controversy for the foreseeable future.

EQUALITY UNDER THE LAW

The catchphrase of nearly every group's claim to a more equal standing in American society has been "equality under the law." When secure in their legal rights, people are positioned to pursue equality in other arenas, such as the economic sector. Americans' claim to legal equality is embodied in a great many laws, a few of which are particularly noteworthy.

Equal Protection: The Fourteenth Amendment

The Fourteenth Amendment, which was ratified in 1868, declares in part that no state shall "deny to any person within its jurisdiction the equal protection of the laws." Through this **equal-protection clause,** the courts have protected groups such as African Americans and women from discrimination by state and local governments.

The Fourteenth Amendment's equal-protection clause does not require government to treat all groups or classes of people the same way in all circumstances. The judiciary allows inequalities that are "reasonably" related to a legitimate government interest. In applying this **reasonable-basis test,** the courts require government only to show that a particular law is reasonable. For example, twenty-one-year-olds can legally drink alcohol but twenty-year-olds cannot. The courts have held that the goal of reducing fatalities from alcohol-related accidents involving young drivers is a valid reason for imposing an age limit on the purchase and consumption of alcohol.

The reasonable-basis test does not apply to racial or ethnic classifications (see Table 5-1). Any law that treats people differently because of race or ethnicity is subject to the **strict-scrutiny test,** under which such a law is presumed unconstitutional unless government can provide overwhelming

table **5-1** LEVELS OF COURT REVIEW FOR LAWS THAT TREAT AMERICANS DIFFERENTLY

Test	Applies To	Standard Used
Strict scrutiny	Race, ethnicity	Suspect category—assumed unconstitutional in the absence of an overwhelming justification
Intermediate scrutiny	Gender	Almost suspect category—assumed unconstitutional unless the law serves a clearly compelling and justified purpose
Reasonable basis	Other categories (such as age and income)	Not suspect category—assumed constitutional unless no sound rationale for the law can be provided

evidence of its necessity. The strict-scrutiny test has virtually eliminated race and ethnicity as permissible classifications when the effect is to place a hardship on members of a racial or ethnic minority. The Supreme Court's position is that race and national origin are **suspect classifications**—in other words, that legal classifications based on race and ethnicity are presumed to have discrimination as their purpose.

The strict-scrutiny test emerged after the 1954 *Brown v. Board of Education of Topeka* ruling and became a basis for invalidating laws that discriminated against black Americans. As other groups, especially women, began to assert their rights more vigorously in the late 1960s and early 1970s, the Supreme Court gave early signs that it might expand the scope of suspect classifications to include gender. In the end, however, the Court announced in *Craig v. Boren* (1976) that sex classifications were permissible if they served "important governmental objectives" and were "substantially" related to the achievement of those objectives.[36] The Court thus placed sex distinctions in an intermediate (or almost suspect) category, to be scrutinized more closely than some other classifications (for example, income or age level) but, unlike racial classifications, justifiable in some instances. In *Rostker v. Goldberg* (1980), for example, the policy of male-only registration for the military draft was upheld on grounds that the exclusion of women from involuntary combat duty serves a legitimate and important purpose.[37]

Nevertheless, rather than giving the government broad leeway to treat men and women differently, the Supreme Court has struck down most of the laws it has recently reviewed that contain sex classifications. A leading case is *United States v. Virginia* (1996), in which the Supreme Court determined that the male-only admissions policy of Virginia Military Institute (VMI), a 157-year-old state-supported college, was unconstitutional. The state had developed an alternative program for women at another college, but the Court concluded that it was no substitute for VMI's unique educational program. (The VMI decision also had the effect of ending the all-male admissions policy of the Citadel, a state-supported military college in South Carolina.)[38]

Equal Access: The Civil Rights Acts of 1964 and 1968

The Fourteenth Amendment prohibits discrimination by government but not by private parties. As a result, for a long period in American history, owners could legally bar black people from restaurants, hotels, and other accommodations, and employers could freely discriminate in their job-hiring practices. Since the 1960s, however, private parties have had much less freedom to discriminate for reasons of race, sex, ethnicity, or religion.

Although women are excluded by law from having to register for the draft, they are eligible to enlist voluntarily in the U.S. military. Shown here is a U.S. woman soldier controlling the crowd on the streets of Mosul, Iraq. Roughly 2 percent of American military casualties in the Iraq conflict have been women.

Accommodations and Jobs   The Civil Rights Act of 1964, which is based on Congress's power to regulate commerce, entitles all persons to equal access to restaurants, bars, theaters, hotels, gasoline stations, and similar establishments serving the general public. The legislation also bars discrimination in the hiring, promotion, and wages of employees of medium-size and large firms. A few forms of job discrimination are still lawful under the Civil Rights Act. For example, an owner-operator of a small business can discriminate in hiring his or her co-workers, and a parochial school can take the religion of a prospective teacher into account.

The Civil Rights Act of 1964 has nearly eliminated the most overt forms of discrimination in the area of public accommodations. Some restaurants and hotels may provide better service to white customers, but outright refusal to serve African Americans or other minority-group members is rare. Such a refusal is a violation of the law and could easily be proved in many instances. It is harder to prove discrimination in job decisions; accordingly, the act has been less effective in rooting out employment discrimination—a subject discussed later in this chapter.

Housing   In 1968, Congress passed civil rights legislation designed to prohibit discrimination in housing. A building owner cannot refuse to sell or rent housing because of a person's race, religion, ethnicity, or sex. An exception is allowed for owners of small multifamily dwellings who reside on the premises.

Despite legal prohibitions on discrimination, housing in America remains highly segregated. Only a third of African Americans live in a neighborhood that is mostly white. One reason is that the annual income of most black families is substantially below that of most white families. Another reason is banking practices. At one time, banks contributed to housing segregation by *redlining*—refusing to grant mortgage loans in certain neighborhoods. This practice drove down the selling prices of homes in these neighborhoods, which led to an influx of African Americans and an exodus of whites. Redlining is prohibited by the 1968 Civil Rights Act, but many of the segregated neighborhoods that it helped create still exist. Studies indicate that minority status is still a factor in the lending practices of some banks. A report of the U.S. Conference of Mayors indicated that, among applicants with average or slightly higher incomes relative to their community, Hispanics and African Americans were about twice as likely as whites to be denied a mortgage.[39]

Equal Ballots: The Voting Rights Act of 1965, as Amended

Free elections are the bedrock of American democracy, yet the right to vote has only recently become a reality for many Americans, particularly African Americans. Although they appeared to have gained that right in 1870 with ratification of the Fifteenth Amendment, southern whites invented a series of devices, including whites-only primaries, poll taxes, and rigged literacy tests, to keep blacks from registering and voting. For example, almost no votes were cast by African Americans in North Carolina between the years 1920 and 1946.[40]

Racial barriers to voting began to crumble in the mid-1940s when the Supreme Court declared that whites-only primary elections were unconstitutional.[41] Two decades later, the Twenty-fourth Amendment outlawed poll taxes. However, the major step toward equal participation by African Americans was passage of the Voting Rights Act of 1965, which forbids discrimination in voting and registration. The legislation empowers federal agents to register voters and to oversee participation in elections. The Voting Rights Act, as interpreted by the courts, also prohibits the use of literacy tests as a registration requirement. The Voting Rights Act had a clear impact on black participation. In the next presidential election, black turnout in the South increased by nearly 20 percent from its previous level.

Congress has renewed the Voting Rights Act several times, most recently in 2006. The act includes a provision that compels states and localities to clear with federal officials any electoral change that has the effect, intended or not, of reducing the voting power of a minority group. One way to reduce the power of a group's votes is to spread members of the group across election districts so that their number in any given district is too small to constitute a voting majority. That situation was at issue in *League of United Latin American Voters v. Perry* (2006), a case involving Texas's twenty-third congressional district, the boundaries of which were drawn in a way that deliberately diluted the power of Hispanic voters. In ordering the state of Texas to redraw the district, the Court said, "The troubling blend of politics and race—and the resulting vote dilution of a group that was beginning to [overcome] prior electoral discrimination—cannot be sustained."[42]

On the other hand, the Court has held that an election district cannot be intentionally shaped to allow a minority group to control it. In three separate cases that were each decided by a 5-4 margin, the Supreme Court ruled that the redistricting of several congressional districts in Texas, North Carolina, and Georgia violated the Fourteenth Amendment because race had been the "dominant" consideration in their creation. The Court held that the redistricting violated the equal-protection rights of white voters and ordered the three states to redraw the districts.[43] However, the Court does permit states to create districts that are dominated by a minority group if the district's boundaries were established for partisan reasons rather than racial or ethnic ones. This ruling came in *Easley v. Cromartie* (2001). At issue was a North Carolina district that was drawn with the goal of creating a safe Democratic district, which resulted in a district with a large proportion of black voters. The Court, which has long allowed partisan redistricting, ruled that if such redistricting incidentally creates a minority-dominated district, as in this case, the action does not violate the Fourteenth Amendment.[44]

EQUALITY OF RESULT

America's disadvantaged groups have made significant progress toward equal rights, particularly during the past few decades. Through acts of Congress and rulings of the Supreme Court, most forms of government-sponsored discrimination—from racially segregated public schools to gender-based

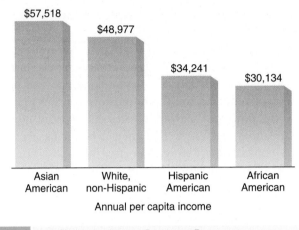

figure   5-5   U.S. FAMILY INCOME, BY RACE AND ETHNICITY

The median income of non-Hispanic white families is substantially higher than that of most other American families. *Source: U.S. Bureau of the Census, 2008.*

pension plans—have been banned. Nevertheless, civil rights problems involve deeply rooted conditions, habits, and prejudices and affect whole categories of people. For these reasons, a new civil rights law rarely produces a sudden and dramatic change in society.

Thus, despite their legal gains, America's traditionally disadvantaged groups are still substantially unequal in their daily lives. The average Hispanic or African American family's annual income, for example, is only about 60 percent of the average non-Hispanic white family's income (see Figure 5-5). Such disparities reflect **de facto discrimination,** discrimination that is a consequence of social, economic, and cultural biases and conditions. This type of discrimination is different from **de jure discrimination,** which is discrimination based on law, as in the case of the state laws that forced black and white children to attend separate schools during the pre-*Brown* period. De facto discrimination is the more difficult type to root out because it is embedded in the structure of society.

Equality of result is the aim of policies intended to reduce de facto discriminatory effects. Such policies are inherently controversial because many Americans believe that government's responsibility extends no further than the removal of legal barriers to equality. This attitude reflects the culture's emphasis on personal *liberty*—the freedom to choose one's associates, employees, neighbors, and classmates. Nevertheless, a few policies—notably affirmative action and busing—have addressed the problem of de facto inequality.

Affirmative Action: Workplace Integration

The difficulty of converting newly acquired legal rights into everyday realities is illustrated by the 1964 Civil Rights Act. Although the legislation prohibited discrimination in employment, women and minorities did not suddenly obtain jobs for which they were qualified. Many employers continued to favor white male employees. Other employers adhered to established employment procedures that kept women and minorities at a disadvantage; membership in many union locals, for example, was handed down from father to son. Moreover, the Civil Rights Act did not require employers to prove that their hiring practices were unbiased. Instead, the burden of proof was on the woman or minority-group member who had been denied a particular job. It was costly and often difficult for individuals to prove in court that their sex or race was the major reason they had not been hired. In addition, a victory in court applied only to the individual in question; it did not help the millions of other women and minorities facing job discrimination.

A broader remedy was obviously required, and the result was the emergence during the late 1960s of affirmative action programs. **Affirmative action** refers to deliberate efforts to provide full and equal opportunities in employment, education, and other areas for members of traditionally disadvantaged groups. Affirmative action requires corporations, universities, and other organizations to establish programs designed to ensure that all applicants are treated fairly. Affirmative action also places a burden of proof on the providers of opportunities, who must demonstrate that any disproportionate granting of opportunities to white males is the result of necessity (such as the nature of the job or the locally available labor pool) and not the result of systematic discrimination against women or minorities.

Few issues in recent decades have sparked more controversy than has affirmative action, a reflection of the public's ambivalence about the policy.[45] The majority of Americans say they *favor* programs that give women and minorities *equal treatment* when applying for jobs, college admission, and the like. The majority also say, however, that they *oppose* programs that would give them *preferential treatment* (see Figure 5-6).

Affirmative Action in the Law

Issues that pit individuals against each other often end up in the courts, and affirmative action is no exception. The policy was first tested before the Supreme Court in *University of California Regents v. Bakke* (1978). Alan Bakke, a white man, was denied admission to a medical school that on the basis of a race-based quota system had admitted several minority-group

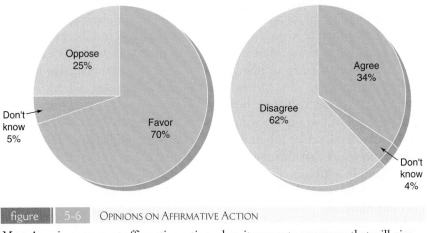

"In order to overcome past discrimination, do you favor or oppose affirmative action programs designed to help blacks, women, and other minorities get better jobs and education?"

"We should make every possible effort to improve the position of blacks and other minorities, even if it means giving them preferential treatment."

Oppose
25%

Don't know
5%

Favor
70%

Agree
34%

Disagree
62%

Don't know
4%

figure   5-6   OPINIONS ON AFFIRMATIVE ACTION

Most Americans support affirmative action when it comes to programs that will give women and minorities an equal chance at opportunities but oppose it when it comes to programs that will give them preferential treatment. *Source: The Pew Research Center for the People and the Press, March 22, 2007.*

applicants with lower admission test scores. Bakke sued, and the Supreme Court ruled in his favor without invalidating the principle of affirmative action. The Court held that quotas were unconstitutional but said that race could be among the factors taken into account in schools' efforts to create a diverse student body.[46] The *Bakke* ruling was followed by a decision that affirmed the use of quotas in a different context. In *Fullilove v. Klutznick* (1980), the Court upheld a congressional spending bill that included the requirement that 10 percent of federal funding for building projects be awarded to minority-owned firms.[47]

These rulings strengthened affirmative action as national policy. However, the appointment of more conservative judges to the Supreme Court during the 1980s narrowed the policy's scope. In 1986, for example, the Court held that preferential treatment for minorities could be justified only in cases of severe discrimination and only when the action did not infringe on white workers' employment rights (for example, if a labor contract specified that seniority would detemine which employees to lay off in the case of job cuts, more-senior white workers could not be laid off in order to enable less-senior minority workers to keep their jobs).[48]

A more substantial blow to affirmative action policy was a 1995 decision, *Adarand v. Pena.* The case arose when Adarand Constructors filed suit over a federal contract that was awarded to a Hispanic-owned company even though Adarand had submitted a lower bid. The Court ruled in Adarand's favor, thereby reversing the *Fullilove* precedent. The Court outlawed rules (such as the 10 percent set-aside of government contracts for minority-owned firms) that give firms an advantage simply because the owners' race is that of a people who have been discriminated against historically. The Court also held that, even in situations where a particular firm has been harmed by discrimination, the remedy must be "narrowly tailored" to the situation—that is, the remedy must be in proportion to the harm done to the firm.[49] *Adarand* marked the end of an era. By holding that affirmative action must be designed to rectify specific acts of discrimination, the Court effectively brought a halt to federal contracts that gave preference to applicants on the basis of race or gender. The Court had earlier halted such contracts at the state and local government levels.

Both advocates and opponents of affirmative action wondered whether race- and gender-based college admission programs would be the next ones struck down by the Supreme Court. In 2003, in what many observers saw as the most important affirmative action ruling since the *Bakke* decision three decades earlier, the Court made its position known. At issue were two University of Michigan affirmative action admission policies: Michigan's point system for undergraduate admission, which granted 20 points (out of a total of 150 possible points) to minority applicants, and its law school admission process, in which race (along with other factors such as work experience and extracurricular activities) was taken into account in admission decisions. The case attracted national attention, including the involvement of major U.S. corporations, which argued that programs such as those at the University of Michigan contributed to their goal of finding well-educated minorities to fill managerial positions.

Opponents of affirmative action hoped that the Court would strike down the Michigan policies, effectively ending the use of race as a factor in college admissions. Indeed, by a 6-3 vote in *Gratz v. Bollinger,* the Supreme Court did strike down Michigan's undergraduate admissions policy because its point system assigned a specific weight to race.[50] However, by a 5-4 vote in *Grutter v. Bollinger,* the Court upheld the law school's program, concluding that it was being applied in a limited and sensible manner and promoted Michigan's "compelling interest in obtaining the educational benefits that flow from a diverse student body." In

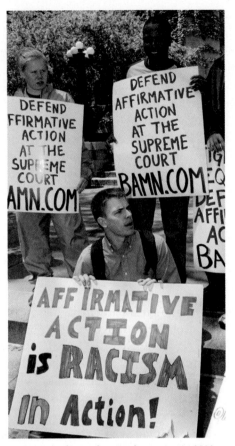

The University of Michigan was the focus of national attention in 2003 as a result of its affirmative action admissions programs. Shown here are demonstrators from both sides of the issue. In its 2003 ruling, the Supreme Court upheld the use of race as a factor in admissions but rejected the use of a "point system" as the method of applying it.

writing for the majority, Justice Sandra Day O'Connor said further that the law school's policy "promotes 'cross-racial understanding,' helps to break down racial stereotypes, and enables [a] better understand[ing of] persons of different races."[51]

Thus, affirmative action remains a part of national education policy. Both sides of the issue recognize, however, that the Supreme Court's narrow 5-4 majority in the 2003 case means that the controversy is not fully settled. Attempts to address the issue of equal opportunity for people of all backgrounds in unique ways have also provoked controversy. An example is a Texas policy on college admissions. Recognizing the disparity in the quality of its public schools and other factors that result in lower average scores on standardized tests for minorities, the state established a policy that guarantees admission at a University of Texas institution to any Texas high school student who graduates in the top 10 percent of his or her class. This approach initially faced little opposition even from critics of affirmative action, but opposition has increased as a result of growing enrollment pressure at Texas's flagship universities and the widening perception that students at weaker high schools have an unfair advantage. The fact is, almost every conceivable method of allocating society's benefits—whether through the public sector or the private sector, and however fair it might at first appear—inevitably leaves some Americans feeling as if they were unfairly treated. At that point, such policies become political issues.[52]

Busing: School Integration

The 1954 *Brown* ruling ended forced segregation of public schools. Government could no longer require minority children to attend separate schools. However, government was not required by the *Brown* decision to compel minority children and white children to attend school together. Fifteen years after *Brown*, because of neighborhood segregation, fewer than 5 percent of America's black children were attending schools that were predominately white. This situation set the stage for one of the few public policies to bring whites into regular contact with blacks: the forced busing of children out of their neighborhoods for the purpose of achieving racial balance in the schools.

In *Swann v. Charlotte-Mecklenburg County Board of Education* (1971), the Supreme Court ruled that the busing of children was an appropriate way to integrate schools that were segregated because past discrimination had contributed to the creation of racially separate neighborhoods.[53] Unlike *Brown*, which affected mainly the South, *Swann* also applied to northern communities where blacks and whites lived separately in part because of discriminatory housing ordinances and real estate practices. *Swann* triggered protests even larger than those accompanying the *Brown* decision. Angry and sometimes violent demonstrations lasting weeks occurred in Charlotte, Detroit, Boston, and other cities.

Forced busing had mixed results. Studies found that busing improved racial attitudes among schoolchildren and improved the performance of minority children on standardized tests without diminishing the performance of white classmates.[54] However, these achievements came at a price. For many children, forced busing meant long hours riding buses each day to and from school. Moreover, busing contributed to white flight to private schools and to the suburbs, which were protected by a 1974 Supreme

Court decision that prohibited busing across school district lines unless those lines had been drawn for the purpose of keeping the races apart.[55] As white students left urban schools, it became harder to achieve racial balance through busing and harder to convince taxpayers to fund these schools adequately.

In the 1990s, the Supreme Court began to allow communities to terminate their busing programs, holding that busing was intended as a temporary rather than a permanent solution to the problem of segregated schools[56] and that communities could devise alternative programs, such as increased spending on neighborhood schools in poorer neighborhoods.[57] Then, in 2007, the Supreme Court took a stand that effectively marks the end of widespread busing. At issue were busing programs that had been established voluntarily (rather than in response to a court order) by the Seattle and Louisville school boards as a means of creating racially diverse student bodies. The programs took race, neighborhood, and student preference into account in assigning students to particular schools. The large majority of students were placed in their school of choice, but some had to attend another school. These arrangements were challenged by several white families whose children did not get their school of choice, and the Supreme Court ruled in their favor, saying they had been denied equal protection under the Fourteenth Amendment.

The Court's opinion was decided by a 5-4 margin with the opposing justices taking starkly different positions. Writing for the majority, Chief Justice John Roberts said, "Before *Brown*, schoolchildren were told where they could and could not go to school based on the color of their skin. The school districts in [Seattle and Louisville] have not carried the heavy burden of demonstrating that we should allow this once again—even for very different reasons." In the dissenting opinion, Justice Stephen Breyer said the ruling is one "the court and the nation will come to regret." Breyer went on to say, "The lesson of history is not that efforts to continue racial segregation are constitutionally indistinguishable from efforts to achieve racial integration. Indeed, it is a cruel distortion of history to compare Topeka, Kansas in the 1950s to Louisville and Seattle in the modern day."[58]

America's public schools have a different makeup than in the pre-Brown era, but the trend in school enrollments is toward increased segregation. As a result of cutbacks in forced busing and white flight to private and suburban schools, America's schools have become less racially diverse (see Figure 5-7). Today, only 30 percent of Hispanic and black children attend a school that is predominately white, compared with 40 percent during the era of widespread busing.

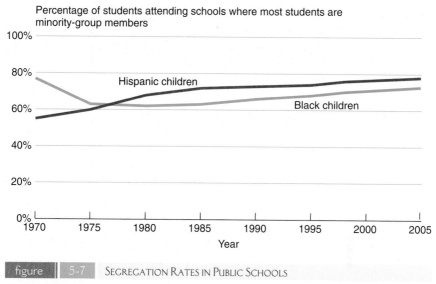

Percentage of students attending schools where most students are minority-group members

figure 5-7 SEGREGATION RATES IN PUBLIC SCHOOLS

In the past two decades, racial and ethnic segregation in America's public schools has increased. More than two-thirds of black and Hispanic children today attend a school in which most of the students are members of a minority group. An increase in the number of non-Hispanic white students attending private schools and a decrease in racial busing are factors in the trend. *Source: U.S. Department of Education, 2008.*

PERSISTENT DISCRIMINATION: SUPERFICIAL DIFFERENCES, DEEP DIVISIONS

In 1944, Swedish sociologist Gunnar Myrdal gained fame for his book *An American Dilemma*, whose title referred to deep-rooted racism in a country that idealized equality.[59] Since then, legal obstacles to the mixing of the races have been nearly eliminated, and public opinion has softened significantly. In the early 1940s, a majority of white Americans believed that black children should not be allowed to go to school with white children; today only a tiny percentage of white Americans hold this opinion. There are also visible signs of racial progress. In the past two decades, increasing numbers of African Americans have attended college, earned undergraduate degrees, obtained jobs as professionals and managers, and moved into suburban neighborhoods.

Nevertheless, true equality for all Americans remains elusive. The realities of everyday American life are still very different for its white and black citizens. For example, a black child born in the United States has more than twice the chance of dying before reaching his or her first birthday than a white child does. The difference in the infant mortality rates of whites and African Americans reflects differences in their nutrition, medical care, and education—in other words, differences in their access to the most basic resources of a modern society.

Equality is a difficult idea in practice because it requires people to shed preconceived notions about how other people think, behave, and feel. Nearly everyone has difficulty seeing beyond superficial differences—whether those differences relate to skin color, national origin, religious preference, sex, or lifestyle—to the shared humanity of people of all backgrounds. Myrdal called discrimination "America's curse." He could have broadened the generalization. Discrimination is civilization's curse, as is clear from the thousands of ethnic, national, and religious conflicts that have marred human history. But America carries a special responsibility because of its high ideals. In the words of Abraham Lincoln, the United States is a nation "dedicated to the proposition that all men are created equal."

SUMMARY   Self-Test www.mhhe.com/pattersonwtp8e

During the past half-century, the United States has undergone a revolution in the legal status of its traditionally disadvantaged groups, including African Americans, women, Native Americans, Hispanic Americans, and Asian Americans. Such groups are now provided equal protection under the law in areas such as education, employment, and voting. Discrimination by race, sex, and ethnicity has not been eliminated from American life, but it is no longer substantially backed by the force of law. This advance was achieved against strong resistance from established interests, which only begrudgingly and slowly responded to demands for equality in law.

Traditionally disadvantaged Americans have achieved fuller equality primarily as a result of their struggle for greater rights. The Supreme Court has been an instrument of change for disadvantaged groups. Its ruling in *Brown v. Board of Education* (1954), in which racial segregation in public schools was declared a violation of the Fourteenth Amendment's equal-protection clause, was a major breakthrough in equal rights. Through its affirmative action and other rulings, such as those providing equal access to the vote, the Court has also mandated the active promotion of social, political, and economic equality. However, because civil rights policy involves large issues concerned with social values and the distribution of society's opportunities and benefits, questions of civil rights are inherently contentious. For this reason, legislatures and executives have been deeply involved in such issues. The history of civil rights includes landmark laws, including the 1964 Civil Rights Act and 1965 Voting Rights Act that were enacted by Congress with the backing of President Lyndon Johnson.

In more recent decades, civil rights issues have receded from the prominence they enjoyed during the 1960s. The scope of affirmative action programs has narrowed, and the use of forced busing to achieve racial integration in America's public schools has been all but eliminated. At the same time, new issues have emerged, including the question of whether same-sex couples will have the same rights as opposite-sex couples and the question of how to treat illegal immigrants, most of whom are Hispanic.

The legal gains of disadvantaged groups over the past half-century have not been matched by material gains. Although progress has been made, it has been slow. Compared with non-Hispanic whites, other Americans lag behind in levels of education, income, and health care. Tradition, prejudice, and the sheer difficulty of social, economic, and political progress stand as formidable obstacles to achieving a more equal America.

KEY TERMS

affirmative action (*p. 179*)

civil rights (*p. 152*)

de facto discrimination (*p. 178*)

de jure discrimination (*p. 178*)

equality of result (*p. 178*)

equal-protection clause (*p. 173*)

equal rights (*p. 152*)

gender gap (*p. 158*)

reasonable-basis test (*p. 173*)

strict-scrutiny test (*p. 173*)

suspect classifications (*p. 174*)

SUGGESTED READINGS

Anderson, Terry H. *The Pursuit of Fairness: A History of Affirmative Action*. New York: Oxford University Press, 2005. A comprehensive look at the affirmative action issue.

Armor, David. *Forced Justice: School Desegregation and the Law*. New York: Oxford University Press, 1996. An evaluation that concludes that the federal courts have overstretched their legal mandate by requiring school integration rather than simply school desegregation.

Blackmon, Douglas A. *Slavery by Another Name: The Re-Enslavement of Black Americans from the Civil War to World War II*. New York: Doubleday, 2008. A historical analysis of the Jim Crow era.

Chang, Gordon H., ed. *Asian Americans and Politics*. Stanford, Calif.: Stanford University Press, 2001. A broad look at the political engagement of Asian Americans.

Garcia, F. Chris, and Gabriel Sanchez. *Hispanics and the U.S. Political System: Moving Into the Mainstream*. Upper Saddle River, N.J.: Prentice-Hall, 2007. A broad examination of Hispanic's growing influence on American politics.

Lawless, Jennifer L., and Richard L. Fox. *It Takes a Candidate: Why Women Don't Run for Office*. New York: Cambridge University Press, 2005. An assessment of why fewer women than men seek public office.

Reeves, Keith. *Voting Hopes or Fears? White Voters, Black Candidates, and Racial Politics in America*. New York: Oxford University Press, 1997. A critical assessment of race and politics in American society.

Rimmerman, Craig A., and Clyde Wilcox. *The Politics of Same-Sex Marriage*. Chicago: University of Chicago Press, 2007. A careful assessment of the political forces surrounding the same-sex marriage issue.

Wilkins, David E. *American Indian Politics and the American Political System.* Lanham, Md.: Rowman & Littlefield, 2006. A comprehensive look at tribal governance and its connection to the American political process.

LIST OF WEBSITES

http://www.airpi.org/   The website of the American Indian Policy Center, which was established by Native Americans in 1992; includes a political and legal history of Native Americans and examines current issues affecting them.

http://www.naacp.org/   The website of the National Association for the Advancement of Colored People (NAACP); includes historical and current information on the struggle of African Americans for equal rights.

http://www.nclr.org/   The website of the National Council of La Raza (NCLR), an organization dedicated to improving the lives of Hispanics; contains information on public policy, immigration, citizenship, and other subjects.

http://www.rci.rutgers.edu/~cawp/   The website of the Center for the American Woman and Politics (CAWP) at Rutgers University's Eagleton Institute of Politics.

POLITICS IN THEORY AND PRACTICE

Thinking: What role have political movements played in securing the legal rights of disadvantaged groups? How has the resulting legislation contributed to a furtherance of these groups' rights?

Participating: Think of a disadvantaged group that you would like to assist. It could be one of the federal government's designated groups (such as Native Americans), one of the other groups mentioned in the chapter (such as the disabled), or some other group (such as the homeless). Contact a college, community, national, or international organization that seeks to help this group and volunteer your assistance. (The Internet provides the names of thousands of organizations, such as Habitat for Humanity, that are involved in helping the disadvantaged.)

Extra Credit

For up-to-the-minute *New York Times* articles, interactive simulations, graphics, study tools, and more links and quizzes, visit the text's Online Learning Center at www.mhhe.com/pattersonwtp8e.

Letter from Birmingham Jail

By Martin Luther King Jr.

Martin Luther King Jr. is the only twentieth-century American to be honored with a national holiday. The civil rights leader was the pivotal figure in the movement to gain legal and political rights for black Americans. The son of a Baptist minister and himself a minister, King used speaking skill and nonviolent protest to galvanize the black community. He was assassinated in Memphis in 1968 as he was preparing to lead a protest march on behalf of the city's sanitation workers.

"Letter from Birmingham Jail" was written in 1963 while King was in the Birmingham, Alabama, city jail. He had been arrested for leading a peaceful protest. While there, he saw a published statement by eight black clergymen questioning his protest activities. They argued that the cause of racial equality was better served by negotiation and delay. King's letter was a reply to their argument.

We know through painful experience that freedom is never voluntarily given by the oppressor; it must be demanded by the oppressed. Frankly, I have yet to engage in a direct-action campaign that was "well timed" in the view of those who have not suffered unduly from the disease of segregation. For years now I have heard the word "Wait!" It rings in the ear of every Negro with piercing familiarity. This "Wait" has almost always meant "Never." We must come to see, with one of our distinguished jurists, that "justice too long delayed is justice denied."

We have waited for more than 340 years for our constitutional and God-given rights. The nations of Asia and Africa are moving with jetlike speed toward gaining political independence, but we still creep at horse-and-buggy pace toward gaining a cup of coffee at a lunch counter. Perhaps it is easy for those who have never felt the stinging dart of segregation to say, "Wait." But when you have seen vicious mobs lynch your mothers and fathers at will and drown your sisters and brothers at whim; when you have seen hate-filled policemen curse, kick and even kill your black brothers and sisters; when you see the vast majority of your twenty million Negro brothers smothering in an airtight cage of poverty in the midst of an affluent society; when you suddenly find your tongue twisted and your speech stammering as you seek to explain to your six-year-old daughter why she can't go to the public amusement park that has just been advertised on television, and see tears welling up in her eyes when she is told that Funtown is closed to colored children, and see ominous clouds of inferiority beginning to form in her little mental sky, and see her beginning to distort her personality by developing an unconscious bitterness toward white people; when you have to concoct an answer for a five-year-old son who is asking: "Daddy, why do white people treat colored people so mean?"; when you take a cross-country drive and find it necessary to sleep night after night in the uncomfortable corners of your automobile because no motel will accept you; when you are humiliated day in and day out by nagging signs reading "white" and "colored"; when your first name becomes "nigger," your middle name becomes "boy" (however old you are) and your last name becomes "John," and your wife and mother are never given the respected title "Mrs."; when you are harried by day and haunted by night by the fact that you are a Negro, living constantly at tiptoe stance, never quite knowing what to expect next, and are plagued with inner fears and outer resentments; when you are forever fighting a degenerating sense of "nobodiness"—then you will understand why we find it difficult to wait. There comes a time when the cup of endurance runs over, and men are no longer willing to be plunged into the abyss of despair. I hope, sirs, you can understand our legitimate and unavoidable impatience.

You express a great deal of anxiety over our willingness to break laws. This is certainly a legitimate concern. Since we so diligently urge people to obey the Supreme Court's decision of 1954 outlawing segregation in the public schools, at first glance it may seem rather paradoxical for us consciously to break laws. One may well ask: "How can you advocate breaking some laws and obeying others?" The answer lies in the fact that there are two types of laws: just and unjust. I would be the first to advocate obeying just laws. One has not only a legal but a moral responsibility to obey just laws. Conversely, one has a moral responsibility to disobey unjust laws. I would agree with St. Augustine that "an unjust law is no law at all."

Now, what is the difference between the two? How does one determine whether a law is just or unjust? A just law is a man-made code that squares with the moral law or the law of God. An unjust law is a code that is out of harmony with the moral law. To put it in the terms of St. Thomas Aquinas: An unjust law is a human law that is not rooted in eternal law and natural law. Any law that uplifts human personality is just. Any law that degrades human personality is unjust. All segregation statutes are unjust because segregation distorts the soul and damages the personality. It gives the segregator a false sense of superiority and the segregated a false sense of inferiority. . . .

Let me give another explanation. A law is unjust if it is inflicted on a minority that, as a result of being denied the right to vote, had no part in enacting or devising the law. Who can say that the legislature of Alabama which set up that state's segregation laws was democratically elected? Throughout Alabama all sorts of devious methods are used to prevent Negroes from becoming registered voters, and there are some counties in which, even though Negroes constitute a majority of the population, not a single Negro is registered. Can any law enacted under such circumstances be considered democratically structured? . . .

I hope you are able to see the distinction I am trying to point out. In no sense do I advocate evading or defying the law, as would the rabid segregationist. That would lead to anarchy. One who breaks an unjust law must do so openly, lovingly, and with a willingness to accept the penalty. I submit that an individual who breaks a law that conscience tells him is unjust, and who willingly accepts the penalty of imprisonment in order to arouse the conscience of the community over its injustice, is in reality expressing the highest respect for law.

Of course, there is nothing new about this kind of civil disobedience. It was evidenced sublimely in the refusal of Shadrach, Meshach and Abednego to obey the laws of Nebuchadnezzar, on the ground that a higher moral law was at stake. It was practiced superbly by the early Christians, who were willing to face hungry lions and the excruciating pain of chopping blocks rather than submit to certain unjust laws of the Roman Empire. To a degree, academic freedom is a reality today because Socrates practiced civil disobedience. In our own nation, the Boston Tea Party represented a massive act of civil disobedience. . . .

Oppressed people cannot remain oppressed forever. The yearning for freedom eventually manifests itself, and that is what has happened to the American Negro. Something within has reminded him of his birthright of freedom, and something without has reminded him that it can be gained. Consciously or unconsciously, he has been caught up by the Zeitgeist, and with his black brothers of Africa and his brown and yellow brothers of Asia, South America and the Caribbean, the United States Negro is moving with a sense of great urgency toward the promised land of racial justice. If one recognizes this vital urge that has engulfed the Negro community, one should readily understand why public demonstrations are taking place. The Negro has many pent-up resentments and latent frustrations, and he must release them. So let him march; let him make prayer pilgrimages to the city hall; let him go on freedom rides—and try to understand why he must do so. . . .

. . . Was not Martin Luther an extremist: "Here I stand; I cannot do otherwise, so help me God." And John Bunyan: "I will stay in jail to the end of my days before I make a butchery of my conscience." And Abraham Lincoln: "This nation cannot survive half slave and half free." And Thomas Jefferson: "We hold these truths to be self-evident, that all men are created equal . . ." So the question is not whether we will be extremists, but what kind of extremists we will be. Will we be extremists for hate or for love?

What's Your Opinion?

When—if at all—do you think it is morally proper to disobey the law? Do you think that Martin Luther King Jr. was justified in using civil disobedience to protest laws that barred black Americans from hotels, restaurants, and other public accommodations? Was it the best course of action?

CHAPTER 6

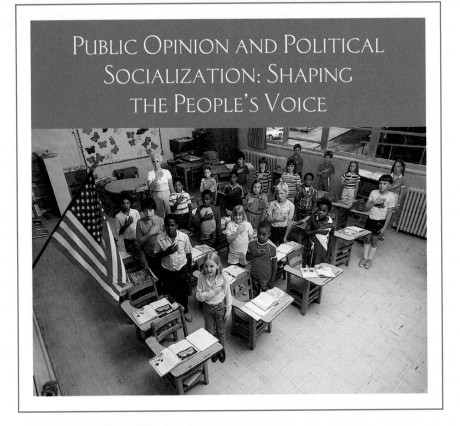

PUBLIC OPINION AND POLITICAL SOCIALIZATION: SHAPING THE PEOPLE'S VOICE

❝ To speak with precision of public opinion is a task not unlike coming to grips with the Holy Ghost. **❞**

V. O. KEY JR.[1]

As the U.S. troop buildup in the Persian Gulf region continued into 2003, Americans were unsure of the best course of action. They had been hearing about Saddam Hussein for years and had concluded that he was a tyrant and a threat. Most Americans expressed a willingness to support a war in Iraq if President George W. Bush deemed it necessary. But Americans had differing opinions on when and whether war should occur. Some wanted to give United Nations inspectors ample time to investigate Iraq's weapons program before a final decision on war was made. Others wanted to delay the decision until the United States could line up international support. Still others supported more immediate action but thought a bombing campaign was preferable to the launching of a ground war that might result in high casualties among U.S. forces. In any case, once the bombs started dropping on Iraq and U.S. ground troops poured into Iraq from their staging base in Kuwait, Americans strongly supported the action. Polls indicated that roughly 70 percent backed President Bush's decision to use military force against Iraq, with 20 percent opposed and 10 percent undecided.

The Iraq war is a telling example of the influence of public opinion on government: public opinion rarely forces officials to take a particular course of action. If President Bush had decided that the Iraq situation could have been resolved through UN weapons inspectors, public opinion would have supported that decision. A majority of Americans would also have supported the president if he had decided that war made sense only if it had broad international support or was limited to an air war.

Although public opinion has a central place in democratic theory, it is seldom an exact guide to policy. As long as the policy seems reasonable, political leaders ordinarily enjoy leeway in choosing a course of action. This chapter discusses public opinion and its influence on U.S. politics. A major theme is that public opinion is a powerful yet inexact force.[2] Government policy cannot be understood apart from public opinion, but it is not a precise determinant of that policy. The main points made in this chapter are these:

- ★ *Public opinion consists of those views held by ordinary citizens that are openly expressed.* Public officials have various means of gauging public opinion but increasingly use public opinion polls for this purpose.

- ★ *The process by which individuals acquire their political opinions is called political socialization.* This process begins during childhood, when, through family and school, Americans acquire many of their basic political values and beliefs. Socialization continues into adulthood, during which peers, political leaders, and the news media are among the major influences.

- ★ *Americans' political opinions are shaped by several frames of reference, including ideology, group attachments, partisanship, and political culture.* These frames of reference are a basis of political consensus in some instances and of political conflict in others.

- ★ *Public opinion has an important influence on government but ordinarily does not directly determine exactly what officials will do.* Public opinion works primarily to place limits on the choices made by officials.

THE NATURE OF PUBLIC OPINION

As representative government took root in the 1700s, political philosophers began to theorize about the public's role in such governments. Jeremy Bentham (1748–1832) was the first English-speaking philosopher to write at length on the subject.[3] Originally an advocate of aristocratic government, Bentham came to believe that "public opinion" had a large and rightful place in governing. He contended that public opinion had the power to ensure that government would rule in a way that brought "the greatest happiness" to the greatest number of people.

Although public opinion is now an everyday political term, it is often used sloppily. A common error is the assumption that "the public"—meaning the whole citizenry—actually has an opinion on nearly every issue of politics. In fact, most issues do not attract the attention of anywhere near a majority of citizens. Agricultural conservation programs, for example, are of keen interest to some farmers, hunters, and environmentalists but of little interest to most people. This pattern is so pervasive that opinion analysts have described America as a nation of *many* publics.[4] Accordingly, a precise definition of the term *public opinion* cannot be based on the assumption that all citizens, or even a majority, are actively interested in and actually hold an opinion on every issue. In this text, **public opinion** will be viewed as the politically relevant opinions held by ordinary citizens that they express openly.[5] This expression need not be verbal. It can also take the form, for example, of a protest demonstration or a vote for one candidate rather than another. The crucial point is that people's private opinions on an issue become public opinion when they become publicly visible.

How Informed Is Public Opinion?

An assumption of democratic politics is that public opinion should control what government does. One problem with a simplistic version of this assumption is that people often have conflicting opinions. In responding to one opinion on an issue, the government is compelled to reject other opinions. People's opinions can also be inconsistent, even contradictory. Polls indicate, for example, that most Americans would like better schools, health care, and other public services while also favoring a reduction in taxes (see Figure 6-1). Which opinion of the people should govern—their desire for more services or their desire for lower taxes?

Another limitation on government by public opinion is that, even on issues of great importance, people's opinions on an issue can be at odds with the reality of that issue. In the buildup to the U.S. invasion of Iraq in 2003, for

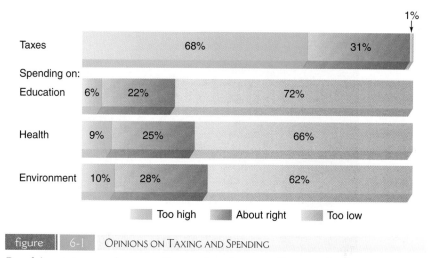

figure 6-1 OPINIONS ON TAXING AND SPENDING

People's opinions can be contradictory. Americans say, for example, that taxes are too high and yet also say, when asked about specific policy areas, that government is spending too little. *Source: National Opinion Research Center, University of Chicago.*

example, polls revealed that more than half of the American public wrongly believed that Iraq had close ties to the al Qaeda terrorist network and that Iraqis were among the nineteen terrorists who had flown airplanes into the World Trade Center and the Pentagon on September 11, 2001. Moreover, despite widespread opposition to the war on the part of most Europeans, Asians, South Americans, and Africans, one in four Americans believed that world opinion favored the war. Americans who held these mistaken views were more inclined to support an invasion of Iraq than were other Americans.[6]

Even many college-educated Americans are uninformed about pub-lic affairs. In 2007, the Intercollegiate Studies Institute surveyed 14,000 first-year and fourth-year college students, giving them a multiple-choice exam to test their "civic literacy." The average college senior had a grade of F, answering only 54 percent of the questions correctly. Only 46 per-cent of the college seniors could identify the phrase "We hold these truths to be self-evident, that all men are created equal" as being part of the Declaration of Independence. On this and the other questions, college freshmen scored even lower than college seniors.[7] An earlier survey of Ivy League students found that one-third could not identify the British prime minister, half could not name both U.S senators from their state, and three-fourths could not identify Abraham Lincoln as the author of the phrase "a government of the people, by the people, and for the people."[8]

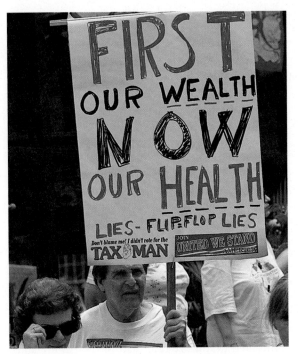

Public opinion includes contradictory elements. According to surveys, for example, most Americans say they want lower taxes but also say they want more public services. At a Boston rally, this demonstrator expresses anger with tax increases while also demanding that government provide more health benefits.

Of course, citizens do not necessarily have to be informed on an issue to have a reasonable opinion about it. Opinions derive mostly from people's values and interests.[9] A person could have a sound opinion on the economy, for example, without a knowledge of the latest economic statistics. Nevertheless, the public's lack of information limits the role that public opinion can play in governing. The choice among policy options sometimes requires an understanding of the causes and consequences of the various options. Citizens frequently lack this type of information.

The Measurement of Public Opinion

Woodrow Wilson once said that he had spent much of his adult life in government and yet had never seen a "government." What Wilson was saying, in effect, was that government is a system of relationships. A government is not a building or a person—it is not tangible in the way that, say, a car or a can of soda is. So it is with public opinion. No one has ever seen a "public opinion," and thus it cannot be measured directly. It must be assessed indirectly.

Election returns are a traditional method of assessing public opinion. Journalists and politicians routinely draw conclusions about what citizens are thinking by how they vote. Letters to the editor in newspapers, email messages to elected officials, and the size of crowds at mass demonstrations are other means of judging public opinion. All these indicators are useful guides for policymakers. None of them, however, is a precise indicator of what the broad public is thinking. Elections offer citizens only a yes-no choice between the candidates, and different voters will have chosen the same candidate for different reasons. As for letter writers and demonstrators, they are nearly always *unrepresentative* of the population as a whole. Fewer than 1 percent of Americans participate each year in a mass demonstration, and fewer than 10 percent write to the president or a member of Congress. Studies have found that the opinions of letter writers and demonstrators are more extreme than those of most citizens.

Public Opinion Polls   In an earlier day, indicators such as elections and letters to the editor were the only means by which public officials could gauge what the public was thinking. Today, they also rely on opinion polls or surveys, which provide a more systematic method of estimating public sentiment.[10]

In a **public opinion poll,** a relatively few individuals—the **sample**—are interviewed in order to estimate the opinions of a whole **population,** such as the residents of a city or a country. If a sufficient number of individuals are chosen at random, their views will tend to be representative—that is, roughly the same as the views held by the population as a whole.

How is it possible to measure the thinking of a large population on the basis of a relatively small sample? How can interviews with, say, one thousand Americans provide a reliable estimate of what millions of them are thinking? The answer is found in the laws of probability. Consider the hypothetical example of a huge jar filled with a million marbles, half of them red and half of them blue. If a blindfolded person reaches into the jar, the probability of selecting a marble of a given color is fifty-fifty. And if one thousand marbles are chosen in this random way, it is likely that about half of them will be red and about half will be blue. Opinion sampling works in the same way. If respondents are chosen at random from a population, their opinions will approximate those of the population as a whole.

Random selection is the key to scientific polling, which is based on *probability sampling*—a sample in which each individual in the population has a known probability of being chosen at random for inclusion. A scientific poll is different from the surveys found on many Internet sites; the individuals who respond to such surveys are selecting themselves for the poll rather than being selected randomly by the pollster. A scientific poll is also different from the "people-in-the-street" interviews that news reporters sometimes conduct. Although a reporter may say that the opinions of those interviewed represent the views of the local population, this claim is clearly faulty. Interviews conducted on a downtown street at the noon hour, for example, will include a disproportionate number of business employees on their lunch break. Housewives, teachers, and factory workers are among the many groups that would be underrepresented in such a sample.

The science of polling is such that the size of the sample, as opposed to the size of the population, is the key to accurate estimates. Although it might be assumed that a much larger sample would be required to poll accurately the people of the United States as opposed to the residents of Georgia or Vermont, the sample requirements are nearly the same. Consider again the example of a huge jar filled with marbles, half of them red and half of them blue. If one thousand marbles were randomly selected, about half would be red and about half would be blue, regardless of whether the jar held one million, 10 million, or 100 million marbles. On the other hand, the size of the sample—the number of marbles selected—does matter. If only ten marbles were drawn, it might happen that five would be of each color but, then again, it would not be unusual for six, seven, or even eight of them to be of the same color. However, if one thousand marbles were drawn, it would be highly unusual for six hundred of the marbles, much less seven or eight hundred of them, to be of the same color.

The accuracy of a poll is expressed in terms of **sampling error**—the degree to which the sample estimates might differ from what the population actually thinks. The larger the sample, the smaller the sampling error, which is usually expressed as a plus-or-minus percentage. For example, a properly drawn sample of one thousand individuals has a sampling error of roughly plus or minus 3 percent. Thus, if 55 percent of a sample of one thousand respondents say they intend to vote for the Republican presidential candidate, then the probability is high that between 52 percent and 58 percent (55 percent plus or minus 3 percent) of all voters actually plan to vote Republican.

The impressive record of the Gallup poll in predicting the outcome of presidential elections indicates that the theoretical accuracy of polls can be matched in practice. The Gallup Organization has polled voters in every presidential election since 1936 (nineteen elections in all) and has erred badly only once: it stopped polling several weeks before the 1948 election and missed a late voter shift that carried Harry Truman to victory.

Problems with Polls Although pollsters assume that their samples are drawn from a particular population, it is seldom the case that everyone in that population has a chance of becoming part of the sample. Only rarely

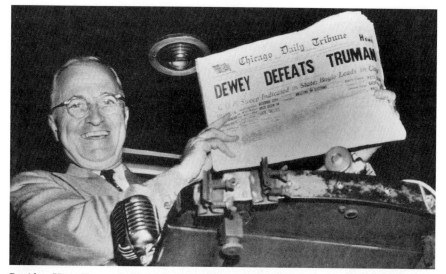

President Harry Truman holds up the early edition *Chicago Tribune* with the headline "Dewey Defeats Truman." The *Tribune* was responding to analysts' predictions that Dewey would win the 1948 election. A Gallup poll a few weeks before the election had shown Dewey with a seemingly insurmountable lead. The Gallup Organization decided that it did not need to conduct another poll closer to the election, a mistake it has not since repeated.

does a pollster have a list of all individuals in a population from which to draw a sample. An expedient alternative is a sample based on telephone numbers. Pollsters use computers to randomly pick telephone numbers, which are then dialed by interviewers to reach households. Within each of these households, a respondent is then randomly selected. Because the computer is as likely to pick one telephone number as any other and because more than 90 percent of U.S. homes have a telephone, a sample selected in this way is assumed to be representative of the population. Nevertheless, some Americans do not have phones, and many of those who are called are not home or refuse to participate. Such factors reduce the accuracy of telephone polling. In fact, although telephone polls continue to provide precise predictions of elections, pollsters are increasingly worried about the future of telephone polling. The percentage of Americans who refuse to participate in telephone surveys has increased sharply in recent decades, and the use of cell phones—which are not included in most computer-based telephone sampling—has risen significantly.

The accuracy of polling is also diminished when respondents are asked about an issue they have not considered. In such instances, interviewees usually offer a response in order not to appear uninformed or uninterested. Scholars label such responses "nonopinions." Almost always, polls on minor issues overestimate the number of people who truly have an opinion on the issue in question.

Less often, respondents will actually have an opinion but not reveal it. On sensitive topics, some interviewees will give what they regard as the socially correct response rather than say what they actually think. A classic example is voter turnout. Although turnout in presidential elections rarely rises above 60 percent, it is not unusual for 75 percent of respondents in postelection polls to claim that they voted. Some of these respondents are not telling the truth, but they prefer to tell the interviewer that they went to the polls rather than admit that they failed to exercise their right to vote.

Respondents are also not always truthful when it comes to expressing opinions that relate to race, gender, ethnicity, and the like. Until recently, in high-profile election campaigns pitting a white candidate against a black candidate, the polls regularly overestimated the black candidate's vote. Some white respondents were apparently reluctant to say they planned to vote for the white candidate because they thought they might be regarded as racist if they said so. The most widely known example occurred in Virginia's 1989 gubernatorial race. Doug Wilder, the Democratic nominee and a black man, had a 10-percentage-point lead in the final polls; he won by less than 1 percent. In more recent elections, such as the 2006 gubernatorial race in Massachusetts, which was won by Duval Patrick, a black man, the polls have predicted the outcome of opposite-race contests with about the same accuracy as same-race contests. However, some analysts thought race might have contributed to the inaccuracy of the polls in New Hampshire's 2008 Democratic presidential primary. After Barack Obama won the Iowa caucuses, his momentum carried into New Hampshire, where all the preelection polls showed him with a comfortable lead in that state's primary. However, to the embarrassment of the pollsters, he lost the primary to Hillary Clinton. Most pollsters argued that the wrongful prediction was the result of the large number of "undecideds" in the preelection polls and the difficulty of predicting which poll respondents would actually vote in the primary. Nevertheless, a few pollsters suggested Obama's race was a factor, given New Hampshire's overwhelming white electorate. In the November general election, however, the polls accurately predicted the size of Obama's victory, suggesting that race is now a negligible factor in the accuracy of election polls.

Question wording can also affect poll results. The way in which an issue is framed, whether it is accompanied by relevant facts, the ordering in which the alternatives are presented, and the precise alternatives offered can all affect people's responses, and thus how the poll's results are interpreted. Consider, for example, the issue of the death penalty as a sentence for murder. Do Americans favor or oppose its use? As it turns out, the answer to this question depends to some extent on how the issue is worded. Respondents in some Gallup polls have been asked: "Are you in favor of the death penalty for a person convicted of murder?" Respondents in other Gallup polls have been asked a different question: "If you could choose between the following two approaches, which do you think is the better penalty for murder—the death penalty or life imprisonment, with absolutely no possibility of parole?" The two questions produce measurably different results. When asked the first question, Americans by roughly two-to-one say they favor the death penalty. When asked the second question, Americans are almost evenly divided on whether the death sentence is the proper penalty.[11]

Despite these and other issues of polling, the poll or survey is the most relied-upon method of measuring public opinion. More than one hundred organizations are in the business of conducting public opinion polls. Some, like the Gallup Organization, conduct polls that are released to the news media by syndication. Most large news organizations also have their own in-house polls; one of the most prominent of these is the CBS News/New York Times poll. Other polling firms specialize in conducting surveys for candidates and officeholders.

POLITICAL SOCIALIZATION: HOW AMERICANS LEARN THEIR POLITICS

Analysts have long been interested in how public opinion originates. The learning process by which people acquire their political opinions, beliefs, and values is called **political socialization.** Just as a language, a religion, or an athletic skill is acquired through a learning process, so too are people's political orientations. For most Americans, the socialization process starts in the family with exposure to the political loyalties and opinions of their parents. The schools later contribute to the process, as do the mass media, friends, work associates, and other agents.

The Process of Political Socialization

The process of political socialization in the United States has two distinguishing characteristics. First, although socialization continues throughout life, most people's political outlook is substantially influenced by their childhood learning. Basic ideas about which political party, the Republicans or the Democrats, is the better one, for example, are often formed uncritically in childhood, in much the same way that beliefs in the superiority of a particular religion—typically, the religion of one's parents—are acquired.

⊕ | HOW THE UNITED STATES COMPARES

National Pride

Americans are justifiably proud of their nation. It is the oldest continuous democracy in the world, an economic powerhouse, and a diverse yet harmonious society. What Americans may not recognize, because it is so much a part of everyday life in America, is the degree to which they are bombarded with messages and symbols of their nation's greatness. Political socialization in the United States is not the rigid program of indoctrination that some societies impose on their people. Nevertheless, Americans receive a thorough political education. Their country's values are impressed on them by every medium of communication: newspapers, daily conversations, television, movies, books, magazines, and so on.

The words and symbols that regularly tell Americans of their country's greatness are important to its unity. In the absence of a common ancestral heritage to bind them, Americans need other methods to instill and reinforce the idea that they are one people. As discussed in Chapter 1, America's political ideals have this effect, as do everyday reminders such as the flying of the flag on homes and private buildings, a practice that is

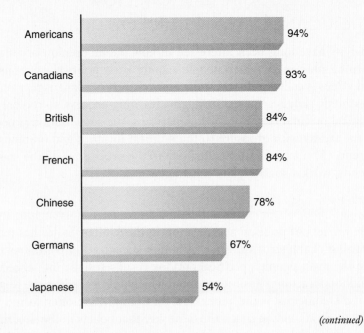

Americans	94%
Canadians	93%
British	84%
French	84%
Chinese	78%
Germans	67%
Japanese	54%

(continued)

almost uniquely American. (Elsewhere, flags are rarely displayed except on public buildings.)

One indicator of Americans' political socialization is the pride they express in their nationality. Americans rank high on this indicator, as shown by the accompanying chart, which is based on polls conducted by the World Values Survey. The percentages are the proportion of respondents in each country that said they were "very proud" or "proud" of their nationality.

A second characteristic of political socialization is that its effect is cumulative. Early learning affects later learning because people have psychological defenses that protect the beliefs they hold. Many people, for example, remain lifelong Republicans or Democrats even as political conditions or their personal lives change in ways that might logically lead them to identify with the other party. Of course, political change can and does occur. Historically, major shifts in partisan orientation have occurred around major upheavals and have been concentrated among younger adults because their beliefs are less firmly rooted than are those of older adults. For example, President Franklin Roosevelt's New Deal, which sought to alleviate the economic hardship of the Great Depression, prompted many younger Republicans, but not many older ones, to shift their loyalty to the Democratic Party.

The Agents of Political Socialization

The socialization process takes place through a variety of **agents of socialization,** including family, schools, mass media, peers, and political leaders and events. It is helpful to consider briefly these agents of socialization and how they affect political learning.

Families The family is a powerful agent of socialization because it has a near-monopoly on the attention of the young child, who places great trust in what a parent says. By the time children reach adulthood, many of the beliefs and values that will stay with them throughout life are firmly in place. Many adults are Republicans or Democrats today because their parents backed that party. They can give all sorts of reasons for preferring their party to the other, but the reasons come later in life. The family also contributes to basic orientations that, while not directly political, have political significance. For example, American families tend to be more egalitarian than families in other nations, and American children often have a voice in family decisions. Basic American values such as equality and individualism have roots in patterns of family interaction.[12]

Schools   The school, like the family, affects children's basic political beliefs. Teachers at the elementary level extol the exploits of national heroes such as George Washington, Abraham Lincoln, and Martin Luther King Jr. and praise the country's economic and political institutions.[13] Although teachers in the middle and high school grades present a more nuanced version of American history, they tend to emphasize the nation's great moments—for example, its decisive role in the two world wars.

U.S. schools are more instrumental in building support for the nation than are the schools in most other democracies. The Pledge of Allegiance, which is recited daily in many U.S. schools, has no equivalent in European countries. Their schools do not open the day by asking students to take an oath of loyalty to the nation. American schools also impart a sense of social equality. Most American children, regardless of family income, attend public schools and study a fairly standard curriculum. In many countries, schoolchildren are separated at an early age, with some placed in vocational classes while others are slotted in college preparatory courses.

Mass Media   The mass media are another powerful socializing agent. Public affairs for most Americans is a second-hand affair, something that is observed through the media rather than witnessed directly. The media's images of society affect what people believe is true of society. Repeated exposure to crime on television, for example, can lead people to believe that society itself is more violent than it actually is. Similarly, news stories that routinely portray politics as a fight between Republicans and Democrats can lead people to think that partisan bickering is what politics is all about.

Peers   Peer groups—friends, neighbors, and coworkers—tend to reinforce what a person already believes. Most people trust the opinions of their friends and associates and are unwilling to deviate too far from what they think. In *The Spiral of Silence*, Elisabeth Noelle-Neumann presents evidence indicating that many individuals are reluctant to express opinions contrary to those of the people around them. If nearly everyone in a group appears to believe, for example, that same-sex marriage should be legal, a person who believes otherwise is likely to remain silent rather than to say it should be illegal. One effect, Noelle-Neumann argues, is to make the prevailing opinion in a group appear to be more firmly and widely held than it actually is.[14]

Political Leaders and Institutions   Citizens look to political leaders and institutions, particularly the president and political parties, as guides to opinion.[15] After the terrorist attacks of September 11, 2001, for example, many Americans were confused about who the enemy was and how America should respond. These views changed dramatically a few days later when President George W. Bush in a televised speech identified al Qaeda as the perpetrators and declared that America would attack Afghanistan if its Taliban government continued to provide them sanctuary. Polls indicated that nine of every ten Americans agreed with Bush's view. However, the ability of political leaders to influence public opinion rests on their credibility. After President Bush led America into a costly war in Iraq on the inaccurate claim that it possessed weapons of mass destruction (WMDs), his political support crumbled, as did his ability to persuade Americans that the war in Iraq was worth the price.

Churches Beginning with the Puritans in the seventeenth century, churches have played a substantial role in shaping Americans' social and political opinions. Most Americans say they believe in God, most attend church at least occasionally, and most belong to a religion that includes teachings on social values. Moreover, most Americans say that religion has answers to many of the problems facing society today. In these and other respects, churches and religion are a more powerful force in the United States than in most other Western nations (see Figure 6-2).

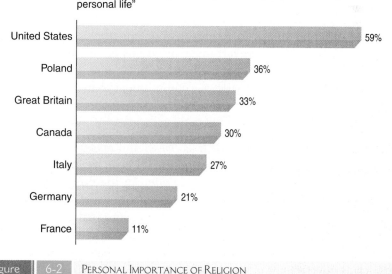

Percentage agreeing that "religion is 'very important' in my personal life"

United States	59%
Poland	36%
Great Britain	33%
Canada	30%
Italy	27%
Germany	21%
France	11%

figure 6-2 PERSONAL IMPORTANCE OF RELIGION

Religion is more important to Americans than to Europeans or Canadians. *Source: Pew Research Center for the People and the Press, 2002.*

Scholars have not studied the influence of churches on political socialization as closely as they have studied the influence of families, schools, peers, or the media.[16] Nevertheless, churches are a significant source of political attitudes, including those related to society's obligations to children, the poor, and the unborn. (The impact of religion is discussed further in a later section of this chapter.)

FRAMES OF REFERENCE: HOW AMERICANS THINK POLITICALLY

What are the frames of reference that Americans acquire in the course of their political socialization? The question is an important one. Shared frames of reference enable people to find common cause. The opinions of millions of Americans would mean little if everyone's view was different. But if enough people think the same way, they may decide to work together to promote their shared interest.

Among the frames of reference through which Americans think about politics are cultural values, ideology, group attachments, and partisanship, as the following discussion will explain.

Cultural Thinking: Common Ideas

As was discussed in Chapter 1, Americans embrace a common set of ideals. Principles such as liberty, equality, and individualism have always meant somewhat different things to Americans but nonetheless are a source of agreement. For example, government programs aimed at redistributing wealth from the rich to the poor are more popular among Europeans than among Americans, who have a deeper commitment to individualism.

Ideological Thinking: The Outlook of Some

Analysts sometimes use words such as *liberal* and *conservative* to describe how ordinary Americans think about politics. These are ideological terms, as are terms such as *socialism* and *communism*. An **ideology** is a consistent pattern of political attitudes that stems from a core belief. A basic belief of socialism, for example, is that society should ensure that everyone's basic economic needs are met. Accordingly, a socialist would support tax and spending policies that redistribute wealth in ways that help the less-affluent, such as government provided health care.

By a strict definition of what constitutes a political ideology—a *consistent* pattern of political attitudes—most Americans do not have one. As illustrated by the earlier example of people who favor steep tax cuts while also want-ing more spending on government services, many citizens hold incompat-ible opinions. Other people have opinions that are generally consistent but include a glaring exception. Most Americans say, for example, that they sup-port free trade between nations, but when their particular job or business is threatened by foreign competition, they oppose it. Farmers provide another example. Compared with most groups, farmers are opposed to welfare pro-grams. On the other hand, farmers strongly favor government spending on crop subsidies and other programs that put money in their pockets. Political scientists have concluded that no more than a fourth of Americans have opin-ions that are consistent enough to meet the definition of a true ideology.[17]

Weaker forms of ideological thinking are more prevalent. Americans differ, for example, in their support of government policies that distribute economic wealth more widely. Those who think government should do more to help the less-well-off are typically described as **economic liberals.** **Economic conservatives,** in contrast, are people who believe that govern-ment should do less in this realm, leaving economic benefits to be distrib-uted to a great extent through the marketplace only.

Opinions on the role of government shift when social issues are involved. Those who think government should do more to promote cultural tradi-tions—for example, by enacting laws that promote certain religious beliefs and practices, such as a ban on abortion or civil unions—are called **social conservatives.** Those who think government should not favor traditional values but should instead leave lifestyle choices to the individual are labeled **social liberals.**

It should be noted that neither conservatives nor liberals hold a consis-tent view on the power of government. Economic conservatives prefer a smaller role for government than do economic liberals. On the other hand, social conservatives prefer a larger role for government than do social lib-erals. Each group wants government to be active or inactive, depending on which posture serves their policy goals. It should also be noted that there is no logical reason why an economic conservative must also be a social con-servative. Although most economic conservatives are socially conservative as well, some are not. In the Rocky Mountain states particularly, many economic conservatives are social liberals. They oppose big government in both the economic and the social realms. The term **liberterian** is used to characterize this combination of attitudes. It is also the case that some economic liberals are social conservatives. They want to use the power of government to achieve economic redistribution and to uphold tradi-tional values. The term **populist** is used to describe this combination of attitudes.

POLITICAL CULTURE

Liberty, Equality, and Self-Government

Americans' Ideologies

In the United States, the key dimensions of political conflict center on the extent of government intervention in the economic marketplace and in the maintenance of traditional values. Government intervention in either sphere has implications for liberty—the amount of freedom you should have in deciding on your lifestyle and in making economic choices. Government intervention in the economic sphere can also affect equality—government has been the principal means of providing economic security for those vulnerable to market forces.

You can test your ideology—and thus in a way your conception of liberty and equality—by asking yourself the two measurement questions used in Gallup surveys:

1. Some people think the government is trying to do too many things that should be left to individuals and businesses. Others think that government should do more to solve our country's problems. Which view is closer to your own?

    a. Government is doing too much.

    b. Government should do more.

2. Some people think the government should promote traditional values in our society. Others think that the government should not favor any particular set of values. Which view is closer to your own?

    a. Government should promote traditional values.

    b. Government should not favor particular values.

If you had been a respondent in a poll that asked these questions, you would have been classified as a *conservative* if you agreed with the first statement of each question (1a and 2a); a *liberal* if you agreed with the second statement of each question (1b and 2b); a *libertarian* if you agreed with the first statement of the first question (1a) and the second statement of the second question (2b); and a *populist* if you agreed with the second statement of the first question (1b) and the first statement of the second question (2a).

Is this the label you normally use when describing your political beliefs? If not, do you think it's a more appropriate label? Why or why not?

Thus, although only a minority of Americans can be classified as true ideologues, ideology can be a useful way to talk about opinion tendencies. Ideological terms help to describe the choices that Americans make and the conflicts that divide them. Beginning with the New Deal, for example, liberal attitudes on economic issues—a preference for government action—dominated. Later, Americans became less trusting of government welfare programs and more worried about their financial cost. Economic conservatism gained strength. Other recent disputes—abortion and immigration to name two—have pitted social conservatives against social liberals.

Group Thinking: The Outlook of Many

For most citizens, groups are a more important frame of reference than is ideology. Many Americans see politics through the lens of the group or groups that define who they are. Farmers, for example, care a lot more about agricultural issues than do members of other groups. And although farmers are more likely than most Americans to oppose government benefit programs, they favor farm subsidies. Their ideological opposition to "big government" suddenly disappears when their own benefits are at issue.

Because of the country's great size, its settlement by various immigrant groups, and its economic pluralism, Americans are a very diverse people. Later chapters examine group tendencies more fully, but it is useful here to mention a few major group orientations: religion, class, region, race and ethnicity, gender, and age.

Religion   Religious beliefs have always been a source of solidarity among group members and a source of conflict with outsiders. As Catholics and Jews came to America in large numbers in the nineteenth and early twentieth centuries, they encountered intense hostility from some Protestants. Today, Catholics, Protestants, and Jews have similar opinions on most policy issues.

Nevertheless, important religious differences remain, although the opposing sides shift as the issues shift.[18] Fundamentalist Protestants and Roman Catholics oppose legalized abortion more strongly than do mainline Protestants and Jews. This split reflects different religious teachings about when human life begins, whether at conception or at a later stage in the development of the fetus. Religious doctrine also affects opinions on poverty programs. Catholics and Jews are more supportive of such programs than Protestants are. An obligation to help the poor is a larger theme in Catholic and Jewish teachings; self-reliance is a larger part of Protestant thought.

The most powerful religious force in contemporary American politics is the so-called religious right, which consists primarily of individuals who see themselves as born-again Christians and who view the Bible as infallible

★ | LEADERS

Franklin D. Roosevelt
(1882–1945)

Historians may differ in where they rank Franklin D. Roosevelt among America's great presidents, but all would place him at the top by one indicator: the ability to lead public opinion. He won the presidency in 1932 during the depths of the Great Depression. FDR's job programs put Americans back to work, and his radio talks—the so-called fireside chats—did much to relieve people's anxieties about the economy and to give them hope of a better day ahead. In 1940, Roosevelt broke with tradition and announced that he would seek a third presidential term. Against the backdrop of war in Europe and continuing economic problems at home, he won the election—though by a narrower margin than in his two previous campaigns. Roosevelt was in office when the Japanese attacked Pearl Harbor on December 7, 1941. It was Roosevelt who again calmed the public, while calling them to action, saying that the Japanese attack was "a day that will live in infamy." Roosevelt won a fourth term in 1944 but died in office of a cerebral hemorrhage as the war was concluding. A distant cousin of President Theodore Roosevelt, FDR came to political prominence as secretary of the navy during World War I and was the Democratic Party's vice presidential nominee in 1920. A year later, he contacted polio and lost full use of his legs, a fact that he kept largely hidden from the public, even as he campaigned successfully for governor of New York and later president of the United States.

truth. Their views on issues such as gay rights, abortion, and school prayer differ significantly from those of the population as a whole. A Time/CNN survey found that born-again Christians are a third more likely than other Americans to agree that "the Supreme Court and the Congress have gone too far in keeping religious and moral values like prayer out of our laws, schools, and many areas of our lives."[19]

Class Economic class has less influence on political opinion in the United States than in Europe, but it is nevertheless related to opinions on certain economic issues. For example, lower-income Americans are more supportive

Economic class as related to jobs and incomes affects Americans' opinions on a range of social and economic issues.

of social welfare programs, business regulation, and progressive taxation than are Americans in higher-income categories.

An obstacle to class-based politics in the United States is that people with similar incomes but differing occupations do not share the same opinions. Support for collective bargaining, for example, is substantially higher among factory workers than among small farmers, service workers, and workers in the skilled crafts, even though the average income of members of all these groups is similar. The interplay of class and opinion is examined more closely in Chapter 9, which discusses interest groups.

Region   For a long period, region nearly defined American politics. The North and South were divided over the issue of race, which spilled over into issues such as education and welfare policy. Racial progress has diminished the regional divide, as has the relocation of millions of Americans from the Northeast and Midwest to the South and West. The policy beliefs of these newcomers tend to be less conservative than those of people native to these regions. Nevertheless, regional differences are still evident on policies such as social welfare, civil rights, and national defense. Residents of the southern, mountain, and Great Plains states have more conservative opinions on these issues than do Americans elsewhere—a reflection of long-standing regional attitudes about government. The differences are large enough that when analysts talk about "red states" (Republican bastions) and "blue states" (Democratic bastions), they basically are referring to regions. The red states are concentrated in the South, Great Plains, and Rocky Mountains. The blue states are found mostly in the Northeast, the northern Midwest, and the West Coast.

Race and Ethnicity   As Chapter 5 pointed out, race and ethnicity have a significant influence on opinions. White and black Americans, for example, differ on issues of integration: blacks more strongly support affirmative action, busing, and other measures designed to promote racial equality and integration. Racial and ethnic groups also differ on economic issues, largely as a result of differences in their economic situations. Blacks and Hispanics are more supportive of public assistance programs, for example, than are non-Hispanic whites. Law enforcement is another area in which different opinions exist. Opinion polls reveal that blacks and Hispanics are less trusting of police and the judicial system than are non-Hispanic whites.

Gender   Although male-female differences of opinion are small on most issues, gender does affect opinion in some policy areas.[20] Women are somewhat more supportive than men of abortion rights and affirmative action. Gallup polls have found, for example, a consistent difference of about 10 percentage points between women and men on support for affirmative action. The difference is even larger on some social welfare issues, such as poverty and education assistance. Compared with men, women have more liberal opinions on these issues, reflecting their greater economic vulnerability and their traditional responsibility for child care. A Washington Post/ABC News poll found, for example, that women were 20 percent more likely than men to favor increased spending for public education.

Women and men also differ in their opinions on the use of military force. In nearly every case, women are less supportive of military action than men are. The terrorist attacks on the World Trade Center and the Pentagon on September 11, 2001, produced an exception to the normal pattern. Men and women were almost equally likely (90 percent and 88 percent, respectively) to favor a military response. But they differ in expected ways when questioned about the Iraq conflict. Women are less likely than men to think that military intervention in Iraq was worthwhile (see Figure 6-3).

Differences such as these contribute to the gender gap discussed in Chapter 5. Women and men do not differ sharply in their political views, but they differ enough to respond somewhat differently to issues, events, and candidates.

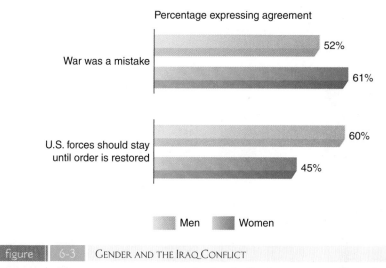

Percentage expressing agreement

War was a mistake — 52% (Men), 61% (Women)

U.S. forces should stay until order is restored — 60% (Men), 45% (Women)

Men   Women

figure 6-3 GENDER AND THE IRAQ CONFLICT

Compared with men, women are somewhat less inclined to support military force as a means of resolving international conflicts. This difference has been evident in polls on support for the Iraq war, as these examples illustrate. *Source: (In order of questions): Gallup poll, August 2007; ABC News/Washington Post poll, November 2005.*

Age Age has always affected opinions, but the gap between young and old is widening. In her book *Young v. Old*, political scientist Susan MacManus notes that the elderly tend to oppose increases in public school funding while supporting increases in social security spending. MacManus predicts that issues of age will increasingly dominate American politics and that the elderly have the political clout to prevail. They vote at higher rates than do young people, are better organized politically (through groups such as the powerful AARP), and are growing in number as a result of lengthened life spans (the so-called graying of America).[21]

Crosscutting Cleavages Although group loyalty can have a powerful impact on people's opinions, this influence is diminished when identification with one group is offset by identification with other groups. In a pluralistic society such as the United States, groups tend to be "crosscutting"—that is, each group includes individuals who also belong to other groups, where they encounter different people and opinions. Crosscutting cleavages encourage individuals to appreciate and understand differences, which leads them toward moderate opinions. By comparison, in societies such as Northern Ireland, where group loyalties are reinforcing rather than crosscutting, opinions are intensified by personal interactions. Catholics and Protestants in Northern Ireland live largely apart from each other, differing not only in their religious beliefs but also in their income levels, neighborhoods of

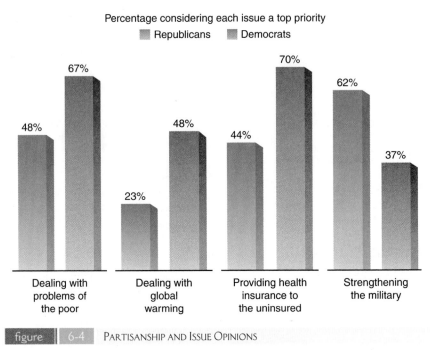

Percentage considering each issue a top priority

■ Republicans   ■ Democrats

Dealing with problems of the poor	Dealing with global warming	Providing health insurance to the uninsured	Strengthening the military

figure | **6-4** | PARTISANSHIP AND ISSUE OPINIONS

Republicans and Democrats differ significantly in their policy opinions and priorities.
Source: Pew Research Center for the People and the Press, 2008.

residence, ethnicities, and loyalties to the government. The result is widespread mistrust between Northern Ireland's Catholics and Protestants.

Partisan Thinking: The Line That Divides

In the everyday world of politics, no source of opinion more clearly divides Americans than that of their partisanship. Figure 6-4 provides examples, but these show only a few of the differences. On nearly every major political issue, Republicans and Democrats have views that are at least somewhat different. In many cases, such as spending programs for the poor, the differences are substantial.

Party identification refers to a person's ingrained sense of loyalty to a political party. Party identification is not formal membership in a party but rather an emotional attachment to a party—the feeling that "I am a Democrat" or "I am a Republican." Scholars and pollsters typically have measured party identification with a question of the following type: "Generally speaking, do you think of yourself as a Republican, a Democrat, an Independent, or what?" About two-thirds of adults call themselves Democrats or Republicans. Of the one-third who prefer the label "Independent," most say they lean toward one party or the other and tend to vote primarily for that party's candidates.

Early studies concluded that party loyalties were highly stable and seldom changed over the course of adult life.[22] Subsequent studies have shown that party loyalties are more fluid than originally believed; they can be influenced by the issues and candidates of the moment.[23] Nevertheless, most adults do not switch their party loyalties easily, and a substantial proportion never waver from their initial commitment to a party, which can often be traced to childhood influences.

★ STATES IN THE NATION

Party Loyalties in the States

The strength of the major parties varies substantially among the states. One indicator of party dominance is the degree to which the party identification of state residents favors one party or the other. In opinion polls, party identification is measured by a question of the following type: "Generally speaking, do you think of yourself as a Republican, a Democrat, an Independent, or what?" The Gallup Organization, using the results of roughly forty thousand interviews it conducted in 2004, estimated the state-by-state distribution of Republican and Democratic identifiers. For the map that follows, a state is classified as Republican if Republican identifiers outnumber Democratic identifiers by 7 percentage points or more. It is classified as Democratic if the reverse is true. The remaining states are classified as competitive. By this indicator, Republican strength is concentrated in the South, the Plains, and the Rockies, while Democratic strength is concentrated in the Northeast and the upper Midwest. Other indicators of party strength, such as control of state elective offices, would result in similar categorizations of the states.

Q: Why is the concentration of Republicans particularly high in some states of the South, the Great Plains, and the Rocky Mountains?

A: The South swung Republican after the Democratic Party took the lead on civil rights in the 1960s. The Great Plains and Rocky Mountain areas have traditionally been Republican, a reflection in part of the rugged individualism that defined their early settlement and contributed to a preference for small government.

(continued)

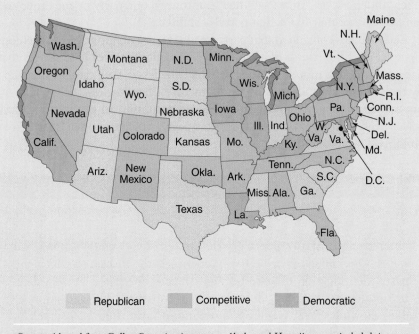

Republican   Competitive   Democratic

*Source: Adapted from Gallup Organization report. Alaska and Hawaii are not included; inter-
views were not conducted in these states.*

Once acquired, partisanship affects how people perceive and interpret
events. An example is the differing opinions of Republicans and Democrats
about U.S. military intervention in Kosovo in 1999 and in Iraq in 2003.
Democrats were more supportive of the first war, while Republicans were
more supportive of the second. While differences in the nature and purpose
of these wars might partially explain this split, partisanship clearly does. The
first of these conflicts was initiated by a Democratic president, Bill Clinton,
while the second was begun by a Republican president, George W. Bush.

For most people, partisanship is not simply blind faith in the party of
their choice. Some Republicans and Democrats know very little about
their party's policies and unthinkingly embrace its candidates. However,
party loyalties are not randomly distributed across the population, but
instead follow a pattern that would be predicted from the parties' his-
tories. The Democratic Party, for example, has been the driving force
behind social welfare and workers' rights policies, while the Republican
Party has spearheaded probusiness and tax reduction policies. The fact
that most union workers are Democrats and most businesspeople are
Republicans is not a coincidence. Their partisanship is rooted in their

economic self-interest.[24] This and other issues of partisanship are examined in more detail at various points later in this book, particularly in Chapters 7, 8, 11, and 12.

THE INFLUENCE OF PUBLIC OPINION ON POLICY

As yet unanswered in our discussion is a central question about public opinion: what impact does it have on government? The question does not have a firm or final answer. In any society of appreciable size, self-government takes place through representative institutions. The people themselves do not directly decide issues of policy, but instead entrust them to elected and

Although public opinion does not always drive government policy, there are times when the impact of public opinion is clearly evident, as in the case of Americans' growing disenchantment with the Iraq conflict as it went beyond the quick ending that President Bush had promised. The public's response encouraged politicians to advocate a scaled-down effort in Iraq. Barack Obama initially centered his 2008 presidential campaign on a withdrawal of U.S. troops from Iraq.

appointed officials. Governing decisions are complex, as are the factors that go into them, including the influence of public opinion.

Some observers claim that officials are relatively insensitive to public opinion—that they are so entrenched in their positions that, however much they claim to serve the people, they actually pay little attention to what ordinary citizens think.[25] This assessment undoubtedly applies to some officials and some issues. However, the most comprehensive study ever conducted on the relationship between public opinion and policy concluded that public opinion does in fact sway government. The study, which examined fifty years of polls and policy decisions, found that when public opinion on an issue changed, policy usually changed in the direction of the change in public opinion. In the case of major issues, this pattern was particularly evident—in such cases, policy typically aligned with public opinion.[26]

However, a more recent study by Lawrence Jacobs and Robert Shapiro found a widening gap between public opinion and policy, apparently because elected officials of both parties have tilted toward the more extreme positions favored by powerful groups within their respective parties (such as the Christian right within the Republican Party and lifestyle liberals within the Democratic Party).[27] Jacobs and Shapiro nonetheless conclude that officials remain sensitive to public opinion on many issues, particularly those that could become campaign issues. As the 2008 election approached, for example, a number of congressional Republicans backed away from their earlier strong support for the war in Iraq. They did not not necessarily call for a quick withdrawal of U.S. forces, but they offered more qualified support for the Iraq mission than previously. Underlying this repositioning were polls showing that the Iraq conflict was unpopular with most voters, enough so that some of them claimed they would vote against any candidate who advocated a large-scale continuing military presence in Iraq.

If elections heighten officials' attention to public opinion, so do particular issues. There are certain actions that officials shy away from for fear of public retribution. Tax hikes are a prime example. Politicians ordinarily will go to great lengths—including borrowing huge amounts of money to shift the problem to future generations—to avoid a major tax increase. Angry taxpayers are officeholders' worst nightmare.

Such examples, however, do not provide an answer to the question of whether public officials are *sufficiently* responsive to public opinion. This question is complicated by the fact that it is partly a normative one—the answer rests on beliefs about the proper relationship between people's opinions and government policies. As we discussed in Chapter 2, some theorists hold that representatives should base their policy decisions on what they believe will best serve the people's interests, while others claim that the people themselves are the best judge of their interests and that it is the representative's duty to pay close heed to the people's demands. The question is also complicated by the fact that politics involves attempts to influence public opinion. Citizens' opinions are not fixed. They can be activated, changed, and crystallized through political action. Political leaders invest enormous amounts of money and time in an effort to get citizens to see things their way.

In fact, one of the best indicators of the power of public opinion is the great effort made by political leaders to harness it in support of their goals. In American politics, popular demand for a policy is a powerful argument for that policy. For this reason and others, great effort is made to organize and represent public opinion through elections (Chapter 7), political parties (Chapter 8), interest groups (Chapter 9), the news media (Chapter 10), and political institutions (Chapters 11–14).

SUMMARY   Self-Test www.mhhe.com/pattersonwtp8e

Public opinion can be defined as those opinions held by ordinary citizens that they openly express. Public officials have many ways of assessing public opinion, such as the outcomes of elections, but they have increasingly come to rely on public opinion polls. There are many possible sources of error in polls, and surveys sometimes present a misleading portrayal of the public's views. However, a properly conducted poll can be an accurate indication of what the public is thinking and can dissuade political leaders from thinking that the views of the most vocal citizens (such as demonstrators and letter writers) are shared by the broader public.

The process by which individuals acquire their political opinions is called political socialization. During childhood, the family and schools are important sources of basic political attitudes, such as beliefs about the parties and the nature of the U.S. political and economic systems. Many of the basic orientations that Americans acquire during childhood remain with them in adulthood, but socialization is a continuing process. Major shifts in opinion during adulthood are usually the consequence of changing political conditions; for example, the Great Depression of the 1930s was the catalyst for wholesale changes in Americans' opinions on the government's economic role. Short-term fluctuations in opinion can result from new political issues and problems. Individuals' opinions in these cases are affected by prior beliefs, peers, political leaders, and the news media. Events themselves are also a significant short-term influence on opinions.

The frames of reference that guide Americans' opinions include cultural beliefs, such as individualism, which affect what people will find politically acceptable and desirable. Opinions can also stem from ideology, although most citizens do not have a strong and consistent ideological attachment. In addition, individuals develop opinions as a result of group orientations—notably, religion, income level, occupation, region, race, ethnicity, gender, and age. Partisanship is perhaps the major source of political opinions; Republicans and Democrats differ in their voting behavior and views on many policy issues.

Public opinion has a significant influence on government but seldom determines exactly what government will do in a particular instance. Public opinion serves to constrain the policy choices of officials. Some policy actions are beyond the range of possibility because the public will not accept change in existing policy or will not seriously consider policy that seems clearly at odds with basic American values. Evidence indicates that officials are at least somewhat attentive to public opinion on highly visible and controversial issues of public policy.

KEY TERMS

agents of socialization (*p. 203*)
economic conservatives
 (*p. 207*)
economic liberals (*p. 207*)
ideology (*p. 206*)
libertarians (*p. 207*)
party identification (*p. 214*)
political socialization (*p. 201*)

population (*p. 197*)
populists (*p. 207*)
public opinion (*p. 194*)
public opinion poll (*p. 197*)
sample (*p. 197*)
sampling error (*p. 198*)
social conservatives (*p. 207*)
social liberals (*p. 207*)

SUGGESTED READINGS

Alvarez, R. Michael, and John Brehm. *Hard Choices, Easy Answers: Values, Information, and American Public Opinion.* Princeton, N.J.: Princeton University Press, 2002. An analysis arguing that what citizens know about politics is assessed in the context of their values and beliefs.

Asher, Herbert. *Polling and the Public,* 7th ed. Washington, D.C.: Congressional Quarterly Press, 2007. A guide to public opinion poll methods and analysis.

Canes-Wrone, Brandice. *Who Leads Whom? Presidents, Policy, and the Public.* Chicago: University of Chicago Press, 2005. A look at recent presidents and their policies in the context of public opinion.

Green, Donald, Bradley Palmquist, and Eric Schickler. *Partisan Hearts and Minds.* New Haven, Conn.: Yale University Press, 2002. An analysis concluding that partisanship powerfully affects how citizens respond to candidates and issues.

Jacobs, Lawrence, and Robert Shapiro. *Politicians Don't Pander.* Chicago: University of Chicago Press, 2000. An analysis concluding that politicians are not driven by polls.

Stimson, James. *Tides of Consent: How Public Opinion Shapes American Politics.* New York: Cambridge University Press, 2004. An analysis of trends in public opinion and their political impact.

Whitaker, Lois Duke, ed. *Voting the Gender Gap.* Urbana: University of Illinois Press, 2008. An edited volume that explores the voting divide between men and women.

Zaller, John R. *The Nature and Origins of Mass Opinion*. New York: Cambridge University Press, 1992. A superb analysis of the nature of public opinion.

LIST OF WEBSITES

http://www.gallup.com/ The website of the Gallup Organization, America's oldest and best known polling organization.

http://www.people-press.org/ The website of the Pew Research Center for the People and the Press; includes an abundance of recent polling results, including cross-national comparisons.

http://www.realclearpolitics.com/ A site that has numerous up-to-date polls from a variety of organizations and on a variety of topics.

http://www.publicagenda.org/ The nonpartisan Public Agenda's site; provides opinions, analyses, and educational materials on current policy issues.

POLITICS IN THEORY AND PRACTICE

Thinking: What factors limit the influence of public opinion on the policy choices of public officials?

Participating: Studies have regularly found that Americans, in relative and in absolute terms, are substantially uninformed about the issues affecting their state, nation, and world. As a result, Americans' opinions about policy issues and problems are not as informed as they could and should be. Citizenship entails responsibilities, one of which is to stay informed about problems and developments that affect the community, the state, and the nation. As an informed citizen, you will be better able to make judgments about policy issues, to choose wisely when voting during elections, and to recognize situations that call for greater personal involvement. Fortunately, you have access to one of the most substantial news systems in the world. News about public affairs is virtually at your fingertips—through your computer, on television, and in the newspaper. Spending only a small amount of time each day following the news will help you to be a more effective and involved citizen.

Extra Credit

For up-to-the-minute *New York Times* articles, interactive simulations, graphics, study tools, and more links and quizzes, visit the text's Online Learning Center at www.mhhe.com/pattersonwtp8e.

The Iraq Syndrome

By John Mueller

Public opinion is a powerful but in-exact force in democratic societies. Rarely is it informed enough and loud enough to force political leaders to take a particular course of action. Public opinion serves mainly to place boundaries on policymakers' choices. The Iraq conflict is a case in point, as Ohio State University professor John Mueller notes in this article from Foreign Affairs *(November/December 2005). Years earlier, Mueller conducted studies of public opinion during the Korean and Vietnam wars, which he uses for comparative pur-poses in this article.*

American troops have been sent into harm's way many times since 1945, but in only three cases—Korea, Vietnam, and Iraq—have they been drawn into sustained ground com-bat and suffered more than 300 deaths in ac-tion. American public opinion became a key factor in all three wars, and in each one there has been a simple association: as casualties mount, support decreases. Broad enthusiasm at the outset invariably erodes.

The only thing remarkable about the current war in Iraq is how precipitously American public support has dropped off. Casualty for casualty, support has declined far more quickly than it did during either the Korean War or the Vietnam War. And if history is any indication, there is little the Bush administration can do to reverse this decline.

More important, the impact of deterio-rating support will not end when the war does. In the wake of the wars in Korea and Vietnam, the American public developed a strong aversion to embarking on such ven-tures again. A similar sentiment—an "Iraq syndrome"—seems to be developing now, and it will have important consequences for U.S. foreign policy for years after the last American battalion leaves Iraqi soil.

The public gave substantial support to the military ventures in Korea, Vietnam, and Iraq as the troops were sent in. In all cases, support decreased as casualties—whether of draftees, volunteers, or reservists—mounted. In each case, the increase in the number of people who considered the venture to be a mistake was steep during the war's early stages, as re-luctant supporters were rather quickly alien-ated; the erosion slowed as approval was re-duced to the harder core. (The dramatic early drop in support for the war in Korea reflected the large number of casualties suffered in the opening phase of that war.)

The most striking thing about the com-parison among the three wars is how much more quickly support has eroded in the case of Iraq. By early 2005, when combat deaths were around 1,500, the percentage of respondents who considered the Iraq war a mistake—over half—was about the same as the percentage who considered the war in Vietnam a mistake at the time of the 1968 Tet offensive, when nearly 20,000 soldiers had already died.

This lower tolerance for casualties is largely due to the fact that the American public places far less value on the stakes in Iraq than it did on those in Korea and Vietnam. The main threats Iraq was thought to present to the United States when troops went in—weapons of mass destruction and support for international terrorism—have been, to say the least, discounted. . . .

When one shifts from questions about whether the war was a "mistake" or "worth it" to ones about whether the United States should get out, much the same pattern holds for Korea, Vietnam, and Iraq: relatively steep declines in support for continuing the war in the early stages, slower erosion later. However, it is close to impossible to judge how many people want to get out or stay the course at any given time because so much depends on how the question is worded. For example, there is far more support for "gradual withdrawal" or "beginning to withdraw" than for "withdrawing" or "immediate withdrawal." Thus in August 2005, The Washington Post [poll] found that 54 percent of respondents favored staying and 44 percent favored withdrawing when the options were posed this way: "Do you think the United States should keep its military forces in Iraq until civil order is restored there, even if that means continued U.S. military casualties, or, do you think the United States should withdraw its military forces from Iraq in order to avoid further U.S. military casualties, even if that means civil order is not restored there?" But in the same month, a Harris poll tallied only 36 percent in support of staying and 61 percent in support of withdrawing when it asked, "Do you favor keeping a large number of U.S. troops in Iraq until there is a stable government there or bringing most of our troops home in the next year?" Still, no matter how the questions are phrased, all the polls have logged increases in pro-withdrawal sentiment over the course of the war. . . .

President George W. Bush, like Lyndon Johnson before him, has made countless speeches explaining what the effort in Iraq is about, urging patience, and asserting that progress is being made. But as was also evident during Woodrow Wilson's campaign to sell the League of Nations to the American public, the efficacy of the bully pulpit is much overrated. The prospects for reversing the erosion of support for the war in Iraq are thus limited. The run-ups to the two wars in Iraq are also instructive in this regard: even though both Presidents Bush labored mightily to sell the war effort, the only thing that succeeded in raising the level of enthusiasm was the sight of troops actually heading into action, which triggered a predictable "rally round the flag" effect. . . .

After the war in Vietnam, there was a strong desire among Americans never to do "that" again. And, in fact, there never was "another Vietnam" during the Cold War. Due to this "Vietnam syndrome," Congress hampered the White House's ability to pursue even rather modest anticommunist ventures in Africa and, to a lesser extent, Latin America (though there was bipartisan support for aiding the anti-Soviet jihad in Afghanistan). Meanwhile, the genocide in Cambodia was studiously ignored in part because of fears that paying attention might lead to the conclusion that American troops should be sent over to rectify the disaster; over most of the course of the genocide, the three major networks devoted a total of 29 minutes of their newscasts to a cataclysm in which millions died.

No matter how the war in Iraq turns out, an Iraq syndrome seems likely. A poll in relatively war-approving Alabama earlier this year, for example, asked whether the United States should be prepared to send troops back to Iraq to establish order there in the event a full-scale civil war erupted after a U.S. withdrawal. Only a third of the respondents favored doing so.

Among the casualties of the Iraq syndrome could be the Bush doctrine, unilateralism, preemption, preventive war, and indispensable-nationhood. Indeed, these once-fashionable (and sometimes self-infatuated) concepts are already picking up a patina of quaintness. Specifically, there will likely be growing skepticism about various key notions: that the United States should take unilateral military action to correct situations or overthrow regimes it considers reprehensible but that present no immediate threat to it, that it can and should forcibly bring democracy to other nations not now so blessed, that it has the duty to rid the world of evil, that having by far the largest defense budget in the world is necessary and broadly beneficial, that international cooperation is of only very limited value, and that Europeans and other well-meaning foreigners are naive and decadent wimps. The United States may also become more inclined to seek international cooperation, sometimes even showing signs of humility. . . .

What's Your Opinion?

What conclusions about the relationship between public opinion and public policy do you draw from Mueller's analysis? Do you think recent developments (Mueller's article was written in late 2005) support or contradict his thesis?

CHAPTER 7

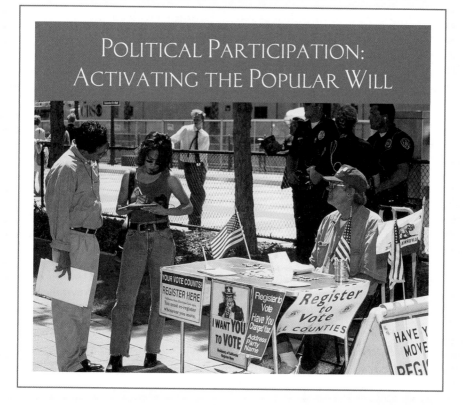

POLITICAL PARTICIPATION:
ACTIVATING THE POPULAR WILL

66 We are concerned in public affairs, but immersed in our private ones. 99

WALTER LIPPMANN[1]

They seemed to come out of nowhere. In the Iowa Democratic caucuses, their numbers were three times greater than in the previous election. In the New Hampshire Democratic primary, their numbers doubled from the 2004 level. In contest after contest in the 2008 Democratic presidential nominating race, young voters, and older ones, too, expressed their sentiments in numbers not seen since the 1970s. A few analysts had predicted that young adults would vote in higher numbers than usual because of their concern with the war in Iraq, but no one had envisioned anything on the scale that occurred. Young adults mostly supported the candidacy of Illinois senator Barack Obama, but New York senator Hillary Clinton had her supporters, too. When all their votes were counted across all the states, the turnout level in the Democratic primaries was that of an earlier era, when young adults voted at much higher rates than they have in recent elections.

Voting is a form of **political participation**—involvement in activities intended to influence public policy and leadership. Political participation involves other activities in addition to voting, such as joining political groups, writing to elected officials, demonstrating for political causes, and giving money to political candidates. Such activities are basic to a properly functioning democratic society. The concept of self-government is based on the idea that ordinary people have a right and a duty to participate in the affairs of state. As it happens, however, political participation in the United States has a different pattern than in most Western democracies, as this chapter will show. The major points made in this chapter are these:

★ *Voter turnout in U.S. elections is low in comparison with that of other democratic nations.* The reasons for this difference include the nature of U.S. election laws, particularly those pertaining to registration requirements and the scheduling of elections.

★ *Most citizens do not participate actively in politics in ways other than voting.* Only a minority of Americans can be classified as political activists. Nevertheless, Americans are more likely than citizens of other democracies to contribute time and money to political and community organizations.

★ *Most Americans make a sharp distinction between their personal lives and public life.* This attitude reduces their incentive to participate and contributes to a pattern of participation dominated by citizens of higher income and education.

VOTER PARTICIPATION

At the nation's founding, **suffrage**—the right to vote—was limited to property-owning males. Tom Paine ridiculed this restriction in *Common Sense*. Observing

Historical
Background

that a man whose only item of property was a jackass would lose his right to vote if the jackass died, Paine asked, "Now tell me, which was the voter, the man or the jackass?" It was not until 1840 that all states extended suffrage to propertyless white males.

Women did not secure the vote until 1920, with the ratification of the Nineteenth Amendment. Decades earlier, Susan B. Anthony had tried to vote in her hometown of Rochester, New York, asserting that it was her right as a U.S. citizen. She was arrested for "illegal voting" and told that her proper place was in the home. By 1920, men had run out of excuses for denying the vote to women. As Senator Wendell Phillips observed, "One of two things is true: either woman is like man—and if she is, then a ballot based on brains belongs to her as well as to him. Or she is different, and then man does not know how to vote for her as she herself does."[2]

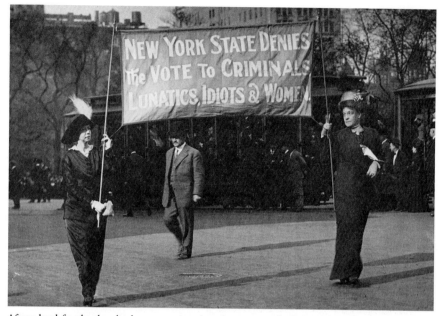

After a hard-fought, decades-long campaign, American women finally won the right to vote in 1920.

African Americans had to wait nearly fifty years longer than women to secure their right to vote. Blacks seemed to have won that right after the Civil War with passage of the Fifteenth Amendment, but as explained in Chapter 5, they were effectively disenfranchised in the South by a number of electoral tricks, including the poll tax, which was a fee of several dollars that had to be paid before a person could register to vote. Because most blacks in the South were too poor to pay it, the poll tax effectively kept many of them from voting. Not until the ratification of the Twenty-fourth Amendment in 1964 was the poll tax outlawed in federal elections. Supreme Court decisions and the Voting Rights Act of 1965 swept away other legal barriers to equal participation by African Americans.

In 1971, the Twenty-sixth Amendment extended voting rights to include citizens eighteen years of age or older. Previously, nearly all states had restricted voting to those twenty-one years of age or older.

Factors in Voter Turnout: The United States in Comparative Perspective

Today nearly any American adult—rich or poor, man or woman, black or white—who is determined to vote can legally and actually do so. Most Americans embrace the symbolism of the vote, saying that they have a duty to vote in elections (see Table 7-1).

| table | 7-1 | OPINIONS ON OBLIGATIONS OF CITIZENS |

Americans rank voting as one of the essential obligations of citizenship.

	Essential Obligation	Very Important Obligation	Somewhat Important	Personal Preference
Treating all people equally regardless of race or ethnic background	57%	33%	6%	4%
Voting in elections	53	29	9	9
Working to reduce inequality and injustice	41	42	12	6
Being civil to others with whom we may disagree	35	45	14	6
Staying informed about news and public affairs	30	42	19	10
Donating blood or organs to help with medical needs	20	37	18	26
Volunteering time to community service	16	42	26	16

Source: Used by permission of the 1996 Survey of American Political Culture, James Davison Hunter and Carol Bowman, Directors, Institute for Advanced Studies in Culture, University of Virginia.

Neverthless, many Americans shirk this duty. Millions choose not to vote regularly, a tendency that sets Americans apart from citizens of most other Western democracies. Since the 1960s, **voter turnout**—the proportion of adult citizens who actually vote in a given election—has averaged about 55 percent in presidential elections (see Figure 7-1). A few presidential elections in this period, including the 2008 election, have resulted in a turnout that is measurably higher than the average, but even in these cases, the nonvoters have outnumbered the voters who backed the winning candidate. Turnout is even lower in the midterm congressional elections that take place between presidential elections. Midterm election turnout

Percentage of eligible adults who voted

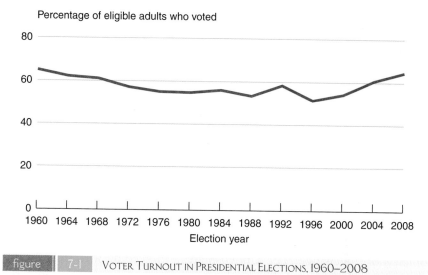

figure 7-1 VOTER TURNOUT IN PRESIDENTIAL ELECTIONS, 1960–2008

After 1960, as indicated by the proportion of voters in the adult-age population, turn-out declined steadily. In the past two decades, turnout has fluctuated, depending on the issues at stake in the particular election. *Source: U.S. Bureau of the Census. Figures based on percent of vote-eligible adults who voted. Figure for 2008 based on preliminary estimates.*

has not reached 50 percent since 1920 and, since 1970, has seldom topped the 40 percent mark. After one midterm election, cartoonist Rigby showed an election clerk eagerly asking a stray cat that had wandered into a polling place, "Are you registered?"[3]

Polling places are even lonelier during local elections. In many cities and towns, barely 20 percent show up to vote in local elections, and the trend has been downward for four decades.[4] Even as the voting rate increased in the 2004 and 2008 presidential elections, it slipped in local elections held in 2005 and 2007.

Nonvoting is more prevalent in the United States than in nearly all other democracies (see "How the United States Compares"). In recent decades, turnout in major national elections has averaged more than 90 percent in Belgium and more than 80 percent in France, Germany, and Denmark.[5] However, the disparity in turnout between the United States and other nations is not as great as these official voting rates suggest. Some nations calculate turnout solely on the basis of eligible adults, whereas the United States has traditionally based its figures on all adults, including legal aliens and other ineligible groups. Nevertheless, even when such statistical disparities are corrected, turnout in U.S. elections is comparatively low.

Contributing to the relatively low turnout in U.S. elections are registration requirements, the frequency of elections, and the political party system.

Registration Requirements   Before Americans are allowed to vote, they must be registered—that is, their names must appear on an official list of eligible voters. **Registration** began around 1900 as a way of preventing voters from casting more than one ballot on Election Day. Multiple balloting had become a tactic of big-city party machines—"vote early and often" was their motto. Although registration reduced illegal voting, it also placed a burden on honest citizens. Because they could now vote only if they took time beforehand to register, those people who forgot or otherwise failed to do so found themselves unable to participate on election day. Turnout in U.S. elections declined steadily after registration was instituted.

Although other democracies also require registration, they place this responsibility on government. In most European nations, public officials have the duty to enroll citizens on registration lists. When someone moves to a new address, for example, the Postal Service will notify registration officials of the change. The United States—in keeping with its individualistic culture—is one of the few democracies in which registration is the individual's responsibility. Moreover, registration rules have traditionally been set by the state governments, and some states make it somewhat dif-

HOW THE UNITED STATES COMPARES

Voter Turnout

The United States ranks near the bottom among the world's democracies in the percentage of eligible citizens who participate in national elections. One reason for the low voter turnout is that individual Americans are responsible for registering to vote, whereas in most other democracies voters are automatically registered by government officials. In addition, unlike some other democracies, the United States does not encourage voting by holding elections on the weekend or by imposing penalties, such as fines, on those who do not participate.

Another factor affecting voter turnout rate in the United States is the absence of a major labor or socialist party, which would serve to bring lower-income citizens to the polls. America's individualist culture and its electoral system (see Chapter 8) have inhibited the establishment of a major labor or socialist party. In democracies where such parties exist, the turnout difference between upper- and lower-income groups is relatively small. In the United States, the gap in the turnout level of lower- and upper-income persons is substantial.

(continued)

Country	Approximate Voter Turnout	Automatic Registration?	Social Democrat, Socialist, or Labor Party?	Election Day a Holiday or Weekend Day?
Belgium	90%	Yes	Yes	Yes
Germany	85	Yes	Yes	Yes
Denmark	85	Yes	Yes	No
Italy	80	Yes	Yes	Yes
Austria	80	Yes	Yes	Yes
France	80	No	Yes	Yes
Great Britain	60	Yes	Yes	No
Canada	60	Yes	Yes	No
Japan	60	Yes	Yes	Yes
United States	55	No	No	No

Source: Developed from multiple sources. Turnout percentages are a rough average of national elections during the past two decades.

ficult for citizens to qualify. Registration periods and locations usually are not highly publicized.[6] Eligibility can also be a problem. In most states, a citizen must reside at an address for a minimum period, usually thirty days, before becoming eligible to register. Scholars estimate that turnout would be roughly 10 percentage points higher in the United States if it had European-style registration.[7]

States with a tradition of lenient registration laws have a higher average turnout rate than other states. Idaho, Iowa, Maine, Minnesota, Montana, New Hampshire, Wisconsin, and Wyoming, which are states that allow people to register at their polling place on election day, have high turnout rates. The states that have the most restrictive registration laws are concentrated in the South, continuing a legacy that traces to the time when black people were kept from voting (see "States in the Nation").

★ ‖ STATES IN THE NATION

Voter Turnout in Presidential Elections

The United States has lower voter turnout than most Western democracies. Within the United States, however, the state-to-state variation is substantial. In a few states, including Minnesota and New Hampshire, nearly seven in ten adults vote in presidential elections. In contrast, there are a few states, including Hawaii and Texas, where barely more than four in ten adults vote.

Q: Why do states in the South and Southwest have relatively low turnout rates?

A: Southern states have more poverty and a tradition of more restrictive registration laws (dating to the Jim Crow era of racial segregation). Both factors are associated with lower voting rates. States with large populations of recent immigrants, including those in the Southwest, also tend to have lower voting rates.

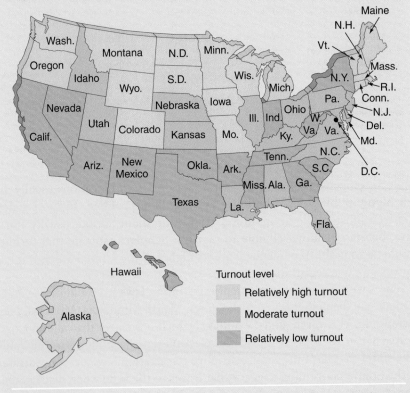

Source: Compiled by author from various sources; based on recent midterm and presidential elections.

In 1993, in an effort to increase registration levels nationwide, Congress enacted a voting registration law known as "motor voter." It requires states to permit people to register to vote when applying for a driver's license or public assistance. Registration is not automatic in these situations; the citizen must voluntarily fill out the registration form. Moreover, the motor voter law does not help citizens who do not drive or do not otherwise have contact with an appropriate state agency. The law has resulted in some new voters but fewer than its proponents envisioned.

A newer device, voter identification cards, will serve to depress voter turnout. Republican-controlled legislatures in several states have enacted laws requiring citizens to have a government-issued photo ID in order to register and vote. These laws are purportedly intended to reduce widespread vote fraud by individual voters, even though scholarly studies have found little evidence to support the claim.[8] Georgia passed such a law, which required citizens without a government-issued photo ID, such as a driver's license or passport, to obtain a voter identification card, which would cost them twenty dollars and expire after five years. To obtain the card, they would need to produce an original birth certificate and other documents and could obtain it only by going to a Department of Motor Vehicles office. Georgia Democrats charged that the law was a blatant attempt to reduce voter turnout among poor people, who are less likely to have a driver's license or passport and less able to afford the fee. After a federal judge invalidated the fee provision, the Georgia legislature eliminated it but retained the photo ID requirement. In 2008, the U.S. Supreme Court ruled on a case involving Indiana's voter identification card law, which is similar to Georgia's. Writing for the Court's 6-3 majority, Justice John Paul Stevens said states have a "valid interest" in improving election procedures and deterring fraud. The Court rejected the argument that the law places an undue burden on the poor. It acknowledged that the law had a partisan element but argued that the law "should not be disregarded simply because partisan interests may have provided one motivation for the votes of individual legislators." In a dissenting opinion, Justice David Souter said the law "threatens to impose nontrivial burdens on the voting rights of tens of thousands of the state's citizens."[9]

Frequency of Elections   Just as America's registration system places a burden on voters, so, too, does its election schedule. The United States holds elections more often than other nations. No other democracy has elections for the lower chamber of its national legislature (the equivalent of the U.S. House of Representatives) as often as every two years, and none schedules elections for chief executive as often as every four years.[10] In addition, most state and local elections in the United States are scheduled separately from federal elections. Over three-fourths of the states elect their governors in nonpresidential election years, and most U.S. cities hold elections of municipal officials in odd-numbered years. Finally, the United States uses primary elections to select the party nominees. In other democracies, party leaders pick them.

Americans are asked to vote two to three times as often as Europeans, which increases the likelihood that they will not participate every time.[11] Moreover, elections in the United States have traditionally been scheduled on Tuesday, forcing most adults to find time before or after work to get to the polls. Many European nations hold their elections on Sunday or declare election day a national holiday, making it easier for working people to vote.

Party Differences   A final contributor to lower voter turnout in the United States is the nation's party system. Most European democracies have three or more significant political parties that have formed along class and social divisions and sometimes along religious and ethnic divisions as well. Labor and social democratic parties abound in Europe, as do middle-class, environmental, and right-wing parties. European voters have a range of choices when they go to the polls and usually can find one that conforms with their views.

The United States has only two major parties, the Republicans and the Democrats. Each has its enthusiastic supporters, yet each party, to get the majority support it needs to win, must have broad support. The Republican and Democratic parties normally try to attract a sizable share of votes from nearly all groups in order to gain the 50 percent or more of the vote they need for victory. As a consequence, the parties sometimes take similar positions on leading issues, reducing the voters' choice. From time to time, the parties are fairly far apart. In the 2008 presidential election, for example, which was waged against the backdrop of the Iraq war and a weak economy, the parties were sharply divided in their positions, and Americans believed a lot was at stake in the choice between the Republicans and Democrats. Voter turnout was relatively high in 2008. In most U.S. elections, however, the differences between the parties are not as pronounced, which leads many people to conclude that the election's outcome will not substantially affect their future or that of the nation.[12] In such cases, turnout is lower than in elections where people think the stakes are high. (Chapter 8 has a fuller discussion of the American two-party system and its consequences.)

Why Some Americans Vote and Others Do Not

Even though turnout is lower in the United States than in other major Western democracies, some Americans vote regularly while others seldom or never vote. Among the explanations for these individual differences are civic attitudes, age, and education and income.

Civic Attitudes   Some Americans have a strong sense of **civic duty**—the belief that they are obliged to participate in public affairs. Citizens who hold this belief tend to be regular voters, often turning out for congressional and state elections as well as presidential elections. Other Americans are beset by **apathy**—a lack of interest in politics. Most of them don't bother to vote, whatever the election. Just as some people would not attend the Super Bowl even if it were free and being played across the street, some Americans would not bother to vote even if a ballot were delivered to their door. Still other Americans refrain from voting because of **alienation**—a feeling of powerlessness rooted in the belief that government doesn't care about people like them. Many of these citizens regard voting as a complete waste of time, convinced that government won't respond to their concerns even if they do go to the polls.

Civic duty and apathy are attitudes that are usually acquired from one's parents. When parents vote regularly and take an active interest in politics, their children usually grow up thinking they have a duty to participate. When parents never vote and show no interest in public affairs, their children are likely to be politically apathetic. Alienation can be traced to childhood socialization, but it often has adult roots. For example, when the Democratic Party took the lead on civil rights issues in the 1960s, some working-class white Democrats felt left out, believing that gains for African Americans would come at their expense. Some of these people switched parties, but a greater number simply stopped voting. Voter turnout among working-class whites dropped sharply in 1968 and in 1972—two presidential elections in which civil rights issues were central.[13]

Age   When viewers tuned into MTV at various times in the 2008 presidential campaign, they might have thought at first that they had selected the wrong channel. Rather than a video of their favorite performer, they saw the presidential candidates urging young people to vote. The candidates had targeted the right audience. Young adults are substantially less likely than middle-aged citizens to vote. Even senior citizens, despite the infirmities of old age, have a far higher turnout rate than do voters under the age of thirty.

In 2004 and again in 2008, turnout among younger voters increased substantially from that of previous recent presidential elections. Underlying this increase was the Iraq war, which mobilized college-educated young adults especially. Most of them opposed the way the Bush administration was conducting the war, and they participated in unusually high numbers.

★ LEADERS

Susan B. Anthony
(1820–1906)

Susan B. Anthony's name is synonymous with women's right to vote—and well it should be. She spent much of her adult life fighting for women's suffrage, even at the risk of arrest. When she was in her twenties, she moved to upstate New York and became politically active. Like many of the women who would lead the movement for women's rights, her first crusade was with the temperance movement, which sought to ban the sale of alcohol because of the hardship alcoholism imposed on women and children. She next joined the abolitionist movement, which sought an end to slavery. After the Civil War, Anthony teamed up with an old friend and fellow activist, Elizabeth Cady Stanton, to demand equal pay and voting rights for women. She twice went to the polls in her hometown of Rochester, New York, to assert her right to vote, and she twice was arrested. By then, Anthony had become a national figure who lectured widely on women's suffrage. She died a decade before women gained the right to vote in the United States, but she, as much as any American, made women's suffrage a reality.

Nevertheless, the voting rate of young adults was still below that of older adults, who are more likely to live in the same residence from one election to the next and thus do not need to reregister in order to vote. Older voters are also more likely to own their homes and to have children, which heightens their sense of having a stake in election outcomes.

Education and Income   College-educated and higher-income Americans have above-average voting rates. They have the financial resources and communication skills that encourage participation and make it personally rewarding. Nevertheless, America is unusual in the degree to which education and income are related to voter participation. Europeans with less education and income vote at only slightly lower rates than those with more education and income. In the United States, however, those with a college degree or in the upper-income level are twice as likely to vote in a

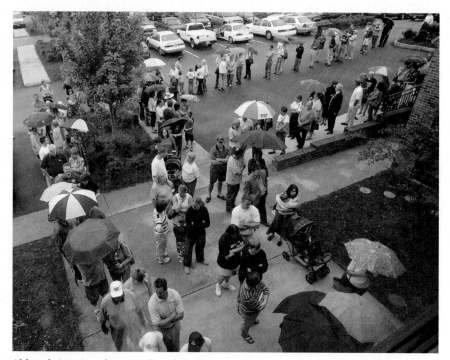

Although Americans have voted in relatively low numbers in recent U.S. elections, the turnout rate increased in 2004 and 2008 in response to the issues of the moment. Here voters stand in a long line waiting to cast their ballot at a polling place in Fort Mill, South Carolina.

presidential election as those who did not finish high school or are in the low-income bracket (see Figure 7-2).

Why the huge difference between the United States and Europe? For one thing, Europeans with less income and education are encouraged to participate by the presence of class-based organizations and appeals—strong socialist or labor parties, politically oriented trade unions, and class-based political ideologies. The United States has never had a major socialist or labor party. Although the Democratic Party represents the working class and the poor to a degree, it is more responsive to middle-class voters, who are a larger share of the electorate and hold the balance of power in U.S. elections.[14] In addition, Americans with less income and education are the people most adversely affected by the country's registration system. Many of them do not own cars or homes and are thus less likely to be registered in advance of an election. They are also less familiar with registration locations and requirements.[15]

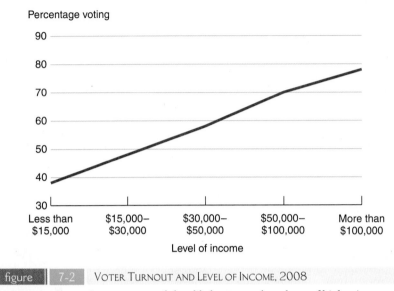

Percentage voting

figure   7-2   VOTER TURNOUT AND LEVEL OF INCOME, 2008

Americans of lower income are much less likely to vote than those of higher income. The gap in these voting rates is greater in the United States than in other western democracies. *Source: U.S. Bureau of the Census.*

CONVENTIONAL FORMS OF PARTICIPATION OTHER THAN VOTING

Most citizens in most democracies vote in elections. No other active form of political participation is as widespread. Nevertheless, voting is a somewhat limited form of involvement. Citizens have the opportunity to vote only at a particular time and only on the choices listed on the ballot. Other activities, such as working on a campaign or joining a civic group, give citizens fuller opportunities to participate.

Campaign and Lobbying Activities

Compared with voting, working for a candidate or attending election rallies requires considerably more time. Not surprisingly, the number of citizens who engage in such activities is relatively small. Nevertheless, the number is higher in the United States than in Europe. A recent study of twenty-three countries found that Americans ranked first in terms of making an effort to influence other voters (see Figure 7-3). One reason Americans are more active in campaigns, even though they vote less, is that they have more opportunities to participate. The United States is a federal system

figure   7-3   CAMPAIGN ACTIVITY

Although Americans are less likely to vote in elections than citizens elsewhere, they are more likely to engage in other campaign activities, such as trying to influence the vote choice of others. *Source: Surveys by Comparative Studies of Electoral Systems, 2001–4. Reported in Russell J. Dalton, "The Myth of the Disengaged American," CSES Report, October 25, 2005, web release. Sixteen other countries were included in surveys; none had a higher participation rate than the United States.*

with campaigns for national, state, and local offices. A citizen who wants to participate can easily find an opportunity at one level of office or another. Most of the European governments are unitary in form (see Chapter 3), which means that there are fewer elective offices and thus fewer campaigns. (Election campaigns are discussed further in Chapter 8.)

Americans are also more likely than Europeans to lobby elected officials. Although most Americans do not write their member of Congress, state legislator, or city councilor, many do so. And they do so in the expectation of a response, even if it is nothing more than a polite letter thanking them for writing. Americans are also more likely than citizens elsewhere to contribute money to support the activities of lobbying groups, such as Greenpeace, Common Cause, the Christian Moral Government Fund, the American Association of Retired Persons, and the National Conservative Political Action Committee. (Lobbying groups are discussed further in Chapter 9.)

Virtual Participation

The introduction of the World Wide Web in the the 1990s opened up an entirely new venue for political participation—the Internet. Through emails, chat rooms, like-minded networks, and the like, the Internet has created participation possibilities previously unimaginable. Although the participation is "virtual" rather than face-to-face, much of it is nonetheless personal in that it involves contact with friends, acquaintances, and activists.

Participation through the Internet has been most evident in presidential campaigns, where virtual participation now far outweighs conventional participation. According to Pew Research Center surveys, huge numbers of Americans send emails to family members, friends, and others in an effort to promote their favorite candidate. Campaign fund-raising through the Internet is also flourishing. In 2004, Howard Dean, though ultimately unsuccessful in his effort to gain the Democratic presidential nomination, raised millions of dollars and attracted thousands of volunteers for his campaign through the Internet. The Internet's potency as a vehicle for citizen-based election politics was even clearer in 2008. Democratic candidate Barack Obama raised more money than his opponents, and most of it was contributed in small amounts through the Internet. He had more than a million contributors and raised more than $300 million online. Never before had a small-donor fund-raising strategy bested the older strategy of raising funds through meetings, dinners, and other contacts with large donors. Obama's personal appeal was a key ingredient; the Internet fund-raising efforts of the other candidates in 2008 were less successful. Internet communication was a key to the Obama campaign's high level of citizen participation—through donations, the emailing of others, and the attending of rallies.

There are other remarkable examples of citizen mobilization through the Internet, few more successful than MoveOn, which claims 2 million "online activists," many of them young people. When MoveOn's organizers make a concerted appeal—whether on behalf of a candidate, a cause, or a bill before Congress—it usually triggers a swift and large response from those in its network.

The full impact of the Web on citizen participation lies in the future. Internet technology will continue to improve, and online use will continue to rise, as will the organizing savvy of Internet operatives.[16] Some analysts believe the Internet will usher in an era of unprecedented citizen involvement and influence. Other analysts are less optimistic, noting that the Internet has hundreds of thousands of websites, most of which have little or nothing to do with public affairs. In the long run, the likely scenario is

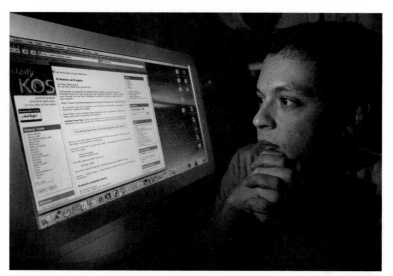

Shown here is Markos Moulitsas Zuniga, who aided in the creation of presidential candidate Howard Dean's "meetups"—supporters connected with one another through the Internet. Zuniga runs a political web log ("blog") called Daily Kos.

that the Internet's mobilizing power will ebb and flow, depending less on further advances in technology than on the urgency of the moment. Over the long course of American democracy, citizens have grown more active when issues have intensified and then settled back down as issues have quieted. The Internet Age is unlikely to be different. (The Internet is discussed further in Chapter 10.)

Community Activities

Many Americans participate in public affairs not through election campaigns but through local organizations such as parent-teacher associations, neighborhood groups, business clubs, church-affiliated groups, and hospital auxiliaries. The actual number of citizens who participate actively in community groups is difficult to estimate, but the number is surely in the tens of millions, reflecting in part a tradition of local participation that dates to colonial times. Moreover, compared with cities and towns in Europe, those in the United States have greater authority over local policies, which gives their residents a reason to participate actively. Because of increased mobility and other factors, Americans may be less tied to their local communities than in the past and therefore less involved in community activity. Nevertheless, Americans are more than twice as likely as Europeans to work together in groups on matters of community concern.[17]

In a widely heralded book titled *Bowling Alone*, Harvard's Robert Putnam claims that America has been undergoing a long-term decline in its **social capital** (the sum of the face-to-face civic interactions among citizens in a society).[18] Putnam attributes the decline to television and other factors that draw people inward and away from participation in civic and political groups. Not all scholars accept Putnam's interpretation of the trend in civic involvement (some indicators point toward a rise in certain types of participation), but no one challenges his claims about the value of civic participation. As the theorist John Stuart Mill (1806–73) noted more than a century ago, community involvement brings people together, builds skills that make them more effective citizens, helps them understand the interests of others, and enables them to protect and promote their interests and those of their community.

UNCONVENTIONAL ACTIVISM: SOCIAL MOVEMENTS AND PROTEST POLITICS

During the era of absolute monarchies, people resorted to protest as a way of expressing displeasure with their rulers. Tax and food riots occurred with some frequency. When democratic governments came into existence, citizens had a regular and less disruptive way to express themselves—through their votes. Voting is double-edged, however. Although the vote gives citizens a degree of control over government, *the vote also gives government control over citizens.*[19] Elected officials can claim that their policies reflect the will of the electorate and must therefore be respected and obeyed, however much they might hurt certain interests in society.

Social movements, or **political movements** as they are sometimes called, are a way for citizens disenchanted with government policy to express their opposition and work to bring about the change they want.[20] These efforts are sometimes channeled through conventional forms of participation, such as political lobbying, but citizens can also take to the streets in protest against government. In 2003, for example, as the Bush administration was preparing for war with Iraq, protest demonstrations were held in many U.S. cities, including Washington and San Francisco. Two percent of adult Americans said they participated in an antiwar demonstration. Many of them were young adults. Participants in social movements are younger on average than nonparticipants, a reversal of the pattern for voting.[21]

Social movements do not always succeed, but they sometimes force government into action. For example, the timing and scope of the landmark 1964 Civil Rights Act and 1965 Voting Rights Act can be explained only as a response by Congress to the pressure created by the civil rights

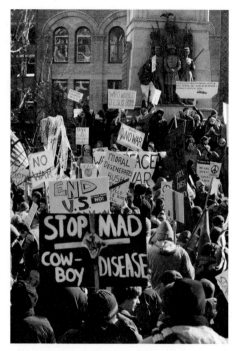

Protesters demonstrate in 2003 against the war in Iraq. Although protest movements are an American tradition, they do not routinely receive strong public support.

movement. Another effective social movement in the 1960s was that of the farmworkers, whose protests led to improved conditions for migrant workers.

Political protests have taken on new forms in recent years. Protest was traditionally a desperate act that began, often spontaneously, when a group had lost hope of succeeding through more conventional methods. Today, however, protest is usually a calculated act—a means of bringing added attention to a cause.[22] These tactical protests often involve a great deal of planning, including, in some instances, the busing of thousands of people to Washington for a rally staged for television. Civil rights, environmental, agricultural, and pro- and anti-abortion groups are among those that have staged tactical protests in Washington in recent years.

Protest politics has a long history in America. Indeed, the United States was founded on a protest movement that sparked a revolution against Britain. Despite this tradition, however, protest activity is less common today in the United States than in many Western democracies (see Figure 7-4). Spain, France, Germany, Sweden, and Ireland are among the countries that have higher rates of participation in political protests.

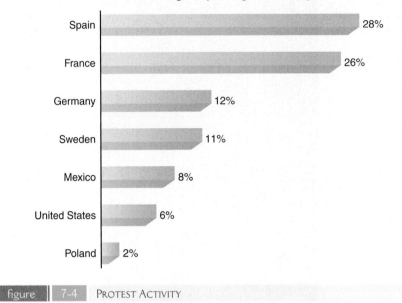

Percentage responding have taken part

Country	Percentage
Spain	28%
France	26%
Germany	12%
Sweden	11%
Mexico	8%
United States	6%
Poland	2%

figure 7-4 PROTEST ACTIVITY

Despite the significance of protest activity in U.S. history, Americans are less likely to protest than are citizens of many other democracies. *Source: Surveys by Comparative Studies of Electoral Systems, 2001–04. Reported in Russell J. Dalton, "The Myth of the Disengaged American," CSES Report, October 25, 2005, web release. Of twenty-three countries surveyed, the United States ranked eighteenth in level of protest activity. Only selected countries are included in this figure.*

Public support for protest activity is also comparatively low in the United States. The Vietnam War protests, which in some cases were accompanied by the burning of draft cards and the American flag, had only marginal public support outside the circle of protesters. When unarmed student protesters at Kent State University and Jackson State University were shot to death in May 1970 by members of the National Guard, many Americans in polls blamed the students, not the guardsmen, for the tragedy. The general public was more accepting of the Iraq war protest in 2003. Even after the fighting had begun, three in every five Americans said they saw the protests as "a sign of a healthy democracy" (see Figure 7-5). Still, almost two in five felt that "opponents of the war should not hold antiwar demonstrations" and half of these said that antiwar demonstrations should be banned entirely. In another poll, about a third of respondents said that protesters were "the kind of people who tend to blame America first."[23] On the other hand, protesters are rarely assaulted by those who disagree with them, and most Americans recognize that protest is part of America's tradition of free expression. In that sense, protest is seen as something to be tolerated, if not admired.

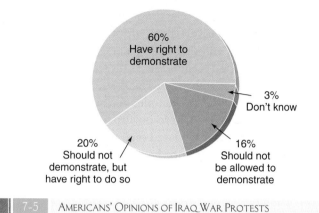

figure 7-5 AMERICANS' OPINIONS OF IRAQ WAR PROTESTS

A majority supported the right of antiwar protesters to demonstrate, although some Americans felt they should not be allowed to do so. *Source: ABC News/Washington Post Poll, March 23, 2003.*

PARTICIPATION AND THE POTENTIAL FOR INFLUENCE

Although Americans claim that political participation is important, many of them do not practice what they preach. Most citizens show little interest in participation except to vote, and a significant minority cannot even be persuaded that voting is worth their time. However, Americans are not completely apathetic: many millions of them contribute to political causes, and more than 100 million vote in presidential elections.

Yet sustained political activism does not engage a large proportion of the public. Moreover, many of those who do participate are drawn to politics by a habitual sense of civic duty rather than by an intense concern with current issues. The emphasis that American culture places on individualism tends to diminish interest in political participation. "In the United States, the country of individualism *par excellence*," William Watts and Lloyd Free write, "there is a sharp distinction in people's minds between their own personal lives and national life."[24] Although wars and severe recessions can lead Americans to take action on a larger scale than is normal, most people under most conditions expect to solve their problems on their own. This is not to say that Americans have a disdain for collective action. In their communities particularly, citizens frequently take part in collective efforts to support a local hospital, improve the neighborhood, and the like. But most Americans tend not to see their personal well-being as being closely linked to partisan political activity.

This tendency contributes to a class bias in American politics. For one thing, it helps maintain a relatively sharp distinction between that which is properly public (political) and that which is properly private (economic). Americans, as political scientist Robert Lane notes, prefer to see benefits distributed primarily through the economic marketplace rather than through the policies of government.[25] For example, access to medical care in the United States, unlike in Europe where government-provided health care is available to all, is to some degree based on a person's ability to pay for it. Roughly 45 million Americans do not have access to adequate health care because they cannot afford health insurance.

Lower-income Americans are a relatively weak force in the nation's politics. They are less likely to have the financial resources and communication skills that encourage participation in politics and make it personally rewarding. Among citizens who are most active in politics, three times as many have incomes in the top third as in the bottom third.[26] This difference is much greater than in other Western democracies, where poorer citizens are assisted through automatic voter registration and by the presence of class-based political organizations. The poor in the United States must arrange their own registration and must choose between two political parties that are attuned primarily to middle-class interests.

Some writers claim that the country is better off if less interested and less knowledgeable citizens—most of whom are near the bottom of the economic ladder—stay home on election day. In a cover story in *Atlantic Monthly*, Robert Kaplan wrote, "The last thing America needs is more voters—particularly badly educated and alienated ones—with a passion for politics."[27] The gist of this age-old argument is that poorer citizens are prone to backing radical leaders and ideas. The problem with this claim is that there is virtually no historical evidence for it; if anything, poorer Americans have been notable for their aversion to class-based radicalism.[28] On the other hand, low turnout can be a problem. In general, the smaller the electorate, the less representative it is of the public as a whole. Polls indicate that the outcomes of elections would in some instances have changed if the turnout had been substantially higher.

And even if greater voter turnout would not have altered the outcomes, campaign platforms are tailored to those who vote. Studies indicate that representatives are more responsive to the demands of participants than to those of nonparticipants. In *Unequal Democracy*, political scientist Larry Bartels shows that elected officials respond to the concerns of their affluent constituents while largely ignoring those of their poor constituents. He presents recent case after recent case where the interests of the affluent have prevailed.[29] Although high-participation groups do not always pursue their own narrow interests, it would be a mistake to conclude that they regularly support policies that benefit others. For example, a turning point in the defeat of President Bill Clinton's health care reform proposal in 1993, which would have extended health care coverage to nearly all Americans, came when middle- and upper-income groups decided that it might increase the cost and reduce the quality of their own medical care. According to Time/CNN polls, support for the Clinton plan dropped from 57 percent to 37 percent between September 1993 and July 1994. Although this decline reflected a loss of support among all groups, the drop was particularly severe among middle- and higher-income people who already had health insurance, through either an individual policy or an employment-related group policy.

In sum, the pattern of individual political participation in the United States parallels the distribution of influence that prevails in the private sector. Those who have the most power in the marketplace also have the most power in the political arena. However, the issue of individual participation is only one piece of the larger puzzle of who rules America and for what purposes. Subsequent chapters will supply additional pieces.

SUMMARY   Self-Test www.mhhe.com/pattersonwtp8e

Political participation is involvement in activities designed to influence public policy and leadership. A main issue of democratic government is the question of who participates in politics and how fully they participate.

Voting is the most widespread form of active political participation among Americans. Yet voter turnout is significantly lower in the United States than in other democratic nations. The requirement that Americans must personally register in order to establish their eligibility to vote is one reason for lower turnout among Americans; other democracies place the burden of registration on government officials rather than on individual citizens. The fact that the United States holds frequent elections also discourages some citizens from voting regularly. Finally, the major American political parties, unlike many of those in Europe, do not routinely and sharply represent the interests of opposing economic classes; thus, the policy stakes in American elections are lower. Some Americans do not vote because they think that policy will not change greatly regardless of which party holds power.

Only a minority of citizens engage in the more demanding forms of political activity, such as work on community affairs or on behalf of a candidate during a political campaign. Nevertheless, the proportion of Americans who engage in these more demanding forms of activity exceeds the proportion of Europeans who do so. Most political activists are individuals of higher income and education; they have the skills and material resources to participate effectively and tend to take a greater interest in politics. More than in any other Western democracy, political participation in the United States is related to economic status.

Social movements are broad efforts to achieve change by citizens who feel that government is not properly responsive to their interests. These efforts sometimes take place outside established channels; demonstrations, picket lines, and marches are common means of protest. Protesters are younger and more idealistic on average than are other citizens, but they are a very small proportion of the population. Despite America's tradition of free expression, protest activities do not have a high level of public support.

Overall, Americans are only moderately involved in politics. While they are concerned with political affairs, they are mostly immersed in their private pursuits, a reflection in part of a cultural belief in individualism. The lower level of participation among low-income citizens has particular significance in that it works to reduce their influence on public policy and leadership.

KEY TERMS

alienation (*p. 235*)

apathy (*p. 235*)

civic duty (*p. 235*)

political participation (*p. 226*)

registration (*p. 230*)

social capital (*p. 242*)

social (political) movements (*p. 242*)

suffrage (*p. 226*)

voter turnout (*p. 228*)

SUGGESTED READINGS

Bartels, Larry. *Unequal Democracy*. Princeton, N.J.: Princteon University Press, 2008. An analysis that shows just how fully lower-income Americans are neglected by policymakers because of their low participation rates.

Bimber, Bruce, and Richard Davis. *Campaigning Online: The Internet in U.S. Elections*. New York: Oxford University Press, 2003. A careful study of citizens' use of the Internet in elections.

Burns, Nancy, Kay Lehman Schlozman, and Sidney Verba. *The Private Roots of Public Action: Gender, Equality, and Public Action*. Cambridge, Mass.: Harvard University Press, 2001. An analysis of gender differences in political participation.

Franklin, Mark N. *Voter Turnout and the Dynamics of Electoral Competition in Established Democracies Since 1945*. New York: Cambridge University Press, 2004. A comparison of voter participation and its correlates in advanced democracies.

Leighley, Jan. *Strength in Numbers: The Political Mobilization of Racial and Ethnic Minorities*. Princeton, N.J.: Princeton University Press, 2001. A study of the factors that motivate blacks and Hispanics to participate.

Patterson, Thomas E. *The Vanishing Voter*. New York: Knopf, 2002. A study of the trends in electoral participation and what might be done to encourage higher participation levels.

Putnam, Robert. *Bowling Alone*. New York: Simon & Schuster, 2000. A provocative analysis of the trend in civic participation.

Zukin, Cliff, Scott Keeter, Molly Andolina, Krista Jenkins, and Michael X. Delli Carpini. *A New Engagement: Political Participation, Civic Life, and the Changing American Citizen*. New York: Oxford University Press, 2006. A comprehensive study concluding that young adults are finding ways other than election politics to exercise citizenship.

LIST OF WEBSITES

http://www.rockthevote.org/ The website of Rock the Vote, an organization dedicated to helping young people realize and utilize their power to affect the civic and political life of their communities.

http://www.electionstudies.org/ The University of Michigan's National Election Studies (NES) site; provides survey data on voting, public opinion, and political participation.

http://www.vanishingvoter.org/ Harvard University's election study site; provides information on voter participation.

http://www.vote-smart.org/ The website of Project Vote Smart; includes information on Republican and Democratic candidates and officials, as well as the latest in election news.

POLITICS IN THEORY AND PRACTICE

Thinking: Why does economic class—differences in people's incomes—make such a large difference in political participation levels? What are the policy consequences of this difference?

Participating: If you are not currently registered to vote, consider registering. You can obtain a registration form from the election board or clerk in your community of residence. There are several websites that contain state-by-state registration information. One such site is https://electionimpact.votenet.com/declareyourself/voterreg. If you are already registered, consider participating in a registration or voting drive on your campus. Although students typically register and vote at relatively low rates, they will often participate if encouraged by other students to do so.

Extra Credit

For up-to-the-minute *New York Times* articles, interactive simulations, graphics, study tools, and more links and quizzes, visit the text's Online Learning Center at www.mhhe.com/pattersonwtp8e.

The Reappearing Voters

By Thomas E. Patterson

The United States ranks low by comparison with other Western democracies in terms of voter turnout. A number of factors, including differences in registration procedures, account for the difference. Yet, as this reading describes, the 2008 presidential primaries set records for turnout, which could be a sign of Americans' renewed interest in election participation. In addition to being the author of this textbook, the writer directed The Vanishing Voter Project at Harvard University, which sought to explain and encourage involvement in U.S. elections.

The possibility that voter participation might be different in 2008 surfaced in the nation's first nominating contest, the Iowa caucuses. The old participation record was 220,000 voters, set in 2000. Turnout in 2008 was far higher and occurred on a bitterly cold January night. More than 350,000 Iowans braved the winter weather to express their preference for the next president of the United States. In yet another sign of things to come, the youth vote—ballots cast by those under 30 years of age—was three times greater than it had been in 2004.

In percentage terms, Iowa's turnout was not earthshaking—only one in six of the eligible adults participated. The Democratic winner, Barack Obama, received the votes of just 4 percent of Iowa's eligible voters. Mike Huckabee, the Republican victor, attracted the support of a mere 2 percent of Iowa

adults. Nevertheless, the 16.3 percent turnout level was not only an all-time Iowa record, it was easily the highest percentage ever recorded for a presidential caucus, and about eight times the average for such contests.

More than a score of primary and caucus turnout records were set in 2008. Total turnout exceeded 30 million voters, eclipsing the old record by more than 10 million. Ohio had a turnout rate of 40.5 percent, which easily eclipsed the previous high of 28.4 percent who voted in 1976. Rhode Island's 28.5 percent topped that state's previous best of 11.5 percent, also set in 1976. So many states set records, in fact, that it is simpler to list those that did not do so. Among the few that failed to reach a new high were California, where 41.7 percent turned out, compared with 46.0 percent in 1964; Wisconsin, where 36.5 percent of the voting-eligible population went to the polls, compared with 48.8 percent in 1972, and Maryland, where the participation rate was 27.3 percent, compared with 29.9 percent in 1964.

Tempering the record-setting was the fact that many of the states that set new records did not have a long record of presidential primaries. Arizona's primary, for example, was only the third such contest in that state. Nevertheless, the overall turnout level across all the primaries was impressive. The overall rate was roughly 30 percent, a 10 percentage point increase over the previous election.

To a degree, the turnout increase had roots in the 2004 campaign. The nominating contests in 2004 did not set records; Bush ran unopposed on the Republican side and turnout quickly collapsed on the Democratic side when it became obvious that John Kerry had a lock on the nomination. However, there was a sharp upturn in turnout in the general election. More than 120 million Americans cast a ballot, the largest number on record. In percentage terms, turnout was far below the historical record, but it was nonetheless the highest since the 1960s. Over 60 percent of the voting-eligible population went to the polls in November. Voting in 2004 was stimulated by concerns over the war in Iraq, a weakening economy, and a polarizing president—the gap in George W. Bush's presidential approval rating between Republicans and Democrats was the highest ever recorded for any president in the history of the Gallup Poll.

These issues carried into the 2008 campaign, which had an added feature. It was the first presidential election since 1952 in which neither the incumbent president nor the incumbent vice president was a candidate, thus assuring a competitive race for the nomination of both parties. Moreover, two of the candidates represented historic firsts. Barack Obama was the first candidate of his race to have a realistic chance of winning a major-party presidential nomination. Hillary Clinton was his female equivalent—the first woman to have a realistic chance.

The unpredictability of the race added to the drama. The outcome of the Republican and Democratic nominating contests was by no means certain in early 2007 when most of the candidates announced they were running. The Democratic lineup, in addition to Obama and Clinton, included John Edwards, the party's 2004 vice-presidential nominee, who had a well-funded campaign and a finely honed campaign message. On the Republican side, John McCain was the early favorite, but he faced strong opposition from his party's conservatives and then had difficulty raising funds, casting doubt on his ability to win the GOP nomination.

The first contests did not have the clear-cut outcome they usually do, which meant the candidates went into Super Tuesday—which, in 2008, included a record twenty-one contests—without a certified frontrunner. These early February contests helped clarify the Republican race. McCain did not run so strongly as to obliterate his opposition, but he took a commanding delegate lead that

put Mitt Romney and Mike Huckabee in enough of a hole that Romney dropped out of the race two days later, while Huckabee limped along before quitting in early March. Even so, the Republican candidates went thirty-eight states into the schedule before McCain emerged unopposed. Not since 1976 had a Republican nominating race been that prolonged. The Democratic race also lasted longer than any such race since 1976, going all the way through the schedule of contests without either Clinton or Obama locking up the delegate votes needed for nomination.

In addition to being treated to a primary season in which nearly every state contest counted, voters experienced a mammoth campaign, particularly on the Democratic side. Clinton and even more so Obama proved to be prodigious fundraisers, which enabled them to mount television and grass-roots campaigns of unprecedented scope. The two Democrats, Obama particularly, showed an ability to bring new voters into the campaign. First-time voters for Obama were disproportionately black or young. Clinton's first-time voters were disproportionately women. In the process, the shape of the nominating electorate, as well as its size, was altered.

Young voters also figured prominently in the 2008 races. Voters under 30 years of age were not overrepresented relative to their numbers in the adult population, but neither were they greatly underrepresented, which is typically the case. They voted at a rate that was only a few percentage points under what it would have been if they had voted in numbers equal to their population share. Obama's candidacy has been widely credited for drawing young adults to the polls in 2008, and there is nothing in the primary election polls to indicate otherwise. In the Democratic primaries, Obama attracted the vote of roughly three in every five young adults.

Participation in the 2008 nominating races will contribute to higher turnout in future elections. The large numbers of first-time voters augurs well for 2012 and beyond. Studies have found that once citizens cast their first ballot, the odds increase they will participate in subsequent elections. There is a caveat, however. As the political scientist Austin Ranney noted, the nominating system, is "consciously designed to maximize participation by persons who are enthusiasts for a particular aspirant *in the year of the convention.*" Ranney's observation speaks to the probable long-term effects of the rise in participation in 2008. The influx of additional voters in 2008 is attributable to the election's unique features: an unpopular war in Iraq, a wobbly economy, the historical firsts represented by the Obama and Clinton candidacies, and competitive races in both parties. When the influence of these factors wanes, which is likely to occur as early as the 2012 campaign, a return to something closer to the normal pattern of presidential nominating races can be expected.

The primary electorate is less stable than the general electorate. The election-to-election variation in turnout for primary elections is much higher than that of general elections. The 2008 nominating contests set record highs that are unlikely to be topped or even approached in the foreseeable future because the power of the combined circumstances that generated extraordinarily high levels of participation in 2008 is unlikely to be equaled any time soon. The participation falloff might even be larger than in past elections. Sandwiched between the upswings in voting in the 2004 and 2008 presidential elections was a small increase in turnout voting in the 2006 midterm elections and a downturn in voting in the 2005 and 2007 local elections—indeed, turnout in 2007 apparently was the lowest in modern times at the local level. This pattern might indicate that today's voters could be more selective than those of earlier generations, choosing to participate or not participate based on their sense of the significance of an election rather than a sense that they should vote at every opportunity.

What's Your Opinion?

Would a change in the structure of the presidential nominating system serve to boost turnout on a permanent basis? Would a national primary, rather than the current system of sequenced state primaries, bring out more voters? Would a national primary have drawbacks that might make it a bad idea, even if it contributed to sustained higher turnout levels?

CHAPTER 8

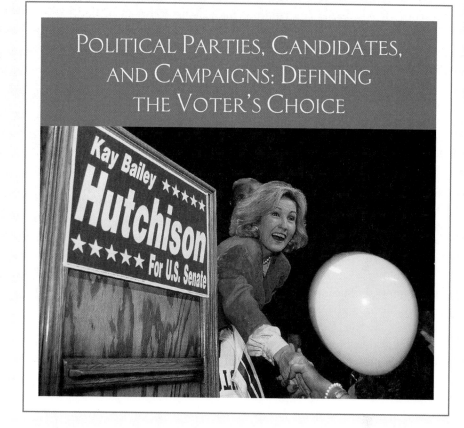

POLITICAL PARTIES, CANDIDATES, AND CAMPAIGNS: DEFINING THE VOTER'S CHOICE

66 Political parties created democracy and . . . modern democracy is unthinkable save in terms of the parties. 99

E. E. SCHATTSCHNEIDER[1]

Nine hundred miles and a week apart, they faced off, each offering its own plan for a better America.

The Democrats met first, in Denver, Colorado. Their 2008 platform included pledges to draw down U.S. forces in Iraq, bring health coverage to millions of uninsured Americans, combat global warming, and create more jobs and higher wages for working families. The Democrats chose Illinois senator Barack Obama, the first African American ever to be chosen for the position, as their presidential nominee. Their vice presidential nominee was Joe Biden, senator from Delaware, who was put on the ticket to deliver northern voters.

The Republicans met in Minnesota's capital city, St. Paul. They selected Arizona senator John McCain as their nominee and Sarah Palin, the governor of Alaska, as his running mate. The Republican platform included promises to keep taxes low, limit abortions, expand parental school choice, stimulate the business sector, and provide the Iraq government with the U.S. military support needed for it to succeed.

The political parties, as their nominees and platforms illustrate, are in the business of offering the voting public a choice. Each party seeks to define itself in a way that will attract majority support. Competition between the parties is the mechanism through which the electorate gets its say in governing. A **political party** is an ongoing coalition of interests joined together in an effort to get its candidates for public office elected under a common label.[2] By offering a choice between policies and leaders, parties give voters a chance to influence the direction of government. "It is the competition of [parties] that provides the people with an opportunity to make a choice," political scientist E. E. Schattschneider wrote. "Without this opportunity popular sovereignty amounts to nothing."[3]

This chapter examines political parties and the candidates who run under their banners. U.S. campaigns are **party-centered politics** in the sense that the Republican and Democratic parties compete across the country election after election. Yet campaigns are also **candidate-centered politics** in the sense that individual candidates devise their own strategies, choose their own issues, and form their own campaign organizations. The following points are emphasized in this chapter:

★ *Political competition in the United States has centered on two parties, a pattern that is explained by the nature of America's electoral system, political institutions, and political culture.* Minor parties exist in the United States but have been unable to compete successfully for governing power.

★ *To win an electoral majority, candidates of the two major parties must appeal to a diverse set of interests.* This necessity has normally led them to advocate moderate and somewhat overlapping policies, although this tendency has weakened in recent years.

★ *U.S. party organizations are decentralized and fragmented.* The national organization is a loose collection of state organizations, which in turn are loose associations of local organizations. This feature of U.S. parties can be traced to federalism and the nation's diversity, which have made it difficult for the parties to act as instruments of national power.

★ *The ability of America's party organizations to control nominations and election to office is weak, which in turn enhances the candidates' role.*

★ *Candidate-centered campaigns are based on money and media and utilize the skills of professional consultants.*

PARTY COMPETITION AND MAJORITY RULE: THE HISTORY OF U.S. PARTIES

Through their numbers, citizens have the potential for great influence, but that potential cannot be realized unless they act together. Parties give them that capacity. When Americans go to the polls, they have a choice between the Republican and Democratic parties. This **party competition** narrows their options to two and in the process enables people with different backgrounds and opinions to unite behind one of the options. In casting a majority of its votes for one party, the electorate chooses that party's candidates, philosophy, and policies over those of the opposing party.

The history of democratic government is synonymous with the history of parties. When the countries of Eastern Europe gained their freedom from the Soviet Union in the early 1990s, one of their first steps toward democracy was the legalization of parties. When the United States was founded over two centuries ago, the formation of parties was also a first step toward the building of its democracy. The reason is simple: it is the competition among parties that gives popular majorities a choice over how they will be governed.[4] If there were no mechanism like the party to enable citizens to act as one, they would be powerless—each too weak to influence government.

The First Parties

America's early leaders mistrusted parties. George Washington in his farewell address warned the nation of the "baneful effects" of parties, and James Madison likened parties to special interests. However, Madison's misgivings about parties gradually gave way to a grudging admiration. He came to realize that parties enabled like-minded people to work together.

Historical Background

America's parties originated in the rivalry within George Washington's administration between Thomas Jefferson, a supporter of states' rights and small landholders, and Alexander Hamilton, a promoter of strong national government and commercial interests (see Figure 8-1). When Hamilton's ideas prevailed in Congress, Jefferson and his followers formed a political party, the Republicans. By adopting this label, which was associated with popular government, the Jeffersonians sought to portray themselves as the rightful heirs to the American Revolution's legacy of self-government.

Hamilton then organized his supporters into a formal party—the Federalists—and in the process created America's first competitive party system. The Federalists took their name from the faction that had supported

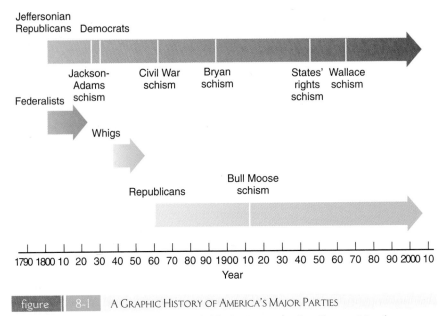

figure   8-1   A GRAPHIC HISTORY OF AMERICA'S MAJOR PARTIES

The U.S. party system has been remarkable for its continuity. Competition between two major parties has been a persistent feature of the system.

ratification of the Constitution, thereby implying that they represented America's governing tradition. However, the Federalists' preoccupation with commercial and moneyed interests fueled Jefferson's claim that the Federalists were bent on establishing a government of the rich and well-born. After Jefferson in the election of 1800 defeated John Adams, who had succeeded Washington as president, the Federalists never again controlled the White House or Congress.

During the so-called Era of Good Feeling, when James Monroe ran unopposed in 1820 for a second presidential term, it appeared as if the political system might operate without parties. Yet by the end of Monroe's second term, policy differences had split the Republicans. The dominant faction, led by Andrew Jackson, retained Jefferson's commitment to the interests of ordinary people. This faction called itself Democratic Republicans, later shortened to Democrats. Thus, the Republican Party of Jefferson is the forerunner of today's Democratic Party rather than of today's Republican Party.

Andrew Jackson and Grassroots Parties

Jackson's goal was to wrest political power from the established elite—all the presidents before him had come from old-line Virginia and Massachusetts families. Jackson wanted a government closer to the people, and he saw the party as the instrument for this transformation, recognizing that it could be used to mobilize them behind like-minded candidates. Whereas Jefferson's party had been well organized only at the leadership level, Jackson sought a party that was built from the bottom up. It would be a **grassroots party.** Jackson's Democratic Party consisted of organizations at the local, state, and national levels, with membership open to all eligible voters. These organizations, along with more liberal suffrage laws, contributed to a nearly fourfold rise in voter turnout during the 1830s.[5] At the peak of Jacksonian democracy, Alexis de Tocqueville wrote, "The People reign in the American political world as the Deity does in the universe."[6]

During this period, a new opposition party, the Whigs, emerged to challenge the Democrats. The Whigs were a catchall party whose followers were united not by a coherent philosophy of their own but by their opposition for one reason or another to Jackson and his followers. However, competition between the Whigs and the Democrats was relatively short-lived. During the 1850s, the slavery issue began to tear both parties apart. The Whig Party withered, and a northern-based new party, calling itself Republican, arose as the main challenger to the Democrats. In the 1860 presidential election, the Democratic Party's northern faction nominated Stephen A. Douglas, who held that the question of whether a new territory would permit slavery was for its voters to decide, while the southern faction nominated John C. Breckinridge, who called for legalized slavery in all territories. The Democratic vote split sharply along regional lines between these two candidates—with the result that the Republican nominee, Abraham Lincoln, who had called for the gradual elimination of slavery, was able to win the presidency with only 40 percent of the popular vote. Lincoln's election prompted the southern states to secede from the Union, which led to the Civil War.

The Civil War was the first and only time in the nation's history that the party system failed to peaceably resolve Americans' political conflicts. The issue of slavery was too explosive to be settled through electoral competition. Every time before and since, Americans have worked out their differences by freely electing the political party they thought would better represent them.[7]

Republicans Versus Democrats: Realignments and the Enduring Party System

After the Civil War, the nation settled into the pattern of competition between the Republican and Democratic parties that has lasted till today. The durability of these two parties is due not to their ideological consistency but to their remarkable ability to adapt during periods of crisis. By abandoning at these crucial times their old ways of doing things, the Republican and Democratic parties have repeatedly remade themselves—with new bases of support, new policies, and new public philosophies.

These periods of great political change are known as *realignments*. A **party realignment** involves four basic elements:

1. The disruption of the existing political order because of the emergence of one or more unusually powerful and divisive issues
2. An election contest in which the voters shift their support strongly in favor of one party
3. A major change in policy brought about through the action of the stronger party
4. An enduring change in the party coalitions, which works to the lasting advantage of the dominant party

Realignments are rare. They do not occur simply because one party wrests control of government from the other. They involve deep and lasting changes in the party system that affect not just the most recent election but later ones as well. By this standard, there have been three clear-cut realignments since the 1850s.

The first of these, the Civil War realignment, brought about a thorough change in the party system. The Republicans replaced the Democrats as the nation's majority party. The Republicans dominated the larger and more populous North, while the Democrats were left with a stronghold in what became known as "the Solid South." During the next three decades, the Republicans held the presidency except for Grover Cleveland's two terms in office and had a majority in Congress for all but four years.

The 1896 election resulted in a second realignment of the Republican-Democratic party system. Three years earlier, an economic panic following a bank collapse had resulted in a severe depression. The Democrat Cleveland was president when the crash happened, and people blamed him and his party. In the aftermath, the Republicans made additional gains in the Northeast and Midwest, solidifying their position as the nation's dominant party. During the four decades between the 1890s realignment and the next one in the 1930s, the Republicans held the presidency except for Woodrow Wilson's two terms and had a majority in Congress for all but six years.

The Great Depression of the 1930s triggered yet another realignment of the American party system. The Republican Herbert Hoover was president during the stock market crash of 1929, and many Americans blamed Hoover, his party, and its business allies for the economic catastrophe

★ | LEADERS

Abraham Lincoln
(1809–65)

Abraham Lincoln had been a member of Congress from Illinois before he was elected to the presidency in 1860. Homely and gangly, Lincoln is regarded by many as America's greatest president for his principled leadership during the Civil War. Lincoln's accomplishments are all the more remarkable in that, unlike earlier presidents, he came from a humble background. His father was a frontiersman, his mother died when he was ten, and he was largely self-schooled. His greatest legacy is the preservation of the American Union. The Emancipation Proclamation and the Gettysburg Address are two of his other legacies. He was assassinated at Ford's Theater in the nation's capital shortly after the start of his second term as president. Lincoln was the first Republican elected to the presidency, and his successful pursuit of victory in the Civil War led to a party realignment that solidified the GOP's status as the nation's majority party.

that followed. The Democrats became the country's majority party. Their political and policy agenda called for an expanded role for the national government. Franklin D. Roosevelt's presidency was characterized by unprecedented policy initiatives in the areas of business regulation and social welfare (see Chapter 3). His election in 1932 began a thirty-six-year period of Democratic presidencies that was interrupted only by Dwight D. Eisenhower's two terms in the 1950s. In this period, the Democrats also dominated Congress, losing control only in 1947–48 and 1953–54.

The reason realignments have such a substantial effect on future elections is that they affect voters' *party identification* (see Chapter 6). Young voters in particular tend to identify with the newly ascendant party and to retain that identity, giving the party a solid base of support for years to come. First-time voters in the 1930s came to identify with the Democratic Party by a two-to-one margin, establishing it as the nation's majority party and enabling it to dominate national politics for the next three decades.[8]

The new order begins: Franklin D. Roosevelt rides to his inauguration with outgoing president Herbert Hoover after the realigning election of 1932.

Today's Party Alignment and Its Origins

A party realignment inevitably loses strength over time as the issues that gave rise to it decline in importance. By the late 1960s, with the Democratic Party divided over the Vietnam War and civil rights, it was apparent that the era of New Deal politics was ending.[9]

The change was most dramatic in the South. The region had been solidly Democratic at all levels since the Civil War, but the Democratic Party's leadership on civil rights angered white conservatives. In the 1964 presidential election, five southern states voted Republican, and the South is now a Republican bastion in presidential politics. The Republican Party also made gains, though more gradually, in elections for other offices in the South. Today most top officials in the region are Republicans.

More slowly and less completely, the northeastern states have become more Democratic. The shift is partly attributable to the growing size of minority populations in the Northeast. But it is also due to the declining influence of the Republican Party's moderate wing, which was concentrated in these states. As southern conservatives became Republican in ever larger numbers, the party's stands on social issues such as abortion and affirmative action tilted toward the right, reducing the party's appeal to the Northeast's progressive Republicans, some of whom shifted their loyalty to the Democratic Party.[10]

Party conflict also extended to federal spending on education, health, and economic security programs. The Democrats, who had started nearly all of these programs, defended them, while Republicans attacked them as being too expensive. Taxing and spending became perennial campaign issues, resulting in a further alignment of liberals against conservatives.

The net result of these changes has been a remaking of the party landscape, but the pattern is not that of a classic party realignment. Rather than occurring abruptly in response to a disruptive issue, as was the case in the 1860s, 1890s, and 1930s realignments, the change has taken place gradually and is the product of several issues rather than an overriding disruptive one. But the cumulative result—a reshuffling of the parties' coalitions and platforms—is similar to that of a realignment. In effect, America's parties have realigned without going through the sudden shock of a realigning election.

The GOP (short for "Grand Old Party" and another name for the Republican Party) has gained the most from these changes in party politics. For three decades after the Great Depression, the GOP was decidedly the weaker party. Since 1968, however, Republicans have held the presidency for over twice as many years as the Democrats. The GOP has had less success at the congressional level, but during the past two decades, it has had roughly the same number of Senate seats and only about 5 percent fewer House seats than the Democrats.

On the other hand, the Republican Party has failed to duplicate the success that the advantaged party enjoyed in the realigments of the 1860s, 1890s, and 1930s. Twice it has appeared to be on the verge of becoming the clearly dominant party, only to fall back because of missteps on the part of top leaders. After winning the presidency in 1968 and 1972, Republican Richard Nixon became embroiled in the Watergate affair and was forced to resign, the first and only president to do so. The Republicans lost a huge number of congressional seats in the 1974 midterm election and did not recover the lost ground until the 1980s. A smaller setback occurred in 1992 when a weak economy enabled Democrat Bill Clinton to defeat incumbent George H. W. Bush in the presidential election. The Republicans won back the presidency in 2000 while also making gains in the 2000 and 2002 congressional elections. However, the Iraq invasion ordered by President George W. Bush in 2003 proved increasingly unpopular, contributing to Republicans' loss of the House and Senate in the 2006 midterm elections and the loss of additional congressional seats and the presidency in the 2008 election.

The Iraq conflict also blunted Republicans' hopes of capturing Americans' partisan loyalties. After trailing the Democrats for years, the Republicans by 2004 had narrowed the partisan gap—Democratic identifiers outnumbered Republican identifiers by only 2 percentage points in the Gallup poll

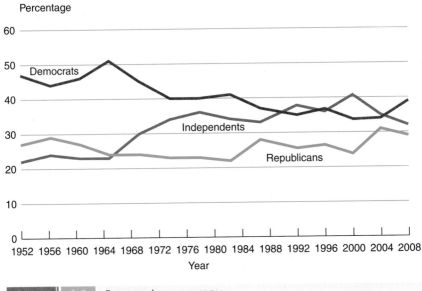

figure 8-2 PARTISAN IDENTIFICATION

After trailing for decades, Republican identifiers nearly reached parity with Democratic identifiers in 2004, only to fall behind again as Iraq and other issues worked to the Democrats' advantage. Of the roughly one-third of voters who describe themselves as Independents, most also say they "lean" toward one of the two major parties. The leaners divide almost evenly between the two parties. *Source: National Election Studies, 1952–2000; Gallup surveys, after 2000.*

(see Figure 8-2). As discontent with Iraq grew, however, the trend reversed, and the Democrats' lead had widened substantially by the 2008 election.[11]

Analysts differ in their opinions on where the party system is heading in the long run. Some predict a period of Republican dominance after the GOP gets past its current problems and is able to refocus the public's attention on the issues that worked for it before the Iraq war disrupted its momentum.[12] Others foresee a resurgent Democratic Party fueled by the increased voting power of Hispanics and young adults, who lean Democratic.[13] One thing is virtually certain: as they have for over 150 years, Americans will continue to look to the Republican and Democratic parties for political leadership. The enduring strength and appeal of the two major parties is a hallmark of American politics.

Parties and the Vote

The power of party is at no time clearer than when, election after election, Republican and Democratic candidates reap the vote of their party's identifiers. In the 2008 presidential election, John McCain had the support of more than 85 percent of Republican Party identifiers, while Barack Obama garnered the votes of more than 85 percent of self-identified Democrats. Major-party candidates do not always do that well with party loyalists, but it is relatively rare—in congressional races as well as in the presidential race—for a party nominee to get less than 80 percent of the partisan vote.

Even the "independents" are less independent than might be assumed. In polls, when asked whether they are a Republican, a Democrat, or an independent, about a third of Americans say they are independents. However, in the follow-up question that asks whether they lean more toward the Republican Party or more toward the Democratic Party, about two in three independents say they lean toward one of the parties. Moreover, most of these independents vote in the direction they lean. In recent presidential elections, more than eight in ten leaners have backed the candidate of the party to which they feel closer. In other words, the number of true independents is no more than about a sixth of the electorate.

There was a period in the 1970s when the number of true independents was larger. It was a time when many otherwise Democrats were disillusioned with their party over the Vietnam War or civil rights, and many otherwise Republicans were disheartened by the Watergate scandal. During this period, there was a sharp rise in the number of voters in federal elections who cast a **split ticket,** that is, voted for one party's presidential candidate and the other party's congressional candidate. Some analysts described this development as a sign of *dealignment*—a weakening of partisanship.[14] Since 1980, however, this kind of ticket splitting has fallen from slightly under 30 percent of voters to an average of less than 20 percent of voters, which is only somewhat above the level of the 1950s (see Figure 8-3).

Nevertheless, some voters in every election are swayed by the issues of the moment. Voters respond to issues both prospectively and retrospectively. **Prospective voting** occurs when the voter chooses a candidate on the basis of what the candidate promises to do if elected. In contrast, **retrospective voting** is based on a judgment about past performance—the situation in which a voter supports the incumbent officeholder or party when pleased with its performance and opposes it when displeased. Retrospective voting is the more common form of issue voting. When things are going poorly with the country, particularly when the economy is bad, voters are inclined to want a change in leadership. In good economic times, incumbents have less to fear. Studies have found, for example, that a weak economy in 1992 contributed to the defeat of incumbent President George H. W. Bush and that a strong economy in 1996 underpinned incumbent President Bill Clinton's successful bid for a second term. The 2008 presidential election was somewhat unusual

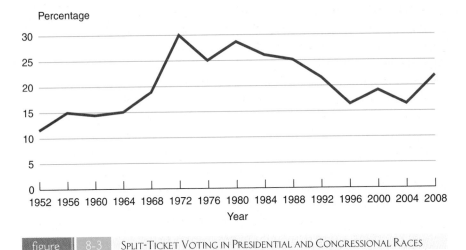

Percentage

figure ‖ **8-3** SPLIT-TICKET VOTING IN PRESIDENTIAL AND CONGRESSIONAL RACES

The level of split-ticket voting, as measured by the percentage who backed one party's candidate for president and the other party's candidate for the House of Representatives, has declined in recent elections. The change reflects an increased level of partisanship among America's voters. *Source: National Election Studies, except 2008 percentage, which is based on exit polls.*

in that two large problems had developed during the George W. Bush's presidency—a weakened economy and an unsettled Iraq situation. Both issues worked to out-party candidate Barack Obama's advantage.

ELECTORAL AND PARTY SYSTEMS

The United States traditionally has had a **two-party system:** Federalists versus Jeffersonian Republicans, Whigs versus Democrats, Republicans versus Democrats. These have not been the only American parties, but they have been the only ones with a realistic chance of acquiring political control. A two-party system, however, is the exception rather than the rule (see "How the United States Compares"). Most democracies have a **multiparty system,** in which three or more parties have the capacity to gain control of government, separately or in coalition. Why the difference? Why are there three or more major parties in most democracies but only two in the United States?

The Single-Member-District System of Election

America's two-party system is due largely to the fact that the nation chooses its officials through plurality voting in **single-member districts.** Each constituency elects a single member to a particular office, such

HOW THE UNITED STATES COMPARES

Party Systems

For nearly 160 years, electoral competition in the United States has centered on the Republican and Democratic parties. By comparison, most democracies have a multiparty system, in which three or more parties receive substantial support from voters. The difference is significant. In a two-party system, the parties tend to have overlapping coalitions and programs, because each party must appeal to the middle-of-the-road voters who provide the margin of victory. In multiparty systems, particularly those with four or more strong parties, the parties tend to separate themselves as each tries to secure the enduring loyalty of voters who have a particular viewpoint.

Whether a country has a two-party or a multiparty system depends on several factors, but particularly the nature of its electoral system. The United States has a single-member, plurality district system in which only the top vote getter in a district gets elected. This system is biased against smaller parties; even if they have some support in a great many races, they win nothing unless one of their candidates places first in an electoral district. By comparison, proportional representation systems enable smaller parties to compete; each party acquires legislative seats in proportion to its share of the total vote. All the countries in the chart that have four or more parties also have a proportional representation system of election.

Number of Competitive Parties

Two	Three	Four or More
United States	Canada (at times)	Belgium
	Great Britain	Denmark
		France
		Germany
		Italy
		Netherlands
		Sweden

as U.S. senator or state representative; the candidate with the most votes (a plurality) in a district wins the office. This system discourages minor parties. Assume, for example, that a minor party received exactly 20 percent of the vote in each of the nation's 435 congressional races. Even though one in five voters nationwide backed the minor party, it would not win any seats in Congress because none of its candidates placed first in any of the 435 single-member-district races. The winning candidate in each race would be the major-party candidate who received the bigger share of the remaining 80 percent of the vote.

By comparison, most European democracies use some form of **proportional representation,** in which seats in the legislature are allocated according to a party's share of the popular vote. This type of electoral system enables smaller parties to compete for power. In the 2005 German elections, for example, the Green Party received 8 percent of the national vote and thereby won 51 seats in the 603-seat Bundestag, the German parliament. If the Greens had been competing under American electoral rules, they would not have won any seats.

Politics and Coalitions in the Two-Party System

The overriding goal of a major American party is to gain power by getting its candidates elected to office. Because there are only two major parties, however, the Republicans or Democrats can win consistently only by attracting majority support. In Europe's multiparty systems, a party can hope for a share of power if it has the firm backing of a minority faction. In the United States, if either party confines its support to a narrow segment of society, it forfeits its chance of gaining control of government.

Seeking the Center American parties, Clinton Rossiter said, are "creatures of compromise."[15] The two parties usually take stands that have broad appeal or at least will not alienate significant blocs of voters. Anytime a party makes a pronounced shift toward either extreme, the political center is left open for the opposing party. Barry Goldwater, the Republican presidential nominee in 1964, proposed the elimination of mandatory social security and said he might consider the tactical use of small nuclear weapons in wars such as the Vietnam conflict—extreme positions that cost him many votes. Eight years later, the Democratic nominee, George McGovern, took positions on Vietnam and income security that alarmed many voters; like Goldwater, he was buried in one of the biggest landslides in presidential history.

It is impossible to understand the dynamics of the U.S. party system without recognizing that the true balance of power in American elections rests with the moderate voters in the center rather than with those who hold more extreme positions. When congressional Republicans mistook their 1994 election victory as a mandate to trim assistance programs for the elderly, the poor, and children, they alienated many of the moderate voters who had contributed to their 1994 victory. These voters wanted "less" government but not a government that punished society's most vulnerable citizens. After weak showings in the 1996 and 1998 elections, congressional Republicans shifted course. They unseated Speaker Newt Gingrich, replacing him with a more pragmatic conservative, Dennis Hastert. "We still need to prove that we can be conservative without being mean," was how one Republican member of Congress described the change in strategy.[16] The adjustment reflects a basic truth about U.S. politics: party ideology is acceptable as long as it is tinged with moderation.

Nonetheless, the Republican and Democratic parties do offer somewhat different alternatives and, at times, a clear choice. When Roosevelt was elected president in 1932, Lyndon Johnson in 1964, and Ronald Reagan in 1980, the parties were relatively far apart in their priorities and programs. Roosevelt's New Deal, for example, was an extreme alternative within the American political tradition and caused a decisive split along party lines. A lesson of these periods is that the center of the American political spectrum can be moved. Candidates risk a crushing defeat by straying too far from established ideas during normal times, but they may do so with some chance of success during turbulent times. The terrorist attacks of September 11, 2001, provided President George W. Bush with just such an opportunity. During his first term, Bush pushed major tax cuts through Congress and also sharply increased defense spending while pursuing an aggressive Middle East policy, backed at every step by congressional Republicans.

When he sought reelection in 2004, Bush pursued the unusual strategy, at least in American politics, of mobilizing his conservative base rather than reaching out to moderates. He won the election, though narrowly. His victory margin was the smallest for a seated president since Woodrow Wilson's reelection in 1916. But Bush's strategy haunted his second term when moderates and independents in increasing numbers turned away from his Iraq policy. When moderates and independents then voted disproportionately Democratic in the 2006 midterm elections, the Republicans lost control of both the House and the Senate. The Bush presidency is a reminder that parties do not always govern toward the center, but it is also a reminder that a party can create trouble for itself by moving away from the center.

Party Coalitions   The groups and interests that support a party are collectively referred to as the **party coalition.** In multiparty systems, each party is supported by a relatively narrow range of interests. European parties tend to divide along class lines, with the center and right parties drawing most of their votes from the middle and upper classes and the left parties drawing most of theirs from the working class. By comparison, America's two-party system requires each party to accommodate a wide range of interests in order to gain the voting plurality necessary to win elections. The Republican and Democratic coalitions are therefore relatively broad. Each includes a substantial proportion of voters of nearly every ethnic, religious, regional, and economic grouping. Only a few groups are tightly aligned with a party. African Americans are the clearest example; they vote about 85 percent Democratic in national elections.

Although the Republican and Democratic coalitions overlap, they are hardly identical (see Figure 8-4). The party coalitions have been forged

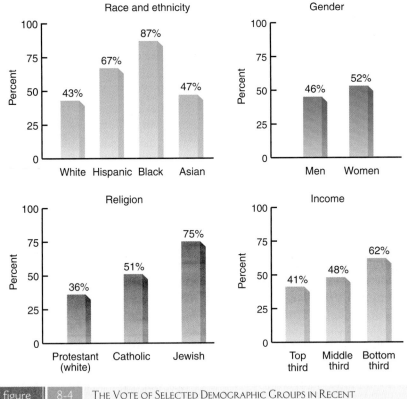

figure   8-4   THE VOTE OF SELECTED DEMOGRAPHIC GROUPS IN RECENT PRESIDENTIAL ELECTIONS

Although the Democratic and Republican coalitions overlap substantially, there are important differences, as illustrated by the Democratic Party's percentage of the two-party vote among some major demographic groups in recent elections. *Source: Compiled by author from NES and other surveys.*

primarily through conflict over the federal government's role in solving social and economic problems. Each party has supported government action to promote economic security and social equality, but the Democrats have favored a greater level of government involvement. Virtually every major assistance program for the poor, the elderly, and low-wage workers since the 1930s has been initiated by the Democrats. Accordingly, the Democratic coalition draws support disproportionately from society's underdogs—blacks, union members, the poor, city dwellers, Hispanics, Jews, and other "minorities."[17] For a long period, the Democratic Party was also the clear choice of the nation's elderly as a result of its support for old-age assistance programs and because the basic political loyalties of the elderly were acquired during the New Deal era, a period favorable to the Democrats. Recently, however, elderly voters have split their vote about evenly between the parties.

The Democratic Party's biggest gains recently have been among women, whose voting pattern traditionally was very similar to that of men. Recent elections, however, have revealed a gender gap (see Chapter 6). Women have voted disproportionately for the Democratic Party, apparently as a result of its positions on issues such as abortion rights, education spending, employment policies, and gun control.

The Republican coalition consists mainly of white middle-class Americans. The GOP has historically been the party of tax cuts and business incentives. It has also been more supportive of traditional values, as reflected, for example, in its opposition to abortion and to civil unions. Not surprisingly, the GOP is strongest in the suburbs and in regions, such as the South, the Great Plains, and the Rocky Mountains, where belief in traditional values and low taxes is prevalent.

The Republican Party has made big gains in recent decades among white fundamentalist Christians, who have been drawn to the GOP by its positions on abortion, school prayer, same-sex marriage, stem cell research, and other social issues.[18] In recent presidential elections, the Republican nominee has garnered the votes of roughly three-fourths of fundamentalist Christians.

Minor (Third) Parties

Although the U.S. electoral system discourages the formation of third parties (or, as they are more properly called, minor parties), the nation has always had them—more than a thousand over its history.[19] Most minor parties have been short-lived, and only a few have had a lasting impact. Only one minor party, the Republican Party, has ever achieved majority status.

Minor parties in the United States have formed largely to promote policies that their followers believe are not being adequately represented by either of the two major parties. A major party is always somewhat captive to its past, which is the source of many of its ideas and most of its followers. When conditions change, major parties can be slow to respond, and a minor party can try to capitalize on neglected issues. Whatever success it achieves, however, is usually short-lived. If a minor party gains a following, one or both major parties typically awaken to its issue, at which time the minor party begins to lose support. Nevertheless, the minor party will have served the purpose of making the major parties more responsive to the public's concerns.

Some minor parties have been virtually "antiparties" in the sense that they arose out of a belief that partisan politics is a corrupting influence. The most influential of these **reform parties** was the Progressive Party, which was as much a political movement as a political party. In the early 1900s, it succeeded in achieving its antiparty agenda in many states and localities. Primary elections, recall elections, nonpartisan elections, initiatives, and popular referendums, discussed in Chapter 2, were among the Progressive's contributions. A more recent reform party was titled just that, the Reform Party. It was created by Ross Perot after he ran as an independent and garnered 19 percent of the vote in the 1992 presidential election (second only to Theodore Roosevelt's 27 percent in 1912 among minor-party candidates). Perot's platform was based on middle-class discontent with the major parties' lack of fiscal restraint. Perot ran again in 1996, this time as the Reform Party's nominee, and won 8 percent of the vote. When Perot chose not to run in 2000, a divisive fight ensued over the Reform Party's nomination, which Pundit Pat Buchanan received. His reactionary platform attracted only 1 percent of the general election vote and nearly wrecked the Reform Party. Since then, it has been trying without much success to rebuild its base.

Historical
Background

Minor parties were at their peak in the nineteenth century, when the party system was still in flux.[20] Many of these parties were **single-issue parties** formed around a lone issue of overriding interest to their followers. The Free Soil Party, which fought the extension of slavery into new territories, and the Greenback Party, which wanted the currency system to be based on paper money rather than gold and silver, are examples. One of these nineteenth-century parties, the Prohibition Party, persisted into the twentieth century and contributed to the ratification in 1919 of the Eighteenth Amendment, which prohibited the manufacture, sale, and transportation of alcoholic beverages (but which was repealed in 1933). Although single-issue parties (for example, the Right to Life Party) exist today, they do not have large followings or much influence. The role that single-issue parties played in the nineteenth century is now played by single-issue interest groups (see Chapter 9).

Although the United States has long had a two-party system, numerous minor parties have surfaced. A few of them have been influential, including the Free Soil Party, which emerged before the Civil War with a platform that called for the abolition of slavery in new states and territories. Shown here is a Free Soil Party poster from the 1848 election. The party's presidential nominee was Martin Van Buren, who had been president from 1837 to 1841 as a member of the Democratic Party.

Other minor parties have been characterized by their ideological commitment to a broad and noncentrist philosophical position, such as redistribution of economic resources. Modern-day **ideological parties** include the Citizens Party, the Socialist Workers Party, and the Libertarian Party, each of which operates on the fringes of American politics. One of the strongest ideological parties in the nation's history was the Populist Party. Its candidate in the 1892 presidential election, James B. Weaver, gained 8.5 percent of the national vote and won twenty-two electoral votes in six western states. The party began as an agrarian protest movement in response to an economic depression and the anger of small farmers over low commodity prices, tight credit, and the high rates charged by railroad monopolies to transport farm goods. The Populists' ideological platform called for government ownership of

the railroads, a graduated income tax, low tariffs on imports, and elimination of the gold standard.[21]

The strongest minor party today is the Green Party, an ideological party
that holds liberal positions on the environment, labor, taxation, social welfare, and other issues. Its 2000 presidential nominee, consumer rights advocate Ralph Nader, received 3 percent of the national vote. According to
polls, Nader (who ran as an Independent in 2004) got most of his support
from voters who otherwise would have backed Democrat Al Gore, thus
tipping the election to the more conservative Republican nominee, George
W. Bush. In 2004, the Green Party decided to compete in the presidential
race, but in a way designed to reduce the chance of tipping the election to
the Republicans. The Green Party rejected Nader's bid for its 2004 nomination, choosing instead Green Party activist David Cobb, a little-known
Texas lawyer. In 2008, the Green Party nominated Cynthia McKinney, an
African American who had been a Democratic member of Congress from
Georgia. Her campaign attracted only limited support.

The most important minor parties have been **factional parties,** created by a split within one of the major parties. Although the Republican
and Democratic parties are normally adept at managing internal divisions,
there have been times when internal conflict has led some of its followers to
break away and form their own party. The most successful of these factional
parties at the polls was Theodore Roosevelt's Bull Moose Party.[22] In 1908,
Roosevelt, after having served eight years as president, declined to seek a
third term and handpicked William Howard Taft for the Republican nomination. When Taft as president showed neither Roosevelt's enthusiasm
for a strong presidency nor his commitment to the goals of the Progressive
movement, Roosevelt challenged Taft for the 1912 Republican nomination but lost out. Backed by Progressive Republicans, Roosevelt proceeded
to form the Bull Moose Party (a reference to Roosevelt's claim that he was
"as strong as a bull moose"). Roosevelt won 27 percent of the presidential
vote to Taft's 25 percent, but the split within Republican ranks enabled
the Democratic nominee, Woodrow Wilson, to win the 1912 presidential
election. The States' Rights Party in 1948 and George Wallace's American
Independent Party in 1968 are other examples of strong factional parties. These parties were formed by white southern Democrats angered
by northern Democrats' support of civil rights for black Americans. Deep
divisions within a party give rise to factionalism and can lead eventually to
a change in its coalition. The conflict over civil rights that began within
the Democratic Party during the late 1940s continued for the next quarter-century, leading many southern whites to shift their party loyalty to
the GOP.

PARTY ORGANIZATIONS

The Democratic and Republican parties have organizational units at the national, state, and local levels. The main purpose of these **party organizations** is the contesting of elections.

The Weakening of Party Organizations

A century ago, party organizations enjoyed almost complete control of nominations and elections. The party organizations still perform all the activities they formerly engaged in. They recruit candidates, raise money, develop policy positions, and canvass for votes. But they do not control these activities as completely as they once did. For the most part, these activities are now directed by the candidates themselves.[23]

Nomination refers to the selection of the individual who will run as the party's candidate in the general election. Until the early twentieth century, nominees were selected by party organizations. To get a party nomination, an individual had to be loyal to the party organization, a requirement that included, if the candidate was elected, a willingness to share with it the spoils of office—government jobs, benefits, and contracts. The party built its organization by handing out these jobs to followers and helping them obtain government services. Some party leaders also used their positions to extort money from building contractors and service providers. New York City's legendary Boss Tweed once charged the city twenty times what a building had actually cost, amassing a huge personal fortune before eventually winding up in jail. Looking for a way to deprive party bosses of their power, reform-minded Progressives argued that control over nominations should rest with ordinary voters rather than with the party organizations (see Chapter 2).

The result was the introduction of the **primary election** (or **direct primary**), which places nomination in the hands of the voters (see Chapters 2 and 12). The candidate who gets the most votes in a party's primary gets its nomination for the general election. In most states, the nominees are chosen in *closed primaries*, in which participation is limited to voters registered or declared at the polls as members of the party whose primary is being held. A number of other states use *open primaries*, a form that allows independents and voters of either party to choose which primary they will vote in, though they cannot choose to vote in both primaries in a given election. A few states use the blanket primary, where voters get a single ballot listing both the Republican and Democratic candidates by office. Each voter can cast only one vote per office but can select a candidate of either party. The top vote-getter in each party becomes its nominee. Louisiana has a

POLITICAL CULTURE

Liberty, Equality, and Self-Government

Political Parties

Historically, political parties have given weight to the voice of ordinary citizens. Their strength is in their numbers rather than in their wealth or status, and political parties give them a means to express that strength through their votes. It is no accident that the Jacksonian Democrats created the first American grassroots party for the purpose of strengthening self-government.

In backing a party, citizens are choosing more than a single officeholder. They are getting a coalition of officeholders committed to a broad agenda of policies and issues. The old adage "vote the person, not the party" is bad advice. To vote for the person is to assume that the individual officeholder wields singular power. But that's not true even in the case of the president. In selecting one presidential candidate over another, Americans are choosing more than the person who will sit behind the desk in the Oval Office. They are also selecting several hundred other executive officers, including the secretary of state, the attorney general of the United States, and the director of the Central Intelligence Agency. The president also nominates all federal judges and justices. The great majority of these individuals, including the judicial officers, will be of the same party as the president. The election of a senator or a representative is also more than a decision about which individual will occupy a seat in Congress. Rarely does a single member of Congress have a decisive voice in legislation. Congress works through collective action, and power resides with the majority party in each chamber. Dozens of important legislative votes are cast in Congress each term. Typically, most Republican members are on one side of the vote and most Democratic members are on the other side.

Accordingly, a vote based on an issue is usually shortsighted. Once in office, a winning candidate will vote on scores of policy issues, not just the one or two issues that were the cornerstone of the election campaign. And what is the best predictor of how the winning candidate will vote on these issues? In nearly every case, the best predictor is the political party to which the officeholder belongs.

If you've been among the Americans who pride themselves on "voting the person, not the party," give some thought to whether it's the most effective way to make a difference as a voter. If you are a party loyalist already, consider taking your commitment a step further. Party organizations at all levels are looking for volunteers, particularly at election time, when they are engaged in registration, canvassing, and get-out-the-vote efforts.

variation on this form in which all candidates are listed on the ballot but are not identified by party; the top two vote-getters, even if of the same party, become the general election candidates.

Primaries hinder the building of strong party organizations. If primaries did not exist, candidates would have to seek nomination through the party organization, and they could be denied renomination if they were disloyal to the party's policy goals. Because of primaries, however, candidates have the option of seeking office on their own, and once elected (with or without the party's help), they can build a personal following that can place them beyond the party's direct control.

In the process of taking control of nominations, candidates also acquire control of most campaign money. At the turn of the twentieth century, when party machines were at their peak, most campaign funds passed through the hands of party leaders. Today, most of the money goes to the candidates directly, without first passing through the parties.

Party organizations were also weakened by the decline of patronage jobs. A century ago, when a party won control of government, it acquired control of nearly all public jobs, which were doled out to loyal party workers. However, as government jobs in the early twentieth century shifted from patronage to the merit system (see Chapter 13), the party organizations controlled many fewer positions. Today, because of the large size of government, thousands of patronage jobs still exist. These government employees help staff the party organizations (along with volunteers), but most of them are indebted to an individual politician rather than to a party organization. Congressional staff members, for example, are patronage employees, but they owe their jobs and their loyalty to their senator or representative, not to their party.

In Europe, where there are no primary elections, the situation is different. Parties control their nominations, and because of this they also control campaign money and workers. A party's candidates are expected to support the national platform if elected. An officeholder who fails to do so is likely to be denied renomination in the next election.

The Structure and Role of Party Organizations

Although the influence of party organizations has declined, parties are in no danger of dying. Candidates and activists need an organization through which to work, and the party meets that need. Moreover, certain activities, such as get-out-the-vote efforts on election day, affect all of a party's candidates and are more efficiently done through the party organization. Indeed, parties have staged a comeback of sorts.[24] National and state party organizations now assist candidates with fund-raising, polling, research, and media production, all essential ingredients of a successful modern campaign.

Structurally, U.S. parties are loose associations of national, state, and local organizations (see Figure 8-5). The national party organizations cannot dictate the decisions made by the state organizations, which in turn do not control the activities of local organizations. However, there is communication between the levels because they all have a stake in the party's success.[25]

Local Party Organizations　In a sense, U.S. parties are organized from the bottom up, not the top down. Of the roughly five hundred thousand

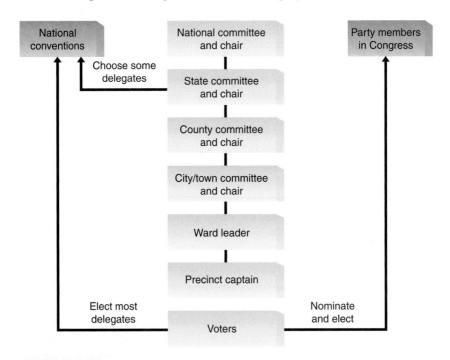

figure ‖ 8-5 FORMAL ORGANIZATION OF THE POLITICAL PARTY

U.S. parties are loosely structured alliances of national, state, and local organizations; most local parties are not as well organized as the chart implies.

elective offices in the United States, fewer than five hundred are contested statewide and only two—the presidency and vice presidency—are contested nationally. All the rest are local offices; not surprisingly, at least 95 percent of party activists work within local organizations.

It is difficult to generalize about local parties because they vary greatly in their structure and activities. Today only a few local party organizations, including the Democratic organizations in Albany, Philadelphia, and Chicago, bear even a faint resemblance to the fabled old-time party machines that, in return for jobs and even welfare services, were able to deliver the vote on election day. In many urban areas, and in most suburbs and towns, the party organizations today do not have enough activists to do organizing work outside the campaign period, at which time—to the extent their resources allow—they conduct registration drives, send mailings or hand out leaflets, and help get out the vote. These activities are not insignificant. Most local campaigns are not well funded, and the party's efforts can tip the balance in a close race.

Local parties tend to concentrate on elections that coincide with local boundaries, such as races for mayor, city council, state legislature, and county offices. Local parties also take part in congressional, statewide, and presidential contests, but in these instances, their role is typically secondary to that of the candidates' personal campaign organizations, which will be discussed later in this chapter.

State Party Organizations   At the state level, each party is headed by a central committee made up of members of local party organizations and local and state officeholders. State central committees do not meet regularly and provide only general policy guidance for the state organizations. Day-to-day operations are directed by a chairperson, who is a full-time, paid employee of the state party. The central committee appoints the chair, but it often accepts the choice of the party's leading politician, usually the governor or a U.S. senator.

The state party organizations engage in activities, such as fund-raising and voter registration, that can improve their candidates' chances of success. State party organizations concentrate on statewide races, including those for governor and U.S. senator, and also focus on races for the state legislature. They play a smaller role in campaigns for national or local offices, and in most states, they do not endorse candidates in statewide primaries.

National Party Organizations   The national Republican and Democratic Party organizations, which are located in Washington, D.C., are structured much like those at the state level: they have a national committee and a national party chairperson.

In 2005, the Democratic Party chose Howard Dean as its national party chair. Most party chairs are not widely known, but Dean was familiar to voters as a result of his strong bid for the 2004 Democratic presidential nomination. The Democrats picked Dean as their chair in hopes that he could boost their fund-raising and grassroots efforts.

The Structure of the National Parties   Although in theory the national parties are run by their committees, neither the Democratic National Committee (DNC) nor the Republican National Committee (RNC) has great power. The RNC (with more than 150 members) and the DNC (with more than 300 members) are too cumbersome and meet too infrequently to oversee party activities. Their power is largely confined to setting organizational policy, such as determining the site of the party's presidential nominating convention and setting the rules governing the selection of convention delegates. They have no power to pick nominees or to dictate candidates' policy positions.

The national party's day-to-day operations are directed by a national chairperson chosen by the national committee, although the committee defers to the president's choice when the party controls the White House. The national chair directs a large staff operation that seeks to build the party's base and promote its presidential and congressional candidates. The RNC and DNC, among other things, run training programs for candidates and their staffs, raise money, seek media coverage of party positions and activities, conduct issue and group research, and send field representatives to help state and local parties with their operations. In some cases, the national parties also try to recruit potentially strong candidates to run in House and Senate races.

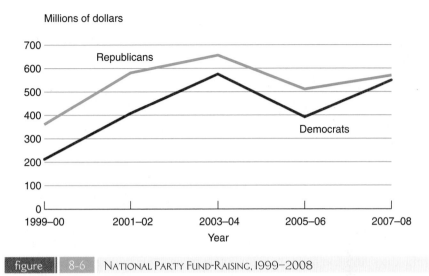

Millions of dollars

figure | 8-6 | NATIONAL PARTY FUND-RAISING, 1999–2008

Over the years, the Republican Party has raised significantly more money than the Democratic Party has. The figures include fund-raising by the DNC, RNC, DCCC, NRCC, DSCC, and NRSC. *Source: Federal Elections Commission. The 2007–2008 data are based on projections from incomplete cycle.*

This model of the national party was created in the 1970s when Republican leaders concluded that an expanded and modernized national organization could contribute to the party's electoral success. The DNC has created a similar organization, but it is less substantial than the RNC's. Modern campaigns, as David Adamany notes, are based on "cash," and Democrats have less of it.[26] In recent election cycles, the Republican national party has usually outspent its Democratic counterpart by a comfortable margin (see Figure 8-6).

Money and the National Parties The parties' major role in campaigns is the raising and spending of money. The RNC and the DNC are major sources of campaign funds, but they are not the only national-level party units involved in fund-raising. There are also House and Senate party campaign committees, which raise funds and provide advice to the party's congressional candidates. These committees consist of the Democratic Congressional Campaign Committee (DCCC), the National Republican Congressional Committee (NRCC), the Democratic Senatorial Campaign Committee (DSCC), and the National Republican Senatorial Committee (NRSC).

A party organization can legally give money directly to a House or Senate candidate. The legal limit is greater for Senate candidates than House candidates and, given the enormous cost of today's campaigns, is not particularly high (about $40,000 in the case of Senate candidates). This funding, along with the money a candidate receives from individual contributors and inter-est groups, which are also subject to strict limits, is termed **hard money**—it goes directly to the candidate and can be spent as he or she chooses.

Limits on party contributions were established when the campaign fi-nance laws were reformed in the 1970s in response to the Watergate scandal. However, a loophole in the laws was exposed when a court ruling allowed the parties to raise and spend unlimited campaign funds provided the funds were not channeled directly to a party's candidates. Thus, whereas a wealthy contributor could legally give a candidate only a limited amount, that same contributor could give an unlimited amount to the candidate's party. These contributions were termed **soft money** in that a party could not hand it over directly to a candidate. But the party could use these contributions to support party activities, such as voter registration efforts, get-out-the-vote drives, and party-centered television ads, that could indirectly benefit its candidates. In some cases, the line between the use of hard and soft money was hard to dis-tinguish. In 1996, for example, the Democratic Party ran a $100-million ad campaign that did not directly urge voters to support Clinton but did include pictures of him and references to his accomplishments as president.

In 2002, Congress closed the loophole through enactment of the Bipartisan Campaign Reform Act (BCRA), which prohibits the national parties from raising or spending soft money. BCRA also bans the state parties from spend-ing soft money in support of candidates for federal office. The Supreme Court upheld these restrictions in a 2003 decision,[27] but a new loophole soon surfaced. The ban on soft money does not fully apply to so-called 527 groups. (Section 527 of the Internal Revenue Code defines the rules governing not-for-profit political groups.) Much of the money that previously would have been contributed to a party organization now finds its way into the hands of 527 groups. Although they are prohibited from attacking a candidate di-rectly, these groups can legally engage in issue advocacy, which has enabled them to mount thinly veiled candidate attacks. During the 2004 presidential election, 527 groups spent more than $100 million. Several of these groups, include MoveOn and Swift Boat Veterans for Truth, were subsequently fined by the Federal Election Commision (FEC), for crossing the line from issue advocacy to candidate advocacy. Swift Boat Veterans for Truth ran televised ads claiming that Democratic nominee John Kerry's Vietnam combat medals, which included the Silver Star and Purple Heart, were fraudulently acquired. The charges, which were shown to be false, were deliberately designed to hurt Kerry's campaign and thus fell outside the realm of issue advocacy.

Like all previous campaign finance legisation, BCRA has been only partially successful in regulating the flow of campaign money.[28] Just as water always runs downhill, money always seems to find its way into election politics.

THE CANDIDATE-CENTERED CAMPAIGN

Party committees have more of a **service relationship** than a power relationship with their party's candidates. Because the party nominees are chosen through primaries, and because many of the potential candidates already have a power base at the local or state level, the national committees are unable to handpick the party nominees. Accordingly, the party organizations tend to back whichever candidate wins the primary. If the candidate then wins the general election, the party at least has denied the office to the opposing party.

Today's campaigns are largely controlled by the candidates, particularly in congressional, statewide, and presidential races. Each candidate has a personal organization, created especially for the campaign and disbanded once it is over. The candidates are entrepreneurs who play what political consultant Joe Napolitan labeled "the election game."[29] The game begins with money—lots of it.

Campaign Funds: The Money Chase

Campaigns for high office are expensive, and the costs keep rising. In 1980, about $250 million was spent on all Senate and House campaigns combined. The figure had jumped to $425 million by 1990. In 2006, the figure easily exceeded $1 billion, more than four times the 1980 level.[30] As might be expected, incumbents have a distinct advantage in fund-raising. They have contributor lists from past campaigns and have the policy influence that donors seek. House and Senate incumbents outspend their challengers by more than two to one.

Because of the high cost of campaigns, candidates spend much of their time raising funds, which come primarily from individual contributors, interest groups (through PACs, discussed in Chapter 9), and political parties. The **money chase** is relentless.[31] A U.S. senator must raise $20,000 a week on average throughout the entire six-year term in order to raise the minimum $6 million it takes to run a competitive Senate campaign in most states. A Senate campaign in a large state can easily exceed that amount. In 2004, despite having a wide lead in the polls over a weak opponent, Barack Obama still spent $10 million on his Senate race in Illinois. House campaigns are less costly, but expenditures of $1 million or more are commonplace. As for presidential elections, even the nominating race is expensive. In 2008, Obama spent more than $200 million during the competitive phase of his campaign for the Democratic nomination. (In presidential races, but not congressional ones, candidates are eligible to receive federal funds, a topic discussed in Chapter 12.)

Organization and Strategy: Hired Guns

The key operatives in today's campaigns are campaign consultants, poll-sters, media producers, and fund-raising and get-out-the-vote specialists. They are **hired guns** who charge hefty fees for their services. "The new king-makers" is the way writer David Chagall characterizes these pros.[32]

These hired guns include campaign strategists who help the candidate to plot and execute a game plan. Over the years, some of these strategists, in-cluding James Carville, Dick Morris, and Roger Ailes, developed legendary reputations. Fund-raising specialists are also part of the new politics. They know how to tap into the networks of large donors and interest groups that contribute to election campaigns and are adept at running targeted direct-mail fund-raising campaigns. The hired guns also include experts who conduct polls and focus groups (the latter are small groups of voters brought together to discuss at length their thoughts on the candidates and issues). Polls and focus groups enable candidates to identify issues and mes-sages that will resonate with voters.[33] Media consultants are another staple of the modern campaign. These experts are adept at producing televised political advertising and creating the "photo-ops" and other staged events that attract news coverage.

The hired guns of the modern campaign are skilled at **packaging** a can-didate—highlighting those aspects of the candidate's partisanship, policy positions, personal background, and personality that are thought most at-tractive to voters. Packaging is not new to politics. Andrew Jackson's self-portrayal in the nineteenth century as "the champion of the people" is an image that any modern candidate could appreciate. What is new is the need to fit the image to the requirements of a world of sound bites, thirty-second ads, and televised debates, and to do it in a persuasive way. In the old days, it was sometimes enough for candidates to drive home the point that they were a Republican or a Democrat, playing on the tendency of voters to choose a candidate on that basis. Party appeals are still critical, but today's voters also want to know about a candidate's personality and policy posi-tions. In their quest for the 2008 Democratic nomination, Barack Obama positioned himself as "the candidate of change," while opponent Hillary Clinton claimed to be "the candidate with experience."

Hired consultants have been a driving force for yet another characteristic of modern campaigns—the tearing down of the opponent.[34] In one sense, negative campaigning is as old as American politics. Thomas Jefferson was the subject of a whispering campaign about his sex life, and Abraham Lincoln was ridiculed by opponents as "a baboon" for his hairy, gangly look and his backwoods roots. But today's version of attack politics is unprecedented

★ STATES IN THE NATION

Public Funding of State Elections

About half the states have public funding of election campaigns. Some of them give the money to political parties, which allocate it to candidates or spend it on party activities such as get-out-the-vote efforts. Other states give funds directly to candidates, although this funding typically is limited to candidates for designated offices, such as governor.

Q: What might explain the fact that there is no clear-cut regional pattern to the public funding of state elections?

A: Public funding of elections is relatively new, so additional states may adopt it in the next decade or two, at which time a regional tendency could emerge. (If your state does not have public funding, do you think it is likely to adopt it anytime soon? Why or why not?)

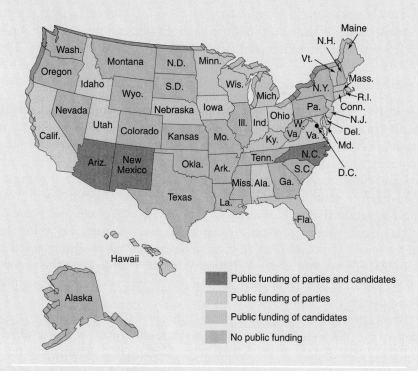

Source: National Conference of State Legislatures, 2008.

in its scale, ubiquity, and sophistication. Professional strategists have concluded that they can win more votes by diminishing the opponent than by
building up their own candidate. In the past three decades, negative television ads have increased threefold, to the point where they now constitute the
large share of political ads.[35] Most campaigns nowadays have a nasty edge,
and the attacks can be downright vicious. In 2002, for example, incumbent
U.S. Senator Max Cleland lost his bid for reelection when his lead in the
polls withered in the face of blistering attacks on his patriotism, including
an ad that showed his face alternately with those of Saddam Hussein and
Osama bin Laden. Cleland's patriotism would have seemed above reproach;
he had lost his legs and right arm in combat in Vietnam. Yet his opponent
seized upon Cleland's vote against a Senate bill creating the Department of
Homeland Security because it did not include the normal protections for
civil service employees. The ad ignored the specifics of Cleland's objection
to the bill, portraying him instead as "soft" on terrorism.

Voter Contacts: Pitched Battle

Today's elections for high office have no historical parallel in their length
and penetration. Candidates start their active campaigning much earlier—
often a year in advance of election day—than they did in times past. The
modern campaign is relentless. Voters are bombarded with messages that
arrive by air, by land, and by Web.

Air Wars The main battleground of the modern campaign is the mass
media, particularly television. Television emerged in the 1960s as the major
medium of presidential and congressional politics and has remained the
dominant medium ever since.

Candidates spend heavily on televised political advertising, which enables them to communicate directly—and on their own terms—with voters. The production and the airing of political ads account for half or more
of campaign spending. Indeed, televised ads are the main reason for the
high cost of U.S. campaigns. In most democracies, televised campaigning
takes place through parties, which receive free air time to make their pitch.
Many democracies even prohibit the purchase of televised advertising time
by candidates (see Table 8-1).

Air wars is the term that political scientist Darrell West applies to candidates' use of televised ads.[36] Candidates increasingly play off each other's
ads, seeking to gain the strategic advantage. Modern production techniques
enable well-funded candidates to get new ads on the air within a few hours'
time, which allows them to rebut attacks and exploit fast-breaking developments, a tactic known as *rapid response*.

| table | 8-1 | TELEVISION CAMPAIGN PRACTICES IN SELECTED DEMOCRACIES |

In many democracies, free television time is provided to political parties, and candidates are not allowed to buy advertising time. The United States provides no free time to parties and allows candidates to purchase air time. Television debates are also a regular feature of U.S. campaigns.

Country	Paid TV Ads Allowed?	Unrestricted Free TV Time Provided?	TV Debates Held?
Canada	Yes	Yes	Yes
France	No	Yes	Yes
Germany	Yes	Yes	Yes
Great Britain	No	Yes	No
Italy	No	Yes	Yes
Netherlands	No	No	Yes
United States	Yes	No	Yes

Candidates also use the press to get their message across, although the amount of news coverage they can get varies widely by location and office. Many House candidates are nearly ignored by their local news media. The New York City media market, for example, includes more than a score of House districts in New York, New Jersey, Pennsylvania, and Connecticut, and candidates in these districts get little or no coverage from the New York media. The presidential campaign, in contrast, gets daily coverage from both national and local media. Between these extremes are Senate races, which always get some news coverage and, if hotly contested, may get heavy coverage.

Debates are also part of the modern media campaign. Debates often attract large and attentive audiences, but they can be risky encounters, because they give viewers a chance to compare the candidates directly. A weak or bumbling performance can hurt a candidate. Some analysts believe, for example, that Al Gore's performance in the first of the 2000 general election debates, when he grimaced and sighed loudly when George W. Bush was talking, cost him the election. Gore had been slightly ahead in the opinion polls but lost his lead immediately after the debate.

Ground Wars Candidates' first priority in a close election is "swing voters"—those voters who conceivably could be persuaded to vote for either side. As election day nears, however, candidates concentrate on getting their supporters to the polls.

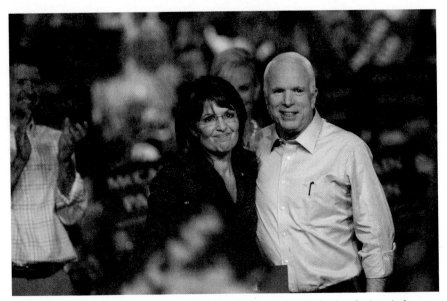

John McCain and Sarah Palin campaign during the 2008 presidential election. In America's candidate-centered system, party nominees have considerable latitude in deciding how they will conduct their campaigns. McCain had a nearly free hand in choosing the little-known Palin as his running mate, instantly making her a major political figure, which is a rare occurrence in a party-centered system.

The get-out-the-vote effort traditionally has been borne by the parties and other organizations, such as labor unions. Although these groups remain the cornerstone of the effort, the candidates are also involved, and increasingly so. As partisanship has intensified in recent years, candidates have found it more difficult to persuade voters to switch sides. It has therefore become important for them to get as many of their supporters as possible to the polls on election day. Some campaign money that formerly would have been spent on televised advertising is now channeled into voter turnout efforts. In the final phase of the 2008 presidential election, millions of potential voters were contacted by phone or in person by the Republican and Democratic campaigns.

Web Wars   New communication technology usually makes its way into campaign politics, and the Internet is no exception. All of the candidates for the 2008 Democratic and Republican nominations, for example, had a website dedicated to providing information, generating public support, attracting volunteers, and raising money. Barack Obama's website was by far the most successful. Through it, he raised tens of millions of dollars and developed a nationwide network of hundreds of thousands of supporters.

Although television is still the principal medium of election politics, some analysts believe that the Internet may eventually overtake it. Email is cheaper than television advertising (and both cheaper and faster than traditional mail). Because it is a targeted medium, the Internet could become the channel through which candidates reach particular voting groups. But the Internet also has some disadvantages relative to television. The most important is that the individual user has greater control over Internet messages. With television, when a political ad appears during a favorite program, most viewers will watch it. An unsolicited message on the Internet is more easily ignored or deleted. Future candidates may conclude that the Internet is the preferred medium for fund-raising and interacting with supporters and that television is the best medium for achieving public recognition and reaching less-interested voters.

PARTIES, CANDIDATES, AND THE PUBLIC'S INFLUENCE

Candidate-centered campaigns have some distinct advantages. First, they can infuse new blood into electoral politics. Candidate recruitment is normally a slow process in party-centered systems. Would-be officeholders pay their dues by working in the party and, in the process, tend to adopt the outlook of those already there. By comparison, a candidate-centered system is more open and provides opportunities for newcomers to gain office quickly. Barack Obama is a case in point. He had run unsuccessfully for the U.S. House of Representatives in 2000 before seeking and getting the Democratic nomination, and then winning, the 2004 U.S. Senate race in Illinois. Barely two years later, Obama announced his candidacy for president of the United States, winning his party's 2008 nomination against the more experienced U.S. Senator Hillary Clinton and then beating the even more experienced U.S. Senator John McCain in the general election. Obama's quick rise from political obscurity to the highest office in the country would be almost unthinkable in a party-centered democracy. Nor is he the only example. In 1976, Jimmy Carter went from being an obscure one-term governor of Georgia to winning the presidency two years later.

Candidate-centered campaigns also lend flexibility to electoral politics. When political conditions and issues change, self-directed candidates quickly

adjust, bringing new ideas into the political arena. Strong party organizations are rigid by comparison. Until the early 1990s, for example, the British
Labour Party was controlled by old-line activists who refused to concede that
changes in the British economy called for changes in the party's trade union-
ist and economic policies. The result was a series of humiliating defeats at the
hands of the Conservative Party that ended only after Tony Blair and other
proponents of "New Labour" successfully recast the party's image.

Also, candidate-centered campaigns encourage national officeholders to
be responsive to local interests. In building personal followings among their
state and district constituents, members of Congress respond to local needs.
Nearly every significant domestic program enacted by Congress is adjusted
to accommodate the interests of states and localities that otherwise would be
hurt by the policy. Members of Congress are not obliged to support the legislative position of their party's majority, and they often extract favors for their
constituents as the price of their support. Where strong national parties exist,
national interests take precedence over local concerns. In both France and
Britain, for example, the pleas of representatives of underdeveloped regions
have often gone unheeded by their party's majority.

In other respects, however, candidate-centered campaigns have some
distinct disadvantages. Often they degenerate into mud-slinging contests,
and they are fertile ground for powerful special-interest groups, which contribute much of the money that underwrites candidates' campaigns. Many
groups give large sums of money to incumbents of both parties, which enables them to insulate themselves from an election's outcome: whether the
Republicans win or the Democrats win, these contributors are assured of
having friends in high places.

Candidate-centered campaigns also weaken accountability by making it
easier for officeholders to deny personal responsibility for government's actions. If national policy goes awry, an incumbent can always say that he or
she is only one vote out of many and that the real problem resides with the
president or with "others" in Congress. The problem of accountability in
the U.S. system is illustrated by the several trillion dollars that have been
added to the national debt since 2000 because of Republican officeholders' insistence on steep tax cuts and huge increases in military spending
and Democratic officeholders' refusal to accept significant cuts in domestic
spending programs. "Running on empty" is how former cabinet secretary
Peter Peterson describes the huge debt being passed along to future generations of Americans that has enabled today's members of Congress to keep
their constituents happy enough to vote them back into office.[37] The problem of accountability is also illustrated by surveys that have asked Americans
about their confidence in Congress. Although most citizens do not have a

high opinion of Congress as a whole, most also say that they have confidence in their local representative in Congress. This paradoxical attitude prevails in so many districts that the net result in most elections is a Congress whose membership is not greatly changed from the previous one (see Chapter 11). In contrast, party-centered campaigns are characterized by collective accountability. When problems occur, voters tend to hold the majority party responsible and invariably vote large numbers of its members out of office.

In sum, candidate-centered campaigns strengthen the relationship between the voters and their individual representative while at the same time weakening the relationship between the full electorate and their representative institutions. Whether this arrangement serves the public's interest is debatable. Nevertheless, it is clear that Americans do not favor party-centered politics. Parties survived the shift to candidate-centered campaigns and will persist, but their organizational heyday has passed. (Congressional and presidential campaigns are discussed further in Chapters 11 and 12, respectively.)

SUMMARY Self-Test www.mhhe.com/pattersonwtp8e

Political parties serve to link the public with its elected leaders. In the United States, this linkage is provided by the two-party system; only the Republican and Democratic parties have any chance of winning control of government. The fact that the United States has only two major parties is explained by several factors: an electoral system—characterized by single-member districts—that makes it difficult for third parties to compete for power; each party's willingness to accept differing political views; and a political culture that stresses compromise and negotiation rather than ideological rigidity.

Because the United States has only two major parties, each of which seeks to gain majority support, their candidates normally tend to avoid controversial or extreme political positions. Sometimes, Democratic and Republican candidates do offer sharply contrasting policy alternatives, particularly during times of crisis. Ordinarily, however, Republican and Democratic candidates pursue moderate and somewhat overlapping policies. Each party can count on its party loyalists, but U.S. elections can hinge on swing voters, who respond to the issues of the moment either prospectively, basing their vote on what the candidates promise to do if elected, or retrospectively, basing their vote on their satisfaction or dissatisfaction with what the party in power has already done.

America's parties are decentralized, fragmented organizations. The national party organization does not control the policies and activities of the state organizations, and these in turn do not control the local organizations. Traditionally, the local organizations have controlled most of the party's workforce because most elections are contested at the local level. Local parties, however, vary markedly in their vitality. Whatever their level, America's party organizations are relatively weak. They lack control over nominations and elections. Candidates can bypass the party organization and win nomination through primary elections. Individual candidates also control most of the organizational structure and money necessary to win elections. The state and national party organizations have recently expanded their capacity to provide candidates with modern campaign services. Nevertheless, party organizations at all levels have few ways of controlling the candidates who run under their banners. They assist candidates with campaign technology, workers, and funds, but they cannot compel candidates' loyalty to organizational goals.

American political campaigns, particularly those for higher office, are candidate centered. Most candidates are self-starters who become adept at "the election game." They spend much of their time raising campaign funds, and they build their personal organizations around hired guns: pollsters, media producers, fund-raisers, and election consultants. Strategy and image making are key components of the modern campaign, as is televised political advertising, which accounts for half or more of all spending in presidential and congressional races.

The advantages of candidate-centered politics include a responsiveness to new leadership, new ideas, and local concerns. Yet this form of politics can result in campaigns that are personality-driven, depend on powerful interest groups, and blur responsibility for what government has done.

Key Terms

air wars (*p. 284*)

candidate-centered politics (*p. 254*)

factional (minor) party (*p. 272*)

grassroots party (*p. 257*)

hard money (*p. 280*)

hired guns (*p. 282*)

ideological (minor) party (*p. 271*)

money chase (*p. 281*)

multiparty system (*p. 264*)

nomination (*p. 273*)

packaging (of a candidate) (*p. 282*)

party-centered politics (*p. 254*)

party coalition (*p. 267*)

party competition (*p. 255*)

party organizations (*p. 273*)

party realignment (*p. 258*)

political party (*p. 254*)

primary election (direct primary) (*p. 273*)

proportional representation (*p. 266*)

prospective voting (*p. 263*)

reform (minor) party (*p. 270*)

retrospective voting (*p. 263*)

service relationship (*p. 281*)

single-issue (minor) party (*p. 270*)

single-member districts (*p. 264*)

soft money (*p. 280*)

split ticket (*p. 263*)

two-party system (*p. 264*)

Suggested Readings

Aldrich, John H. *Why Parties? The Origin and Transformation of Political Parties in America*. Chicago: University of Chicago Press, 1995. An insightful analysis of what parties are and how they emerge and develop.

Buell, Emmett H., Jr., and Lee Sigelman. *Attack Politics: Negativity in Presidential Campaigns Since 1960.* Lawrence: University Press of Kansas, 2008. A look at how negative politics has come to pervade campaigns.

Flanigan, William H., and Nancy H. Zingale. *Political Behavior of the American Electorate*, 11th ed. Washington, D.C.: Congressional Quarterly Press, 2005. An overview of Americans' electoral behavior.

Geer, John. *In Defense of Negativity.* Chicago: University of Chicago Press, 2006. A provcative and award-winning analysis of televised political ads.

Greenberg, Stanley B. *The Two Americas: Our Current Political Deadlock and How to Break It.* New York: Thomas Dunne Books, 2004. An assessment of party politics in today's America.

Hershey, Marjorie Randon. *Party Politics in America*, 13th ed. New York: Longman, 2009. A well-written, thorough analysis of U.S. political parties.

Hillygus, D. Sunshine, and Todd G. Shields. *The Persuadable Voter: Wedge Issues in Presidential Campaigns.* Princeton, N.J.: Princeton University Press, 2008. A careful analysis of the use of wedge issues, such as abortion, in campaign strategy.

Patterson, Kelly D. *Political Parties and the Maintenance of Liberal Democracy.* New York: Columbia University Press, 1996. A systematic look at the effects of political parties on American government and politics.

Sifreg, Micah L. *Spoiling for a Fight: Third-Party Politics in America.* New York: Routledge, 2003. An analysis of America's third parties and their impact on the two-party system.

Stonecash, Jeffrey. *Class and Party in American Politics.* Boulder, Colo.: Westview Press, 2001. An insightful analysis that argues that class is still very much a part of America's party politics.

West, Darrell M. *Air Wars: Television Advertising in Election Campaigns, 1952–2004*, 5th ed. Washington, D.C.: Congressional Quarterly Press, 2005. A thorough study of the role of televised advertising in election campaigns.

LIST OF WEBSITES

http://www.democrats.org/ The Democratic National Committee's site; provides information on the party's platform, candidates, officials, and organization.

http://www.greenparties.org/ The Green Party's site; contains information on the party's philosophy and policy goals.

http://www.rnc.org/ Home page of the Republican National Committee; offers information on Republican leaders, policy positions, and organizations.

http://www.jamescarvillesoffice.com/ The website of James Carville, one of the nation's top campaign consultants.

POLITICS IN THEORY AND PRACTICE

Thinking: Why are elections conducted so differently in the United States than in European democracies? Why are the campaigns so much longer, more expensive, and more candidate-centered?

Participating: Consider becoming a campaign or political party volunteer. The opportunities are numerous. Parties and candidates at every level from the national on down seek volunteers to assist in organizing, canvassing, fund-raising, and other activities. As a college student, you have communication and knowledge skills that would be valuable to a campaign or party organization. You might be pleasantly surprised by the tasks you are assigned.

Extra Credit

For up-to-the-minute *New York Times* articles, interactive simulations, graphics, study tools, and more links and quizzes, visit the text's Online Learning Center at www.mhhe.com/pattersonwtp8e.

GOP Has Lock on South, and Democrats Can't Find Key

By Ronald Brownstein

In recent decades, America's political party system has undergone a slow and partial realignment that has substantially altered the political landscape. The clearest case is the American South. Once staunchly Democratic, it has become solidly Republican. In a December 15, 2004, article, Los Angeles Times *national political correspondent Ronald Brownstein concluded on the basis of voting returns from the 2004 presidential election that the Democratic party has little prospect of reversing the situation. Following is an abbreviated version of his article.*

The generation-long political retreat of Democrats across the South is disintegrating into a rout.

President Bush dominated the South so completely in last month's presidential election that he carried nearly 85% of all the counties across the region—and more than 90% of counties where whites are a majority of the population, according to a *Times* analysis of election results and census data.

The *Times'* analysis which provides the most detailed picture yet of the vote in Southern communities, shows that Bush's victory was even more comprehensive than his sweep of the region's 13 states would suggest.

His overwhelming performance left Sen. John F. Kerry clinging to a few scattered islands of support in a region that until the 1960s provided the foundation of the Democratic coalition in presidential politics. Kerry won fewer Southern counties than any Democratic nominee since the Depression except Walter F. Mondale in 1984 and George S. McGovern in 1972, according to data assembled by the *Times* and Polidata, a firm that specializes in political statistics.

In Southern counties without a substantial number of African American or Latino voters, Bush virtually obliterated Kerry. Across the 11 states of the old Confederacy, plus Kentucky and Oklahoma, whites constitute a majority of the population in 1,154 counties. Kerry won 90 of them. By contrast, Bill Clinton won 510 white-majority counties in the South eight years ago.

"We are out of business in the South," said J. W. Brannen, the Democratic Party chairman in Russell County, Ala., the only white-majority county in the state that Kerry carried.

The results underscore the enormity of the challenge facing Democrats as they try to rebuild their Southern support. Most ominously for them, the patterns suggest that under Bush, the GOP is solidifying its hold not just on Southern white conservatives but white moderates as well, a trend also apparent in exit polls of Southern voters on election day. "As the older white moderates leave the scene, they are being replaced with younger moderates more willing to vote Republican," said Merle Black, a political scientist at Atlanta's Emory University and the author of several books on Southern politics.

Compounding the Democratic dilemma is the growing tendency of Southern whites who vote Republican for president to support GOP candidates down the ballot. In 1984, Ronald Reagan won slightly more counties across the South than Bush did this year; but after Reagan's landslide, Republicans held 12 of the 26 U.S. Senate seats in the region. After Bush helped the GOP win six open Southern Senate seats last month, Republicans now hold 22 of the 26 Senate seats in the 13 states.

That is the most either party has controlled in the region since Democrats also won 22 in 1964—ironically, the election in which the white backlash against the Civil Rights Act allowed the GOP to make its first inroads into the South.

Forty years later, under a Southern Republican president, the South has become an electoral fortress for the GOP. Outside the South, Democrats hold more House and Senate seats and won many more electoral college votes than the GOP last month. But the GOP's advantage in the region has been large enough to overcome those deficits and create Republican majorities in both chambers of Congress and the electoral college. And the magnitude of November's Republican sweep last month suggests the GOP advantage across the region is expanding.

"I don't think that for 50 years we're going to be a Republican section of the country," said former Democratic National Committee Co-Chairman Donald L. Fowler of South Carolina. "I really believe we have the potential to turn a lot of this around in a decade. But it will take constructive, directed, consistent work to do it. It's just not going to happen by itself. We're in too big a hole."

Politically, the South includes 13 states: Alabama, Arkansas, Florida, Georgia, Kentucky, Louisiana, Mississippi, North Carolina, Oklahoma, South Carolina, Tennessee, Texas and Virginia. Together they cast 168 electoral college votes, more than three-fifths of the 270 required for election.

Many political analysts see Bush's commanding performance across the region— and Republican gains in other elections during his presidency—as the fourth wave in the GOP's Southern ascendance.

The GOP, which was founded in the 1850s as a Northern party opposed to the expansion of slavery, won very few Southern states in presidential races for a full century after the Civil War. Democrat Franklin D. Roosevelt won every Southern state in all four of his presidential campaigns.

Republican President Dwight D. Eisenhower had some Southern success in the 1950s. But the GOP planted its first lasting roots in the region amid the white backlash against the passage of the Civil Rights and Voting Rights acts under Democratic President Lyndon B. Johnson in the mid-1960s.

Opposition to the new civil rights laws, and to such follow-on initiatives as affirmative action and school busing for racial integration, powered the first wave of GOP gains in the South. But the party expanded its appeal by courting Southern whites with conservative messages on such nonracial issues as taxes, national defense and moral values. That second advance reached a crescendo during Ronald Reagan's two elections. "Reagan's presidency was the turning point in the evolution of a competitive, two-party electorate in the South," Black and his brother, Earl Black, wrote in their 2002 book, *The Rise of Southern Republicans.*

For the next decade, Democrats remained competitive enough for Southerner Bill Clinton to capture five Southern states in 1992. But the disenchantment over Clinton's chaotic first two years fueled a third wave of GOP Southern gains. In their midterm landslide of 1994, Republicans for the first time captured the majority of House and Senate seats from the South. As Clinton pursued a more centrist course after 1994, Democrats stanched their congressional losses in the South and even regained some governorships. In 1996, Clinton again won five Southern states.

But under Bush, the GOP is on the march again. In the Senate, Republicans have increased the number of seats they hold in the 13 Southern states from 18 before Bush took office to 22. (The GOP has now won the last 10 open-seat Senate races in the South.) In the House, Republicans have stretched their advantage in the Southern states from 27 seats before Bush took office to 40 today. "This is a cumulative process that has gained critical momentum in the past four years," said Karl Rove, Bush's chief political advisor.

Analyzing the results at the county level illustrates Bush's dominance vividly. In 2000, Bush won 1,047 counties across the South and held then-Vice President Al Gore to 294, according to Polidata. This year, Bush won 1,124 counties and held Kerry to 216, according to Polidata figures based on preliminary election results.(The South had one fewer county this year than in 2000 because two jurisdictions merged in Virginia.)

Those numbers represent a catastrophic decline for the Democrats since the 1990s, when Clinton won more than 650 counties in each of his presidential victories. Bush has become the first candidate since Franklin D. Roosevelt in 1940 and 1944 to carry more than 1,000 Southern counties twice.

What's Your Opinion?

Do you believe, as does South Carolina's Fowler, that Democrats can "turn a lot of this around in a decade"? Or do you think he's being wildly optimistic about the Democratic Party's prospects in the South? Why?

CHAPTER 9

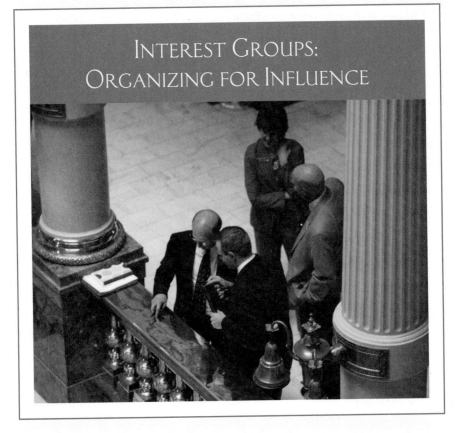

INTEREST GROUPS: ORGANIZING FOR INFLUENCE

66 The flaw in the pluralist heaven is that the heavenly chorus sings with a strong upper-class bias. 99

E. E. SCHATTSCHNEIDER[1]

Senior-citizen groups launched their attack within hours of President George W. Bush's 2005 State of the Union address. Bush had specified for the first time key components of his social security reform plan: workers would be able to funnel a third of their social security taxes into private individual investment accounts, and benefits on the remaining two-thirds would be scaled back. For their part, current retirees and workers fifty-five years of age or older would be exempt from benefit reductions. These reforms, Bush said, would save social security from going "bankrupt" in 2042, the year when benefit payouts were projected to exceed incoming revenue if no change was made in the system.

Led by the American Association of Retired Persons (AARP), the seniors' lobby assailed the plan and orchestrated a campaign involving tens of thousands of angry calls, letters, telegrams, and faxes from retirees to their congressional representatives. The AARP poured nearly $10 million into newspaper advertisements—"If we feel like gambling, we'll play the slots"—attacking Bush's proposal to partially privatize social security. Seniors groups found an ally in congressional Democrats. Senate minority leader Harry Reid (D-Nev.) called Bush's plan "social security roulette." "Democrats are all for giving Americans more of a say and more choices when it comes to their retirement savings," Reid declared. "But that doesn't mean taking Social Security's guarantee and gambling with it. And that's coming from a senator who represents Las Vegas." Within days, opinion polls showed declining support for Bush's plan. Over the next several months, public support for his proposal continued to fall, and by summer the plan had no chance of gaining congressional approval.

The AARP's campaign against Bush's social security initiative suggests why interest groups are both admired and feared. On the one hand, groups have a legitimate right to express their views on public policy issues. It is entirely appropriate for senior citizens or other groups—whether farmers, consumers, business firms, or college students—to promote their interests through collective action. In fact, the *pluralist* theory of American politics (see Chapter 1) holds that society's interests are most effectively represented through group action.

On the other hand, groups can wield too much power. If a group gets its way at an unreasonable cost to the rest of society, the public interest is harmed. When Bush announced his intention to reform social security, most Americans felt that some kind of change was needed. Bush did not help his cause by proposing a change—the creation of private retirement accounts—that was more closely aligned with his belief in the marketplace than with his stated goal of protecting social security from bankruptcy. Economists calculated that Bush's plan might actually cost more money than it would save. Nevertheless, the time seemed ripe for a fruitful debate on the future of social security. Did AARP and its group allies, in pursuit of their own agenda, needlessly derail that debate?

Opinions might differ as to the answer to this question, but there is no doubt that groups have considerable influence over public policy. Indeed, most observers believe that group influence has increased in recent decades. The situation has been described as the rise of **single-issue politics:** groups have organized around nearly every conceivable policy issue, with each group pressing its demands to the utmost through lobbying and other forms of political pressure.

An **interest group**—also called a "faction," "pressure group," or "special interest"—has two characteristics: an organized membership and the pursuit of policy goals that stem from its members' shared interest. Thus, a bridge club or an amateur softball team is not an interest group because it does not seek to influence the political process. In contrast, organizations such as the Association of Wheat Growers, the National Organization for Women, the World Wildlife Fund, and the National Rifle Association are interest groups because each is an organized entity and each seeks to further its members' interests through political action.

Interest groups are similar to political parties in some respects, but the two types of organizations differ in important ways.[2] Major political parties address a broad range of issues so as to appeal to diverse blocs of voters. Parties exist to contest elections. They change their policy positions as the voters' preferences change. For the party, the winning of elections is almost everything. Interest groups, in contrast, focus on specific issues of direct concern to their members. A group may involve itself in elections, but its purpose is to influence public policy in its area of interest and on behalf of its members.

This chapter examines the degree to which various interests in American society are represented by organized groups, the process by which interest groups exert influence, and the costs and benefits of group politics with respect to the public good. The main points made in the chapter are these:

★ *Although nearly all interests in American society are organized to some degree, those associated with economic activity, particularly business enterprises, are by far the most thoroughly organized.* Their advantage rests on their superior financial resources and on the fact that they offer potential members private goods (such as wages and jobs).

★ *Groups that do not have economic activity as their primary function often have organizational difficulties.* These groups pursue public or collective goods (such as a safer environment) that are available even to individuals who are not group members, so individuals may choose not to pay the costs of membership.

★ *Lobbying and electioneering are the traditional means by which groups communicate with and influence political leaders.* Recent developments, including grassroots lobbying and PACs, have heightened interest groups' influence.

★ *The interest-group system overrepresents business interests and higher-income groups and fosters policies that serve a group's interest more than the public interest.* Thus, although groups are an essential part of the policy process, they also distort that process.

THE INTEREST-GROUP SYSTEM

In the 1830s, the Frenchman Alexis de Tocqueville wrote that the "principle of association" was nowhere more evident than in America.[3] It is a description that still holds. Americans are more likely than citizens of other nations to join organized groups (see "How the United States Compares"). Nevertheless, Americans are not equally well connected to groups. Some individuals have the skills, money, contacts, or time to participate in group politics; others do not. Moreover, some groups are inherently more attractive to potential members than others and thus find it easier to organize. Groups also differ in their financial resources and thus in their capacity for political action.

Therefore, a first consideration in regard to group politics in America is the issue of how thoroughly various interests are organized. Interests that are highly organized stand a good chance of having their views heard by policymakers. Those that are poorly organized run the risk of being ignored.

Economic Groups

No interests are more fully or effectively organized than those that have economic activity as their primary purpose. Corporations, labor unions, farm groups, and professional associations, among others, exist primarily for economic purposes—to make profits, provide jobs, improve pay, or protect an occupation. For the sake of discussion, we will call such organizations **economic groups**. Almost all such organizations engage in political activity as a means of promoting and protecting their economic interests. An indicator of this is the fact that Washington lobbyists who represent economic groups outnumber those of all other groups by more than two to one.

The predominance of economic interests was predicted in *Federalist* No. 10, in which James Madison declared that property is "the most common and durable source of factions." Stated differently, nothing seems to matter quite so much to people as their economic self-interest.

Types of Economic Groups Most economic groups are of four general types: business groups, labor groups, agricultural groups, and professional groups.

Business Groups More than half of all groups formally registered to lobby Congress are business organizations. Virtually all large corporations and many smaller ones are politically active. Business firms are also represented through associations such as the U.S. Chamber of Commerce, which includes nearly 3 million businesses of all sizes. Other business

Groups: "A Nation of Joiners"

"A nation of joiners" is how the Frenchman Alexis de Tocqueville described the United States during his visit to this country in the 1830s. Tocqueville was stunned by the group and community activity he saw, suggesting that Europeans would find it hard to comprehend. "The political activity that pervades the United States," said Tocqueville, "must be seen to be understood."

Today, Americans still are more actively involved in groups and community causes than are Europeans. Some observers, including Robert Putnam, believe that group activity in the United States is in decline (*Bowling Alone*, 2000). Even if that is true, Americans are more engaged in groups than citizens elsewhere. Among the reasons are the nation's tradition of free association, the openness of American society, and the prominence of religion and public education. Much of the nation's group life revolves around its churches and its schools.

Another reason is the structure of the U.S. political system. Because of federalism and the separation of powers, the American system offers numerous points at which groups can try to influence public policy. If unsuccessful with legislators, groups can turn to executives or to the courts. If thwarted at the national level, groups can turn to state and local governments. By comparison, the governments of most other democratic nations are not organized in ways that facilitate group access and influence. France's unitary government, for example, concentrates power at the national level.

Such differences are reflected in citizens' participation rates. Americans are more likely to belong to groups than are the French, Italians, British, or Germans, as the accompanying figures from the World Values Survey indicate.

	No group	1–3 groups	4 or more groups
United States	18%	63%	19%
Germany	33%	60%	7%
Great Britain	46%	45%	9%
Italy	59%	40%	◄1%
France	61%	35%	4%

Percentage belonging to: ■ No group ■ 1–3 groups ■ 4 or more groups

Source: World Values Survey Association, 2008.

associations, such as the American Petroleum Institute, are confined to a single trade or industry.

Business interests have an advantage that economist Mancur Olson called "the size factor."[4] It might be thought that in a democracy the interests of groups with large memberships would nearly always prevail over the interests of small groups. However, as Olson points out, small groups are ordinarily more united on policy issues and often have more resources, enabling them to win out against large groups. Business groups in a particular industry are usually few in number and tend to work together to influence government on issues of joint interest. In contrast, taxpayers, though they number in the tens of millions and could be powerful if they joined together, have no real interest in paying dues to a taxpayers' group that would lobby on their behalf. In 2008, these differences came together in ways that conceivably hurt taxpayers while helping financial institutions, such as JP Morgan Chase. At issue was a government bailout aimed at protecting major investment banks from bankruptcy as a result of their purchase of mortgage-backed securities, which had declined sharply in value as the U.S. housing market weakened. With the backing of policymakers in the Federal Reserve and the Treasury Department, as well as President Bush and some of the top congressional leaders, the banking industry narrowly succeeded in persuading Congress to pass legislation that provided the Treasury Department with $700 billion in taxpayers' money to buy mortgage-related securities from troubled financial institutions in order to keep them afloat, even though it was their purchase of risky high-yield investments that had led them to the point of bankruptcy.

Labor Groups   Since the 1930s, organized labor has been politically active on a large scale. Its goal has been to promote policies that benefit workers in general and union members in particular. Although there are some major independent unions, such as the United Mine Workers and the Teamsters, the dominant labor group is the AFL-CIO, which has its national headquarters in Washington, D.C. The AFL-CIO has 9 million members in its roughly fifty affiliated unions, which include the International Brotherhood of Electrical Workers, the Sheet Metal Workers, and the Communications Workers of America.

At one time, about a third of the U.S. workforce was unionized, but today only about one in eight workers belongs to a union. Skilled and unskilled laborers have historically been the core of organized labor, but their numbers are decreasing while the numbers of professionals, technicians, and service workers are increasing. Professionals have shown little interest in union organization, perhaps because they identify with management or consider themselves economically secure. Service workers and technicians are also

★ | LEADERS

James Madison
(1751–1836)

James Madison has been called the "father of the Constitution." Madison himself rejected that label, saying that the Constitution was the work of "many heads and many hands." Nevertheless, of the Framers, Madison was the best political theorist and saw most clearly how government could be structured as a control on the misuse of political power.
His *Federalist* No. 10, which deals with the problem of interest groups, is regarded by some as the finest political essay ever penned by an American. Later, Madison assisted Thomas Jefferson in forming a political party that aimed to promote ordinary citizens as opposed to the rich and powerful—the forerunner of today's Democratic Party. He served as secretary of state during Jefferson's presidency and, in 1808, succeeded Jefferson as president. Europe was in the midst of the Napoleonic Wars, and Madison was unsuccessful in maintaining America's neutrality. In 1812, the British invaded Washington, D.C., burning the Capitol and forcing Madison to flee to Maryland. The British withdrew and later were defeated by General Andrew Jackson at New Orleans, leading Americans to claim victory in the War of 1812. Madison completed his second presidential term in 1817. After leaving office, he spoke out often against the growing states'-rights sentiment in the South that eventually would plunge the nation into the Civil War over the issue of slavery. On his deathbed, Madison said he wished for nothing more than preservation of the Union.

difficult for unions to organize because they work closely with managers and, often, in small offices.

Nevertheless, unions have made inroads in their efforts to organize service and public employees. Teachers, hotel workers, police officers, firefighters, social workers, and restaurant employees are among the service and public employee groups that have become increasingly unionized. In fact, the nation's largest unions today are those that represent service and public employees rather than skilled and unskilled laborers (see Table 9-1).

table	9-1	THE LARGEST LABOR UNIONS, 1950 AND 2000

The largest labor unions today represent service and public employees; fifty years ago, the largest unions represented skilled and unskilled workers.

1950	2000
1. United Auto Workers	1. National Education Association
2. United Steel Workers	2. International Brotherhood of Teamsters
3. International Brotherhood of Teamsters	3. United Food and Commercial Workers International
4. United Brotherhood of Carpenters & Joiners	4. American Federation of State, County, & Municipal Employees
5. International Association of Machinists	5. Service Employees International

Source: U.S. Department of Labor.

Agricultural Groups   Farm organizations represent another large economic lobby. The American Farm Bureau Federation is the largest of the farm groups, with more than 4 million members. The National Farmers Union, the National Grange, and the National Farmers Organization are smaller farm lobbies. Agricultural groups do not always agree on policy issues. For instance, the Farm Bureau sides with agribusiness and owners of large farms, while the Farmers Union promotes the interests of smaller "family" farms.

There are also numerous specialty farm associations, including the Association of Wheat Growers, the American Soybean Association, and Associated Milk Producers. Each association acts as a separate lobby, seeking to obtain policies that will serve its members' particular interest.

Professional Groups   Most professions have lobbying associations. Among the most powerful of these groups is the American Medical Association (AMA), which, with nearly three hundred thousand members, represents about half the nation's physicians. The AMA has consistently opposed any government policy that would limit physicians' independence. Other professional groups include the American Bar Association (ABA) and the American Association of University Professors (AAUP).

An Organizational Edge   One reason for the abundance of economic groups is their access to financial resources. Political lobbying does not come cheap. If a group is to make its views known, it normally must have

This 1873 lithograph illustrates the benefits of membership in the National Grange, an agricultural interest group.

a headquarters, an expert staff, and communication facilities. Economic groups pay for these things with money generated by their economic activity. Corporations have the greatest built-in advantage. They do not have to charge membership dues or conduct fund-raisers to support their lobbying. Their political money comes from their business profits.

Some economic groups rely on dues rather than profits to support their lobbying, but they have something of economic value to exchange for these dues. Labor unions, for example, offer their members, in return for dues, access to higher-paying jobs. Such groups offer what is called a **private (individual) good**—a benefit, such as a job, that is given directly to a particular individual. An important feature of a private good is that it can be withheld. If an individual is unwilling to pay organizational dues, the group can refuse to provide the benefit it offers.

Citizens' Groups Economic groups do not have a monopoly on lobbying. There are a great number of other interest groups, which are referred to collectively as **citizens' groups** (or **noneconomic groups**). Group members in this category are joined together not by a material incentive—such as jobs, higher wages, or profits—but by a **purposive incentive,** the satisfaction of contributing to what they regard as a worthy goal or purpose.[5] Whether a group's purpose is to protect the environment, return prayer to the public schools, or feed the poor at home or abroad, there are citizens who are willing to participate simply because they believe the cause is a worthy one.

However, citizens' groups find it harder than economic groups to raise the money necessary for lobbying. These groups do not generate profits or fees as a result of economic activity. Moreover, the incentives they offer prospective members are not exclusive. As opposed to the private or individual goods provided by many economic groups, most noneconomic groups offer **collective (public) goods** as an incentive for membership. Collective goods are, by definition, benefits that belong to all; they cannot be granted or withheld on an individual basis. The air people breathe and the national forests people visit are examples of collective goods. They are available to one and all, those who do not pay dues to a clean-air group or a wilderness preservation group as well as those who do.

The Free-Rider Problem   The shared characteristic of collective goods creates what is called the **free-rider problem:** individuals can receive the good even when they do not contribute to the group's effort. Take the case of National Public Radio (NPR). Although NPR's programs are funded primarily through listeners' donations, those who do not contribute can listen to the programs. These noncontributors are free riders: they receive the benefit without paying for it. About 90 percent of regular listeners to NPR do not contribute to their local station.

In a purely economic sense, as economist Mancur Olson noted, it is not rational for an individual to contribute to a group when its benefit can be obtained for free.[6] Moreover, the dues paid by any single member are too small to affect the group's success one way or another. Why pay dues to an environmental group when any improvements in the air, water, or wildlife from its lobbying efforts are available to everyone and when one's individual contribution is too small to make a real difference? Although many people do join such groups anyway, the free-rider problem is one reason citizens' groups are less fully organized than economic groups.

The free-rider problem has been lessened, but not eliminated, in recent decades by advances in communication that enable citizens' groups to more easily contact prospective members. Computer-assisted direct mail is one of these advances. Group organizers buy mailing lists and flood the mails with computer-typed "personal" letters asking recipients to pay a small annual membership fee. For some individuals, a fee of $25–50 annually represents no great sacrifice and offers the satisfaction of supporting a cause in which they believe. Until the computer era, citizens' groups had great difficulty identifying and contacting potential members, which is one reason the number of such groups was so much smaller in the past than today.

The Internet is also a boon to citizens' groups. Nearly every such group of any size has its own website and email list. MoveOn is an example of the Internet's organizing capacity. MoveOn was started by a handful of liberal activists working out of a garage. By 2004, they had created an Internet network that linked hundreds of thousands of citizens who could be mobilized in support of liberal candidates and causes. MoveOn raised more than $3 million in 2006 for Democratic candidates while also launching a massive get-out-the-vote effort in the election's closing days that helped the Democrats capture control of Congress. In 2008, it used its fund-raising capacity to assist Barack Obama in the Democratic presidential primaries, contributing to his victory over Hillary Clinton.

Despite such examples, the organizational muscle in American politics rests primarily with economic groups. They have an edge on citizens' groups in nearly every respect—money, solidarity, and control (see Table 9-2).

table 9-2 ADVANTAGES AND DISADVANTAGES HELD BY ECONOMIC AND CITIZENS' GROUPS

Compared with economic groups, citizens' groups have fewer advantages and more disadvantages.

Economic Groups	Citizens' Groups
Advantages	*Advantages*
Economic activity provides the organization with the resources necessary for political action.	Members are likely to support leaders' political efforts because they joined the group in order to influence policy.
Individuals are encouraged to join the group because of economic benefits they individually receive (e.g., wages).	*Disadvantages*
Disadvantages	The group has to raise funds, especially for its political activities.
Persons within the group may not support leaders' political efforts because they did not join the group for political reasons.	Potential members may choose not to join the group because they get collective benefits even if they do not join (the free-rider problem).

Types of Citizens' Groups Most citizens' groups are of three general types: public-interest groups, single-issue groups, and ideological groups.

Public-Interest Groups Groups that claim to represent the broad interests of society call themselves public-interest groups. The label is somewhat misleading. The leaders of these groups are not chosen by the public at large, and the issues they target are ones of their own choosing. Moreover, people have different opinions on what constitutes the "public interest." Nevertheless, there is a basis for distinguishing the so-called public-interest groups from economic groups: the latter seek direct material benefits for their members, while the former seek benefits that are less tangible and more widely shared. For example, the National Association of Manufacturers, an economic group, seeks policies favorable to large corporations, while the League of Women Voters, a public-interest group, seeks policies—such as simplified voter registration—that benefit the broader public.

More than half of the currently active public-interest groups were established after 1960. Prominent examples are the state-level Public Interest Research Groups (PIRGs), such as NYPIRG (New York), CALPIRG (California), and TexPIRG (Texas). Virtually every state now has a PIRG, which usually has chapters on college campuses. Drawing on their network of researchers, students, and advocates, they lobby on behalf of such issues as product safety and political reform.

Single-Issue Groups A single-issue group is organized to influence policy in just one area. Notable current examples are the National Rifle Association and the various right-to-life and pro-choice groups that have formed around the issue of abortion. The number of single-issue groups has risen sharply in the past three decades, and these groups now pressure government on almost every conceivable issue, from nuclear arms to day care centers to drug abuse.

Environmental groups are sometimes classified as public-interest groups, but they can also be classified as single-issue organizations in that most of them seek to influence public policy in a specific area, such as pollution reduction, wilderness preservation, or wildlife protection. The Sierra Club, one of the oldest environmental groups, was formed in the 1890s to promote the preservation of scenic areas. Also prominent are the National Audubon Society, the Wilderness Society, the Environmental Defense Fund, Greenpeace U.S.A., and the Izaak Walton League. Since 1960, membership in environmental groups has more than tripled as a result of the public's increased concern about environmental protection.[7]

The Internet has made it easier for citizens' groups to organize and increase their membership. One of the most successful examples is MoveOn. It was founded by a small group of liberal activists, including Wes Boyd and Joan Blades, shown here standing outside their home in California.

Ideological Groups   Single-issue groups have an issue-specific policy agenda. In contrast, ideological groups have a broad agenda that derives from a philosophical or moral position. An example is the Christian Coalition of America, which describes itself as "America's leading grassrooots organization defending our godly heritage." The group addresses a wide range of issues, including school prayer, abortion, and television programming. Ideological groups on both the left and the right have increased substantially in number since the 1960s.

Some ideological groups are formed squarely around a political philosophy. The American Conservative Union (ACU) is the largest conservative organization and lobbies on issues like taxation and national defense. MoveOn is a liberal counterpart to the ACU, as is Americans for Democratic Action (ADA). One of the oldest ideological groups in the country, the ADA was founded in the 1940s to promote civil rights and working-class interests. Groups such as the National Organization for Women (NOW) and the National Association for the Advancement of Colored People (NAACP) can also be classified generally as ideological groups. Although they represent particular demographic groups, they do so across a wide range of issues. For example, NOW addresses issues ranging from jobs to reproduction to political representation.

A Special Category of Interest Group: Governments

While the vast majority of organized groups represent private interests, some represent governments. Most states and major cities have at least one

Washington lobbyist. Intergovernmental lobbying also occurs through groups such as the Council of State Governments, the National Governors Conference, the National Association of Counties, the National League of Cities, and the U.S. Conference of Mayors. These organizations sometimes play a significant role in national policy debates. For example, as Congress was preparing in 2006 to renew and amend the antiterrorism legislation that had gone into effect in 2001, the National Governors Conference and the U.S. Conference of Mayors lobbied heavily to ensure that the changes reflected state and local concerns, including the adequacy of federal funding.

Foreign governments also lobby in Washington. Arms sales, foreign aid, immigration, and trade practices are among the U.S. policies they target.[8] However, foreign governments are prohibited from engaging in certain lobbying activities, including contributions to U.S. election campaigns.

INSIDE LOBBYING: SEEKING INFLUENCE THROUGH OFFICIAL CONTACTS

Modern government is an inviting target for interest groups. Modern government is involved in so many issues—business regulation, income maintenance, urban renewal, cancer research, and energy development, to name only a few—that hardly any interest in society could fail to benefit significantly from having influence over federal policies or programs. Moreover, modern government is action-oriented. Officials are more inclined to solve problems than let them fester. When forest fires in California, Arizona, and other western states destroyed property worth millions in 2008, the federal government granted large sums to meet the clean-up and other costs of the affected states, localities, and residents.

Groups seek government's support through **lobbying,** a term that refers broadly to efforts by groups to influence public policy through contact with public officials. Lobbying is big business in America. A section of the nation's capital, known as K Street, is populated almost completely by lobbying firms. There are more than twenty thousand Washington lobbyists, and according to official records, they spend more than $1 billion annually on lobbying activities. The actual amount is higher, but no one is quite sure by how much. Lobbying is regulated by the Honest Leadership and Open Government Act of 2007 (which amended the Lobbying Disclosure Act of 1995), which defines who must register as a lobbyist and what lobbying activities and expenditures must be reported. The act was further amended in 2007 to tighten some of its provisions, but it is still the case that some Washington lobbying efforts never become part of the public record.

Interest groups rely on two main lobbying strategies, which have been labeled "inside lobbying" and "outside lobbying."[9] Each strategy involves communication with public officials, but the strategies differ in what is communicated and who does the communicating. This section discusses **inside lobbying,** which is based on group efforts to develop and maintain close ("inside") contacts with policymakers. (Outside lobbying is described in the next section.)

Acquiring Access to Officials

Inside lobbying seeks to give a group direct access to officials in order to influence their decisions. Access is not the same as influence, but it can be a first step in gaining influence. Without access, a group might never have an opportunity to make its position known to policymakers.[10] The importance of access is evident, for example, in the high salaries that former members of Congress can command when they become lobbyists. It is unusual for a seated member of Congress to deny a former member a chance to stop by the congressional office to discuss a group's position on pending legislation. Although former congressional members are prohibited for a period after leaving office from lobbying Congress, they are free to do so thereafter and typically represent groups with which they had close ties while in office.

Lobbying once depended significantly on tangible inducements, sometimes including bribes. This old form of lobbying survives, but modern lobbying generally involves subtler methods than simply slipping a cash-filled envelope to a public official. Lobbyists concentrate on supplying policymakers with information that supports the group's position on pending policy.[11] For the most part, inside lobbying is directed at policymakers who are inclined to support the group rather than at those who have opposed it in the past. This tendency reflects both the difficulty of persuading opponents to change long-held views and the advantage of working through trusted officials. Thus, union lobbyists work mainly with pro-labor officeholders, just as corporate lobbyists work mainly with policymakers who support business interests.

Money is the essential ingredient of inside-lobbying efforts. The American Petroleum Institute, for example, with its abundant financial resources, can afford a downtown Washington office staffed by lobbyists, petroleum experts, and public relations specialists who help the oil companies maintain access to and influence with legislative and executive leaders. Many groups spend upward of $1 million annually on lobbying. One of the top spenders, the American Hospital Association (AHA), invested more than $10 million on lobbying in 2008. Other groups get by on much less,

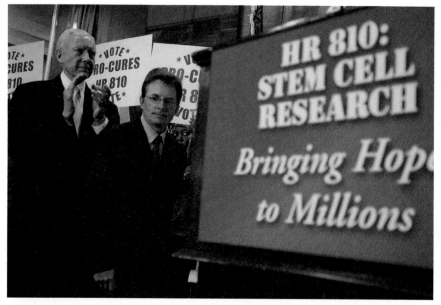

Inside lobbying involves contacts with policymakers. Shown here are actor Michael J. Fox and Senator Orrin Hatch (R-Utah) at an event staged to persuade Congress to enact legislation expanding federal support for stem cell research. Congress passed the legislation, but it was vetoed by President George W. Bush.

but it is hard to lobby effectively on a tiny budget. Given the costs of maintaining a Washington lobby, the domination by corporations and trade associations is understandable. These economic groups have the money to retain high-priced lobbyists, while many other interests do not.

Lobbying Congress   The targets of inside lobbying are officials of all three government branches—legislative, executive, and judicial. The benefits of a close relationship with members of Congress are the most obvious. With support in Congress, a group can obtain the legislative help it needs to achieve its policy goals. By the same token, members of Congress can benefit from working closely with lobbyists. The volume of legislation facing Congress is heavy, and members rely on trusted lobbyists to identify bills that deserve their attention. When Republican lawmakers took control of Congress in 1995, they invited corporate lobbyists to participate directly in drafting legislation affecting business. Congressional Democrats complained loudly, but Republicans said they were merely getting advice from those who best understood business's needs and noted that Democrats had worked closely with organized labor when they were in power.

Lobbyists' effectiveness depends in part on their reputation for fair play. Lobbyists are expected to play it straight. Said one congressman, "If any [lobbyist] gives me false or misleading information, that's it—I'll never see him again."[12] Bullying is also frowned upon. During the debate over the North American Free Trade Agreement in 1993, the AFL-CIO threatened to compaign against congressional Democrats who supported the legislation. The backlash from Democrats on both sides of the issue was so intense that the union backed down on its threat. The safe lobbying strategy is the aboveboard approach: provide information, rely on longtime allies among members of Congress, and push steadily but not too aggressively for legislative goals.

Lobbying Executive Agencies   As the scope of federal policy has widened, lobbying of the executive branch has increased in importance. Bureaucrats make key administrative decisions and develop policy initiatives that the legislative branch later makes into law. By working closely with executive agencies, groups can influence policy decisions at the formulation and implementation stages. In return, groups can help agencies by backing them when their programs and budgets are being reviewed for renewal by Congress and the White House.

Nowhere is the link between groups and the bureaucracy more evident than in the regulatory agencies that oversee the nation's business sectors. For example, the Food and Drug Administration (FDA), which regulates the nation's pharmaceutical companies, relies on them for much of the information used in deciding whether new drugs are safe enough to be put on the market. The FDA is sometimes cited as an example of "agency capture." The capture theory suggests that regulatory agencies pass through a series of phases that constitute a life cycle. When an agency is first created in response to a marketplace problem, it vigorously regulates the targeted industry to make it more responsive to the public interest, but as the agency gets older, its oversight weakens until at best it protects the status quo and at worst it falls captive to the very industry it is supposed to regulate. The FDA exploded into the news in 2004 when the arthritis drug Vioxx was taken off the market after it was discovered that users had abnormally high rates of stroke and heart attack. The FDA apparently had been lax in reviewing the drug's safety, and some within the agency complained they had been pressured by top officials and drug companies not to find safety problems with drugs.[13] Vioxx was generating $2.5 billion a year in sales for Merck, the pharmaceutical company that had invented and patented it.

Studies indicate that the capture theory describes only some agencies—and then only some of the time. Agencies selectively cooperate with or oppose interest groups, depending on which strategy better suits agency purposes. Agency officials are aware that they can lose support in Congress, which controls agency funding and program authorization, if they show too much favoritism toward an interest group.[14] In response to the Vioxx controversy, as well as similar problems with other new drugs, Congress passed legislation in 2007 that forced the FDA to toughen its pre- and post-marketing drug safety testing.

Lobbying the Courts   Judicial rulings in areas such as education and civil rights have made interest groups recognize that the courts can be a way for them to obtain their policy goals.[15] Interest groups have several judicial lobbying options, including efforts to influence the selection of federal judges. Right-to-life groups have pressured Republican administrations to make opposition to abortion a prerequisite for nomination to the federal bench. Democratic administrations have in turn faced pressure from pro-choice groups in their judicial nominations.[16] Groups also use lawsuits to bring about policy change. For some organizations, such as the American Civil Liberties Union (ACLU), legal action is the primary means of lobbying. The ACLU often takes on unpopular causes, such as the free-speech rights of fringe groups. Such causes have little chance of success in legislative bodies but may prevail in a courtroom.

As interest groups increasingly resort to legal action, they often find themselves facing one another in court. Environmental litigation groups such as the Earthwise Legal Defense Fund and the Environmental Defense Fund have frequently sued oil, timber, and mining corporations.

Webs of Influence: Groups in the Policy Process

To get a fuller picture of how inside lobbying works, it is helpful to consider two policy processes—iron triangles and issue networks—in which many groups are enmeshed.

Iron Triangles   An **iron triangle** consists of a small and informal but relatively stable set of bureaucrats, legislators, and lobbyists who seek to develop policies beneficial to a particular interest. The three "corners" of one such triangle are the Department of Agriculture (bureaucrats), the agriculture committees of Congress (legislators), and farm groups such as the Associated Milk Producers and the Association of Wheat Growers (lobbyists). Together they determine many of the policies affecting farmers. Although the support of other players, including the president and a majority in Congress, is needed to enact new policies, they often defer to the judgment of the agricultural triangle, whose members are most familiar with farmers' needs.

A group in an iron triangle has an inside track to those legislators and bureaucrats who are best positioned to help it. And because the group has

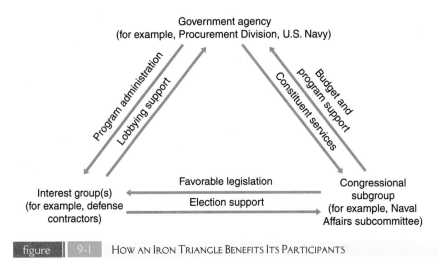

figure 9-1 How an Iron Triangle Benefits Its Participants

An iron triangle works to the advantage of each of its participants: an interest group, a congressional subgroup, and a government agency.

something of value to offer in return, the relationships tend to be "ironclad." The group provides lobbying support for the agency's funding and programs and makes campaign contributions to its congressional allies. Agricultural groups, for example, contribute millions of dollars to congressional campaigns, most of which goes to the reelection campaigns of House and Senate agriculture committee members. Figure 9-1 summarizes the benefits that flow to each member of an iron triangle.

Issue Networks   Iron triangles represent the pattern of influence in only certain policy areas and are less common now than in the past. A more frequent pattern of influence today is the **issue network**—an informal grouping of officials, lobbyists, and policy specialists (the "network") who come together *temporarily* around a policy problem (the "issue").

Issue networks are a result of the increasing complexity of policy problems. Participants must have an intimate knowledge of the issue at hand in order to engage it effectively. Thus, unlike iron triangles, where a participant's position is everything, an issue network is built around specialized interests and knowledge. On any given issue, the participants might come from a variety of executive agencies, congressional committees, interest groups, and institutions such as universities or think tanks. Compared to iron triangles, issue networks are less stable. As the issue develops, new participants may join the debate and old ones may drop out. Once the issue is resolved, the network disbands.[17]

An example of an issue network is the set of participants who would come together over the issue of whether a large tract of old forest should be opened to logging. A few decades ago, that issue would have been settled in an iron triangle consisting of the timber companies, the U.S. Forest Service, and relevant members of the House and Senate agriculture committees. But as forestlands have diminished and environmental concerns have grown, such issues can no longer be contained within the cozy confines of an iron triangle. Today, an issue network would form that included logging interests, the U.S. Forest Service, House and Senate agriculture committee members, research scientists, and representatives of environmental groups, the housing industry, and animal-rights groups. Unlike the old iron triangle, which was confined to like-minded interests, this issue network would include opposing interests (for example, the loggers and the environmentalists). And unlike an iron triangle, the issue network would dissolve once the issue that brought the parties together was resolved.

Issue networks, then, differ substantially from iron triangles. In an iron triangle, a common interest brings the participants together in a long-lasting and mutually beneficial relationship. In an issue network, an immediate issue brings the participants together in a temporary network that is based on their ability to knowledgeably address the issue and where they play out their separate interests before disbanding once the issue is settled.

Despite these differences, iron triangles and issue networks do have one thing in common: they are arenas in which organized groups exercise influence. The interests of the general public may be taken into account in these webs of power, but the interests of the participating groups are foremost.

Outside Lobbying: Seeking Influence Through Public Pressure

Although an interest group may rely solely on inside lobbying, this approach is not likely to be successful unless the group can demonstrate that it represents an important constituency. Accordingly, groups also engage in **outside lobbying,** which involves bringing constituency ("outside") pressure to bear on policymakers (see Table 9-3).[18]

Constituency Advocacy: Grassroots Lobbying

One form of outside pressure is **grassroots lobbying**—that is, pressure designed to convince government officials that a group's policy position has popular support. No group illustrates grassroots lobbying better than the AARP (American Association of Retired Persons). With more than 30 million

| table 9-3 | TACTICS USED IN INSIDE AND OUTSIDE LOBBYING STRATEGIES |

Inside and outside lobbying are based on different tactics.

Inside Lobbying	Outside Lobbying
Developing contacts with legislators and executives Providing information and policy proposals to key officials Forming coalitions with other groups	Encouraging group members to write, phone, or email their representatives in Congress Seeking favorable coverage by news media Encouraging members to support particular candidates in elections Targeting group resources on key election races Making PAC contributions to candidates

members and a staff of sixteen hundred, the AARP is a powerful lobby on retirement issues such as social security and Medicare. When major legislation affecting retirees is pending, the AARP swings into action. Congress receives more mail from members of the AARP than it does from members of any other group. The AARP's support was instrumental, for example, in the enactment in 2003 of a controversial prescription drug program for the elderly. Until the AARP's last-minute endorsement, the program seemed headed for a narrow defeat in Congress.

Electoral Action: Votes and PAC Money

An "outside" strategy can also include election activity. "Reward your friends and punish your enemies" is a political adage that loosely describes how interest groups view elections. The possibility of campaign opposition from a powerful group can restrain an officeholder. Opposition from the 3-million-member National Rifle Association, for example, is a major reason the United States has lagged behind other Western societies in its handgun control laws, despite polls indicating that a majority of Americans favor such laws.

Interest groups gain influence by contributing money to candidates' campaigns. As one lobbyist said, "Talking to politicians is fine, but with a little money they hear you better."[19] Members of Congress sometimes get into hot water by listening to lobbyists while also taking contributions

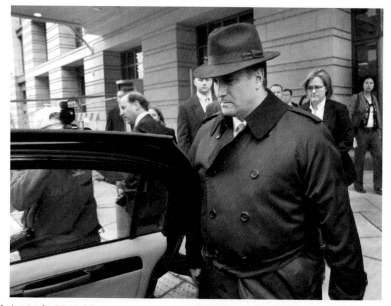

Lobbying in the United States rests on access, information, persuasion, and mutual support. Occasionally, lobbying is a shadier business in which favors are granted that skirt the laws governing lobbying. In 2005, news broke that a prominent Washington lobbyist, Jack Abramoff, had engaged in possibly illegal deals with a number of legislative and executive officials. It did not help Abramoff's case that he had lavished expensive trips on some officials. Controversy surrounding his relationship with Abramoff prompted House majority leader Tom DeLay to resign his congressional seat. Abramoff is shown here leaving federal court in Washington in 2006.

from them. When it was alleged in 2005 that lobbyist Jack Abramoff had cheated some of his clients while also lavishing campaign donations on members of Congress in return for favorable legislation, it sent a shock wave through Washington. Several members of Congress quickly returned Abramoff's campaign donations in the hope that doing so would insulate them from the corruption scandal. A casualty of the Abramoff affair was Representative Tom DeLay (R-Tex.), who lost his post as House majority leader when his close relationship with Abramoff became known. Abramoff had funneled hundreds of thousands of dollars, some of it of questionable legality, to DeLay for political purposes.

A group's election contributions are funneled through its **political action committee (PAC).** A group cannot give organizational funds (such as corporate profits or union dues) to candidates, but through its PAC, a group can solicit voluntary contributions from members or employees and then donate this money to candidates. A PAC can back as many candidates as it wants but is legally limited in the amount it can contribute to a single candidate. The ceiling is $10,000 per candidate—$5,000 in the primary

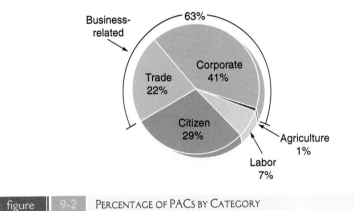

Most PACs represent business. Corporate and trade association PACs make up 63 percent of the total. *Source:* Federal Election Commission, 2008.

campaign and $5,000 in the general election campaign. (These financial limits apply to candidates for federal office. State and local campaigns are regulated by state laws, and some states allow PACs to make unlimited contributions to individual candidates.)

There are more than four thousand PACs, and PAC contributions account for roughly a third of total contributions to congressional campaigns. Their role is less significant in presidential campaigns, which are bigger in scale and depend largely on individual contributors.

More than 60 percent of all PACs are associated with businesses (see Figure 9-2). Most of these are corporate PACs, such as the Ford Motor Company Civic Action Fund, the Sun Oil Company Political Action Committee (Sunpac), and the Coca-Cola PAC. The others are tied to trade associations, such as RPAC (National Association of Realtors). The next-largest set of PACs consists of those linked to citizens' groups (that is, public-interest, single-issue, and ideological groups), such as the liberal People for the American Way and the conservative National Conservative Political Action Committee (NCPAC). Labor unions, once the major source of group contributions, now account for less than 10 percent of PACs.

PACs contribute roughly eight times as much money to incumbents as to their challengers. PACs recognize that incumbents are likely to win and thus to remain in positions of power. One PAC director, expressing a common view, said, "We always stick with the incumbent when we agree with them both."[20] To some extent, the tendency of PACs to back incumbents has blurred long-standing partisan divisions in campaign funding. Business interests are especially pragmatic. Although they tend to favor Republican candidates, they are reluctant to anger Democratic incumbents. The result

Limits on PAC Contributions

Elections of state officials (such as governors and state legislators) are regulated by state law rather than by federal law. In federal elections, PACs can contribute to as many candidates as they like, but they cannot contribute more than $10,000 ($5000 in the primary and $5000 in the general election) to a particular candidate. Some states place no limits on how much money a PAC can contribute to a state or local candidate. Of the states that limit PAC contributions, only New York and Nevada allow contributions in excess of $10,000.

Q: Why might states located to the west of the Mississippi River (which runs down the eastern borders of Minnesota, Iowa, Missouri, Arkansas, and Louisiana) place fewer limits on PAC contributions than other states?

A: A possible explanation is that the political cultures of the western-most states, as a result of their frontier heritage, are less accepting of government regulation of any kind.

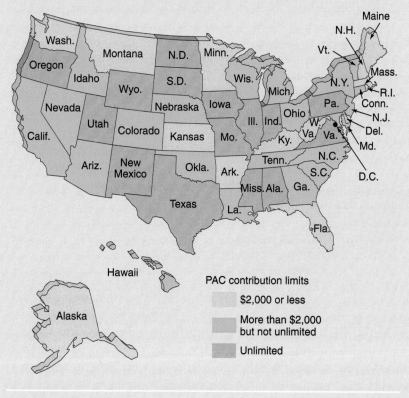

PAC contribution limits

- $2,000 or less
- More than $2,000 but not unlimited
- Unlimited

Source: National Conference of State Legislatures, 2008.

is that Democratic incumbents, particularly in House races, have received substantial support over the years from business-related PACs.[21] Other PACs, of course, are less pragmatic. The Christian Moral Government Fund, for example, backs only candidates who take conservative stands on issues such as school prayer and abortion.

PAC influence has been hotly debated. Advocates of PACs claim that groups have a right to be heard, including the right to express themselves with money. Advocates also note that PACs raise their money through contributions by small donors and are therefore a better system of campaign finance than one based on wealthy donors. On the other hand, critics complain that PACs give interest groups—economic groups particularly—far too much influence on Congress.[22]

Although members of Congress deny that they are unduly influenced by PACs, there is no question that PACs give interest groups a level of access to lawmakers that ordinary citizens lack. Nevertheless, Congress is unlikely in the foreseeable future to pass legislation that would outlaw PACs. The fact is, most members of Congress are unwilling to eliminate a source of campaign funds that helps them to stay in office.

THE GROUP SYSTEM: INDISPENSABLE BUT BIASED

As noted in the chapter's introduction, pluralist theory holds that organized groups are a source of sound governance. On one level, this claim is beyond dispute. Without groups to carry their message, most of society's interests would find it difficult to get government's attention and support. Yet the issue of representation is also a question of whether all interests in society are fairly represented through the group system, and here the pluralist argument is less compelling.

The Contribution of Groups to Self-Government: Pluralism

Group activity is an essential part of self-government. An obstacle to popular sovereignty is the difficulty that public officials have in trying to discover what the people want from government. To discern their wishes, lawmakers consult public opinion polls, meet with constituents, and assess election results. Lobbying activities are also a clue to what people are seeking. Moreover, government does not exist simply to serve majority interests. The fact that most people are not retirees or labor union members or farmers or college students or Hispanics does not mean that the concerns of such "minorities" are unworthy of attention. And what better instrument exists for promoting their interests than lobbying groups working on their behalf?

Some pluralists even question the usefulness of terms such as the *common good* and the *collective interest*. If people disagree on society's goals and priorities, as they always do, how can it be said that people have a "common" or "collective" interest? As an alternative, pluralists contend that the common good ultimately is best served by a process that serves a wide array of separate interests. Thus, if manufacturing interests prevail on one issue, environmentalists on another, farmers on a third, minorities on a fourth, and so on until a great many interests are served, the collective interest of society will have been promoted. Pluralists also note that the promotion of the special interest often works to the benefit of others. Tax incentives for corporations that encourage research and capital investment, for example, can result in better products and additional jobs.

Finally, interest groups often take up issues that are neglected by the political parties. Party leaders typically shy away from issues, such as affirmative action or immigration, on which the party's voters disagree. Such issues would get less notice if not for the groups that promote them. And when groups succeed in drawing attention to these issues, they can sometimes force the parties to address them as well. In this sense, as political scientist Jack Walker noted, the party and group systems together produce a more responsive type of politics than would be the case if the other system somehow did not exist.[23]

Flaws in Pluralism: Interest-Group Liberalism and Economic Bias

Although pluralist theory includes compelling arguments, it also has some questionable aspects. Political scientist Theodore Lowi points out that there is no concept of society's collective interest in a system that gives special interests the ability to determine the policies affecting them.[24] The basis of decision making in such cases is not rule by the majority but rule by a minority—whichever special interest has the most clout in a policy area. Moreover, it cannot be assumed that what a lobbying group wants is what most people would want. Consider the case of the federal law that required auto dealers to list the known defects of used cars on window stickers. The law was repealed after an extensive lobbying campaign financed by contributions of more than $1 million by the National Association of Automobile Dealers to the reelection campaigns of members of Congress.

Lowi uses the term **interest-group liberalism** to describe the tendency of officials to support the policy demands of the interest group or groups that have a special stake in a policy. It is "liberal" in the sense that

Republican and Democratic lawmakers alike are in the habit of catering to
interest groups. Each party has it favorites—for example, business does better when Republicans are in power, and labor does better when Democrats
are in power. But neither party is "conservative" in the sense of being reluctant to use the power of government to promote the narrow interests of
particular groups. One effect is a weakening of majority rule. Rather than
policymaking by the majority acting through its elected representatives, interest-group liberalism involves policymaking by narrow segments of society acting on their own behalf with the help of lawmakers. Another adverse
effect is an inefficient use of society's resources: groups get what they want,
whether or not their priorities match those of society as a whole.

Another flaw in the pluralist argument resides in its claim that the group
system is representative. Although pluralists acknowledge that well-funded
interests have more influence, they say that the group process is relatively
open and few interests are entirely left out. This claim contains an element
of truth, but it is not the full truth. As this chapter has shown, organization is an unequally distributed resource. Economic interests, particularly
corporations, are the most highly organized, and studies indicate that group
politics works chiefly to the advantage of monied interests.[25] Of course, economic groups do not dominate everything, nor do they operate unchecked.
Many of the citizen groups formed since the 1960s were created as checks
on the power of corporate lobbies. Environmental groups are an example.
Although some of them, including the Sierra Club, have existed for a century or longer, most of them are more recent in origin and work to shield the
environment from threats posed by business activity. Activist government
has also brought the group system into closer balance; the government's
poverty programs have spawned groups that seek to protect these programs.
Nevertheless, nearly two-thirds of all lobbying groups in Washington are
business-related. The interest-group system is biased toward America's economically oriented groups, particularly its corporations.

The group system is similarly slanted toward the interests of upper-mid-
dle-class Americans. Affluent Americans have the money, communication
skills, and savvy to participate effectively in special-interest politics. The
poor, minorities, women, and the young are greatly underrepresented in the
group system. A lack of organization does not ensure an interest's failure, just
as the existence of organization does not guarantee success. However, organized interests are obviously in a better position to promote their views.

The business and class bias of the group system is especially significant
because the most highly organized interests are those least in need of government's help. Corporations and affluent citizens already control the largest
share of society's resources. The lobbying system magnifies their advantage.

POLITICAL CULTURE
Liberty, Equality, and Self-Government

Interest Groups

Rarely is the tension between liberty and equality more evident than in the activities of interest groups. "Liberty is to faction what air is to fire," wrote James Madison in *Federalist* No. 10. Madison was lamenting the self-interested behavior of factions or, as they are called today, interest groups. Yet Madison recognized that the only way to suppress this behavior was to destroy the liberty that allows people to organize.

Interest groups tend to strengthen the already powerful and thus contribute to political inequality. As political scientist E. E. Schattschneider said, the group system "sings with a strong upper-class bias."

Numerous efforts have been made to harness the power of groups without infringing on Americans' rights of free expression, assembly, and petition. Laws have been enacted that require lobbyists to register, report their lobbying expenditures, and identify the issues on which they are working. Other laws restrict group contributions to candidates for public office. Yet nothing in the end seems to be all that effective in harnessing the self-interested actions of groups.

Do you think there is an answer to "Madison's dilemma"? Or are the excesses of group politics simply one of the costs of living in a free society?

A Madisonian Dilemma

James Madison recognized the dilemma inherent in group activity. Although he worried that interest groups would have too much political influence, he argued in *Federalist* No. 10 that a free society must allow the pursuit of self-interest. Unless people can promote the separate opinions that stem from differences in their needs, values, and possessions, they are not a free people.

Ironically, Madison's constitutional solution to the problem of factions has become part of the problem. The American system of checks and balances, with a separation of powers at its core, was designed to prevent a majority faction from trampling on the interests of smaller groups. Indeed, throughout the nation's history, majorities have been frustrated in their efforts to exercise power by America's elaborate system of divided government, which makes it relatively easy for a determined minority to block action by the majority.

This same system, however, makes it relatively easy for minority factions—or, as they are called today, special-interest groups—to gain government support. If they can get the backing of even a small number of well-placed policymakers, as in the case of iron triangles, they are likely to get many of the benefits they seek. Because of the system's division of power, they have numerous points at which to exert influence. Often, they need only to find an ally in one place, whether that be a congressional committee or an executive agency or a federal court, to get at least some of what they seek. And once they obtain a government benefit, it is likely to endure. Benefits are hard to eliminate because concerted action by the executive branch and both houses of Congress is usually required. If a group has strong support in even a single institution, it usually can fend off attempts to eliminate a policy or program that serves its interest. Such support ordinarily is easy to acquire, because the group has resources—information, money, and votes—that officeholders want. (Chapters 11 and 13 discuss further the issue of interest-group power.)

SUMMARY   Self-Test www.mhhe.com/pattersonwtp8e

A political interest group is composed of a set of individuals organized to promote a shared concern. Most interest groups owe their existence to factors other than politics. These groups form for economic reasons, such as the pursuit of profit, and maintain themselves by making profits (in the case of corporations) or by providing their members with private goods, such as jobs and wages. Economic groups include corporations, trade associations, labor unions, farm organizations, and professional associations. Collectively, economic groups are by far the largest set of organized interests. The group system tends to favor interests that are already economically and socially advantaged.

Citizens' groups do not have the same organizational advantages as economic groups. They depend on voluntary contributions from potential members, who may lack interest and resources or who recognize that they will get the collective good from a group's activity even if they do not participate (the free-rider problem). Citizens' groups include public-interest, single-issue, and ideological groups. Their numbers have increased dramatically since the 1960s despite their organizational problems.

Organized interests seek influence largely by lobbying public officials and contributing to election campaigns. Using an inside strategy, lobbyists develop direct contacts with legislators, government bureaucrats, and members of the judiciary in order to persuade them to accept the group's perspective on policy. Groups also use an outside strategy, seeking to mobilize public support for their goals. This strategy relies in part on grassroots lobbying—encouraging group members and the public to communicate their policy views to officials. Outside lobbying also includes efforts to elect officeholders who will support group aims. Through political action committees (PACs), organized groups now provide nearly a third of all contributions received by congressional candidates.

The policies that emerge from the group system bring benefits to many of society's interests and often serve the collective interest as well. But when groups can essentially dictate policies, the common good is rarely served. The majority's interest is subordinated to group (minority) interests. In most instances, the minority consists of individuals who already enjoy a substantial share of society's benefits.

KEY TERMS

citizens' (noneconomic) groups (*p. 305*)

collective (public) goods (*p. 305*)

economic groups (*p. 299*)

free-rider problem (*p. 305*)

grassroots lobbying (*p. 315*)

inside lobbying (*p. 310*)

interest group (*p. 297*)

interest-group liberalism (*p. 321*)

iron triangle (*p. 313*)

issue network (*p. 314*)

lobbying (*p. 309*)

outside lobbying (*p. 315*)

political action committee (PAC) (*p. 317*)

private (individual) goods (*p. 304*)

purposive incentive (*p. 305*)

single-issue politics (*p. 297*)

SUGGESTED READINGS

Berry, Jeffrey M. *The New Liberalism: The Rising Power of Citizen Groups.* Washington, D.C.: Brookings Institution, 2000. An exploration of the influence that citizen groups exercise.

Browne, William P. *Cultivating Congress: Constituents, Issues, and Interests in Agriculture Policymaking.* Lawrence: University Press of Kansas, 1995. An analysis of the limits of "iron triangles" as a description of congressional policymaking.

Grossman, Gene M., and Elhanan Helpman. *Interest Groups and Trade Policy.* Princeton, N.J.: Princeton University Press, 2002. An examination of the impact of groups' campaign and lobbying activities on trade policy.

Herrnson, Paul S., Ronald G. Shaiko, and Clyde Wilcox, eds. *The Interest Group Connection: Electioneering, Lobbying, and Policymaking in Washington,* 2nd ed. Washington, D.C.: CQ Press, 2004. Essays and commentaries on groups and officials and the linkages between them.

Lowery, David, and Holly Brasher. *Organized Interests and American Government.* New York: McGraw-Hill, 2004. An overview of interest-group politics.

Lowi, Theodore J. *The End of Liberalism,* 2d ed. New York: Norton, 1979. A thorough critique of interest groups' influence on American politics.

Olson, Mancur, Jr. *The Logic of Collective Action*, rev. ed. Cambridge, Mass.: Harvard University Press, 1971. A pioneering analysis of why some interests are more fully and easily organized than others.

Rozell, Mark J., Clyde Wilcox, and David Madland. *Interest Groups in American Campaigns*, 2nd ed. Washington, D.C.: Congressional Quarterly Press, 2005. An assessment of the election role of interest groups.

LIST OF WEBSITES

http://www.fec.gov/ The Federal Election Commission site; offers information on elections, voting, campaign finance, parties, and PACs; also includes a citizens' guide to campaign contributions.

http://www.pirg.org/ The Public Interest Research Group (PIRG) site; PIRG has chapters on many college campuses, and the site provides state-by-state policy and other information.

http://www.sierraclub.org/ The website of the Sierra Club, one o f the oldest environmental protection interest groups, which promotes conservation; provides information on its activities.

http://www.townhall.com/ The website of the American Conservative Union (ACU); includes policy and political information, and has a lively chat room.

POLITICS IN THEORY AND PRACTICE

Thinking: Why are there so many more organized interests in the United States than elsewhere? Why are so many of these groups organized around economic interests—particularly business interests?

Participating: Consider contributing to a citizens' interest group. Such groups depend on members' donations for operating funds. Citizens' groups cover the political spectrum from right to left and touch on nearly every conceivable public issue. You will not have difficulty locating a group through the Internet that has policy goals consistent with your beliefs and values. If you are interested in contributing your time instead, some citizens groups (for example, PIRG) have college chapters that might provide opportunities for you to work on issues of personal interest.

Extra Credit

For up-to-the-minute *New York Times* articles, interactive simulations, graphics, study tools, and more links and quizzes, visit the text's Online Learning Center at www.mhhe.com/pattersonwtp8e.

The Lobbying Game Today

By Jonathan D. Salant

_____

Lobbying is a natural part of the political process but nowhere is it more prominent than in the United States. More than twenty thousand lobbyists work in Washington, D.C., spending upward of $2 billion annually to impress their views on federal officials. In this 2006 article, which was published in the journal of the Carl Albert Congressional Research and Studies Center at the University of Oklahoma, Jonathan Salant, a reporter with Bloomberg News, describes congressional lobbying and the influence patterns resulting from it.

Capitol Hill lobbyists have traditionally served as a source of information for lawmakers and their staffs. In recent years, they have become an important source of campaign contributions as well as a coveted place for officials to land once their terms have expired.

The traditional role of lobbyist has been to advocate, letting a lawmaker or staff member know how a proposal would affect the corporation or interest group employing him or her. A good lobbyist supplies unbiased details that the lawmaker can use in deciding whether to support or oppose the particular provision. . . .

In recent years, newspapers have reported that lobbyists have gone beyond advocating a particular position to helping draft the legislation itself. Representative Rahm Emanuel (D-Ill.), the chairman of the Democratic Congressional Campaign Committee, has decried what he calls the "blurring of the line between lobbying and writing legislation."

Lobbying is big business in Washington, its growth mirroring the increase in the federal budget. Between 1999 and 2005, the amount of money spent on lobbying by companies, trade associations and other interest groups grew to $2.4 billion from $1.5 billion, a 60 percent increase, according to PoliticalMoneyLine, an independent group that tracks lobbying, During the same period, the federal budget rose to $2.5 trillion from $1.7 trilion, a 47 percent boost, according to the Congressional Budget Office.

"The size and scope of government is just staggering," said John Feehery, a former spokesman for House Speaker Dennis Hastert (R-Ill.), and now executive vice president of the Motion Picture Association of America. "If you want to get your share, you need a lobbyist. That's how you do it. As long as there's more money there's going to be a need for people in Washington to be hired to get it."

What do companies get for that money? Bloomberg News examined the 20 largest publicly traded federal contractors using data from the Federal Contracts Database, PoliticalMoneyLine, and Dwight L. Morris and Associates (which analyzes Federal Election Commission filings). The idea was to see how much companies spent to influence lawmakers versus how much they received in federal contracts.

The nation's largest federal contactor, Lockheed Martin Corp., received $39.8 billion in federal contracts in 2003-04; During the same period, the company spent $15.8 million on lobbying expenses and campaign donations. The ratio of contracts to expenditures was $2,517 to $1.

"It's an investment strategy," former House Appropriations Committee Democratic spokesman David Sirora said. "We shouldn't blame companies for spending a lot of money on lobbying because it's an investment strategy. We should blame those lawmakers who we the public empower to spend our dollars for selling off that power in exchange for campaign cash. That's the problem."

Lawmakers say they approve government spending on the merits, not on who's doing the lobbying. "For every one [project] that we will agree to, you'll find two or three we do not agree to," said Representative C.W. (Bill) Young (R-Fla.), the chairman of the House Appropriations defense subcommittee. "I don't deal with the lobbyist. What I tell the lobbyist to do is bring in the CEO or the project manager so I can deal directly with the people involved."

When they're not trying to influence lawmakers, lobbyists are helping them raise money. Lobbyists serve as treasurers of campaign committees or political action committee for almost 80 lawmakers, according to the Center for Public Integrity, a watchdog group. They also host fundraisers for lawmakers; in one week in April, while House committees drafted lobbying legislation, there were at least four fundraisers sponsored by lobbyists.

Republican lobbyist Jack Abramoff (who pleaded guilty in January to conspiring to corrupt public officials), his associates, and Indian tribal clients contributed $1.4 million to 171 lawmakers between 2001 and 2004, two-thirds to Republicans. During his time at the lobbying firm of Greenberg Traurig LLP, the firm's political action committee donations rose from $183,851 in 2000 to $360,185.

Overall, campaign donations from lobbyists rose to $18.5 million in 2006 from $7.5 million in 1996. Federal Election Commission records show.

"Because campaign donations are the way that lobbyists believe they can get access, the campaign fianance system keeps rolling along untouched," said Rogan Kersh,

a political science professor (now scrving as associate dean at New York University) who teaches courses on lobbying. "Members of Congress are terrified they're going to be knocked off by a challenger. The lobbyists fuel the process and give money to those already in office". . . .

Lobbyists also play prominent roles in obtaining earmarks—local projects inserted into legislation—for clients.

The number of earmarks has increased from 4,126 in 1994, the last year the Democrats controlled both houses of Congress, to 15,569 in 2006, according to the Congressional Research Service.

At least 46 former House Appropriations Committee aides registered as lobbyists after leaving their congressional jobs since 1998, according to records compiled by the Center for Public Integrity. That compared with 36 for the House Ways and Means Committee and 34 for the House Energy and Commerce panel.

One lobbying firm that has hired former appropriations staff members is PMA Group of Arlington, Virginia, whose founder, Paul Magliocchetti, and six other employees once worked for the committee. The firm got 66 special projects worth $119 million for its clients inserted into defense spending legislation for the fiscal year that began Oct. 1, according to Taxpayers for Common Sense, an advocacy group that favors less government spending.

The Washington-based firm Van Scoyoc Associates Inc. employed three former appropriations staff members and got 18 special projects worth $66 million in the defense measure, according to Taxpayers for Common Sense records.

"The revolving door allows these lobbyists to exploit the relationships they have with lawmakers that can hand out billions and billions of dollars," said Alex Knott, political editor for the Center for Public Integrity.

Stu Van Scoyoe, president of the firm that bears his name, said former congressional aides give his clients the technical knowledge they need, such as the proper format for a funding request, and can anticipate objections and address them to prevent an allocation from being rejected.

"The appropriations staffers tend to be very much into the details, very much green eyeshades type of people," Van Scoyoc said. "Having people who are currently knowledgeable in programs and in the details of programs is always an advantage."

Former top-level staff members can lawfully lobby their former committee after a one-year waiting period. Lower-level staff members can lobby immediately after leaving their congressional job.

One lawmaker who writes spending legislation said former appropriations aides have an advantage in securing funds because they know the process.

"Obviously, they're more knowledgeable because of their experience, but they don't have any undue influence," said Representative Harold Rogers, a Kentucky Republican who chairs the appropriations homeland security subcommittee. "If you know your subject, you're usually more successful."

The Appropriations Committee's top two staff members had left the congressional payroll and worked as lobbyists before joining staff of panel Chairman Jerry Lewis of California. Committee staff director Frank Cushing left the panel in 2003 to lobby for defense contractors, and rejoined it in 2005.

Jeffrey Shockey initially worked for Lewis from 1991 to 1999, and later worked for a lobbying firm in which Lewis's longtime friend, former Republican Representative Bill Lowery of California, is a partner. Shockey became deputy director of the Appropriations Committee staff in 2005.

Appropriations Committee spokesman John Scofield said Cushing and Shockey returned to the Appropriations Committee because they wanted to work for Lewis. "These guys gave up good situations and high-paying jobs to do public service," Scofield said.

The House this year passed new rules to identify the lawmakers who request earmarks. The rules expire at the end of the year.

That was the only ethics reform passed. When Congress considered stronger legislation, some lobbyists began lobbying against the measure.

"No matter how well-intentioned a reform effort may be, it will be meaningless to the American people if we first don't begin by talking about enforcement of the current rules," said Paul Miller, president of the American League of Lobbyists, in testimony to the Senate Homeland Security and Government Affairs Committee in January.

On Election Day 2006, three House Republicans with ties to Republican lobbyist Jack Abramoff, who pleaded guilty to conspiring to corrupting public officials, lost their reelection campaigns. Three seats vacated by Republicans who resigned because of ethical problems also fell to the Democrats. A CNN exit poll found 42 percent of voters saying ethics were an "extremely important" factor in their vote.

What's Your Opinion?

What limits, if any, would you place on lobbying? Would you change, for example, "the revolving door" restrictions governing lobbying by individuals that have worked in Congress? Do you think such changes would substantially or only slightly diminish the influence of lobbyists?

CHAPTER 10

THE NEWS MEDIA: COMMUNICATING POLITICAL IMAGES

66 The press in America . . . determines what people will think and talk about an authority that in other nations is reserved for tyrants, priests, parties, and mandarins. 99

THEODORE H. WHITE[1]

The news flashed across America. Eliot Spitzer, governor of New York, had been caught paying for a high-priced call girl. Using the alias George Fox, Spitzer had checked into the Mayflower hotel in Washington, D.C., where he was scheduled to testify at a congressional hearing the next morning on the bond crisis spreading through the financial markets. Unbeknown to Spitzer, the FBI had wiretapped his phone, seeking to account for suspicious money transfers from his New York bank account. In the process, they discovered that Spitzer—known to the prostitution ring as Client No. 9—was wiring the money to pay for a rendezvous with a call girl. After being contacted by the FBI and informed that his calls had been taped, Spitzer called a press conference and, with his wife at his side, apologized for his actions. Two days later, with the story still in the headlines and facing mounting pressure to resign, Spitzer stepped down as New York's governor, saying that he did not want his "private failings to disrupt the public's work." Spitzer concluded his brief resignation speech by noting: "Over the course of my public life, I have insisted—I believe correctly—that people, regardless of their position or power, take responsibility for their conduct. I can and will ask no less of myself."

Spitzer was elected governor in 2006, after having made a reputation for ferreting out Wall Street corruption as state attorney general. Ironically, he had also prosecuted prostitution rings. However, nothing that Spitzer had done previously—not as attorney general, not as gubernatorial candidate, and not as governor—had generated anywhere near the headlines accompanying the revelation that he had paid for the services of a prostitute. It was front-page news throughout the country, the lead story on television newscasts, and the leading topic of conversation on talk shows and Internet blogs. It was also grist for the late-night television shows. On his program, after noting that Spitzer might have used campaign funds to pay for the prostitute, Conan O'Brien quipped: "To be fair, [he] did get her vote."

Although reporters sometimes compare the news to a mirror held up to reality, the news is more accurately described as a refracted version of reality. The **news** is mainly an account of obtruding events, particularly those that are *timely* (new or unfolding developments rather than old or static ones), *dramatic* (striking developments rather than commonplace ones), and *compelling* (developments that arouse people's emotions).[2] These tendencies have their origins in a number of factors, the most significant of which is that news organizations aim to make a profit. Accordingly, they seek news stories that will attract a large audience. Thus, compared with Spitzer's sexual liaison, his work as a top public official was less newsworthy. It was part of the ongoing business of government and did not lend itself to the vivid storytelling of a sex scandal.

News organizations and journalists are referred to collectively as the **press** or the **news media**. The press includes broadcast networks (such as ABC and NPR), cable networks (such as CNN and Fox), newspapers (such as the *Chicago Tribune* and *Dallas Morning News*), news magazines (such as *Time* and *Newsweek*), and Internet sites that provide news and commentary (such as Instapundit and the Drudge Report). The U.S. news system has been undergoing substantial changes. For decades the news system was monopolized by broadcast television and daily newspapers. They are still the dominant players, but over the past quarter-century, they have lost audience and influence to cable news, talk radio, and Internet sites, a point that will be addressed later in the chapter.

After getting caught paying for a prostitute, New York governor Eliot Spitzer, with his wife by his side, announces his resignation from office. The scandal generated far more news coverage than anything Spitzer had done in office, including his efforts to weed out Wall Street corruption. The news media, as their coverage of Spitzer illustrates, presents a refracted version of reality, where sensational developments typically get more attention than the day-to-day policy problems that have a larger effect on Americans' lives.

This chapter examines the news media's role in the American political system. The chapter will argue that the press is a key intermediary between Americans and their leaders, but it will also argue that the press is a different kind of intermediary than either the political party or the interest group, which seek to represent particular interests in society. Most news organizations do not aim to represent particular interests. They do claim, with some justification, to serve the public interest by keeping people informed about public affairs. Yet their news coverage is driven as much by a need to attract an audience in order to sell advertising, which finances their operations. Accordingly, the news tends to focus on sensational events that will catch people's attention rather than on ordinary developments that are ultimately more important in people's lives. This chapter will explore this and other aspects of the press and its news coverage. The main ideas presented in the chapter are these:

★ *The American press was initially tied to the nation's political party system (the partisan press) but gradually developed an independent position (the objective press).* In the process, the news shifted from a political orientation, which emphasizes political values and ideas, to a journalistic orientation, which stresses newsworthy information and events.

★ *In recent years, traditional news organizations have faced increased competition for people's attention from cable and the Internet, which has contributed to audience fragmentation and the rise of opinionated journalism.*

★ *The news media have several functions—signaling (the press brings relevant events and problems into public view), common-carrier (the press serves as a channel through which leaders and citizens can communicate), watchdog (the press scrutinizes official behavior for evidence of deceitful, careless, or corrupt acts), and partisan (the press promotes particular interests and values).* The traditional media contribute mainly to the first three functions while the "new" news media contribute mainly to the last one.

★ *The news audience has been shifting and fragmenting, partly as a result of new technology and partly because young adults are less likely than older ones to have a daily news habit.* One consequence has been a widening information gap between America's better-informed and less-informed citizens.

HISTORICAL DEVELOPMENT: FROM THE NATION'S FOUNDING TO TODAY

Democracy thrives on a free flow of information.[3] Communication enables a free people to keep in touch with one another and with officials, a fact not lost on America's early leaders. Alexander Hamilton persuaded John Fenno to start a newspaper, the *Gazette of the United States*, as a means of publicizing the policies of George Washington's administration. To finance the paper, Hamilton, as secretary of the treasury, granted it the Treasury Department's printing contracts. Hamilton's political rival, Thomas Jefferson, dismissed the *Gazette's* reporting as "pure Toryism" and convinced Philip Freneau to start the *National Gazette* as an opposition paper. Jefferson, as secretary of state, gave Freneau the authority to print State Department documents.

Early newspapers were printed a page at a time on flat presses, a process that limited production and kept the cost of each copy beyond the reach

Historical Background

of ordinary citizens. Leading papers such as the *Gazette of the United States* had fewer than fifteen hundred readers and could not have survived without party support. Not surprisingly, the "news" they printed was laden with partisanship.[4] In this era of the **partisan press**, publishers openly backed one party or the other.

Technological innovation in the early 1800s helped bring about the gradual decline of the partisan newspaper. With the invention of the telegraph, editors had access to timely information on events outside the local area, which led them to substitute news stories for opinion commentary. Creation of the hand-cranked rotary press was equally important because it enabled publishers to print their newspapers more cheaply and quickly. The *New York Sun* was the first paper to take advantage of the new technology. The *Sun* reduced the price of its daily paper from six cents to a penny, and its daily circulation rose from one thousand to ten thousand in less than a year.[5] Increased circulation meant increased advertising revenue, which helped to free newspapers from their dependence on government printing contracts.

By the late nineteenth century, helped along by the invention of newsprint and power-driven presses, many American newspapers were printing fifty thousand or more copies a day, and their large circulations enabled them to charge high prices for advertising. The period marked the height of newspapers' power and the low point in their sense of public responsibility. A new style of reporting—"yellow journalism"—had emerged as a way of boosting circulation. It was "a shrieking, gaudy, sensation-loving, devil-may-care kind of journalism which lured the reader by any possible means."[6] A circulation battle between William Randolph Hearst's *New York Journal* and Joseph Pulitzer's *New York World* may have contributed to the outbreak of the Spanish-American War through sensational (and largely inaccurate) reports on the cruelty of Spanish rule in Cuba. A young Frederic Remington (who later became a noted painter and sculptor), working as a news artist for Hearst, planned to return home because Cuba appeared calm and safe, but Hearst cabled back: "Please remain. You furnish the pictures and I'll furnish the war."[7]

The Objective-Journalism Era

The excesses of yellow journalism led some publishers to consider ways of reporting the news more responsibly. One step was to separate the newspaper's advertising department from its news department, thus reducing the influence of advertisers on news content. A second development was a new model of reporting called **objective journalism**, which was based on the reporting of "facts" rather than opinions and was "fair" in that it presented both sides of partisan debate. A chief advocate of this new form of journalism was Adolph Ochs of the *New York Times*. Ochs bought the *Times* in 1896, when its circulation was 9,000; four years later, its readership had grown to 82,000. Ochs told his reporters that he "wanted as little partisanship as possible . . . as few judgments as possible."[8] The *Times* gradually acquired a reputation as the country's best newspaper. Objective reporting was also promoted through newly formed journalism schools, such as those at Columbia University and the University of Missouri. Within a few decades, objective journalism was entrenched at most American newspapers.

Yellow journalism was characterized by its sensationalism. William Randolph Hearst's *New York Journal* whipped up public support for a war in Cuba against Spain through inflammatory reporting on the sinking of the battleship *Maine* in Havana Harbor in 1898.

Until the twentieth century, the print media were the only form of mass communication. By the 1920s, however, hundreds of radio stations were broadcasting throughout the nation. At first the government did not regulate radio broadcasting. The result was chaos. A common problem was that nearby stations often used the same or adjacent radio frequencies, interfering with each other's broadcasts. Finally, in 1934, Congress passed the Communications Act, which regulated broadcasting and created the Federal Communications Commission (FCC) to oversee the process. Broadcasters had to be licensed by the FCC, and because the number of available broadcasting frequencies was limited, licensees had to be evenhanded in their political coverage. Section 315 of the Communications Act imposed on broadcasters an "equal time" restriction, which prohibited them from selling or giving airtime to a political candidate without offering to sell or give an equal amount of airtime to other candidates for the same office. (An exception was later made for election debates; broadcast-ers can televise them even if third-party candidates are excluded.)

Television followed radio, and by the late 1950s, more than 90 percent of American homes had a TV set. In this period, the FCC imposed a second restriction—the Fairness Doctrine—on broadcasters. The Fairness Doctrine required broadcasters to "afford reasonable opportunity for the discussion of conflicting views of public importance." Broadcasters were pro-hibited from using their news coverage to promote one party or issue position at the expense of another. In effect, the objective-reporting model practiced voluntarily by the newspapers was imposed by law on broadcasters.

The Rise of the "New" News

During the era of objective journalism, the news was not entirely devoid of partisanship. Although broadcasters were prohibited by law from editori-alizing, newspapers were not. Most of them backed one political party or the other on their editorial and opinion (op-ed) pages. Nevertheless, it was difficult to tell from their news pages which party they backed editorially. Nearly all of them highlighted the same national stories each day, and if a high-ranking public official got embroiled in a scandal or policy blunder, they played it up, whether the official was a Republican or a Democrat.

The introduction of cable television did not at first change this pattern. Cable television is transmitted by privately owned wire rather than broad-cast over the public airways and therefore did not have to comply with the Fairness Doctrine. Nevertheless, when the media mogul Ted Turner started CNN in 1980, he chose to abide by it, instructing his correspon-dents to pursue a path of partisan neutrality. He sought to attract view-ers through round-the-clock news and live on-the-scene reports. Turner's marketing idea worked. CNN's audience and reputation ballooned when-ever a major event occurred. In 1991, for example, Americans were riveted to CNN's live coverage from Baghdad as the first American bombs of the Persian Gulf War began falling on that city.

When CNN was launched in 1980, barely more than 10 percent of American homes had cable service. Within a decade, however, the number exceeded 50 percent, which led the FCC to rescind the Fairness Doctrine. The FCC reasoned that the scarcity argument was no longer compelling be-cause cable had greatly increased the number of available channels. Broadcast stations were suddenly free to cover politics in ways of their choosing.

Radio stations were the first to respond to the change. They had previ-ously been required to air a liberal talk show if they aired a conservative one. The reverse was also true. As a consequence, most station owners had chosen not to broadcast political talk shows. After the Fairness Doctrine was eliminated, however, scores of radio stations switched from playing music to airing political talk shows, and today, radio listeners in every market have access to such programming. Cable television, too, provides partisan talk shows, a trend that began when the billionaire media mogul Rupert Murdoch launched Fox News in 1996. He hired Roger Ailes, a Republican political consultant, to run Fox News, instructing him to devise a format appealing to political conservatives. Ailes hired several conservative talk show hosts, including Bill O'Reilly. Within a relatively few years, bouyed by a largely Republican audience, Fox News had surpassed CNN as the most heavily watched cable news network.

In the 1990s, the Internet emerged as yet another source of news and political commentary. Unlike a newspaper, broadcast station, or cable company, where the capital investment can run into the tens or even hundreds of millions of dollars, the Internet has a low cost of entry. Anyone with a

Elimination of the Fairness Doctrine led to the emergence of Christian broadcasting as a political forum. Although Christian broadcasting, led by Pat Robertson's Christian Broadcasting Network, was widely heard and watched in some parts of the country, it was constrained in its political commentary by the Fairness Doctrine. Once that obstacle was removed, however, Robertson and other conservative Christian broadcasters changed their programming to include political appeals. Robertson even ran for public office himself, entering the 1988 race for the Republican presidential nomination. Robertson is pictured here hosting his television program, *The 700 Club*.

computer and technical savvy can create a website or blog devoted to news and public affairs. Thousands of such sites exist. Their sheer number and the stunning success of some of them—the Drudge Report, Instapundit, Daily Kos, and Boing Boing, to name a few—have created an important "new" news media. Such sites resemble political talk radio in that they freely mix news and partisanship.

THE POLITICS OF NEWS

The news media are Americans' window onto the world of politics. For most people, politics is largely a second-hand experience, something they observe through the media rather than directly. The media are not, however, the main source of citizens' political *opinions*. Party loyalties, group attachments, and social networks are more important sources. On the other hand, people's political *perceptions* derive largely from the media. People's mental pictures of events and policy problems, and even their images of political institutions and leaders, stem primarily from what they see and hear through the news media.

The news media operate as *gatekeepers*. Out of the countless possibilities each day, they determine which events will be covered and which ones will not. These selections, in turn, will influence what citizens are thinking and talking about. What determines these selections? What determines whether something will make the news, and thus become known to the public, or will not make the news, and thus remain largely out of sight except to those directly affected?

As it happens, journalists' selections are channeled by four functions—the signaling, common-carrier, watchdog, and partisan functions—that the media perform. We'll look first at the signaling function.

The Signaling Function

The media's responsibilities include a **signaling function**. The media seek to alert the public to important developments as soon as possible after they happen—a state visit to Washington by a foreign leader, a bill that has just been passed by Congress, a change in the nation's unemployment level, or a terrorist bombing in a foreign capital.

The U.S. media are well equipped to play a signaling role. They are poised to converge on any major news event anywhere in the nation and nearly anywhere in the world. The signaling function is performed largely by the traditional media—the wire services, the daily newspapers, and the television networks. They are staffed and organized to cover events and consequently are the source of most breaking news. Occasionally, an event enters the news stream through the Internet. It was bloggers who first recognized that a racially laden comment by Senate Republican leader Trent Lott in 2002 was big news—big enough that it would eventually force Lott to resign his leadership post. Nevertheless, hundreds of news stories enter the news stream daily, and the great bulk of them are generated by traditional news outlets.

A Common Version of Reality   In their capacity as signalers, the media have the power to focus the public's attention. The term **agenda setting** has been used to describe the media's ability to influence what is on people's minds.[9] By covering the same events, problems, issues, and leaders—simply by giving them space or time in the news—the media place them on the public agenda. The press, as Bernard Cohen notes, "may not be successful much of the time in telling people what to think, but it is stunningly successful in telling them what to think about."[10]

Even when "media reality" does not match "objective reality," it can have a powerful effect on what people think is true. A classic example occurred in the early 1990s when local television newscasts, in an attempt to bolster sagging ratings, upped their crime coverage. "If it bleeds it leads" became the mantra of local TV news. Meanwhile, the national media were playing up several high-profile murder cases, including the arrest of serial killer Joel Rifkin, who murdered eighteen women in New York, and the kidnap-murder of 12-year-old Polly Klaas in California. Crime was the most heavily reported national issue, overshadowing all others, even the timely topics of health care reform and the economy. The effect on public opinion was dramatic. In the previous decade, no more than 5 percent of Americans had believed at any time that crime was the country's biggest problem. By 1994, however, more than 40 percent of Americans said that crime was the top issue facing the nation. Politicians got caught up in the public's anxiety. Lawmakers rushed to enact tough new sentencing policies and spent more money to build new prisons than at any time in the nation's history. The irony was that the actual level of crime in America was *declining* during this period. According to U.S. Justice Department statistics, the rate of violent crime had dropped by 5 percent since 1990.[11]

The press is a powerful agenda setter in part because nearly all major news organizations focus on the same stories and interpret them in pretty much the same way. In view of the freedom and great number of news organizations—there are roughly fifteen hundred daily newspapers and a thousand local television outlets in the United States—it might be expected that Americans would be exposed to widely different versions of national news. The opposite is true. Each day, newspapers and broadcast outlets from coast to coast tend to present the same national news, thus conveying the sense that the news, somehow, *is* reality.

Objective journalism, which inclines news outlets to refrain from using the news as a device for promoting a particular viewpoint, is a reason the national news is everywhere pretty much the same. Unlike some European news systems, where journalism norms allow and even encourage reporters to present the news through a partisan lens, American reporters are expected to treat the political parties and their leaders in a balanced way. They do not always do so, but in their quest for balance, American reporters tend toward a common interpretation of political developments, as opposed to a Republican version or a Democratic version.

Another reason the news everywhere in the United States is pretty much the same is that news outlets rely on the wire services for most of their national coverage. Most U.S. news organizations lack the resources to gather news outside their own location and rely for this coverage on the wire services, particularly the Associated Press (AP), which has three thousand reporters stationed throughout the country and the world to gather news stories and transmit them to subscribing news organizations. More than 95 percent of the nation's dailies (as well as most broadcast stations) subscribe to the AP, which, because it serves the full range of American news outlets, studiously avoids partisanship in preparing its stories. A few U.S. newspapers—including the *New York Times*, *Wall Street Journal*, *Los Angeles Times*, *Washington Post*, and *Chicago Tribune*—have large enough reporting staffs to generate their own national coverage. Nevertheless, these papers, too, give similar coverage to the same top stories each day. They differ mostly in their feature, follow-up, and investigative reports, most of which appear on the inside pages rather than on the front page.

Local television stations also depend on outside sources for their national news coverage. Television production is hugely expensive, which limits the ability of local stations to produce anything except local news. For their national coverage, they rely on video feeds from the leading television networks—ABC, CBS, NBC, CNN, Fox, and MSNBC. Even the national networks have a similar lineup of stories. Most network newcasts are a half hour in length, with ten minutes devoted to advertising. With so little time for news, the day's top stories tend to dominate the newscasts of all networks. Moreover, network correspondents cover the same beats and rely on many of the same sources, which leads them to report more or less the same things. After filming a congressional hearing, for example, network correspondents are likely to agree on what was most newsworthy about it—often a testy exchange between a witness and one of the committee members.

Informing the Public, or Attracting an Audience?   The signaling function of the press is sometimes called its informing function, but the latter

★ | STATES IN THE NATION

In the News, or Out?

Most of the news that reaches Americans, no matter where they live, originates with a handful of news outlets, such as NBC News. This coverage, however, concentrates on events in a few places. The map shows the relative frequency with which each of the fifty states was mentioned on NBC News during a one-year period.

Q: Why do some states get more coverage than other states?

A: The heavily covered states are usually the more populous ones, which increases the likelihood that a newsworthy event will occur. In NBC's case, coverage is also heavier in states where one of its news bureaus is located. NBC has bureaus in New York, Washington, Los Angeles, Dallas, Atlanta, Chicago, and Boston.

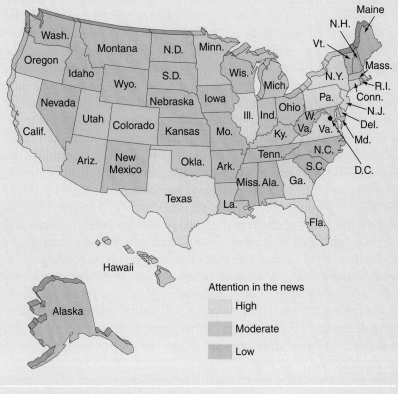

Source: Data compiled by the author from Nexis.

is a much less accurate description of how the media operate. Although news organizations take seriously their responsibility to inform the public, the more pressing concern is a need "to attract and hold a large audience for advertisers."[12] Without ad revenue, nearly all U.S. news organizations would go out of business. Only a few news outlets—an example is National Public Radio, which depends on listener contributions—support themselves through something other than commercial advertising.

The very definition of news—what it is and what it is not—is built around the need to attract an audience.[13] The news is intentionally shortsighted. Each day, journalists must have new stories to tell, ones that are different from yesterday's. The continuing need for fresh stories leads journalists to cover what they call "hard events"—developments that have taken a clear and definable shape within the past twenty-four hours.[14] Without a hard event to lend it form and immediacy, an issue is likely to go unreported. For example, although few developments in the post–World War II era had a bigger impact on U.S. politics than the northward trek of southern blacks, it was rarely mentioned in the news. As African Americans in the late 1940s and 1950s moved into the northern cities by the hundreds each day, white people, pushed by racial fears and pulled by the lure of the suburbs, moved out in equally large numbers. Within a few decades, the political, social, and economic landscape of urban America had been substantially altered—a transformation that was rarely the subject of news coverage. Columnist George Will wryly noted that a ribbon should have been stretched across the Mason-Dixon line as the one-millionth African American crossed it on the way north; the breaking of the ribbon would have given the media a "peg" on which to hang the story of urban America's extraordinary transformation.[15]

At the same time, policy issues and problems do not change much from day to day, and thus are not considered particularly newsworthy. The first time that a top politician talks about a major policy issue, it is likely to be reported, and it may even make the front page. Thereafter, its news value is small; it is "old news." The 2008 presidential nomination contest between Barack Obama and Hillary Clinton, for example, was waged largely in the context of their different levels of experience and their opposing positions on the invasion of Iraq. These differences were not, however, the main focus of the candidates' news coverage. Journalists focused instead on the latest poll results, delegate counts, accusations, gaffes, tactics, and the like. These were the "new" developments in the Democratic race and therefore what journalists saw as "news."[16]

The press's need for novelty also explains why sensational crimes and wayward celebrities get so much attention. In 2008, an ambulance was called to the home of the singer Britney Spears, who was distraught over a child custody dispute with her ex-husband, Kevin Federline. Photos taken by journalists parked outside her residence, along with aerial video provided by television news stations, showed Spears being taken from her home on a stretcher, surrounded by paramedics. The pictures were flashed across the country—the latest episode in the ongoing Spears media saga.

Of course, serious issues do get some coverage. But the mix of news stories is designed as much to attract an audience as to inform it. Not surprisingly, studies have found that news exposure does not lead to exceptionally high levels of political information.[17] As might be expected, people who pay close attention to the news are better informed on the issues than those who pay little or no attention. Nevertheless, Americans are not exceptionally well informed about public affairs. Some European news systems are less advertising oriented (see "How the United States Compares"), and their audiences are somewhat better informed. A study of seven Western countries found, for example, that Americans ranked next to last (ahead of only Spaniards) in their ability to correctly identify prominent world leaders and developments.[18]

The Watchdog Function

The American press takes responsibility for exposing incompetent, hypocritical, and corrupt officials. In this **watchdog function,** the press stands ready to expose officials who violate accepted legal, ethical, or performance standards. The American news media have rightfully been called a fourth branch of government—part of the political system's checks on abuses of power.

The norms of objective journalism foster watchdog reporting. Although journalists are expected to fairly treat opposing political views, there is no norm that would limit criticism of officials who abuse the public trust. American journalists also operate within a system that provides substantial press freedom. Unlike British journalists who are barred from reporting what the government designates as "official secrets," American journalists operate under the principle of "no prior restraint," which holds that government cannot stop a news story unless it can convince a court that it would gravely harm the nation (see Chapter 4). Thus, it was an American news outlet, the Drudge Report, which reported that Britain's Prince Harry was serving as a British army officer in Afghanistan. Some British journalists were aware of the assignment but had accepted a government ban on reporting it. After the Drudge Report revealed his combat status, he was removed from Afghanistan so that he and his unit would not be targeted by hostile forces there.

The U.S. press is also unusual in the degree to which it is free from libel judgments (see Chapter 4). It is nearly impossible for a U.S. official

How the United States Compares

Public Broadcasting

Public broadcasting got off to a slow start in the United States. Unlike the case in Europe, where public broadcasting networks (such as Britain's BBC) were created at the start of the radio age, the U.S. government handed control of broadcasting to commercial networks, such as NBC and CBS. By the time Congress decided in the 1960s that public broadcasting was needed, the commercial networks were so powerful that they convinced Congress to assign it second-class status. Public broadcasting was poorly funded and was denied access to the most powerful broadcast frequencies. In fact, most television sets in the 1960s had tuners that could not dial in the stations on which public broadcast programs were aired. Not surprisingly, public broadcasting faltered at the beginning and still operates in the shadow of commercial broadcasting.

Nevertheless, public broadcasting does have a success story—National Public Radio (NPR). Over the past two decades, NPR's audience has quadrupled. Each week, more than 20 million Americans listen to NPR, many of them on a regular basis. NPR's growth is a stark contrast to what has happened to commercial newscasts during the same period. The combined audience of the ABC, CBS, and NBC evening newscasts is now half that of the early 1980s. NPR has built its audience through a strategy opposite to that of the commercial networks. As the news audiences of these networks declined in the face of widening competition from cable television, they "softened" their newscasts—boosting entertainment content in the hope of luring viewers away from cable programs. Former Federal Communication Commission chairman Newton Minow derided the change as "pretty close to tabloid." In contrast, NPR has held to the notion that news is news and not also entertainment. Although NPR carries features, they are typically tied to news developments. Studies indicate that NPR's audience is more politically interested and informed than any other broadcast news audience. Many of its listeners are refugees from the broadcast network news they used to watch but now find to be lacking in substance.

Despite NPR's success, public broadcasting in the United States is but a small part of the total news system, and the consequences are substantial. In countries like Britain, Germany, and Japan, where public

(continued)

broadcasting is well funded, it sets a standard for high-quality news that conditions the public to prefer it and to expect it from other news providers as well. In the United States, public broadcasting depends on stories reported first by commercial outlets, where the profit motive can lead to news based more on its audience appeal than its social relevance. Accordingly, many Americans have become accustomed to, and even prefer, news produced for its entertainment value. "Amusing ourselves to death" is communication scholar Neil Postman's description of this kind of news.

to win a libel suit against a newspaper, magazine, or broadcast organization even in situations where his or her reputation has been harmed by false allegations. In Britain, where libel judgments are more easily obtained, journalists have to be more judicious in alleging that officials have been guilty of misconduct.

American journalists have not always vigorously fullfilled their watchdog function. One such period was the early phase of the Cold War between the United States and the Soviet Union. When Senator Joseph McCarthy (R-Wisc.) in the early 1950s falsely claimed that hundreds of Americans in the State Department, Hollywood, and the universities were subversive communists, the press served as a megaphone for his wild charges, sometimes with sensational headlines. Only after Republican President Dwight D. Eisenhower and leading members of Congress spoke out against McCarthy did the press flatly reject his trumped-up claims. There were noteworthy exceptions, including CBS's famed Edward R. Murrow, but the press by and large failed in its watchdog role during the McCarthy era.

After the terrorist attacks of September 11, 2001, the news media also stepped back from their watchdog role. Press criticism of political leaders and institutions fell sharply, as journalists sought to contribute to a newfound sense of national unity and purpose. NBC News outfitted its peacock logo with stars and stripes following the World Trade Center and Pentagon attacks, and computer-generated flags festooned the other networks. Although there was some critical reporting during the lead-up to the 2003 invasion of Iraq, news organizations did not vigorously scrutinize the Bush administration's arguments on the need for war. Moreover, nearly all the major news organizations "embedded" correspondents in U.S. combat units, virtually guaranteeing that the early phase of the war would get favorable coverage.[19]

The Iraq invasion was an exception, however. Journalists are normally skeptical of politicians' motives and actions, an outlook that deepened during

★ LEADERS

Ida Tarbell
(1857–1944)

Watchdog reporting in the United States traces to the Progressive Era of the early 1900s, when the partisan journalism of the nation's early decades began to yield to objective journalism. The objective model obliged journalists to remain neutral on partisan issues but did not prohibit them from aggressively pursuing corruption, favoritism, abuse, and incompetence, whether in the public or the private sector. The early watchdog journalists were known as Muckrakers, and several of them, including Upton Sinclair and Lincoln Steffens, gained fame through their exposés. Sinclair even attacked the newspaper industry itself, claiming in *The Brass Check* that it routinely ignored the corrupt practices of firms that advertised heavily in the newspaper. No muckraker had a bigger impact, however, than Ida Tarbell, who in the two-volume *The History of the Standard Oil Company* (1904) exposed the predatory practices of John D. Rockefeller in building his oil empire. Tarbell's book led the federal government to use the Sherman Anti-Trust Act to break up Rockefeller's firm, Standard Oil of New Jersey. Much of the material in Tarbell's two-volume book appeared earlier in *McClure's*, a widely circulated magazine of the period that also published pieces by other muckrakers. A native Pennsylvania, Tarbell first gained recognition after moving to Paris where she wrote on Europe for American magazines. She returned to the United States a decade before publication of her book on Rockefeller, taking a job with *McClure's*. During her lifetime, she was one of America's most famous women, though she declined requests that she take a leadership role in the women's suffrage movement. Her best-selling books included biographies of Napoleon Bonaparte and Abraham Lincoln.

the Vietnam War. A turning point was the *New York Times*'s publication in 1970 of the so-called Pentagon Papers—classified documents revealing that government had deceived the public by claiming that the war in Vietnam was going well when in fact it was going badly. The Nixon administration tried to block publication of the documents but was overruled by the Supreme report typically includes a contrary statement or action by another official, usually of the opposite party.

Second, although news typically originates in the words and actions of political leaders, they do not monopolize the news, particularly on television. TV news is now more journalist-centered than it is newsmaker-centered.[23] In an effort to keep their viewers tuned in, television newscasts use a fast-paced format in which each story has multiple pieces woven together in story form, with the journalist acting as the storyteller. One indicator of this format is the "shrinking sound bite" in presidential campaigns. In the 1960s, a candidate's sound bite (the length of time within a television story that a candidate speaks without interruption) was more than forty seconds on average.[24] In recent campaigns, the average sound bite has been less than ten seconds, barely enough time for the candidate to utter a long sentence (see Figure 10-1). It is the journalists, not the candidates, who do most of the talking. For every minute that Barack Obama and John McCain spoke on the network evening newscasts during the 2008 presidential campaigns, the journalists who were covering them spoke for more than five minutes.[25] Most of the time that Obama and McCain could be seen on the evening news with their mouth moving, their voice could not be heard; the journalist's voice was the audible one.

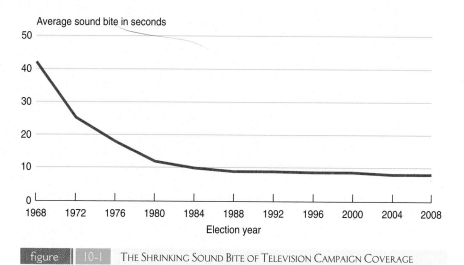

figure 10-1 THE SHRINKING SOUND BITE OF TELEVISION CAMPAIGN COVERAGE

The average length of time that presidential candidates are shown speaking without interruption on broadcast television newscasts has declined sharply in recent elections. *Source: Adapted from Daniel C. Hallin, "Sound Bite News: Television Coverage of Elections 1968–1988." Journal of Communication 42 (Spring 1992): 6. The 1992–2008 data are from the Center for Media and Public Affairs.*

Journalists also say different things than public officials do. Whereas officials talk mainly about policy problems and issues, journalists talk mainly about the "game" of politics. They focus on political strategy and infighting, portraying politics as a struggle for personal power and competitive advantage. Journalists could present politics in the context of policy problems and debates, but they choose instead to present it in the context of its strategic aspects. For the journalist, the strategic context has two advantages over the policy frame. First, the give-and-take among political leaders is more easily observed and reported than are policy positions and conditions. Second, the political game is a reliable source of fresh material. Policy problems and issues do not change much from day to day, but the political game is constantly in motion.[26]

Communication scholars use the term **framing** to describe the way in which events are cast. Framing is a process of selecting certain aspects of reality and making them the most salient part of the communication, thereby conveying a particular interpretation of a situation.[27] Although the strategic game is a natural part of politics, it is an ever larger part of the news about politics because it is the frame through which journalists construct most of their political stories. In effect, the press "depoliticizes" issues, treating them more as objects of competition than as objects of serious debate.[28] The impact of this type of political coverage is substantial. Studies have found that most Americans believe that politicians spend too much time fighting among themselves and that politicians will say almost anything in order to get elected or hold onto power.[29] Although these perceptions are not entirely attributable to journalists' frame of reference, it is a major contributor.

The Partisan Function

Traditionally, the **partisan function**—acting as an advocate for a particular viewpoint or interest—has been the responsibility of political leaders, political institutions, and political organizations. Today, however, the news media—particularly the newer media—also function in that capacity.

Traditional Media: Mostly Neutral   During the era of the partisan press, newspapers sought to guide their readers' opinions. In the presidential election campaign of 1896, for example, the *San Francisco Call*, a Republican newspaper, devoted 1,075 column-inches of photographs to the Republican ticket of McKinley-Hobart and only 11 inches to their Democratic opponents, Bryan and Sewell.[30] San Francisco Democrats had their own bible, the Hearst-owned *Examiner*, which touted William Jennings Bryan as the savior of working men. The emergence of objective journalism brought an end to that style of reporting. Rather than slanting the news to favor the

Republican or Democratic side, journalists sought to give their audience both sides, leaving it to them to decide which one was better.

The traditional media—the daily newspapers and broadcast networks—still operate largely in this way. Of course, newspapers have long distinguished their news pages from their editorial pages. Their commitment to two-sided news reporting does not extend to their editorializing. Most newspapers side editorially with the Republican Party, though this tendency varies with national conditions. In the 2000 presidential race, for example, George W. Bush was endorsed by many more daily papers than was his Democratic opponent, Al Gore.[31] In the 2004 race, however, newspaper endorsements split more closely between Bush and the Democratic nominee, John Kerry. Some newspapers that had backed Bush in 2000 deserted him in 2004, citing the deteriorating Iraq situation as the reason.[32]

The traditional broadcast television networks—ABC, CBS, and NBC—do not endorse candidates and say they are unbiased, a claim that is sometimes disputed, particularly by conservatives. In a best-selling recent book, a former network correspondent, Bernard Goldberg, accused the networks of having a liberal agenda.[33] Such allegations are not completely baseless. Until recently, for example, the concerns of evangelical Christians were rarely a subject of broadcast news except in the context of conflict-ridden issues like creationism and abortion. There is also the fact that most broadcast news journalists, as well as most journalists generally, lean Democratic in their personal beliefs.[34]

Scholarly studies indicate, however, that the level of bias in network newscasts is small. In fact, the television-age president with the worst press coverage was a Democrat, Bill Clinton. The Center for Media and Public Affairs found that Clinton's negative coverage exceeded his positive coverage in every quarter of every year of his two-term presidency—a dubious record that no president before or since has equaled.[35]

Instead of a partisan bias, scholars have highlighted a different tendency—the networks' preference for the negative. Michael Robinson concluded that broadcast journalists have a "negativist, contentious" outlook on politics.[36] The networks' preference for "bad news" can be seen, for example, in their coverage of presidential candidates. Virtually every nominee since the 1980s has received mostly negative coverage during the course of the campaign. "Bad news" has characterized network coverage of Democratic and Republican nominees alike. In any given election, one of the nominees gets more favorable coverage than the other, but not by much and not with any partisan regularity.[37]

The news turned negative after Vietnam and Watergate—developments that convinced journalists that politicians could not be trusted—and has largely stayed that way. Studies of news coverage in the 1990s found, for

The publication of photos showing the abuse of Iraqi prisoners by U.S. soldiers undermined the U.S. government's claim that allegations about prisoner abuse were exaggerated. The press was acting in its watchdog role when it published the photos and reported on conditions in U.S. military prisons in Iraq. The news coverage led to a congressional investigation.

example, that every high-profile agency except the Department of Defense had received more negative than positive coverage. The State Department's coverage was only 13 percent positive, and the Justice Department's coverage was just 10 percent favorable.[38] The legislative branch has fared no better. Press coverage of Congress has been steadily negative since the 1970s, regardless of which party controlled Congress or how much or little was accomplished. "Over the years," concluded scholar Mark Rozell, "press coverage of Congress has moved from healthy skepticism to outright cynicism."[39]

The networks' negativity helps to explain why they are widely perceived as biased. Research has found that negative news is perceived differently by those who support and those who oppose the politician being criticized. Opponents tend to see the criticism as valid while supporters tend to see it as unjustified and therefore biased. This reaction is heightened when people see an attack on television as opposed to reading about it in a newspaper.[40] It is not surprising, then, that Democrats during Bill Clinton's presidency tended to think that the networks favored the Republicans while Republicans during George W. Bush's presidency tended to think that the networks favored the Democrats. Such findings do not mean that the networks are completely unbiased, for they are not. The findings do indicate, however, that much of the perceived bias is in the eye of the beholder.[41]

Scholars have found a correlation between the tone of news coverage and Americans' trust and confidence in political leaders and institutions. The University of Pennsylvania's Joseph Cappella and Kathleen Hall Jamieson demonstrated, for example, that negative messages bring out feelings of mistrust of politicians and political institutions. "The effect," Cappella and Jamieson write, "occurs for broadcast as well as print news."[42] For their part, journalists acknowledge a negative slant but say that Americans are best served when the press errs on the side of criticism, even if that criticism is sometimes unfair or exaggerated. As CNN correspondent Bob Franken put it, "We historically are not supposed to be popular, and it's almost our role to be the bearer of bad news."[43]

Talk Shows: Mostly Conservative   The broadcast networks' partisan bias—real and perceived—has been an issue for conservatives at least since 1970 when Republican Vice President Spiro Agnew called the networks "nattering nabobs of negativism." Nevertheless, Republicans could only pressure the networks to cover politics differently in that there was no realistic alternative. Cable television and the rescinding of the Fairness Doctrine changed that situation by providing a host of new options, including partisan talk shows.

On both radio and television, most of the successful partisan talk shows have been hosted by conservatives. The host with the largest audience is radio's Rush Limbaugh. In the top twenty-five radio markets, Limbaugh's show has more listeners, in all age groups, than the listenership of all the top liberal talk shows combined. Limbaugh built his following in the early 1990s with attacks on Bill Clinton, whom Limbaugh variously characterized as a draft-dodger, womanizer, and wimp. When Republicans in the 1994 midterm elections won control of both the House and Senate for the first time in four decades, Limbaugh's contribution was widely heralded. "Operation Restore Democracy" was Limbaugh's label for his months-long radio campaign to get GOP candidates elected, and political conservatives went to the polls in unusually high numbers, prompting analysts to call Limbaugh the Republicans' "electronic precinct captain."

The success of Limbaugh's radio show led Roger Ailes, a Republican political consultant, to create a television version. However, Limbaugh's television talk show never caught on, and it folded in 1996 after a four-year run. Rubert Murdoch then hired Ailes to run a new television network, Fox News. Murdoch reasoned that conservatives, because of discontent with the established networks, would respond to a conservative alternative. Fox's newscasts concentrate on top stories but give them a conservative touch. For example, although Fox did not ignore the postdebate polls in

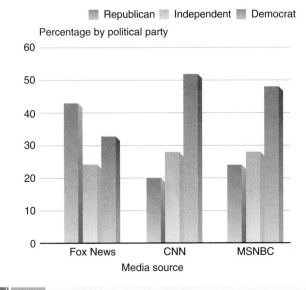

Republican Independent Democrat

Percentage by political party

figure | 10-2 | CABLE TELEVISION NEWS VIEWERS, BY PARTY IDENTIFICATION

As indicated by where people say they get most of their cable news, Republicans prefer Fox News while Democrats choose CNN or MSNBC. *Source: Adapted from data in "State of the Media 2008," a report of the Project for Excellence in Journalism. Percentages based only on poll respondents who identified as Republicans, Democrats, or Independents.*

2004 indicating that most Americans thought John Kerry had outdebated George W. Bush each time, Fox carried fewer debate-related stories than the other networks and was the only network to portray Bush more favorably than Kerry during the debate period.[44] Fox's talk show hosts—including Sean Hannity and Bill O'Reilly, who has the highest-rated political talk show on cable television—tilt toward the conservative side. Like the audience for political talk radio, the Fox News television audience is disproportionately Republican (see Figure 10-2). CNN's audience, which was roughly balanced between Republicans and Democrats until Fox News came along, is now heavily Democratic, as is that of MSNBC, the third-ranked cable network.

CNN and MSNBC have responded to Fox's ratings success by installing talk show hosts who lure their audiences through partisan or hard-edged appeals. MSNBC's lineup is liberal, featuring Keith Olbermann and Rachel Maddow, as well as Chris Matthews, a former Democratic congressional staffer who is critical of both parties but aims his sharpest barbs at the Republicans. CNN has a more balanced lineup that includes conservative Glenn Beck, along with the less predictable but no less assertive Lou Dobbs, who has the larger audience of the two. Dobbs is perhaps best described as a populist. He rails against illegal immigrants—which appeals to conservatives—but also rails against wealthy interests and Iraq policy—which appeals to liberals.

The news outlet with the largest liberal following is National Public Radio (NPR). Its weekly audience of 20 million listeners rivals Limbaugh's, although its format is different. NPR's newscasts are based on breaking stories from AP and other news outlets, and they present a balanced view of the two parties. NPR's appeal to liberals is based on its talk shows, which, though neutral in tone, tend to focus on issues of particular concern to liberals, such as global warming.

The most popular of the stridently liberal talk shows rely on political satire to make their point. In fact, the most prominent of these shows—*The Daily Show*, *The Colbert Report*, and *Real Time with Bill Maher*—are televised on entertainment channels (Comedy Central and HBO) rather than news channels. Jon Stewart's *Daily Show*, seen by more than a million viewers each night, has the largest following. Like Limbaugh's radio talk show, which soared in the 1990s when Limbaugh feasted off the actions of Democratic President Bill Clinton, Stewart's show rose in popularity as his attacks on the policies of Republican President George W. Bush became sharper. In a telling episode, Stewart looked blankly at the television screen for seemingly endless seconds before blurting out "Please say, please say, you're kidding me." This comment followed a videotape of Bush's national security advisor, Condoleezza Rice, admitting to Congress that she had read a classified document titled "Bin Laden Determined to Attack Inside the United States" a month before the September 11, 2001, terrorist attacks on the World Trade Center and the Pentagon. Rice had earlier claimed that no one in the Bush administration could possibly have foreseen the attacks.

The Internet: Mostly Liberal   Although the First Amendment protects each individual's right to press freedom, this right in practice was once reserved for a tiny few. Journalist A. J. Liebling wrote that freedom of the press belongs to those with the money to own a broadcast station or newspaper.[45]

Today, because of the Internet, freedom of the press is enjoyed by a larger number of Americans than ever before. Although access to the Internet is no substitute for owning a newspaper or a television station, it does provide ordinary citizens with an opportunity to be part of the news system. Through their websites, citizens can post news and information about public affairs, harangue officials, argue for public policies, and mobilize the support of others. The Internet has reduced the barriers to public communication to a level not seen since colonial days, when pamphleteers dominated political communication. The most influential pamphleteer was Thomas Paine, whose pamphlet *Common Sense* sold over a hundred thousand copies and mobilized American opposition to British rule. "We have the power to begin the world over again," wrote Paine, who also penned the famous line "These are the times that try men's souls."

The Internet has been a boon to political mobilizers. During the 2008 presidential campaign, Barack Obama used his opposition to the Iraq war, his oratorical skill, and the power of the Internet to go from relative obscurity to the White House. Obama's campaign raised roughly $600 million, much of it through Internet contributions of less than $250. The Internet was also the medium for one of the most successful citizen-led efforts in history—a global movement that succeeded in getting nearly one hundred countries to sign an international treaty banning the use of land mines. Its organizer, Jody Williams, was awarded the Nobel Peace Prize.

The Internet has a capacity that traditional media lack: the ability to interact with its followers. During the 2008 presidential nominating campaigns, TechCrunch, which has nearly a half million unique monthly visitors, polled its readers on their preferences for the Democratic and Republican nominees. TechCrunch then endorsed Barack Obama for the Democratic nomination and John McCain for the Republican nomination, urging its readers to support them with votes and campaign contributions.

When it comes to news, however, the Internet's significance is harder to pinpoint. Because the cost of entry is low, there are literally thousands of websites where news is regularly posted and examined. However, Internet news is characterized by what analysts call "the long tail." When news-based websites are arrayed by the number of visitors to each site, there are a few heavily visited sites on one end and many lightly visited sites on the other end—"the long tail." As it happens, most of the heavily visited sites are those of the traditional media, including CNN.com, nytimes.com, and MSNBC.com. In addition, most of the other heavily visited sites, such as Google News, republish news gathered and reported first by the established media. In other words, most Americans who go to the Internet for news are seeing news generated by the same sources they otherwise rely on for news.

Occasionally, a major story will originate on the Internet. Bloggers were the first to identify as forgeries the government documents CBS's Dan Rather presented during the 2004 campaign as proof that President George W. Bush had shirked his National Guard duties in the early 1970s. Within months, Rather was forced to retire prematurely as anchor of the *CBS Evening News.* Rather's departure was a source of glee for many in the blogging community. Whether liberal or conservative, bloggers tend to

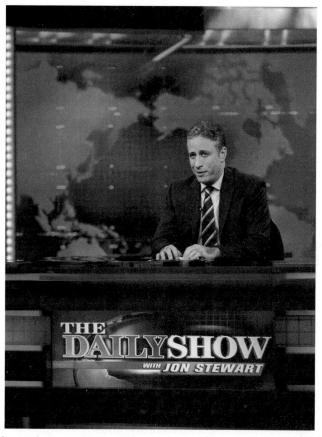

Unlike talk shows, where conservative viewpoints dominate, Internet blogs and comedy-based shows are bastions of liberal sentiment. Show here is *The Daily Show*'s Jon Stewart, who hosts a left-leaning news and comedy program.

share a disdain for the mainstream press, which they accuse of everything from bias to irrelevance.

The special contribution of Internet-based news is that it provides an outlet for opinion, through the news commentary of bloggers and Internet users. Unlike most of the successful talk-radio programs, however, most of the successful blogs have a liberal bias. One of the largest of these sites is the *Huffington Post*, which was started by activist Arianna Huffington. Launched in 2005 as a moderately liberal site, it soon changed into an unabashedly liberal site that made President Bush its primary target. The site has more than 7 million unique visitors each month, which ranks it ahead of the news sites of several major news organizations, including CBS and the *Los Angeles Times*.

The Internet is in its early years as a news medium, so it is hazardous to guess whether initial tendencies will continue. But with Americans increasingly looking to the Internet for information, including news, it is safe to say that the Internet's importance will continue to grow.[46]

ATTENTION TO NEWS

The U.S. news system now has more outlets—including newspapers, television stations, talk shows, and bloggers—than at any time in its history. The news system also provides a wider variety of content—everything from straight news to partisan harangues—than ever before. Although it might be assumed, as a result, that Americans are more attentive and more informed about public affairs than ever before, that is not the case. The same media system that makes news available on demand at any time also makes it relatively easy for people without an interest in news to avoid it. America today has many citizens who consume copious amounts of news. It also has many citizens who consume almost none.

The Shrinking Audience for News

The 1980s were the turning point in the shape of the news audience. Until then, and for nearly two centuries, the news audience had been enlarging. Rising literacy rates, increased urbanization, and less-expensive newspapers had widened the audience during the nineteenth century. The introduction of radio news in the early twentieth century, and the emergence of television news a few decades later, further expanded the daily news audience.

The attractiveness of television was critical to the last phase of this expansion. Americans were nearly obsessed with television in its early years and would watch most anything available. In most television markets at the dinner hour, the only choices available to viewers were the the ABC newscast, the CBS newscast, and the NBC newscast. Viewers who were intent on watching television in this time slot had no alternative but to sit through the news. They constituted an "inadvertent news audience"—brought to the news less by a strong preference for it than by an addiction to television.[47]

The television news audience at its peak was enormous. At the dinner hour, most television sets in America were turned on, and 85 percent of these sets were tuned to the news. This exposure rubbed off on the children. The evening news was a ritual in many families, and though the children might have preferred something else, they, too, watched it. By the time many of these children finished school, many of them had acquired a television news habit of their own.

Television's capacity to generate an interest in news declined sharply in the 1980s with the rapid spread of cable. Viewers no longer had to sit through the news while waiting for entertainment programming to appear. Television news did not lose most of its regular viewers, but it did lose its ability to develop an interest in news among adults who preferred entertainment programming. And its capacity to generate news interest in children was greatly diminished. Fewer of their parents were watching the dinner-hour news, and even if they were watching, the children, as a Kaiser Family Foundation study revealed, were usually in another room watching entertainment shows.[48]

To be sure, some Americans were getting more news than was possible in earlier times. Round-the-clock news was available to anyone with cable TV. Yet cable also made it possible for people to avoid the news with ease. And large numbers of Americans, mostly younger adults, abandoned news for movies, sitcoms, comedy shows, and other cable programs.[49] The result was a steady decline in the broadcast news audience. Some of the drop was attributable to viewers who shifted to cable news. Even when they are accounted for, however, the absolute proportion of Americans watching television news on a daily basis dropped significantly. Newspaper circulation also declined, partly because cable TV was taking up more and more of people's media time and partly because fewer people had a daily news habit.

Age and Attention to News

Today, the daily audience for news consists disproportionately of older adults. Compared with adults thirty years of age or younger, those over fifty are three times more likely to follow public affairs closely through a newspaper—meaning they read a newspaper nearly every day and pay reasonably close attention to the news pages while doing so. The disparity is not as great with television news, but it is still a substantial one. Older adults are roughly twice as likely as young adults to watch television news almost daily and to sit through most of the newscast while doing so. Age differences shrink for Internet-based news but do not disappear. Even though older adults are somewhat less likely than young adults to access the Web, they make greater use of it as a news source. In fact, roughly half of young adults pay little or no attention on a regular basis to any news source.[50]

Of course, citizens do not have to avail themselves of every conceivable source of news in order to stay abreast of the daily news. Daily exposure to a single news medium can be sufficient. However, compared with one in two older adults, fewer than one in four young adults follow the news closely on a daily basis through at least one news source (see Figure 10-3). In fact, nearly half of young adults pay little or no attention on a regular basis to news.

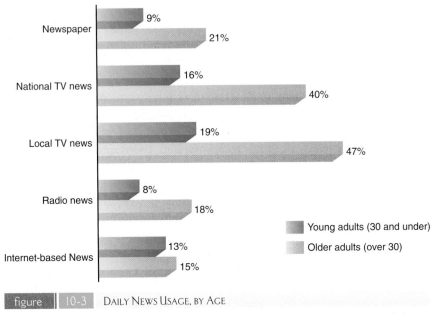

figure | 10-3 DAILY NEWS USAGE, BY AGE

Most older adults follow the news closely on a daily basis, whereas most young adults do not. *Source: Survey by Shorenstein Center on the Press, Politics, and Public Policy (Harvard University), 2007. To be classified as a daily user, a respondent had to follow the news on a daily basis in a medium and attend to it for more than a few minutes while doing so. Respondents were asked about five mediums: newspaper, national TV, local TV, radio, and the Internet.*

A few decades ago, the news habits of younger and older adults were similar. In the late 1950s, for example, 53 percent of those in the 21–29 age group regularly read news coverage of national politics, compared with 61 percent in the 30–44 age group, 60 percent in the 45–60 age group, and 57 percent of those over 60. From this evidence, Martin Wattenberg in his recent book *Is Voting for Young People?* concludes, "Young, middle aged, and old alike took in newspaper coverage at about the same rate." Wattenberg found a similar pattern for television news. Young adults were less likely in the 1960s to watch the nightly news, but not by a wide margin. "There was little variation in news viewing habits by age," Wattenberg writes. "TV news producers could hardly write off young adults, given that two out of three said they had watched such broadcasts every night."[51]

The widening age gap in news consumption has been accompanied by a widening age gap in possession of political information. Wattenberg found that, until the early 1970s, young adults were actually more knowledgeable about current events and leaders than senior citizens, which he attributed largely to differences in education. Most older citizens of that time had not graduated from high school. Since the 1980s, and increasingly so, young adults have been less informed than older ones. In 2004, for example, whereas adults sixty-five years of age and older could answer correctly 55 percent of factual questions about politics contained in the National Election Studies (NES) survey, adults under thirty years of age could answer only 36 percent of the questions accurately. In fact, young adults scored lower than all other age groups on every NES question, whether it was identification of current political leaders, information about the presidential candidates, knowledge of which party controlled Congress, or basic civic facts. The chapter of Wattenberg's book in which these findings are presented is pointedly titled, "Don't Ask Anyone Under 30."[52]

Although some analysts suggest that the Internet will lead young Americans back to the news, there is no evidence to date to support that view. Although, like television, the Internet has it addicts, the sites they choose to visit are largely determined by the interests they bring to the Web. A 2006 Pew Research Center study indicates that the Internet is not even particularly powerful in strengthening the news habit of those who use the Internet as a news source. Compared with the typical newspaper reader or television news viewer, the typical Internet-news user spends many fewer minutes per day attending to the medium's news. Even the on-demand feature of Internet news can work against the formation of an online news habit because it breaks the link between ritual and habit. Newspaper reading, for example, is a morning ritual for some Americans—the almost unthinking stroll to the door or curb to retrieve the paper, followed by the almost unthinking opening of the paper to the preferred section. As the scholars Maria Len Rios and Clyde Bentley note, online news exposure is less fixed by time, place, and routine—elements that strengthen a habit.

The Internet cannot be faulted for the decline in news interest among young Americans. Other factors, including a weakening of the home as a place where news habits are acquired, underlie this development. Notwithstanding the cartoon father with his nose buried in the paper after a day at work, news exposure in the home was once a family affair. The newspaper sections were shared, as was the space around the radio or in front of the television set. Today, media use is largely a solitary affair, contributing to the tendency of media use to reinforce interests rather than to create new ones, including an interest in news.

MEDIA AND THE PUBLIC IN THE INTERNET AGE

The news media today are a greatly different political intermediary than they were only a few decades ago, and the political consequences are substantial.

The old media system was dominated by a few powerful news organizations—the broadcast networks in particular. They had a huge daily audience, enabling them to alert Americans of all ages and classes to the same events. They also provided a platform for political leaders who, through a single statement or event, could reach tens of millions of citizens. And because these media reported developments in a largely nonpartisan way, the political translation of these developments rested almost solely with political parties and interest groups, enhancing their political roles.

Today's media system is markedly different. The traditional media are still major players, but their audiences are smaller and their influence is diminished. Moreover, as they have struggled to hold onto their audience, they have "softened" their news—infusing it with more stories about celebrities, crime, and the like. The relentless search for attention-grabbing

The Internet has opened up the media system, allowing citizens, groups, and leaders to communicate more powerfully than was possible during the not-so-distant era when news organizations almost totally controlled the instruments of mass communication. Shown here is a web page of Rock the Vote, an organization dedicated to helping young adults to register and vote.

stories has always blunted the news media's ability to provide the citizens with a clear understanding of what is broadly at issue in politics. Journalist Walter Lippmann put it plainly:

> The press is no substitute for [political] institutions. It is like the beam of a searchlight that moves restlessly about, bringing one episode and then another out of darkness into vision. Men cannot do the work of the world by this light alone. They cannot govern society by episodes, incidents, and interruptions.[53]

Lippman was writing in a slower media age. Today the "episodes, incidents, and interruptions" occur with remarkable speed, threatening the public's ability to focus on what is truly important politically. The 2008 Democratic presidential nominating race is a case in point. Even though there were major issues in that race—Iraq, the economy, and health care, to name only three—the news of the Obama-Clinton contest was filled with dozens of small controversies, as journalists seized on every misstep by the candidates or their advisers in search of new stories. Everything from Obama's minister to Clinton's trip to the Balkans a decade earlier became headline news, distracting the voters from the real issues separating the candidates.

Partisanship is also a larger part of today's news because the newer media— cable TV and the Internet—rely on it to build their audiences. If Americans were once exposed to a more or less common version of the news, they no longer are. Those citizens who depend for their news on blogs, cable programs, or talk radio get versions laden with partisan arguments. As political scientist Markus Prior shows in *Post-Broadcast Democracy*, today's media system contributes to partisan polarization. Many of the new media outlets play up partisan differences, exhalting their side while tearing down the opposing side. To be sure, the heightened partisan polarization in the electorate (Chapter 8), Congress (Chapter 11), and the presidency (Chapter 12) owes mainly to factors outside the media. Nevertheless, the current media system exacerbates partisan differences, pushing Americans further apart on key issues.

The new media system also contributes to another widening divide— the information gap between America's better-informed and less-informed citizens. The information gap, of course, is not new. At no time in the nation's history have nearly all citizens been well informed about public affairs. However, the gap is widening because today's news system makes it easier for citizens without an intrinsic interest in news to avoid it. When using the media, people can easily bypass the news if it holds little or no appeal. That development might prove to be the most important consequence of the new media system. For if citizens cannot be prompted to follow news of public affairs, the nation will one day face the larger challenge of how to maintain self-government when huge numbers of citizens know little to nothing about the policy choices their country faces.

SUMMARY   Self-Test www.mhhe.com/pattersonwtp8e

In the nation's first century, the press was allied closely with the political parties and helped the parties mobilize public opinion. Gradually, the press freed itself from this partisan relationship and developed a form of reporting, known as objective journalism, that emphasizes fair and accurate accounts of newsworthy developments. That model still governs the news reporting of the traditional media—daily newspapers and broadcasters—but does not hold for the newer media—radio talk shows, cable TV talk shows, and Internet blogs. Although some of them cover politics in the traditional way, many of them transmit news through a partisan lens.

The press performs four basic functions. First, in their signaling function, journalists communicate information to the public about breaking events and new developments. This information makes citizens aware of developments that impact on their lives. However, because of the media's need to attract an audience, breaking news stories often focus on developments, such as celebrity scandals, that have little to do with issues of politics and government. In a second function, that of watchdog, the press acts to protect the public by exposing deceitful, careless, or corrupt officials. Third, the press functions as a common carrier in that it provides political leaders with a channel for addressing the public. Increasingly, however, the news has centered nearly as much on the journalists themselves as on the newsmakers they cover. Finally, the press functions as a partisan advocate. Although the traditional media perform this function to a degree, the newer media—the talk shows and blogs—specialize in it. Their influence has contributed to a rising level of political polarization in the United States.

The news audience has changed substantially in the past few decades. Daily newspapers and broadcast news have lost audience to cable television and the Internet. At the same time, the emergence of cable television and the Internet has made it easier for citizens to avoid news when using the media. Although some citizens today consume more news than was possible at an earlier time, other citizens—young adults in particular—consume less news than was typical at an earlier time. A consequence is that young adults are less informed politically relative to both older adults and to earlier generations of young adults.

KEY TERMS

agenda setting (*p. 339*)
common-carrier function (*p. 348*)
framing (*p. 350*)
news (*p. 331*)
objective journalism (*p. 334*)

partisan function (of the press) (*p. 350*)
partisan press (*p. 333*)
press (news media) (*p. 331*)
signaling (signaler) function (*p. 338*)
watchdog function (*p. 343*)

SUGGESTED READINGS

Baum, Matthew. *Soft News Goes to War.* Princeton, N.J.: Princeton University Press, 2003. A study of the impact of soft-news coverage of war.

Bennett, W. Lance, Regina G. Lawrence, and Steven Livingston. *When the Press Fails: Political Power and the News Media from Iraq to Katrina.* Chicago: University of Chicago Press, 2008. A revealing account of news coverage, particularly during the buildup to the Iraq conflict.

Bimber, Bruce A., and Richard Davis. *Campaigning Online: The Internet in U.S. Elections.* New York: Oxford University Press, 2003. A careful study of Internet use in election campaigns.

Farnsworth, Stephen J., and S. Robert Lichter. *The Mediated Presidency: Television News and Presidential Governance.* Latham, Md.: Rowman & Littlefield, 2006. An empirical study of television coverage of the presidency.

Hamilton, James T. *All the News That's Fit to Sell.* Princeton, N.J.: Princeton University Press, 2004. A careful study of the economic influences on news content.

Mindich, David T. Z. *Tuned Out: Why Americans Under 40 Don't Follow the News.* New York: Oxford University Press, 2005. A look at the news habits of young adults.

Overholser, Geneva, and Kathleen Hall Jamieson. *The Press.* New York: Oxford University Press, 2005. A comprehensive survey of U.S. journalism and news.

Patterson, Thomas E. *Out of Order.* New York: Vintage Books, 1994. An analysis of how election news coverage has changed in recent decades.

Prior, Markus. *Post-Broadcast Democracy: How Media Choice Increases Inequality in Political Involvement and Polarizes Elections.* New York: Cambridge University Press, 2007. A thoughtful assessment of how the new media system is widening the information and partisan divides.

LIST OF WEBSITES

http://www.cmpa.com/ The website for the Center for Media and Public Affairs (CMPA), a nonpartisan organization that analyzes news coverage on a continuing basis, provides analyses of news content that are useful to anyone interested in the media's political coverage.

http://www.drudgereport.com/ The website through which Matt Drudge (The Drudge Report) has challenged the traditional media's control of the news.

http://www.fcc.gov/ The Federal Communications Commission (FCC) website; provides information on broadcasting regulation and current issues.

http://www.newslink.org/ A website that provides access to more than a thousand news organizations, including most U.S. daily newspapers.

POLITICS IN THEORY AND PRACTICE

Thinking: Why does almost every U.S. news outlet, despite having the freedom to say nearly anything it wants, cover virtually the same national stories in virtually the same way as other news organizations?

Participating: Before the Internet opened new channels of communication, freedom of the press, which is granted by the First Amendment to all Americans, was enjoyed for the most part only by the very few who owned or worked in the news media. With the Internet, the opportunity for citizen communication, though not unlimited, is greater than at any time in the nation's history. Take advantage of the opportunity. Meetup.com is one of literally thousands of Internet sites where you can participate in discussion forums about politics and issues. A more ambitious alternative is to start your own web log. Blogging is time consuming but allows you to create an agenda of news, information, and opinion—an activity previously reserved for newspaper editors and broadcast producers. Either of these options will enable you to make your voice heard and also help you to hone your citizenship skills—the ability to communicate, to defend your own views, and to learn what others think.

Extra Credit

For up-to-the-minute *New York Times* articles, interactive simulations, graphics, study tools, and more links and quizzes, visit the text's Online Learning Center at www.mhhe.com/pattersonwtp8e.

To Publish, or Not to Publish?

By Alex Jones

In late 2005 and again in 2006, the New York Times *released stories telling of secret U.S. surveillance programs that were part of the war on terrorism. Two programs exposed by the* Times *possibly were outside the law, while the third program seemed within the law. Should the* Times *have revealed any of the classified programs, particularly the third one? The question goes to the heart of the role of the free press in a democratic society. Is a democracy better served by a press that aggressively exposes the actions of government, or is it better served by a press that follows the government's judgment about what the American people should or should not know? This question is addressed in this essay by Alex Jones, director of the Joan Shorenstein Center on the Press, Politics, and Public Policy at Harvard University's Kennedy School of Government. He argues that the press serves the public interest when it errs on the side of openness. (A revised and abbreviated version of this essay was developed in collaboration with four communication school deans— Geoffrey Cowan of the University of Southern California, John Lavine of Northwestern University, Nicholas Lemann of Columbia University, and Orville Schell of the University of California, Berkeley—and published jointly in their names in 2006.)*

Most Americans want their government to be held accountable, which is the *raison d'etre* of watchdog journalism. At the same time, they do not want the press to disclose their government's vital secrets.

Since 9/11, serious news organizations have wrestled with the enduring problem of performing the press's vital watchdog role while also honoring citizenship responsibilities. The issue is once again front and center because of June 23rd articles, published by the *New York Times, Los Angeles Times* and *Wall Street Journal,* describing the government's efforts to track terrorist financing information. The *New York Times* has attracted most of the outrage because it took the lead in investigating the system.

For citizens, the dilemma comes down to choosing between the risk that would result from disclosure and the parallel risk of being kept in the dark, as the government often prefers. As the director of a center charged with imparting the values of responsible journalism to the next generation of reporters and editors, I favor disclosure when there are not very strong reasons for withholding information.

It is appropriate that Americans should be concerned when news organizations publish information that the President of the United States and others in authority have strongly urged not be published. No sane citizen would wish for the media to provide terrorists with information that would be likely to endanger American lives.

President Bush has denounced the *Times* in exceptionally harsh language, and on June 29 the House of Representatives formally condemned the paper. Some critics of the *Times* have termed its actions as treasonous and called for criminal charges under the Espionage Act. One conservative commentator told the *San Francisco Chronicle* that she would happily send Bill Keller, the paper's executive editor, to the gas chamber.

Keller has characterized the decision to publish the information as a "close call," which makes this an especially important moment to examine the proper balance between the press's watchdog role and its obligation to keep legitimate secrets whose exposure would badly damage the national interest.

The public has repeatedly expressed its support for the press's watchdog role, while also excoriating the media for bias and other faults. In a 2004 survey by the University of Missouri, 83 percent of respondents agreed with the statement that "it is important for journalists to press for access to information about our government, even when officials would like to keep it quiet." In the same poll, about the same number of people said that they see "social or political bias in news coverage." Clearly, the public wants the press to keep a sharp lookout, but wants the job performed responsibly. We share this sentiment.

Walking the line between its watchdog and its citizenship roles requires the press to exercise an independent judgment, and at times to defy the government. In the case of the stories about financial data under question, the government's main concern seemed to be that hitherto cooperative banks might stop cooperating if the *Times* disclosed the existence of their financial tracking system. So far that has apparently not happened. For many Americans, however, the possibility of damage to terrorist surveillance should have been sufficient justification for the *Times* to remain silent. Why, they ask, should the press take such a chance?

There are situations in which that chance should not be taken. For instance, we agree with Porter Goss, the former director of the Central Intelligence Agency, that it was wrong for the *Washington Times* in 1998 to disclose that the C.I.A. was listening in on Osama bin Laden's satellite phone. We think it equally clear that Robert Novak's column should not have unmasked Valerie Plame as a covert C.I.A. agent.

Yet, as a general rule, we believe that if it is a close call, and there is no good reason to believe that the story will put American lives at risk, the press should publish because far more damage will be done to a democratic society by keeping important information away from the American people than by leveling with them.

In our society, there is inevitable tension between liberty and security, but the two are interdependent. A knowledgeable public strengthens security in most circumstances, and makes government accountable. Similarly, excessive secrecy undermines security by treating real secrets and faux secrets the same, thus diluting a sense of urgency when information truly needs protecting. We know from our history that the government often claims to be concerned about national security when its actual concern is that disclosure will prove politically or personally embarrassing. The documents that came to be known as the Pentagon Papers in 1971 told how Presidents Eisenhower, Kennedy, and Johnson had all misled the American people regarding our role in Vietnam. Many of the documents were classified to keep their contents out of the public's view for political reasons.

The nation's founders adopted the First Amendment for the express purpose of making it more difficult for government to shield itself from the kind of careful, if often unwelcome, scrutiny that a democracy requires. For the same reason, Congress passed the Freedom of Information Act, and many states enacted Sunshine Laws to forestall government's tendency to prefer acting behind closed doors.

In the wake of 9/11, national security understandably became the top priority, and a new climate of caution regarding information was a sensible response to a sophisticated terrorist foe. President Bush's response was to declare a "war on terror" and has since claimed almost limitless powers that he views as inherently granted the president in time of war by the Constitution. Such extraordinary presidential power, in the context of what seems likely to be a permanent state of war, is unprecedented. The wise men who forged our nation created checks and balances and spoke passionately about the need for a free and independent press out of fear that too much power in any one branch of government would be dangerous.

The Bush administration has been excessively aggressive in restricting access to information on grounds of national security. There is an unmistakable pattern of limiting what Americans may reasonably know. For example, earlier this year historians complained that intelligence agencies were removing previously declassified historical documents from libraries and archives on the grounds of national security. Some of these papers dated from as far back as the Korean War; many had already been cited multiple times in books.

In general, the Bush Administration has sought to conduct much if not most of the war on terror in secret, and it has been able to do so with little oversight from Congress, which would normally be a key check on power. When the press has played such an oversight role, it has often been harshly criticized. For instance, a few months ago President Bush denounced the *Times* for revealing the National Security Agency's program of monitoring international telephone calls by Americans without first getting warrants, as a law passed by Congress required. In that case, the president rebuked the *Times* for revealing a classified secret. For most observers, however, the most important secret that was revealed, was that the president had ignored Congressional accountability and the statutory process that had been established.

The F.B.I. was summoned to conduct an aggressive effort to discover the source of the information. The F.B.I. even conducted a probe into the papers of columnist Jack Anderson after his death, which prompted a rebuke from the Senate Judiciary Committee and a number of journalists are under subpoena in cases where their sources are being sought. There is concern that journalists' phone records are going to be made available to the government, again on the basis of national security concerns.

A proper balance between disclosure and secrecy is in the nation's interest, but that balance has tilted in a direction that threatens to weaken watchdog reporting at a time when it is badly needed.

Despite the rhetoric of their fiercest critics, most news organizations—and most journalists—take secrets very seriously. Indeed, in a number of cases since 9/11, the *Times* has forgone publication of information at the request of the Bush Administration. In the case of the article on domestic eavesdropping, the *Times* held the story for a year before publishing it only after it felt that the issues raised were of great importance.

We believe that the extraordinary power of the presidency at this moment in history mandates more scrutiny by the public rather than less. Yet, Attorney General Alberto R. Gonzales has said publicly that he would consider prosecuting journalists for publishing classified information. Such an action would be devastating to the right of citizens to know what their government is doing in their name. The drumbeat for such extreme action appears to be an effort to intimidate and cow the press from probing dark corners.

We subscribe to the vision of Carl C. Magee, a crusading journalist whose Albuquerque, N.M., newspaper infuriated another president in the 1920s with revelations in the Teapot Dome scandal. Forced to close his paper after being driven into bankruptcy, Magee emerged two months later with another newspaper. Emblazoned on the front page was a new motto, borrowed from Dante: Give Light and the People Will Find Their Way."

What's Your Opinion?

Do you share Alex Jones's view of press responsibility when it comes to issues of national security? Is the nation best served by a press that leans toward revealing what officials would like to keep hidden from the public? Under what conditions do you think it might be inappropriate for the press to publish information about classified government programs?

CHAPTER 11

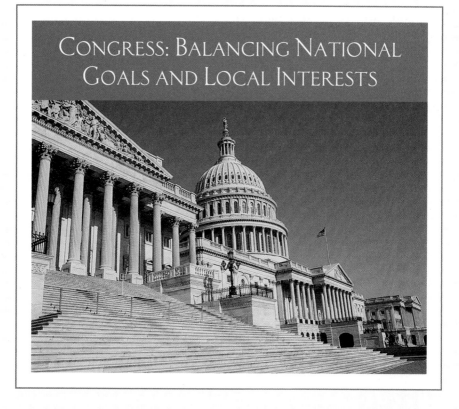

CONGRESS: BALANCING NATIONAL
GOALS AND LOCAL INTERESTS

❝ There are two Congresses. . . . The tight-knit complex world of Capitol Hill is a long
way from [the member's district], in perspective and outlook as well as in miles. ❞

ROGER DAVIDSON AND WALTER OLESZEK[1]

In September 2005, Congress faced the question of how to come up with the billions of dollars that would be required to rebuild New Orleans and the other Gulf Coast communities devastated by hurricane Katrina.

One option was to trim the $286-billion transportation bill that Congress had enacted a little more than a month earlier. In it were hundreds of pork-barrel projects that members of Congress had secured for their home states and districts. One such project was a bridge that came to be known as "the bridge to nowhere." Nearly the length of the Golden Gate Bridge, it would link the town of Ketchikan, Alaska (population 9,000) to Gravina Island (population 50). Its inclusion in the transportation bill was due to the power of its sponsor, Representative Don Young (R-Alaska), who chaired the House Transportation and Infrastructure Committee that oversaw the legislation. Congressman Young's project was only the most salient example. Virtually every member of Congress, House and Senate alike, had put something into the transportation bill that served constituent interests.

When commentators proposed that the projects be canceled and the money spent instead on Katrina relief, the response from Congress was a deafening no. Almost no member stepped forward to say that his or her pet project should be shelved. When a reporter asked Representative Young whether he was willing to cancel the Ketchikan-Gravina bridge, he replied, "They can kiss my ear! That's the dumbest thing I've ever heard." Young later relented, but the money for the bridge, rather than being spent in the Gulf Coast area, was shuttled to Alaska transportation officials to use on other projects in their state.

The story of Katrina and the 2005 transportation bill illustrates the dual nature of Congress. It is both a lawmaking institution for the country and a representative assembly for states and districts.[2] Members of Congress have a duty to serve both the interests of their constituencies and the interests of the nation as a whole. The nation's needs sometimes come first, but not always. Senators and representatives depend on the voters back home to win reelection, and they seldom miss an opportunity to serve their interests.[3]

The Framers of the Constitution established Congress as the leading branch of the national government. Congress is the first institution defined in the Constitution. Moreover, Article I does not simply give to Congress the lawmaking powers of government. It grants Congress, and Congress alone, this power: "All legislative powers herein granted shall be invested in a Congress, which shall consist of a Senate and House of Representatives." Congress is granted the authority even to decide the form and function of the executive departments and the lower courts. No executive agency or lower court can exist except as authorized by Congress.

The positioning of Congress as the first among equals in a system of divided powers reflected the Framers' trust in representative institutions. Congress was to be the branch where the interests of the people, through the House of Representatives, and the interests of the states, through the Senate, would find their fullest expression, a rejection of the European monarchical model of executive supremacy. Of course, the Framers had an innate mistrust of political power and were not about to give Congress free rein. The president and the courts were granted significant checks on legislative power. Yet the government's lawmaking and representation functions, which are in combination the signature functions of a republic, were granted to Congress.

The Framers' vision of how the federal branches would operate has not withstood fully the test of time, as this chapter and subsequent chapters on the presidency and the judiciary will show. Nevertheless, an accounting of the

★ | LEADERS

Henry Clay
(1777–1852)

In the 1950s, the Senate appointed a committee to identify its most distinguished former members. Henry Clay was named the best U.S. senator in the country's history. Clay also served in the House, rising to the level of Speaker and holding the post longer than anyone else in the nineteenth century. Clay was a reknowned orator, rivaled in the Senate only by Massachusett's Daniel Webster and South Carolina's John C. Calhoun. The three men were called the "Great Triumvirate," though they were hardly of like mind politically. Clay, the moderate, sought to bridge the widening gulf between North and South. During debate over the Compromise of 1850, which he helped forge in an effort to save the Union, Clay said, "I know no North, no South, no East, no West." A person of contradictions, Clay was a slave owner and yet spoke out against slavery. Clay eventually emancipated nearly all of his slaves, arguing that gradual emancipation was the only thing that would save the Union. Clay's ambition was to become president of the United States, an office he sought three times, coming closest in 1844, when he lost narrowly to James K. Polk. A native of Kentucky, his influence on his home state was said to be felt even after his death in 1852. Although Kentucky was a slaveholding state, it remained in the Union when other slaveholding states seceded after Abraham Lincoln's election as president in 1860. During his liftime, Clay had called secession an act of "treason."

U.S. political institutions starts naturally with Congress. This chapter examines that institution, beginning with congressional election and organization and concluding with congressional policymaking. The points emphasized in the chapter are these:

★ *Congressional elections tend to have a strong local orientation and to favor incumbents.* Congressional office provides incumbents with substantial resources (free publicity, staff, and legislative influence) that give them (particularly House members) a major advantage in election campaigns.

However, incumbency also has some liabilities that contribute to turn-over in congressional membership.

★ *Leadership in Congress is provided by party leaders, including the Speaker of the House and the Senate majority leader.* Party leaders are in a more powerful position today than a few decades ago because the party caucuses have become more cohesive.

★ *The work of Congress is done mainly through its committees and subcommittees, each of which has its separate leadership and policy jurisdiction.* The committee system of Congress allows a broad sharing of power and leadership, which serves the power and reelection needs of Congress's members but fragments the institution.

★ *Congress lacks the direction and organization required to provide consistent leadership on major national policies, but it is well organized to handle policies of relatively narrow scope.* At times, Congress takes the lead on broad national issues, but ordinarily it does not do so.

★ *Congress's policymaking role is based on three major functions: lawmaking, representation, and oversight.*

CONGRESS AS A CAREER: ELECTION TO CONGRESS

In the nation's first century, service in Congress was not a career for most of its members. Before 1900, at least a third of the seats in Congress changed hands at each election. Most members left voluntarily. Because travel was slow and arduous, serving in the nation's capital meant spending months away from one's family. Moreover, the national government was not the center of power that it is today; many politicians preferred to serve in state capitals.

The modern Congress is a different kind of institution. Most of its members are professional politicians, and a seat in the U.S. Senate or House is as high as most of them can expect to rise in politics. The pay (about $170,000 a year) is reasonably good, and the prestige of their office is substantial, particularly if they serve in the Senate. A lengthy career in Congress is the goal of most of its members.

The chances of sustaining a career in Congress are high. Getting elected to Congress is difficult, but staying there is relatively easy. In recent decades, roughly 95 percent of House incumbents and 85 percent of Senate incumbents seeking another term have been reelected (see Figure 11-1). These figures slightly overestimate incumbents' success rate. A few incumbents each term retire from Congress rather than face a challenger they

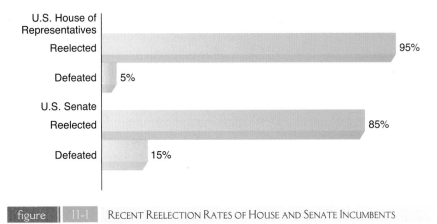

figure 11-1 RECENT REELECTION RATES OF HOUSE AND SENATE INCUMBENTS

Congressional incumbents have a very good chance of winning another term, as indicated by the reelection rates of U.S. representatives and senators who sought reelection during the five congressional elections from 2000 to 2008.

fear will beat them. On balance, however, incumbents have a commanding edge over their opponents. Most of them, particularly those in the House, win reelection by a margin of 20 percentage points or higher.

Using Incumbency to Stay in Congress

One reason incumbents run so strongly is that many congressional districts and some states are so lopsidedly Democratic or Republican that candidates of the stronger party seldom lose. In Utah and Kansas, for example, residents who identify themselves as Republicans outnumber by a wide margin residents who identify themselves as Democrats. Massachusetts and California are examples of states where the Democrats hold a commanding majority. However, whether their constituency is lopsided or competitive, incumbents have several built-in advantages over their challengers.

The Service Strategy: Taking Care of Constituents   An incumbent promotes his or her reelection prospects by catering to the **constituency:** the body of citizens eligible to vote in the incumbent's state or district. Members of Congress pay attention to constituency opinions when choosing positions on legislation, and they work hard to get their share of **pork-barrel projects** (a term referring to legislation that funds a special project for a particular locale, such as a new highway or hospital). They also respond to their constituents' individual needs, a practice known as the **service strategy.** Whether a constituent is seeking information about a government program, expressing an opinion about pending legislation, or looking for help in obtaining a federal benefit, the representative's staff is ready to assist.

Congressional staffers spend most of their time not on legislative matters but on constituency service and public relations—efforts that pay
off on election day.[4] Each House member receives an office allowance
of roughly $800,000 a year with which to hire no more than eighteen
permanent staff members.[5] Senators receive allowances that range between $2 million and $4 million a year, depending on the population size
of the state they represent. Smaller-state senators tend to have staffs in
the range of thirty people while larger-state senators have staffs closer in
number to fifty people.[6] Each member of Congress is also permitted several free mailings annually to constituent households, a privilege known
as the "*frank.*" These mailings, along with press releases and other public
relations efforts, help incumbents build name recognition and constituent support—major advantages in their reelection campaigns.

Campaign Fund-Raising: Raking in the Money   Incumbents also have a
decided advantage when it comes to raising campaign funds. Congressional
elections are expensive because of the high cost of polling, TV advertising, and other modern techniques (see Figure 11-2). Today a successful
House campaign in a competitive district costs more than a million dollars.

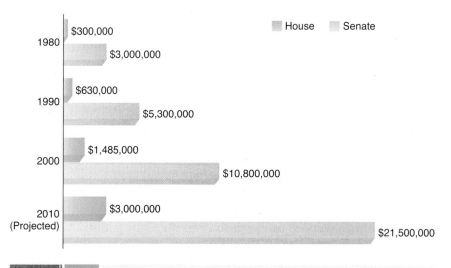

| | House | Senate |

| 1980 | $300,000 |
| | $3,000,000 |

| 1990 | $630,000 |
| | $5,300,000 |

| 2000 | $1,485,000 |
| | $10,800,000 |

| 2010 (Projected) | $3,000,000 |
| | $21,500,000 |

figure   11-2   CONGRESSIONAL CAMPAIGN EXPENDITURES, BY DECADE

Each decade, the cost of running for congressional office has risen sharply as campaign
techniques—TV advertising, opinion polling, and so on—have become more elaborate and sophisticated. The increase in spending can be seen from a comparison of the
approximate average spending by both candidates per House or Senate seat at ten-year
intervals, beginning in 1980. Roughly speaking, the cost has doubled each decade,
which is the basis for the 2010 projection. *Source: Federal Election Commission.*

The price of victory in competitive Senate races is much higher, rang-ing from several million dollars in small states to $20 million or more in larger states. Rarely do incumbents say they had trouble raising enough money to conduct an effective campaign. Challengers, however, usually say their fund-raising fell far short of what they needed.[7] However, chal-lengers, though they still trail incumbents, find it easier to attract funds when they have a chance of winning. In the 2006 midterm election, with political conditions working in their favor, Democratic challengers had a much easier time raising money than they did in the 2002 midterms, when the issues favored the Republicans.

Incumbents' past campaigns and constituent service enable them to develop mailing lists of potential contributors. Individual contributions, most of which are $100 or less, account for about 60 percent of all funds raised by congressional candidates and are obtained mainly through fund-raising events and direct-mail solicitation. Incumbents also have an edge with political action committees (PACs), which are the fund-raising arm of interest groups (see Chapter 9). Most PACs are reluctant to op-pose an incumbent unless the candidate clearly is vulnerable. More than 85 percent of PAC contributions in recent elections have been to incum-bents; their challengers received less than 15 percent (see Figure 11-3).

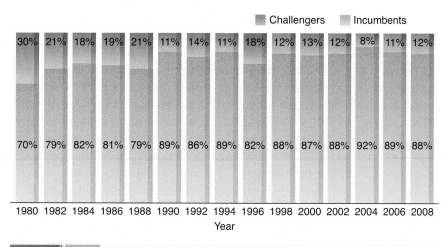

figure 11-3 ALLOCATION OF PAC CONTRIBUTIONS BETWEEN INCUMBENTS AND CHALLENGERS IN CONGRESSIONAL RACES THAT INCLUDED AN INCUMBENT, 1980–2008

In allocating campaign contributions, PACs favor incumbent members of Congress over their challengers by a wide margin. *Source: Federal Elections Commission. Figures for 2008 based on preliminary data.*

"Anytime you go against an incumbent, you take a minute and think long and hard about what your rationale is," said Desiree Anderson, director of the Realtors PAC.[8] (A race without an incumbent—called an **open-seat election**—usually brings out a strong candidate from each party and involves heavy spending, especially when the parties are closely matched in the state or district.)

Redistricting: Favorable Boundaries for House Incumbents   House members, but not senators, have a final advantage in winning reelection. Because incumbents are hard to unseat, they are always a force to be reckoned with, a fact that is blatantly apparent during redistricting. Every ten years, after each population census, the 435 seats in the House of Representatives are reallocated among the states in proportion to their population. This process is called **reapportionment.** States that have gained population since the last census may acquire additional House seats, while those that have lost population may lose seats. New York was among the states that lost one or more House seats as a result of the 2000 census; Arizona was among the states that gained one or more seats. (The Senate is not affected by population change, because each state has two senators regardless of its size.)

The responsibility for redrawing House election districts after a reapportionment—a process called **redistricting**—rests with the state governments. States are required by law to make their districts as nearly equal in population as possible. There are many ways, however, to divide a state into districts of nearly equal size, and the party in power in the state legislature will draw the new district boundaries in ways that favor candidates of its party—a process called **gerrymandering.** The party's incumbents will be given districts packed with enough of the party's voters to ensure their reelection. What about the other party's incumbents? The safest tactic in this case is to place them in districts with overwhelming numbers of voters of their own party, assuring them of an easy victory but also reducing the number of voters of that party in other districts and placing that party at a disadvantage in these other races.

For a small number of House incumbents, redistricting threatens their reelection. When a state loses a congressional seat or seats, there may be fewer seats than there are incumbents who plan to seek another term. In this case, incumbents can end up running against each other. Moreover, the party in control of the state legislature might conclude that a particular incumbent of the opposite party can be beaten and will redraw the boundaries of the incumbent's district to the incumbent's disadvantage. Turnover in House seats typically is higher in the first election after redistricting than in subsequent elections. The newly redrawn districts include some voters who are unfamiliar with the incumbent, diminishing one advantage incumbents ordinarily enjoy over their challengers. By and large, however, incumbents do not suffer greatly from redistricting, and the great majority of them wind up in districts that virtually assure their reelection. After the 2000 census, no more than 60 of the 435 House districts were competitive in the sense that they had a relatively close balance of Republican and Democratic voters. The rest were heavily Republican or heavily Democratic.

Pitfalls of Incumbency

Incumbency is not without its risks. In addition to the outside possibility that a House member will be placed in an unfavorable district as a result of reapportionment, potential pitfalls for Senate and House members alike include disruptive issues, personal misconduct, and variation in turnout, as well as strong challengers.

Disruptive Issues   Most elections are not waged in the context of disruptive issues, but when they are, incumbents are at greater risk. When voters are angry about existing political conditions, they are more likely to believe that those in power should be tossed out of office. In the 1994 midterm elections, when the public was upset over the economy and Democratic President Bill Clinton's leadership, more than 10 percent of congressional incumbents—more than twice the usual percentage and virtually all of them Democrats—were defeated, enabling the Republicans to gain control of the House and Senate. The 2006 midterm election, which was waged in the context of Republican President George W. Bush's leadership of an unpopular war in Iraq, also saw the defeat of more than twice the usual number of incumbents. This time, virtually all of them were Republicans, enabling the Democrats to seize control of both chambers. A prominent victim was Pennsylvania Senator Rick Santorum, who, as chair of the Republican Senate Conference, was the third-ranking member of the Republican Senate leadership. Easily reelected six years earlier, Santorum was defeated by Bob Casey, Pennsylvania's state treasurer.

Personal Misconduct   Members of Congress can also fall prey to scandal. Life in Washington can be fast-paced, glamorous, and expensive, and some members of Congress get caught up in influence peddling, sex scandals, and other forms of misconduct. Roughly a fourth of House incumbents who lost their bid for reelection in the past two decades were shadowed by ethical questions. "The first thing to being reelected is to stay away from scandal, even minor scandal," says political scientist John Hibbing.[9] Even top congressional leaders are not immune to the effects of scandal,

When Massachusetts was redistricted in 1812, Governor Elbridge Gerry had the lines of one district redrawn in order to ensure that a candidate of his party would be elected. Cartoonist Elkanah Tinsdale, noting that the strangely shaped district resembled a salamander, called it a "Gerry-mander."

as illustrated by the experience of former House majority leader Tom DeLay. Accused of questionable fund-raising and deal making, DeLay resigned his House seat in 2006. Another House Republican, Florida's Mark Foley, also resigned in 2006. He was discovered to have sent sexually explicit email messages to underage male congressional interns. The Foley scandal was particularly damaging to his party because it occurred within weeks of the November election, placing the GOP on the defensive at an inopportune time.

Turnout Variation: The Midterm Election Problem   Typically, the party holding the presidency loses seats in the midterm congressional elections, particularly in the House of Representatives. In only four of the last twenty-five midterm elections (including those in 1998 and 2002) has the president's party gained seats. The 2006 midterm election, when the Republicans lost seats, fit the typical pattern.

The tendency is attributable partly to the drop-off in turnout that accompanies a midterm election. The electorate in a presidential election is substantially larger than the midterm electorate. People who vote only in the presidential election tend to have weaker party affiliation and to be more responsive to the issues of the moment. These issues are likely to favor one party, which contributes to the success not only of its presidential candidate but also of its congressional candidates. In the subsequent midterm election, many of these voters stay home while those who do go to the polls vote largely along party lines. Accordingly, the congressional candidates of the president's party do not get the boost they enjoyed in the previous election, and House seats are lost as a result.[10] The pattern also can be explained by the tendency of voters to frame their view of national politics in terms of their opinion of the president's performance. Presidents usually lose popularity after taking office as a result of tough policy choices or the emergence of new problems. As the president's support declines, so does the voters' inclination to support congressional candidates from the president's party.[11]

Strong Challengers: A Particular Problem for Senators   Incumbents, particularly those in the Senate, are also vulnerable to strong challengers. Except for the presidency, the Senate is the highest rung of the political ladder. Governors and House members are frequent challengers for Senate seats, and they have the electoral base, reputation, and experience to compete effectively. Moreover, the U.S. Senate lures wealthy challengers. Maria Cantwell spent $10 million of her own money to defeat Senator Slade Gorton in the state of Washington's Senate race in 2000. Cantwell made her fortune as an executive with RealNetworks, a high-tech company. Running again in 2006, Cantwell found herself in a tighter-than-expected race, partly because her opponent, Mike McGavick, was himself a millionaire executive.

House incumbents have less reason to fear strong challengers. A House seat often is not attractive enough to induce prominent local politicians, such as mayors or state legislators, to risk their political careers in a challenge to an incumbent.[12] As a result, House incumbents frequently face weak opponents with little or no government or political experience. However, the dynamic changes somewhat when the electorate is angry and wants a change in leadership. Then the party not in power has an easier time convincing potentially strong challengers to run. In 1994, when the political mood favored the Republicans, the GOP fielded a relatively strong slate of challengers, which contributed to its success in unseating Democratic incumbents. In 2006, with the parties' roles reversed, the Democrats fielded an unusually strong group of challengers and picked up House seats.

Safe Incumbency and Representation

Although incumbents can and do lose their reelection bids, they normally win easily. An effect is to reduce Congress's responsiveness to political change. Research indicates that incumbents tend to hold relatively stable policy positions during their time in office.[13] Thus, because few congressional

★ ‖ STATES IN THE NATION

Women in the State Legislatures

Women have had more success in gaining election to state legislatures than to Congress, partly because there is more turnover and less incumbency advantage at the state level, which creates more opportunities for newcomers to run and to win. More than one in five state legislators are women, a fourfold increase since 1970. The state of Vermont, with more than 35 percent, has the highest proportion of women legislators. South Carolina, with fewer than 10 percent, has the lowest.

Q: Why do the northeastern and western regions have the most women legislators?

A: The northeastern and western regions have a higher proportion of college-educated women in the workforce than do other regions. College-educated women are more likely to run for public office and to actively support those who do run.

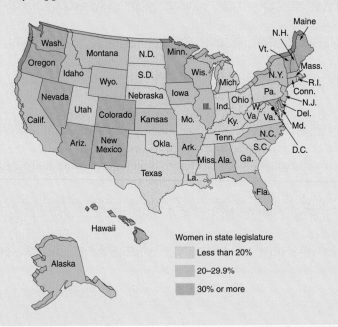

Source: Created from data gathered by the Center for the American Woman and Politics (CAWP); National Information Bank on Women in Public Office; and Eagleton Institute of Politics, Rutgers University, 2008.

seats normally change hands during an election, Congress normally does not change its direction all that much from election to election.

Safe incumbency weakens the public's influence on Congress. Democracy depends on periodic shifts in power between the parties to bring public policy into closer alignment with public opinion. In European democracies, incumbents tend to win or lose depending on their political party's popularity, which can change markedly from one election to the next; shifts in popularity can produce huge changes in the number of legislative seats controlled by the various parties. In the United States, incumbents often are able to overcome an adverse political climate through constituency service and other advantages of their office. In 1980, for example, the U.S. economy was beset by high levels of inflation and unemployment, but the Democrats nonetheless held onto their majority in the House of Representatives because most of the party's incumbents had enough cushion to win despite the fact that most Americans thought the country was headed in the wrong direction. A similar public mood produced a very different result in Britain's 1997 election. The governing Conservative Party went into the election with a 343-273 seat advantage over the Labour Party in the House of Commons but emerged with only 165 seats compared to Labour's 419.

It is worth noting that national legislators in other democracies do not have the large personal staffs or the travel and publicity budgets that members of Congress have. Nor do national legislators elsewhere enjoy anywhere near the inside track to campaign funding that members of Congress enjoy.

Who Are the Winners in Congressional Elections?

The Constitution places only a few restrictions on who can be elected to Congress. House members must be at least twenty-five years of age and have been a citizen for at least seven years. For senators, the age and citizenship requirements are thirty years and nine years, respectively. Senators and representatives alike must be residents of the state from which they are elected.

But if the formal restrictions are minimal, the informal limits are substantial. Congress is not a microcosm of the population. Although lawyers constitute less than 1 percent of the population, they make up a third of Congress. Attorneys enter politics in large numbers in part because of the central place of law in government and also because seeking elective office is a good way— even if a candidate loses—to build up a law practice. Along with lawyers, professionals such as business executives, educators, bankers, and journalists account for more than 90 percent of congressional membership.[14] Blue-collar workers, clerical employees, and homemakers are seldom elected to Congress.

Farmers and ranchers are not as rare; a fair number of House members from rural districts have agricultural backgrounds.

Finally, members of Congress are disproportionately white and male. Although the number of minority-group members and women in Congress is twice that of two decades ago, each of them accounts for only about 15 percent of the members (see Chapter 5). Safe incumbency is a major obstacle to their election to Congress.[15] In open-seat races in which they have run, they have won about half the time. However, they have been no more successful than other challengers in dislodging congressional incumbents. In elections to state and local office, where incumbency is less important, women and minority candidates have made greater inroads (see "States in the Nation").

PARTY LEADERSHIP IN CONGRESS

The House and Senate are organized along party lines. (Table 11-1 shows the party composition in Congress during the past two decades.) Members of Congress from each party meet periodically in a **party caucus** to plan strategy and discuss their legislative goals. At the start of each two-year congressional term, the party caucus is also the venue in which party members choose their **party leaders.**

House Leadership

The Constitution specifies that the House of Representatives will be presided over by a Speaker, elected by its members. In practice, this means the Speaker will be a member of the majority party, because it has enough

table 11-1	THE NUMBER OF DEMOCRATS AND REPUBLICANS IN THE HOUSE OF REPRESENTATIVES AND SENATE, 1999–2010					
	1999–2000	**2001–2**	**2003–4**	**2005–6**	**2007–8**	**2009–10**
House						
Democrats	212*	213	208	203	235*	256
Republicans	223	222	227	232	200	179
Senate						
Democrats	45*	51*	49	45	51*	57
Republicans	55	49	51	55	49	43

*Chamber not controlled by the president's party. Senate and House members who are independents are included in the total for the party with which they caucused.

votes to elect one of its own to the post. Thus, when the Democrats took control of the House after the 2006 election, Nancy Pelosi, the Democrats' leader in the chamber, replaced Republican Dennis Hastert as Speaker. Pelosi is the first woman ever to serve as leader of either the House or the Senate.

The Speaker of the House is sometimes said to be the second-most-powerful official in Washington, after the president. The Speaker is active in developing the party's positions on issues and in persuading party members in the House to support these positions. Although the Speaker cannot force party members to support the party's program, they look to the Speaker for leadership. The Speaker also has certain formal powers, including the right to speak first during House debate on legislation and the power to recognize members—that is, give them permission to speak from the floor. Because the House places a time limit on floor debate, not everyone has a chance to speak on a given bill, and the Speaker can sometimes influence legislation simply by exercising the power to decide who will speak and when. The Speaker also chooses the chairperson and the majority-party members of the powerful House Rules Committee, which controls the scheduling of bills for debate. Legislation that the Speaker wants passed is likely to reach the floor under conditions favorable to its enactment; for example, the Speaker may ask the Rules Committee to delay sending a bill to the floor until there is enough support for its passage. The Speaker also has other ways of influencing the work of the House. The Speaker assigns bills to committees, places time limits on the reporting of bills out of committees, and assigns members to conference committees. (The importance of these powers over committee action will become apparent later in this chapter.)

The Speaker is assisted by the House majority leader and the House majority whip, who are also chosen by the majority party's members. The majority leader acts as the party's floor leader, organizing the debate on bills and lining up legislative support. The whip has the job of informing party members when critical votes are scheduled. As voting is getting under way on the House floor, the whip will sometimes stand at a location that is easily seen by party members and let them know where the leadership stands on the bill by giving them a thumbs-up or thumbs-down signal.

The minority party also has its House leaders. The House minority leader heads the party's caucus and its policy committee and plays the leading role in developing the party's legislative positions. The minority leader is assisted by a minority whip.

Senate Leadership

In the Senate, the most important party leadership position is that of the majority leader, who heads the majority-party caucus. The majority leader's role is much like that of the Speaker of the House in that the Senate majority leader formulates the majority party's legislative agenda and encourages party members to support it. Like the Speaker, the Senate majority leader chairs the party's policy committee and acts as the party's voice in the chamber. The majority leader is assisted by the majority whip, who sees to it that members know when important votes are scheduled and ensures that the party's strongest advocates on a legislative measure are present for the debate. The Senate also has a minority leader and a minority whip, whose roles are comparable to those performed by their counterparts in the House.

Unlike the Speaker of the House, the Senate majority leader is not the chamber's presiding officer. The Constitution assigns this responsibility to the vice president of the United States. However, because the vice president is allowed to vote in the Senate only to break a tie, the vice president normally is not in the Senate chamber unless support for a bill is so closely divided that a tie vote appears possible. The Senate has a president pro tempore, who, in the absence of the vice president, has the right to preside over the Senate. President pro tempore is largely an honorary position that by tradition is held by the majority party's senior member. In any case, the presiding official has limited power, because each senator has the right to speak at any length on bills under consideration.

The Senate's tradition of unlimited debate stems mainly from its small size (only 100 members, compared with the House's 435 members). Senators like to view themselves as the equals of all others in their chamber and thus are less inclined than House members to take direction from their leadership. For this reason and others, the Senate majority leader has less influence over what the Senate does than the House Speaker has over the House's actions.

The Power of Party Leaders

Because the reelection of senators and representatives depends largely on their own efforts, they have a considerable degree of independence from their congressional leaders. Although the Speaker of the House and the Senate majority leader, as well as their counterparts in the minority party, wield considerable influence they cannot, unlike party leaders in European legislatures, require their members to follow their lead (see "How the United States Compares"). Accordingly, the power of Senate and House leaders rests heavily on the trust placed in them by the members of their party. If they are adept at promoting ideas and building coalitions, they can

🌐 HOW THE UNITED STATES COMPARES

Legislative Leadership and Authority

The U.S. House and Senate are separate and coequal chambers, each with its own leadership and rules. This type of legislative structure is not found in most democracies. Many democracies, for example, have a single legislative chamber, which is apportioned by population. If the United States had an equivalent legislature, it would consist only of the House of Representatives.

Even democracies that have bicameral (two-chamber) legislatures tend to structure them differently than the U.S. Congress is structured. The U.S. Senate is apportioned strictly by geography: there are two senators from each state. Germany is among the democracies that have a chamber organized along geographical lines, but Germany's upper house (the Bundesrat) differs from the U.S. Senate. Each of the German states (known as Länder) has at least three representatives in the Bundesrat, but the more populous states have more than three representatives.

Moreover, in most bicameral legislatures, one legislative chamber has substantially less power than the other. In the British Parliament, for example, the House of Lords in some instances can slow down legislation that is passed by the House of Commons but cannot stop it from becoming law. In the German Parliament, the Bundesrat has a voice on constitutional policy issues but not on most national policy issues, and its vote can in some cases be overridden by the population-based chamber (the Bundestag). In the United States, the Senate and House are equal in their legislative powers; without their joint agreement, a law cannot be enacted.

The U.S. Congress is fragmented in other ways as well: it has elected leaders with limited formal powers, a network of relatively independent and powerful committees, and members who are free to follow or ignore other members of their party. It is not uncommon for a fourth or more of a party's legislators to vote against their party's position on important legislative issues. In contrast, European legislatures have a centralized power structure: top leaders have substantial authority, the committees are weak, and the parties are unified. European legislators are expected to support their party unless granted permission to vote otherwise on a particular bill. Legislative leadership is much easier to exercise in Europe's hierarchical parliaments than in America's "stratarchical" Congress.

(continued)

Country	Form of Legislature
Canada	One house dominant
France	One house dominant
Germany	One house dominant (except on certain issues)
Great Britain	One house dominant
Israel	One house only
Japan	One house dominant
Mexico	Two equal houses
Sweden	One house only
United States	Two equal houses

exercise considerable power within their chamber. By the same token, their power can evaporate if they make a mistake that hurts their party. In 2002, Republican Senate leader Trent Lott of Mississippi resigned his post after he placed his party at the center of an unwanted controversy by publicly praising the South's segregated past.

Party leaders are in a more powerful position today than a few decades ago as a result of changes in the composition of the congressional parties. The GOP's once substantial progressive faction has been eclipsed by its conservative wing. At the same time, the Democratic Party's conservative wing, represented by its southern lawmakers, has virtually disappeared. As congressional Republicans have become more alike in their thinking and further apart from congressional Democrats, each group has found it easier to band together and stand against the opposing party.[16] Accordingly, the party leaders, working through the party caucuses, have found it easier to bring their party's lawmakers together on legislative issues. This heightened unity is evident in the pattern of *roll-call votes* (votes on which each member's vote is officially recorded, as opposed to voice votes, where the members simply say "aye" or "nay" in unison and the presiding officer indicates which side prevails without tallying individual members' positions). Over the past three decades, party-line voting on roll calls has increased considerably (see Figure 11-4). In the 1970s, roll-call votes generally did not

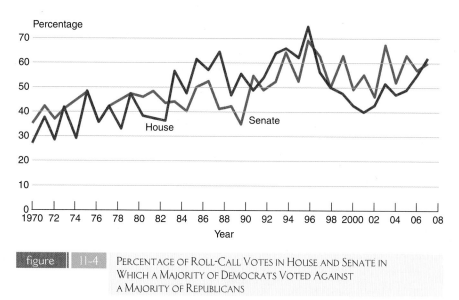

figure   11-4   PERCENTAGE OF ROLL-CALL VOTES IN HOUSE AND SENATE IN WHICH A MAJORITY OF DEMOCRATS VOTED AGAINST A MAJORITY OF REPUBLICANS

Democrats and Republicans in Congress are often on opposite sides of issues; party-line voting has been relatively high since the 1980s. *Source:* Congressional Quarterly Weekly, *various dates.*

pit most Republicans against most Democrats. More recently, most roll-call votes have divided along party lines.

Nevertheless, most party members are secure in their reelection prospects and thus are not compelled to go along with the party leadership. Moreover, members of Congress have their own policy goals, which do not always accord with those of the party leadership. Some members also have close ties to the special interests that back their campaigns and want to help them out, which can put them at odds with the party leadership on particular issues.

THE COMMITTEE SYSTEM

Most of the work in Congress is conducted through **standing committees,** which are permanent committees with responsibility for a particular area of public policy. At present there are twenty standing committees in the House and sixteen in the Senate (see Table 11-2). Both the House and the Senate, for example, have a standing committee that handles foreign policy issues. Other important standing committees are those that deal with agriculture, commerce, the interior (natural resources and public lands), defense, government spending, labor, the judiciary, and taxation. House committees, which average about thirty-five to forty members each, are about twice the

| table | 11-2 | THE STANDING COMMITTEES OF CONGRESS |

House of Representatives	Senate
Agriculture	Agriculture, Nutrition, and Forestry
Appropriations	Appropriations
Armed Services	Armed Services
Budget	Banking, Housing, and Urban Affairs
Education and Labor	Budget
Energy and Commerce	Commerce, Science, and Transportation
Financial Services	Energy and Natural Resources
Foreign Affairs	Environment and Public Works
Homeland Security	Finance
House Administration	Foreign Relations
Judiciary	Health, Education, Labor, and Pensions
Natural Resources	Homeland Security and Governmental Affairs
Oversight and Government Reform	Judiciary
Rules	Rules and Administration
Science and Technology	Small Business and Entrepreneurship
Small Business	Veterans' Affairs
Standards of Official Conduct	
Transportation and Infrastructure	
Veterans' Affairs	
Ways and Means	

size of Senate committees. Each standing committee has legislative authority in that it can draft and rewrite proposed legislation and can recommend to the full chamber the passage or defeat of the legislation it considers.

Most of the standing committees have subcommittees, which specialize in some aspect of the committee's work. Altogether there are about two hundred House and Senate subcommittees, each of which has a defined jurisdiction. The House Foreign Affairs Committee, for instance, has seven subcommittees: Africa and Global Health; Asia, the Pacific, and the Global Environment; Europe; International Organizations, Human Rights, and Oversight; Middle East and South Asia; Terrorism, Nonproliferation, and Trade; and Western

Hemisphere. Each House and Senate subcommittee has about a dozen members. These few individuals do most of the work and have a leading voice in the disposition of bills in their policy area.

Congress could not possibly handle its workload without the help of its committee system. About ten thousand bills are introduced during each two-year session of Congress. The sheer volume of legislation would paralyze the institution if it did not divide the work among its various standing committees, each of which has its own staff. Unlike the members' personal staffs, which concentrate on constituency relations, the committee staffs perform an almost entirely legislative function. They help draft legislation, organize hearings, and participate in altering bills within the committee.

In addition to its permanent standing committees, Congress also has a number of *select committees*, which are created for a specific time period and purpose. A current example is the Senate Select Committee on Intelligence, which oversees the work of intelligence agencies, such as the CIA. Congress also has *joint committees*, composed of members of both houses, that perform advisory functions. The Joint Committee on the Library, for example, oversees the Library of Congress, the largest library in the world. Finally, Congress has **conference committees**—joint committees formed temporarily to work out differences in House and Senate versions of a particular bill. The role of conference committees is discussed more fully later in the chapter.

Committee Jurisdiction

The 1946 Legislative Reorganization Act requires that each bill introduced in Congress be referred by the party leaders to the proper committee. An agricultural bill introduced in the Senate must be assigned to the Senate Agriculture Committee, a bill dealing with foreign affairs must be sent to the Senate Foreign Relations Committee, and so on. This requirement is a major source of each committee's power. Even if its members are known to oppose certain types of legislation, bills clearly within its **jurisdiction**—the policy area in which it is authorized to act—must be sent to it for deliberation.

In some cases, however, jurisdiction is subject to disputed. Which House committee, for example, should handle a major bill addressing the role of financial institutions in global trade? The Financial Services Committee? The Commerce Committee? The International Relations Committee? All committees seek legislative influence, and each is jealous of its jurisdiction, so a bill that overlaps committee boundaries can provoke a "turf war" over which committee will handle it.[17] Party leaders can take advantage of these situations by shuttling a bill to the committee that is most likely to handle it in the way they would like. But because party leaders depend on the committees for support, they cannot regularly ignore a committee that has a strong claim to a bill. At times, party leaders have responded by dividing up a bill, handing over some of its provisions to one committee and other provisions to a second committee.

Committee Membership

Each committee has a fixed number of seats, and the majority party holds most of them. The ratio of Democrats to Republicans on each committee is approximately the same as the ratio in the full House or Senate, but there is no fixed rule on this matter, and the majority party decides what the ratio will be (mindful that at the next election it could become the chamber's minority party). Members of the House typically serve on only two committees. Senators often serve on four, although they can sit on only two major committees, such as Foreign Relations and Finance.

At the start of each new term, the parties decide which of their members will serve on each committee, though reelected members by tradition are allowed to stay on committees on which they have been serving. (An exception occurs when a party loses control of the Senate and House, which will lead it also to lose committee seats, in which case some of its reelected members get bumped.) Because each committee has a fixed number of seats, a committee must have a vacancy before a new member can be appointed. Most vacancies occur after an election as a result of the retirement or defeat of committee members. Each party has a special committee in each chamber that decides who will fill committee vacancies. Several factors influence these decisions, including members' preferences. Most newly elected members of Congress ask for and receive assignment to a committee on which they can serve their constituents' interests and at the same time enhance their reelection prospects. For example, when Amy Klobuchar was elected to the Senate in 2006 from Minnesota, a state that depends heavily on the farm sector, she asked for and received an appointment to the Senate Agriculture Committee, which oversees this sector. Klobuchar's political base was in the Twin Cities area, and her position on the agricultural committee has enabled her to strengthen ties to the state's rural voters. Members of Congress also prefer membership on one of the more prestigious committees, such as the Senate Foreign Relations Committee and the House Ways and Means (taxation) Committee. A seat on these committees is coveted because they deal with vital issues, such as taxes and international affairs. Factors such as members' party loyalty, willingness to work hard on committee business, and length of congressional service weigh heavily in the determination of appointments to these key committees.[18]

Subcommittee assignments are handled differently. The members of each party on a committee decide who among them will serve on each of its subcommittees. The members' preferences and seniority, as well as the interests of their constituencies, are key influences on subcommittee assignments.

Committee Chairs

Each committee (as well as each subcommittee) is headed by a chairperson. The position of committee chair is a powerful one. The chair schedules committee meetings, determines the order in which committee bills are considered, presides over committee discussions, directs the committee's majority staff, and can choose to lead the debate when a committee bill reaches the floor of the chamber for a vote by the full membership.

Committee chairs are always members of the majority party and usually the party member with the most **seniority** (consecutive years of service) on the committee. Seniority is based strictly on time served on a committee, not on time spent in Congress. Thus, if a member switches committees, the years spent on the first committee do not count toward seniority on the second one. The seniority system has advantages: it reduces the number of power struggles that would occur if the chairs were decided each time by open competition, it places committee leadership in the hands of experienced members, and it enables members to look forward to the reward of a position as chair after years of service on the same committee.

The seniority system is not absolute, however, and is less controlling than in the past. There was a period when seniority was a strict rule, which led to abuses. Although most chairs were responsive to the concerns of other members, some were dictatorial. Howard Smith, an arch segregationist, chaired the House Rules Committee from 1955 to 1965 and used his position to keep civil rights legislation from reaching the House floor for a vote. During that era, a committee could not meet unless its chair called it into session, and Smith would leave Washington for his Virginia farm when a civil rights bill came to the Rules Committee, returning only if committee members agreed to withdraw the bill from consideration. Abuses by Smith and other imperious chairs led to reforms in the 1970s that reduced the power of committee chairs. Seniority was no longer an absolute rule, and a committee majority was given the power to call a committee into session if the chair refused to do so.

Committees and Parties: Who Is in Control?

In one sense, committees are an instrument of the majority party, in that it controls most of each committee's seats and appoints its chair. In another sense, each committee is a power in its own right. Committees have been

Nancy Pelosi, House Democratic leader since 2002 and Speaker of the House since 2007, is the first woman in U.S. history to lead a major party in Congress. First elected to Congress in 1987 from a northern California district, Pelosi quickly made a reputation for herself as a diligent legislator and tenacious bargainer. Her father also served in the House of Representatives and later served five terms as mayor of Baltimore, where she grew up. Pelosi is shown here with other House Democratic leaders to highlight a bill that had just been passed by the House of Representatives.

described at "little legislatures," each secure in its jurisdiction, membership, and leadership, and each wielding considerable control over the legislation it handles.

Committees serve to decentralize power in Congress and to meet individual members' power and reelection needs. Less than a dozen members hold a party leadership position, but several hundred serve as committee or subcommittee chairs or are "ranking members," which is the term for the minority party's committee and subcommittee leaders. In these positions, they exercise authority, often in ways that serve local constituencies or personal policy agendas—actions that may or may not be fully consistent with the party leadership's overall goals. The result is an institution very different from European parliaments, where power is concentrated in the top party leadership (an arrangement reflected even in the name for rank-and-file members: "backbenchers").

This characteristic of Congress reflects a fundamental fact. House and Senate members owe their election to their own efforts, as much as to the party's efforts, and consequently have the independence to act somewhat as they please and have an incentive to respond to constituency interests when these run counter to their party's national agenda. In 2007, when Democratic Senate leaders sought to unite their party's members behind comprehensive immigration reform, which would have allowed illegal aliens to remain in the country as guest workers and placed some of them in line for citizenship, nearly every Democratic senator from a state with strong anti-immigrant sentiment voted against the reform bill.

In an effort to strengthen the party's role, Republicans when taking control of Congress in 1995 sought to reduce the power of committees and their chairs. The Republicans passed over some senior party members in selecting the committee chairs and placed term limits on the rest. After six years, a chair or ranking member must relinquish the post. Each chair was to use the position's power to promote the goals of the party as opposed to those of individual committee members. When the Democrats took over Congress in 2007, they left the term limits in place. And in fact, during the past dozen or so years, as will be discussed at length later in the chapter, the political parties have had unusually strong control over the legislative agenda, though less than that of the parties in European legislatures.

The balance between party power and committee power, however, is an ongoing issue. The institution is at once a place for conducting the nation's business and a venue for promoting constituency interests. At times, the balance has tipped toward the committees and their leadership. At other times, it has tipped toward the parties and their leadership. At all times, there has been an attempt to achieve a workable balance of the two. The distinguishing feature of congressional power is its division among the membership, with provision for added power—sometimes more and sometimes less—in the hands of the top party leaders.

HOW A BILL BECOMES LAW

Parties, party leaders, and committees are critical actors in the legislative process. Their roles and influence, however, vary with the nature of the legislation under consideration.

Committee Hearings and Decisions

The formal process by which bills become law is shown in Figure 11-5. A **bill** is a proposed legislative act. Many bills are prepared by executive agencies, interest groups, or other outside parties, but members of Congress

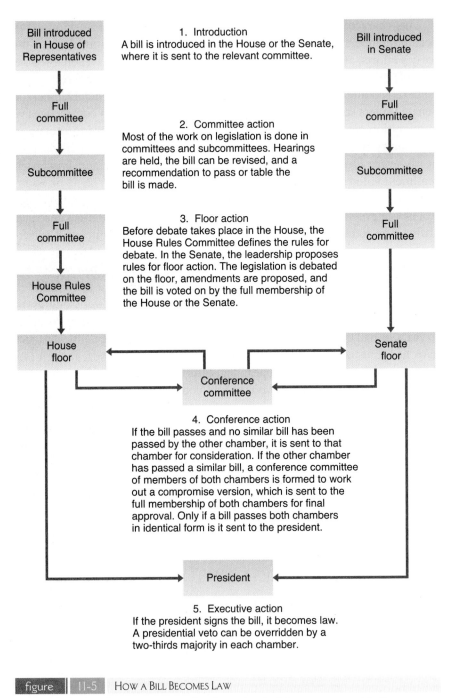

figure   11-5   HOW A BILL BECOMES LAW

Although the legislative process can be short-circuited in many ways, this diagram describes a normal way a bill becomes law.

also draft bills, and only they can formally submit a bill for consideration by their chamber. Once a bill is introduced by a member of the House or Senate, it is given a number and a title and is then sent to the appropriate committee, which assigns it to one of its subcommittees. Less than 10 percent of the bills that committees consider reach the floor for a vote; the others are "killed" when committees decide that they do not warrant further consideration and table them. The full House or Senate can overrule committee decisions, but this rarely occurs.

The fact that committees kill more than 90 percent of the bills submitted in Congress does not mean that committees exercise 90 percent of the power in Congress. A committee rarely decides fully the fate of legislation that is important to the majority party or its leadership. Most bills die in committee because they are of little interest to anyone other than a few members of Congress or are so poorly conceived that they lack merit. Some bills are not even supported by the members who introduce them. A member may submit a bill to appease a powerful constituent group and then quietly inform the committee to ignore it.

If a bill appears to have merit, the subcommittee will schedule hearings on it. The subcommittee invites testimony on the proposed legislation from lobbyists, administrators, and experts. After the hearings, if the subcommittee still feels that the legislation is needed, members recommend the bill to the full committee, which can hold additional hearings. In the House, both the full committee and a subcommittee can "mark up," or revise, a bill. In the Senate, markup usually is reserved for the full committee.

From Committee to the Floor

If a majority of the committee vote to recommend passage of the bill, it is referred to the full chamber for action. In the House, the Rules Committee has the power to determine when the bill will be voted on, how long the debate on the bill will last, and whether the bill will receive a "closed rule" (no amendments will be permitted), an "open rule" (members can propose amendments relevant to any of the bill's sections), or something in between (for example, only certain sections of the bill will be subject to amendment). The Rules Committee has this scheduling power because the House is too large to operate effectively without strict rules for the handling of legislation by the full chamber. The rules are also a means by which the majority party controls legislation. When they controlled the House in the period before 1995, Democrats employed closed rules to prevent Republicans from proposing amendments to major bills, a tactic House Republicans said they would forgo when they took control in 1995. Once in control, however, the Republicans applied closed rules to a number of major bills. The tactic was too effective to ignore.

On most House bills, only a small number of legislators are granted the opportunity to speak on the floor. In most cases, the decision as to who will speak is delegated to the bill's chief sponsor and one of the bill's leading opponents.

The Senate also has a rules committee, but it has much less power than in the House. In the Senate, the majority leader, usually in consultation with the minority leader, schedules bills. All Senate bills are subject to unlimited debate unless a three-fifths majority of the full Senate votes for **cloture**, which limits debate to thirty hours. Cloture is a way of defeating a Senate **filibuster**, which is a procedural tactic whereby a minority of senators can block a bill by talking until other senators give in and the bill is withdrawn from consideration or altered to fit opponents' demands. In late 2005, for example, Senate Democrats used the filibuster to block a vote on renewal of the USA Patriot Act, saying that they would allow it to come to a vote only if Republicans agreed to add protections of privacy rights. Three months later, Senate Democrats got the changes they wanted, and the bill passed by an overwhelming majority.

In the Senate, members can propose any amendment to any bill. That is not true in the House, where proposed amendments must directly relate to the bill's contents. Senate amendments do not have to be germane to the bill's provisions. For example, a senator may propose an antiabortion amendment to a bill dealing with defense expenditures. Such amendments are called **riders.**

Leadership and Floor Action

Committee action is usually decisive on bills that address small issues. If a majority of committee members favor such a bill, it normally is passed by the full chamber, often without amendment. In a sense, the full chamber merely votes to confirm or modify decisions made previously by committees and subcommittees. Of course, these units do not operate in a vacuum. In making its decisions, a committee takes into account the fact that its action can be reversed by the full chamber, just as a subcommittee recognizes that the full committee can overrule its decision.[19] Partisanship also serves as a check on committee action. When a committee's vote is sharply divided along party lines, other members may conclude that they need to look more closely at the bill before deciding whether to vote for it.

On major bills, the majority party's leaders (particularly in the House) have increasingly set the agenda.[20] They shape the bill's broad content and work closely with the relevant committee during the bill's committee phase. Once the bill clears the committee, they often assume leadership of the floor debate. In these efforts, they depend on the ongoing support of their party's members. To obtain it, they consult their members informally and through the party caucus. **Party discipline**—the willingness of a party's House or Senate members to act as a unified group—is increasingly important in congressional action and is the key to party leaders' ability to shape major legislation. (The role of parties in Congress is discussed further in the section on Congress's representation function.)

Conference Committees and the President

For a bill to pass, it must have the support of a simple majority (50 percent plus one) of the House or Senate members voting on it. To become law, however, a bill must be passed in identical form by both the House and the Senate. About 10 percent of all bills that pass both chambers—the proportion is larger for major bills—differ in important respects in their House and Senate versions. These bills are referred to conference committees to resolve the differences. Each conference committee is formed temporarily for the sole purpose of handling a particular bill; its members are usually appointed from the House and Senate standing committees that drafted the bill. The conference committee's job is to develop a compromise version, which then goes back to the House and Senate floors for a vote. There it can be passed, defeated, or returned to conference, but not amended.

A bill that is passed in identical form by the House and the Senate is not yet a law. The president also plays a role. If the president signs the bill, it becomes **law.** If the president exercises the **veto,** the bill is sent back to Congress with the president's reasons for rejecting it. Congress can override a veto by a two-thirds vote of each chamber; the bill then becomes law without the president's signature. A bill also becomes law if Congress is in session and the president fails to sign or veto the bill within ten days (Sundays excepted). However, if Congress has concluded its term and the president fails to sign a bill within ten days, the bill does not become law. This last situation, called a pocket veto, forces Congress in its next term to start over from the beginning: the bill again must pass both chambers and again is subject to presidential veto.

CONGRESS'S POLICYMAKING ROLE

The Framers of the Constitution expected that Congress, as the embodiment of representative government, would be the institution to which the people looked for policy leadership. During most of the nineteenth century,

table	11-3	THE MAJOR FUNCTIONS OF CONGRESS

Function	Basis and Activity
Lawmaking	Through its constitutional grant to enact law, Congress makes the laws authorizing federal programs and appropriating the funds necessary to carry them out.
Representation	Through its elected constitutional officers—U.S. senators and representatives—Congress represents the interests of constituents and the nation in its deliberations and its lawmaking.
Oversight	Through its constitutional responsibility to see that the executive branch carries out the laws faithfully and spends appropriations properly, Congress oversees and sometimes investigates executive action.

Congress had that stature. Aside from a few strong leaders such as Andrew Jackson and Abraham Lincoln, presidents did not play a major legislative role (see Chapter 12). However, as national and international forces combined to place greater leadership and policy demands on the federal government, the president became a vital part of the national legislative process. Today Congress and the president substantially share the legislative effort, although their roles differ greatly.[21]

Congress's policymaking role revolves around its three major functions: lawmaking, representation, and oversight (see Table 11-3). In practice, the three functions overlap, but they are conceptually distinct.

The Lawmaking Function of Congress

Under the Constitution, Congress is granted the **lawmaking function:** the authority to make the laws necessary to carry out the powers granted to the national government. The constitutional powers of Congress are substantial; they include the power to tax, to spend, to regulate commerce, and to declare war. However, whether Congress takes the lead in the making of laws depends heavily on the type of policy at issue.

Broad Issues: Fragmentation as a Limit on Congress's Role   Congress is structured in a way that can make agreement on large issues difficult to obtain. Congress is not one house but two, each with its own authority and constituency base. Neither the House nor the Senate can enact legislation without the other's approval, and the two chambers are hardly two versions of the same thing. California and North Dakota have exactly the same representation in the Senate, but in the House, which is apportioned by population, California has fifty-three seats compared to North Dakota's one.

Congress also includes a lot of lawmakers: 100 members of the Senate and 435 members of the House. They come from different constituencies and represent different and sometimes opposing interests, which leads to disagreements. Nearly every member of Congress, for example, supports the principle of global free trade. Yet when it comes to specific trade provisions, members often disagree. Foreign competition means different things to manufacturers who produce automobiles, computer chips, or underwear; it means different things to farmers who produce corn, sugar, or grapes; and it means different things to firms that deal in international finance, home insurance, or student loans. And because it means different things to different people in different parts of the country, members of Congress who represent these areas have conflicting views on when free trade makes sense.

Even when the majority party's members are more or less united, Congress can struggle to take decisive action. The Democrats found themselves in this position after they took control of the House and Senate in the 2006 election. Most of the Democrats had campaigned against the large-scale U.S. military commitment in Iraq, and they joined together on votes to reduce the American presence there. In every case, however, their efforts were blocked either by President Bush's veto, which required a two-thirds vote in each chamber to override, or by the Senate rule requiring sixty votes to invoke cloture. The fact was, the Democrats' congressional majority—which was barely over 50 percent in the Senate and not all that much larger in the House—was far too slim for them to override a presidential veto or secure cloture. Opinion polls indicated growing dissatisfaction with the performance of congressional Democrats, but in truth, they lacked the legislative votes to prevail.

For such reasons, Congress often has difficulty taking the lead on broad issues of national policy. A legislative institution can easily lead on such issues only if it grants this authority to its top leader. But Congress does not have a single leader. The House has its separate leaders, as does the Senate. Moreover, although the rise in party discipline in Congress has strengthened the role of the chambers' leaders, the fact remains that House and Senate members of the same party are still literally free to go their separate ways if they so choose. As a result, Congress sometimes struggles when faced with the task of developing a comprehensive policy response to broad national issues. In 2008, for example, Congress addreseed the renewal of legislation pertaining to terrorist surveillance. The Senate backed the bill sought by the White House while the House Democratic leaders objected to a provision granting retroactive immunity to telecom companies that had provided private phone records to the government under the original legislation. This objection proved a big enough obstacle that the existing program expired. Although subsequent negotiations eventually resulted in the program's renewal, the split between the House and Senate and the split within the House among its members produced deadlock, despite wide agreement among lawmakers on the urgency of the legislation.

As an institution, the presidency is better suited to the task of providing leadership on major national issues. First, whereas Congress's authority is divided, executive power is vested constitutionally in the hands of a single individual—the president. Unlike congressional leaders, who must bargain with their members when taking a stand on legislation, the president does not have to negotiate with other executive officials in taking a position. Second, whereas members of Congress tend to see issues mainly from the perspective of their state or district, the president tends to see them from a national perspective.

News coverage also tilts national policy leadership toward the president. On national television news, the presidency gets twice the coverage of Congress, which, when it is covered, is frequently portrayed as simply responding to presidential initiatives. Former House Speaker Thomas P. "Tip" O'Neill once said that if there was only one thing he could accomplish as Speaker it would be to persuade the news media that Congress is a branch of government coequal with the president. Congress established C-SPAN, which carries House and Senate proceedings on cable television, in hopes that it would put the institution more into the national spotlight. Whatever C-SPAN's other effects, it has done little to make Americans look first to Congress for leadership on national policy issues.

Presidential leadership means that Congress normally will pay attention to White House proposals, not that it will adopt them. Congress typically accepts a presidential initiative only as a starting point in its deliberations. It may reject the proposal outright—particularly when the president is from the opposing party—but any such proposal provides Congress with a tangible bill to focus on. If the proposal is at all close to what a congressional majority would regard as acceptable, Congress will use it as a baseline from which to make changes that will bring it in line with the thinking of the congressional majority. (The legislative roles of Congress and the president are discussed further in Chapter 12.)

In its lawmaking activities, Congress has the support of three congressional agencies. One is the Congressional Budget Office (CBO), which was created as part of the Budget Impoundment and Control Act of 1974. Its two hundred fifty employees provide Congress with general economic projections, overall estimates of government expenditures and revenues, and specific estimates of the costs of proposed programs. (The budgetary process is described more fully in later chapters.)

A second congressional agency is the Government Accountability Office (GAO). With three thousand employees, the GAO is the largest congressional agency. Formed in 1921, it has primary responsibility for overseeing executive agencies' spending of money that has been appropriated by Congress. The programs that the executive agencies administer are authorized and funded by Congress. The GAO's responsibility is to ensure that executive agencies operate in the manner prescribed by Congress.

The third and oldest congressional agency is the Congressional Research Service (CRS). It has a staff of one thousand employees and operates as a nonpartisan reference agency. It conducts research and responds to information requests from congressional committees and members.

Congress in the Lead: Fragmentation as a Policymaking Strength
Congress occasionally takes the lead on large issues. Labor legislation, environmental law, federal aid to education, and urban development are policy areas in which Congress has frequently taken the initiating role.[22] Social welfare is not such an area generally, but the Welfare Reform Act of 1996, which dramatically altered the shape of public assistance to the poor, was a congressional initiative (see Chapter 3). Nevertheless, Congress does not routinely develop broad policy programs and carry them through to passage. "Congress remains organized," James Sundquist notes, "to deal with narrow problems but not with broad ones."[23]

Not surprisingly, then, the great majority of the hundreds of bills that Congress considers each session deal with narrow issues. Congress has the leading role in the disposition of these particular bills, which are handled largely through the standing committees. The same fragmentation that makes it difficult for Congress to take the lead on broad issues makes it easy for Congress to tackle scores of narrow issues simultaneously. Most of the legislation passed by Congress is "distributive"—that is, it confers benefits on a particular group while spreading the costs across the taxpaying public. Veterans' benefits are one example. Such legislation, because it directly benefits a particular constituency, is a type of policy that members of Congress prefer to support. The cost of any such policy is spread so widely that taxpayers are unlikely to notice. On the other hand, the benefit is targeted so precisely that the recipients will notice and appreciate the help. Such policies are also the type that Congress, through its committee system, is organizationally best suited to handle. Most committees parallel a major constituent interest, such as agriculture, commerce, labor, or veterans.

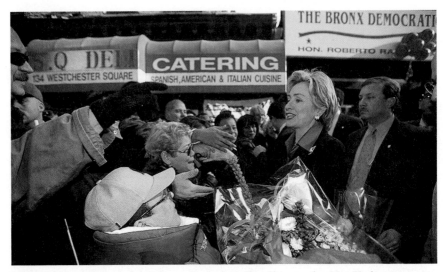

Hillary Clinton is the only first lady to seek elective office. She moved to New York to compete in the state's Senate race, which she won. She won reelection in 2006 and then launched her campaign for the 2008 Democratic presidential nomination.

The Representation Function of Congress

In the process of making laws, the members of Congress represent various interests within American society, giving them a voice in the national legislature. The proper approach to the **representation function** has been debated since the nation's founding. A recurrent issue has been whether the main concern of a representative should be the interests of the nation as a whole or those of his or her own constituency. These interests overlap to some degree but rarely coincide exactly. Policies that are of benefit to the full society are not always equally advantageous to particular localities and can even cause harm to some constituencies.

Representation of States and Districts   The choice between national and local interests is not a simple one, even for a legislator who is inclined toward either orientation. To be fully effective, members of Congress must be reelected time and again, a necessity that compels them to pay attention to local demands. Yet, as part of the nation's legislative body, no member can easily ignore the nation's needs. In making the choice, most members of Congress, on narrow issues at least, tend toward a local orientation.[24] Opposition to gun control legislation, for example, is much stronger among members of Congress representing rural areas where hunting weapons are commonplace.

Local representation also occurs through the committee system. Although studies indicate that committee members' preferences are not radically different from those of the full House or Senate,[25] representatives and senators typically sit on committees and subcommittees with policy jurisdictions that coincide with their constituents' interests. For example, farm-state legislators dominate the membership of the House and Senate Agriculture Committees, and westerners dominate the Interior Committees (which deal with federal lands and natural resources, most of which are concentrated in the West). Committees are also the site of most of the congressional **logrolling**—the practice of trading one's vote with another member so that both get what they want. It is not uncommon, for example, for Agriculture Committee members from livestock-producing states of the North to trade votes with committee members from the South, where crops such as cotton, tobacco, and peanuts are grown.

Nevertheless, representation of constituency interests has its limits. Constituents have little interest in most issues that come before Congress. Whether Congress should appropriate a few million dollars in foreign aid to Chad or Bolivia is not the sort of issue that local residents know and care about. Moreover, members of Congress often have no choice but to go against the wishes of a significant portion of their constituency. The interests of workers and employers in a district or state, for example, can differ considerably.

Of course, constituent groups are not the only groups that get legislators' support. The nation's capital is filled with powerful lobbies that contribute funds to congressional campaigns. These lobbying groups sometimes have as much influence with a member of Congress as do interest groups in the member's home state or district.

Representation of the Nation Through Parties   When a clear-cut and vital national interest is at stake, members of Congress can be expected to respond to that interest. With the economy showing signs of a recession in early 2008, Congress quickly enacted legislation that provided most taxpayers a rebate of several hundred dollars in the hope that they would spend it, thereby giving the economy a boost. The House voted 380-34 in favor of the tax rebate, while the Senate vote was 81-16.

In most cases, however, members of Congress, though agreeing on a need for national action, disagree on the course of action. Most Americans believe, for example, that the nation's education system requires strengthening. The test scores of American schoolchildren on standardized reading, math, and science examinations are substantially below those of children in many other industrial democracies. This situation creates pressure for political action. But what action is necessary and desirable? Does more money have to be funneled into public schools, and if so, which level of government—federal, state, or local—should provide it? Or does the problem rest with teachers? Should they be subject to higher certification and performance standards? Or is the problem a lack of competition for excellence? Should schools be required to compete for students and the tax dollars they represent? Should private schools be part of any such competition, or would their participation wreck the public school system? There is no general agreement on such issues. The quality of America's schools is of vital national interest, and quality schools would serve the common good. But the means to that end are the subject of endless dispute.

In Congress, debates over national goals occur primarily along party lines. Republicans and Democrats have different perspectives on national issues because their parties differ philosophically and politically. In the end-of-the-year budget negotiations in 1998 and 1999, for example, Republicans and Democrats were deadlocked on the issue of new funding to hire thousands of public school teachers. The initiative had come from President Clinton and was supported by congressional Democrats. But it was opposed by congressional Republicans, who objected to spending federal (as opposed to state and local) funds for that purpose and who also objected to the proposed placement of the new teachers (most of whom would be placed in overcrowded schools, most of which are in Democratic constituencies). Democrats and Republicans alike agreed that more teachers were needed, but they disagreed on how that goal should be reached. In the end, through concessions in other areas, President Bill Clinton and the congressional Democrats obtained federal funding for new teachers, but it was done so through an intensely partisan process.

Partisanship has a large influence on the president's relationship with Congress.[26] Presidents serve as legislative leaders not so much for the whole Congress as for members of their own party. Opposition and support for presidential initiatives usually divides along party lines. Accordingly, the White House's success in getting its intiatives through Congress has depended on which party controls it (see Chapter 12).

In short, any accounting of representation in Congress that minimizes the influence of party is faulty. If constituency interests drive the thinking of many members of Congress, so do partisan values. In fact, constituent and partisan influences are often difficult to separate in practice. In the case of conflicting interests within their constituencies, members of Congress naturally side with those that align with their party. When local business and labor groups take opposing sides on issues before Congress, for example, Republican members tend to back business's position, while Democratic members tend to line up with labor.

The Oversight Function of Congress

Although Congress enacts the nation's laws and appropriates the funds to implement them, the administration of these laws is entrusted to the executive branch. Congress has the responsibility to see that the executive branch carries out the laws faithfully and spends the money properly, a supervisory activity referred to as the **oversight function** of Congress.[27]

Oversight is carried out largely through the committee system of Congress and is facilitated by the parallel structure of the committees and the executive bureaucracy: the House and Senate judiciary committees oversee the work of the Department of Justice, the House and Senate Agriculture Committees monitor the Department of Agriculture, and so on. The Legislative Reorganization Act of 1970 spells out each committee's responsibility for overseeing its parallel agency:

> Each standing committee shall review and study, on a continuing basis, the application, administration, and execution of those laws, or parts of laws, the subject matter of which is within the jurisdiction of that committee.

Most federal programs must have their funding renewed every year, a requirement that gives Congress leverage in its ongoing oversight function. If an agency has acted improperly, Congress may reduce the agency's appropriation or tighten the restrictions on the way its funds can be spent. A major difficulty is that the House and Senate Appropriations Committees must review nearly the entire federal budget, a task that limits the amount of attention they can give any particular program.

Oversight is a challenging task. The biggest obstacle to effective oversight is the sheer magnitude of the task. With its hundreds of agencies and thousands of programs, the federal bureaucracy is beyond comprehensive scrutiny. If congressional committees were to try to monitor all the bureaucracy's activities, they would have no time to do anything else. Although Congress is required by law to maintain "continuous watchfulness" over programs, oversight normally is not pursued aggressively unless members of Congress are annoyed with an agency, have discovered that a legislative authorization is being grossly abused, or are reviewing a program for possible major changes.

When an agency is suspected of serious abuses, a committee is likely to hold hearings. Except in cases involving *executive privilege* (the right to withhold confidential information affecting national security), executive branch officials must testify at these hearings if asked to do so. If they refuse, they can be cited for contempt of Congress, a criminal offense. Congress's investigative power is not listed in the Constitution, but the judiciary has upheld this power, and Congress uses it routinely.

POLITICAL CULTURE

Liberty, Equality, and Self-Government

Congress

To the Framers of the Constitution, Congress was the first branch of government. It was through their representatives in Congress that the people would have their say on national policy. Congress was expected to be at once the symbol and the instrument of self-government. As Alexander Hamilton expressed it, "Here, sir, the people govern!"

Some analysts wonder whether that claim is as valid today as it has been in the past. The modern Congress is filled with careerists, who have the capacity to hold onto their offices indefinitely. This diminishes the ability of citizens, through their votes, to change the direction of Congress. Moreover, today's election campaigns run more on money than on citizen volunteers. While most congressional campaign money comes from small citizen contributions, significant amounts come from groups that have more access to members of Congress than do ordinary citizens. When in office, members of Congress work closely—some say too closely—with powerful lobbies.

Political scientists have not studied representative-constituency relations closely enough over a long enough time to say whether the public's influence on Congress has been declining. There is observational evidence to suggest that it has declined, but there is also evidence to the contrary, such as the increased use of polls by members of Congress as a means of determining where their constituents stand on issues of policy.

What's your sense of Congress? Do you feel its members are sufficiently in tune with constituent opinion? Regardless of how you feel, can you think of ways to bring members of Congress into closer alignment with the people they serve? How desirable is it to have a close alignment of public sentiment and congressional action? (You might find it helpful to review the distinction made in Chapter 2 between representatives as the public's trustees and representatives as the public's delegates.)

Congress's zeal for oversight increases substantially when the White House is the target, provided that it's in the opposite party's hands. When hearings were held in 2006 on National Security Agency (NSA) wiretaps that were ordered by President Bush without judicial approval, the Republican-controlled Congress limited the proceedings. Congressional

Republicans did not want to stage hearings that day after day would produce headlines damaging to Bush. However, after the Republicans lost control of Congress in 2007, they were powerless to prevent congressional Democrats from holding high-profile hearings. Congressional Democrats held hearing after hearing that pilloried Bush's policy.

CONGRESS: TOO MUCH PLURALISM?

Congress is an institution divided between service to the nation and service to the separate constituencies within it. Its members have responsibility for the nation's laws, yet for reelection they depend on the voters of their states and districts and are highly responsive to constituency interests. This latter focus is facilitated by the committee system, which is organized around particular interests. Agriculture, labor, education, banking, and commerce are among the interests represented through this system. It is hard to conceive of a national legislature structured to respond to special interests more closely than is the Congress of the United States.

Pluralists admire this feature of Congress. They argue that the United States has a majoritarian institution in the presidency and that Congress is a place where a *diversity* of interests is represented. Critics reject this view, saying that Congress is sometimes so responsive to particular interests that it neglects the broader national interest. This criticism is blunted from time to time by a strong majoritarian impulse in Congress. The current period is one of those moments. The high level of party discipline in recent years, coupled with the widening ideological gap between the parties, has placed Congress at the center of national debate on Iraq, immigration, health care, and other large issues.

Yet Congress cannot easily be an institution that is highly responsive both to diverse interests and to the national interest. These interests often conflict, as the difficulty of getting agreement on immigration reform illustrates. Although nearly all members of Congress believe illegal immigration is a pressing national issue, a legislative solution has been difficult to achieve because immigration provokes sharply different views in various states and localities, depending on how they are affected by it. Members of Congress from states and districts where anti-immigration sentiment is strong are reluctant, however they might feel personally, to back legislation that runs counter to this sentiment. This inherent tension between congressional members' national role and their local electoral base has been replayed many times in U.S. history. In a real sense, the strengths of Congress are also its weaknesses. Those features of congressional election and organization that make Congress responsive to local constituencies are often the very ones that make it difficult for Congress to act as an instrument of national policy. The perennial challenge for members of Congress is to find a workable balance between what Roger Davidson and Walter Oleszek call the "two Congresses": one embodied by the Capitol in Washington, and the other by the members' separate districts and states.[28]

SUMMARY   Self-Test www.mhhe.com/pattersonwtp8e

Members of Congress, once elected, are likely to be reelected. Members of Congress can use their office to publicize themselves, pursue a service strategy of responding to the needs of individual constituents, and secure pork-barrel projects for their states or districts. House members gain a greater advantage from these activities than do senators, whose larger constituencies make it harder for them to build close personal relations with voters and whose office is more likely to attract strong challengers. Incumbency does have some disadvantages. Members of Congress must take positions on controversial issues, may blunder into political scandal or indiscretion, must deal with changes in the electorate, or may face strong challengers; any of these conditions can reduce members' reelection chances. By and large, however, the advantages of incumbency far outweigh the disadvantages. Incumbents' advantages extend into their reelection campaigns: their influential positions in Congress make it easier for them to raise campaign funds from PACs and individual contributors.

Congress is a fragmented institution. It has no single leader; rather, the House and Senate have separate leaders, neither of whom can presume to speak for the other chamber. The principal party leaders of Congress are the Speaker of the House and the Senate majority leader. They share leadership power with committee and subcommittee chairpersons, who have influence on the policy decisions of their committee or subcommittee.

It is in the committees that most of the day-to-day work of Congress is conducted. Each standing committee of the House or the Senate has jurisdiction over congressional policy in a particular area (such as agriculture or foreign relations), as does each of its subcommittees. In most cases, the full House and Senate accept committee recommendations about the passage of bills, although amendments to bills are quite common and committees are careful to take other members of Congress into account when making legislative decisions. Congress is a legislative system in which influence is widely dispersed, an arrangement that suits the power and reelection needs of its individual members. However, partisanship is a strong and binding force in Congress. It is the basis on which party leaders are able to build support for major legislative initiatives. On this type of legislation, party leaders and caucuses, rather than committees, are the central actors.

The major function of Congress is to enact legislation. Yet the role it plays in developing legislation depends on the type of policy involved. Because of its divided chambers and committee structure, as well as the concern of its members with state and district interests, Congress, through its party leaders and caucuses, only occasionally takes the lead on broad national issues; Congress instead typically looks to the president for this leadership. Nevertheless, presidential initiatives are passed by Congress only if they meet its members' expectations and usually only after a lengthy process of compromise and negotiation. Congress is more adept at handling legislation that deals with problems of narrow interest. Legislation of this sort is decided mainly in congressional committees, where interested legislators, bureaucrats, and groups concentrate their efforts on issues of mutual concern.

A second function of Congress is the representation of various interests. Members of Congress are highly sensitive to the state or district they depend on for reelection. They do respond to overriding national interests, but for most of them local concerns generally come first. National or local representation often operates through party representation, particularly on issues that divide the Democratic and Republican parties and their constituent groups.

Congress's third function is oversight—the supervision and investigation of the way the bureaucracy is implementing legislatively mandated programs. Although oversight is a difficult process, it is an important means of legislative control over the actions of the executive branch.

Key Terms

bill (*p. 395*)
cloture (*p. 398*)
conference committees (*p. 391*)
constituency (*p. 375*)
filibuster (*p. 378*)
gerrymandering (*p. 378*)
jurisdiction (of a congressional
  committee) (*p. 391*)
law (as enacted by Congress) (*p. 399*)
lawmaking function (*p. 400*)
logrolling (*p. 405*)
open-seat election (*p. 378*)
oversight function (*p. 407*)

party caucus (*p. 384*)
party discipline (*p. 399*)
party leaders (*p. 384*)
pork-barrel projects (*p. 375*)
reapportionment (*p. 378*)
redistricting (*p. 378*)
representation function (*p. 404*)
rider (*p. 398*)
seniority (*p. 393*)
service strategy (*p. 375*)
standing committees (*p. 389*)
veto (*p. 399*)

Suggested Readings

Burden, Barry C. *Personal Roots of Representation*. Princeton, N.J.: Princeton University Press, 2007. An analysis that reveals how representatives' personal preferences affect their legislative votes.

Dwyre, Diana, and Victoria Farrar-Myers. *Legislative Labyrinth: Congress and Campaign Finance Reform*. Washington, D.C.: Congressional Quarterly Press, 2001. An inside look at the mix of Congress and campaign money.

Herrnson, Paul S. *Congressional Elections: Campaigning at Home and in Washington*, 5th ed. Washington, D.C.: Congressional Quarterly Press, 2008. A study arguing that members of Congress run two campaigns, one at home and one in Washington.

Quirk, Paul J., and Sarah A. Binder, eds. *The Legislative Branch*. New York: Oxford University Press, 2005. A comprehensive set of essays on Congress by many of the best congressional scholars.

Sidlow, Edward. *Challenging the Incumbent: An Underdog's Undertaking*. Washington, D.C.: Congressional Quarterly Press, 2003. A fascinating case study of the difficulties faced by those who dare to challenge an incumbent.

Sinclair, Barbara. *Unorthodox Lawmaking: New Legislative Processes in the U.S. Congress*, 2nd ed. Washington, D.C.: Congressional Quarterly Press, 2000. A detailed analysis of the American legislative process.

Smith, Steven S., Jason M. Roberts, and Ryan J. Vander Wielen. *The American Congress*. New York, NY: Cambridge University Press, 2007. An insightful and comprehensive examination of Congress.

Strahan, Randall. *Leading Representatives: The Agency of Leaders in the Politics of the U.S. House*. Baltimore, Md.: Johns Hopkins University Press, 2007. A study arguing that congressional leaders are powerful in their own right.

LIST OF WEBSITES

http://www.usafmc.org/default.asp?pagenumber=8 The website of the United States Association of Former Members of Congress, which has a "Congress to Campus" program that upon request brings former congressional members to campuses for talks.

http://thomas.loc.gov/ The Library of Congress site, named after Thomas Jefferson; provides information about the congressional process, including the status of pending legislation.

http://www.house.gov/ The U.S. House of Representatives' website; has information on party leaders, pending legislation, and committee hearings, as well as links to each House member's office and website.

http://www.senate.gov/ The U.S. Senate's website; is similar to that of the House and provides links to each senator's website.

POLITICS IN THEORY AND PRACTICE

Thinking: How does the structure of Congress (for example, its two chambers and its committee system) affect its policymaking role?

Participating: Each year, thousands of college students serve as interns in Congress or a state legislature. Many internships are unpaid, but students can ordinarily receive college credit for the experience. Internships are not always a great adventure. Many legislative interns envision themselves contributing ideas and research that might influence public policy only to find that they are answering letters, developing mailing lists, or duplicating materials. Nevertheless, few interns conclude that their experience has been a waste of time. Most find it rewarding and, ultimately, memorable. Information about internships can be obtained from the American Political Science Association (www.apsa. org). In addition, there are organizations in Washington that arrange internships in Congress and the executive agencies. These organizations frequently charge a fee for their services, so you might want to contact a legislative office or executive agency directly. It is important to make your request as early as possible in the college year, because some internship programs have deadlines and nearly all offices receive more requests than they can accommodate. You could also check with the student services office at your college or university. Some of these offices have information on internship programs and can be of assistance.

Extra Credit

For up-to-the-minute *New York Times* articles, interactive simulations, graphics, study tools, and more links and quizzes, visit the text's Online Learning Center at www.mhhe.com/pattersonwtp8e.

Running for Congress, Staying in Congress

By Paul S. Herrnson

_____

In this essay, University of Maryland Professor Paul Herrnson discusses the nature of congressional campaigns and the decisive role incumbency plays in their outcome. Once elected, members of Congress use the resources of their office to solidify their hold on that office. An effect is a warping of both the electoral process and the legislative process.

In order to win a congressional election or even to be remotely competitive, candidates must compete in two campaigns: one for votes and one for resources. The campaign for votes is the campaign that generally comes to mind when people think about congressional elections. It requires a candidate to assemble an organization and to use that organization to target key groups of voters, select a message they will find compelling, communicate that message, and get supporters to the polls on election day.

The other campaign, which is based largely in Washington, D.C., requires candidates to convince the party operatives, interest group officials, political consultants, and journalists who play leading roles in the nation's political community that their races will be competitive and worthy of support. Gaining the backing of these various individuals is a critical step in attracting the money and campaign services that are available in the nation's capital and

in other wealthy urban centers. These resources enable the candidate to run a credible campaign back home. Without them, most congressional candidates would lose their bids for election. . . .

Candidates, not political parties, are the major focus of congressional campaigns, and candidates, not parties, bear the ultimate responsibility for election outcomes. These characteristics of congressional elections are striking when viewed from a comparative perspective. In most democracies, political parties are the principal contestants in elections, and campaigns focus on national issues, ideology, and party programs and accomplishments. In the United States, parties do not run congressional campaigns nor do they become the major focus of elections. Instead, candidates run their own campaigns, and parties contribute money or election services to some of them. Parties also may advertise or mobilize voters on behalf of candidates. A comparison of the terminology commonly used to describe elections in the United States with that used in Great Britain more than hints at the differences. In the United States, candidates are said to *run* for Congress, and they do so with or without party help. In Britain, by contrast, candidates are said to *stand* for election to Parliament, and their party runs most of the campaign. The difference in terminology only slightly oversimplifies reality.

Unlike candidates for national legislatures in most other democracies, U.S. congressional candidates are self-selected rather than recruited by party organizations. They must win the right to run under their party's label through a participatory primary, caucus, or convention, or by scaring off all opposition.

. . . Although they talk about the competition and are, indeed, wary of it, congressional incumbents, particularly House members, operate in a political setting that works largely to their benefit. . . . [I]ncumbents enjoy significant levels of name recognition and voter support, are able to assemble superior campaign organizations, and can draw on their experience in office to speak knowledgeably about issues and claim credit for the federally financed programs and improvements in their state or district. Incumbents also tend to get favorable treatment from the media. Moreover, most can rely on loyal followers from previous campaigns for continued backing: supporters at home tend to vote repeatedly for incumbents, and supporters in Washington and the nation's other wealthy cities routinely provide incumbents with campaign money.

Things look different from the typical challenger's vantage point. Most challengers, particularly those with some political experience, recognize that most of the cards are stacked against an individual who sets out to take on an incumbent. Little in the setting in which most congressional campaigns take place favors the challenger. Most challengers lack the public visibility, money, and campaign experience to wage a strong campaign. Moreover, because those who work in and help finance campaigns recognize the strong odds against challengers, they usually see little benefit in helping them. As a result, high incumbent success rates have become a self-fulfilling prophecy. Senate reelection rates ranged from 55 percent to almost 97 percent between 1950 and 2002. Between 1982 and 2002 almost 4 percent of all Senate incumbents had no major-party opponent, and just over half of those involved in contested races won by 60 percent or more of the two-party vote. Only 16 percent of all senators seeking reelection in 2000 and 2002 were defeated. Between 1950 and 2002, House incumbents enjoyed an overall reelection rate of better

than 93 percent; the 2000 and 2002 elections returned to Congress roughly 98 percent and 96 percent, respectively, of those who sought to keep their jobs. Even during the tidal wave that swept away thirty-four Democrats in the House in the 1994 elections, just over 90 percent of all House incumbents who sought to remain in office did so. With some important exceptions, most experienced politicians wait until an incumbent retires, runs for another office, or dies before running for office. Thus, many House seats fail to attract meaningful competition. . . .

Many explanations exist for the relative lack of competition in House elections. Some districts are so dominated by one party that few individuals of the other party are willing to commit their time, energy, or money to running for office. In many cases, the tradition of one-party dominance is so strong that virtually all the talented, politically ambitious individuals living in the area join the dominant party. When an incumbent in these districts faces a strong challenge, it usually takes place in the primary, and the winner is all but guaranteed success in the general election.

Uncompetitive House districts are often the product of the redistricting process. In states where one party controls both the governorship and the state legislature, partisan gerrymandering is often used to maximize the number of House seats the dominant party can win. In states where each party controls at least some portion of the state government, compromises are frequently made to design districts that protect congressional incumbents. Party officials and political consultants armed with computers, election returns, and demographic statistics can "pack" and "crack" voting blocs in order to promote either of these goals. The result is that large numbers of congressional districts are designed to be uncompetitive. In 2002, for example, only three of California's fifty-three House elections were decided by a margin of less than twenty points, and one of those seats might not have been competitive if scandal-plagued Gary Condit had not lost the Democratic primary. States that use nonpartisan commissions, which often ignore incumbency, tend to produce more competitive House races. In contrast to the situation in California, four of Iowa's five House seats were decided by fewer than fifteen points.

The desire of incumbents to retain their seats has changed Congress in ways that help discourage electoral competition. Most of those who are elected to Congress quickly understand that they will probably never hold a higher office because there are too few of such offices to go around. Like most people, they do everything in their power to hold on to their jobs. Congress has adapted to the career aspirations of its members by providing them with resources that can be used to increase their odds of reelection. Free mailings, WATS lines, Internet web sites, district offices, and subsidized travel help members gain visibility among their constituents. Federal "porkbarrel" projects also help incumbents win the support of voters. Congressional aides help members write speeches, respond to constituent mail, resolve problems that constituents have with executive branch agencies, and follow the comings and goings in their bosses' districts. These perquisites of office give incumbents tremendous advantages over challengers. They also discourage experienced politicians who could put forth a competitive challenge from taking on an entrenched incumbent.

The dynamics of campaign finance have similar effects. Incumbents have tremendous fundraising advantages over challengers, especially among PACs and wealthy individual donors. Many incumbents build up large war chests to discourage potential challengers from running against them. With the exception of millionaires and celebrities, challengers who decide to contest a race against a member of the House or Senate typically find they are unable to raise the funds needed to mount a viable campaign.

What's Your Opinion?

As a citizen, are you troubled by a congressional election system in which incumbents have an overwhelming edge over challengers? What are the advantages and disadvantages of this arrangement? What steps, if any, would you take to reduce incumbents' electoral advantage?

CHAPTER 12

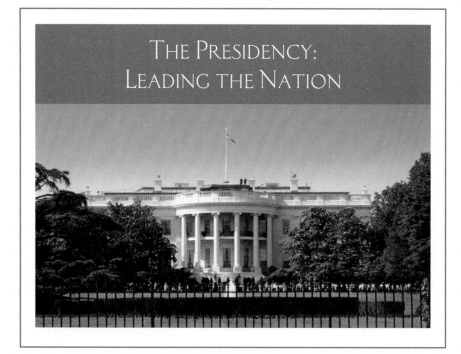

THE PRESIDENCY: LEADING THE NATION

66 [The president's] is the only voice in national affairs. Let him once win the admiration and confidence of the people, and no other single voice will easily overpower him. **99**

WOODROW WILSON[1]

George W. Bush was sinking in the polls. The economy was weakening, and the newly elected Bush was being criticized for not doing enough to reverse the downturn. Bush was also getting heat for the defection of Senator James Jeffords of Vermont, which cost Republicans control of the Senate. The news media had given him the honeymoon period traditionally accorded a new president, but they were now turning on him.

Everything changed on September 11, 2001. After the terrorist attacks on the World Trade Center and the Pentagon, Americans rallied around their president. Bush vowed that America would not rest until the terrorists were brought to justice. His presidential approval rating reached 96 percent, the highest level ever recorded. Not even Franklin Roosevelt had received approval ratings that high during the Second World War. During the next two years, buoyed by public support, Bush led the nation into wars in Afghanistan and Iraq as part of his "war on terrorism."

Three years later, everything had changed again for President Bush. The U.S. invasion of Iraq was followed by problems the Bush administration had not anticipated. Ongoing civil strife, continued attacks on U.S. forces, a failure to find weapons of mass destruction, abuses of Iraqi prisoners by U.S. soldiers, and the escalating financial cost of Iraq's reconstruction were eroding his public support. Bush was able to win reelection in 2004, but his victory was by the smallest margin for an incumbent since Harry Truman's victory in 1948. Bush's reelection gave him a boost in the opinion polls, but it was short-lived. By early 2005, his approval rating was dropping again, and it eventually fell below 30 percent, one of the lowest levels ever recorded.

The Bush story is but one in the saga of the ups and downs of the modern presidency. Lyndon Johnson's and Richard Nixon's dogged pursuit of the Vietnam War led to talk of "the imperial presidency," an office so powerful that constitutional checks and balances were no longer an effective constraint on it. Within a few years, because of the undermining effects of Watergate and of changing international conditions during the Ford and Carter presidencies, the watchword became "the imperiled presidency," an office too weak to meet the nation's demands for executive leadership. Ronald Reagan's policy successes prior to 1986 renewed talk heard in the Roosevelt and Kennedy years of "a heroic presidency," an office that is the inspirational center of American politics. After the Iran-Contra scandal in 1986, Reagan was more often called a lame duck. The first George Bush's handling of the Gulf crisis—leading the nation in 1991 into a major war and emerging from it with a stratospheric public approval rating—bolstered the heroic conception of the office. A year later, Bush was defeated in his campaign for a second term. Bill Clinton overcame a fitful start to his presidency to become the first Democrat since Franklin D. Roosevelt in the 1930s to win reelection. As Clinton was launching an aggressive second-term policy agenda, however, he got entangled in an affair with a White House intern, Monica Lewinsky, that led to his impeachment by the House of Representatives and weakened his claim to national leadership.

No other political institution has been subject to such varying characterizations as the modern presidency. One reason is that the formal powers of the office are modest, and so presidential power changes with national conditions, political circumstances, and the personal capacities and policy choices of the office's occupant.[2] The American presidency is always a central office in that its occupant is a focus of national attention. Yet the presidency is not an inherently powerful office, in the sense that presidents routinely get what they want. Presidential power is conditional. It depends on the president's own abilities but even more on

The conditional nature of presidential power was evident during George W. Bush's presidency. In 2001, his presidential approval rating soared above 90 percent, and his influence over national policy was substantial. In the final years of his presidency, Bush's approval rating was below 40 percent, and his ability to lead Congress and public opinion was greatly diminished.

circumstances—on whether the situation demands strong leadership and whether the political support for that leadership exists. When conditions are favorable, the president is powerful. When conditions are adverse, the president is vulnerable.

This chapter examines the roots of presidential power, the presidential selection process, the staffing of the presidency, and the factors associated with the success and failure of presidential leadership. The main ideas of this chapter are these:

★ *Public expectations, national crises, and changing national and world conditions have required the presidency to become a strong office.* Underlying this development is the public support the president acquires from being nationally elected.

★ *The modern presidential election campaign is a marathon affair in which self-selected candidates must plan for a strong start in the nominating contests and center their general-election strategies on media, issues, and a baseline of support.* The lengthy campaign process strengthens the public's belief that the presidency is at the center of the U.S. political system.

★ *The modern presidency could not operate without a large staff of assistants, experts, and high-level managers, but the sheer size of this staff makes it impossible for the president to exercise complete control over it.*

★ *The president's election by national vote and position as sole chief executive ensure that others will listen to the president's ideas; but to lead effectively, the president must have the help of other officials and, to get their help, must take their interests into account.*

★ *Presidential influence on national policy is highly variable.* Whether presidents succeed or fail in getting their policies enacted depends heavily on the force of circumstance, the stage of their presidency, partisan support in Congress, and the foreign or domestic nature of the policy issue.

FOUNDATIONS OF THE MODERN PRESIDENCY

The writers of the Constitution knew what they wanted from a president—national leadership, statesmanship in foreign affairs, command in time of war or insurgency, enforcement of the laws—but they could devise only general phrases to describe the president's constitutional authority. Compared with Article I, which enumerates Congress's specific powers, Article II of the Constitution contains relatively general statements on the president's powers.[3]

Historical
Background

Over the course of American history, each of the president's constitutional powers has been extended in practice beyond the Framers' intention. For example, the Constitution grants the president command of the nation's military, but only Congress can declare war. In *Federalist* No. 69, Alexander Hamilton wrote that a surprise attack on the United States was the only justification for war by presidential action. Nevertheless, presidents have sent troops into military action abroad more than two hundred times. Of the more than a dozen wars included in that figure, only five were declared by Congress.[4] All of America's most recent wars—the Korean, Vietnam, Persian Gulf, Balkans, Afghanistan, and Iraq conflicts—have been fought by presidential order rather than by a congressional declaration of war.

The Constitution also empowers the president to act as diplomatic leader with the authority to appoint ambassadors and to negotiate treaties with other countries, subject to approval by a two-thirds vote of the Senate. The Framers anticipated that Congress would define the nation's foreign policy objectives, while the president would oversee their implementation. However, the president gradually became the principal architect of U.S. foreign policy and has even acquired the power to make treatylike arrangements with other nations, in the form of executive agreements. In 1937, the Supreme Court ruled that executive agreements, signed and approved only by the president, have the same legal status as treaties, although Congress can cancel executive agreements with which it disagrees.[5] Since World War II, presidents have negotiated over ten thousand executive agreements—more than ten times the number of treaties ratified by the Senate during the same period.[6]

The Constitution also vests "executive power" in the president. This power includes the responsibility to execute the laws faithfully and to appoint major administrators, such as heads of the various departments of the executive branch. In *Federalist* No. 76, Hamilton indicated that the president's real authority as chief executive was to be found in this appointive capacity. Presidents have indeed exercised substantial power through their appointments, but they have found their administrative authority—the power to execute the laws—to be of greater significance, because it enables them to interpret the meaning of these laws. President Ronald Reagan used his executive power to *prohibit* the use of federal funds by family-planning clinics that offered abortion counseling. President Bill Clinton exerted the same power to *permit* the use of federal funds for this purpose. The same act of Congress was the basis for each of these actions. The act authorizes the use of federal funds for family-planning services, but it neither requires nor prohibits their use for abortion counseling, enabling the president to decide this issue.

Finally, the Constitution provides the president with legislative authority, including use of the veto and the opportunity to recommend proposals to Congress. The Framers expected this authority to be used in a limited way. George Washington acted as the Framers anticipated: he proposed only three legislative measures and vetoed only two acts of Congress. Modern presidents have assumed a more active legislative role. They regularly submit proposals to Congress, and most of them have not hesitated to veto legislation they find disagreeable.

The presidency, for many reasons, is a more powerful office than the Framers envisioned. But two features of the office in particular—*national election* and *singular authority*—have enabled presidents to make use of changing demands on government to claim the position of leader of the

★ ‖ LEADERS

George Washington
(1732–99)

George Washington, the nation's first president and its greatest in the minds of some historians, was born into a Virginia planter family. As a child, he excelled as a horseman, a skill that along with family connections earned him an officer's commission. He was involved in the first major skirmish of the French and Indian War. His daring and bravery under fire—two horses were shot out from under him as he rallied troops who had fled in the face of the enemy—made him a national hero. When the American colonies a decade later declared their independence from Britain, he was the natural choice to lead the Continental Army. Throughout the six-year Revolutionary War, Washington avoided pitched battles, knowing that his poorly equipped soldiers were no match for British regulars. Finally, in 1781, his forces trapped the British army at Yorktown and with the help of French naval vessels scored a decisive victory that ended the war. Some of his countrymen thought Washington should be named king, but he dismissed the idea, saying America was a new type of nation. He retired to his Mount Vernon plantation, only to grow increasingly worried by the growing discord among the states and the inability of Congress to govern effectively.

In 1787, Washington presided over the Philadelphia convention that drafted a constitution that became the basis for a stronger central government. Following ratification of the Constitution, Washington was elected president by unanimous vote of the Electoral College. He recognized that his presidency would define future ones. In a letter to James Madison, Washington wrote, "It is devoutly wished on my part that these precedents may be fixed on true principles." Washington pushed for a strong national government, believing that it could keep the nation from devolving into sectional rivalries. He also kept the United States out of foreign entanglements, believing the new country was too weak militarily to play such a role. Washington could have been elected to a third term, but he stepped down after two terms, stating

(continued)

that the presidency was a citizen's office, not a monarchal one. It was a precedent that all presidents adhered to until Franklin Roosevelt ran for and won a third term in 1940 at a time when the country was confronting the twin threats of economic depression and war. Roosevelt's presidency prompted Congress to initiate the Twenty-second Amendment to the Constitution, which limits a president to two terms in office.

American people. It is a claim that no other elected official can routinely make, and it is a key to understanding the role and power of the president.

Asserting a Claim to National Leadership

The first president to forcefully assert a claim to popular leadership was Andrew Jackson, who had been swept into office in 1828 on a tide of pub-

Historical Background

lic support that broke the hold of the upper classes on the presidency. Jackson used his popular backing to challenge Congress's claim to national policy leadership, contending that he was "the people's tribune."

However, Jackson's view was not shared by most of his successors during the nineteenth century, because national conditions did not routinely call for strong presidential leadership. The prevailing conception was the **Whig theory,** which held that the presidency was a limited or constrained office whose occupant was confined to the exercise of expressly granted constitutional authority. The president had no implicit powers for dealing with national problems but was primarily an administrator, charged with carrying out the will of Congress. "My duty," said President James Buchanan, a Whig adherent, "is to execute the laws . . . and not my individual opinions."[7]

Theodore Roosevelt rejected the Whig tradition upon taking office in 1901. He attacked the business trusts, pursued an aggressive foreign policy, and pressured Congress to adopt progressive domestic policies. Roosevelt embraced the **stewardship theory,** which calls for an assertive presidency that is confined only at points specifically prohibited by law. As "steward of the people," Roosevelt said, he was permitted "to do anything that the needs of the Nation demanded unless such action was forbidden by the Constitution or by the laws."[8]

Roosevelt's image of a strong presidency was shared by Woodrow Wilson, but his other immediate successors reverted to the Whig notion of the limited presidency.[9] Herbert Hoover's restrained conception of the presidency prevented him from acting decisively during the devastation of the Great Depression. Hoover said that he lacked the constitutional authority to establish public relief programs for jobless Americans. However, Hoover's successor, Franklin D. Roosevelt, shared the stewardship theory of his distant cousin Theodore Roosevelt, and FDR's New Deal signaled the end of the limited presidency. As FDR's successor, Harry Truman, wrote in his memoirs, "The power of the President should be used in the interest of the people and in order to do that the President must use whatever power the Constitution does not expressly deny him."[10]

Today the presidency is an inherently strong office. The modern presidency becomes a more substantial office in the hands of a confident individual like George W. Bush, but even a less forceful person like Jimmy Carter is expected to act assertively. This expectation not only is the legacy of former strong presidents but also stems from changes that have occurred in the federal government's national and international policy responsibilities.

The Need for Presidential Leadership of an Activist Government

During most of the nineteenth century (the Civil War being the notable exception), the United States did not need a strong president. The federal government's policymaking role was small, as was its bureaucracy. Moreover, the nation's major issues were of a sectional nature (especially the North-South split over slavery) and thus were suited to action by Congress, which represented state interests. The U.S. government's role in world affairs was also small. As these conditions changed, however, the presidency also changed.

Foreign Policy Leadership The president has always been the nation's foreign policy leader, but the role initially was a rather undemanding one. The United States avoided entanglement in the turbulent affairs of Europe and was preoccupied with westward expansion. By the end of the nineteenth century, however, the nation was seeking a world market for its goods. President Theodore Roosevelt advocated an American economic empire and looked south toward Latin America and west toward Hawaii, the Philippines, and China for new markets (the "Open Door" policy). However, the United States' tradition of isolationism remained a powerful influence on national policy. The United States fought in World War I but immediately thereafter demobilized its armed forces. Over President Woodrow Wilson's objections, Congress then voted against the entry of the United States into the League of Nations.

World War II fundamentally changed the nation's international role and the president's role in foreign policy. In 1945 the United States emerged

Harry S Truman's presidency was characterized by bold foreign policy initiatives. He authorized the use of nuclear weapons against Japan in 1945, created the Marshall Plan as the basis for the economic reconstruction of postwar Europe, and sent U.S. troops to fight in Korea in 1950. Truman is shown here greeting British Prime Minister Winston Churchill at a Washington airport in early 1952.

as a global superpower, a giant in world trade, and the recognized leader of the noncommunist world. The United States today has a military presence in nearly every part of the globe and an unprecedented interest in trade balances, energy, and other international issues affecting the nation.

The effect of these developments on America's political institutions has been one-sided.[11] Because of the president's constitutional authority as chief diplomat and military commander and the special demands of foreign policy leadership, the president, not Congress, has taken the lead in addressing the nation's increased responsibilities in the world. Foreign policy requires singleness of purpose and, at times, fast action. Congress—a large, divided, and unwieldy institution—is poorly suited to such a response. In contrast, the president, as sole head of the executive branch, can act quickly and speak authoritatively for the nation as a whole in its relations with other nations. This capacity has rarely been more evident than after the terrorist attacks of September 11, 2001. The initiative in the war on terrorism rested squarely with the White House. President Bush decided on the U.S. response to the attacks and took the lead in obtaining international support for U.S. military, intelligence, and diplomatic initiatives. Congress backed these actions enthusiastically. The joint resolution that endorsed Bush's decision to attack the Taliban government in Afghanistan passed unanimously in the Senate and with only a single dissenting vote in the House. In reality, however, Congress had little choice but to support whatever policies Bush chose. Americans wanted decisive action and were looking to the president, not to Congress, for leadership.

In other situations, Congress is less compliant. In recent decades, it has contested presidential positions on issues such as global trade and international human rights. Nevertheless, the president is clearly the leading voice in U.S. foreign policy. (The changing shape of the world and its implications for presidential power and leadership are discussed more fully later in the chapter.)

Domestic Policy Leadership   The change in the president's domestic leadership role has also been substantial. Throughout most of the nineteenth

Historical Background

century, Congress jealously guarded its constitutional powers, making it clear that it was in charge of domestic policy. James Bryce wrote in the 1880s that Congress paid no more attention to the president's views on legislation than it did to the editorial positions of newspaper publishers.[12]

By the early twentieth century, however, the national government was taking on regulatory and policy responsibilities imposed by the nation's transition from an agrarian to an industrial society, and the executive branch was growing ever larger. In 1921, Congress conceded that it lacked the centralized authority to coordinate the growing national budget and enacted the Budget and Accounting Act, which provided for an executive budget. Federal departments and agencies would no longer submit their annual budget requests directly to Congress. Instead, the president would develop the various agencies' requests into a comprehensive budgetary proposal, which then would be submitted to Congress as a starting point for its deliberations.

During the Great Depression of the 1930s, Franklin D. Roosevelt's New Deal responded to the public's demand for economic relief with a broad program that required a level of policy planning and coordination beyond the capacity of Congress. In addition to public works projects and social welfare programs, the New Deal made the government a partner in nearly every aspect of the nation's economy. If economic regulation was to work, unified and continuous policy leadership was needed, and only the president could routinely provide it.

Presidential authority has continued to grow since Roosevelt's time. In response to pressures from the public, the national government's role in areas such as education, health, welfare, safety, and protection of the environment has expanded greatly, which in turn has created additional demands for presidential leadership.[13] Large government, with its emphasis on comprehensive planning and program coordination, has favored executive authority at the expense of legislative authority. All democracies have seen a shift in power from their legislature to their executive. In Britain, for example, the prime minister has taken on responsibilities that once belonged to the cabinet or to Parliament.

CHOOSING THE PRESIDENT

Historical
Background

As the president's policy and leadership responsibilities changed during the nation's history, so did the process of electing presidents. The changes do not parallel each other exactly, but they are related both politically and philosophically. As the presidency drew ever closer to the people, their role in selecting the president grew ever more direct.[14] The United States in its history has had four systems of presidential selection, each more "democratic" than its predecessor (see Table 12-1).

table 12-1 THE FOUR SYSTEMS OF PRESIDENTIAL SELECTION

Selection System	Period	Features
1. Original	1788–1828	Party nominees are chosen in congressional caucuses. Electoral College members act somewhat independently in their presidential voting.
2. Party convention	1832–1900	Party nominees are chosen in national party conventions by delegates selected by state and local party organizations. Electoral College members cast their ballots for the popular-vote winner in their respective states.
3. Party convention, primary	1904–68	As in system 2, except that a *minority* of national convention delegates are chosen through primary elections (the majority still being chosen by party organizations).
4. Party primary, open caucus	1972–present	As in system 2, except that a *majority* of national convention delegates are chosen through primary elections.

The delegates to the constitutional convention of 1787 feared that popular election of the president would make the office too powerful and accordingly devised an electoral vote system (the so-called Electoral College). The president was to be chosen by electors picked by the states, with each state entitled to one elector for each of its members of Congress (House and Senate combined). This system was changed after the election in 1828 of Andrew Jackson, who believed that the people's will had been denied four years earlier when he got the most popular votes but failed to gain an electoral majority. Jackson was unable to persuade Congress to support a constitutional amendment that would have eliminated the Electoral College, but he did obtain the next-best alternative: he persuaded the states to link their electoral votes to the popular vote. Under Jackson's reform, which is still in effect today, each party in a state has a separate slate of electors who gain the right to cast a state's electoral votes if their party's candidate places first in the state's popular voting. Thus, the popular vote for the candidates directly affects their electoral vote, and one candidate is likely to win both forms of the presidential vote. Since Jackson's time, only Rutherford B. Hayes (in 1876), Benjamin Harrison (in 1888), and George W. Bush (in 2000) have won the presidency after having lost the popular vote.

Jackson also championed the national convention as a means of nominating the party's presidential candidate (before this time, nominations were made by party caucuses in Congress and in state legislatures). The parties' strength was at the grass roots, among the people, and Jackson saw the convention process as a means of bringing the citizenry and the presidency closer together. Since Jackson's time, presidential nominees have been formally chosen at national party conventions. Each state party sends delegates to the national convention, and these delegates select the party's nominee.

Jackson's system of presidential nomination remained fully intact until the early twentieth century, when the Progressives devised the primary election as a means of curbing the power of the party bosses (see Chapter 2). State party leaders had taken control of the nominating process by handpicking their states' convention delegates. The Progressives sought to give voters the power to select the delegates. Such a process is called an *indirect primary*, because the voters are not choosing the nominees directly (as they do in House and Senate races) but rather are choosing delegates who in turn select the nominees.

However, the Progressives were unable to persuade most states to adopt presidential primaries, which meant that party leaders continued to control enough of the delegates to pick the nominees. That arrangement held until 1968 when Democratic Party leaders ignored the strength of anti-Vietnam

War sentiment in the primaries and nominated Vice President Hubert Humphrey, who had not entered a single primary and was closely identified with the Johnson administration's Vietnam policy. After Humphrey narrowly lost the 1968 general election to Richard Nixon, reform-minded Democrats forced changes in the nominating process. The new rules gave rank-and-file party voters more control by requiring states to choose their delegates through either primary elections or **open party caucuses** (meetings open to any registered party voter who wants to attend). Although the Democrats initiated the change, the Republicans also were affected by it. Most states that adopted a presidential primary in order to comply with the Democrats' new rules also required Republicans to select their convention delegates through a primary.

Today it is the voters in state primaries and open caucuses who play the decisive role in the selection of the Democratic and Republican presidential nominees.[15] A state's delegates are awarded to candidates in accordance with how well they do in the state's primary or caucus. Thus, to win the majority of national convention delegates necessary for nomination, a candidate must place first in a lot of states and do at least reasonably well in most of the rest. (About forty states choose their delegates through a primary election; the others use the caucus system.)

In sum, the presidential election system has changed from an elite-dominated process to one based on voter support. This arrangement has strengthened the presidency by providing the office with the reserve of power that popular election confers on democratic leadership.

The Primary Elections

The fact that voters pick the party nominees has opened the nominating races to any politician with the energy and resources to run a major national campaign. Nominating campaigns, except those in which an incumbent president is seeking reelection, typically attract a half-dozen contenders. The 2008 nominating races drew an even larger number—roughly ten candidates for each party.

Candidates have no choice but to start early and campaign hard. A key to success in the nominating campaign is **momentum**—a strong showing in the early contests that leads to a buildup of public support in subsequent ones. Nobody—not the press, not donors, not the voters—has an interest in candidates who are at the back of the pack. No candidate in recent decades has got off to a lousy start in the first few contests and then picked up enough steam to come anywhere near to winning the nomination. All the advantages rest with the fast starters. They get more attention from the press, more money from contributors, and get more consideration by the voters. Not surprisingly, presidential contenders strive to do well in the early contests, particularly the first caucuses in Iowa and the first primary in New Hampshire. In 2008, Barack Obama's successful quest for the Democratic presidential nomination began with a victory in Iowa. John McCain lost there, but a win a few days later in New Hampshire's primary started the momentum that carried him to the Republican nomination.

Money, always a critical factor in elections, has become increasingly important in the past three decades because states have moved their primaries and caucuses to the early weeks of the nominating period in order to increase their influence on the outcome. Within the first month of the 2008 nominating period, more than half the states held their primary or caucus. To compete effectively in so many contests over such a short period, candidates need money—lots of it. A candidate can be in only one place at a time, so the campaign must be carried to other voters through costly televised political advertising. Observers estimate that it takes at least $40 million to run a strong nominating campaign, and possibly a lot more than that for a candidate who does not have substantial name recognition and public support before the campaign begins. In nearly every nominating race from 1984 to 2008, the winner was the candidate who had raised the most money before the start of the primaries.

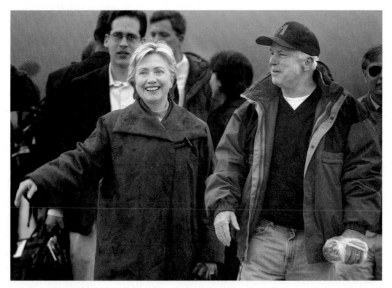

The modern presidential campaign is a marathon event that formally lasts nearly a year and speculatively is always under way. Shown here are Hillary Clinton and John McCain shortly before they entered the race for their respective party's presidential nomination.

Candidates in primary elections receive federal funding if they meet the eligibility criteria. The Federal Election Campaign Act of 1974 (as amended in 1979) provides for federal matching funds. Under the program, the government matches the first $250 of each private donation received by a primary election candidate, provided the candidate raises at least $5,000 in individual contributions of up to $250 in at least twenty states. This provision is designed to restrict matching funds to candidates who can show that they have a reasonable amount of public support. In addition, any candidate who receives matching funds must agree to limit expenditures for the nominating phase to a set amount overall (roughly $50 million in 2008) and in particular states (the 2008 limits in Iowa and New Hampshire, for example, were roughly $1.4 million and $800,000, respectively). The limits are adjusted upward each election year to account for inflation. Taxpayers fund the matching program by checking a box on their income-tax return allocating $3 of their taxes to it.

Until the 2000 election, when George Bush declined matching funds so that he could raise unrestricted amounts of money for his nominating campaign, candidates had routinely accepted matching funds, which meant they had to abide by the spending limits. In 2004, Bush again turned down matching funds, as did the two leading Democratic contenders, Howard Dean and John Kerry. In 2008, an even larger number of candidates declined public funds. Obama was easily the most successful of these candidates, raising in excess of $300 million for his nominating campaign—more than four times the amount he would have been allowed if he had accepted matching funds.

As candidates have increasingly declined public funding, there have been calls to raise the allowable spending limit under public financing, perhaps to as high as $100 million. Otherwise, observers say, the only candidates who will accept matching funds will be those with no chance of victory. This development would defeat the purpose of public funding, which is to free candidates from the obligations that come from accepting contributions from private groups and individuals.

The National Party Conventions

The summertime national party conventions mark the end of the nominating campaign. In an earlier era, the convention was where the nomination was actually decided. State party delegations would come together at their convention to bargain and choose among potential nominees. Since 1972, when the delegate selection process was changed, the leading candidate in every case has acquired enough delegates in the primaries to lock up the nomination before the convention begins. Nevertheless, the convention is a major event. It brings together the delegates elected in the state caucuses and primaries, who then approve a party platform and formally nominate the party's presidential and vice presidential candidates.

By tradition, the choice of the vice presidential nominee rests with the presidential nominee. In 2008, Obama selected Delaware senator Joe Biden, who had extensive foreign policy experience, to be his running mate. For his part, McCain picked little-known Alaska governor Sarah Palin, whose forceful acceptance speech at the Republican convention transformed her from a curiosity into a major force in the McCain campaign. She helped energize the party's supporters and drew huge crowds at campaign stops during the general election—a feat unprecedented in the recent annals of vice presidential nominees. (As Table 12-2 indicates, roughly a third of recent presidents reached that office after serving first as vice president.)

The Campaign for Election

The winner in the November general election is certain to be either the Republican or the Democratic candidate. Two-thirds of the nation's voters identify with the Republican or Democratic Party, and most Independents lean toward one or the other of them. As a result, the major-party presidential nominees have a built-in source of votes. Even Democrat George McGovern, who had the lowest level of party support in the past half-century, was backed in 1972 by 60 percent of his party's identifiers.

Because the Democratic and Republican nominees have this huge advantage, a third-party candidate has no realistic hope of victory. Even Ross Perot, who in 1992 ran the most successful third-party campaign in nearly a century, was able to garner only a fifth of the vote. On the other hand, third-party candidates have sometimes caused problems for a major party by siphoning votes away from its nominee. In 2000, third-party candidate Ralph Nader drew 4 percent of the popular vote, most of it from voters who indicated that they otherwise would have backed Al Gore, the Democratic nominee. If Nader had not been in the race, Gore, rather than George W. Bush, would have won the 2000 presidential election.

Election Strategy   The candidates' strategies in the general election are shaped by many considerations, including the constitutional provision that each state shall have electoral votes equal in number to its representation in Congress. Each state thus gets two electoral votes for its Senate representation and a varying number of electoral votes depending on its House representation. Altogether, there are 538 electoral votes (including 3 for the District of Columbia, even though it has no voting representatives in

| table | 12-2 | THE PATH TO THE WHITE HOUSE |

President	Years in Office	Highest Previous Office	Second Highest Office
Theodore Roosevelt	1901–8	Vice president*	Governor
William Howard Taft	1909–12	Secretary of war	Federal judge
Woodrow Wilson	1913–20	Governor	None
Warren G. Harding	1921–24	U.S. senator	Lieutenant governor
Calvin Coolidge	1925–28	Vice president*	Governor
Herbert Hoover	1929–32	Secretary of commerce	War relief administrator
Franklin D. Roosevelt	1933–45	Governor	Assistant secretary of Navy
Harry S Truman	1945–52	Vice president*	U.S. senator
Dwight D. Eisenhower	1953–60	None (Army general)	None
John F. Kennedy	1961–63	U.S. senator	U.S. representative
Lyndon Johnson	1963–68	Vice president*	U.S. senator
Richard Nixon	1969–74	Vice president	U.S. senator
Gerald Ford	1974–76	Vice president*	U.S. representative
Jimmy Carter	1977–80	Governor	State senator
Ronald Reagan	1981–88	Governor	None
George Bush	1989–92	Vice president	Director, CIA
Bill Clinton	1993–2000	Governor	State attorney general
George W. Bush	2001–2008	Governor	None
Barack Obama	2009–	U.S. senator	State senator

Became president on death or resignation of incumbent.

Congress). To win the presidency, a candidate must receive at least 270 votes, an electoral majority. (If no candidate receives a majority, the election is decided in the House of Representatives. No president since John Quincy Adams in 1824 has been elected in this way. The procedure is defined by the Constitution's Twelfth Amendment, which is reprinted in the appendixes.)

The importance of the electoral votes is magnified by the existence of the **unit rule:** all the states except Maine and Nebraska grant all their electoral votes as a unit to the candidate who wins the state's popular vote. For this reason, candidates are concerned with winning the most populous states, such as California (with 55 electoral votes), Texas (34), New York (31), Florida (27), Pennsylvania (21), Illinois (21), Ohio (20), Michigan (17), and Georgia, New Jersey, and North Carolina (15 each).

Even more so than a state's size, however, the closeness of the vote in a state dictates how much attention it will get from the candidates. Because of the unit rule, a state that is lopsidedly Democratic or Republican will be ignored. Its electoral votes are already locked up. Thus, the fall campaign becomes a fight over the toss-up states or, as they have come to be called, the battleground states. In 2008, only a third of the states were seen by the Obama and McCain campaigns as states that realistically could be won by either candidate. The two candidates spent nearly all their money and time in the battleground states during the closing months of the campaign. Other states might just as well have been located in Canada for the attention they received from the candidates.

At campaign's end, electoral votes and not popular votes determine the winner (see "States in the Nation"). In 2000, George W. Bush was elected with 271 electoral votes, two more than required, even though he received 550,000 fewer popular votes than Al Gore. Bush was the first president since Benjamin Harrison in 1888 to win the presidency despite losing the popular vote.

Media and Money The modern presidential campaign is a media campaign. At one time, candidates relied heavily on party organization and rallies to carry their messages to the voters, but now they rely on the media, particularly television. Candidates strive to produce the pithy ten-second sound bites that the television networks prefer to highlight on the evening newscasts. They also rely on the power of the "new media," making appearances on programs such as *Larry King Live* and *The Daily Show* and creating their own websites.

The television campaign includes political advertising. Televised commercials are by far the most expensive part of presidential campaigns, accounting for about half the candidates' general election expenditures. Most of this advertising is shown in the battleground states, with the result that Americans in these locations are bombarded with ads while those living elsewhere see relatively few. In most recent campaigns, televised ads have been the main vehicle by which candidates have attacked their opponents. Unlike the news coverage they receive, candidates fully control the content of their ads, enabling them to craft unflattering, one-sided portrayals of their opponent.[16]

Television is also the forum for the major confrontation of the fall campaign: the presidential debates. The first televised debates took place in 1960 between John Kennedy and Richard Nixon, and an estimated 100 million people watched at least one of their four debates. Televised debates resumed in 1976 and have become a fixture of presidential campaigns. Debates can influence voters' assessments of the candidates, though they have only occasionally had a large effect on the race. The 2008 Obama-McCain debates were typical in this respect. Most Americans judged Obama to have won all three debates. However, the polls indicated that the debates did not greatly affect the candidates' support, perhaps because voters were concerned with the widening financial crisis, which helped Obama's candidacy.

The highlight of the general election campaign is the televised debates between the Republican and Democratic nominees. Shown here is a scene from one of the McCain-Obama debates in 2008.

★ STATES IN THE NATION

Electoral Vote Strategy in the 2008 Election

The Constitution of the United States specifies that the president is to be chosen by electoral votes. The candidate receiving a majority of the electoral vote, even if receiving fewer popular votes than the opponent, becomes president. The Constitution further specifies that states have authority to determine how their electors will be chosen. Today, all states except two (Maine and Nebraska, which give one electoral vote to the winner of each congressional district and two electoral votes to the statewide winner), give all of their electoral votes to the popular-vote winner in the state. This winner-take-all feature of the electoral vote system leads presidential candidates to focus on toss-up states—those that conceivably could be won by either party.

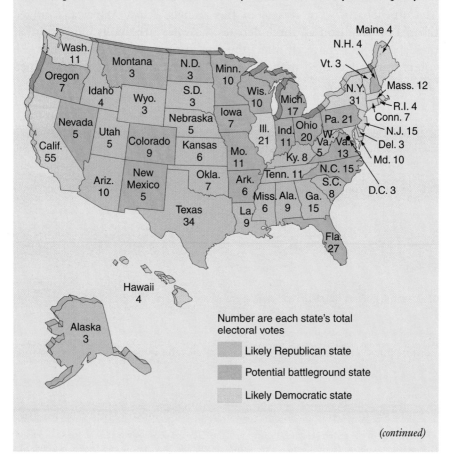

Number are each state's total electoral votes

Likely Republican state

Potential battleground state

Likely Democratic state

(continued)

These so-called battleground states are the only ones where the candidates spend any appreciable amount of time and money. One-sided states—those that are strongly enough Republican or Democratic to be safely in one candidate's grasp—are more or less ignored during the fall campaign.

As the Obama and McCain campaigns began the 2008 general election, their strategists targeted the states where the popular vote might possibly go either way. The accompanying map identifies these potential battleground states, as well as those that were conceded to the other party. As the campaign drew ever closer to the November election, the Obama and McCain campaigns further narrowed their strategies, pouring most of their resources into the half-dozen or so states where the race was closest.

The Republican and Democratic nominees are each eligible for federal funding of their general election campaigns even if they did not accept it during the primaries. The amount for the general election was set at $20 million in 1975 and has been adjusted for inflation in succeeding elections. The figure for the major-party nominees in 2008 was roughly $85 million. The only string attached to this money is that candidates who accept it can spend no additional funds on their campaigns (although each party is allowed to spend some money—in 2008, roughly $5 million—on behalf of its nominee).

Candidates can choose not to accept public funds, in which case the amount they spend is limited only by their ability to raise money privately. However, all major-party nominees since 1976 had accepted federal funding in the general election until Barack Obama, after having promised to run on public funds, opted out in 2008. Other candidates for the presidency qualify for a proportional amount of federal funding if they receive at least 5 percent of the vote and do not spend more than $50,000 of their own money on the campaign.

The Winners The Constitution specifies that the president must be at least thirty-five years old, be a natural-born U.S. citizen, and have been a U.S. resident for at least fourteen years. Yet the holding of high public office is nearly a prerequisite for gaining the presidency. Except for four army generals, all presidents to date have served previously as vice presidents, members of Congress, state governors, or top federal executives. Historians have developed rankings of the presidents, and if one thing is clear from these rankings, it is that there is no template for a successful presidency. The best presidents have differed considerably in their backgrounds, as have the worst ones. Of the four army generals, for example, one of them (George Washington) is ranked as a "great" president while another (Dwight Eisenhower) is seen as "near great." The other two (Zachary Taylor and Ulysses S. Grant) are rated "below average" by historians.

Until Obama's election in 2008, all presidents had been white. No woman has won the presidency, though it is only a matter of time before the nation has its first woman president. Until the early 1950s, a majority of Americans polled said they would not vote for a woman for president. Today, fewer than 10 percent hold this view. A similar change of opinion preceded John Kennedy's election to the presidency in 1960. Kennedy was the nation's first Catholic president and only the second Catholic to receive a major party's nomination.

STAFFING THE PRESIDENCY

When Americans go to the polls on election day, they have in mind the choice between two individuals, the Democratic nominee and the Republican nominee. In effect, however, they are choosing a lot more than a single executive leader. They are also picking a secretary of state, the director of the FBI, the chair of the Federal Reserve Board, and a host of other executives. Each of these is a presidential appointee.

Presidential Appointees

A president's ability to make executive appointments is a significant source of power. For one thing, modern policymaking rests on a deep understanding of policy issues and also on knowledge of how to successfully guide proposals through policy channels. Many presidential appointees have these skills. Further, the president cannot be in a hundred places at once—but the president's appointees can be. They extend the president's influence into the huge federal bureaucracy by overseeing those agencies they are appointed to head. Not surprisingly, the president seeks to appoint individuals who are members of the same political party and are committed to the Administration's policy goals.

The Executive Office of the President   The key staff organization is the Executive Office of the President (EOP), created by Congress in 1939 to provide the president with the staff necessary to coordinate the activities of the executive branch.[17] The EOP has since become the command center of the presidency. Its exact configuration is determined by the president, but some of its organizational units have carried over from one president to the next. These include the White House Office (WHO), which consists of the president's closest personal advisers; the Office of Management and Budget (OMB), which consists of experts who formulate and administer the federal budget; and the National Security Council (NSC), which advises the president on foreign and military affairs.

The Vice President The Constitution assigns all executive authority to the president, and none to the vice president. Earlier presidents typically refused to delegate significant duties to their vice presidents, which diminished the office's appeal. Nomination to the vice presidency was refused by many leading politicians, including Daniel Webster and Henry Clay. Said Webster, "I do not propose to be buried until I am really dead."[18] When he assumed the presidency in 1977, Jimmy Carter redefined the vice presidency, giving his vice president, Walter Mondale, an office in the West Wing of the White House and assigning him significant policy responsibilities. The vice president is now entrenched in the West Wing and is supported by an administrative staff (the Office of the Vice President) of a dozen people, including a domestic policy adviser and a national security policy adviser.

The change owes partly to the control that recent presidential nominees have had in selecting their running mate. They have tended to choose someone they trust or who fills a deficit in their background. Carter had never served in Washington, which was a reason he selected Mondale, an experienced and widely admired U.S. senator. Obama selected Joe Biden as his running mate in 2008 in part because of Biden's foreign policy expertise, an area in which Obama was weak. Biden's lengthy experience in the Senate was also counted on to be of help in getting Obama's legislative proposals through Congress.

George W. Bush may have given his vice president, Dick Cheney, too large a role in his administration. Much of the policy advice and information that Bush received was channeled through Cheney, enabling him to cast it to fit his objectives.[19] Among other things, Cheney was a chief architect of the Iraq invasion and other policies that weakened Bush's presidency, including warrantless wiretapping and the harsh treatment of enemy detainees (see Chapter 4). Cheney successfully fought attempts by congressional investigative committees to secure memos and other material that might have revealed more fully his role in Bush administration policies.

The White House Office Of the EOP's other organizational units, the White House Office serves the president most directly and personally. The units within the WHO include the Communications Office, the Office of the Press Secretary, the Office of the Counsel to the President, and the Office of Legislative Affairs. As these names suggest, the WHO consists of the president's personal assistants, including close personal advisers, press agents, legislative and group liaison aides, and special assistants for domestic and international policy. They work in the White House, and the president can hire and fire them at will. These personal assistants do much of the legwork for the president and serve as a main source of advice. Most of them are skilled at developing political strategy and communicating with the public, Congress, state and local governments, key groups, and the news media. Because of their proximity to the president, they are among the most powerful individuals in Washington.

Policy Experts　　The president is also served by the policy experts in the EOP's other organizations. These include economists, legal analysts, national security specialists, and others. The president is advised on economic issues, for example, by the National Economic Council (NEC). The NEC gathers information to develop indicators of the economy's strength and applies economic theories to various policy alternatives. Modern policymaking cannot be conducted in the absence of such expert knowledge and advice.

The President's Cabinet　　The heads of the fifteen executive departments, such as the Department of Defense and the Department of Agriculture, constitute the president's **cabinet.** They are appointed by the president, subject to confirmation by the Senate. Although the cabinet once served as the president's main advisory group, it has not played this role since Herbert Hoover's administration. As national issues have become increasingly complex, the cabinet has become outmoded as a policymaking forum: department heads are likely to be well informed only about issues in their particular area. Accordingly, cabinet meetings are no longer the scene of lengthy deliberations on how the president should respond to major policy issues. These discussions now take place between the president and top presidential advisers. Nevertheless, cabinet members, as individuals who head major departments, are important figures in any administration. The president chooses them for their prominence in politics, business, government, or the professions.[20] The office of secretary of state is generally regarded as the most prestigious cabinet post.

Other Presidential Appointees　　In addition to cabinet secretaries, the president appoints the heads and top deputies of federal agencies and commissions. Altogether, the president appoints a few thousand executive officials. However, most of these appointees are selected at the agency level or are part-time workers. This still leaves nearly seven hundred full-time appointees who serve the president more or less directly, a much larger number than are appointed by the chief executive of any other democracy.[21]

Presidents rely on trusted advisers in making critical policy decisions. During the Cuban missile crisis in 1962, this group of advisers to President John F. Kennedy helped him decide on a naval blockade as a means of forcing the Soviet Union to withdraw its missiles from Cuba.

The Problem of Control

Although the president's appointees are a huge asset, they can also be a liability: because they are so numerous, the president has difficulty controlling all that they do. President Truman had a wall chart in the Oval Office listing more than one hundred officials who reported directly to him; he often told visitors, "I cannot even see all of these men, let alone actually study what they are doing."[22] Since Truman's time, the number of bureaucratic agencies has more than doubled, compounding the problem of presidential control over subordinates.[23]

The problem of presidential control is most severe in the case of appointees who work outside the White House, in the departments and agencies. The loyalty of agency heads and cabinet secretaries often is split between a desire to promote the president's goals and an interest in boosting themselves or the agencies they lead. In 2005, when Hurricane Katrina devastated New Orleans, FEMA director Michael Brown, a Bush appointee, took the lead even though he had no appreciable experience with disaster relief. Intent on taking full control, Brown ignored the chain of command, withholding information from his immediate superior, the Homeland Security secretary, thereby making a coordinated relief effort harder to accomplish. Brown's incompetence was initially obscured by the scale of the disaster. Two days into the relief effort, President Bush said publicly, "Brownie, you're doing a heck of a job." Several days later, however, Brown's missteps had become clear and were headline news, leading the White House to force him to resign.

Lower-level appointees within the departments and agencies pose a different type of problem. The president rarely, if ever, sees them, and they typically are political novices (most have fewer than two years of government experience) and are not very knowledgeable about policy. These appointees are often "captured" by the agency in which they work because they depend on the agency's career bureaucrats for advice. (Chapter 13 examines further the relationship between presidential appointees and career bureaucrats.)

In sum, the modern presidential office is a double-edged sword. Presidents today have greater responsibilities than their predecessors, and this increase in responsibilities expands their opportunities to exert power. At the same time, the range of these responsibilities is so broad that presidents must rely on staff who may or may not act in the president's best interests. The modern president's recurring problem is to find some way of making sure that appointees place the interests of the presidency ahead of all others. (The subject of presidential control of the executive branch is discussed further in Chapter 13.)

FACTORS IN PRESIDENTIAL LEADERSHIP

The president operates within a system of separate institutions that share power (see "How the United States Compares"). Significant presidential action normally depends on the approval of Congress, the cooperation of the bureaucracy, and sometimes the acceptance of the judiciary. Because other officials have their own priorities, presidents do not always get their way. Congress in particular—more than the courts or the bureaucracy—holds the key to presidential success. Without congressional authorization and funding, most presidential proposals are nothing but ideas, empty of action.

Whether a president's initiatives succeed or fail depends substantially on several factors, including the force of circumstance, the stage of the president's term, the nature of the particular issue, the president's support in Congress, and the level of public support for the president's leadership. The remainder of this chapter examines each of these factors.

The Force of Circumstance

During his first months in office and in the midst of the Great Depression, Franklin D. Roosevelt accomplished the most sweeping changes in domestic policy in the nation's history. Congress moved quickly to pass nearly

HOW THE UNITED STATES COMPARES

Systems of Executive Policy Leadership

The United States instituted a presidential system in 1789 as part of its constitutional checks and balances. This form of executive leadership was copied in Latin America but not in Europe. European democracies adopted parliamentary systems, in which executive leadership is provided by a prime minister, who is a member of the legislature. In recent years, some European prime ministers have campaigned and governed as if they were a singular authority rather than the head of a collective institution. France in the 1960s created a separate chief executive office but retained its parliamentary form of legislature.

The policy leadership of a president can differ substantially from that of a prime minister. As a singular head of an independent branch of government, a president does not have to share executive authority but nevertheless depends on the legislative branch for support. By comparison, a prime minister shares executive leadership with a cabinet, but once agreement within the cabinet is reached, he or she is almost assured of the legislative support necessary to carry out policy initiatives.

Presidential System	Presidential/ Parliamentary System	Parliamentary System
Mexico	Finland	Australia
United States	France	Belgium
Venezuela	Russia	Canada
		Germany
		Great Britain
		Israel
		Italy
		Japan
		Netherlands
		Sweden

every New Deal initiative he proposed. In 1964 and 1965, Lyndon Johnson pushed landmark civil rights and social welfare legislation through Congress on the strength of the civil rights movement, the legacy of the assassinated President Kennedy, and large Democratic majorities in the House and Senate. When Ronald Reagan assumed the presidency in 1981, inflation and high unemployment had greatly weakened the national economy and created a mood for change, enabling Reagan to persuade Congress to support some of the most substantial taxing and spending changes in history.

From such presidencies has come the popular impression that presidents single-handedly decide national policy. However, each of these periods of presidential dominance was marked by a special set of circumstances: a decisive election victory that gave added force to the president's leadership, a compelling national problem that convinced Congress and the public that bold presidential action was needed, and a president who was mindful of what was expected and who vigorously advocated policies consistent with those expectations.

When conditions are favorable, the power of the presidency is remarkable. The problem for most presidents is that conditions normally are not conducive to strong leadership. Political scientist Erwin Hargrove suggests that presidential influence depends largely on circumstance.[24] Some presidents serve in periods when resources are scarce or when important problems are surfacing in American society but have not yet reached a critical point. Such situations, Hargrove contends, work against the president's efforts to accomplish significant policy change. In 1994, reflecting on the constraints of budget deficits and other factors beyond his control, President Clinton said he had no choice but "to play the hand that history had dealt" him. Stark reality also confronted Obama when he assumed the presidency in 2009. A large budget deficit complicated his campaign promise to spend heavily on health care and education.

The Stage of the President's Term

If conditions conducive to great accomplishments occur infrequently, it is nonetheless the case that nearly every president has favorable moments. Such moments often come during the first months in office. Most newly elected presidents enjoy a **honeymoon period** during which Congress, the press, and the public anticipate initiatives from the Oval Office and are more predisposed than usual to support them. Not surprisingly, presidents have put forth more new programs in their first year in office than in any subsequent year. James Pfiffner uses the term *strategic presidency* to refer to a president's need to move quickly on priority items in order to take advantage of the policy momentum gained from the election.[25] Later in their terms, presidents tend to be less successful in presenting initiatives and getting them enacted. They may run out of good ideas, get caught up in scandal, or exhaust their political resources; further, the momentum of their election is gone, and sources of opposition have emerged. Even highly successful presidents like Johnson and Reagan have had weak records in their final years. Franklin Roosevelt began his presidency with a remarkable period of achievement—the celebrated "Hundred Days"—but during his last six years in office, few of his major domestic proposals were enacted.

An irony of the presidency, then, is that presidents are usually most powerful when they are least knowledgeable—during their first months in office. These months can, as a result, be times of risk as well as times of opportunity. An example is the Bay of Pigs fiasco during the first year of John Kennedy's presidency, in which a U.S.-backed invasion force of anticommunist Cubans was easily defeated by Fidel Castro's army.

The Nature of the Issue: Foreign or Domestic

In the 1960s, political scientist Aaron Wildavsky wrote that although the nation has only one president, it has two presidencies: one domestic and one foreign.[26] Wildavsky was referring to Congress's greater tendency to defer to presidential leadership on foreign policy issues than on domestic policy issues. He had in mind the broad leeway Congress had granted Truman, Eisenhower, Kennedy, and Johnson in their foreign policies. Wildavsky's thesis is now regarded as a somewhat time-bound conception of presidential influence. Today, many of the same factors that affect a president's domestic policy success, such as the partisan composition of Congress, also affect foreign policy success.

Nevertheless, presidents still have somewhat of an advantage when the issue is foreign policy, because they have more authority to act on their own and are more likely to receive support from Congress.[27] The clash between powerful interest groups that occurs over many domestic issues is less prevalent in the foreign policy area. Additionally, the president is recognized by other nations as America's voice in world affairs, and members of Congress sometimes will defer to the president in order to maintain America's credibility abroad. In some cases, presidents literally decide the direction of foreign policy. In their 2008 race, Obama and McCain took sharply opposing positions on the U.S. military presence in Iraq. Obama's victory meant a more substantial drawdown of U.S. troops than McCain had proposed.

Presidents also have leverage in foreign and defense policy because of their special relationship with the defense, diplomatic, and intelligence agencies, sometimes called "presidential agencies." Other agencies that are responsive to the president are sometimes even more receptive to Congress; the Department of Agriculture, for example, often is more concerned with having the support of farm-state senators and representatives than with having the president's backing. The defense, diplomatic, and intelligence agencies, however, are different in that their missions are closely tied to the president's constitutional authority as commander-in-chief and chief diplomat. In the buildup to the Iraq war, for example, the defense and intelligence agencies operated in ways that promoted President Bush's stand on the need to confront Saddam Hussein militarily. Only later did Congress discover that the intelligence information it had been provided, as well as the assessments it had been given by the Defense Department on the level of military force required to invade and pacify Iraq, had been tailored to suit Bush's plans.

Relations with Congress

Although the power of the presidency is not nearly as extensive as some Americans assume, presidents' ability to influence the agenda of national debate is unrivaled, reflecting their unique claim to represent the whole country. Whenever the president directs attention to a particular issue, members of Congress take notice. But will they take action? The answer is sometimes yes and sometimes no, depending in part on whether the president takes their concerns into account.

Seeking Cooperation from Congress   As the center of national attention, presidents can start to believe that their ideas should prevail over those of Congress. This reasoning invariably gets any president into trouble. Jimmy Carter had not held national office before he was elected president in 1976 and thus had no clear understanding of how Washington operates.[28] Soon after taking office, Carter deleted from his budget nineteen public works projects that he believed were a waste of taxpayers' money, ignoring the determination of members of Congress to obtain federally funded projects for their constituents. Carter's action set the tone for a conflict-ridden relationship with Congress.

In order to get the help of members of Congress, the president must respond to their interests as they respond to those of the president.[29] The most basic fact about presidential leadership is that it takes place in the context of a system of divided powers. Although the president gets most of the attention, Congress has most of the constitutional authority in the American system, and presidents must get the cooperation of Congress to achieve their legislative goals.

President Lyndon Johnson addresses a joint session of Congress in 1965. Johnson had an extraordinary record of success with Congress, which adopted the great majority of his legislative proposals. Johnson had the good fortune of working with a Congress controlled—by a wide margin—by his own party.

Even the president's most direct legislative tool, the veto, has limits. Congress can seldom muster the two-thirds majority in each chamber required to override a presidential veto, so the threat of a veto can make Congress bend to the president's demands. Yet, as presidential scholar Richard Neustadt argued, the veto is as much a sign of presidential weakness as it is a sign of strength, because it arises when Congress refuses to go along with the president's ideas.[30] An example is the first veto cast by George W. Bush. Until then, Bush was on track to join Thomas Jefferson as the only two-term president not to veto a bill. In 2006, however, Bush vetoed a bill that would have expanded federal support for embryonic-stem-cell research. He had announced his opposition to such research early in his presidency and was successful for a time in getting congressional Republicans to back him. As Bush's popularity plummeted in 2005, however, some congressional Republicans separated themselves from the president out of concern for their reelection chances. Enough Republicans defected on the stem-cell bill to get it through Congress, setting the stage for Bush's veto. Bush was further weakened when his party lost control of the House and Senate in the 2006 midterm elections. He increasingly resorted to actual and threatened vetoes in dealing with Congress.

Congress is a constituency that all presidents must serve if they expect to have its support. Neustadt concluded that presidential power, at base, is "the power to persuade."[31] Like any singular notion of presidential power, Neustadt's has limitations. Presidents at times have the power to command and to threaten. They can also appeal directly to the American people as a means of pressuring Congress. But Congress can never be taken for granted. Theodore Roosevelt expressed the wish that he could "be the president and Congress, too," if only for a day, so that he would have the power to enact as well as to propose laws.

Benefiting from Partisan Support in Congress   For most presidents, the next best thing to being "Congress, too" is to have a Congress filled with members of their own party. The sources of division within Congress are many. Legislators from urban and rural areas, wealthier and poorer constituencies, and different regions of the country often have very different views of the national interest. To obtain majority support in Congress, the president must find ways to overcome these differences.

No source of unity is more important to presidential success than partisanship. Presidents are more likely to succeed when their own party controls Congress (see Figure 12-1). Between 1954 and 1992, each Republican president—Eisenhower, Nixon, Ford, Reagan, and Bush—had to contend with a Democratic majority in one or both houses of Congress. Congress passed a smaller percentage of the initiatives supported by each of these presidents than those supported by any Democratic president of the period: Kennedy, Johnson, or Carter. In his first two years in office, backed by Democratic majorities in the House and Senate, more than 85 percent of the bills Clinton supported were enacted into law. After Republicans took control of Congress in 1995, Clinton's legislative success rate sank below 40 percent. George W. Bush suffered a similar fate when control of Congress shifted from the Republicans to the Democrats in 2007. Bush had a legislative success rate of 81 percent in 2006, but it fell to 38 percent in 2007—a sharp illustration of how presidential power depends on which party controls Congress.

Colliding with Congress   On rare occasions, presidents have pursued their goals so zealously that Congress has been compelled to take steps to curb their use of power.

The ultimate sanction of Congress is its constitutional power to impeach and remove the president from office. The House of Representatives decides

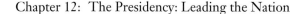

figure 12-1 PERCENTAGE OF BILLS PASSED BY CONGRESS ON WHICH THE PRESIDENT ANNOUNCED A POSITION, 1953–2007

In most years, presidents have been supported by Congress on a majority of policy issues on which they have taken a stand. Presidents fare better when their party controls Congress. *Source: Congressional Quarterly Weekly Report, various dates.*

by majority vote whether the president should be impeached (placed on trial), and the Senate conducts the trial and then votes on the president's case, with a two-thirds vote required for removal from office. In 1868, Andrew Johnson came within one Senate vote of being removed from office for his opposition to Congress's harsh Reconstruction policies after the Civil War. In 1974, Richard Nixon's resignation halted congressional proceedings on the Watergate affair that almost certainly would have ended in his impeachment and removal from office.

The specter of impeachment arose again in 1998 when the House of Representatives by a vote of 258 to 176 authorized an investigation of President Clinton's conduct. He was accused of lying under oath about his relationship with intern Monica Lewinsky and of obstructing justice by trying to conceal the affair. The gravity of the allegations was leavened by the circumstances. The charges had grown out of an extramarital affair rather than a gross abuse of executive power, and though Americans disapproved of Clinton's behavior, most of them did not think it constituted "treason, bribery, or other high crimes and misdemeanors," the Constitution's basis for impeachment and removal from office. Not surprisingly, congressional Republicans and Democrats differed sharply on the impeachment issue. At all formal stages of the process—the House vote to authorize an inquiry, the House vote on the articles of impeachment, and the Senate vote on whether to remove the president—the vote was divided largely along party lines. In the end, Clinton was acquitted by the Senate, but his legacy will forever be tarnished by his impeachment by the House.

The gravity of an impeachment action makes it an unsuitable basis for curbing presidential power except in rare instances. More often, Congress has responded legislatively to what it sees as unwarranted assertions of executive power. An example is the Budget Impoundment and Control Act of 1974, which prohibits a president from indefinitely withholding funds that have been appropriated by Congress. The legislation was enacted in response to President Nixon's practice of withholding funds from programs he disliked. A similar controversy erupted in 2006 when it was revealed that President Bush had used so-called signing statements to challenge the constitutionality of more than seven hundred bills. These statements, appended to a bill when the president signs it, are meant to indicate that the president does not necessarily plan to abide by particular provisions of a law. Although Bush was not the first president to use this device, he had attached signing statements to more bills than all of his predecessors combined and had done so in secrecy. Even congressional Republicans expressed concerned about the practice. At Senate Judiciary Committee hearings, Senator Arlen Specter (R-Penn.), chair of the committee, argued that presidents do not have the authority to pick and choose among legislative provisions, approving those they like and disregarding the rest. The president's choice is to accept or reject a bill in its entirety. Said Specter, "The president has the option under the Constitution to veto or not." [32]

Congress's most significant historical effort to curb presidential power is the War Powers Act. During the Vietnam War, Presidents Johnson and Nixon repeatedly misled Congress, supplying it with intelligence estimates that painted a falsely optimistic picture of the military situation. Believing the war was being won, Congress regularly voted to provide the money necessary to keep it going. However, congressional support changed abruptly in 1971 with publication in the *New York Times* of classified documents (the so-called Pentagon Papers) that revealed the Vietnam situation to be much worse than Johnson and Nixon had claimed.

To prevent future presidential wars, Congress in 1973 passed the War Powers Act. Nixon vetoed the measure, but Congress overrode his veto. The act does not prohibit the president from sending troops into combat, but it does require the president to notify Congress of the reason for committing combat troops within forty-eight hours of their deployment. The act also specifies that hostilities must end within sixty days unless Congress extends the period; gives the president an additional thirty days to withdraw the troops from hostile territory, although Congress can shorten this period; and requires the president to consult with Congress whenever feasible before sending troops into a hostile situation.

Every president since Nixon has claimed that the War Powers Act infringes on his constitutional power as commander in chief, and each has refused to accept it fully. The Supreme Court has not ruled on the constitutionality of the War Powers Act, leaving open the question of whether it is a substantial constraint on the president's war-making powers.

Thus, the effect of presidential efforts to circumvent congressional authority has been to heighten congressional opposition. Even if presidents gain in the short run by acting on their own, they undermine their capacity to lead in the long run if they fail to keep in mind that Congress is a coequal branch of the American governing system.

Public Support

Every recent president has had the public's confidence at the start of his term of office. When asked in polls whether they "approve or disapprove of how the president is doing his job," a majority of Americans have expressed approval during the first months of the president's term. Sooner or later, however, all **presidential approval ratings** have slipped below this high point, and several recent presidents have left office with a rating below 50 percent (see Table 12-3).

Public support affects a president's ability to achieve policy goals. Presidential power rests in part on a claim to national leadership, and the legitimacy of that claim is roughly proportional to the president's public support. With public backing, the president's leadership cannot easily be dismissed by other Washington officials. When the president's public support sinks, officials are less inclined to accept presidential leadership. Congress's response to George W. Bush's leadership illustrates the pattern. In the early years of his presidency, Bush got from the Congress nearly everything he asked for, a reason that five years elapsed before he cast his first veto. As his popularity declined, however, congressional inaction on or opposition to his major proposals became nearly the rule. Among the casualties were Bush's social security and immigration reform proposals.

Events and Issues The public's support for the president is affected by national and international conditions. Threats from abroad tend to produce

| table | 12-3 | PERCENTAGE OF PUBLIC EXPRESSING APPROVAL OF PRESIDENT'S PERFORMANCE |

Presidential approval ratings generally are higher at the beginning of the term than at the end.

President	Years in Office	Average During Presidency	First-Year Average	Final-Year Average
Harry Truman	1945–52	41%	63%	35%
Dwight Eisenhower	1953–60	64	74	62
John Kennedy	1961–63	70	76	62
Lyndon Johnson	1963–68	55	78	40
Richard Nixon	1969–74	49	63	24
Gerald Ford	1974–76	46	75	48
Jimmy Carter	1977–80	47	68	46
Ronald Reagan	1981–88	53	58	57
George H. W. Bush	1989–92	61	65	40
Bill Clinton	1993–2000	57	50	60
George W. Bush	2001–08	51	68	33

Source: Averages compiled from Gallup polls.

a patriotic "rally 'round the flag" reaction that initially creates widespread support for the president. Every foreign policy crisis in the past four decades has followed this pattern. Americans were deeply divided in 2003 over the wisdom of war with Iraq, but when the fighting began, President Bush's approval rating rose. However, ongoing crises can erode a president's support if they are not resolved successfully or soon. Bush's approval rating jumped above 70 percent with the invasion of Iraq in 2003 but then fell steadily as U.S. casualties mounted. By 2006, his approval rating had fallen below 40 percent, and his party suffered heavy losses in that year's midterm election.

Historically, presidents' public support has rested mainly on the strength of the economy. Economic downturns invariably reduce the public's confidence in the president.[33] Ford, Carter, and the first President Bush lost their reelection bids when their popularity plummeted after the economy swooned. In contrast, Clinton's popularity rose in 1995 and 1996 as the economy strengthened, contributing to his reelection in 1996. The irony, of course, is that presidents do not actually have that much control over the economy. If they did, it would always be strong.

The Televised Presidency A major advantage that presidents enjoy in their efforts to nurture public support is their access to the media, particularly television. Only the president can expect the networks to provide free air time on occasion, and in terms of the amount of news coverage, the president and top presidential advisers receive twice as much coverage as all members of Congress combined.

Political scientist Samuel Kernell calls it "going public" when the president bypasses inside bargaining with Congress and promotes "himself and his policies by appealing to the American public for support."[34] Such appeals are at least as old as Theodore Roosevelt's use of the presidency as a "bully pulpit," but they have increased substantially in recent years. As the president's role has moved from administrative leader to policy advocate and agenda setter, public support has become increasingly important to presidential success. Television has made it easier for presidents to go public with their programs, though the public's response depends partly on the president's rhetorical skill. Ronald Reagan was called "the Great Communicator" because of his skilled use of television to mobilize public support.

However, presidents cannot count on favorable press coverage. Journalists are adept at putting their own spin on what political leaders say and tend to play up adverse developments. For example, although presidents get some credit in the press when the economy is doing well, they get mounds of negative coverage when the economy is doing poorly. They also get hammered whenever there is a whiff of wrongdoing within the Administration. In 2004, for example, informed sources claimed that the Bush administration had targeted Iraq long before it ordered an invasion of that country. Secretary of Defense Donald Rumsfeld reportedly wanted to bomb Iraq immediately after the terrorist attacks of September 11, 2001, even though there was no evidence linking Iraq to the attacks. Rumsfeld was quoted by a White House insider as saying "There aren't any good targets in Afghanistan and there are lots of good targets in Iraq." The allegations were front-page news for days on end, putting the Bush administration on the defensive.

The Illusion of Presidential Government Presidents have no choice but to try to counter negative press coverage with their own version of events. President George W. Bush did exactly that by scheduling blocks of interviews with journalists from local and regional news outlets to say that the real story of the Iraq effort—the success story of reopened schools, restored oil production, and renewed hope for the Iraqi people—was not being told by the Washington press corps. Bush accused national reporters of focusing only on the death and destruction in Iraq.

Such efforts can carry a president only so far, however. No president can fully control his communicated image, and national conditions ultimately have the largest impact on a president's public support. No amount of public relations can disguise adverse developments at home or abroad. Indeed, presidents run a risk by building up their images through public relations. By thrusting themselves into the limelight, presidents contribute to the public's belief that the president is in charge of the national government, a perception political scientist Hugh Heclo calls "the illusion of presidential government."[35] If they are as powerful as they project themselves to be, they will be held responsible for policy failures as well as policy successes.

Because the public expects so much from its presidents, they get too much credit when things go well and too much blame when things go badly. Therein lies an irony of the presidential office. More than from any constitutional grant, more than from any statute, and more than from any crisis, presidential power derives from the president's position as the sole official who can claim to represent the entire American public. Yet because presidential power rests on a popular base, it erodes when public support declines. The irony is that the presidential office typically grows weaker as problems mount. Just when the country most needs effective leadership, strong leadership often is hardest to achieve.[36]

SUMMARY   Self-Test www.mhhe.com/pattersonwtp8e

The presidency has become a much stronger office than the Framers envisioned. The Constitution grants the president substantial military, diplomatic, legislative, and executive powers, and in each case the president's authority has increased measurably over the nation's history. Underlying this change is the president's position as the one leader chosen by the whole nation and as the sole head of the executive branch. These features of the office have enabled presidents to claim broad authority in response to the increased demands placed on the federal government by changing global and national conditions.

During the course of American history, the presidential selection process has been altered in ways intended to make it more responsive to the preferences of ordinary people. Today, the electorate has a vote not only in the general election but also in the selection of party nominees. To gain nomination, a presidential hopeful must gain the support of the electorate in state primaries and open caucuses. Once nominated, the candidates receive federal funds for their general election campaigns, which today are based on televised appeals.

Although the campaign tends to personalize the presidency, the responsibilities of the modern presidency far exceed any president's personal capacities. To meet their obligations, presidents have surrounded themselves with large staffs of advisers, policy experts, and managers. These staff members enable the president to extend control over the executive branch while at the same time providing the information necessary for policymaking. All recent presidents have discovered, however, that their control of staff resources is incomplete and that some things others do on their behalf can work against what they are trying to accomplish.

As sole chief executive and the nation's top elected leader, presidents can always expect that their policy and leadership efforts will receive attention. However, other institutions, particularly Congress, have the authority to make presidential leadership effective. No president has come close to winning approval of all the programs he has placed before Congress, and the presidents' records of success have varied considerably. The factors in a president's success include whether national conditions that require strong leadership from the White House are present and whether the president's party has a majority in Congress.

To hold onto an effective leadership position, the president depends on the backing of the American people. Recent presidents have made extensive use of the media to build support for their programs, yet they have had difficulty maintaining that support throughout their terms of office. A major reason is that the public expects far more from its presidents than they can deliver.

KEY TERMS

cabinet (*p. 440*)
honeymoon period (*p. 444*)
momentum (in campaigns) (*p. 429*)
open party caucuses (*p. 429*)

presidential approval ratings (*p. 451*)
stewardship theory (*p. 423*)
unit rule (*p. 434*)
Whig theory (*p. 423*)

SUGGESTED READINGS

Campbell, James E. *The American Campaign: U.S. Presidential Campaigns and the National Vote.* College Station, Tex.: Texas A&M University Press 2008. An analysis that reveals the predictability of presidential campaign outcomes.

Entman, Robert M. *Projections of Power: Framing News, Public Opinion, and U.S. Foreign Policy.* Chicago: University of Chicago Press, 2003. An assessment of the president's power to set the news agenda.

Jones, Charles O. *The Presidency in a Separated System.* Washington, D.C.: Brookings Institution Press, 2005. A careful analysis of president-Congress relations.

Milkis, Sidney, and Michael Nelson. *The American Presidency: Origins and Development, 1776–2002*, 5th ed. Washington, D.C.: Congressional Quarterly Press, 2007. A thoughtful assessment of the factors and conditions that have molded the presidential office.

Neustadt, Richard E. *Presidential Power and the Modern Presidents: The Politics of Leadership from Roosevelt to Reagan.* New York: Free Press, 1990. The classic analysis of the limitations on presidential power.

Pika, Joseph A., and John Anthony Maltese. *The Politics of the Presidency*, 7th ed. Washington, D.C.: Congressional Quarterly Press, 2008. An insightful look at the leadership skills demanded of presidents.

Schlesinger, Arthur M., Jr. *The Imperial Presidency*. Boston: Mariner Books, 2004. An analysis of the modern presidency by a Pulitzer Prize–winning historian.

Skowronek, Stephen. *Presidential Leadership in Political Time: Reprise and Reappraisal*. Lawrence: University of Kansas Press, 2008. An assessment of how conditions of the time have affected presidents' role and power.

List of Websites

http://www.ibiblio.org/lia/president A site with general information on specific presidents and links to the presidential libraries.

http://www.ipl.org/ref/POTUS A site that profiles the nation's presidents, their cabinet officers, and key events during their time in office.

http://www.usa.gov/ A site that gives information on the presidency and the Executive Office of the President, as well as links to key executive agencies and organizations.

http://www.whitehouse.gov/ The White House's home page; has an email guest book and includes information on the president, the vice president, and current White House activities.

Politics in Theory and Practice

Thinking: Why is presidential power "conditional"—that is, why is it affected so substantially by circumstance, the makeup of Congress, and popular support? (The separation of powers should be part of your answer.)

Participating: Consider writing a letter or sending an email to the president or a top presidential appointee that expresses your opinion on an issue that is currently the object of executive action. You can inform yourself about the administration's policy or stance on the issue through the website of the White House (www.whitehouse.gov) or of the agency in question (for example, the State Department's site, www.state.gov).

Extra Credit

For up-to-the-minute *New York Times* articles, interactive simulations, graphics, study tools, and more links and quizzes, visit the text's online learning center at www.mhhe.com/pattersonwtp8e.

Presidential Power

By Richard Cheney

When George W. Bush took office in-2001, his vice president, Dick Cheney, helped persuade him to take a forceful view of the presidency. Cheney believed that Congress had encroached on the powers of the president, particularly in the realm of national security but also in the areas of executive secrecy and administrative discretion. Cheney's view prevailed. The White House claimed broad authority in its pursuit of the war on terrorism and the handling of enemy combatants, on several occasions refusing to provide Congress with executive memos dealing with policy decisions. President Bush also made extensive use of "signing statements," which indicated points at which he thought legislation passed by Congress infringed on executive authority. Vice President Cheney's fullest public statement on the question of presidential power came during a December 2005 press conference that he held on Air Force Two (the-vice president's plane) while traveling with reporters to the Middle East. Following is a transcript of that press conference.

REPORTER: Sir, if I could ask you to step back for a moment, there has been a lot written and talked about recently about executive power, the power of the presidency. You have a really interesting perspective on this having served in the Ford White House, which arguably was the point at which presidential power had reached its absolute nadir. And I'm curious how that experience has shaped your view of presidential powers. . . .

CHENEY: Yes, I do have the view that over the years there had been an erosion of presidential power and authority that [is] reflected in a number of developments [including] the War Powers Act, which many people believe is unconstitutional. It's never really been tested. We sort of have an understanding when we commit force that the U.S., the government, the executive branch will notify the Congress, but making it clear we're not doing it [in response to] the War Powers Act, in fact. It has never been tested. It will be tested at some point. I am one of those who believe that was an infringement upon the authority of the President. The [Impoundment] and Control Act, back in the '70s, passed during the Ford administration that limited the President's authority to impound funds, a series of things [like] Watergate—a lot of the things around Watergate and Vietnam, both, in the '70s— served to erode the authority, I think, the President needs to be effective especially in a national security area. If you want reference to an obscure text, go look at the minority views that were filed with the Iran-Contra Committee; the Iran Contra Report in about 1987. Nobody has ever read them, but part of the argument in Iran Contra was whether or not the President had the authority to do what was done in the Reagan years. And those of us in the minority wrote minority views, but they were actually authored by a guy working for me, for my staff, that I think are very good in laying out a robust view of the President's prerogatives with respect to the conduct of especially foreign policy and national security matters. It will give you a much broader perspective. I served in the Congress for 10 years. I've got enormous regard for the other body, [Article] I of the Constitution, but I do believe that, especially in the day and age we live in, the nature of the threats we face, it was true during the Cold War, as well as I think what is true now, the President of the United States needs to have his constitutional powers unimpaired, if you will, in terms of the conduct of national security policy. That's my personal view.

In other areas, in the perspective looking at issues that come up during this administration, one of those was the Energy Task Force. My belief is that the President is entitled to and needs to have unfiltered advice in formulating policy, that he ought to be able to seek the opinion of anybody he wants to, and that he should not have to reveal, for example, to a member of Congress who he talked to that morning. That issue was litigated all the way up to the Supreme Court, and we won—ultimately referred back to the D.C. Circuit where we got a unanimous opinion supporting our position. So when you're asking about my view of the presidency, yes, I believe in a strong, robust executive authority. And I think the world we live in demands it. And to some extent, that we have an obligation as an administration to pass on the offices we hold to our successors in as good a shape as we found them.

REPORTER: Do you think the pendulum is in the right place now?

CHENEY: I do think it's swung back. If you look at it from a historical standpoint, the presidency in the late 1800s was a relatively weak organization, a relatively weak institution. I describe Teddy Roosevelt as a strong President—to some extent, maybe Woodrow Wilson. F.D.R. really established a sense of the modern presidency during

the Depression and World War II. And of course, World War II changed circumstances so that instead of demobilizing at the end of the war, we maintained robust military forces afterwards because of the Cold War. Circumstances change. I think you're right, probably the end of the next administration, you had the nadir of the modern presidency in terms of authority and legitimacy, then a number of limitations that were imposed in the aftermath of Vietnam and Watergate. But I do think that to some extent now, we've been able to restore the legitimate authority of the presidency.

REPORTER: Do you think the NSA thing [secret wiretaps of conversations that were not authorized by a judge] will reignite that debate then? . . .

CHENEY: It's important that you be clear that we're talking about individuals who are al Qaeda or have an association with al Qaeda, who we have reason to believe are part of that terrorist network. There are two requirements, and that's one of them. It's not just random conversations. If you're calling Aunt Sadie in Paris, we're probably not really interested. . . .

REPORTER: But aren't you concerned that because of that, this place where you are right now, where you feel comfortable in terms of presidential power could swing the other way, that there could be a backlash, and then Congress would impose even more restrictions on the executive branch?

CHENEY: No, I think when the American people look at this, they will understand and appreciate what we're doing and why we're doing it. It's not an accident that we haven't been hit in four years. There's a temptation for people to sit around and say, well, gee, that was just a one-off affair, they didn't really mean it. Bottom line is we've been very active and very aggressive defending the nation and using the tools at our disposal to do that. That ranges from everything to going into Afghanistan and closing down the terrorist camps, rounding up al Qaeda wherever we can find them in the world, to an active robust intelligence program, putting out rewards, the capture of bad guys, and the Patriot Act. . . .

Either we're serious about fighting the war on terror or we're not. Either we believe that there are individuals out there doing everything they can to try to launch more attacks, to try to get ever deadlier weapons to use against, or we don't. The President and I believe very deeply that there's a hell of a threat, that it's there for anybody who wants to look at it. And that our obligation and responsibility given our job is to do everything in our power to defeat the terrorists. And that's exactly what we're doing.

But if there's anything improper or inappropriate in that, my guess is that the vast majority of the American people support that, support what we're doing. They believe we ought to be doing it, and so if there's a backlash pending, I think the backlash is going to be against those who are suggesting somehow that we shouldn't take these steps in order to protect the country.

What's Your Opinion?

Do you share Vice President Cheney's view of presidential power? Should the president have nearly unlimited discretion, relative to Congress and the courts, to deal with threats to national security?

CHAPTER 13

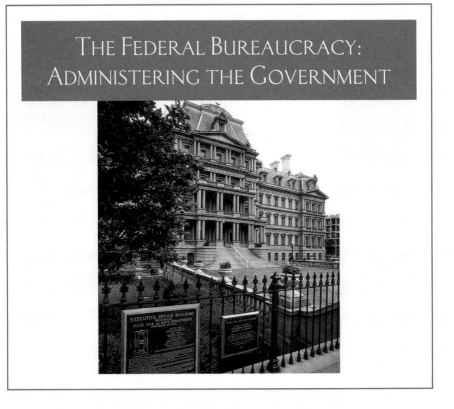

THE FEDERAL BUREAUCRACY: ADMINISTERING THE GOVERNMENT

> ❝ [No] industrial society could manage the daily operations of its public affairs without bureaucratic organizations in which officials play a major policymaking role. ❞
>
> NORMAN THOMAS[1]

Early on the morning of September 7, 1993, a truck pulled up to the south lawn of the White House and unloaded pallets stacked with federal regulations. The display was the backdrop for a presidential speech announcing the completion of the National Performance Review or, as it is commonly called, NPR. The federal regulations piled atop the pallets symbolized bureaucratic red tape, and the NPR was the Clinton administration's initiative to make government more responsive.

The origins of the NPR were plain enough. For years, the federal bureaucracy had been derided as being too big, too expensive, and too intrusive. These charges gained strength as federal budget deficits increased and the public became increasingly dissatisfied with the performance of the government in Washington. Reform attempts in the 1970s and 1980s had not stemmed the tide of federal deficits or markedly improved the bureaucracy's performance. Clinton campaigned on the issue of "reinventing government" and acted swiftly on the promise. Vice President–elect Al Gore was placed in charge of the NPR. He assembled more than two hundred career bureaucrats, who knew firsthand how the bureaucracy operated, and organized them into "reinventing teams." The NPR's report included 384 specific recommendations grouped into four broad imperatives: reducing red tape, putting customers first, empowering administrators, and cutting government back to basic services.[2]

The NPR was the most recent in a lengthy list of major efforts to remake the federal bureaucracy. The NPR was different in its particulars, but its claim to improve administration while saving money was consistent with the claims of earlier reform panels, including the Brownlow, Hoover, and Volcker commissions.[3] Like those efforts, the NPR addressed an enduring issue of American politics: the bureaucracy's efficiency, responsiveness, and accountability.

Modern government would be impossible without a large bureaucracy. It is the government's enormous administrative capacity that makes it possible for the United States to have ambitious programs such as space exploration, social security, interstate highways, and universal postal service. Yet the bureaucracy also poses special problems. Even those who work in federal agencies agree that the bureaucracy can be unresponsive, wasteful, and self-serving.

As one of thousands of services provided by the federal bureaucracy, the National Hurricane Service monitors hurricane activity and provides early warning to affected coastal areas.

This chapter examines both the need for bureaucracy and the problems associated with it. The chapter describes the bureaucracy's responsibilities, organizational structure, and management practices. The chapter also explains the "politics" of the bureaucracy. Although the three constitutional branches of government impose a degree of accountability on the bureaucracy, its sheer size confounds their efforts to control it fully. The main points discussed in this chapter are these:

★ *Bureaucracy is an inevitable consequence of complexity and scale.* Modern government could not function without a large bureaucracy. Through authority, specialization, and rules, bureaucracy provides a means of managing thousands of tasks and employees.

★ *The bureaucracy is expected simultaneously to respond to the direction of partisan officials and to administer programs fairly and competently.* These conflicting demands are addressed through a combination of personnel management systems—the patronage, merit, and executive leadership systems.

★ *Bureaucrats naturally take an "agency point of view," seeking to promote their agency's programs and power.* They do this through their expert knowledge, support from clientele groups, and backing by Congress or the president.

★ *Although agencies are subject to oversight by the president, Congress, and the judiciary, bureaucrats exercise considerable power in their own right.*

FEDERAL ADMINISTRATION: FORM, PERSONNEL, AND ACTIVITIES

For many Americans, the word *bureaucracy* brings to mind waste, mindless rules, and rigidity. This image is not unfounded, but it is one-sided. Bureaucracy is a highly effective form of organization. Although Americans tend to equate bureaucracy with the federal government, bureaucracy is found wherever there is a need to manage large numbers of people and tasks. All large-scale, task-oriented organizations—public and private—are bureaucratic in form.[4] General Motors is a bureaucracy, as is every university. The state governments are also every bit as "bureaucratic" as the federal government (see "States in the Nation").

In formal terms, **bureaucracy** is a system of organization and control that is based on three principles: hierarchical authority, job specialization, and formalized rules. These features are the reason bureaucracy, as a form of organization, is the most efficient means of getting people to

★ ‖ STATES IN THE NATION

The Size of State Bureaucracies

Although the federal bureaucracy is often criticized as being "too big," it is actually smaller on a per capita basis than even the smallest state bureaucracy. There are 83 federal employees for every 1,000 Americans. Illinois, with 103 state employees for every 1,000 residents, has the smallest state bureaucracy on a per capita basis. Hawaii has the largest—428 state employees per 1,000 residents.

Q: What do the states with larger per capita bureaucracies have in common?

A: In general, the least populous states, especially those that are larger geographically, have larger bureaucracies on a per capita basis. This pattern reflects the fact that a state, whatever its population, has basic functions (such as highway maintenance and policing) that it must perform.

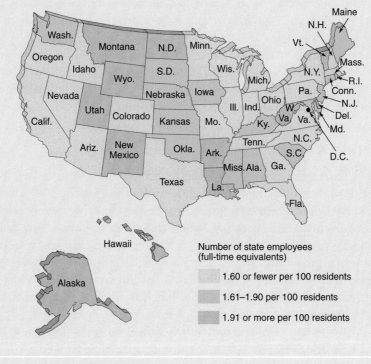

Number of state employees
(full-time equivalents)

□ 1.60 or fewer per 100 residents

□ 1.61–1.90 per 100 residents

□ 1.91 or more per 100 residents

Source: U.S. Bureau of the Census, 2008.

work together on tasks of great magnitude. **Hierarchical authority** refers to a chain of command whereby the officials and units at the top of a bureaucracy have authority over those in the middle, who in turn control those at the bottom. Hierarchy speeds action by reducing conflict over the power to make decisions: those higher in the organization have authority over those below them. **Job specialization** refers to explicitly defined duties for each job position and to a precise division of labor within the organization. Specialization yields efficiency because each individual concentrates on a particular job and thereby becomes proficient at the tasks it involves. **Formalized rules** are the standardized procedures and established regulations by which a bureaucracy conducts its operations. Formalized rules enable workers to make quick and consistent judgments because decisions are based on preestablished rules rather than on elaborate case-by-case assessments.

These same organizational characteristics are also the source of bureaucracy's pathologies. Administrators perform not as whole persons but as parts of an organizational entity. Their behavior is governed by position, specialty, and rule. At its worst, bureaucracy grinds on, heedless of the interests of its members or their clients. Fixed rules can become an end unto themselves, as anyone who has applied for a driver's license or a student loan knows all too well.

If bureaucracy is an indispensable condition of large-scale organization, gross bureaucratic inefficiency and unresponsiveness are not. At least that is the assumption underlying efforts to strengthen the administration of government, a topic examined later in this chapter.

The Structure of the Federal Bureaucracy

The U.S. federal bureaucracy has roughly 2.5 million employees, who have the responsibility for administering thousands of programs. The president and Congress get far more attention in the news, but the bureaucracy has the more immediate impact on Americans' everyday lives. The federal bureaucracy performs a wide range of functions; for example, it delivers the daily mail, maintains the national forests, administers social security, enforces environmental protection laws, develops the country's defense systems, provides foodstuffs for school lunch programs, and regulates the stock markets.

The U.S. federal bureaucracy is organized along policy lines. One agency handles veterans' affairs, another specializes in education, a third is responsible for agriculture, and so on. No two units are exactly alike. Nevertheless, most of them take one of five general forms: cabinet

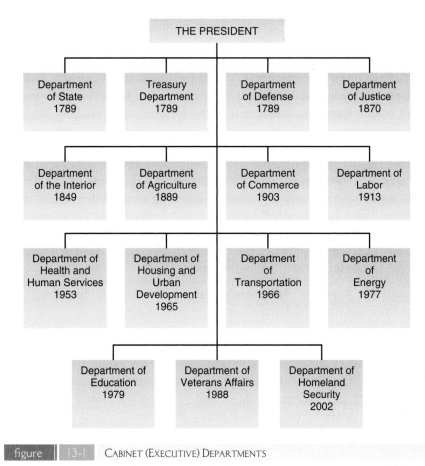

figure   13-1   CABINET (EXECUTIVE) DEPARTMENTS

Each executive department is responsible for a general policy area and is headed by a secretary or, in the case of Justice, the attorney general, who serves as a member of the president's cabinet. Shown is each department's year of origin. (The Office of the Attorney General was created in 1789 and became the Justice Department in 1870.)

department, independent agency, regulatory agency, government corporation, or presidential commission.

Cabinet Departments   The major administrative units are the fifteen **cabinet (executive) departments** (see Figure 13-1). Except for the Department of Justice, which is led by the attorney general, the head of each department is its secretary (for example, the secretary of defense), who also serves as a member of the president's cabinet.

Cabinet departments vary greatly in their visibility, size, and importance. The Department of State, one of the oldest and most prestigious departments, is also one of the smallest, with approximately 25,000 employees. The Department of Defense has the largest workforce, with more than 600,000 civilian employees (apart from the more than 1.4 million uniformed active service members). The Department of Health and Human Services has the largest budget; its activities account for more than a fourth of all federal spending, much of it in the form of social security benefits. The Department of Homeland Security is the newest department, dating from 2002.

Each cabinet department has responsibility for a general policy area, such as defense or law enforcement. This responsibility is carried out within each department by semiautonomous operating units that typically carry the label "bureau," "agency," "division," or "service." The Department of Justice, for example, has thirteen such operating units, including the Federal Bureau of Investigation (FBI), the Civil Rights Division, the Tax Division, and the Drug Enforcement Administration (DEA).

Independent Agencies   **Independent agencies** resemble the cabinet departments but typically have a narrower area of responsibility. They include organizations such as the Central Intelligence Agency (CIA) and the National Aeronautics and Space Administration (NASA). The heads of these agencies are appointed by and report to the president but are not members of the cabinet. In general, the independent agencies exist apart from cabinet departments because their placement within a department would pose symbolic or practical policy problems. NASA, for example, could conceivably be located in the Department of Defense, but such positioning would suggest that the space program exists solely for military purposes and not also for civilian purposes such as space exploration and satellite communication.

Regulatory Agencies   **Regulatory agencies** are created when Congress recognizes the need for ongoing regulation of a particular economic activity. The Securities and Exchange Commission (SEC), which oversees the stock and bond markets, is a regulatory agency. So is the Environmental Protection Agency (EPA), which monitors and prevents industrial pollution. Table 13-1 lists some of the regulatory agencies and other noncabinet units of the federal bureaucracy.

Some regulatory agencies, particularly the older ones (such as the SEC), are headed by a commission of several members who are nominated by the president and confirmed by Congress but who are not subject to removal after they are appointed to office. Commissioners serve for a fixed number of years, a legal stipulation intended to make them "independent" of political pressure. However, the newer regulatory agencies (such as the EPA)

table 13-1	SELECTED U.S. REGULATORY AGENCIES, INDEPENDENT AGENCIES, GOVERNMENT CORPORATIONS, AND PRESIDENTIAL COMMISSIONS
Central Intelligence Agency	National Foundation on the Arts and the Humanities
Commission on Civil Rights	National Labor Relations Board
Consumer Product Safety Commission	National Railroad Passenger Corporation (Amtrak)
Environmental Protection Agency	National Science Foundation
Equal Employment Opportunity Commission	National Transportation Safety Board
Export-Import Bank of the United States	Nuclear Regulatory Commission
Farm Credit Administration	Occupational Safety and Health Review Commission
Federal Communications Commission	Office of Personnel Management
Federal Deposit Insurance Corporation	Peace Corps
Federal Election Commission	Securities and Exchange Commission
Federal Maritime Commission	Selective Service System
Federal Reserve System, Board of Governors	Small Business Administration
Federal Trade Commission	U.S. Arms Control and Disarmament Agency
General Services Administration	U.S. Information Agency
National Aeronautics and Space Administration	U.S. International Trade Commission
National Archives and Records Administration	U.S. Postal Service

Source: The U.S. Government Manual.

lack this independence. They are headed by a single presidential appointee who can be removed at the president's discretion.

Beyond their executive functions, regulatory agencies have legislative and judicial functions. They issue regulations and judge whether individuals or organizations have complied with them. The SEC, for example, can impose fines and other penalties on business firms that violate regulations pertaining to the trading of stocks and bonds.

Government Corporations **Government corporations** are similar to private corporations in that they charge clients for their services and are governed by a board of directors. However, government corporations receive federal funding to help defray operating expenses, and their directors are

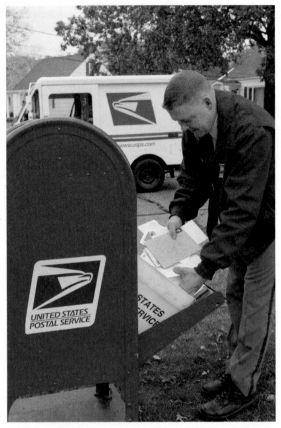

The U.S. Postal Service is regarded by analysts as the best entity of its kind anywhere. It delivers more mail to more addresses than any other postal administration in the world, and does so inexpensively and without undue delay. Yet, like many other government agencies, it is often criticized for its inefficiency and ineptness.

appointed by the president with Senate approval. The largest government corporation is the U.S. Postal Service, with roughly 700,000 employees. Other government corporations include the Federal Deposit Insurance Corporation (FDIC), which insures savings accounts against bank failures, and the National Railroad Passenger Corporation (Amtrak), which provides passenger rail service.

Presidential Commissions   **Presidential commissions** provide advice to the president. Some of them are permanent bodies; examples include the Commission on Civil Rights and the Commission on Fine Arts. Other presidential commissions are temporary and disband after making recommendations on specific issues. An example is the President's Commission to Strengthen Social Security, which was created by President Bush in 2001 to study possible ways of reforming social security.

Federal Employment

The roughly 2.5 million civilian employees of the federal government include professionals who bring their expertise to the problems involved in governing a large and complex society, service workers who perform such tasks as the typing of correspondence and the delivery of mail, and middle and top managers who supervise the work of the various federal agencies.

More than 90 percent of federal employees are hired by merit criteria, which include educational attainment (in the case, for example, of lawyers and engineers), employment experience, and performance on competitive tests (such as the civil service and foreign service examinations). The merit system is intended to protect the public from inept or biased administrative practices that could result if partisanship were the employment criterion.

Federal employees are underpaid in comparison with their counterparts in the private sector. The large majority of federal employees have a GS (Graded Service) job ranking. The regular civil service rankings range from GS-1 (the lowest rank) to GS-15 (the highest). College graduates who enter the federal service usually start at the GS-5 level, which provides an annual salary of roughly $27,000 for a beginning employee. With a master's degree, employees begin at level GS-9 with a salary of roughly $40,000 a year. Federal employees' salaries increase with rank and length of service. Public employees receive substantial fringe benefits, including full health insurance, secure retirement plans, and generous vacation time and sick leave.

Public service has its drawbacks. Federal employees can form labor unions, but their unions by law have limited authority: the government maintains full control of job assignments, compensation, and promotion. Moreover, the Taft-Hartley Act of 1947 prohibits strikes by federal employees and permits the firing of striking workers. When federal air traffic controllers went on strike anyway in 1981, they were fired by President Reagan. There are also limits on the partisan activities of civil servants. The Hatch Act of 1939 prohibited them from holding key positions in election campaigns. In 1993, Congress relaxed this prohibition but retained it for certain high-ranking career bureaucrats.

Government employment is overseen by two independent agencies. The Office of Personnel Management supervises the hiring and job classification of federal employees. The Merit Service Protection Board handles appeals of career civil servants who have been fired or who face other disciplinary action.

The Federal Bureaucracy's Policy Responsibilities

The Constitution mentions executive departments but does not grant them any powers. Their authority derives from grants of power to the three constitutional branches: Congress, the president, and the courts. Nevertheless, the bureaucracy is far more than an administrative extension of the three branches. It exercises considerable power of its own.

Administrative agencies' main job is **policy implementation**—that is, the carrying out of decisions made by Congress, the president, and the courts. Although implementation has been described as "mere administration," it is in fact a creative activity. In the course of their work, administrators develop policy ideas that they then bring to the attention of the White House or Congress. Administrative agencies also make policy in the process of determining how to implement congressional, presidential, and judicial decisions. The Telecommunications Act of 1996, for example, had as its stated goal "to promote competition and reduce regulation in order to secure lower prices and higher quality services for American telecommunication consumers and encourage the rapid deployment of new telecommunications technologies." Although the act included specific provisions, its implementation was left largely to the Federal Communications Commission (FCC) to determine. The FCC ruled, for example, that regional telephone companies (the Bell companies) had to open their networks to AT&T and other competitors at wholesale rates far below what they were charging their retail customers, which enabled these other carriers to compete with the Bell companies for local phone customers. Through this ruling, the FCC was responding to its legislative mandate "to promote competition." However, it was the FCC rather than Congress that determined the wholesale rates and competitors' access to Bell's customers. Such *rulemaking*—establishing how a law will work in practice—is the chief way administrative agencies exercise power over policy.[5]

Agencies also are charged with the delivery of services—carrying the mail, processing welfare applications, approving government loans, and the like. Such activities are governed by rules, and in most instances the rules determine what gets done. But some services give agency employees enough discretion that laws can be applied arbitrarily, a situation that Michael Lipsky describes as "street-level bureaucracy."[6] For example, FBI agents pursue organized crime more vigorously than they pursue white-collar crime, even though the laws do not say that white-collar crime should be treated more lightly.

In sum, administrators exercise discretion in carrying out their responsibilities. They initiate policy, develop it, evaluate it, apply it, and decide whether others are complying with it. The bureaucracy does not simply administer policy; it also *makes policy.*

Development of the Federal Bureaucracy: Politics and Administration

Agencies are responsible for programs that serve society, yet each agency was created and is maintained in response to partisan interests. Each agency thus confronts two simultaneous but incompatible demands: that it administer programs fairly and competently and that it respond to partisan demands.

Historically, this conflict has worked itself out in ways that have made the organization of the modern bureaucracy a blend of the political and the administrative. This dual line of development is reflected in the mix of management systems that characterizes the bureaucracy today—the patronage, merit, and executive leadership systems.

Small Government and the Patronage System

The federal bureaucracy originally was small (three thousand employees in 1800, for instance). The federal government's role was confined mainly to defense and foreign affairs, currency and interstate commerce, and the delivery of the mail. The nation's first six presidents, from George Washington through John Quincy Adams, believed that only distinguished men should be entrusted with the management of the national government. Nearly all top presidential appointees were men of education and political experience, and many of them were members of socially prominent families. They often remained in their positions year after year.

Historical Background

The nation's seventh president, Andrew Jackson, did not share his predecessors' admiration for the social elite. In Jackson's view, government would be more responsive to the public if it were administered by ordinary people of good sense.[7] Jackson also believed that top administrators should remain in office only for short periods to ensure a steady influx of fresh ideas that were consistent with the president's. Jackson's **patronage system** was popular with the general public but opposed by elites, who labeled it a **spoils system**—a device for giving government jobs to friends and party hacks. Although this depiction was not entirely accurate in the case of Jackson's appointees, it was true of those of several later presidents, who extended patronage to all levels of administration without much regard for its impact on governance.

Growth in Government and the Merit System

In the latter part of the 1800s, the federal government began to grow rapidly in size (see Figure 13-2), largely because rapid economic growth was placing new demands on it. Farmers were among the groups clamoring for help from government, and Congress in 1889 created the Department of Agriculture. Business and labor interests also pressed their claims, and in 1903, Congress established the Department of Commerce and Labor to "promote the mutual interest" of the nation's firms and workers. (The separate interests of business and labor proved stronger than their shared concerns, and thus in 1913, Commerce and Labor became separate departments.)

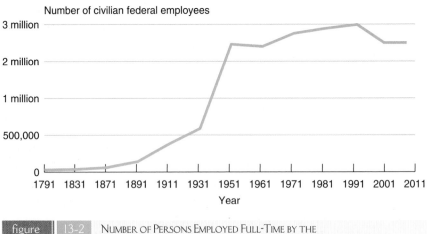

figure ‖ 13-2   NUMBER OF PERSONS EMPLOYED FULL-TIME BY THE
FEDERAL GOVERNMENT

The federal bureaucracy grew slowly until the 1930s, when an explosive growth began in the number of programs that required ongoing administration by the federal government. *Source:* Historical Statistics of the United States and Statistical Abstract of the United States, 1986, 322; recent figures from U.S. Office of Personnel Management. Figure excludes uniformed military personnel.

As government expanded, the need for a more skilled and experienced workforce became apparent. Movement away from the patronage system got a boost when Charles Guiteau, a disappointed officeseeker, assassinated President James A. Garfield in 1881. Two years later, Congress passed the Pendleton Act, which established a **merit (civil service) system** whereby certain federal employees were hired through competitive examinations or by virtue of having special qualifications, such as training in a particular field. The transition to a career civil service was gradual. Only 10 percent of federal positions in 1885 were filled on the basis of merit. But the pace accelerated when the Progressives championed the merit system as a way of eliminating partisan graft and corruption in the administration of government (see Chapter 2). By 1920, as the Progressive Era was concluding, more than 70 percent of federal employees were merit appointees. Since 1950, the proportion of merit employees has never dipped below 80 percent.[8]

The administrative objective of the merit system is **neutral competence.**[9] A merit-based bureaucracy is "competent" in the sense that employees are hired and retained on the basis of their skills, and it is "neutral" in the sense that employees are not partisan appointees and are expected to be of service to everyone, not just those who support the incumbent president. Although the merit system contributes to impartial and proficient administration, it has its own biases and inefficiencies. Career bureaucrats tend to place their agency's interests ahead of those of other agencies and typically oppose efforts to trim their agency's programs. They are not partisans in a Democratic or Republican sense, but they are partisan in terms of protecting their own agencies, as will be explained more fully later in the chapter.

Big Government and the Executive Leadership System

As problems with the merit system surfaced after the early years of the twentieth century, reformers looked to a strengthened presidency—**an executive leadership system**—as a means of coordinating the bureaucracy's activities to increase its efficiency and responsiveness.[10] The president was to provide the general leadership that would overcome agency boundaries. As Chapter 12 describes, Congress in 1939 provided the president with some of the tools needed for improved coordination of the bureaucracy. The Office of Management and Budget (OMB) was created to give the president the authority to coordinate the annual budgetary process. Agencies were required to prepare their budget proposals under the direction of the president, who then submitted the overall budget to Congress for its approval and modification. The president was also authorized to develop the Executive Office of the President, which oversees the agencies' activities on the president's behalf.

Like the merit and patronage systems, the executive leadership system has brought problems as well as improvements to the administration of government. In practice, the executive leadership concept can give the president too much leverage over the bureaucracy and thereby weaken Congress's ability to act as a check on presidential power. A case in point is the intelligence estimates the Bush administration gave Congress while seeking a congressional resolution authorizing a military attack on Iraq. The Bush administration said that the CIA had discovered that Iraq had weapons of mass destruction (WMDs) and was prepared to use them to attack U.S. interests. In his 2003 State of the Union address, President Bush said, "The dictator of Iraq is not disarming. To the contrary, he is deceiving." In a speech to the United Nations, Secretary of State Colin Powell claimed, "The facts on Iraq's behavior demonstrate . . . that Saddam Hussein and his regime are concealing their efforts to produce more weapons of mass destruction."

Yet "the facts" proved othewise. In testimony before Congress in 2004, the chief U.S. weapons inspector in Iraq, David Kay, said that his team had failed to uncover evidence of WMDs in Iraq. This and other revelations produced heated debate over who was to blame for the faulty claim. Did the blame rest largely with the intelligence agencies or with the White House, which had pressured the intelligence agencies to make a strong case for war with Iraq. Many observers blamed both, concluding that the White House had overstated the evidence and that the intelligence agencies had been too eager to tell the White House what it wanted to hear.

Thus, the executive leadership system, like the patronage and merit systems, is not foolproof. It can make bureaucratic agencies overly dependent on the presidency, thereby distorting their activities and reducing congressional checks on executive power. Nevertheless, the executive leadership system is a necessary part of an overall strategy for the effective handling of the bureaucracy. At its best, the system imposes principles of effective management—such as eliminating wasteful duplication—on the work of government agencies.

The federal bureaucracy today embodies aspects of all three systems—patronage, merit, and executive leadership—a situation that reflects the tensions inherent in governmental administration. The bureaucracy is expected to carry out programs fairly and competently (the merit system), but it is also expected to respond to political forces (the patronage system) and to operate efficiently (the executive management system). Table 13-2 summarizes the strengths and weaknesses of each of these administrative systems.

table 13-2	STRENGTHS AND WEAKNESSES OF MAJOR SYSTEMS FOR MANAGING THE BUREAUCRACY	
System	**Strengths**	**Weaknesses**
Patronage	Makes the bureaucracy more responsive to election outcomes by allowing the president to appoint some executive officials.	Gives executive authority to individuals chosen for their partisan loyalty rather than for their administrative or policy expertise; can favor interests that supported the president's election.
Merit	Provides for *competent* administration in that employees are hired on the basis of ability and allowed to remain on the job and thereby become proficient, and provides for *neutral* administration in that civil servants are not partisan appointees and are expected to work in an evenhanded way.	Can result in fragmented, unresponsive administration because career bureaucrats are secure in their jobs and tend to place the interests of their particular agency ahead of those of other agencies or the nation's interests as a whole.
Executive leadership	Provides for presidential leadership of the bureaucracy in order to make it more responsive and to coordinate and direct it (left alone, the bureaucracy tends toward fragmentation).	Can upset the balance between executive and legislative power and can make the president's priorities, not fairness or effective management, the basis for administrative action.

THE BUREAUCRACY'S POWER IMPERATIVE

A common misperception is that the president, as the chief executive, has the sole claim on the bureaucracy's loyalty. In fact, Congress also has reason to claim ownership because it is the source of the bureaucracy's programs and funding. One presidential appointee asked a congressional committee whether it had any problem with his plans to reduce one of his agency's programs. The committee chairman replied, "No, you have the problem, because if you touch that bureau I'll cut your job out of the budget."[11]

The U.S. system of separate institutions sharing power encourages each institution to guard its turf. In addition, the president and members of Congress differ in their constituencies and thus in the interests to which they are most responsive. For example, although the agricultural sector is just one of many concerns of the president, it is of vital interest to senators and representatives from farm states. Finally, because the president and Congress are elected separately, the White House and one or both houses of Congress may be in the hands of opposing parties. Since 1968, this source of executive-legislative conflict has been more the rule than the exception.

If agencies are to operate successfully in this system, they must seek support where they can find it—if not from the president, then from Congress. In other words, agencies have no choice but to play politics.[12] Any agency that sits by idly while other agencies seek support from the White House and Congress is certain to lose out.

The Agency Point of View

Administrators tend to look out for their agency's interests, a perspective that is called the **agency point of view.** This perspective comes naturally to most high-ranking civil servants. More than 80 percent of top bureaucrats reach their high-level positions by rising through the ranks of the same agency.[13] As one top administrator said when testifying before the House Appropriations Committee, "Mr. Chairman, you would not think it proper for me to be in charge of this work and not be enthusiastic about it . . . would you? I have been in it for thirty years, and I believe in it."[14] Studies confirm that bureaucrats believe in the importance of their agency's work. One study found, for example, that social welfare administrators are three times as likely as other civil servants to believe that social welfare programs should be a high policy priority.[15]

Professionalism also cements agency loyalties. High-level administrative positions have increasingly been filled by scientists, engineers, lawyers, educators, physicians, and other professionals. Most of them take jobs in an agency whose mission they support, as in the case of the aeronautical engineers who work for NASA or the doctors who work for the National Institutes of Health (NIH).

Sources of Bureaucratic Power

In promoting their agency's interests, bureaucrats rely on their specialized knowledge, the support of interests that benefit from the programs they run, and the backing of the president and Congress.

⊕ HOW THE UNITED STATES COMPARES

Educational Backgrounds of Bureaucrats

To staff its bureaucracy, the U.S. government tends to hire persons with specialized educations to hold specialized jobs. This approach heightens the tendency of bureaucrats to take the agency point of view. By comparison, Great Britain tends to recruit its bureaucrats from the arts and humanities, on the assumption that general aptitude is the best qualification for detached professionalism. The continental European democracies also emphasize detached professionalism, but in the context of the supposedly impartial application of rules. As a consequence, high-ranking civil servants in Europe tend to have legal educations. The college majors of senior civil servants in the United States and other democracies reflect these tendencies.

College Major of Senior Civil Servants	Norway	Germany	Great Britain	Italy	Belgium	United States
Natural science/ engineering	8%	8%	26%	10%	20%	32%
Social science/ humanities/ business	38	18	52	37	40	50
Law	38	63	3	53	35	18
Other	16	11	19	—	5	—
	100%	100%	100%	100%	100%	100%

Adapted from The Politics of Bureaucracy, 5th ed, by B. Guy Peters. Copyright © 2001 by Routledge. Printed by permission of Thomsen Publishing Services.

The Power of Expertise   Most of the policy problems that the federal government confronts do not lend themselves to simple solutions. Whether the issue is space travel or hunger in America, expert knowledge is essential to the development of effective public policy. Much of this expertise is held by bureaucrats. They spend their careers working in a particular policy area, and many of them have had scientific, technical, or other specialized training (see "How the United States Compares").[16]

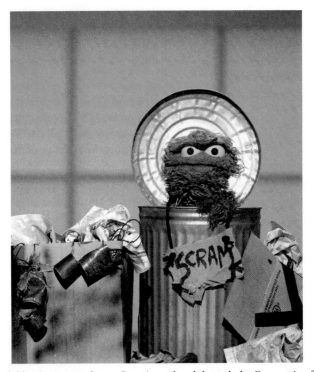

The popular children's program *Sesame Street* is produced through the Corporation for Public Broadcasting, a government agency that gains leverage in budgetary deliberations from its public support. Shown here in a photo of a display at the Smithsonian National Museum of American History is Oscar the Grouch, a *Sesame Street* puppet whose home is a garbage can.

By comparison, elected officials are generalists. To some degree, members of Congress do specialize through their committee work, but they rarely have the time or the inclination to acquire a commanding knowledge of a particular issue. The president's understanding of policy issues is even more general. Not surprisingly, the president and members of Congress rely on the bureaucracy for policy advice and guidance.

All agencies acquire some power through their careerists' expertise. No matter how simple a policy issue may appear at first, it invariably involves more complexity than meets the eye. A recognition that the United States has a trade deficit with China, for example, can be the premise for policy change, but this recognition does not begin to address basic issues such as the form the new policy might take, its probable cost and effectiveness, and its links to other issues, such as America's standing in Asia. Among the officials most likely to understand these issues are the career bureaucrats in the Commerce Department and the Federal Trade Commission.

The Power of Clientele Groups   Most agencies have **clientele groups**—special interests that benefit directly from an agency's programs. Clientele groups assist agencies by placing pressure on Congress and the president to support those programs from which they benefit.[17] For example, when House Speaker Newt Gingrich threatened in 1995 to "zero out" funding for the Corporation for Public Broadcasting, audience members and groups such as the Children's Television Workshop wrote, called, faxed, and cajoled members of Congress, saying that programs like *Sesame Street* and *All Things Considered* were irreplaceable. Within a few weeks, Gingrich had retreated from his position, saying that a complete cessation of funding was not what he had in mind.

In general, agencies both assist and are assisted by the clientele groups that depend on the programs they administer.[18] Many agencies were created for the purpose of promoting particular interests in society. For example, the Department of Agriculture's career bureaucrats are dependable allies of farm interests year after year. The same cannot be said of the president, Congress as a whole, or either political party, all of whom must balance farmers' demands against those of other interests.

The Power of Friends in High Places   Although members of Congress and the president sometimes appear to be at war with the bureaucracy, they need it as much as it needs them. An agency's resources—its programs, expertise, and group support—can assist elected officials in their efforts to achieve their goals. When President George W. Bush in 2001 announced plans for a war on terrorism, he needed the help of careerists in the CIA and the Department of Defense to make his efforts successful. At a time when other agencies were feeling the pinch of a tight federal budget, these agencies received new funding.

Bureaucrats also seek favorable relations with members of Congress. Congressional support is vital because agencies' funding and programs are established through legislation. Agencies that offer benefits to major constituency interests are particularly likely to have close ties to Congress. In some policy areas, more or less permanent alliances—iron triangles—form among agencies, clientele groups, and congressional subcommittees. In other policy areas, temporary issue networks form among bureaucrats, lobbyists, and members of Congress. As explained in Chapters 9 and 11, these alliances are a means by which an agency can gain support from key legislators and groups.

BUREAUCRATIC ACCOUNTABILITY

Even though most Americans say that they have a favorable impression of their most recent personal experience with the bureaucracy (as, say, when a senior citizen applies for social security), they have an unfavorable impression of the bureaucracy as a whole. Along with citizens of other democracies, they see the programs of government bureaucracies as wasteful and inefficient. This view is overly harsh. In areas such as health care and retirement insurance, government bureaucracies are actually more efficient than private organizations. In other areas, efficiency is an inappropriate standard for government programs. The most efficient way to administer government loans to college students, for example, would be to give money to the first students who apply and then close down the program when the money runs out. However, college loan programs, like many other government programs, operate on the principles of fairness and need, which require that each application be judged on its merits.

Studies indicate that the U.S. bureaucracy compares favorably to government bureaucracies elsewhere. "Some national bureaucracies," writes Charles Goodsell, "may be roughly the same [as the U.S. bureaucracy] in quality of overall performance, but they are few in number."[19] Of course, not all U.S. agencies have strong performance records. The Immigration and Naturalization Service (INS) is one agency that has been chronically mismanaged. Yet the performance of many U.S. agencies is superior to that of their counterparts in other industrialized democracies. The U.S. Postal Service, for example, has an on-time and low-cost record that few postal services can match.

Nevertheless, it is easy to see why most Americans hold a relatively unfavorable opinion of the federal bureaucracy. Americans have traditionally mistrusted political power, and the bureaucracy is the symbol of "big government." It is also a convenient target for politicians who claim that "Washington bureaucrats" are wasting taxpayer money. (The irony is that the bureaucracy has no power to create programs or authorize spending; these decisions are made by Congress and the president.)

Adapting the requirements of the bureaucracy to those of democracy is challenging. Bureaucracy is the antithesis of democracy. Bureaucrats are unelected and hold office indefinitely, and they make decisions based on fixed rules rather than on debate and deliberation. This situation raises the question of **bureaucratic accountability**—the degree to which bureaucrats are held accountable for the power they exercise. Bureaucratic accountability occurs primarily through oversight by the president, Congress, and the courts.[20]

Accountability Through the Presidency

The president can only broadly influence, not directly control, the bureaucracy. "We can outlast any president" is a maxim of bureaucratic politics. Each agency has its clientele and its congressional supporters as well as statutory authority for its existence and activities. No president can unilaterally elimi-nate an agency or its funding or programs. Nor can the president be indiffer-ent to the opinions of career civil servants—not without losing their support and expertise in developing and implementing presidential policy objectives.

To encourage the bureaucracy to act responsibly, the president can apply management tools that have developed out of the "executive leadership" concept discussed earlier in this chapter. These tools include reorganiza-tion, presidential appointments, and the executive budget.

Reorganization   The bureaucracy's extreme fragmentation—its hundreds of separate agencies—makes presidential coordination of its activities dif-ficult. Agencies pursue independent and even contradictory paths, resulting in an undetermined amount of waste and duplication of effort. For example, more than one hundred governmental units are responsible for different pieces of federal education policy.

All recent presidents have tried to streamline the bureaucracy and make it more accountable. Such changes seldom greatly improve things, but they can produce marginal gains.[21] For George W. Bush, the challenge came after the terrorist attacks on the World Trade Center and the Pentagon. Breakdowns in the FBI and CIA had undermined whatever chance there might have been to prevent the attacks. These agencies had neither shared nor vigorously pursued the intelligence information they had gathered. Bush decided, and Congress agreed, that a reorganization of the FBI and CIA, as well as the creation of the Department of Homeland Security (DHS), was necessary. Nevertheless, neither the White House nor Congress was under the illusion that this reorganization would fully correct the coordination problems plaguing the agencies accountable for responding to external and internal threats to Americans' safety.[22]

Indeed, the DHS failed miserably in its first big test after the reorganiza-tion. That test came not from terrorists but from Hurricane Katrina, which slammed into the Gulf Coast in 2005, killing hundreds of Americans and dis-placing tens of thousands. One of DHS's agencies, the Federal Emergency Management Agency (FEMA), has responsibility for coordinating disaster response efforts, and its response by all accounts was disorganized and inad-equate. At times, FEMA appeared to know less than the news media about what was happening in the Gulf area. Its communication and transportation systems broke down, resulting in long delays in providing relief assistance. FEMA's director, Michael Brown, did not even keep his boss, DHS secretary Michael Chertoff, informed of his actions, telling Congress months later that doing so would have been "a waste of time" because the DHS did not have the needed resources. Brown was fired two weeks into the relief effort, and

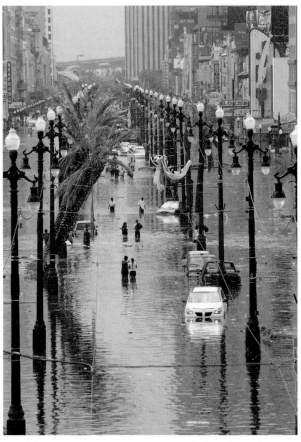

The devastation caused by Hurricane Katrina in 2005 overwhelmed the capacity of the nation's governments, leading to widespread criticism of officials at all levels. Shown here is New Orleans' famed Canal Street, covered by floodwaters.

some observers felt that Chertoff's job was saved only to avoid the appearance that the entire department was in disarray.

Presidential Appointments   Although there is almost no direct confrontation with a bureaucrat that a president cannot win, the president does not have time to deal personally with every troublesome careerist or to ensure that the bureaucracy has complied with every presidential order. The president relies on political appointees in federal agencies to ensure that directives are followed.

The power of presidential appointees is greater in those agencies where wide latitude exists in the making of decisions. Although the Social Security Administration (SSA) has a huge budget and makes monthly payments to more than 40 million Americans, the eligibility of recipients is determined by fixed rules. The head of the SSA does not have the option, say, of granting a retiree an extra $100 a month because the retiree is facing financial hardship. In contrast, most regulatory agencies have discretion over regulatory policy, and the heads of these agencies have latitude in their decisions. For example, President Ronald Reagan's appointee to chair the Federal Trade Commission (FTC), James Miller III, was a strong-willed economist who shared Reagan's belief that consumer protection policy had gone too far and was adversely affecting business interests. In Miller's first year as head of the FTC, the commission dropped one-fourth of its pending cases against business firms.[23] Overall, enforcement actions declined by half during Miller's tenure compared with that of his predecessor.

However, as noted in Chapter 12, there are limits to what a president can accomplish through appointments. High-level presidential appointees number in the hundreds, and their turnover rate is high: the average appointee remains in the Administration for less than two years before moving on to other employment.[24] No president can keep track of all appointees, much less instruct them in detail on all intended policies. Moreover, many presidential appointees have little knowledge of the agencies they head, which makes it difficult for them to exercise control. FEMA's fired director, Michael Brown, was appointed to head the agency because of his political connections. He had little management experience and virtually no disaster relief experience before taking up his post at FEMA.

The Executive Budget   Faced with the difficulty of controlling the bureaucracy, presidents have come to rely heavily on their personal bureaucracy, the Executive Office of the President (EOP).

In terms of presidential management, the key unit within the EOP is the Office of Management and Budget (OMB). Funding, programs, and regulations are the mainstays of every agency, and the OMB has substantial influence on each of these areas. No agency can issue a major regulation without the OMB's verification that the regulation's benefits outweigh its costs, and no agency can propose legislation to Congress without the OMB's approval. However, the OMB's greatest influence over agencies derives from its budgetary role. At the start of the annual budget cycle, the OMB assigns each agency a budget limit in accord with the president's instructions. The agency then develops a proposed budget, which is reviewed and revised by the OMB before being included in the budget package that the president sends to Congress (see Table 13-3).

In most cases, an agency's overall budget does not change much from year to year, indicating that a significant portion of the bureaucracy's activities persist regardless of who sits in the White House or Congress. It table 13-3 THE BUDGETARY PROCESS

Bureaucratic agencies are funded through a process that assigns significant roles to the president and Congress, as well as to the agencies themselves. The annual federal budget allocates the hundreds of billions of dollars that support federal agencies and programs. This table provides a simplified step-by-step summary of the process.

1. In the calendar year preceding enactment of the budget, the Office of Management and Budget (OMB) instructs each agency to prepare its budget request within guidelines established by the White House.

2. Agencies work out their budget proposals in line with White House guidelines and their own goals. Once completed, agency proposals are sent to the OMB for review and adjustment to fit the president's goals.

3. In January, the president submits the adjusted budget to Congress.

4. The president's budget is reviewed by the Congressional Budget Office (CBO) and is referred to the House and Senate Budget and Appropriations Committees. The Budget Committees in each chamber then set expenditure ceilings in particular areas, which are voted upon by the members of Congress. Once set (usually in April), the budget ceilings establish temporary limits within which the Appropriations Committees must act.

5. Through subcommittee hearings, the House and Senate Appropriations Committees meet with agency heads and adjust the president's budgetary recommendations to fit congressional goals. Once the Appropriations Committees have completed their work, the proposals are submitted to the full House and Senate for a vote. Differences in the House and Senate versions are reconciled in conference committee.

6. The legislation is sent to the president for approval or veto. Before this point, the White House and Congress will have engaged in intense negotiations to resolve differences in their priorities. If the White House is satisfied with the outcome of the bargaining, the president can be expected to sign the legislation.

7. The new budget takes effect October 1, unless Congress has not completed its work by then or the president exercises the veto. If agreement has not been reached by this date, temporary funding (authorized by Congress and approved by the president) is required to keep the government in operation until a permanent budget can be enacted. If temporary funding is not provided, a shutdown of nonessential government services occurs.

must be noted, however, that the bulk of federal spending is for programs such as social security that, although enacted in the past, enjoy the continuing support of the president, Congress, and the public.

Accountability Through Congress

Congress has powerful means of influencing the bureaucracy. All agencies depend on Congress for their existence, authority, programs, and funding.

The most substantial control that Congress exerts on the bureaucracy is through its power to authorize and fund programs. Without authorization and funding, a program simply does not exist, regardless of the priority an agency claims it deserves. Congress can also void an administrative decision through legislation that instructs the agency to follow a different course of action. However, Congress lacks the time and expertise to work out complex policies down to the last detail.[25] The government would grind to a halt if Congress tried to define fully how federal programs will be designed and run.

Congress also exerts some control through its oversight function, which involves monitoring the bureaucracy's work to ensure its compliance with legislative intent.[26] However, as noted in Chapter 11, oversight is a difficult and relatively unrewarding task, and members of Congress ordinarily place less emphasis on oversight than on their other major duties. Only when an agency has clearly stepped out of line is Congress likely to take decisive corrective action by holding hearings to ask tough questions and to warn of legislative punishment.

Because oversight is burdensome, Congress has shifted much of the responsibility to the Government Accountability Office (GAO). The GAO's primary function once was to keep track of the funds spent within the bureaucracy; it now also monitors whether policies are being implemented as Congress intended. The Congressional Budget Office (CBO) carries out oversight studies as well. When the GAO or CBO uncovers a major problem with an agency's handling of a program, it notifies Congress, which can then take corrective action.

Bureaucrats generally are kept in check by an awareness that misbehavior can trigger a response from Congress. Nevertheless, oversight cannot correct mistakes or abuses that have already occurred. Recognizing this limit on oversight, Congress has devised ways to constrain the bureaucracy *before* it acts. The simplest method is to draft laws that contain very specific provisions that limit bureaucrats' options in implementing policy. Another restrictive device is the **sunset law,** which establishes a specific date when a law will expire unless it is reenacted by Congress. Advocates of sunset laws see them as a means to counter the bureaucracy's reluctance to give up programs that

★ LEADERS

Herbert Hoover
(1874–1964)

Herbert Hoover was president when the Wall Street Crash of 1929 propelled the United States into the Great Depression. Convinced that the free market would correct itself and bring a recovery, Hoover stood by as Americans lost their jobs and their homes until 1932 when they voted him out of office. For such reasons, Hoover is not ranked among the country's top presidents. However, he has been described as the finest bureaucrat America has ever produced. He was in China during the Boxer Rebellion and used the engineering skills he had been taught at Stanford to build barricades that protected his work crew from marauding gangs. He was in London when World War I broke out and was asked to head a relief effort to help 10 million food-starved Belgians. Although Belgium was sandwiched between the British and German armies, Hoover's organizing skills enabled him to dispatch the food, trucks, and ships to get the job done. When the United States entered the war in 1917, Hoover became U.S. Food Administrator, charged with supplying food to the U.S. military and its allies without starving the American public in the process. Hoover developed a campaign—"Food Will Win the War"—that asked Americans to eat less. "Meatless Mondays" was part of it. Domestic food consumption declined by a sixth, enabling the United States to triple its shipments abroad. After the war, Hoover headed the American Relief Organization that was the main supplier of food for more than 300 million people in nearly two dozen countries. Hoover's food packets were the origin of the CARE packages.

When Warren Harding was elected president in 1920, Hoover was appointed to head the Commerce Department, which took on the task of eliminating waste and duplication in industry—for example, by standardizing the size of nuts, bolts, and other parts. He brought statistical methods into the department, arguing that policy decisions should be based on precise analysis, not guesswork. In 1927, Hoover

(continued)

oversaw the nation's response to a devastating Mississippi River flood. A year later, Hoover was elected to the presidency. After his White House years, Hoover stayed active in public life. Presidents Roosevelt and Truman placed him in charge of food and famine relief efforts during and after World War II. In the 1950s, at the request of President Eisenhower, he chaired the first and second Hoover Commissions, which proposed ways to improve the bureaucracy.

have outlived their usefulness. Because members of Congress usually want the programs they create to last far into the future, however, most legislation does not include a sunset provision.

Accountability Through the Courts

The bureaucracy is also overseen by the judiciary. Legally, the bureaucracy derives its authority from acts of Congress, and an injured party can bring suit against an agency on the grounds that it has failed to carry out a law properly. Judges can then order an agency to change its application of the law.[27]

However, the courts have tended to support administrators if their actions seem at all consistent with the laws they are administering. The Supreme Court has held that agencies can apply any reasonable interpretation of statutes unless Congress has specifically stated something to the contrary and that agencies in many instances have wide discretion in deciding whether to enforce statutes.[28] These positions reflect the need for flexibility in administration. The bureaucracy and the courts would both grind to a halt if judges regularly second-guessed bureaucrats' decisions. The judiciary promotes bureaucratic accountability primarily by encouraging administrators to act responsibly in their dealings with the public and by protecting individuals from the bureaucracy's worst abuses. In 1999, for example, a federal court approved a settlement in favor of African American farmers who demonstrated that the Department of Agriculture had systematically favored white farmers in granting federal farm loans.[29]

Accountability Within the Bureaucracy Itself

A recognition of the difficulty of ensuring adequate accountability of the bureaucracy through the presidency, Congress, and the courts has led to the development of mechanisms of accountability within the bureaucracy itself. Two measures—whistle-blowing and demographic representativeness—are particularly noteworthy.

Whistle-Blowing   Although the bureaucratic corruption that is rampant in some countries is relatively uncommon in the United States, a certain amount of waste, fraud, and abuse is inevitable in a bureaucracy as big as that of the federal government. **Whistle-blowing,** the act of reporting instances of official mismanagement, is a potentially effective internal check. To encourage whistle-blowers to come forward with their information, Congress enacted the Whistle Blower Protection Act to protect them against retaliation. Federal law also provides whistle-blowers with financial rewards in some cases.

Nevertheless, whistle-blowing is not for the faint-hearted. Many federal employees are reluctant to report instances of mismanagement because they fear retaliation. Their superiors might claim that they are malcontents or find subtle ways to punish them. Even their fellow employees are unlikely to think highly of "tattletales."

Accordingly, whistle-blowing sometimes does not occur until an employee has left an agency or quit government service entirely. A case in point is former CIA intelligence official John Kiriakou, who said in 2007 that the CIA had used waterboarding to interrograte Abu Zubaydah, a high-ranking leader of Al Qaeda. It was the first such admission by a CIA operative and prompted some CIA officials to demand an FBI investigation of Kiriakou. They withdrew the request upon realizing that an investigation would result in further disclosures that could embarrass the CIA or compromise its mission. (Waterboarding is an interrogation technique in which the person is strapped down with the head inclined downward. Water is then poured over the face, leading to inhalation and a sense of drowning and pending death. The technique was once considered a war crime by the U.S. government and violates the Geneva Conventions on the treatment of detainees.)

Demographic Representativeness   Although the bureaucracy is an unrepresentative institution in the sense that its officials are not elected by the people, it can be representative in the demographic sense. If bureaucrats were a demographic microcosm of the general public, they presumably would treat the various groups and interests in society more fairly.[30]

At present, the bureaucracy is not demographically representative at its top levels (see Table 13-4). About three in every five managerial and professional positions are held by white males. However, the employment status of women and, to a lesser extent, minorities has improved in recent decades, and top officials in the bureaucracy include a greater proportion of women and minorities than is found in Congress or the judiciary. Moreover, if all employees are considered, the federal bureaucracy comes reasonably close to being representative of the nation's population.

| table | 13-4 | FEDERAL JOB RANKINGS (GS) OF VARIOUS DEMOGRAPHIC GROUPS |

Women and minority-group members are underrepresented in the top jobs of the federal bureaucracy, but their representation has been increasing.

	Women's Share		Blacks' Share		Hispanics' Share	
Grade Level*	**1982**	**2002**	**1982**	**2002**	**1982**	**2002**
GS 13–15 (highest ranks)	5%	32%	5%	10%	2%	4%
GS 9–12	20	46	10	16	4	7
GS 5–8	60	67	19	26	4	9
GS 1–4 (lowest ranks)	78	69	23	28	5	8

In general, the higher-numbered grades are managerial and professional positions, and the lower-numbered grades are clerical and manual labor positions.
Source: Office of Personnel Management, 2008.

Demographic representativeness is only a partial answer to the problem of bureaucratic accountability. A fully representative civil service would still be required to play agency politics. The careerists in, say, defense agencies and welfare agencies are similar in their demographic backgrounds, but they differ markedly in their opinions about policy. Each group believes that the goals of its agency should take priority. The inevitability of an agency point of view is the most significant of all political facts about the U.S. federal bureaucracy.

REINVENTING GOVERNMENT?

In *Reinventing Government*, David Osborne and Ted Gaebler argue that the bureaucracy of today was created in response to earlier problems, particularly those spawned by the Industrial Revolution and a rampant spoils system. They claim that the information age requires a different kind of administrative structure, one that is leaner and more responsive. Osborne and Gaebler assert that government should set program standards but should not necessarily take on all program responsibilities. If, for example, a private firm can furnish meals to soldiers at U.S. army posts at a lower cost than the military can provide them, it should be contracted to provide the meals. Osborne and Gaebler also say that administrative judgments should be made at the lowest bureaucratic level feasible. If, for example, Department of Agriculture field agents have the required knowledge to make a certain type of decision, they should be empowered to make it rather than being required to get permission from superiors. Finally, Osborne and Gaebler argue that the bureaucracy should focus on outputs (results) rather than inputs (dollars spent). Federal loans to college students, for example, should be judged by how many students stay in college as a result of these loans rather than by how much money is doled out.[31]

These ideas informed the Clinton administration's National Performance Review (described in this chapter's introduction). Even though the Bush administration decided not to continue the initiative, the NPR's impact is felt through laws and administrative practices established during its tenure. An example is a law that requires agencies to systematically measure their performance by standards such as efficiency, responsiveness, and outcomes.

Some analysts question whether government bureaucracy can or even should be reinvented. They have asked, for example, whether the principles of decentralized management and market-oriented programs are as sound as their advocates claim. A reason for hierarchy is to ensure that decisions made at the bottom of the bureaucracy are faithful to the laws enacted by Congress. Free to act on their own, lower-level administrators, as they did under the spoils system, might favor certain people and interests over others.[32] There is also the issue of the identity of the "customers" in a market-oriented administration.[33] Who are the Security and Exchange Commission's customers? Are they firms, brokerage houses, or shareholders? Won't some agencies inevitably favor their more powerful customers at the expense of their less powerful ones?

Furthermore, there are practical limits on how much the federal bureaucracy can be trimmed. While some activities can be delegated to states and localities and others can be privatized, most of Washington's programs cannot be reassigned. National defense, social security, and Medicare are but three examples, and they alone account for well over half of all federal spending. In addition, the outsourcing of tasks to private contractors does not necessarily result in smaller government or reduced waste. Many contracts are a better deal for the private firms awarded them than for taxpayers. In one case, the GAO found that a contractor was charging the government $86 per sheet for plywood that normally sold for $14 a sheet. Nor does outsourcing necessarily result in better performance. When the space shuttle *Columbia* disintegrated upon reentry in 2003, some analysts suggested that the tragedy was rooted in NASA's decision to assign many of the shuttle program's safety checks to private contractors in order to cut costs.

Thus, although the current debate over the functioning of the federal bureaucracy is unique in its specific elements, it involves long-standing issues. How can the federal government be made more efficient and yet accomplish all that Americans expect of it? How can it be made more responsive and yet act fairly? How can it be made more creative and yet be held accountable? As history makes clear, there are no easy or final answers to these questions.

SUMMARY   Self-Test www.mhhe.com/pattersonwtp8e

Bureaucracy is a method of organizing people and work, based on the principles of hierarchical authority, job specialization, and formalized rules. As a form of organization, bureaucracy is the most efficient means of getting people to work together on tasks of great magnitude and complexity. It is also a form of organization that is prone to waste and rigidity, which is why efforts are always being made to "reinvent" it.

The United States could not be governed without a large federal bureaucracy. The day-to-day work of the federal government, from mail delivery to provision of social security to international diplomacy, is done by the bureaucracy. Federal employees work in roughly four hundred major agencies, including cabinet departments, independent agencies, regulatory agencies, government corporations, and presidential commissions. Yet the bureaucracy is more than simply an administrative giant. Administrators exercise considerable discretion in their policy decisions. In the process of implementing policy, they make important policy and political choices.

Each agency of the federal government was created in response to political demands on national officials. Because of its origins in political demands, the administration of government is necessarily political. An inherent conflict results from two simultaneous but incompatible demands on the bureaucracy: that it respond to the preferences of partisan officials and that it administer programs fairly and competently. This tension is evident in the three concurrent personnel management systems under which the bureaucracy operates: patronage, merit, and executive leadership.

Administrators are actively engaged in politics and policymaking. The fragmentation of power and the pluralism of the American political system result in a contentious policy process, which leads government agencies to compete for the power required to administer their programs effectively. Accordingly, civil servants tend to have an agency point of view: they seek to advance their agency's programs and to repel attempts by others to weaken their position. In promoting their agency, civil servants rely on their policy expertise, the backing of their clientele groups, and the support of the president and Congress.

Administrators are not elected by the people they serve, yet they wield substantial independent power. Because of this, the bureaucracy's accountability is a central issue. The major checks on the bureaucracy are provided by the president, Congress, and the courts. The president has some power to reorganize the bureaucracy and the authority to appoint the political head of each agency. The president also has management tools (such as the executive budget) that can be used to limit administrators' discretion. Congress has influence on bureaucratic agencies through its authorization and funding powers and through various devices (including sunset laws and oversight hearings) that hold administrators accountable for their actions. The judiciary's role in ensuring the bureaucracy's accountability is smaller than that of the elected branches, but the courts do have the authority to force agencies to act in accordance with legislative intent, established procedures, and constitutionally guaranteed rights.

Nevertheless, administrators are not fully accountable. They exercise substantial independent power, a situation not easily reconciled with democratic values. Because of this, and also because of the desire to make the bureaucracy more efficient, there have been numerous efforts over time to reform the bureaucracy. The most recent such effort includes contracting out the work of government to private firms. Like all such efforts, this latest reinvention has solved some problems while creating new ones—an indication of the immensity of the challenge.

KEY TERMS

agency point of view (*p. 476*)
bureaucracy (*p. 462*)
bureaucratic accountability (*p. 480*)
cabinet (executive) departments (*p. 465*)
clientele groups (*p. 479*)
demographic representativeness
 (*p. 489*)
executive leadership system (*p. 473*)
formalized rules (*p. 464*)
government corporations (*p. 467*)
hierarchical authority (*p. 464*)

independent agencies (*p. 466*)
job specialization (*p. 464*)
merit (civil service) system (*p. 473*)
neutral competence (*p. 473*)
patronage system (*p. 472*)
policy implementation (*p. 470*)
presidential commissions (*p. 468*)
regulatory agencies (*p. 466*)
spoils system (*p. 472*)
sunset law (*p. 485*)
whistle-blowing (*p. 488*)

SUGGESTED READINGS

Aberbach, Joel D., and Bert A. Rockman. *In the Web of Politics: Two Decades of the U.S. Federal Executive*. Washington, D.C.: Brookings Institution, 2000. An evaluation of the federal bureaucracy and its evolving nature.

Du Gay, Paul. *The Values of Bureaucracy*. New York: Oxford University Press, 2005. An insightful analysis of how bureaucracies work and the values they embody.

Huber, Gregory A. *The Craft of Bureaucratic Neutrality: Interests and Influence in Governmental Regulation of Occupational Safety*. New York: Cambridge University Press, 2007. An argument that claims political neutrality is the best political strategy, as well as the proper administrative approach, for agencies.

Ketti, Donald F. *System Under Stress: Homeland Security and American Politics*. Washington, D.C.: Congressional Quarterly Press, 2007. An award-winning study of executive reorganization that focuses on the Department of Homeland Security.

Meier, Kenneth J., and Laurence J. O'Toole, Jr. *Bureaucracy in a Democratic State.* Baltimore, Md.: Johns Hopkins University Press, 2006. A careful assessment of the relationship between bureaucracy and democracy.

Osborne, David, and Ted Gaebler. *Reinventing Government: How the Entrepreneurial Spirit Is Transforming the Public Sector.* New York: Addison-Wesley, 1992. The book that Washington policymakers in the 1990s regarded as the guide to transforming the bureaucracy.

Page, Edward C., and Bill Jenkins. *Policy Bureaucracy: Government with a Cast of Thousands.* New York: Oxford University Press, 2005. An assessment of the bureaucracy as a policymaking institution.

Sagini, Meshack M. *Organizational Behavior: The Challenges of the New Millennium.* Lanham, Md.: University Press of America, 2001. A comprehensive assessment of bureaucratic structures and behaviors.

LIST OF WEBSITES

http://www.census.gov/ The website of the Census Bureau, the best source of statistical information on Americans and the government agencies that administer programs affecting them.

http://www.whistleblower.org/ The Government Accountability Project's website is designed to protect and encourage whistle-blowers by providing information and support to federal employees.

http://www.whitehouse.gov/government/cabinet.html A website that lists the cabinet secretaries and provides links to each cabinet-level department.

POLITICS AND THEORY IN PRACTICE

Thinking: What are the major sources of bureaucrats' power? What mechanisms for controlling that power are available to the president and Congress?

Participating: If you are considering a semester or summer internship, you might want to look into working for a federal, state, or local agency. Compared with legislative interns, executive interns are more likely to get paid and to be given significant duties. (Many legislative interns spend the bulk of their time answering phones or responding to mail.) Internship information can often be obtained through an agency's website. You should apply as early as possible; some agencies have application deadlines. You might even consider a career in government. President John F. Kennedy said that government is "the highest calling." Although this view is not widely shared today, government service can be a satisfying career. A 2002 study by Harvard's Kennedy School of Government found that public-sector managers get more intrinsic satisfaction from their work, which focuses on improving public life, than do private-sector managers. For people who want to pursue a government career, a first step is often a master's degree program in public administration or public policy. Many of these programs require only a year of study after the bachelor's degree. For an entry-level employee with a master's degree rather than a bachelor's degree, the initial salary is 40 percent higher. Appointees with master's degrees enter the civil service at a higher rank (GS-9 rather than GS-5) and are placed in positions that entail greater responsibility than those assigned to newly hired appointees with bachelor's degrees. Those who enter the civil service at the higher rank also are more likely to advance to top positions as their careers develop.

Extra Credit

For up-to-the-minute *New York Times* articles, interactive simulations, graphics, study tools, and more links and quizzes, visit the text's Online Learning Center at www.mhhe.com/pattersonwtp8e.

Hurricane Katrina: A Nation Unprepared

By Senate Committee on Homeland
Security and Governmental Affairs

———————

*As a form of organization, bureau-
cracy is unrivaled in its capacity to
undertake large-scale operations.
Yet it is a relatively inflexible form
of organization that can falter when
circumstances require a quick and
adaptive response. By all accounts,
the American bureaucracy failed
when hurricane Katrina hit the Gulf
Coast states in 2005. The following
selection is from a Senate committee's assessment of local, state, and
federal response to that catastrophic
event. It is a story of poor planning,
poor communication, poor coordination, poor execution, and poor leadership. The problem was not solely
a bureaucratic one. It was also the
result of political failure and of the
unprecedented scale of one of the
worst natural disasters in modern
U.S. history. Nevertheless, the human
and property loss was much larger
than it would have been had the bureaucratic response at all levels been
more effective.*

Hurricane Katrina was an extraordinary act
of nature that spawned a human tragedy. It
was the most destructive natural disaster in

American history, laying waste to 90,000
square miles of land, an area the size of the
United Kingdom. In Mississippi, the storm
surge obliterated coastal communities and
left thousands destitute. New Orleans was
overwhelmed by flooding. All told, more
than 1,500 people died. Along the Gulf
Coast, tens of thousands suffered without
basic essentials for almost a week.

But the suffering that continued in the
days and weeks after the storm passed did
not happen in a vacuum; instead, it continued longer than it should have because of—
and was in some cases exacerbated by—the
failure of government at all levels to plan,
prepare for and respond aggressively to the
storm. These failures were not just conspic-
uous; they were pervasive. . . .

While authorities recognized the need
to begin search-and-rescue missions even
before the hurricane winds fully subsided,
other aspects of the response were hin-
dered by a failure to quickly recognize the
dimensions of the disaster. These problems
were particularly acute at the federal level.
The Homeland Security Operations Center
(HSOC)—charged with providing reliable
information to decision makers including the
Secretary and the President—failed to create
a system to identify and acquire all available, relevant information, and as a result
situational awareness was deeply flawed.
With local and state resources immediately
overwhelmed, rapid federal mobilization of
resources was critical. Yet reliable information on such vital developments as the levee
failures, the extent of flooding, and the presence of thousands of people in need of life-
sustaining assistance at the New Orleans

Convention Center did not reach the White House, Secretary Chertoff, or other key officials for hours, and in some cases more than a day. [Michael] Brown [head of the Federal Emergency Management Agency (FEMA)], then in Louisiana, contributed to the problem by refusing to communicate with Secretary Chertoff, opting instead to pass information directly to White House staff. Moreover, even though senior DHS [Department of Homeland Security] officials did receive on the day of landfall numerous reports that should have led to an understanding of the increasingly dire situation in New Orleans, many indicated they were not aware of the crisis until sometime Tuesday morning.

DHS was slow to recognize the scope of the disaster or that FEMA had become overwhelmed. On the day after landfall, DHS officials were still struggling to determine the "ground truth" about the extent of the flooding despite the many reports it had received about the catastrophe; key officials did not grasp the need to act on the less-than-complete information that is to be expected in a disaster. DHS leaders did not become fully engaged in recovery efforts until Thursday, when in Deputy Secretary Michael Jackson's words, they "tried to kick it up a notch"; after that, they did provide significant leadership within DHS (and FEMA) as well as coordination across the federal government. But this effort should have begun sooner. . . .

Overwhelmed by Katrina, the city and state [had] turned to FEMA for help. On Monday, [Louisiana] Governor [Kathleen] Blanco asked Brown for buses, and Brown assured the state the same day that 500 buses were en route to assist in the evacuation of New Orleans and would arrive within hours. In spite of Brown's assurances and the state's continued requests over the course of the next two days, FEMA did not direct the U.S. Department of Transportation to send buses until very early on Wednesday, two days after landfall, and the buses did not begin to arrive at all until Wednesday evening and not in sig-

nificant numbers until Thursday. Concerned over FEMA's delay in providing buses—and handicapped by the Louisiana Department of Transportation and Development's utter failure to make any preparation to carry out its lead role for evacuation under the state's emergency plan—Governor Blanco directed members of her office to begin locating buses on Tuesday and approved an effort to commandeer school buses for evacuation on Wednesday. But these efforts were too little, too late. Tens of thousands of people were forced to wait in unspeakably horrible conditions until as late as Saturday to be evacuated. . . .

Problems with obtaining, communicating and managing information plagued many other aspects of the response as well. FEMA lacked the tools to track the status of shipments, interfering with the management of supplying food, water, ice and other vital commodities to those in need across the Gulf Coast. So too did the incompatibility of the electronic systems used by federal and state authorities to manage requests for assistance, which made it necessary to transfer requests from the state system to the federal system manually.

Supplies of commodities were especially problematic. Federal shipments to Mississippi did not reach adequate levels until 10 days after landfall. The reasons for this are unclear, but FEMA's inadequate "surge capacity"—the ability to quickly ramp up the volume of shipments—is a likely cause. In both Mississippi and Louisiana, there were additional problems in getting the supplies the "last mile" to individuals in need. Both states planned to make supplies available for pickup at designated distribution points, but neither anticipated the problems people would face in reaching those points, due to impassable roads or other issues. And in Louisiana, the National Guard was not equipped to assume this task. One of Louisiana's greatest shortages was portable toilets, which were requested for the Superdome but never arrived there, as more than 20,000 people were forced to reside inside the Superdome without working plumbing for nearly a week. . . .

By Tuesday afternoon, the New Orleans Superdome had become overcrowded, leading officials to turn additional refugees away. Mayor [Ray] Nagin then decided to open the Morial Convention Center as a second refuge of last resort inside the city, but did not supply it with food or water. Moreover, he communicated his decision to open the Convention Center to state and federal officials poorly, if at all. That failure, in addition to the delay of shipments due to security concerns and DHS's own independent lack of awareness of the situation, contributed to the paucity of food, water, security, or medical care at the Convention Center, as a population of approximately 19,000 gathered there. Those vital commodities and services did not arrive until Friday, when the Louisiana National Guard, assisted by National Guard units from five other states, brought in relief supplies provided by FEMA, established law and order, and then evacuated the Convention Center on Saturday within eight hours. . . .

Federal law-enforcement assistance was too slow in coming, in large part because the two federal Departments charged under the NRP [National Response Plan] with providing such assistance—DHS and the Department of Justice (DOJ)—had done almost no pre-storm planning. In fact, they failed to determine even well into the post-landfall period which of the two departments would assume the lead for federal law enforcement. . . . As a result, later in the week, as federal law-enforcement officers did arrive, some were distracted by a pointless "turf war" between DHS and DOJ over which agency was in the lead. In the end, federal assistance was crucial, but should have arrived much sooner.

What's Your Opinion?

From the information provided here, what do you think was the major source of the failure of government to respond adequately to Katrina: was it mostly a bureaucratic failure, mostly a political failure, or mostly a consequence of the scale of the problem? Are there large lessons about the nature of bureaucracy that you would derive from the Katrina response, recognizing that Katrina was a rare occurrence as opposed to a routine event?

CHAPTER 14

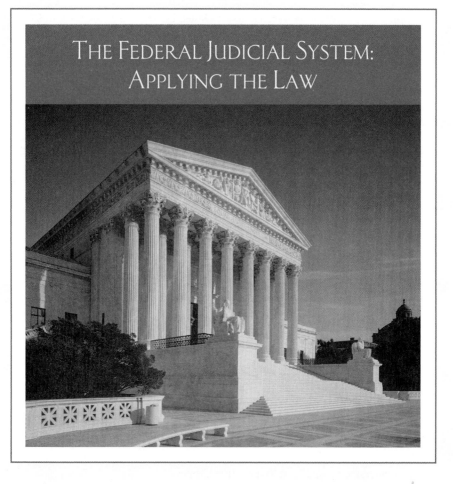

THE FEDERAL JUDICIAL SYSTEM:
APPLYING THE LAW

" It is emphatically the province and duty of the judicial department to say what the law is. Those who apply the rule to particular cases, must of necessity expound and interpret that rule. If two laws conflict with each other, the courts must decide on the operation of each. **"**

JOHN MARSHALL[1]

Through its rulings in *Parents v. Seattle School District* (2007) and *Meredith v. Jefferson County Board of Education* (2007), the Supreme Court effectively ended the use of forced busing of schoolchildren as a means of integrating public schools. At issue were busing programs that the Seattle and Louisville school boards had adopted voluntarily (rather than in response to court order) as a means of creating racially diverse schools. The programs took

race, neighborhood, and student preference into account in school place-
ments. The large majority of students were placed in their school of choice,
but some were assigned elsewhere, an arrangment challenged by white parents whose children did not get their school of choice.

The Supreme Court ruled in their favor, saying their children had been
denied the equal protection guaranteed by the Fourteenth Amendment.
In doing so, the Court reversed longstanding positions. Busing as a means
of integrating public schools dated to the early 1970s, when the Supreme
Court ruled that it was an acceptable means of overcoming the effects of
past discrimination.[2] The Fourteenth Amendment's equal protection clause
had a longer history, having been invoked for the first time in *Brown v.
Board of Education* (1954), which outlawed state laws forcing black children
to attend separate schools from whites.[3]

The Court's rulings in the Seattle and Louisville cases were decided
by a 5-4 vote with the opposing justices taking starkly different positions. Writing for the majority, Chief Justice John Roberts said, "Before
Brown, schoolchildren were told where they could and could not go to
school based on the color of their skin. The school districts in these
cases have not carried the heavy burden of demonstrating that we should
allow this once again—even for very different reasons." Roberts concluded: "The way to stop discrimination on the basis of race is to stop
discriminating on the basis of race." In his dissenting opinion, Justice
John Paul Stevens said there was "a cruel irony" in the majority's use of
the *Brown* decision as an argument against voluntary efforts to achieve
school integration.[4]

The Court's rulings illustrate three key points about court decisions. First,
the judiciary is an important policymaking body. Some of its rulings are as
consequential as a law of Congress or an executive order of the president.
Second, the judiciary has considerable discretion in its rulings. The Seattle
and Lousiville school rulings were not based on any literal reading of the law
or else the justices would have been in full agreement on the proper ruling.
Third, the judiciary is a political as well as legal institution. The busing rulings were a product of contending political forces, had political content, and
were decided by political appointees.

This chapter describes the federal judiciary and the work of its judges
and justices. Like the executive and legislative branches, the judiciary is
an independent branch of the U.S. government, but unlike the two other
branches, its top officials are not elected by the people. The judiciary is not
a democratic institution, and its role is different from and, in some areas,
more contentious than the roles of the executive and legislative branches.

This chapter explores this issue in the process of discussing the following main points:

★ *The federal judiciary includes the Supreme Court of the United States, which functions mainly as an appellate court; courts of appeals, which hear appeals; and district courts, which hold trials.* Each state has a court system of its own, which for the most part is independent of supervision by the federal courts.

★ *Judicial decisions are constrained by applicable constitutional law, statutory and administrative law, and precedent.* Nevertheless, political factors have a major influence on judicial appointments and decisions; judges are political officials as well as legal ones.

★ *The judiciary has become an increasingly powerful policymaking body in recent decades, raising the question of the judiciary's proper role in a democracy.* The philosophies of judicial restraint and judicial activism provide different answers to this question.

THE FEDERAL JUDICIAL SYSTEM

The Constitution establishes the judiciary as a separate and independent branch of the federal government. The Constitution provides for the Supreme Court of the United States but gives Congress the power to determine the number and types of lower federal courts.

Federal judges are nominated and appointed to office by the president, subject to confirmation by majority vote in the Senate. Unlike the office of president, senator, or representative, the Constitution places no age, residency, or citizenship requirements on the office of federal judge. Nor does the Constitution require judges to have legal training, though by tradition they do. Once seated on the bench, as specified in the Constitution, they "hold their offices during good behavior." This has meant, in effect, that federal judges serve until they die or voluntarily retire. No Supreme Court justice and only a handful of lower-court judges have been removed through impeachment and conviction by Congress, the method of early removal provided for by the Constitution.

The argument for life tenure for federal judges was forcefully made by Alexander Hamilton in *Federalist* No. 78. Responding to arguments by anti-Federalists that unelected, life-appointed judges would be a threat to the republic, Hamilton argued that the judicial branch would be the weakest of the three branches because it had no way to force the other two branches to comply with its rulings. Its authority would rest instead on "judgment"—the reasonableness and evenhandedness of its decisions. The best way to ensure that judicial decisions met this standard, Hamilton claimed, was to grant life tenure to federal judges so that they would be free of immediate political pressure and owe allegiance only to the rule of law.

The Supreme Court of the United States

The Supreme Court of the United States is the nation's highest court. The chief justice of the United States presides over the Supreme Court and, like the eight associate justices, is nominated by the president and is subject to Senate confirmation.

Article III of the Constitution grants the Supreme Court both original and appellate jurisdiction. A court's **jurisdiction** is its authority to hear cases of a particular type. **Original jurisdiction** is the authority to be the first court to hear a case. The Supreme Court's original jurisdiction includes legal disputes involving foreign diplomats and cases in which the opposing parties are state governments. The Court in its history has convened

The Supreme Court's Louisville and Seattle busing decisions in 2007 effectively ended the use of forced busing as a means of integrating public schools, an illustration of the power of the judiciary.

as a court of original jurisdiction only a few hundred times and has rarely done so in recent decades.

The Supreme Court does its most important work as an appellate court. **Appellate jurisdiction** is the authority to review cases that have already been heard in lower courts and are appealed to a higher court by the losing party; these higher courts are called *appeals courts* or *appellate courts*. The Supreme Court's appellate jurisdiction extends to cases arising under the Constitution, federal law and regulations, and treaties. The Court also hears appeals involving legal controversies that cross state or national boundaries. Appellate courts, including the Supreme Court, do not retry cases; rather, they determine whether a trial court acted in accord with applicable law.

Selecting and Deciding Cases   The Supreme Court's power is most apparent when it declares another institution's action to be unconstitutional. This power, called **judicial review**, was first asserted by the Supreme Court in *Marbury v. Madison* (1803), when the Court rebuked both the president and Congress (see Chapter 2). It is a power that the Supreme Court has used sparingly. During its history, it has invoked judicial review in roughly fifteen hundred cases.[5] About 90 percent of these cases have involved actions by state and local governments. Only about 10 percent of the cases have involved action by Congress or the president, an indication that the Supreme Court does not routinely seek confrontations with the other branches of the federal government.

Although judicial review is the most dramatic application of the Supreme Court's power, its primary responsibility is to establish legal precedents that will guide the decisions of lower courts. A **precedent** is a judicial decision that serves as a rule for settling subsequent cases of a similar nature. Lower courts are expected to follow precedent—that is, to resolve cases of a like nature in ways consistent with upper-court rulings.

The Supreme Court's ability to set legal precedent is strengthened by its control over the cases it will hear. Nearly all cases that reach the Supreme Court do so after the losing party in a lower-court case has requested a Supreme Court hearing, which occurs only if at least four of the nine justices agree to hear it. If they do so, a **writ of certiorari** is granted, whereby the lower court is asked to submit a transcript of the case for the Supreme Court to review. Each year roughly eight thousand parties apply for certiorari, but the Court grants certiorari to fewer than a hundred cases.

The Supreme Court is most likely to grant certiorari when the U.S. government through the solicitor general (the high-ranking Justice Department official who serves as the government's lawyer in Supreme Court cases) requests it.[6] The solicitor general tracks cases in which the federal government is a party. When the government loses a case in a lower court, the solicitor general decides whether to appeal it to the Supreme Court. Such cases often make up half or more of the cases the Court hears in a term.

The Supreme Court seldom accepts a routine case, even if the justices believe that a lower court has made a mistake. The Court's job is not to correct the errors of other courts but to resolve substantial legal issues. This broad standard essentially means that a case must center on an issue of significance not merely to the parties involved but to the nation. As a result, most cases heard by the Court raise major constitutional issues, affect the lives of many Americans, address issues that are being decided inconsistently by the lower courts, or involve rulings that conflict with a previous Supreme Court decision. When the Court does accept a case, chances are that most of the justices disagree with the lower court's ruling. About three-fourths of the Supreme Court's decisions have reversed the judgments of lower courts.[7]

Once the Supreme Court accepts a case, it sets a date on which the attorneys for the two sides will present their oral arguments. Strict time limits, usually thirty minutes per side, are imposed on these presentations. Although the oral arguments are a time for the lawyers to highlight their key points and for the justices to raise questions,[8] these arguments are usually less decisive than the lengthy written **brief** each side submits, which contains its full argument.

The oral session is also less important than the **judicial conference** that follows, which is attended only by the nine justices and in which they discuss and vote on the case. The conference's proceedings are secret, which allows the justices to speak freely about a case and to change their minds as the discussion unfolds.[9]

Issuing Decisions and Opinions   After a case has been decided in conference, the Court prepares and issues its ruling, which consists of a decision and one or more opinions. The **decision** indicates which party the Court supports and by how large a margin. The **opinion** explains the reasons behind the decision. The opinion is the most important part of a Supreme Court ruling because it contains the justices' legal reasoning. For example, in the landmark *Brown* opinion, the Court held that government-sponsored school segregation was unconstitutional because it violated the Fourteenth Amendment provision that guarantees equal protection under the law to all citizens. This opinion became the legal basis by which communities throughout the southern states were ordered by lower courts to end their policy of segregating public school students by race.

When a majority of the justices agree on the legal basis of a decision, the result is a **majority opinion**. In some cases there is no majority opinion because

John Marshall
(1755–1835)

John Marshall served thirty-four years as chief justice of the Supreme Court, the longest tenure in that position in U.S. history. Marshall had served for a time as John Adams's secretary of state and in the House of Representatives before being appointed chief justice by Adams. Before Marshall's tenure, the Supreme Court was perceived as a feeble branch of the federal government. Marshall changed that notion. An ardent nationalist who saw himself as a guardian of federal authority, Marshall steered the Court through a series of decisions that established it as a powerful institution and helped lay the foundation for a strong Union. The Supreme Court's ruling in *McCulloch v. Maryland* (1819) affirmed the claims that national law was supreme over conflicting state law and that the federal government's powers were not narrowly constrained by the Constitution.

Despite philosophical differences with the presidents who succeeded Adams, Marshall dominated the Court throughout his long tenure, persuading newly appointed justices to back him on key constitutional issues. Marshall saw himself as a Framer of the Constitution, acting as the ongoing architect of the work begun in Philadelphia during the summer of 1787. Although Marshall was a distant cousin of Thomas Jefferson, the two men were bitter opponents. Marshall's first landmark decision, *Marbury v. Madison* (1803), which established the principle of judicial review, was a rebuke to President Jefferson's executive authority. Their ongoing dispute peaked in 1807 at the trial of Aaron Burr, who was justly accused of treason by the Jefferson administration. Marshall presided over the trial and acquitted Burr, ruling that the word of a single eyewitness was insufficient grounds for conviction.

a majority of the justices agree on the decision but cannot agree on the legal basis for it. The result in such cases is a **plurality opinion,** which presents the view held by most of the justices who side with the winning party. Another type of opinion is a **concurring opinion**, a separate view written by a justice who votes with the majority but disagrees with its reasoning.

Justices on the losing side can write a **dissenting opinion** to explain their reasons for disagreeing with the majority position. Sometimes these dissenting arguments have later become the majority opinion. In a 1942 dissenting opinion, Justice Hugo Black wrote that defendants in state felony trials should have legal counsel even if they cannot afford to pay for it. Two decades later, in *Gideon v. Wainwright* (1963), the Court adopted Justice Black's position.[10]

When part of the majority, the chief justice decides which justice will write the majority opinion. Otherwise, the senior justice in the majority determines the author. Chief justices have often given themselves the task of writing the majority opinion in important cases. John Marshall did so often; *Marbury v. Madison* (1802) and *McCulloch v. Maryland* (1819) were among the opinions he wrote (see Chapters 2 and 3). The justice who writes the Court's majority opinion has the responsibility to express accurately the majority's reasoning. The vote on a case is not considered final until the opinion is written and agreed upon, so plenty of give-and-take can occur during the writing stage.[11] In rare cases, the writing stage has produced a change in the Court's decision. In *Lee v. Weisman* (1992), a case involving prayer at a public school graduation, Justice Anthony Kennedy originally sided with the four justices who said the prayer was allowable. While writing the 5-4 majority opinion, Kennedy found that he could not make a persuasive case for that position. He switched sides, resulting in a 5-4 majority the other way.

Other Federal Courts

There are more than one hundred federal courts but only one Supreme Court, and its position at the top of the judicial system gives the Supreme Court unparalleled importance. It is a mistake, however, to conclude that the Supreme Court is the only court that matters. Judge Jerome Frank once wrote of the "upper-court myth," which is the view that appellate courts, and in particular the Supreme Court, are the only truly significant judicial arena and that lower courts just dutifully follow the rulings handed down by courts at the appellate level.[12] The reality is very different, as the following discussion explains.

U.S. District Courts   The lowest federal courts are the district courts (see Figure 14-1). As noted above, there are nearly one hundred federal district courts altogether—at least one in every state and as many as four in some states. District court judges, who number about seven hundred in all, are appointed by the president with the consent of the Senate. Except for the small number of cases heard by the Supreme Court in its original jurisdiction, the federal district courts are the chief trial courts of the federal system. Nearly all criminal and civil cases arising under federal law are

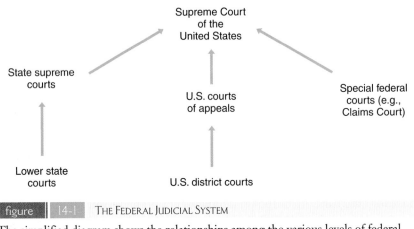

The simplified diagram shows the relationships among the various levels of federal courts and between state and federal courts. The losing party in a case can appeal a lower-court decision to the court at the next-highest level, as the arrows indicate. Decisions normally can be moved from state courts to federal courts only if they raise a constitutional question.

argued first in the district courts. They are the only courts in the federal system where the two sides present their case to a jury for a verdict. Cases at this level are typically presided over by a single judge.

Lower federal courts unquestionably rely on and follow Supreme Court decisions in their own rulings. The Supreme Court reiterated this requirement in a 1982 case, *Hutto v. Davis:* "Unless we wish anarchy to prevail within the federal judicial system, a precedent of this Court must be followed by the lower federal courts no matter how misguided the judges of those courts may think it to be."[13] However, the idea that lower courts are rigidly bound to Supreme Court rulings is part of the upper-court myth. District court judges might misunderstand the Supreme Court's position and deviate from it for that reason. In addition, the facts of a case before a district court are seldom identical to those of a case settled by the Supreme Court. The lower-court judge must decide whether a different legal judgment is appropriate. Finally, it is not unusual for the Supreme Court to issue a general ruling that is ambiguous enough to give lower courts some flexibility in deciding similar cases that come before them.

Most federal cases end with the district court's decision; the losing party does not appeal the decision to a higher court. This fact is another indication of the highly significant role of district court judges.

U.S. Courts of Appeals   When cases are appealed from district courts, they go to a federal court of appeals. These appellate courts are the second level of the federal court system. Courts of appeals do not use juries. Ordinarily, no new evidence is submitted in an appealed case; rather, appellate courts base their decisions on a review of lower-court records. Appellate judges act as supervisors in the legal system, reviewing trial court decisions and correcting what they consider to be legal errors. Facts (that is, the circumstances of a case) found by district courts are ordinarily presumed to be correct.

The United States has thirteen courts of appeals, each of which serves a "circuit" comprised of between three and nine states, except for the circuit that serves the District of Columbia only and the U.S. Court of Appeals for the Federal Circuit, which specializes in appeals involving patents and international trade (see Figure 14-2). Between four and twenty-six judges sit on each court of appeals, but each case usually is heard by a panel of three judges. On rare occasions, all the judges of a court of appeals sit as a body (*en banc*) in order to resolve difficult controversies, typically ones that have resulted

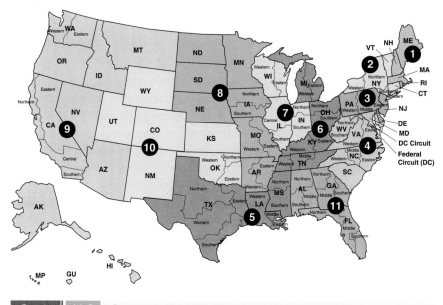

figure   14-2   GEOGRAPHIC BOUNDARIES OF U.S. COURTS OF APPEALS

The United States has thirteen courts of appeals, each of which serves a "circuit." Eleven of these circuit courts serve anywhere from three to nine states, as the map shows. The other two are located in the District of Columbia: the Court of Appeals for the District of Columbia and the Court of Appeals for the Federal Circuit, which specializes in appeals involving patents and international trade. Within each circuit are federal trial courts, most of which are district courts. Each state has at least one district court within its boundaries. Larger states like California (which has four district courts, as can be seen on the map) have more than one. *Source: Administrative Office of the U.S. Courts.*

in conflicting decisions within the same circuit. Each circuit is monitored by a Supreme Court justice, who normally takes the lead in reviewing appeals originating in that circuit. Conflict or inconsistency in how the different circuits are applying a law can lead the Supreme Court to review such cases.

Courts of appeals offer the only real hope of reversal for many appellants, because the Supreme Court hears so few cases. The Supreme Court reviews less than 1 percent of the cases heard by federal appeals courts.

Special U.S. Courts   In addition to the Supreme Court, the courts of appeals, and the district courts, the federal judiciary includes a few specialty courts. Among them are the U.S. Claims Court, which hears cases in which the U.S. government is being sued for damages; the U.S. Court of International Trade, which handles cases involving appeals of U.S. Customs Office rulings; and the U.S. Court of Military Appeals, which hears appeals of military courts-martial. Some federal agencies and commissions also have judicial powers (for example, the issuing of fines), and their decisions can be appealed to a federal court of appeals.

The State Courts

The American states are separate governments within the U.S. political system. The Tenth Amendment protects each state in its sovereignty, and each state has its own court system. Like the federal courts, state court systems have trial courts at the bottom level and appellate courts at the top.

Each state decides for itself the structure of its courts and the method of selecting judges. In some states judges are appointed by the governor, but in most states judgeships are *elective offices.* The most common form involves competitive elections of either a partisan or a nonpartisan nature. Other states use a mixed system called the *merit plan* (also called the "Missouri Plan" because Missouri was the first state to use it) under which the governor appoints a judge from a short list of acceptable candidates provided by a judicial selection commission. The judge selected must then periodically be reviewed by the voters, who, rather than choosing between the judge and an opponent, simply decide by a "yes" or "no" vote whether the judge should be allowed to stay in office (see "States in the Nation").

Besides the upper-court myth, there exists a "federal court myth," which holds that the federal judiciary is the most significant part of the judicial system and that state courts play a subordinate role. This view also is inaccurate. More than 95 percent of the nation's legal cases are decided in state courts. Most crimes (from shoplifting to murder) and most civil controversies (such as divorces and business disputes) are defined by state or local law. Moreover, nearly all cases that originate in state courts end there. The

★ | STATES IN THE NATION

Principal Methods of Selecting State Judges

The states use a variety of methods for selecting the judges on their highest court, including the merit plan, election, and political appointment. The states that appoint judges grant this power to the governor, except in Virginia, Connecticut, and South Carolina, where the legislature makes the choice.

Q: What might explain why several states in the middle of the nation use the merit plan for selecting judges?

A: The merit plan originated in the state of Missouri. Innovations in one state sometimes spread to adjacent states that have similar political cultures.

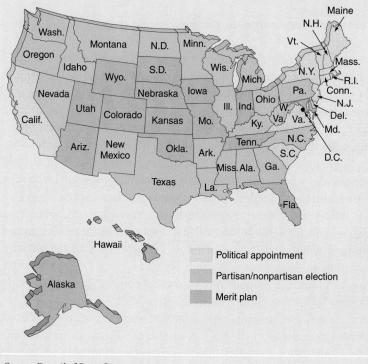

Political appointment

Partisan/nonpartisan election

Merit plan

Source: Council of State Governments.

Texas solicitor general Ted Cruz presents a case before the Supreme Court of Texas. It is one of two high courts in the state and has final say in civil and juvenile cases. The other high court in Texas is the Court of Criminal Appeals, which hears appeals of criminal cases. Each court has nine judges, elected to staggered six-year terms. More than 95 percent of the nation's legal cases are decided entirely by state courts, a refutation of the federal court myth, which wrongly holds that the federal courts are all that matter in the end. The United States has a federal system of government, and the division of power between the national and state governments affects the courts as well as other governing institutions.

federal courts don't come into the picture because the case does not involve a federal issue.

In state criminal cases, after a person has been convicted and after all avenues of appeal in the state court system have been exhausted, the defendant can seek a writ of habeas corpus from a federal court on grounds that a state court made a decision that contravened a provision of the U.S Constitution—as, for example, in a claim that the suspect's Fifth Amendment right to remain silent was violated by state officials (see Chapter 4). If the federal court accepts such an appeal, it ordinarily confines itself to the federal aspects of the matter, such as whether the defendant's constitutional rights were in fact violated. In addition, the federal court accepts the facts determined by the state court unless such findings are clearly in error. Federal courts are also disinclined, when a provision of federal law does not clearly resolve a case, to substitute their own interpretation of a state's constitution for the interpretation provided by the state court. In short, legal and factual determinations of state courts can bind the federal courts—a clear contradiction of the federal court myth.

However, issues traditionally within the jurisdiction of the states can become federal issues through the rulings of federal courts. In its *Lawrence v. Texas* decision in 2003, for example, the Supreme Court invalidated state laws that made it illegal for consenting adults of the same sex to engage in private sexual relations.[14] Earlier, the Court had held that states had the authority to decide whether to prohibit such acts.[15] Lawrence had appealed his conviction in state court as a violation of the due process clause of the Fourteenth

Amendment. The fact that he grounded his appeal in federal law allowed his case to be heard in federal court. And when the Supreme Court then decided in his favor on the basis of the Fourteenth Amendment, federal law became the governing authority in such cases.

FEDERAL COURT APPOINTEES

The quiet dignity of the courtroom and the lack of fanfare with which a court delivers its decisions give the impression that the judiciary is as far removed from the world of politics as a governmental institution can possibly be. In reality, federal judges and justices are political officials who exercise the authority of a separate and powerful branch of government. All federal jurists bring their political views with them to the courtroom and have regular opportunities to promote their political beliefs through the cases they decide. Not surprisingly, the process by which federal judges are appointed is a partisan one.

The Selection of Supreme Court Justices and Federal Judges

The formal method for appointments to the Supreme Court and to the lower federal courts is the same: the president nominates, and the Senate confirms or rejects. Beyond that basic similarity, however, lie significant differences.

Supreme Court Nominees   A Supreme Court appointment is a real opportunity for a president.[16] Most justices retain their positions for many years, enabling presidents to influence judicial policy through their appointments long after they have left office. The careers of some Supreme Court justices provide dramatic testimony to the enduring nature of judicial appointments. For example, Franklin D. Roosevelt appointed William O. Douglas to the Supreme Court in 1939, and for thirty years after Roosevelt's death in 1945, Douglas remained a strong liberal influence on the Court.

Presidents invariably seek nominees who share their political philosophy, but they also must take into account a nominee's acceptability to others. Every nominee is closely scrutinized by the legal community, interested groups, and the media; must undergo an extensive background check by the FBI; and then must gain the approval of a Senate majority. Within the Senate, the key body is the Judiciary Committee, whose members have responsibility for conducting hearings on judicial nominees and recommending their confirmation or rejection by the full Senate.

Nearly 20 percent of presidential nominees to the Supreme Court have been rejected by the Senate on grounds of judicial qualification, political

The justices of the U.S. Supreme Court pose for a photo. From left, they are: Anthony Kennedy, Stephen Breyer, John Paul Stevens, Clarence Thomas, Chief Justice John Roberts, Ruth Bader Ginsburg, Antonin Scalia, Samuel Alito, David Souter.

views, personal ethics, or partisanship. Most of these rejections occurred before 1900, and partisan politics was the main reason. Today a nominee with strong professional and ethical credentials is less likely to be blocked for partisan reasons alone. An exception was Robert Bork, whose 1987 nomination by President Reagan was rejected primarily because of intense opposition to his judicial philosophy from Senate Democrats. On the other hand, nominees can expect confirmation if they have personal integrity and a solid legal record and also show during Senate confirmation hearings the temperament and reasoning expected of a Supreme Court justice. The nomination of John Roberts in 2005 to be chief justice is a case in point. He faced tough questioning during Senate hearings, but nothing startlingly new or disturbing came out, and he was confirmed by a 78-22 vote. Senate hearings held a few months later on the nomination of Samuel Alito, whose past record raised more issues than did that of Roberts, went less smoothly, but he nonetheless was confirmed by a 58-42 vote.

Lower-Court Nominees   The president normally delegates to the deputy attorney general the task of identifying potential nominees for lower-court judgeships, a process that includes seeking recommendations from U.S. senators of the president's party, and sometimes House members as well.

Senatorial courtesy, a tradition that dates back to the 1840s, holds that a senator from the state in which a vacancy has arisen should be consulated on the choice of the nominee if the senator is of the same party as the president.[17] If not consulted, the senator involved can request that confirmation be denied, and other senators will normally grant the request as a "courtesy" to their colleague.

Although the president does not become as personally involved in selecting lower-court nominees as in naming potential Supreme Court justices, lower-court appointments are collectively a significant factor in the impact of a president's administration. Recent presidents have appointed on average more than one hundred judges during a four-year term of office.

Justices and Judges as Political Officials

Presidents generally manage to appoint jurists who have a similar political philosophy. Although Supreme Court justices are free to make their own decisions, their legal positions can often be predicted from their background. A study by judicial scholar Robert Scigliano found that about three of every four appointees have behaved on the Supreme Court approximately as presidents could have expected.[18] Of course, a president has no guarantee that a nominee will fulfill his hopes. For example, Justices Earl Warren and William Brennan proved to be more liberal than President Dwight D. Eisenhower had anticipated. Asked whether he had made any mistakes as president, Eisenhower replied, "Yes, two, and they are both sitting on the Supreme Court."[19]

The Role of Partisanship   Presidents nearly always choose members of their own party as Supreme Court nominees. The same is true of lower-court judgeships. More than 90 percent of recent district and appeals court nominees have been members of the president's political party.[20]

This fact does not mean that federal judges and justices engage in blatant partisanship while on the bench. They are officers of a separate branch of government and prize their judicial independence. All Republican appointees do not vote the same way on cases, nor do all Democratic appointees. Nevertheless, partisanship influences judicial decisions. A study of the voting records of appellate court judges, for example, found that Democratic appointees were more likely than Republican appointees to side with parties that claimed their civil rights or civil liberties had been violated.[21]

Other Characteristics of Judicial Appointees   In recent years, increasing numbers of federal justices and judges have had prior judicial experience; the assumption is that such individuals are best qualified for appointment to the

| table | 14-1 | JUSTICES OF THE SUPREME COURT, 2008 |

Most recent appointees held an appellate court position before being nominated to the Supreme Court.

Justice	Year of Appointment	Nominating President	Position Before Appointment
John Paul Stevens	1975	Ford	Judge, U.S. Court of Appeals
Antonin Scalia	1986	Reagan	Judge, U.S. Court of Appeals
Anthony Kennedy	1988	Reagan	Judge, U.S. Court of Appeals
David Souter	1990	G. H. W. Bush	Judge, U.S. Court of Appeals
Clarence Thomas	1991	G. H. W. Bush	Judge, U.S. Court of Appeals
Ruth Bader Ginsburg	1993	Clinton	Judge, U.S. Court of Appeals
Stephen Breyer	1994	Clinton	Judge, U.S. Court of Appeals
John Roberts Jr.*	2005	G. W. Bush	Judge, U.S. Court of Appeals
Samuel Alito Jr.	2006	G. W. Bush	Judge, U.S. Court of Appeals

*Chief Justice.

federal bench. Most recent appellate court appointees have been district or state judges or have worked in the office of the attorney general.[22] Elective office (particularly a seat in the U.S. Senate) was once a common route to the Supreme Court,[23] but recent justices have typically held an appellate court judgeship before their appointment (see Table 14-1).

White males are greatly overrepresented on the federal bench, just as they dominate in Congress and at the top levels of the executive branch. However, the number of women and minority-group members appointed to federal judgeships has increased significantly in recent decades. The number of such appointees has varied according to which party controls the presidency. Women and minority-group members are key constituencies of the Democratic Party; not surprisingly, Democratic presidents have appointed more judges from these groups than have Republican presidents (see Figure 14-3). Of President Bill Clinton's appointees, for example, roughly 30 per-

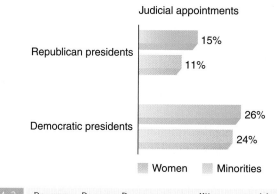

Judicial appointments

figure **14-3** POLITICAL PARTIES, PRESIDENTS, AND WOMEN AND MINORITY JUDICIAL APPOINTEES

Reflecting differences in their parties' coalitions, recent Republican and Democratic presidents have quite different records in terms of the percentage of their judicial appointees who have been women or minority-group members. *Source: Various sources. Data based on appointees of Presidents Carter, Reagan, G. H. W. Bush, Clinton, and G. W. Bush.*

cent were women and 25 percent were members of racial or ethnic minority groups, compared with 20 percent in each category for George W. Bush.

The Supreme Court is less demographically representative than are the lower courts. Of the nine current justices, only one (Ruth Bader Ginsburg) is a woman, and only one (Clarence Thomas) is a minority-group member. The historical pattern is even more one-sided. Until 1916, when Louis D. Brandeis was appointed to the Court, no Jewish justice had ever served. Prior to the twentieth century, only one Catholic, Roger Taney, had served on the Court. Thurgood Marshall in 1967 was the first black justice, and Sandra Day O'Connor in 1981 was the first woman justice. Antonin Scalia in 1986 was the Court's first justice of Italian descent. No person of Hispanic or Asian descent has been appointed to the Supreme Court. Of the Court's current members, five are Catholic, the first time ever that a majority of the justices have not been Protestants.

THE NATURE OF JUDICIAL DECISION MAKING

Federal judges and justices are political officials: they constitute one of three coequal branches of the national government. Yet, unlike members of Congress or the president, judges make their decisions within the context of a legal process. As a consequence, their discretionary power is less than that of elected officials. Article III of the Constitution bars a federal court from issuing a decision except in response to an actual case presented to it. As federal judge David Bazelon noted, a judge "can't wake up one morning and simply decide to give a helpful little push to a school system, a mental hospital, or the local housing agency."[24]

Judicial decisions are also restricted in scope. Technically, a court ruling is binding only on the parties involved. Its broader impact depends on the willingness of others to accept it. If a court were to decide, for example, that a school was bound by law to spend more on programs for the learning disabled, the ruling would extend to other schools in the same situation only if those schools voluntarily complied or were forced by subsequent court action to do so. By comparison, if Congress were to pass legislation granting funds for programs for the learning disabled, all eligible schools would receive the funding.

Another major restriction on the courts is the law itself. Although a president or Congress can make almost any decision that is politically acceptable, the judiciary must justify its decisions in terms of existing provisions of the law. When asked by a friend to "do justice," Justice Oliver Wendell Holmes Jr. said that the law, rather than his inclination, was his guide.[25] In applying the law, judges engage in a creative legal process that requires them to identify the facts of the case, determine and sometimes formulate the relevant legal principles or rules, and then apply these to the case at hand.

The Constraints of the Facts

A basic distinction in any legal case is between "the facts" and "the laws." The **facts** of a case, as determined by trial courts, are the relevant circumstances of a legal dispute or offense. In the case of a person accused of murder, for example, key facts would include evidence about the murder and whether the rights of the accused were respected by police in the course of their investigation. The facts of a case are crucial because they determine which law or laws apply to the case. A murder case cannot be used as an occasion to pronounce judgment on freedom of religion, for example.

The Constraints of the Law

In deciding cases, the judiciary is also constrained by existing **laws.** To use an obvious comparison, the laws that apply to a case of alleged murder differ from those that apply to a case of alleged shoplifting. A judge must treat a murder case as a murder case, applying to it the laws that define murder and the penalties that can be imposed when someone is found guilty of that crime.

Laws fall into three broad categories—civil, criminal, and procedural. **Civil law** governs relations with and between private parties. Marriage, divorce, business contracts, and property ownership are examples of relations covered by civil law. In all states but Massachusetts, for example, civil law limits marriage to a man and a woman; same-sex couples in these states are prohibited by law from marrying. In this example, civil law defines the basis for a legally binding contract. Civil law also applies to disputes between private parties. The courts ordinarily do not get involved in such disputes unless the parties themselves cannot resolve their differences. For example, a dispute in which a homeowner alleges that an insurance company has failed to pay a policy claim could end up in court if they cannot settle it themselves. The losing party in a civil suit might be ordered to pay or otherwise compensate the other party but would not face jail unless he or she refuses to comply with a court order, which can be a punishable offense. Government can also be a party to a civil suit, as when the IRS sues a taxpayer in a dispute over how much the taxpayer owes the government.

Criminal law deals with acts that government defines as illegal and that can result in a fine, imprisonment, or other sanction. Murder, assault, shoplifting, and drunk driving are examples of acts that are covered by criminal law. The government is always a party to a criminal law case; the other party is the individual alleged to have broken the law. (Legal relationships between government and private parties, whether criminal or civil, are defined as *public law. Private law* refers to the legal rights and relationships between private parties.)

Procedural law refers to rules that govern the legal process. In some cases, these rules apply to government, as in the example of the obligation of police to inform suspects of their right to an attorney and to remain silent. In other cases, the rules apply to private parties. For example, in some states, a homeowner cannot take an insurance company to court over a policy claim without first having that claim heard, and possibly resolved, by an arbitration board.

There are three sources of law that constrain the courts: the Constitution, legislative statutes (and the administrative regulations derived from them), and precedents established by previous court rulings (see Table 14-2).

The Constitution and Its Interpretation   The Constitution of the United States is the nation's highest law, and judges and justices are sworn to uphold it. When a case raises a constitutional issue, a court has the duty to apply the Constitution to the case. For example, the Constitution prohibits the states from printing their own currency. If a state decided that it would do so anyway, a federal judge would be obligated to rule against the practice.

Nevertheless, constitutional provisions are open to interpretation in some cases. For example, the Fourth Amendment of the Constitution protects

table	14-2	SOURCES OF LAW THAT CONSTRAIN THE DECISIONS OF THE FEDERAL JUDICIARY

Federal judges make their decisions in the context of law, which limits their discretion. The Constitution, statutes, and precedents are major constraints on the judiciary.

U.S. Constitution: The federal courts are bound by the provisions of the U.S. Constitution. The sparseness of its wording, however, requires the Constitution to be applied in the light of present circumstances. Thus, judges are accorded some degree of discretion in their constitutional judgments.

Statutory law: The federal courts are constrained by statutes and by administrative regulations derived from the provisions of statutes. Most laws, however, are somewhat vague in their provisions and often have unanticipated applications. As a result, judges have some freedom in deciding cases based on statutes.

Precedent: Federal courts tend to follow precedent (or stare decisis), which is a legal principle developed through earlier court decisions. Because times change and not all cases have a clear precedent, judges have some discretion in their evaluation of the way earlier cases apply to a current case.

individuals against "unreasonable searches and seizures," but the meaning of "unreasonable" is not specified. Judges must decide upon its meaning in particular situations. Take, for example, the question of whether wiretapping, which was not invented until 150 years after ratification of the Fourth Amendment, is included in the prohibition on unreasonable searches and seizures. Reasoning that the Fourth Amendment was intended to protect individuals from government snooping into their private lives, judges have ruled that indiscriminate wiretapping is unconstitutional.

Statutes and Administrative Laws, and Their Interpretation   The vast majority of cases that arise in courts involve issues of statutory and administrative law rather than constitutional law. Statutory law is legislative (statute) law. *Administrative law* is based on *statutory law* but is set by government agencies rather than by legislatures. Administrative law consists of the rules, regulations, and judgments that agencies make in the process of implementing and enforcing statutory law.

All federal courts are bound by federal statutory and administrative laws, as well as by treaties, and judges must work within the confines of these laws. A company that is charged with violating an air pollution law, for example, will be judged within the context of that law—what it permits and what it prohibits, and what penalties apply if the company is found to have broken the law. When hearing such a case, judges will often try to determine whether the meaning of the statute or regulation can be determined by common sense (the "plain meaning rule"). The question for the judge is what the law or regulation was intended to safeguard (such as clean air). The law or regulation in most cases is clear enough that when the facts of the case are considered, the decision is fairly predictable. Not all cases, however, are clear-cut in their facts or in the applicable law or laws. Where, for example, do college admissions programs that take race into account cross the line from legal to illegal by placing too much weight on race? In such instances, courts have no choice but to exercise their judgment.

Legal Precedents (Previous Rulings) and Their Interpretation   The U.S. legal system developed from the English common-law tradition, which includes the principle that a court's decision on a case should be consistent with previous judicial rulings. This principle, known as precedent, reflects the philosophy of stare decisis (Latin for "to stand by things that have been settled"). Precedent holds that principles of law, once established, should be applied in subsequent similar cases. Judges and justices often cite past rulings as justification for their decisions in the cases before them.

Precedent is important because it gives predictability to the application of law. Government has an obligation to make clear what its laws are and how they are being applied. If courts routinely ignored how similar cases had been decided in the past, they would create confusion and uncertainty about what is lawful and what is not. A business firm that is seeking to comply with environmental protection laws, for example, can develop company policies that will keep the company safely within the law if court decisions in this area are consistent. If courts routinely ignored precedent, a firm could unintentionally engage in an activity that a court might conclude was unlawful.

POLITICAL INFLUENCES ON JUDICIAL DECISIONS

Although judicial rulings are constrained by existing laws, judges nearly always have some degree of discretion in their decisions.[26] The Constitution is a sparsely worded document and must be adapted to new and changing situations. The judiciary also has no choice at times but to impose meaning on statutory law. Congress cannot always anticipate specific applications of a legislative act, and in these cases it relies on general language to describe the act's purpose. The judiciary must decide what this language means in the context of a specific case arising under the act. Precedent is even less precise as a guide to decisions in that it is specific to particular cases. A new case may differ in important ways from its closest precedent or rest at the intersection of competing precedents.

The Supreme Court's ruling in *Faragher v. City of Boca Raton* (1998), involving sexual harassment in the workplace, illustrates the ambiguity that can exist in the law. The Court developed its ruling in the context of the antidiscrimination provisions of the Civil Rights Act of 1964. However, the act itself contains no description of, or even reference to, job-related sexual harassment. Nevertheless, the act does prohibit workplace discrimination, and the Court was unwilling to dismiss sexual harassment as an irrelevant form of job-related discrimination. In judging the case, the Court had to determine for itself which actions in the workplace are instances of harassment and which are not. In this sense, the Court was "making" law; it was deciding how legislation enacted by Congress applied to behavior that Congress had not specifically addressed when it wrote the legislation.[27]

In sum, judges have leeway in their decisions. As a consequence, their rulings reflect not only legal influences but political ones. Political influences can come from both outside and inside the judicial system.

Outside Influences on Court Decisions

The courts can and do make unpopular choices, but in the long run, judicial decisions must be seen as fair if they are to be obeyed. In other words, the judiciary cannot ignore the expectations of the general public, interest groups, and elected representatives.

Public Opinion and Interest Groups   Judges are responsive to public opinion, although much less so than are elected officials. In some cases, for example, the Supreme Court has tailored its rulings in an effort to gain public support or reduce public resistance. In the *Brown* case, the justices, recognizing that school desegregation would be an explosive issue in the South, required only that desegregation take place "with all deliberate speed" rather than immediately or on a fixed timetable. The Supreme Court typically has stayed close enough to public opinion to avoid massive public resistance to its decisions.[28]

The courts also respond to interest groups, primarily through rulings in the lawsuits filed by them. Some groups rely on lawsuits as their primary political strategy because their issues are more likely to be decided favorably in a court than through an elected institution. An example is

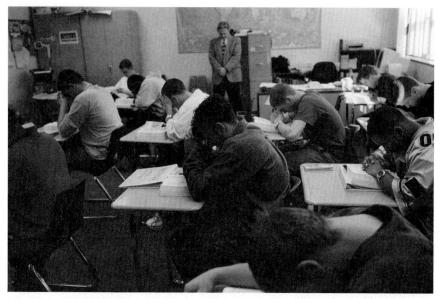

The Supreme Court's power is never more evident than when its strikes down a law passed by Congress or a state legislature on grounds that it violates the Constitution. Over the years, the Court has invalidated a number of state laws that have sought to promote religion in public schools. The Court considers the issue of religion in the schools to be an issue of individual rights rather than of majority rule.

the American Civil Liberties Union (ACLU), which has filed hundreds of lawsuits over the years on issues of individual rights. In 2006, for example, the ACLU filed suit against the Bush administration over its wiretapping of individuals' phone and email messages without obtaining a court order, claiming such action to be a violation of the First and Fourth Amendments. A group can also try to influence the courts by filing an amicus curiae ("friend of the court") brief in which it presents its views on a case in which it is not one of the parties directly involved (see Chapter 9).[29] Groups' influence on the courts has increased in recent decades as a result of both a sharp rise in group activity and the use of more sophisticated judicial strategies. Groups carefully select the cases they pursue, choosing those with the greatest chance of success. They also carefully pick the courts in which they file, because some judges are more sympathetic than others to their particular issue.

Congress and the President   Groups and the general public also make an impact on the judiciary indirectly, through their elected representatives. Both Congress and the president have powerful means of influencing the federal judiciary.

Congress is constitutionally empowered to establish the Supreme Court's size and appellate jurisdiction and can rewrite legislation that it feels the judiciary has misinterpreted. Meanwhile, the president is responsible for enforcing court decisions and has some influence over the issues that come before the courts. Under President Ronald Reagan, for instance, the Justice Department pushed lawsuits that challenged the legality of affirmative action. Judicial appointments also provide the president and Congress with opportunities to influence the judiciary's direction. When Democrat Bill Clinton took office in 1993, more than a hundred federal judgeships were vacant. The first President Bush had expected to win reelection and had not moved quickly to fill vacancies as they arose. As it became apparent that he might lose the election, the Democrat-controlled Congress delayed action on his appointments. This enabled Clinton to fill many of the positions with loyal Democrats. The tables were turned in 2001. Senate Republicans had slowed action on Clinton nominees, enabling George W. Bush to appoint Republicans to existing vacancies when he took office.

In recent decades, the judicial appointment process has been unusually contentious, reflecting both the growing partisanship in Congress (see Chapter 11) and the widening range of issues (everything from abortion to the environment) being fought out in the courts. Nevertheless, the influence of elected officials on the judiciary is never total. Judges prize their independence. The fact that they hold their appointments indefinitely allows them to resist undue pressure from the elected branches of government. In 2004, for example, the Supreme Court, though it was filled with Republican appointees, rejected the Bush administration's claim that U.S. citizens charged with terrorism can be jailed indefinitely without a judicial hearing (see Chapter 4).

Inside Influences: The Justices' Own Political Beliefs

Although the judiciary symbolizes John Adams's characterization of the U.S. political system as "a government of laws, and not of men," judicial rulings are affected by the political beliefs of the men and women who sit on the courts.[30] Most Supreme Court justices do not change their views greatly during their tenure. As a result, major shifts in the Court's positions usually occur when its membership changes. The appointment of Samuel Alito to the Court in 2006 appears to have marked such a shift. Although the justice he replaced, Sandra Day O'Connor, usually voted with the Court's four most conservative justices, she did not invariably do so. She cast the deciding vote, for example, in the 2003 University of Michigan case that upheld affirmative action (see Chapter 5) and in a 2001 Nebraska case that upheld the use of partial-birth abortion when the mother's life is endangered. In contrast, Alito cast the deciding vote in the 2007 Seattle and Lousiville school integration decisions and in the 2007 decision to uphold a congressional ban on the use of partial-birth abortion. These and other Alito decisions prompted liberal and conservative observers alike to say that the Court had swung solidly to the right. Even one of the Supreme Court justices admitted as much. "It is not often in the law," wrote Justice Stephen Breyer, "that so few have so quickly changed so much."[31]

Studies by Jeffrey Segal and Harold Spaeth show that justices generally vote in line with their political attitudes.[32] Nonunanimous decisions of the Supreme Court frequently divide along the same political lines. In most such recent decisions, for example, justices Antonin Scalia and Clarence Thomas, who are Republican appointees, have been opposed by justices Breyer and Ruth Bader Ginsburg, the Court's two Democratic appointees.[33] It is true, of course, that disputes that reach the Supreme Court are anything but clear-cut. If they were, they would have been settled in the lower federal courts. Nevertheless, Supreme Court decisions are a mix of law and politics.

Arguably, partisanship was never more evident than in the Supreme Court's *Bush v. Gore* (2000) decision that blocked a manual recount of the Florida presidential vote in 2000, thereby assuring the election of the Republican nominee, George W. Bush.[34] The five justices in the majority—Chief Justice William Rehnquist and associate justices Sandra Day O'Connor, Anthony Kennedy, Antonin Scalia, and Clarence Thomas—were all Republican appointees and were the same justices who in previous decisions had deferred to state authority and had opposed new applications of the Fourteenth Amendment's equal protection clause. Yet they rejected the authority of the Florida high court, which had ordered a statewide manual recount of the vote. They also employed a never-before-used application of the equal protection clause, ruling that the recount could not go forward because no uniform standard for counting the ballots existed. Justice John Paul Stevens, who thought the Florida high court had acted properly in ordering a recount, accused the Court's majority of devising a ruling based on their partisan desires rather than on the law. Stevens noted that different standards for casting and counting ballots are used throughout the country, even within the same state. Stevens argued that the Supreme Court's majority had ignored "the basic principle, inherent in our Constitution and our democracy, that every legal vote should be counted."[35] Some observers suggested that if Bush had been trailing in the Florida vote, the Court's majority would have come up with reasons why a recount was required.

HOW THE UNITED STATES COMPARES

Judicial Power

U.S. courts are highly political compared to the courts of most other democracies. Because U.S. courts operate in a constitutional system of divided powers, they are required to rule on conflicts between state and nation or between the executive and the legislative branches, which thrusts the judiciary into the middle of political conflicts. It should not be surprising, then, that federal judges and justices are appointed through an overtly political process in which partisan views and activities are major considerations. Many federal judges, particularly at the district level, have no significant prior judicial experience.

The pattern is different in most European democracies, where judgeships tend to be career positions. Individuals are appointed to the judiciary at an early age and then work their way up the judicial ladder largely on the basis of seniority. Partisan politics does not play a large role in judicial appointments.

The power of U.S. courts is nowhere more evident than in the exercise of judicial review—the voiding of a legislative or executive action on the grounds that it violates the Constitution. Judicial review was invented in the United States when, in *Marbury v. Madison* (1803), the Supreme Court declared an act of Congress unconstitutional. Some democracies, including Great Britain, still do not allow broad-scale judicial review, but most democracies now provide for it.

In the so-called American system of judicial review, all judges can declare a law invalid when it conflicts with constitutional provisions. By comparison, the so-called Austrian system restricts judicial review to a special constitutional court. Judges in other courts cannot declare a law void on the grounds that it is unconstitutional: they must apply the law as it is written. In the Austrian system, moreover, constitutional decisions can be made in response to requests for judicial review by elected officials when they are considering legislation. In the American case, judges can act only within the framework of actual legal cases; thus, their rulings are made only after laws have been enacted.

JUDICIAL POWER AND DEMOCRATIC GOVERNMENT

The issue of judicial power is heightened by the fact that federal judges are not elected.[36] The principle of self-government asserts that law-making majorities have the power to decide society's policies. Because the United States has a constitutional system that places checks on the will of the majority, the judiciary clearly has a key role in the system. Nevertheless, there is a basic issue of **legitimacy**—the proper authority of the judiciary in a governing system based on the principle of majority rule.

The Limits of Judicial Power

The judiciary's power has been a source of controversy throughout the nation's history, but the controversies have seldom been livelier than during recent decades. The judiciary at times has acted almost legislatively by defining broad social policies, such as abortion, busing, affirmative action, church-state relations, and prison reform. During the 1990s, for example, the prison systems in forty-two states were operating under federal court orders that mandated improvements in health care or reductions in overcrowding. Through such actions the judiciary has restricted the policymaking authority of the states, has narrowed legislative discretion, and has made judicial action an effective political strategy for certain interests.[37]

The judiciary has become more extensively involved in policymaking for many of the same reasons that Congress and the president have been thrust into new policy areas and become more deeply involved in old ones. Social and economic changes have required government to play a larger role in society, and this development has generated a seemingly endless series of new legal controversies. Environmental pollution, for example, was not a major issue until the 1960s; since then, it has been the subject of numerous court cases.

Nevertheless, judges are not elected by the voters to make law. They are appointed and charged with applying the law. How far should judges go in asserting their interpretations of the law, as opposed to those put into effect by the people's elected representatives? There are competing schools of thought on this issue, none of which is definitive. The Constitution is silent on the question of how it should be interpreted, which has left the judiciary's proper role open to dispute. Nevertheless, it is instructive to review briefly some of the competing theories.

Debating the Judiciary's Proper Role

The doctrine of **judicial restraint** holds that judges should broadly defer to precedent and to decisions made by legislatures. The restraint doctrine holds that in nearly all cases public issues should be decided by elected lawmakers and not appointed judges. The role of judges is to apply the law rather than redefine it. According to the doctrine of judicial restraint, judges should refrain from declaring a law to be unconstitutional unless it clearly conflicts with the Constitution. Advocates of judicial restraint say that when judges substitute their views for those of elected representatives, they undermine the fundamental principle of self-government—the right of popular majorities, through their representatives, to decide the policies by which they will be governed.[38] Deference to Congress or a state legislature recognizes that legislation results from striking a balance between contending interests and that elected representatives, not judges, are in the best position to determine the proper balance. Advocates also claim that restraint serves to maintain public confidence in the judiciary, thereby increasing the likelihood of **compliance** with its decisions—that is, acceptance of and obediance to court rulings.[39]

In contrast, the doctrine of **judicial activism** holds that judges should actively interpret the Constitution, statutes, and precedents in light of established principles when elected representatives fail to act in clear accord with these principles. Although advocates of judicial activism acknowledge the importance of majority rule, they claim that the courts should not be subservient to the decisions of elected officials when core principles are at issue. Judges should not hesitate to override precedent or law when it conflicts with constitutional principles or fails to meet society's vital needs.

Over its history, the Supreme Court has had many proponents of each doctrine. Chief Justice John Marshall was an activist who used the Court to enlarge the judiciary's power and to promote the national government (see Chapters 2 and 3). Judicial review—the most substantial form of judicial power—is not explicitly granted by the Constitution but was claimed through Marshall's opinion in *Marbury v. Madison*. Associate Justice Oliver Wendell Holmes Jr. was Marshall's philosophical opposite, favoring judicial restraint. One of the nation's most influential jurists, Holmes wrote of the need for the judiciary to defer to the elected branches except when they blatantly overstep their authority.[40] Holmes wrote the opinion in *Schenck v. United States* (1919) that upheld a congressional restriction on free speech, despite the First Amendment admonition that Congress shall pass "no law . . . abridging the freedom of speech." Holmes argued that the law in question was aimed at "substantive evils that Congress has a right to prevent" (see Chapter 4).[41]

I was sentenced to the state Penitentiary by the Circuit Court of Bay County, State of Florida. The present proceeding was commenced on a petition for a Writ of Habeus Corpus to the Supreme Court of the State of Florida to vacate the sentence, on the grounds that I was made to stand Trial without the aid of counsel, and, at all times of my incarceretion. The said Court refused To appoint counsel and therefore deprived me of Due process of law, and violate my rights in the Bill of Rights and the constitution of the United states.

5th day of Jan 1962 Petitioner

Notary Public

Gideon's Letter to the Supreme Court
John F. Davis, Clerk, Supreme Court of the United States

The handwritten letter that Clarence Gideon (insert) sent to the Supreme Court in 1962. The letter led eventually to the *Gideon* decision, in which the Court held that states must provide poor defendants with legal counsel (see Chapter 4). Seen by many people at the time as judicial activism, the ruling is now fully accepted.

The Supreme Court as a whole has at times been activist and at other times been restrained. Although judicial activism is sometimes associated with liberal justices, history indicates that justices' partisanship is not a precise predictor of their judicial philosophy. The conservative-dominated Supreme Court in the period between the Civil War and the Great Depression was an activist judiciary, striking down most state and congressional legislation aimed at economic regulation (see Chapter 3). Simlarly, the liberal-dominated Supreme Court in the period after World War II was an activist judiciary, striking down state legislative acts by the dozen in expanding the civil liberties of the criminally accused (see Chapter 4) and the civil rights of black Americans (see Chapter 5). The recent Supreme Court has also been an activist court. In the past dozen years, the Supreme Court has struck down more acts of Congress than were invalidated during the entire previous half-century.[42] Walter Dellinger, a former U.S. solicitor general, said of the Court: "[It] doesn't defer to government at any level. [It] is confident it can come up with the right decisions, and it believes it is constitutionally charged with doing so."[43]

Liberal and conservative justices can be distinguished more clearly by their views on how to interpret the Constitution. **Originalism theory,** a prominent philosophy of conservatives, holds that the Constitution should be interpreted in the way that a reasonable person would have viewed it at the time it was written.[44] Originalists emphasize the wording of the law,

POLITICAL CULTURE
Liberty, Equality, and Self-Government

The Judiciary

The French writer Alexis de Tocqueville observed that there is barely a political controversy in America that sooner or later does not become also a judicial issue. Abortion, age-related discrimination, and Internet content are but a few of the recent examples.

Americans know less about the judiciary than about the elected branches of their government—Congress and the presidency. Nevertheless, when it comes to the protection of their liberty, the judiciary is key. Its power to protect personal freedom is most evident when the Supreme Court strikes down actions taken by elected officials. In most cases, the target of Supreme Court action is not the Congress or the president, but state and local officials. The Supreme Court has struck down well over a thousand state laws and local ordinances, most of which have involved issues of personal freedom, as in *Near v. Minnesota* (freedom of the press) and *Gideon v. Wainwright* (the right to an attorney, even if the defendant is too poor to hire one). That the actions of state and local governments would more often prompt judicial review is hardly surprising. There are fifty state governments and thousands of local governments, compared with a single federal government. Moreover, state and local governments have most of the responsibility for law enforcement and public order, which is where individual rights most frequently collide with authority.

Imagine, as was originally the case, that the Supreme Court had no authority to rule on Bill of Rights issues arising from state and local action. Do you think you would have less liberty in that situation? Why or why not?

arguing that words of the Framers can be plainly understood whereas their intent is hard to determine. The judge's task then is to determine the original meaning of the Constitution's words and, once that is done, to apply that meaning to the case at hand. Current Supreme Court justice Antonin Scalia is an avowed originalist: "You figure out what [the Constitution] was understood to mean when it was adopted and that's the end of it." The difficult part, Scalia claims, comes in trying to figure out what the words meant to those who wrote and ratified them. "It requires immersing oneself in the political and intellectual atmosphere of the time—somehow placing out of mind knowledge that we have which an earlier age did not."[45]

An opposing theory, embraced more often by liberal justices than conservative ones, is the notion that the Constitution is a living document that should be interpreted in light of changing circumstances. Proponents of the **living constitution theory** claim that the Framers, by inserting essential principles and general propositions into the Constitution, intended it to be an adaptable instrument. They cite the preamble of the convention's Committee of Detail, which says the Constitution "ought to be accommodated to times and events." Current Supreme Court justice Stephen Breyer embraces this view, saying that the judiciary should be intent on promoting in today's world the kind of government the Constitution was meant to establish. "The Constitution," Breyer argues, "provides a framework for the creation of democratically determined solutions, which protect each individual's basic liberties and assures that individual equal respect by government, while securing a democratic form of government."[46]

These disputes are philosophical ones. As indicated, the Constitution does not specify a method by which judges should arrive at their decisions. Nevertheless, the disputes are important because they address the question of the role that judges ought to play in a governing system based on the often-conflicting concepts of majority rule and individual rights. The United States is a constitutional democracy that recognizes both the power of the majority to rule and the claim of the minority to protection of its rights. The judiciary was not established as the nation's final authority on all things relating to the uses of political power. Yet the judiciary was established as a coequal branch of government charged with responsibility for protecting individual rights and constraining political authority. The issue of how far the courts should go in asserting their authority is an open one, but it is also an important one for students of American government to ponder.

SUMMARY   Self-Test www.mhhe.com/pattersonwtp8e

At the lowest level of the federal judicial system are the district courts, where most federal cases begin. Above them are the federal courts of appeals, which review cases appealed from the lower courts. The U.S. Supreme Court is the nation's highest court. Each state has its own court system, consisting of trial courts at the bottom and one or two appellate levels at the top. Cases originating in state courts ordinarily cannot be appealed to the federal courts unless a federal issue is involved, and then the federal courts can choose to rule only on the federal aspects of the case. Federal judges at all levels are nominated by the president, and if confirmed by the Senate, they are appointed by the president to the office. Once on the federal bench, they serve until they die, retire, or are removed by impeachment and conviction.

The Supreme Court is unquestionably the most important court in the country. The legal principles it establishes are binding on lower courts, and its capacity to define the law is enhanced by the control it exercises over the cases it hears. However, it is inaccurate to assume that lower courts are inconsequential (the upper-court myth). Lower courts have considerable discretion, and the great majority of their decisions are not reviewed by a higher court. It is also inaccurate to assume that federal courts are far more significant than state courts (the federal court myth).

The courts have less discretionary authority than elected institutions do. The judiciary's positions are constrained by the facts of a case and by the laws as defined through the Constitution, statutes and government regulations, and legal precedent. Yet existing legal guidelines are seldom so precise that judges have no choice in their decisions. As a result, political influences have a strong impact on the judiciary. It responds to national conditions, public opinion, interest groups, and elected officials, particularly the president and members of Congress. Another political influence on the judiciary is the personal beliefs of judges, who have individual preferences that are evident in the way they decide issues that come before the courts. Not surprisingly, partisan politics plays a significant role in judicial appointments.

In recent decades, the Supreme Court has issued broad rulings on individual rights, some of which have required governments to take positive action on behalf of minority interests. As the Court has crossed into areas traditionally left to lawmaking majorities, the legitimacy of its rulings has been questioned. Advocates of judicial restraint claim that the justices' personal values are inadequate justification for exceeding the proper judicial role; they argue that the Constitution entrusts broad issues of the public good to elective institutions and that judicial activism ultimately undermines public respect for the judiciary. Judicial activists counter that the courts were established as an independent branch and should not hesitate to promote new principles when they see a need, even if this action brings them into conflict with elected officials.

KEY TERMS

appellate jurisdiction (*p. 502*)

brief (*p. 503*)

civil law (*p. 516*)

compliance (*p. 526*)

concurring opinion (*p. 504*)

criminal law (*p. 517*)

decision (*p. 503*)

dissenting opinion (*p. 505*)

facts (of a court case) (*p. 516*)

judicial activism (*p. 526*)

judicial conference (*p. 503*)

judicial restraint (*p. 526*)

judicial review (*p. 502*)

jurisdiction (of a court) (*p. 501*)

laws (of a court case) (*p. 516*)

legitimacy (of judicial power) (*p. 525*)

living constitution theory (*p. 529*)

majority opinion (*p. 503*)

opinion (of a court) (*p. 503*)

original jurisdiction (*p. 501*)

originalism theory (*p. 527*)

plurality opinion (*p. 504*)

precedent (*p. 502*)

procedural law (*p. 517*)

senatorial courtesy (*p. 513*)

writ of certiorari (*p. 502*)

SUGGESTED READINGS

Davis, Richard. *Electing Justices: Fixing the Supreme Court Nomination Process.* New York: Oxford University Press, 2005. An examination of the now-contentious process through which Supreme Court justices are nominated and confirmed.

Gillman, Howard. *Votes That Counted: How the Court Decided the 2000 Presidential Election.* Chicago: University of Chicago Press, 2001. An accounting of the *Bush v. Gore* ruling.

Hansford, Thomas G., and James F. Spriggs II. *The Politics of Precedent on the Supreme Court.* Princeton, N.J.: Princeton University Press, 2006. An examination of how the Court interprets precedent to suit new situations and goals.

Maltzman, Forest, Paul Wahlbeck, and James Spriggs. *The Collegial Game: Crafting Law on the U.S. Supreme Court.* New York: Cambridge University Press, 2000. A fascinating look at the strategic considerations that go into Supreme Court justices' interactions and decisions.

McGuire, Kevin T. *Understanding the Supreme Court: Cases and Controversies.* New York: McGraw-Hill, 2002. An overview of Supreme Court decisions and approaches to legal disputes.

O'Brien, David M. *Storm Center: The Supreme Court in American Politics,* 7th ed. New York: Norton, 2005. A thorough assessment of the Supreme Court.

Sandler, Ross, and David Schoenbord. *Democracy by Decree: What Happens When Courts Run Government.* New Haven, Conn.: Yale University Press, 2003. A critical evaluation of the courts' growing policy role.

Segal, Jeffrey A., and Harold J. Spaeth. *The Supreme Court and the Attitudinal Model Revisited.* New York: Cambridge University Press, 2002. A study of inter-justice agreement on Supreme Court decisions that reveals the importance of political attitudes in the Court's rulings.

LIST OF WEBSITES

http://www.cnn.com/CRIME/ A website that allows you to take the facts of actual court cases, examine the law and the arguments, and then decide each case for yourself.

http://www.fjc.gov/ The home page of the Federal Judicial Center, an agency created by Congress to conduct research and provide education on the federal judicial system.

http://www.lib.umich.edu/govdocs/fedjudi.html A University of Michigan web page that provides detailed information on the federal judicial system.

http://www.law.cornell.edu The Cornell University Legal Information Institute's website, includes full-text versions of historic and recent Supreme Court decisions, as well as links to state constitutions and other subjects.

POLITICS IN THEORY AND PRACTICE

Thinking: Which philosophy—judicial restraint or judicial activism—comes closer to your own thinking about the proper role of the courts? Does your support for restraint or activism depend on whether a judicial decision conforms to your own preference on the issue in question?

Participating: The right to a jury trial is one of the oldest features—dating to the colonial period—of the American political experience. Jury trials also offer the average citizen a rare opportunity to be part of the governing structure. Yet Americans increasingly shirk jury duty. When summoned, many of them find all sorts of reasons why they should be excused from jury duty. In some areas of the country, the avoidance rate exceeds 50 percent. Some citizens even give up their right to vote because they know that jurors in their area are selected from names on voter registration lists. There are reasons, however, to look upon jury duty as an opportunity as well as a responsibility. Studies indicate that citizens come away from the jury experience with a fuller appreciation of the justice system. Jurors acquire an understanding of the serious responsibility handed to them when asked to decide upon someone's guilt or innocence. The legal standard in American courts—"guilty beyond a reasonable doubt"—is a solemn one. The fairness of the jury system also requires full participation by the community. Studies show that jurors' life experiences can affect the decisions they reach. If everyone on a jury is from the same background and one that is different from the defendant's, the odds of a wrongful verdict increase. "A jury of one's peers" should mean just that—a jury of individuals who, collectively, represent the range of groups in the community. If you are called to serve on a jury, you should answer the call. You would want nothing less from others if you or one of your family members or friends were the person on trial.

Extra Credit

For up-to-the-minute *New York Times* articles, interactive simulations, graphics, study tools, and more links and quizzes, visit the text's Online Learning Center at www.mhhe.com/pattersonwtp8e.

Judicial Interpretation

By William J. Brennan Jr.

As a legal institution, the Supreme Court operates within the framework of laws. But how fully binding on the Court is the law? In a speech delivered at Georgetown University, the late Justice William Brennan discussed this issue in the context of the Constitution's provisions. Brennan explained the difficulty of discerning the Framers' intentions, beginning with the fact that they frequently disagreed among themselves on the meaning of particular constitutional provisions. He argued that the Constitution cannot mean whatever a momentary majority wants it to mean and claimed that some of its principles (such as checks and balances) are unmistakable. Nevertheless, he embraced the view that the Constitution was meant to be a flexible document that can and must be adapted to meet America's changing needs. Brennan served on the Supreme Court for three decades.

The Constitution is fundamentally a public text—the monumental charter of a government and a people—and a Justice of the Supreme Court must apply it to resolve public controversies. For, from our beginning, a most important consequence of the constitutionally created separation of powers has been the American habit, extraordi-

nary to other democracies, of casting social, economic, philosophical and political questions in the form of lawsuits, in an attempt to secure ultimate resolution by the Supreme Court. . . . Not infrequently, these are the issues upon which contemporary society is most deeply divided. They arouse our deepest emotions. The main burden of my twenty-nine terms on the Supreme Court has thus been to wrestle with the Constitution in this heightened public context, to draw meaning from the text in order to resolve public controversies.

Two other aspects of my relation to this text warrant mention First, constitutional interpretation for a federal judge is, for the most part, obligatory. When litigants approach the bar of court to adjudicate a constitutional dispute, they may justifiably demand an answer. Judges cannot avoid a definitive interpretation because they feel unable to, or would prefer not to, penetrate to the full meaning of the Constitution's provisions. Unlike literary critics, judges cannot merely savor the tensions or revel in the ambiguities inhering in the text—judges must resolve them.

Second, consequences flow from a Justice's interpretation in a direct and immediate way. A judicial decision respecting the incompatibility of Jim Crow with a constitutional guarantee of equality is not simply a contemplative exercise in defining the shape of a just society. It is an order—supported by the full coercive power of the state—that the present society change in a fundamental aspect: . . . More than the litigants may be affected. The course of vital social, economic and political currents may be directed.

These . . . defining characteristics of my relation to the constitutional text—its public nature, obligatory character, and consequentialist aspect—cannot help but influence the way I read that text. When Justices interpret the Constitution they speak for their community, not for themselves alone. The act of interpretation must be undertaken with full consciousness that it is, in a very real sense, the community's interpretation that is sought. Justices are not platonic guardians appointed to wield authority according to their personal moral predilections. Precisely because coercive force must attend any judicial decision to countermand the will of a contemporary majority, the Justices must render constitutional interpretations that are received as legitimate. The source of legitimacy is, of course, a wellspring of controversy in legal and political circles. At the core of the debate is what the late Yale Law School Professor Alexander Bickel labeled "the countermajoritarian difficulty." Our commitment to self-governance in a representative democracy must be reconciled with vesting in electorally unaccountable Justices the power to invalidate the expressed desires of representative bodies on the ground of inconsistency with higher law. . . .

There are those who find legitimacy in fidelity to what they call "the intentions of the Framers." In its most doctrinaire incarnation, this view demands that Justices discern exactly what the Framers thought about the question under consideration and simply follow that intention in resolving the case before them. It is a view that feigns self-effacing deference to the specific judgments of those who forged our original social compact. But in truth it is little more than arrogance cloaked as humility. It is arrogant to pretend that from our vantage we can gauge accurately the intent of the Framers on application of principle to specific, contemporary questions. All too often, sources of potential enlightenment such as records of the ratification debates provide sparse or ambiguous evidence of the original intention. Typically, all that can be gleaned is that the Framers themselves did not agree about the

application or meaning of particular constitutional provisions, and hid their differences in cloaks of generality. Indeed, it is far from clear whose intention is relevant—that of the drafters, the congressional disputants, or the ratifiers in the states—or even whether the idea of an original intention is a coherent way of thinking about a jointly drafted document drawing its authority from a general assent of the states. And apart from the problematic nature of the sources, our distance of two centuries cannot but work as a prism refracting all we perceive. One cannot help but speculate that the chorus of lamentations calling for interpretation faithful to "original intention"—and proposing nullification of interpretations that fail this quick litmus test—must inevitably come from persons who have no familiarity with the historical record. . . .

Another, perhaps more sophisticated, response to the potential power of judicial interpretation stresses democratic theory: because ours is a government of the people's elected representatives, substantive value choices should by and large be left to them. This view emphasizes not the transcendent historical authority of the Framers but the predominant contemporary authority of the elected branches of government. . . .

The view that all matters of substantive policy should be resolved through the majoritarian process has appeal under some circumstances, but I think it ultimately will not do. Unabashed enshrinement of majority would permit the imposition of a social caste system or wholesale confiscation of property so long as a majority of the authorized legislative body, fairly elected, approved. Our Constitution could not abide such a situation. It is the very purpose of a Constitution—and particularly of the Bill of Rights—to declare certain values transcendent, beyond the reach of temporary political majorities. The majoritarian process cannot be expected to rectify claims of minority right that arise as a response to the outcomes of that very majoritarian process. . . .

Faith in democracy is one thing, blind faith quite another. Those who drafted our Constitution understood the difference. One cannot read the text without admitting that it embodies substantive value choices; it places certain values beyond the power of any legislature. Obvious are the separation of powers; the privilege of the Writ of Habeas Corpus; prohibition of Bills of Attainder and *ex post facto* laws; prohibition of cruel and unusual punishments; the requirement of just compensation for official taking of property; the prohibition of laws tending to establish religion or enjoining the free exercise of religion; and, since the Civil War, the banishment of slavery and official race discrimination. With respect to at least such principles, we simply have not constituted ourselves as strict utilitarians. While the Constitution may be amended, such amendments require an immense effort by the People as a whole.

To remain faithful to the content of the Constitution, therefore, an approach to interpreting the text must account for the existence of these substantive value choices, and must accept the ambiguity inherent in the effort to apply them to modern circumstances. . . .

We current Justices read the Constitution in the only way that we can: as Twentieth Century Americans. We look to the history of the time of framing and to the intervening history of interpretation. But the ultimate question must be, what do the words of the text mean in our time? For the genius of the Constitution rests not in any static meaning it might have had in a world that is dead and gone, but in the adaptability of its great principles to cope with current problems and current needs.

Source: From William J. Brennan Jr., "*Judicial Interpretation.*" Address to the Text and Teaching Symposium, Georgetown University, October 12, 1985.

What's Your Opinion?

Justice Brennan's view of constitutional interpretation emphasizes the principles embedded in the Constitution and a need to apply these principles to contemporary problems. Do you agree with this view? Why or why not?

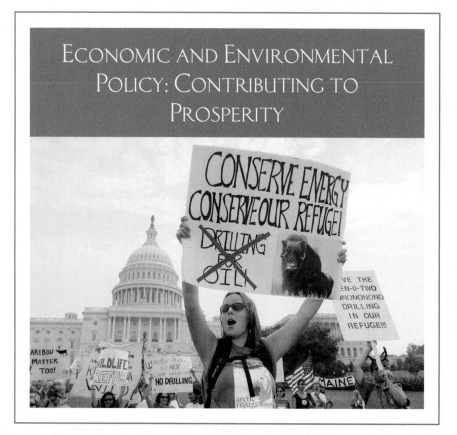

CHAPTER 15

ECONOMIC AND ENVIRONMENTAL POLICY: CONTRIBUTING TO PROSPERITY

66 We the people of the United States, in order to . . . insure domestic tranquility . . . 99

PREAMBLE, U.S. CONSTITUTION

The financial markets in 2008 were downright scary. The U.S. dollar, long the standard of international trade, was weakening dramatically due to excessive consumer and government spending. The stock market, too, was shaky. A few weeks into the year, it had shed all of the gains of the previous year, and then headed lower. The housing market was in turmoil. Home values were dropping at a record pace, as were foreclosures, as homeowners with subprime adjustable rate mortgages increasingly found it difficult to make their monthly payments. Some economists predicted that the United States was entering its steepest downturn since the Great Depression of the 1930s.

Few economists, however, predicted another Great Depression. The reason was simple enough. Back in the early 1930s, there were no government programs in place to stabilize and stimulate the economy. Moreover, the response to the 1929–31 drop in stock prices had worsened the situation. Businesses had cut back on production, investors had fled the stock market, depositors had withdrawn their bank savings, and consumers had slowed their spending—all of which had accelerated the downward spiral. In 2008, on the other hand, government programs were in place to protect depositors' savings, slow the drop in home and stock prices, and steady the economy through adjustments in interest rates and government spending. Among the government initiatives was an economic stimulus bill that gave tax rebates to more than 130 million American households in the expectation they would spend the money, thereby giving the economy a boost.

This chapter examines economic and environmental policy. As was discussed in the first chapter, public policy is a decision by government to follow a course of action designed to produce a particular result. In this vein, economic policy centers on the promotion and regulation of economic interests and, through fiscal and monetary actions, on economic growth and stability. Although the private decisions of firms and individuals are the main force in the American economic system, these decisions are influenced by government policy. Washington seeks to maintain high productivity, employment, and purchasing power; regulates business practices that otherwise would harm the environment or result in economic inefficiency and inequity; and promotes economic interests. The main ideas presented in this chapter are these:

★ *Through regulation, the U.S. government imposes restraints on business activity for the purpose of promoting economic efficiency and equity.* This regulation is often the cause of political conflict, which is both ideological and group-centered.

★ *Through regulatory and conservation policies, the U.S. government seeks to protect and preserve the environment from the actions of business firms and consumers.*

★ *Through promotion, the U.S. government helps private interests achieve their economic goals.* Business in particular benefits from the government's promotional efforts, including, for example, tax breaks and loans.

★ *Through its taxing and spending decisions (fiscal policy), the U.S. government seeks to maintain a level of economic supply and demand that will keep the economy prosperous.*

★ *Through its money supply decisions (monetary policy), the U.S. government— through the Fed—seeks to maintain a level of inflation consistent with sustained, controllable economic growth.*

THE PUBLIC POLICY PROCESS

Government action in the economic sector is part of the **public policy process**—the political interactions that lead to the emergence and resolution of public policy issues. Before examining economic policy, it is helpful to describe the process through which it and other types of policy are developed.

Political scientists have identified three stages that together make up the policy process (see Figure 15-1). The first stage—problem recognition—refers to the emergence of issues. The second stage—policy formation—refers to the formulation and enactment of a policy response to the problem. The third stage—policy implementation—refers to the carrying out of policy.

Problem Recognition

Policy problems stem from conditions of society—the employment rate, the quality of the schools, the security of the nation, the safety of the streets, and so on. Yet only certain conditions will be seen as problems of a *public* nature. Even life-threatening conditions can worsen for years without people thinking of them as anything but a personal problem. Obesity is an example. Americans did not gain dozens of pounds overnight. Rather, over the course of several decades, they slowly got heavier to the point where obesity was a leading cause of poor health. Only recently, after research studies revealed the scope of the problem, have Americans begun to think of obesity as a public policy problem.

In some cases **problem recognition** happens suddenly, even shockingly, as in the case of the terrorist attacks of September 11, 2001, when hatred of the United States by extremist elements abroad—a condition—erupted into a threat to America's long-term security—a policy problem. Yet it ordinarily takes time for people to realize that they have a problem requiring

Problem Recognition	Policy Formation	Policy Implementation
Stage in which conditions in society become seen as policy problems	Stage in which a policy or program is formulated and adopted	Stage in which the adopted policy is put in place and evaluated

figure   15-1   THE PUBLIC POLICY PROCESS

The public policy process refers to the political interactions that lead to the emergence and resolution of public policy issues. The process includes three somewhat distinct stages.

attention. During World War II, Americans of all races fought together against Nazi Germany and its racist ideology. But when the war ended, white Americans initially acted as if nothing in their own society needed correcting. Black Americans knew better. They were still by law shuttled off to separate and inferior public schools and denied entry to white hospitals, restaurants, and theaters. The contradiction was simply too large to be ignored. Within a decade, America had begun to dismantle its system of government-imposed racial segregation.

Policy problems come to public attention in a variety of ways. Interest groups, members of Congress, political parties, and the news media are among the actors that set the policy agenda. By highlighting a problem day after day, for example, the news media can convince people that something needs to be done about it. No agenda setter, however, has a more direct influence than does the president. Even a single presidential pronouncement can trigger a policy response. The AIDS crisis in Africa was far from Americans' minds until January 28, 2003. That evening, in his State of the Union address, President George W. Bush declared that Africa's problem could no longer be ignored. Within months, Congress had appropriated $1.4 billion to fight AIDS in Africa.

Policy Formation

After a policy problem is recognized, the question of how to address it arises. What is the proper policy response? **Policy formation**—the development of a policy for dealing with the problem—is seldom easy.

For one thing, an array of actors are likely to want a say in what gets done. Such actors will include elected officials but could also include interest groups, citizens, and civic organizations. At times, a small set of actors is able to limit what the political scientist E. E. Schattschneider called the "scope of conflict,"[1] thereby effectively deciding among themselves what gets done. Iron triangles (see Chapter 9) are an arrangement of this type. More commonly, the scope of conflict widens, subjecting policymakers to a broader set of influences and forcing them to accommodate a variety of interests.

In addition, because society is complex, most policy problems are intertwined with other problems and issues, and thus cannot be resolved without also taking them into account. Consider, for example, the question of whether government price supports for corn should be increased as a way of easing the economic pressures on corn farmers. Although a subsidy would clearly help corn growers, there are other interests that may or may not be helped by it. How would a subsidy impact on consumers, on farmers' decisions about which crops to plant, on ethanol production, and on the federal deficit? How might such a subsidy affect even foreign policy? Other countries have corn growers who compete in the world market with America's farmers. If U.S. growers are provided a subsidy, they can sell their corn at a lower price, giving them an advantage over other sellers in the world market. Faced with that prospect, foreign governments might decide to subsidize their own corn growers, possibly triggering a trade war. As far-fetched as this example might seem, it approximates what happened in 2006 at the international round of trade talks. After five years of negotiation among scores of countries, the talks collapsed, partly because the United States refused to reduce its hefty farm subsidies.

The complexity of modern policymaking has created an entire industry— that of the policy analyst. Thousands of scholars, consultants, and policy specialists are engaged in formulating solutions to policy problems. Most economic policy, for example, is designed by trained economists. Politicians also formulate policy. They lack the analytic tools of the policy specialists but have their own strength: they have a sense of what other politicians will support. When President Lyndon Johnson decided in 1965 to tackle the issue of public health, some of his advisers wanted him to propose to Congress a government-paid universal health care system like those of Europe. Knowing that congressional conservatives would block it, Johnson pursued a more limited objective that he believed Congress would accept. The result was Medicare and Medicaid, which offer government-provided health care to the elderly and poor, respectively.

Policy formation in the United States takes place through a system of divided powers. To become law, a bill must get majority support in the House and in the Senate and be signed by the president. Unless there is solid support at each stage for the bill, it is unlikely to pass. For this reason, most policies enacted by Congress are the product of considerable bargaining and compromise, and are typically modest in scope. As the political scientist Aaron Wildavsky noted, incremental policies—those that depart only somewhat from existing policy—are the characteristic output of the U.S. policy process.[2]

Policy Implementation

Once a policy is adopted, it has to be put into effect. This stage is the **policy implementation** phase. Responsibility for implementation rests mainly with bureaucrats, who are charged with carrying out the law (see Chapter 13).

It is often assumed that, once a policy has been formulated, the implementation of that policy is clear-cut. The assumption is sometimes warranted.

When Congress in 2008 authorized rebates to taxpayers as a means of stimulating the economy, the implementation—getting the rebate checks into the hands of taxpayers—was time consuming but straightforward. The rebates were based on the income tax returns that had been filed earlier in the year; those taxpayers that met the eligibility criteria were identified by the Internal Revenue Service and received a rebate.

In most cases, however, policy implementation is an open-ended process. Bureaucratic agencies have to decide exactly how a policy will be put into action. In doing so, they may encounter resistance from interests that are adversely affected by the policy. Even interests that benefit from the policy are likely to want a say in how it is carried out. Agencies may also have to take into account local differences when implementing policy. Legislation aimed at improving local transportation poses different implementation problems in Manhattan than in rural Mississippi. And sometimes a bureaucratic agency lacks the resources to implement a policy in the way it was envisioned. When a prescription drug benefit was added to Medicare in 2006, for example, the eligibility rules established by Congress were so intricate that many retirees could not on their own determine how best to obtain the benefit. The bureaucrats in charge of the program were flooded with requests for assistance and lacked the manpower to meet the demand, resulting in delayed or improper responses to the benefit applications of hundreds of thousands of retirees.

Policy evaluation is part of the implementation stage. Sometimes the question of whether a policy is working can be answered in specific terms, such as whether the construction of a new stretch of federal highway is on time and within budget. Many policies, however, are hard to evaluate. An example is foreign economic aid. Economic development in poor countries is subject to so many factors that it is difficult to assess the impact of assistance grants. In such cases, policy evaluation usually centers on how well the program is being administered—for example, whether the money is being channeled to the right places or is finding its way into the pockets of corrupt officials.

In summary, the public policy process is a set of analytically distinct stages that problems go through on their way to some sort of resolution. The problem recognition stage is when conditions in society become seen as public policy problems; the policy formation stage is when a solution is settled upon in the form of a policy or program; and the policy implementation stage is when the adopted policy is put into place and its effectiveness assessed.

We turn now to a particular area of policy—the economy. The discussion will start with regulatory policy and conclude with an explanation of government's efforts to maintain a stable economy.

GOVERNMENT AS REGULATOR OF THE ECONOMY

An **economy** is a system of production and consumption of goods and services that are allocated through exchange. When a shopper buys food at a store, that transaction is one of the millions of economic exchanges that make up the economy.

In *The Wealth of Nations* (1776), Adam Smith advanced the doctrine of **laissez-faire economics,** which holds that private individuals and firms should be allowed to make their own production and distribution decisions. Smith reasoned that firms will supply a good when there is a demand for it (that is, when people are willing and able to buy it). Smith argued that the desire for profit is the "invisible hand" that guides supply decisions in a capitalist system. He acknowledged that the doctrine of laissez-faire capitalism has limits. Certain areas of the economy, such as roadways, are natural monopolies and are better run by government than by private firms. Government is also needed to impose order on private transactions by regulating banking, currency, and contracts. Otherwise, Smith argued, the economy should be left in private hands.

Communism is an alternative to capitalism. In *Das Kapital* (*Capital,* 1867), Karl Marx argued that a free-market system is exploitative because employees work for a wage below the value they add to the market price of the goods they produce. They do the work while the owners reap the profits from their labor. Marx proposed a collective economy in which the workers are also the owners. The former Soviet Union and its satellite countries attempted a variation of the model—firms were put under collective ownership, although ordinary workers had little say in their operation. The Soviet model collapsed because it proved to be an inefficient method for allocating capital and labor and for coordinating the supply of goods with the demand for them.

Today, free-market systems dominate the world economy, although they are mixed systems rather than the pure laissez-faire systems that Smith envisioned. They are called *mixed economies* because, though they center on private firms and transactions, they also assign a substantial role to government. The U.S. economy is no exception. The U.S. government owns some industry (for example, the Tennessee Valley Authority, which produces electricity) and provides some welfare services (for example, the Medicare program). However, in comparison, say, with the Scandinavian countries, where government provides health care to all citizens and controls a number of major industries, including the airlines, the U.S. economy

Microsoft's Bill Gates speaks to an audience about his firm's international scope. Microsoft's large market share and restrictive access policies have made it a target of antitrust action in the United States and abroad. Antitrust policy is designed to improve the efficiency of the market through regulatory action. When a firm is able to control a market, it can charge artificially high prices, which reduces efficiency. Buyers pay more for a good than they would in a market where firms have to compete by offering their product at a price where customers will select it over a competitor's product.

relies more heavily on the free market to make its production, distribution, and consumption decisions.

One way the U.S. government participates in the economy is through the **regulation** of privately owned businesses.[3] U.S. firms are not free to act as they please but rather operate within the constraint of government regulation, which is designed to promote either economic *efficiency* or *equity* (see Table 15-1).

Efficiency Through Government Intervention

Economic efficiency results when firms fulfill as many of society's needs as possible while using as few of its resources as possible.[4] **Efficiency** refers to the relationship of inputs (the labor and material that go into making a product or service) to outputs (the product or service itself). The greater the output for a given input, the more efficient the production process.

| table | 15-1 | THE MAIN OBJECTIVES OF REGULATORY POLICY |

The government intervenes in the economy to promote efficiency and equity.

Objective	Definition	Representative Actions by Government
Efficiency	Fulfillment of as many of society's needs as possible at the cost of as few of its resources as possible. The greater the output for a given input, the more efficient the process.	Preventing restraint of trade; requiring producers to pay the costs of damage to the environment; reducing restrictions on business that cannot be justified on a cost benefit basis.
Equity	When the outcome of an economic transaction is fair to each party.	Requiring firms to bargain in good faith with labor; protecting consumers in their purchases; protecting workers' safety and health.

Preventing Price Fixing   Adam Smith and other classical economists argued that the free market is the optimal means of achieving efficiency. Producers will try to use as few resources as possible in order to keep their prices low so that customers will buy their products. To compete, less efficient producers will have to find a way to cut their production costs or be forced out of business.

However, the assumption that efficiency is inherent in free markets is flawed. The same incentive—the profit motive—that drives producers to keep prices low can drive them to seek a monopoly on a good or to conspire with other producers to fix its price at an artificially high level. If they succeed in this effort, they do not have to be concerned with efficiency because consumers who want or need a good will have no choice but to buy it from them for the asking price.

Price fixing was prevalent in the United States in the late nineteenth century when large trusts came to dominate many areas of the economy, including the oil, steel, railroad, and sugar industries. Railroad companies, for example, had no competition on short routes and charged such high rates that many farmers went broke because they could not afford to ship their crops to markets. In 1887, Congress enacted the Interstate Commerce Act, which created the Interstate Commerce Commission (ICC) and charged it with regulating railroad practices and fares.

Business competition today is regulated by a wide range of federal agencies, including, for example, the Federal Trade Commission (FTC), the Food and Drug Administration (FDA), and the Antitrust Division of the Justice Department. The goal of regulatory activity is to protect consumers by preserving market competition. This does not mean in all cases that government will take action to increase the number of competitors in a particular sector of the economy. The government is inclined to accept concentrated ownership in the oil, automobile, and other industries where the capital costs are so high that it is difficult for small firms to operate, much less compete.[5] Government acceptance of corporate giants also reflects the realization that market competition is no longer simply an issue of domestic firms. For example, the major U.S. automakers—Chrysler, Ford, and General Motors—compete for customers not only with each other but with Asian and European auto manufacturers.

Making Business Pay for Indirect Costs   Economic inefficiencies also result when businesses or consumers fail to pay the full costs of resources used in production. Consider companies whose industrial wastes seep into nearby lakes and rivers. The price of these companies' products does not reflect the cost to society of the resulting water pollution. Economists label these unpaid costs **externalities.**

Until the 1960s, the federal government did not require firms to pay such costs. The impetus to begin doing so came not only from lawmakers but also from the scientific community and environmental groups. The Clean Air Act of 1963 and the Water Quality Act of 1965 required industry to install antipollution devices to keep the discharge of air and water pollutants within specified limits. In 1970, Congress created the Environmental Protection Agency (EPA) to monitor firms and ensure their compliance with federal regulations governing air and water quality and the disposal of toxic wastes. (Environmental policy is discussed more fully later in the chapter.)

Deregulation   Although government regulation is intended to increase economic efficiency, it can have the opposite effect if it unnecessarily increases the cost of doing business.[6] Firms have to expend work hours to monitor and implement government regulations, which in some instances (for example, pollution control) also require companies to buy and install expensive equipment. These costs are efficient to the degree that they produce commensurate benefits. Yet if government places excessive regulatory burdens on firms, they waste resources in the process of complying. The result is higher-priced goods that are more expensive for consumers and less competitive in the domestic and global markets (see "How the United States Compares").

In response to this problem, Congress in 1995 enacted legislation that prohibits administrators in some instances from issuing a regulation unless they can demonstrate that its benefits will outweigh its cost. A more concerted response has been **deregulation**—the rescinding of regulations already in force for the purpose of improving efficiency. This process began in 1977 with passage of the Airlines Deregulation Act, which eliminated government-set airfares and, the requirement that airlines provide service to smaller-sized cities. The change had the intended effect: airfares declined, and competition between airlines increased on routes between larger-sized cities. Congress followed airline deregulation with partial deregulation of the trucking, banking, energy, and communications industries, among others.

Reductions in regulation, however, can be carried too far.[7] Underregulation can result in harmful business practices. The profit motive can lead firms and their executives to act recklessly or illegally.

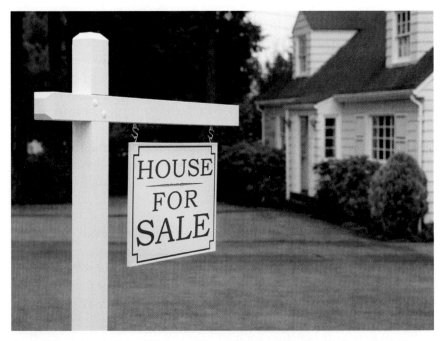

A meltdown in the subprime mortgage sector contributed to falling home prices and a rise in foreclosures. This development rippled through the economy and the financial markets, contributing to an economic downturn in 2008.

HOW THE UNITED STATES COMPARES

Global Economic Competitiveness

The United States ranked first on the World Economic Forum's 2007–8 global economic competitiveness index. The World Economic Forum (WEF) is a private economic research organization that bases its rankings on factors such as a nation's corporate management, finance, institutional openness, government regulation, public infrastructure, science and technology, and labor. Its rankings also reflect the results of an annual survey of roughly ten thousand business executives from around the globe who are asked about their experiences in dealing with various countries and markets.

The United States has been at or near the top of the WEF's rankings for a number of years. It has consistently ranked higher than major economic rivals such as Germany and Japan, whose management, regulatory, and finance systems are more rigid, reducing their capacity to respond flexibly to the global marketplace. The United

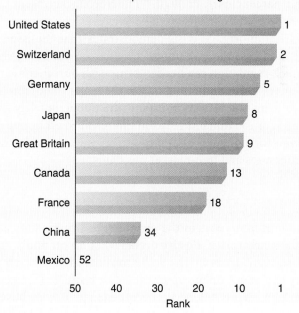

Growth competitiveness ranking

Country	Rank
United States	1
Switzerland	2
Germany	5
Japan	8
Great Britain	9
Canada	13
France	18
China	34
Mexico	52

(continued)

States ranks particularly high on the quality of its technology, management, and finance. A weakness is its labor practices. U.S. workers enjoy fewer protections and benefits (such as health care coverage) than do their counterparts in many other industrialized societies. The 2007–8 survey was conducted before U.S. financial markets declined due to the subprime mortgage crisis and other economic problems.

Companies are more likely to engage in questionable practices when weak regulation leads them to believe they can get away with it. Such was the case with the subprime mortgage crisis that surfaced in 2007. Mortage firms lured marginally qualified homebuyers with low interest rates and small down payments. When the price of homes then began to decline and home buyers were unable to keep up with their mortgage payments, many of them defaulted. The result was a crisis in the financial markets that required a government bailout. In 2008, the U.S. government felt compelled to provide banking and investment firms roughly $1 trillion in loans and buyouts to keep them afloat. Expressing a view held by many Democratic and Republican leaders, Barack Obama said that government had failed to regulate Wall Street closely enough. "The free market," said Obama, "was never meant to be a free license to take whatever you can get."

The subprime mortgage crisis demonstrates that the issue of business regulation is not a simple question of whether or not to regulate. On one hand, too much regulation can burden firms with bureaucratic red tape and costly implementation requirements. On the other hand, too little regulation can give firms the leeway to exploit the public unfairly or recklessly. Either too little or too much regulation can result in economic inefficiency. The challenge for policymakers is to strike the proper balance between regulatory measures and free-market mechanisms.

Equity Through Government Intervention

The government intervenes in the economy to bring equity as well as efficiency to the marketplace. **Equity** occurs when an economic transaction is fair to each party.[8] A transaction can be considered fair if each party enters into it freely and is not unknowingly at a disadvantage (for example, if the seller knows a product is defective, equity requires that the buyer also know of the defect).

An early equity initiative was the creation of the Food and Drug Administration (FDA) in 1907. Because consumers often cannot tell whether foods and drugs are safe to consume, the FDA works to keep adulterated foods and dangerous or ineffective drugs off the market. In the 1930s, financial reforms were among the equity measures enacted under the New Deal. The Securities and Exchange Act of 1934 and the Banking Act of 1934 were designed in part to protect investors and savers from dishonest or imprudent brokers and bankers. The New Deal also provided greater equity for organized labor, which previously had been in a weak position in its dealings with management. The Fair Labor Standards Act of 1938, for example, established a minimum wage and placed limits on the use of child labor.

The 1960s and 1970s produced the greatest number of equity reforms. Ten federal agencies, including the Consumer Product Safety Commission, were established to protect consumers, workers, and the public from harmful business activity. Among the products declared to be unsafe in the 1960s and 1970s were cigarettes, lead paint, and leaded gasoline. The benefits have been substantial. Lead, for example, can cause brain damage in children. In the period since lead paint and leaded gasoline have been banned, the average level of lead in children's blood has dropped by 75 percent.[9]

The Politics of Regulatory Policy

Economic regulation has come in waves, as changes in national conditions have produced bursts of social awareness. The first wave came during the Progressive Era, when reformers sought to stop the unfair business practices of the new monopolies, such as the railroads. The second wave came during the Great Depression, when reformers sought to regulate financial and labor markets.

Although businesses fought the Progressive and New Deal reforms, their opposition was lessened in the long term by the fact that most of the resulting regulation applied to a particular industry rather than to firms of all types. This pattern makes it possible for a regulated industry to gain influence with those officials responsible for regulating it. By cultivating close ties to the FDA, for example, pharmaceutical companies have managed to obtain faster clearance to market new drugs, which are a main source of their profits.[10] In some cases, the FDA's fast-track approval process has been harmful to consumers. The anti-inflammatory drug Vioxx, for example, had to be withdrawn from the market in 2004 after it was found to increase the risk of heart attacks and strokes. Although not all industries have as much leverage as the drug firms with their regulators, it is generally true that industries have not been greatly hampered by the older form of regulation and in many cases have benefited from it.

The third wave of regulatory reform, in the 1960s and 1970s, differed from the Progressive and New Deal phases in both its form and its politics. This third wave has been called the era of "new social regulation" because of the broad social goals it addressed in three policy areas: environmental protection, consumer protection, and worker safety. Most of the regulatory agencies established during the third wave have larger mandates than those created earlier. They have responsibility not for a single industry but for firms of all types, and their policy scope covers a wide range of activities. The Environmental Protection Agency (EPA), for example, is charged with regulating environmental pollution of almost any kind by almost any firm.

Because newer agencies such as the EPA have a wide-ranging clientele, no one firm or industry can easily influence agency policy to a great extent. There is also strong group competition within some of the newer regulatory spheres. For example, business lobbies must compete with environmental groups such as the Sierra Club and Greenpeace for influence with the EPA.[11] The firms regulated by the older agencies, in contrast, typically face no powerful competition in their lobbying activities. Broadcasters, for example, are virtually unopposed in most of their efforts to influence the Federal Communications Commission (FCC). Although television viewers and radio listeners have a stake in FCC decisions, they are not well enough organized to lobby it effectively.

Unlike the older agencies that are run by a commission whose members serve for fixed terms and cannot be removed during their term of office, some of the newer agencies, including the EPA, are headed by a single director who is appointed by the president with Senate approval and is subject to immediate removal by the president. This arrangment also weakens the link between the regulatory agency and the firms it regulates. An agency head who gives favorable treatment to a firm risks removal if the president disapproves.

GOVERNMENT AS PROTECTOR OF THE ENVIRONMENT

Few changes in public opinion and policy during recent decades have been as dramatic as those relating to the environment. Most Americans today recycle some of their garbage, and roughly two-thirds say they are either an active environmentalist or sympathetic to environmental concerns. In the 1960s, few Americans sorted their trash, and few could have answered a polling question that asked them whether they were an "environmentalist." The term was not commonly used, and most people would not have understood its meaning.

The publication in 1962 of Rachel Carson's *The Silent Spring* helped launch the environmental movement.[12] Written at a time when the author was dying of breast cancer, *Silent Spring* revealed the threat to birds and animals of pesticides such as DDT. Carson's appearance at a Senate hearing contributed to legislative action that produced the 1963 Clean Air Act and the 1965 Water Quality Act. They were the first major federal laws designed to protect the nation's air, water, and ground from pollution. Today, environmental protection extends to nearly two hundred harmful forms of emission.

Conservationism: The Older Wave

Although antipollution policy is relatively new, the government has been involved in land conservation for more than a century.[13] The first national park was created at Yellowstone in 1872 and, like the later ones, was established to preserve the nation's natural heritage for generations to come. The national park system serves more than 100 million visitors each year and includes a total of 80 million acres, an area larger than every state except Alaska, Texas, California, and Montana. The national parks are run by the National Park Service, an agency within the Department of Interior. Another agency, the U.S. Forest Service, located within the Department of Agriculture, manages the national forests, which cover an area more than twice the size of the national parks. They too have been preserved in part to protect America's natural heritage.

However, the nation's parks and forests are subject to a "dual use" policy. They are nature preserves and recreation areas, but they are also rich in natural resources—minerals, timber, and grazing lands. The federal government sells permits to ranchers, logging companies, and mining firms that give them the right to take some of these resources, a policy that can place their interests in conflict with those of conservationists. A case in point is Alaska's Arctic National Wildlife Refuge. The refuge is home to numerous species, including caribou and moose, but it also contains substantial oil and natural gas reserves. Oil companies have long wanted to drill in this wilderness area, while environmental groups have sought to prohibit drilling. Over the past few decades, the Arctic National Wildlife Refuge has periodically

★ ‖ LEADERS

Rachel Carson
(1907–64)

Born on a farm near Pittsburgh, Rachel Carson had hoped to become a writer but switched to biology as an undergraduate and went on to earn a master's degree in zoology at Johns Hopkins University. She then started work on a doctorate, but the untimely death of her father and the need to take care of her mother ended this pursuit. In 1936, while working part-time at the U.S. Bureau of Fisheries (later the U.S. Fish and Wildlife Services), she learned of a full-time position that was opening up and decided to take the civil service exam, an uncommon ambition at the time for a woman. Carson outscored all the men who took the exam with her and was awarded the position.

In her job, Carson worked on scientific journals but sought a wider audience. She astonished even herself when *The Atlantic Monthly* accepted an article she had submitted. The article led to a book contract with Simon and Schuster, but the resulting book sold poorly. Undeterred, she continued to publish articles in popular magazines and won the 1952 National Book Award for her second book, *The Sea Around Us*. However, it was *The Silent Spring*, published in 1962, that brought her lasting fame. Even before the book was released, chemical companies were threatening lawsuits and seeking to undermine her argument by portraying her as mentally unstable and scientifically untrained. The Department of Agriculture also came out against her, labeling as false her charge that the insecticide DDT was a carcinogen and environmental threat. Despite the attacks, *The Silent Spring* became a huge bestseller and led to invitations for Carson to testify before Congress. Her book and congressional testimony contributed to passage of the first federal safe air and water legislation. Tragically, at the height of her fame, Carson was fatally stricken with breast cancer. In 1981, she was posthumously awarded the Presidential Medal of Freedom, the nation's highest civilian award.

The federal government's environmental efforts include programs designed to conserve nature through the protection of forests and other natural assets. Shown here is a scene from Yellowstone National Park.

been the focus of intense political debate and lobbying. President Bill Clinton threatened to veto any bill that would open the area to drilling. President George W. Bush, in contrast, proposed to open the area to drilling as part of his program to increase the nation's energy supplies.

As the debate over Alaska's Artic National Wildlife Refuge reveals, conservation is more than an issue of protecting nature's unspoiled beauty. Also involved is the protection of species that need their natural habitat to survive. Some species, such as the deer and the raccoon, adapt easily to human encroachment. Other species are threatened by it. These species are covered by the Endangered Species Act (ESA) of 1973; it directs federal agencies to protect threatened and endangered species and authorizes programs that will preserve natural habitats. Hundreds of mammals, birds, fishes, insects, and plants are currently on the ESA's protection list.

Disputes have arisen between ESA administrators and those individuals and firms that depend on natural resources for their jobs and profits. The northern spotted owl, which inhabits the forests of Oregon and Washington, was at the center of one of these controversies. The spotted owl nests in old-growth trees that are prized by the logging industry. Federal administrators, citing the ESA, banned logging in the owl's habitat. The ensuing legal battle ended with a compromise in which logging was permitted in some old-growth timber areas and prohibited in others. Although this outcome left neither side fully satisfied, it is typical of how most such disputes are settled. More recently, federal officials have emphasized cooperative relationships with private parties. They are eligible for grants if they act to protect threatened and endangered species. In 2006, for example, a Wyoming association received a $120,000 federal grant to dredge a creek that a rare species of trout travels to get to its traditional spawning area.

Environmentalism: The Newer Wave

The pivotal decade in the federal government's realization that Americans needed protection from the harmful effects of air, water, and ground pollutants was the 1960s. The period was capped by the first Earth Day. Held in the spring of 1970, it was the brainchild of Senator Gaylord Nelson (D-Wis.), who had devoted nearly ten years to finding ways to increase public interest in environmental issues. With Earth Day, Nelson succeeded to a degree not even he could have imagined: ten thousand grade schools and high schools, two thousand colleges, and one thousand communities participated in the event, which included public rallies and environmental cleanup efforts. Earth Day has been held every year since 1970 and is now a worldwide event.

Environmental Protection   The year 1970 also marked the creation of the Environmental Protection Agency. Within a few months, the EPA was issuing new regulations at such a rapid pace that business firms had difficulty keeping track of all the mandates, much less complying fully with them. Corporations eventually found an ally in President Gerald Ford, who in a 1975 speech claimed that business regulation was costing $150 billion annually, or $2,000 for every American family.[14] Although Ford's estimate exceeded that of economic analysts, his point was not lost on policymakers or the public. The economy was in a slump, and the costs of complying with the new regulations were slowing an economic recovery. Polls indicated a decline in public support for regulatory action.

Since then, environmental protection policy has not greatly expanded, but neither has it greatly contracted. The emphasis has been on the effective administration of laws put into effect in the 1960s and 1970s. The EPA particularly was granted a broad mandate from Congress to protect America's air and water. In a 2001 decision, for example, the Supreme Court ruled unanimously that public health is the only thing that the EPA should take into account in establishing air quality standards; the costs to industry are not to be considered.[15] The Court went further in 2007 by ordering the EPA to act on carbon emissions. The Bush administration claimed that the EPA could choose for itself which actions to take and not to take. By a 5-4 vote, the Supreme Court ruled that the EPA had to comply with its legislative mandate: "Under the clear terms of the Clean Air Act, EPA can avoid taking further action only if it determines that greenhouse gases do not contribute to climate change. . . ."[16]

Environmental regulation has led to dramatic improvements in air and water quality. Pollution levels today are far below their levels of the 1960s, when yellowish-gray fog ("smog") hung over cities like Los Angeles and New York and when bodies of water like the Potomac River and Lake Erie were open sewers. In the past four decades, toxic waste emissions have been cut by half, hundreds of polluted lakes and rivers have been revitalized, energy efficiency has increased, food supplies have been made safer, and urban air pollution has decreased by more than 60 percent.[17]

Progress has been slower in cleaning up badly contaminated toxic waste sites. These sites can contaminate local water supplies and become a health hazard. Abnormally high cancer rates have been found in the vicinity of some of these sites. In the 1980s, Congress established the so-called Superfund program to rid these sites of their contaminants. However, the cleanup process has been slow and contentious. Firms that caused the pollution are liable for some of the cleanup costs, but many of these firms are no longer in business, have since been purchased by other companies, or lack the money. Firms that could pay have often chosen instead to fight the issue in court, further delaying the cleanup. To date, only about half of the sites targeted by the Superfund program as posing serious hazards have been cleaned up.

Energy Policy and Global Warming   No environmental issue has received more attention recently than global warming. The scientific community has been warning for more than a decade that carbon emissions are creating a "greenhouse effect" (the trapping of heat in the atmosphere). The result has been a rise in the earth's temperatures and in ocean levels, as a result of melting of the polar ice caps.

Until recently, some political leaders dismissed the evidence, saying repeatedly that "more research was needed." Today, few politicians openly question the existence of global warming. Political leaders disagree, however, on what should be done about it. Global warming can be retarded only by carbon emission reductions that in some cases require costly technological innovations and would slow economic growth. So far in the United States, the progrowth side has had the upper hand. The United States is the single largest source of worldwide carbon emissions

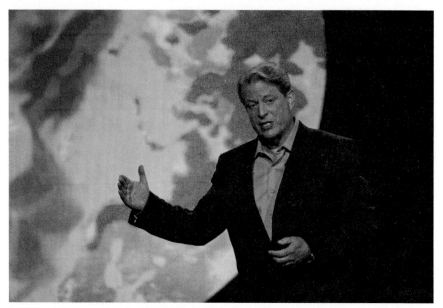

In 2007, Al Gore received the Nobel Prize for his efforts to awaken policymakers around the globe to the dangers of global warming. His documentary film on climate change, *An Inconvenient Truth*, received an Oscar. Gore was vice president during the Clinton administration, and though he received more popular votes in the 2000 presidential election, Gore lost the presidency when George W. Bush garnered a majority of the electoral vote.

(see Figure 15-2), and U.S. policymakers have resisted demands at home and from abroad for substantial new restrictions on air pollution. In 2002, for example, President Bush declared that the United States would not participate in the Kyoto agreement, a multinational effort to reduce the emission of greenhouse gases.

Even critics of Bush's action acknowledged that the Kyoto agreement was problematic. It imposed light burdens on some countries and heavy burdens on others, including the United States. Nevertheless, support is growing among Republican and Democratic leaders alike for a substantial response to the problem of global warming. Energy conservation through a steep hike in the tax on gasoline would be a short-term answer, but it is unlikely that America's consumers would embrace it or that officeholders would risk their political careers by voting for it. The price of gasoline is already a hot issue because of the rise in the world price of oil. Instability in the Middle East, a weakening of the value of the dollar, and increased demand for oil in China and India helped push oil prices in 2008 above $140 a barrel—eight times the price of a few years earlier. And as the price of

Tons of CO$_2$ per capita annually

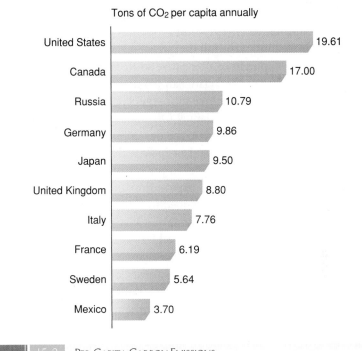

United States — 19.61
Canada — 17.00
Russia — 10.79
Germany — 9.86
Japan — 9.50
United Kingdom — 8.80
Italy — 7.76
France — 6.19
Sweden — 5.64
Mexico — 3.70

figure 15-2 PER CAPITA CARBON EMISSIONS

Americans emit more carbon dioxide into the atmosphere on a per capita basis than do the people of other countries. Carbon dioxide is the major cause of global warming and is a by-product of the burning of fossil fuels, such as coal and oil. *Source: OECD, 2008.*

oil rose, so did the price of gasoline; in some places, it reached $4 a gallon, far more than Americans are accustomed to paying.

In addition to its impact on oil prices, worldwide economic growth is accelerating the rate at which carbon emissions are being spewed into the atmosphere, exacerbating the problem of global warming. The situation spurred passage in 2007 of the Energy Independence and Security Act, which had the backing of President Bush and large majorities in the Senate and House. The legislation mandated higher fuel-efficiency standards for vehicles for the first time in three decades, requires a fivefold increase over fifteen years in the production of renewable fuels such as ethanol, and set a goal of eliminating incandescent light bulbs within a decade. House Speaker Nancy Pelosi (D-Calif.) described the bill as "a moment of change." President Bush said the legislation was a "major step . . . toward confronting global climate change."

However, Congress and the White House were unable to reach agreement on subsidies for alternative energy sources such as wind, solar, and geothermal power, and provisions of the bill that would have provided tens of billions of dollars toward development of alternative sources were dropped from consideration. This deletion evoked criticism from environmental groups, who have pressured policymakers to move more quickly on alternative sources. In the 2008 presidential campaign, Barack Obama adopted that position, proposing initiatives designed to speed up the development of alternative energy sources. John McCain also advanced proposals that would provide federal funding and tax incentives for the development of such sources. However, McCain also proposed aggressive oil exploration, including opening up additional offshore areas to drilling. "We need to drill, drill, drill," said McCain, prompting protests from environmentalists. Obama subsequently endorsed offshore drilling, though on a more limited basis.

In the years ahead, Americans will increasingly have to make trade-offs between environmental protection, energy costs, and economic growth. To a degree, they are prepared to make them. Polls indicate that a majority of Americans would support further environmental regulation even if the result is slower economic growth. However, in part because of their greater resistance to government regulation and to taxes (including the gas tax), Americans are less willing to make the trade-offs than are Canadians, the Japanese, or most Western Europeans (see Figure 15-3).

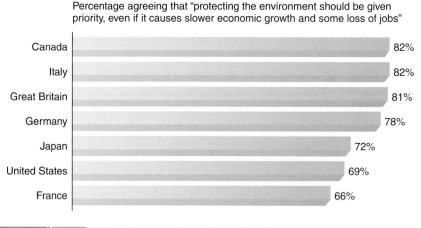

Percentage agreeing that "protecting the environment should be given priority, even if it causes slower economic growth and some loss of jobs"

Country	Percentage
Canada	82%
Italy	82%
Great Britain	81%
Germany	78%
Japan	72%
United States	69%
France	66%

figure 15-3 OPINIONS ON THE ENVIRONMENT AND ECONOMIC GROWTH

Majorities in industrialized democracies support environmental protection, even if it means somewhat slower economic growth. However, Americans are somewhat less likely than citizens elsewhere to accept this trade-off. *Source: The Pew Research Center for the People and the Press, Global Attitudes Survey, 2002.*

GOVERNMENT AS PROMOTER OF ECONOMIC INTERESTS

The U.S. government has always made important contributions to the nation's economy. Congress in 1789 gave a boost to the nation's shipping industry by placing a tariff on goods brought into the United States on foreign ships, thereby encouraging importers to use American ships. Since that first favor, the U.S. government has provided thousands of direct benefits to economic interests. The following sections provide examples of a few of these benefits.

Promoting Business

American business is not opposed to government regulation as such. Corporations object only to regulatory policies that hurt their interests. At various times and in different ways, as in the case of the FCC and broadcasters, some regulatory agencies have promoted the interests of the very industries they are supposed to regulate in the public interest.

Providing loans and tax breaks is another way that government promotes business. Firms receive loan guarantees, direct loans, tax credits for capital investments, and tax deductions for capital depreciation. Over the past forty years, the burden of federal taxation has shifted dramatically from corporations to individuals. A few decades ago, the revenues raised from taxes on corporate income were roughly the same as the revenues raised from taxes on individual income. Today, individual taxpayers carry a much heavier burden. Some analysts do not regard the change as particularly significant, arguing that higher corporate taxes would be passed along to the public anyway in the form of higher prices for goods and services.

The most significant contribution that government makes to business is the traditional services it provides, such as education, transportation, and defense. Colleges and universities, which are funded primarily by governments, furnish business with most of its professional and technical workforce and with much of the basic research that goes into product development. The nation's roadways, waterways, and airports are other public-sector contributions without which business could not operate. In short, America's business has no bigger booster than government.

Promoting Labor

Laissez-faire thinking dominated government's approach to labor well into the twentieth century. The governing principle, developed by the courts a century earlier, held that workers had limited rights of collective action.

Union activity was regarded as interference with the natural supply of labor and the free setting of wages. Government's hostility toward labor was evident, for example, in the use of police and soldiers during the late 1800s to break up strikes.

The 1930s brought major changes. The key legislation was the National Labor Relations Act of 1935, which guaranteed workers the right to bargain collectively and prohibited business from discriminating against union employees and from unreasonably interfering with union activities. Government has also aided labor over the years by legislating minimum wages and maximum work hours, unemployment benefits, safer and more healthful working conditions, and nondiscriminatory hiring practices. Although government support for labor extends beyond these examples, it is not nearly as extensive as its assistance to business. America's culture of individualism has resulted in public policies that are less favorable to labor than are policies in European countries.

Promoting Agriculture

Until well into the twentieth century, most Americans still lived on farms and in small rural communities. Agriculture was America's dominant business and was assisted by the government's land policies. The Homestead Act of 1862, for example, opened government-owned lands to settlement, creating spectacular "land rushes" by offering 160 acres of government land free to each family that staked a claim, built a house, and farmed the land for five years.

Farm programs today provide assistance to both small farmers and large commercial enterprises (agribusinesses) and cost the federal government billions of dollars annually. A major goal of this spending is to eliminate some of the risks associated with farming. Weather, world markets, and other factors can radically affect crop and livestock prices, and federal programs are designed to protect farmers from adverse developments.

Experience has shown that the agricultural sector benefits from government intervention. In 1996, Congress passed legislation that trimmed long-standing crop subsidy and crop allocation programs. The goal was to let the free market largely determine the prices farmers would get for their crops and to let farmers themselves decide on the crops they would plant. The result was a depressed farm economy—prices fell sharply because of the surplus production of particular crops. In 2002, Congress abandoned the free-market approach. Crop subsidies were increased and expanded to include more crops. Then, in 2008, Congress overrode a presidential veto to enact a five-year, $300-billion farm bill that puts farmers in line for hefty government assistance in future years. At present, federal payments account for more than a fourth of net agricultural income, making America's farmers among the most heavily subsidized anywhere in the world.

FISCAL POLICY: GOVERNMENT AS MANAGER OF THE ECONOMY, I

Until the 1930s, the U.S. government adhered to the prevailing free-market theory and made no attempt to regulate the economy as a whole. The economy, which was regarded as largely self-regulating, was fairly prosperous, but it collapsed periodically, resulting in widespread unemployment.

The greatest economic collapse in the nation's history—the Great Depression of the 1930s—finally brought an end to traditional economics. President Franklin D. Roosevelt's government spending and job programs, designed to stimulate the economy and put Americans back to work, heralded the change.[18] Although Roosevelt's use of government policy as an economic stimulus was highly controversial, today it is accepted practice. Government is expected to pursue policies that will foster economic growth and stability.

Taxing and Spending Policy and Politics

The government's efforts to maintain a thriving economy are made mainly through its taxing and spending decisions, which together are referred to as its **fiscal policy** (see Table 15-2).

The annual federal budget is the basis of fiscal policy. Thousands of pages in length, the budget allocates federal expenditures among government programs and identifies the revenues—taxes, social insurance receipts, and

table 15-2   FISCAL POLICY: A SUMMARY

Taxing and spending levels can be adjusted in order to affect economic conditions.

Problem	Fiscal Policy Actions
Low productivity and high unemployment	Demand side: increase spending Supply side: cut business taxes
Excess production and high inflation	Decrease spending Increase taxes

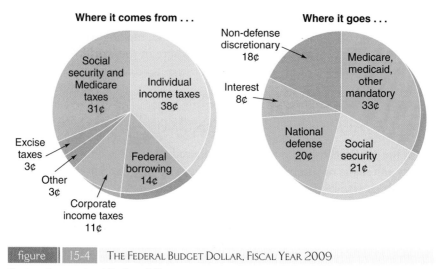

Where it comes from . . .

- Social security and Medicare taxes 31¢
- Individual income taxes 38¢
- Excise taxes 3¢
- Other 3¢
- Corporate income taxes 11¢
- Federal borrowing 14¢

Where it goes . . .

- Non-defense discretionary 18¢
- Interest 8¢
- Medicare, medicaid, other mandatory 33¢
- National defense 20¢
- Social security 21¢

figure 15-4   THE FEDERAL BUDGET DOLLAR, FISCAL YEAR 2009

Source: Congressional Budget Office.

borrowed funds—that will be used to pay for these programs (see Figure 15-4). From one perspective, the budget is the national government's allocation of costs and benefits. Every federal program benefits some interest, whether it be farmers who get price supports, defense firms that obtain military contracts, or retirees who receive monthly social security checks. From another standpoint, that of fiscal policy, the budget is a device for stimulating or dampening economic growth. Through changes in overall levels of spending and taxing, government can help keep the economy running smoothly.

Fiscal policy has origins in the economic theories of John Maynard Keynes. In *The General Theory of Employment, Interest, and Money* (1936), Keynes noted that employers naturally become cautious during an economic downturn and cut back on production and the number of workers. Challenging the traditional idea that government should also cut back during a downturn, Keynes claimed that a downturn can be shortened only by increased government spending. Keynes said that government should engage in **deficit spending**—spending more than it gets from taxes—which can be accomplished through the borrowing and printing of money. By placing additional money in the hands of consumers, government can stimulate spending, which in turn will stimulate production and create jobs, thereby promoting an economic recovery.[19]

According to Keynesian theory, the level of the government's response should be commensurate with the severity of the problem. During an

economic depression—an exceptionally steep and sustained downturn in the economy—the government should engage in massive new spending programs to hasten the recovery. During an **economic recession,** which is a less severe downturn, government spending should also be increased but by a smaller amount.

Demand-Side Stimulation   Keynes's theory focused on government's efforts to stimulate consumer spending. This **demand-side economics** emphasizes the consumer "demand" component of the supply–demand equation. When the economy is sluggish, the government by increasing its spending can place additional money in consumers' hands. With more money to spend, consumers buy more goods and services. This increase in demand stimulates businesses to produce more goods and hire more workers. In this way, government spending contributes to economic recovery. This rationale was the basis for the tax rebates that more than 100 million Americans received in 2008. The economy had slowed dramatically, and President Bush and Congress responded by sending checks totaling $150 billion to taxpayers, urging them to spend their rebate. Most of the money was in fact spent within a few months, giving the economy a much needed boost.

The tax rebates were not the government's only contribution in 2008 to reversing the economic downturn. Since the 1930s, federal spending has been at permanently high levels. Each month, for example, roughly 40 million Americans receive a social security check from the government. In turn, they spend it on food, clothing, housing, entertainment, and other goods and services. They pump billions of dollars each month into the U.S. economy, which creates jobs and income for millions of other Americans. And social security is only one—albeit the largest—of numerous federal spending programs. Each day, the federal government spends about $5 billion, more than the typical large corporation pumps into the economy during an entire year. The U.S. economy thus has a constant demand-side stimulus: government spending on an ongoing and massive scale.

Although increased spending is a tool that government can employ to alleviate a severe economic crisis, it is a tool that needs to be applied sensibly. Excessive spending results in a **budget deficit**—the situation where the federal government spends more in a year than it receives in tax and other revenues. The shortfall increases the **national debt,** which is the total cumulative amount that the U.S. government owes to creditors. At present, the national debt exceeds $9 trillion, which requires enormous expenditures just to pay the interest on it. Interest payments on the national debt are roughly the total of all federal income taxes paid by Americans living

figure 15-5   THE FEDERAL BUDGET DEFICIT/SURPLUS

The federal government ran a budget deficit until 1998, at which time a surplus that was expected to last for years emerged. In 2001, however, the surplus quickly disappeared as a result of an economic downturn, costs associated with the war on terrorism, and a cut in federal taxes. *Source: Office of Management and Budget, 2008. Figure for 2008 based on preliminary estimates.*

west of the Mississippi. Only rarely in recent decades has the U.S. government had a **balanced budget** (the situation where revenues are equal to government expenditures) or a **budget surplus** (the situation where the federal government receives more in tax and other revenues than it spends). The usual situation has been a budget deficit, which is also the outlook for the foreseeable future (see Figure 15-5).

Supply-Side Stimulation   A fiscal policy alternative to demand-side stimulation is **supply-side economics,** which emphasizes the business (supply) component of the supply-demand equation. Supply-side theory was a cornerstone of President Ronald Reagan's economic program. He believed that economic growth could occur as easily from stimulation of the business sector as from stimulation of consumer demand. "Reaganomics" included substantial tax breaks for businesses and upper-income individuals.[20] Supply-side theory was also the basis of President George W. Bush's economic initiatives, which included sharp cuts in the tax rate on individuals, with most of the gains going to high-income taxpayers, and a reduction in the **capital-gains tax,** the tax that individuals pay on gains in capital investments such as property and stocks. Under Bush, the capital-gains tax rate, which had been 28 percent, fell to 15 percent, and the highest marginal rate on individual income fell to 35 percent, down from 39 percent.

Supply-side measures are designed to encourage investment in business expansion and capital markets, creating economic growth that results in increases in employment and income. As jobs and wages increase, so does consumer spending, furthering the economic growth.

As with demand-side stimulation, supply-side policy can be taken too far. Both Reagan and Bush argued that the increased business activity resulting from their tax cuts would soon produce the additional revenues needed to offset the loss of revenue from the cuts. Although the Reagan and Bush tax cuts provided an economic boost, the loss of revenue in each case was greater than the gain in revenue from the resulting economic growth. As a consequence, the tax cuts contributed to increases in the budget deficit and the national debt.[21] In Bush's case, the tax cuts in combination with the costs of the Iraq war drove the U.S. budget deficit to record highs, threatening to cancel any long-term contribution the tax cuts might have made to economic growth.[22] During congressional testimony, outgoing Federal Reserve chairman Alan Greenspan warned that the budget deficits were "unsustainable" and a severe threat to the long-term health of the U.S. economy. (Bush's tax cuts are discussed further in Chapter 16.)

Controlling Inflation   High unemployment and low productivity are only two of the economic problems that government is called on to solve. Another is **inflation**—an increase in the average level of prices of goods and services. Before the late 1960s, inflation was a minor problem—a less than 4 percent annual rate. But inflation rose sharply during the last years of the Vietnam War and remained high throughout the 1970s, reaching a postwar record rate of 13 percent in 1979. The effects were substantial. Prices were rising but personal income was stagnant. Many Americans were forced to cut back on basics, such as food and medical care. Personal and business bankruptcies rose sharply as a result of rising costs and skyrocketing loan rates. The interest rates on business and home loans topped 15 percent—up from 5 percent a few years earlier.

Since the early 1980s, the annual inflation rate has been more manageable, and public concern with inflation has receded. Nevertheless, recent developments, including sharp increases in consumer and government debt, have weakened the U.S. dollar, which could trigger another inflationary period in the near future. To fight inflation, government applies policies exactly the opposite of those used to fight unemployment and low productivity. By cutting spending or raising personal income taxes, government can take money from consumers, thus reducing demand and dampening prices. (The main policy tool for addressing inflation is monetary policy, which is discussed later in the chapter.)

Partisan Differences   Partisan politics is a component of fiscal policy. Working-class Americans are a significant part of the Democratic coalition and are usually the first and most deeply affected by rising unemployment. Accordingly, Democratic leaders have usually responded to a sluggish economy with increased government spending (demand-side fiscal policy), which offers direct help to the unemployed and stimulates consumption. Virtually every increase in federal unemployment benefits during the past fifty years, for example, has been initiated by Democratic officeholders.

Republican leaders are more likely to see an economic downturn through the eyes of business firms. Republicans in Washington typically have sought ways to stimulate business activity as a means of economic recovery. Thus, Republicans have usually resisted large increases in government spending (with the exception of defense spending) as a response to a sluggish economy. Such spending requires government to borrow money, which leads to upward pressure on interest rates. This pressure in turn raises business costs, because firms must pay higher interest rates for the money they borrow.

Tax policy also has partisan dimensions. Democratic policymakers have typically sought tax policies that help working-class and lower-middle-class Americans. Democrats have favored a **graduated (or progressive) personal income tax,** in which the tax rate increases significantly as income rises. Republicans have preferred to keep taxes on upper incomes at a relatively low level, contending that this policy encourages the savings and investment that foster economic growth (supply-side fiscal policy). These differences are evident, for example, in the Economic Growth and Tax Relief Reconciliation Act of 2001. Proposed by President Bush, the legislation contained a huge tax cut for upper-income taxpayers. In Congress, the bill had the support of 90 percent of Republicans and only 20 percent of Democrats.[23] Then, in the 2008 presidential campaign, Democratic nominee Barack Obama vowed to rescind the Bush tax cut and raise taxes on upper incomes, while Republican nominee John McCain promised to preserve the cut. (Tax policy is discussed further in Chapter 16.)

The Budgetary Process

The president and Congress jointly determine fiscal policy, mainly through the annual budgetary process. The Constitution grants Congress the power to tax and spend, but the president, as chief executive, plays a major role in shaping the budget (see Chapter 12). In reality, the budgetary process involves give-and-take between Congress and the president as each tries to exert influence over the final budget.[24]

The budgetary process is an elaborate one, as might be expected when billions of dollars in federal spending are at issue. From beginning to end, the process lasts a year and a half (see Figure 15-6). The process begins in the executive

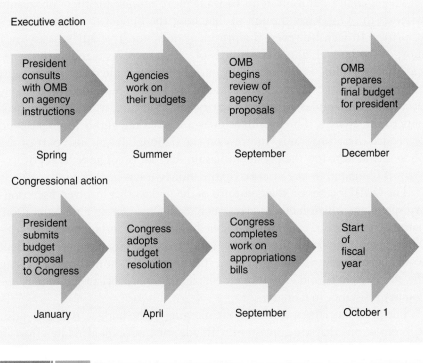

Executive action

| President consults with OMB on agency instructions | Agencies work on their budgets | OMB begins review of agency proposals | OMB prepares final budget for president |

Spring   Summer   September   December

Congressional action

| President submits budget proposal to Congress | Congress adopts budget resolution | Congress completes work on appropriations bills | Start of fiscal year |

January   April   September   October 1

figure 15-6 FEDERAL BUDGETARY PROCESS

The budget begins with the president's instructions to the agencies and ends when Congress enacts the budget. The entire process spans about eighteen months.

branch when the president, in consultation with the Office of Management and Budget (OMB), establishes general budget guidelines. The OMB is part of the Executive Office of the President (see Chapter 12) and takes its directives from the president. Hundreds of agencies and thousands of programs are covered by the budget, and the OMB uses the president's directives to issue the instructions that will guide each agency's budget preparations. For example, each agency is assigned a budget ceiling within which it must work.

The agencies receive these instructions in the spring and then work through the summer to develop a detailed agency budget, taking into account their existing programs and any new proposals. These agency budgets then go to the OMB in September for a full review that invariably includes further consultation with each agency. The agency budgets are then finalized and combined into the full budget. Throughout, the OMB stays in touch with the White House to ensure that the budget items conform to the president's objectives.

The agencies naturally tend to want more money for their programs, whereas the OMB has the job of matching the budget to the president's priorities. In fact, however, the president does not have any real say over most of the budget, about two-thirds of which involves mandatory spending. This spending is authorized by current law, and the government must allocate and spend the money unless the law itself is rescinded, an unlikely occurrence. Examples are social security and Medicare, which provide benefits to the elderly. The president does not have the authority to suspend or reduce these programs. Interest on the national debt is also part of the budget, and here too the president has no real option. The federal government is obligated to pay interest on the money it has borrowed.

The OMB focuses on the one-third of the budget that involves discretionary spending, which includes areas such as defense, foreign aid, education, national parks, space exploration, public broadcasting, and highways. In reality, even a large part of this spending is not truly discretionary. No president would even consider slashing defense spending to almost nothing or closing the national parks, and even modest cuts in a discretionary program may encounter resistance in Congress.

The president, then, works on the margins of the budget, trying to push it in directions that are consistent with administration goals. The effort in many policy areas consists of a modest increase or decrease in spending compared with the previous year. There are always a few areas, however, where the president will attempt a more dramatic adjustment. In each of his budgets, for example, President Bush asked for large increases in defense spending to assist in the war on terrorism and to pay for the Iraq war and reconstruction.

In January, the president transmits the full budget to Congress. This budget is just a proposal, because Congress alone has the constitutional power to appropriate funds. During Congress's work on the budget, the president's recommendations undergo varying degrees of change. The priorities of a majority in Congress are never exactly those of the president, even when they are members of the same party. When they are members of opposite parties, their priorities may differ greatly.

Upon reaching Congress, the president's budget proposal goes first to the House and Senate budget committees. Their job is to establish overall spending and revenue levels. Once they have settled on these levels, the full House and Senate vote on them. Once approved, the levels are a blueprint for the rest of Congress's work on the budget.

The House and Senate Appropriations Committees take over at this point. They are the most important part of congressional deliberations on the budget. The House Appropriations Committee through its subcommittees has

★ STATES IN THE NATION

Federal Taxing and Spending: Winners and Losers

Fiscal policy (the federal government's taxing and spending policies) varies in its effect on the states. The residents of some states pay a lot more in federal taxes than they receive in benefits. The biggest loser is New Jersey, whose taxpayers get back in federal spending in their state only $0.61 for every dollar they pay in federal taxes. Nevada taxpayers ($0.65 for every dollar) are the next-biggest losers. In contrast, the residents of some states get back more from federal spending programs than they contribute in taxes. The biggest winners are New Mexico and Mississippi, whose taxpayers get back $2.03 and $2.02, respectively, in federal spending in their states for every dollar they pay in federal taxes.

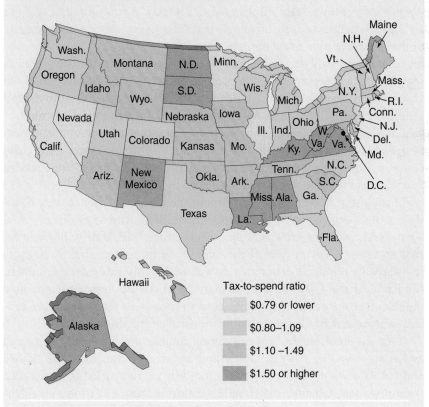

Tax-to-spend ratio
- $0.79 or lower
- $0.80–1.09
- $1.10–1.49
- $1.50 or higher

Source: Adapted from Tax Foundation Calculations, 2007.

(continued)

Q: Why are most of the "losers" in the northeastern section of the country?

A: The federal taxes that originate in a state reflect its wealth, and the northeastern states are generally the wealthier ones. Because they are wealthier, they also get less federal assistance for programs designed to help lower-income people and areas. Finally, most federal lands and military installations—sources of federal money—lie outside the northeastern region.

the primary task of reviewing the budget items, a review that includes hearings with each federal agency. There are ten such subcommittees, each of which has responsibility for a substantive area, such as defense or agriculture. Agency budgets invariably are changed at this stage. A subcommittee may cut an agency's budget because it believes that the agency's work is not a priority or that the agency has asked for more funds than it needs. Or the subcommittee may decide to increase an agency's budget beyond what the president has requested. The subcommittees' recommendations are then submitted to the House Appropriations Committee for final review and submission to the full House for a vote. The Senate Appropriations Committee and its subcommittees conduct a similar review, but the Senate is a smaller body, and its review of agency requests is normally less thorough. To some degree, the Senate committee and its subcommittees serve as a "court of appeals" for agencies that have had their budget requests reduced by the House.

Throughout this process, members of the House and Senate rely heavily on the Congressional Budget Office (CBO), which, as discussed in Chapter 11, is the congressional equivalent of the OMB. If the CBO believes that an agency has misjudged the amount of money needed to meet its legislatively required programs, it will make this information known. Similarly, if the CBO concludes that the OMB has miscalculated how much the government can be expected to receive in taxes and other revenues, members of Congress will be notified of the discrepancy.

After the work of the appropriations committees has been completed and is approved by the full House and Senate, differences in the Senate and House versions of the appropriations bill are reconciled in conference committee (see Chapter 11). The legislation is then sent to the president for approval or veto. The threat of a presidential veto can be enough to persuade Congress to accept many of the president's recommendations. In the end, the budget inevitably reflects both presidential and congressional priorities. Neither branch ever gets everything it wants, but each branch always gets some of what it wants.

Once the budget has been passed by both the House and the Senate and is signed by the president, it takes effect on October 1, the starting date of the federal government's fiscal year. If agreement on the budget has not been reached by October 1, temporary funding is required in order to maintain government operations. In late 1995, President Clinton and the Republican Congress deadlocked on budgetary issues to such an extent that they could not even agree on temporary funding. Their standoff twice forced a brief shutdown of nonessential government activities.

MONETARY POLICY: GOVERNMENT AS MANAGER OF THE ECONOMY, II

Fiscal policy is not the only instrument of economic management available to government; another is **monetary policy,** which is based on adjustments in the amount of money in circulation (see Table 15-3). Monetarists, as economists who emphasize monetary policy are called, contend that the money supply is the key to sustaining a healthy economy. Their leading theorist, the American economist Milton Friedman, held that supply and demand are best controlled through the money supply.[25] Too much money in circulation contributes to inflation because too many dollars

table 15-3	MONETARY POLICY: A SUMMARY OF THE FED'S ROLE

The money supply can be adjusted in order to affect economic conditions.

Problem	Monetary Policy Actions by Federal Reserve
Low productivity and high unemployment (requiring an increase in the money supply)	Decrease interest rate on loans to member banks Decrease cash reserve that member banks must deposit in Federal Reserve System
Excess productivity and high inflation (requiring a decrease in the money supply)	Increase interest rate on loans to member banks Increase cash reserve that member banks must deposit in Federal Reserve System

are chasing too few goods, which drives up prices. Too little money in circulation results in a slowing economy and rising unemployment, because consumers lack the ready cash and easy credit required to push up spending levels. Monetarists believe in increasing the money supply when the economy needs a boost and decreasing the supply when it needs to be slowed down.

The Fed

Control over the money supply rests not with the president or Congress but with the Federal Reserve Board System (known as "the Fed"). Created by the Federal Reserve Act of 1913, the Fed has a board of governors whose seven members serve for fourteen years, except for the chair and vice chair, who serve for four years. All members are appointed by the president, subject to Senate approval. The Fed regulates all national banks and those state banks that meet certain standards and elect to become members of the Federal Reserve System.

The Fed decides how much money to add to or subtract from the economy, seeking a balance that will permit steady growth without causing an unacceptable level of inflation. One way the Fed affects the money supply is by raising or lowering the cash reserve that member banks are required to deposit with the Federal Reserve. This reserve is a proportion of each member's total deposits. By increasing the reserve rate, the Fed takes money from member banks and thereby takes it out of circulation. When the Fed lowers the reserve rate, banks have more money available to loan to consumers and investors.

A second and more visible way the Fed affects the money supply is by lowering or raising the interest rate that member banks are charged when they borrow from the Federal Reserve. When the Fed raises the interest rate, banks also tend to raise the rate they charge for new loans, which discourages borrowing and thus reduces the amount of money entering the economy. Conversely, by lowering the interest rate, the Fed encourages firms and individuals to borrow from banks, which increases the money supply. The Fed's interest-rate adjustments are often front-page news because they are a signal of the strength of the economy and thus affect the decisions of consumers and firms. As the economy slowed down in 2008, for example, the Fed began a series of adjustments that dropped the interest rate by several percentage points, which enabled member banks to lower their rates, thereby making loans more affordable for firms and consumers.

Economists debate the relative effectiveness of monetary policy and fiscal policy, but monetary policy has one obvious advantage: it can be implemented more quickly than fiscal policy. The Fed can adjust interest and reserve rates on short notice, thus providing the economy with a psychological boost to go along with the financial effect of a change in the money supply. In contrast, changes in fiscal policy usually take months to implement. Congressional action is relatively slow, and new taxing and spending programs ordinarily require a preparation period before they can be put into effect. Five months elapsed, for example, before the tax rebate checks authorized by Congress in early 2008 actually reached the taxpayers.

The Politics of the Fed

The greater flexibility of monetary policy has positioned the Fed as the institution with primary policy responsibility for keeping the U.S. economy on a steady course. The Fed's power can easily be exaggerated. The U.S. economy is subject to a lot of influences, of which the money supply is only one. Nevertheless, the Fed is a vital component of U.S. economic policy.[26]

At the time the Fed was created in 1913, economists had not yet "invented" the theory of monetary policy, and the Fed had no role in the management of the nation's economy. It now plays a large role, which raises important questions about the power it wields. One question is the issue of representation: whose interests does the Fed serve, those of the public as a whole or those of the banking sector? The Fed is not a wholly impartial body. Although it makes decisions in the context of economic theories and projections, it is "the bankers' bank" and as such is protective of monied interests. In 2008, the Fed stepped in with loans to financial institutions to prevent them from bankruptcy as a result of their holdings in shaky mortgage-related securities. The Fed justified its intervention by saying that the financial markets might otherwise collapse, adversely affecting every American. What was immediately clear, however, was that taxpayers were being forced to subsidize the banks. A related question is the issue of accountability: should the Fed, an unelected body, have so much power? Though appointed by the president, members of the Federal Reserve Board are not subject to removal. They serve for fixed terms and are relatively insulated from political pressures, including the changes that take place through elections. Of course, the Fed, as a banking institution, has a vested interest in a healthy economy (too much inflation erodes banks' returns on loans; too much unemployment decreases demand for loans) and thus operates within its own system of checks and balances. Nevertheless, the restraints on the Fed are weaker than those on popularly elected institutions.

Regardless, the Fed is part of the new way of thinking about the federal government and the economy that emerged during the Great Depression of the 1930s. Prior to that time, the federal government's economic role was largely confined to the provision of a limited number of public services, such as the currency and mail delivery. Roosevelt's New Deal permanently changed the government's role. Through its economic management and regulatory activities, the government has assumed an ongoing role in the economy, contributing to its stability and efficiency. The results are impressive. In the roughly three-quarters of a century that the U.S. government has played a significant policy role, the American economy has progressed at a relatively steady pace. There have been recessions, but none of them has been remotely like the devastating depressions of earlier times, a testimony to the soundness of economic theory and of its application by policymakers. (The economic policies of the federal government in the areas of social welfare and national security are discussed in the next two chapters.)

SUMMARY   Self-Test www.mhhe.com/pattersonwtp8e

Although private enterprise is the main force in the American economic system, the federal government plays a significant role through its policies to regulate, promote, and stimulate the economy.

Regulatory policy is designed to achieve efficiency and equity, which require the government to intervene, for example, to maintain competitive trade practices (an efficiency goal) and to protect vulnerable parties in economic transactions (an equity goal). Many of the regulatory decisions of the federal government, particularly those of older agencies (such as the Food and Drug Administration), are made largely in the context of group politics. Business lobbies have an especially strong influence on the regulatory policies that affect them. In general, newer regulatory agencies (such as the Environmental Protection Agency) have policy responsibilities that are broader in scope and apply to a larger number of firms than those of the older agencies. As a result, the policy decisions of newer agencies are more often made in the context of party politics. Republican administrations are less vigorous in their regulation of business than are Democratic administrations.

Business is the major beneficiary of the federal government's efforts to promote economic interests. A large number of programs, including those that provide loans and research grants, are designed to assist businesses, which are also protected from failure through measures such as tariffs and favorable tax laws. Labor, for its part, obtains government assistance through laws concerning matters such as worker safety, the minimum wage, and collective bargaining. Yet America's individualistic culture tends to put labor at a disadvantage, keeping it less powerful than business in its dealings with the government. Agriculture is another economic sector that depends substantially on government's help, particularly in the form of income stabilization programs such as those that provide crop subsidies.

The U.S. government pursues policies that are designed to protect and conserve the environment. A few decades ago, the environment was not a policy priority. Today, there are many programs in this area, and the public has become an active participant in efforts to conserve resources and prevent exploitation of the environment. The continuing challenge is finding a proper balance between the nation's natural environment, its economic growth, and its energy needs.

Through its fiscal and monetary policies, Washington attempts to maintain a strong and stable economy—one characterized by high productivity, high employment, and low inflation. Fiscal policy is based on government decisions in regard to spending and taxing, which are aimed at either stimulating a weak economy or dampening an overheated (inflationary) economy. Fiscal policy is worked out through Congress and the president and consequently is responsive to political pressures. However, because it is difficult to raise taxes or cut programs, the government's ability to apply fiscal policy as an economic remedy is limited. Monetary policy is based on the money supply and works through the Federal Reserve, which is headed by a board whose members hold office for fixed terms. The Fed is a relatively independent body, a fact that has given rise to questions as to whether it should play such a large role in influencing national economic policy.

KEY TERMS

balanced budget (*p. 564*)

budget deficit (*p. 563*)

budget surplus (*p. 564*)

capital-gains tax (*p. 564*)

deficit spending (*p. 562*)

demand-side economics (*p. 563*)

deregulation (*p. 546*)

economic depression (*p. 563*)

economic recession (*p. 563*)

economy (*p. 542*)

efficiency (*p. 543*)

equity (in relation to economic policy) (*p. 548*)

externalities (*p. 546*)

fiscal policy (*p. 561*)

graduated personal income tax (*p. 566*)

inflation (*p. 565*)

laissez-faire doctrine (*p. 542*)

monetary policy (*p. 571*)

national debt (*p. 563*)

policy formation (*p. 539*)

policy implementation (*p. 540*)

problem recognition (*p. 538*)

public policy process (*p. 538*)

regulation (*p. 543*)

supply-side economics (*p. 564*)

SUGGESTED READINGS

Duncan, Richard. *The Dollar Crisis: Causes, Consequences, Cures*, rev. ed. New York: John Wiley, 2005. A look at the problem of budget and trade deficits.

Jones, Bryan D., and Walter Williams. *The Politics of Bad Ideas: The Great Tax-Cut Delusion and the Decline of Good Government in America*. New York: Longman, 2008. A critique of the idea that tax cuts are the key to economic prosperity.

Lindbloom, Charles E. *The Market System: What It Is, How It Works, and What to Make of It.* New Haven, Conn.: Yale University Press, 2001. A clear analysis of the advantages and disadvantages of the market system.

Mayer, Martin. *Fed: The Inside Story of How the World's Most Powerful Financial Institution Drives the Markets.* New York: Free Press, 2001. A look at the Fed's impact on the economy and politics.

McChesney, Robert. *The Problem of the Media.* New York: Monthly Review Press, 2004. A scathing critique of media regulation.

Rosenbaum, Walter A. *Environmental Politics and Policy*, 6th ed. Washington, D.C.: Congressional Quarterly Press, 2004. A comprehensive examination of the politics of environmental policy.

Schick, Allen. *The Federal Budget*, 3rd ed. Washington, D.C.: The Brookings Insitution Press, 2007. An explanation of the federal budgetary process.

Sheingate, Adam D. *The Rise of the Agricultural Welfare State.* Princeton, N.J.: Princeton University Press, 2003. A penetrating analysis of farm policy in the United States, France, and Japan.

LIST OF WEBSITES

http://www.federalreserve.gov/default.htm The Federal Reserve System website; describes the Fed, provides information about its current activities, and has links to some of the Fed's national and international information sources.

http://www.epa.gov/ The Environmental Protection Agency (EPA) website; provides information on environmental policy and regulations, EPA projects, and related subjects.

http://www.ftc.gov/ The website of the Federal Trade Commission, one of the older regulatory agencies; describes the range of the FTC's activities.

http://www.whitehouse.gov/OMB The home page of the Office of Management and Budget; contains a summary of the annual federal budget and describes the OMB's operations and responsibilities.

POLITICS IN THEORY AND PRACTICE

Thinking: What are the tools of fiscal policy and monetary policy? What are the advantages and disadvantages of each of these two approaches to managing the economy?

Participating: The environment is a policy area where individual citizens can make a difference by reducing waste and pollution. If you have a car, you will burn significantly less fuel if you accelerate and drive more slowly. Choosing a fuel-efficient car, keeping your car properly tuned, walking rather than driving short distances to stores, and living closer to work or school are other ways to cut gas consumption. In your residence, the simplest steps are to use lights sparingly and keep the thermostat lower during cold periods and higher during hot periods. Smaller but meaningful savings can be achieved through simple things such as using low-flow shower heads and replacing incandescent bulbs with fluorescent lights, which require less energy and last longer. Even a change in eating habits can make a difference. Frozen convenience foods are wasteful of energy. They are cooked, frozen, and then cooked again—not to mention the resources used up in packaging. Fresh foods are more nutritious and less wasteful. And if you prefer bottled water to tap water, consider using a water filter system instead. Nearly all of the cost of bottled water is due to the plastic container, which is a non-biodegradable petroleum product. The recycling of paper, plastics, and bottles also conserves natural resources. However, the recycling process itself requires the use of energy. By cutting back on your use of recyclables and by recycling those you do use, you will contribute twice over to a cleaner environment.

Extra Credit

For up-to-the-minute *New York Times* articles, interactive simulations, graphics, study tools, and more links and quizzes, visit the text's Online Learning Center at www.mhhe.com/pattersonwtp8e.

Global Warming

By Al Gore

In 2006, an unlikely subject became a box-office hit. On its opening weekend, it had the highest average box-office take per screening of any documentary film in history. The movie was An Inconvenient Truth *narrated by Al Gore, the former vice president and presidential nominee. For several years previously, Gore had been presenting a slide show on global warming to audiences around the country, trying to raise public awareness of the problem. Following is an excerpt of what Gore said during a presentation at New York City's Beacon Theater on January 15, 2004. The event was sponsored by MoveOn, a liberal organization that relies on the Internet to mobilize its followers.*

[T]he vast majority of the most respected environmental scientists from all over the world have sounded a clear and urgent alarm. The international community—including the United States—began a massive effort several years ago to assemble the most accurate scientific assessment of the growing evidence that the earth's environment is sustaining severe and potentially irreparable damage from the unprecedented accumulation of pollution in the global atmosphere. In essence, these scientists are telling the people of every nation that global warming caused by human activities is becoming a serious threat to our common future. I am also troubled that the Bush/ Cheney Administration does not seem to hear the warnings of the scientific community in the same way that most of us do.

Here is what we are talking about: Even though the earth is of such vast size, the most vulnerable part of the global environment is the atmosphere—because it is surprisingly thin—as the late Carl Sagan used to say: like a coat of varnish on a globe. I don't think there is any longer a credible basis for doubting that the earth's atmosphere is heating up because of global warming. So the evidence is overwhelming and undeniable. Global Warming is real. It is happening already and the anticipated consequences are unacceptable. But it is important to understand that this crisis is actually just a symptom of a deeper underlying cause.

Yet in spite of the clear evidence available all around us, there are many who still do not believe that Global Warming is a problem at all. And it's no wonder: because they are the targets of a massive and well-organized campaign of disinformation lavishly funded by polluters who are determined to prevent any action to reduce the greenhouse gas emissions that cause global warming, out of a fear that their profits might be affected if they had to stop dumping so much pollution into the atmosphere.

And wealthy right-wing ideologues have joined with the most cynical and irresponsible companies in the oil, coal and mining industries to contribute large sums of money to finance pseudo-scientific front groups that specialize in sowing confusion in the public's mind about global warming. They issue one misleading "report" after another, pretending that there is significant disagreement in the legitimate scientific community in areas where there is actually a broad-based consensus. The techniques they use were pioneered years earlier by the tobacco industry in its long campaign to create uncertainty in the public's mind about the health risks caused by tobacco smoke. Indeed, some of the very same scientific camp-followers who took money from the tobacco companies during that effort are now taking money from coal and oil companies in return for their willingness to say that global warming is not real.

In a candid memo about political strategy for Republican leaders, pollster Frank Luntz expressed concern that voters might punish candidates who supported more pollution, but offered advice on the key tactic for defusing the issue. The Bush Administration has gone far beyond Luntz' recommendations, however, and has explored new frontiers in cynicism by time and time again actually appointing the principal lobbyists and lawyers for the biggest polluters to be in charge of administering the laws that their clients are charged with violating. Some of these appointees have continued to work very closely with the outside pseudo-scientific front groups even though they are now on the public payroll.

Two Attorneys General have now publicly accused officials in the Bush White House Council on Environmental Quality of conspiring with one of the outside groups to encourage the filing of a lawsuit as part of a shared strategy to undermine the possibility of government action on Global Warming. Vice President Cheney's infamous "Energy Task Force" advised lobbyists for polluters early in the new administration that there would be no action by the Bush White House on Global Warming and then asked for their help in designing a totally meaningless "voluntary" program. . . .

The problem is that our world is now confronting a five-alarm fire that calls for bold moral and political leadership from the United States of America. With such leadership, there is no doubt that we could solve the problem of global warming. After all, we brought down communism, won wars

in the Pacific and Europe simultaneously, enacted the Marshall Plan, found a cure for polio and put men on the moon. When we set our sights on a visionary goal and are unified in pursuing it, there is very little we cannot accomplish. . . .

Instead of spending enormous sums of money on an unimaginative and retread effort to make a tiny portion of the Moon habitable for a handful of people, we should focus instead on a massive effort to ensure that the Earth is habitable for future generations. If we make that choice, the U.S. can strengthen our economy with a new generation of advanced technologies, create millions of good new jobs, and inspire the world with a bold and moral vision of humankind's future.

We are now at a true fork in the road. And in order to take the right path, we must choose the right values and adopt the right perspective. My friend the late Carl Sagan, whose idea it was to take this picture of the Earth, said this: "Look again at that dot. That's here. That's home. That's us. On it everyone you love, everyone you know. Everyone you ever heard of, every human being who ever WAS lived out their lives. The aggregate of our joy and suffering, thousands of confident religions, ideologies and economic doctrines, every hunter and forager, every hero and coward, every creator and destroyer of civilization, every king and peasant, every young couple in love, every mother and father, hopeful child inventor and explorer, every teacher of morals, every corrupt politician, every "superstar," every "supreme leader," every saint and sinner in the history of our species lived there—on a mote of dust suspended in a sunbeam.

"The Earth is a very small stage in a vast cosmic arena. Think of the rivers of blood spilled by all those generals and emperors, so that, in glory and triumph, they could become the momentary masters of a fraction of a dot. Think of the endless cruelties visited by the inhabitants of one corner of this pixel on the scarcely distinguishable inhabitants of some other corner, how frequent their misunderstandings, how eager they are to kill one another, how fervent their hatreds. Our posturings, our imagined self-importance, the delusion that we have some privileged position in the Universe, are challenged by this point of pale light. . . .

"The Earth is the only world known so far to harbor life. There is nowhere else, at least in the near future, to which our species could migrate. Visit, yes. Settle, not yet. Like it or not, for the moment the Earth is where we make our stand. There is perhaps no better demonstration of the folly of human conceits than this distant image of our tiny world. To me, it underscores our responsibility to deal more kindly with one another, and to preserve and cherish the pale blue dot, the only home we've ever known."

What's Your Opinion?

Do you share former Vice President Gore's concern with global warming? Do you share his interpretation of the scientific evidence and of the Bush administration's position on the issue? What do you think is the appropriate trade-off between environmental protection and economic growth, given that any substantial effort to reduce global warming would involve policies that would slow economic growth somewhat in the near term?

CHAPTER 16

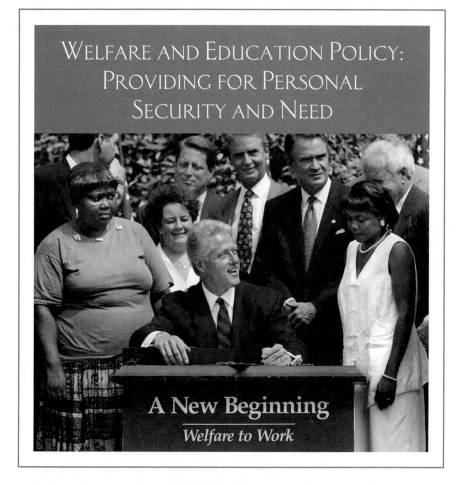

WELFARE AND EDUCATION POLICY:
PROVIDING FOR PERSONAL
SECURITY AND NEED

A New Beginning
Welfare to Work

66 We the people of the United States, in order to . . . promote the general welfare . . . 99

PREAMBLE, U.S. CONSTITUTION

As the Welfare Reform Act came up for renewal in 2002, there was cause for both hope and fear. The original legislation had been a stunning success. By the late 1990s, the number of people on the welfare rolls had been cut almost in half. In only three states—Hawaii, Rhode Island, and New Mexico—was the drop less than 20 percent (see "States in the Nation"). The trend defied what had been called welfare policy's "reverse gravity" law: welfare rolls that went up but never came down. Two factors accounted for the change. One was the booming national economy. As more Americans got jobs, the demand for welfare decreased. The second factor was the 1996

★ ‖ STATES IN THE NATION

The Declining Number of Families on Welfare

The welfare rolls in the United States peaked in March 1994. After that, the number of American families on welfare dropped precipitously, which analysts attributed to both the surge in the U.S. economy and the 1996 welfare reform bill that instituted new work rules. Between 1994 and 2002, welfare cases fell by 57 percent. The biggest drop (89 percent) was in Wisconsin. The smallest (7 percent) was in Hawaii. The decline in each state during this period is shown in the map below.

Q: What might explain the state-to-state variation in the decline in the welfare rolls?

A: States that had weaker economies in the early 1990s had bigger drops in their welfare rolls in the latter part of the 1990s. These states had more laid-off workers on welfare, and as the economy strengthened, many of these unemployed workers found jobs.

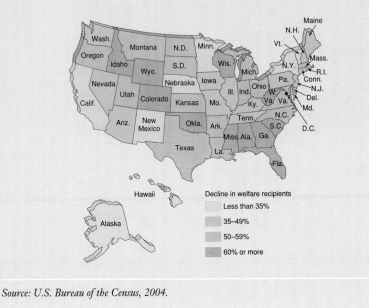

Source: U.S. Bureau of the Census, 2004.

Welfare Reform Act, which limited the length of eligibility for benefits and required that able-bodied recipients find work or risk loss of benefits.

The situation in 2002 was starkly different. Those welfare recipients who had found work were the ones easiest to place in jobs. Many of those still unemployed lacked the education, skill, or temperament to find and hold a job. Moreover, the economy had weakened, and welfare rolls were starting to rise even as government revenues were declining. "At the beginning of welfare reform, we had the happy circumstance of a booming economy, low unemployment, falling welfare caseloads, and the states having the money to give more help to the poor, especially the working poor," said Sharon Parrott of the Center on Budget and Policy Priorities. "Now, everything is going the other way. Caseloads are rising, the value of the federal block grant is down, and state budgets are in catastrophic shape."[1]

The 2002 debate in Congress reflected these new realities. Yet it also brought out old differences. Congressional Republicans wanted to increase pressure on the states to move more people off welfare and into work; they also argued for strict adherence to the eligibility rules, tight controls on federal spending, and increased work hours for welfare recipients. Congressional Democrats sought more funding for day care, education, and job-training programs; they also wanted to give the states more latitude in their administration of the welfare program. The differences were substantial enough to create a months-long deadlock between the Republican-controlled House and the Democratic-controlled Senate. "By stalling on . . . welfare reform," said Bill Thomas (R-Calif.) of the House Committee on Ways and Means, "the Senate is shaping their legacy—inaction." Senate majority leader Tom Daschle (D-S. Dak.) was unbending, vowing to hold out until the Republicans agreed to "strong child care provisions."[2]

Social welfare policy is an area in which opposing philosophies of government collide. Some people, like Senator Daschle, hold that government should provide substantial assistance to those Americans who are less equipped to compete effectively in the marketplace. Others, like Representative Thomas, hold that welfare payments, except to those who are indisputedly unfit to work, discourage personal effort and create welfare dependency.

America's federal system of government is also a source of conflict over welfare policy. Welfare was traditionally a responsibility of state and local governments. Only since the 1930s has the federal government played a major role by providing some of the funding and imposing restrictions on the use of the money. The strictness of federal guidelines and the amount that the federal government should contribute to welfare spending are contentious issues.

This chapter examines the social problems that federal welfare programs are designed to alleviate and describes how these programs operate. It also addresses public-education policies. This chapter seeks to provide an informed basis for understanding issues of social welfare and education and to show why disagreements in these areas are so substantial. These issues involve hard choices that inevitably require trade-offs between federal and state power and between the values of individual self-reliance and egalitarian compassion. The main points of the chapter are these:

★ *Poverty is a large and persistent problem in America, deeply affecting about one in seven Americans, including many of the country's most vulnerable— children, female-headed families, and minority-group members.* Social welfare programs have reduced the extent of poverty in the United States.

★ *Welfare policy has been a partisan issue, with Democrats taking the lead on government programs to alleviate economic insecurity and Republicans acting to slow down or reverse these initiatives.*

★ *Social welfare programs are designed to reward and foster self-reliance or, when this is not possible, to provide benefits only to those individuals who are truly in need.* U.S. welfare policy is not based on the assumption that every citizen has a right to material security.

★ *Americans favor social insurance programs (such as social security) over public assistance programs (such as food stamps).* As a result, most social welfare expenditures are not targeted toward the nation's neediest citizens.

★ *A prevailing principle in the United States is equality of opportunity, which in terms of policy is most evident in the area of public education.* America invests heavily in its public schools and colleges.

POVERTY IN AMERICA: THE NATURE OF THE PROBLEM

In the broadest sense, social welfare policy includes any effort by government to improve social conditions. In a narrower sense, which is the way the term generally will be used in this chapter, social welfare policy refers to government programs that help individuals meet basic human needs, including food, clothing, and shelter.

The Poor: Who and How Many?

Americans' social welfare needs are substantial. Although Americans are far better off economically than most of the world's peoples, poverty is a significant and persistent problem in the United States. The government defines the **poverty line** as the annual cost of a thrifty food budget for an urban family of four, multiplied by three to include the cost of housing, clothes, and other necessities. Families whose incomes fall below that line are officially considered poor. In 2007, the poverty line was set at an annual

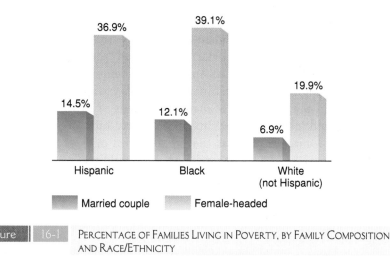

figure | 16-1 | PERCENTAGE OF FAMILIES LIVING IN POVERTY, BY FAMILY COMPOSITION AND RACE/ETHNICITY

Poverty is far more prevalent among female-headed households and African American and Hispanic households. *Source: U.S. Bureau of the Census, 2008.*

income of roughly $20,000 for a family of four. One in eight Americans—roughly 35 million people, including more than 10 million children—live below the poverty line. If they could all join hands, they would form a line stretching from New York to Los Angeles and back again.

America's poor include individuals of all ages, races, religions, and regions, but poverty is concentrated among certain groups. Children are one of the largest groups of poor Americans. One in every five children lives in poverty. Most poor children live in families with a single parent, usually the mother. In fact, as can be seen from Figure 16-1, a high proportion of Americans residing in families headed by divorced, separated, or unmarried women live below the poverty line. These families are at a disadvantage because most women earn less than men for comparable work, especially in nonprofessional fields. Women without higher education or special skills often cannot find jobs that pay significantly more than the child-care expenses they incur if they work outside the home. Single-parent, female-headed families are roughly five times as likely as two-income families to fall below the poverty line, a situation referred to as "the feminization of poverty."[3]

Poverty is widespread among minority-group members. Compared with whites, twice as many African Americans and Hispanics live below the poverty line. Poverty is also geographically concentrated. Although poverty is often portrayed as an urban problem, it is somewhat more prevalent in rural areas. About one in seven rural residents—compared with one in nine urban residents—lives in a family with income below the poverty line. The urban figure is misleading, however, in that the level of poverty is very high in some inner-city areas. Suburbs are the safe haven from poverty. Because suburbanites are far removed from it, many of them have no sense of the impoverished condition of what Michael Harrington called "the other America."[4]

The "invisibility" of poverty in America is evident in polls showing that most Americans greatly underestimate the number of poor in their country. Nothing in the daily lives of many Americans or in what they see on television would lead them to think that poverty rates are uncommonly high. Yet the United States has the highest level of poverty among the advanced industrialized nations, and its rate of child poverty is more than twice the average rate of the other countries (see "How the United States Compares").

Living in Poverty: By Choice or Chance?

Many Americans hold to the idea that poverty is largely a matter of choice—that most low-income Americans are unwilling to make the effort to hold a responsible job and get ahead in life. In his book *Losing Ground*, Charles Murray argues that America has a permanent underclass of unproductive citizens who prefer to live on welfare and whose children receive little educational encouragement at home and grow up to be copies of their parents.[5] There are, indeed, many such people in America. They number in the millions. They are the toughest challenge for policymakers because almost nothing about their lives equips them to escape from poverty and its attendant ills.

Yet most poor Americans are in their situation as a result of circumstance rather than choice. After reviewing the extensive research on the causes of poverty and examining data that tracked individuals over periods of time, economists Signe-Mary McKernan and Caroline Ratcliffe concluded that most of the poor are poor only for a while, and then for reasons largely beyond individual control—such as a job layoff or desertion by the father—rather than because they prefer not to work.[6] When the U.S. economy goes into a tailspin, the impact devastates many families. The U.S. Department of Labor estimated in early 2008 that the pending economic recession could eventually cause several million workers to lose their jobs. Moreover, a full-time job does not guarantee that a family will rise above the poverty line. A family of four with one employed adult who works forty hours a week at $7 an hour (roughly the minimum wage) has an annual income of about $14,000, which is $6,000 below the poverty line. Millions of Americans—mostly household workers, service workers, unskilled laborers, and farmworkers—are in this position. The U.S. Bureau of Labor Statistics estimates that roughly 10 percent of full-time workers do not earn enough to lift their family above the poverty line.[7]

HOW THE UNITED STATES COMPARES

Children Living in Poverty

The United States has the highest child poverty rate among industrialized nations. One in five American children lives in poverty; in most other industrialized nations, the number is fewer than one in ten. These numbers are from the Office of Economic Development, which defines as being in poverty any household with an income less than half that of the median household.

The United States ranks at the top in part because its income is less evenly distributed. As a consequence, the United States has the highest percentage of both rich and poor children in the industrialized world. In addition, the United States spends less on government assistance for the poor. Without government help, for example, the child poverty rates in the United States and France would be about equal. Through its governmental programs, France has reduced the rate to just over 7 percent. Through its welfare programs, the United States reduces the rate only somewhat.

Child poverty in the United States is made worse by the relatively large number of single-parent families, although Sweden, which has a similarly large number of such families, has one of the world's lowest rates of child poverty.

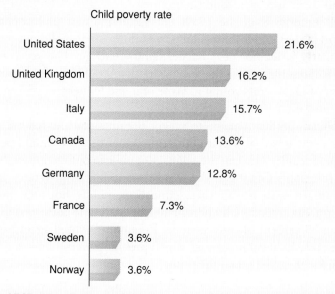

Child poverty rate

Country	Rate
United States	21.6%
United Kingdom	16.2%
Italy	15.7%
Canada	13.6%
Germany	12.8%
France	7.3%
Sweden	3.6%
Norway	3.6%

Source: OECD, 2008. Figures are from various years depending on the availability of country-level data.

The Politics and Policies of Social Welfare

At one time in the nation's history, the federal government was not involved in social welfare policy. Poverty and other welfare problems were deemed to fall within the powers reserved to the states by the Tenth Amendment and to be adequately addressed by them, even though they did not offer substantial welfare services. Individuals were expected to fend for themselves, and those unable to do so were usually supported by relatives and friends.

Historical Background

This approach reflected the idea of **negative government,** which holds that government governs best by staying out of people's lives, giving them as much freedom as possible to determine their own pursuits and encouraging them to become self-reliant.

The Great Depression changed that outlook. The unemployment level reached 25 percent, and many of those with jobs were working for pennies. Americans looked to the federal government for help. Franklin D. Roosevelt's New Deal brought economic relief in the form of public jobs and assistance programs and changed opinions about the federal government's welfare role.[8] This new attitude reflected a faith in **positive government**—the idea that government intervention is necessary in order to enhance personal liberty and security when individuals are buffeted by economic and social forces beyond their control.

Not all Americans of the 1930s embraced the new philosophy. Most Republican leaders and loyalists clung to traditional ideas about self-reliance and free markets. Democrats spearheaded the change. The key vote in the House of Representatives on the Social Security Act of 1935, for example, had 85 percent of Democrats voting in favor of it and 99 percent of Republicans voting against it.[9]

Republicans gradually came to accept the idea that the federal government has a role in social welfare but argued that the role should be kept as small as practicable. Thus, in the 1960s, Republican opposition to President Lyndon Johnson's Great Society was substantial. His programs included federal initiatives in health care, education, public housing, nutrition, and other areas traditionally dominated by state and local governments. More than 70 percent of congressional Republicans voted against the 1965 Medicare and Medicaid programs, which provide government-paid medical assistance for the elderly and the poor.

In contrast, the 1996 Welfare Reform Act, which was designed to cut welfare rolls and costs, had the overwhelming support of congressional

Republicans, while a majority of congressional Democrats voted against it. Republicans embraced it because it limited the time that recipients would be eligible to receive welfare benefits and because it gave the states greater control over the welfare program.

Although the Republican and Democratic parties have been at odds on social welfare issues, they have also had reason to work together. Millions of Americans depend on the federal government to provide benefits to ease the loss of income caused by retirement, disability, unemployment, and the like. Some social welfare spending, such as federal grants for health research, benefits society broadly. Other spending directly helps individuals. **Transfer payments** are government benefits given directly to individual recipients, such as the monthly social security checks that retirees receive. Most programs that support individuals are **entitlement programs,** meaning that any individual who meets the criteria for eligibility is entitled to the benefit. For example, upon reaching the legal retirement age, any senior citizen who has paid social security taxes for the required amount of time is entitled to receive social security benefits. In this sense, entitlement programs have the same force of law as taxes. Just as individuals are required by law to pay taxes on the income they earn, they are entitled by law to receive government benefits for which they qualify.

Individual-benefit programs fall into two broad groups: social insurance programs and public assistance programs. Social insurance programs enjoy broader public support, are more heavily funded, and provide benefits to individuals of all income levels. Public assistance programs have less public support, receive less funding, and are restricted to people of low income. The next two sections discuss these two types of programs.

Social Insurance Programs

More than 40 million Americans receive monthly benefits from social insurance programs—including social security, Medicare, unemployment insurance, and workers' compensation. The two major programs, social security and Medicare, cost the federal government more than $800 billion per year. Such programs are labeled **social insurance** because eligibility is restricted to individuals who paid special payroll taxes during their working years.

Social Security The main social insurance program is social security for retirees. The program began with passage of the Social Security Act of 1935 and is funded through payroll taxes on employees and employers (currently set at 6.2 percent). Franklin D. Roosevelt emphasized that retiring workers would receive an insurance benefit that they had

★ | LEADERS

Lyndon B. Johnson
(1908–1973)

Aside from Franklin D. Roosevelt, no American left a larger social welfare legacy than President Lyndon B. Johnson. LBJ's Great Society programs include Medicare and Medicaid, as well as increased federal spending in areas such as education, childhood nutrition, and poverty alleviation. A Democrat from Texas, Johnson served first in the House of Representatives and then in the Senate, where he quickly rose through the ranks to become Senate majority leader in the 1950s. In 1960, John F. Kennedy picked Johnson to be his running mate, hoping that Johnson could deliver Texas to the Democratic column. Texas did vote Democratic, which gave Kennedy a narrow victory in the Electoral College. Ascending to the presidency when Kennedy was assassinated in 1963, Johnson won a landslide election victory in 1964. Backed by huge Democratic majorities in Congress, he then won enactment of his Great Society programs. Johnson was also instrumental in passage of the 1964 Civil Rights Act and the 1965 Voting Rights Act. He had grown up in a poor area of Texas, which contributed to his desire to use government to help the disadvantaged. However, Johnson also presided over the escalation of the Vietnam War, which tarnished his legacy. He had intended to seek reelection in 1968, and likely would have won a narrow victory, but the war had created a deep split within the Democratic Party. In a nationally televised speech, Johnson announced he would not seek or accept his party's 1968 presidential nomination, saying he intended to devote the remainder of his presidency to ending the Vietnam War. The goal eluded him, and he returned to Texas, where he died of a heart attack shortly before his successor, Richard Nixon, concluded a truce ending U.S. involvement in Vietnam.

earned through their payroll taxes, not a handout from the government. In part because of this method of financing, the social security program has broad public support.[10] Opinion polls indicate that the large majority of Americans favor current or higher levels of social security benefits for the elderly. Social security is one of the few welfare programs run entirely by the federal government. Washington collects the payroll taxes that fund the program and sends monthly checks directly to the nearly 40 million social security recipients, who receive on average about $1,000 a month.

Although people qualify for social security by paying payroll taxes during their working years, the money they receive upon retirement is funded by payroll taxes on current workers' salaries. This arrangement poses a long-term threat to the viability of the social security program because people are living longer than they once did. Three decades from now, about one in five Americans will be over age sixty-five, at which time—unless changes are made in the social security program—there will not be enough workers to pay for retiree benefits.

In 2005, President George W. Bush proposed a partial privatization of social security as an answer to the long-term problem. Workers would have been allowed to place roughly a third of social security tax payments into private, individual stock market accounts. Bush claimed that individuals would get a greater return on their money through the stock market, thereby reducing what government would need to pay when workers retired. Bush's proposal was attacked by congressional Democrats and by powerful groups including the American Association of Retired Persons (AARP), who argued that Bush's proposal would expose retirees to the risks of the stock market. Critics also said that the Bush plan would make the solvency problem worse, not better. Payroll taxes that otherwise would have been used to offset payments to retirees would have been diverted into private accounts. Bush's plan failed to win congressional approval, but a need to overhaul social security remains. At some point, as happened in the 1980s, a bipartisan commission is likely to be formed to develop a compromise solution that will preserve America's commitment to its elderly retirees.

Unemployment Insurance   The 1935 Social Security Act provides for unemployment benefits for workers who lose their jobs involuntarily. Unemployment insurance is a joint federal-state program. The federal government collects the payroll taxes that fund unemployment benefits, but states have the option of deciding whether the taxes will be paid by both employees and employers or by employers only (most states use the latter option). Individual states also set the tax rate, conditions of eligibility, and benefit level, subject to minimum standards established by the federal government. Although unemployment benefits vary widely among states, they average $350 a week, somewhat more than a third of what an average worker makes while employed. The benefits in most cases are terminated after twenty-six to thirty-nine weeks.

The unemployment program does not have the broad public support that social security enjoys. This situation reflects the widespread assumption that the loss of a job, or the failure to find a new one right away, is often a personal failing. Unemployment statistics indicate otherwise. For example, U.S. Bureau of Labor statistics reveal that of those workers who lost their jobs in 2001, only 13 percent were fired or quit voluntarily. The rest became unemployed because of either a temporary layoff or the permanent elimination of a job position.

Medicare   After World War II, most European democracies created government-paid health care systems, and President Harry Truman, a Democrat, proposed a similar program for Americans. The American Medical Association (AMA) called Truman's plan "un-American" and vowed to mobilize local physicians to campaign against members of Congress who supported "socialized medicine." Truman's proposal never came to a vote in Congress. In 1961, President John F. Kennedy, also a Democrat, proposed a health care program restricted to social security recipients, but the AMA, the insurance industry, and congressional conservatives succeeded in blocking the plan.[11]

The 1964 elections swept a tide of liberal Democrats into Congress, and the result was Medicare. Enacted in 1965, the program provides medical assistance to retirees and is funded primarily through payroll taxes. Medicare is based on the insurance principle, and because of this, it has gained as much public support as social security. Medicare does not cover all hospital, nursing home, or physicians' fees, but enrollees in the program have the option of paying an insurance premium for fuller coverage of these fees. Enrollees who cannot afford the additional premium can apply to have the government pay it. In 2006, a prescription drug benefit was added to the Medicare program, though it has restrictions that limit the benefits primarily to retirees who either are too poor to afford prescription drugs or have very high prescription drug costs. Retirees not in these categories receive a small benefit from the program but are required to pay most of the cost of their prescription drugs.

At some point soon, Congress will have to overhaul the Medicare program. The rising cost of medical care and the growing number of elderly have combined to threaten the solvency of the program; it is projected to run out of money within a decade unless new revenues and cost-cutting measures are devised. Among the options under consideration are increased payroll taxes, more cost sharing by recipients, more use of managed-care options, and further reductions in government payments to doctors and hospitals.

Public Assistance Programs

Unlike social insurance programs, **public assistance** programs are funded through general tax revenues and are available only to the financially needy. Eligibility for these programs is established by a **means test;** that is, applicants must prove that they are poor enough to qualify for the benefit. Once they have done so, they are entitled to the benefit, unless their personal situation changes or government legislates different eligibility criteria. These programs often are referred to as "welfare," and the recipients as "welfare cases."

Americans are far less supportive of public assistance programs than they are of social insurance programs. Americans tend to look upon social insurance benefits as having been "earned" by the recipient, while they see public assistance benefits as "handouts." Because of their individualistic culture, Americans are less inclined than Europeans to believe that government should provide substantial help to the poor (see Figure 16-2). Support for public assistance programs also is weakened by Americans' perception that the government is already spending vast amounts on welfare. A poll found that Americans believe public assistance programs to be the second costliest item in the federal budget. These programs actually rank much farther down the list. In fact, the federal government spends hundreds of billions of dollars more on its two major social insurance programs—social security and Medicare—than it does on all public assistance programs combined.

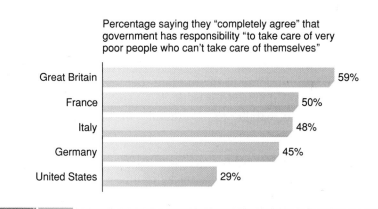

Percentage saying they "completely agree" that government has responsibility "to take care of very poor people who can't take care of themselves"

Great Britain	59%
France	50%
Italy	48%
Germany	45%
United States	29%

figure 16-2 OPINIONS ON GOVERNMENT'S RESPONSIBILITY FOR THE POOR

Compared to Europeans, Americans are much less likely to believe that government has a responsibility for the poor. *Source: The Pew Research Center for the People and the Press, Global Attitudes Survey, 2002.*

Supplemental Security Income (SSI) is a combined federal-state program that provides public assistance to blind and disabled people.

Supplemental Security Income   A major public assistance program is Supplemental Security Income (SSI), which originated as federal assistance to the blind and elderly poor as part of the Social Security Act of 1935. By the 1930s, most states had begun or were considering such programs. Although the federal legislation was designed to replace their efforts, the states have retained a measure of control over benefits and eligibility and are required to provide some of the funding. Because SSI recipients (who now include the disabled in addition to the blind and elderly poor) have obvious reasons for their inability to provide fully for themselves, this public assistance program is not widely criticized.

Temporary Assistance for Needy Families (TANF)   Before passage of the 1996 Welfare Reform Act (discussed in the chapter's introduction), needy American families had an open-ended guarantee of cash assistance. As long as their income was below a certain level, they were assured of government support. The program (Aid for Families with Dependent Children, or AFDC for short) was created in the 1930s as survivors' insurance to assist children whose fathers had died prematurely. Relatively small at the outset, the program became controversial as Americans increasingly linked it to welfare dependency and irresponsibility. AFDC was an entitlement program, which meant that any single parent (and in some states two parents) living in poverty could claim the benefit and keep it for as long as a dependent child was in the household. Some AFDC recipients were content to live on this assistance, and in some cases their children also grew up to become AFDC recipients, creating what was called "a vicious cycle of poverty." By 1995, AFDC was supporting 14 million Americans at an annual cost of more than $15 billion.

The 1996 Welfare Reform Act abolished AFDC, replacing it with the program titled Temporary Assistance for Needy Families (TANF). TANF's goal is to reduce long-term welfare dependency by limiting the length of time recipients can receive assistance and by giving the states an incentive to place welfare recipients into jobs. Each state is given an annual federal bloc grant that it uses to help poor families meet their subsistence needs and to develop programs that will help the parents find employment. The state programs operate within strict federal guidelines, including the following:

- Americans' eligibility for federal cash assistance is limited to no more than five years in their lifetime.
- Within two years, the head of most families on welfare must find work or risk the loss of benefits.
- Unmarried teenage mothers qualify for welfare benefits only if they remain in school and live with a parent or legal guardian.
- Single mothers lose a portion of their benefits if they refuse to cooperate in identifying for child support purposes the father of their children.

Although states can grant exceptions to some of the rules (for example, an unmarried teenage mother who faces sexual abuse at home is permitted to live elsewhere), the exceptions are limited. States can even choose to impose more restrictive rules in some areas. For example, states have the option of denying increased benefits to unwed mothers who give birth to another child.

So far, TANF has been relatively successful. The percentage of families on public assistance has declined significantly since passage of the 1996 Welfare Reform Act. The biggest challenge facing the states has been creating welfare-to-work programs that qualify people for jobs secure enough to free them from welfare dependency. Most welfare recipients who have found employment since 1996 had enough skills that they required little or no job training from the state. In contrast, most of those who have been unable to find long-term employment have limited education and few job-related skills.[12]

Food Stamps   The Food Stamps program, which took its present form in 1961, is fully funded by the federal government. The program provides an **in-kind benefit**—not cash, but food stamps that can be spent only on grocery items.

Food stamps are available only to people who qualify on the basis of low income. The program is intended to improve the nutrition of poor families by enabling them to purchase qualified items—mainly foodstuffs—with food stamps. Some critics say that food stamps stigmatize their users by making it obvious to onlookers in the checkout line that they are "welfare cases." More prevalent criticisms are that the program is too costly and that too many undeserving people receive food stamps.

Subsidized Housing   Low-income persons are also eligible for subsidized housing. Most of the federal spending in this area is on rent vouchers, an in-kind benefit. The government gives the individual a monthly rent payment voucher, which the individual gives in lieu of cash to the landlord, who then hands the voucher over to the government in exchange for cash. About 5 million households annually receive a federal housing subsidy.

The U.S. government spends much less on public housing than it gives in tax breaks to homeowners, most of whom are middle- and upper-income Americans. Homeowners are allowed tax deductions for their mortgage interest payments and their local property tax payments. The total of these tax concessions is three times as much as is spent by the federal government on housing for low-income families.

Medicaid   When Medicare, the health care program for the elderly, was created in 1965, Congress also established Medicaid, which provides health care for poor people who are already on welfare. It is considered a public assistance program, rather than a social insurance program like Medicare, because it is based on need and funded by general tax revenues. Roughly 60 percent of Medicaid funding is provided by the federal government, and about 40 percent by the states. More than 20 million Americans receive Medicaid assistance.

Medicaid is controversial because of its costs. As health care costs have spiraled far ahead of the inflation rate, so have the costs of Medicaid. It absorbs roughly half of all public assistance dollars spent by the U.S. government and has forced state and local governments to cut other services to meet their share of the costs. "It's killing us" is how one local official described the impact of Medicaid on his community's budget.[13] As is true of other public assistance programs, Medicaid has been criticized for supposedly helping too many people who could take care of themselves if they tried harder. This belief is contradicted, ironically, by the situation faced by many working Americans. There are roughly 45 million Americans living in families with incomes that are too high to qualify them for Medicaid but too low to cover the cost of health insurance.[14]

Culture, Welfare, and Income

Surveys repeatedly show that most Americans are convinced that people on welfare could get along without if they tried. As a consequence, there is constant political pressure to reduce welfare expenditures and to weed out undeserving recipients. The result is a welfare system that is both inefficient, in that much of the money spent on welfare never reaches the intended recipients, and inequitable, in that less than half of social welfare spending goes to the people who need it the most.[15]

Inefficiency and Inequity   The United States has the most inefficient welfare system in the Western world. Because of the unwritten principle that the individual must somehow earn or be in absolute need of assistance, the U.S. welfare system is heavily bureaucratic. For example, the 1996 welfare reform bill—which limits eligibility to families with incomes below a certain level and, in most instances, to families with a single parent living in the home—requires that the eligibility of each applicant be checked periodically by a caseworker. This procedure makes such programs doubly expensive; in addition to making payments to recipients, the programs must pay local caseworkers, supervisors, and support staffs (see Figure 16-3). These costs do not include the costs of the state and federal agencies that oversee the programs.

The bureaucratic costs of welfare are substantially lower in Europe because most European countries have unitary rather than federal systems, which eliminates a layer of government, and also because eligibility is more often universal, as in the case of government-paid health care. Caseworkers do not have to pore over records to determine who is and who is not eligible for medical treatment—everyone is.[16]

figure   16-3   THE CUMBERSOME ADMINISTRATIVE PROCESS BY WHICH WELFARE RECIPIENTS GET THEIR BENEFITS

European welfare programs are also more equitable in the sense that the major beneficiaries are those individuals most in need, unlike the case in the United States. The federal government spends far more on social security and Medicare, which assist rich and poor alike, than it spends in total on all public assistance programs, which help only the needy. Of course, social insurance programs do help many who are needy. Monthly social security checks keep millions of Americans, mostly widows, out of poverty; about one-fourth of America's elderly have no significant monthly income aside from what they receive from social security. Nevertheless, families in the top fifth of the income population receive more in federal social insurance benefits than is spent on TANF, food stamps, and housing subsidies combined.

Income and Tax Measures   The American political culture's emphasis on individualism is also evident in its tax and income policies. Economic redistribution—the shifting of money from the more affluent to the less affluent—is an aspect of these policies, but it is a relatively small component.

The United States has substantial income inequality (see Figure 16-4). Americans in the top fifth by income receive half of total U.S. income, while those in the bottom fifth get less than a twentieth. The imbalance is greater than that in any other industrialized democracy. One reason is that income taxes are not used for economic redistribution to the extent that they are in other democracies. In 2008, the top tax rate in the United States was 35 percent and applied to net income above $335,000. Income below that level is taxed at lower rates. Thus, a taxpayer with a net income of $500,000 pays the 35 percent rate on the amount above $335,000 and lower rates on the

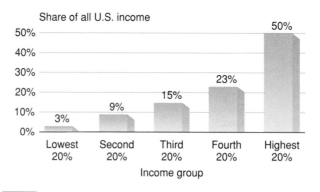

figure 16-4 INCOME INEQUALITY IN THE UNITED STATES

The United States has the highest degree of income inequality of any industrialized democracy. Citizens in the top fifth by income get half of all income; those in the bottom fifth get less than a twentieth of all income. *Source: U.S. Bureau of the Census, 2008.*

rest. In Europe, a top rate of 50 percent is not uncommon, and the top rate starts at a lower income level than in the United States.

The U.S. tax code also includes tax breaks for upper-income individuals, such as the deduction for mortgage interest on a vacation home. Moreover, the well-to-do escape social security taxes on a large part of their income. The social security tax is a flat rate of about 6 percent that begins with the first dollar earned and stops completely after roughly $100,000 in earnings. Thus, individuals earning less than $100,000 pay social security taxes on every dollar they make, while those earning more than $100,000 pay no social security taxes on the dollars they make over this amount.

The net result is that the **effective tax rate** (the actual percentage of a person's income spent to pay taxes) of high- and middle-income Americans is not greatly different. When all taxes (including personal income taxes, social security taxes, state sales taxes, and local property taxes) are combined, the average American family's effective tax rate is about three-fourths that of a family with an income over a million dollars. In Europe, where tax breaks for the well-to-do are few, the effective tax rate for high-income taxpayers is substantially greater than that for average taxpayers.[17] Of course, although well-to-do Americans pay relatively low taxes, the fact that they earn a lot of money means that they contribute the large share of tax revenues in absolute dollars. The top 10 percent of U.S. earners pay about half the personal income taxes received by the federal government. On the other hand, they keep much more of what they earn than do high-income taxpayers elsewhere.

In recent decades, taxes on the wealthy have been reduced considerably, a development that began during the Reagan administration and continued under George W. Bush. Arguing that high taxes on the wealthy stunted economic growth (see Chapter 15), Bush persuaded Congress to enact phased-in tax cuts that sharply reduced taxes on high incomes. Capital-gains taxes were slashed, and marginal tax rates on personal income were reduced. The savings to Americans in the top 1 percent of income is $54,493 per year, compared with an average of $67 for those in the bottom 20 percent and $611 for those in the middle 20 percent. In terms of total dollars, less than 1 percent of the cuts are for those in the bottom fifth by income, while those in the middle fifth get 8 percent of the cuts and those in the top fifth receive 75 percent of the cuts.[18]

Portions of this tax cut are scheduled to be phased out in 2010 unless Congress decides to renew them, which made them an issue in the 2008 presidential campaign. Democratic nominee Barack Obama came out against renewal of the tax cuts, saying that they benefited the wealthy at the expense of the middle class. Republican nominee John McCain supported renewal, saying that continuation of the tax cuts would spur economic growth.

Although America's wealthiest individuals have been the major beneficiaries of recent tax policy, the nation's poorest working families have also received tax relief through the Earned Income Tax Credit (EITC). One of Democrat Bill Clinton's first acts as president was to expand EITC eligibility, and today about 10 million low-income American families receive an EITC payment each year. The maximum yearly payment to any family is roughly $4,500, and eligibility is limited to families that include a wage earner. EITC payments occur when the wage earner files a personal income tax return. Those whose incomes are low enough receive an EITC payment, the amount of which depends on the level of their income and whether they have dependents. The EITC program is now the federal government's largest means-tested cash assistance program. According to U.S. Census Bureau calculations, the EITC lifts about a third of low-income Americans above the poverty line. Moreover, because EITC payments are based on income tax returns, the program does not require a costly bureaucracy of caseworkers. EITC payments are processed at the same time and in the same way as tax refunds for employees who have paid too much in withholding.

EDUCATION AS EQUALITY OF OPPORTUNITY

Although the Earned Income Tax Credit is subject to budgetary and political pressures, it enjoys more support than most assistance programs. The reason is simple: EITC is tied to employment. Only those who work are eligible to receive the payment. Polls that span more than a half century reveal that Americans have consistently favored work-based assistance to welfare payments as the answer to poverty. Work is believed to foster initiative and accountability; welfare "handouts" are believed to breed dependency and irresponsibility.

At the same time, Americans believe that people should have a fighting chance to succeed in the job market. Although few Americans would support economic equality for all, most Americans endorse the principle of **equality of opportunity**—the idea that people should have a reasonable chance to succeed if they make the effort. The concept includes a commitment to equality in the narrow sense that everyone should have a fair chance to get ahead. But it is a form of equality shaped by liberty because the outcome—personal success or personal failure—depends on what individuals do with that opportunity. The expectation is that people will end up differently—some will make a good living and some will be poor. It is sometimes said that equality of opportunity gives individuals an equal chance to become unequal.

Equality of opportunity is an ideal. Americans obviously do not start life on an equal footing. It was said of one successful American politician, whose father before him was a successful politician and a millionaire, that "he was born on third base and thought he hit a triple."[19] Some Americans are born into privilege, and others start life in such abject poverty that they realistically have no chance of escaping it. Nonetheless, equality of opportunity is more than a catchphrase. It is the philosophical basis for a number of government programs, none more so than public education.

Public Education: Leveling Through the Schools

During the nation's first century, the question of a free education for all children was a divisive issue. Wealthy interests feared that an educated public would challenge their power. Egalitarians, on the other hand, saw education as a means of enabling ordinary people to get ahead. The egalitarians won out. Public schools sprang up in nearly every community and were open free of charge to children who could attend.[20]

Today, as discussed in Chapter 1, the United States invests more heavily in public education at all levels than does any other country. The curriculum in American schools is also relatively standardized. Unlike those countries that divide children even at the grade school level into different tracks that lead ultimately to different occupations, the United States aims to educate all children in essentially the same way. Of course, public education is not a uniform experience for American children. The quality of education depends significantly on the wealth of the community in which a child resides. The Supreme Court has upheld this arrangement, saying that states are obliged to give all children an "adequate" education as opposed to an "equal" one across all communities.

The United States does have a federal education program, Head Start, dedicated to helping poor children. Established in the 1960s during the Johnson administration, it provides preschool education to low-income children in order to help them succeed when they begin kindergarten. At no time in its history, however, has the Head Start program been funded at a level that would allow all eligible children to participate. The low point was reached in the 1980s, when there was only enough money to allow the enrollment of one in ten of those eligible. Today, less than half of all eligible children get to participate.

Nevertheless, the United States through its public schools educates a broad segment of the population. Arguably, no country in the world has made an equivalent effort to give children, whatever their parents' background, an

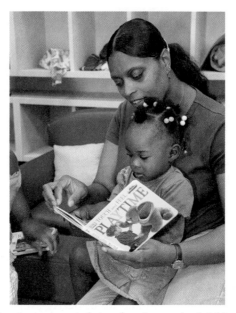

The Head Start education program is designed to give preschool children from poorer homes a better chance to succeed when they enter kindergarten.

equal opportunity in life through education. Per-pupil spending on public elementary and secondary schools is roughly twice as high in the United States as it is in the nations of Western Europe. America's commitment to broad-based education extends to college. The United States is far and away the world leader in terms of the proportion of adults receiving a college education.[21]

The nation's education system preserves both the myth and the reality of an equal-opportunity society. The belief that success can be had by anyone who works for it could not be sustained if the education system were tailored for a privileged elite. And educational attainment is related to personal success, at least as measured by annual incomes. In fact, the gap in income between those with and those without a college education is greater now than at any time in the country's history.

Public School Issues

Because America's public schools play such a key role in creating an equal-opportunity society, they are closely scrutinized. Parents of schoolchildren are not shy about saying what they think of their local schools. Interestingly, parents tend to rate their own children's schools more highly than they rate other schools. A national survey found that two-thirds of parents gave their children's schools a grade of A or B but only a fourth gave the nation's schools as a whole a grade that high.[22]

POLITICAL CULTURE
Liberty, Equality, and Self-Government

Education Policy

Public education has never been a uniform experience for American children. Cities in the late nineteenth century neglected the education of many immigrant children, who were thereby placed at a permanent disadvantage. During the first half of the twentieth century, southern public schools for black children were designed to keep them down, not lift them up. Today, many children in poorer neighborhoods attend overcrowded and understaffed public schools.

Nevertheless, the nation's public schools have been the primary means by which Americans of all nationalities, colors, creeds, and income levels have been brought together. At no time in most Americans' lives are they as thoroughly immersed in a socially diverse environment as when, as children and adolescents, they attend public schools.

America's broad-based system of public education stems from a melding of its egalitarian and individualistic traditions. Leon Sampson, a nineteenth-century socialist, noted the stark difference between the philosophy of public education in the United States and that in Europe. "The European ruling classes," he wrote, "were open in their contempt for the proletariat. But in the United States equality, and even classlessness, the creation of wealth for all and political liberty were extolled in the public schools." Sampson concluded that American schools embodied a unique conception of equality. Everyone was being trained in much the same way so that each person would have the opportunity to succeed. "It is," he said, "a socialist conception of capitalism."

Of course, a great deal of ethnic, racial, and class segregation still exists in the schools. For example, in some suburban schools few of the children come from families earning less than $75,000 a year. And in some urban schools few of the children come from families earning more than $25,000 a year. Yet, were it not for public schools, America would be a substantially more stratified society, both in terms of one's classmates while in school and in terms of one's prospects for success after leaving school.

Public education in America was called "the great leveler" when it began in the early nineteenth century. Since then it has earned that label.

The issues facing public schools are far-ranging. Disorder in the schools is a major issue in some communities. So is student performance on standardized tests—U.S. students do not even score in the top ten internationally on tests in science or math. Few policy issues are more contentious, however, than proposals to reallocate money among schools. School choice is one such issue. Under this policy, the public schools compete for students, and schools that attract the most students are rewarded with the largest budgets. Advocates of the policy claim that it forces school administrators and teachers to do a better job and gives students the option of leaving a school that is performing poorly.[23] Parents favor such a policy by a wide margin, unless their children are harmed by it. Poor children in particular often have little choice but to attend the nearest school because their parents are unable to transport them to a better but more distant school.[24]

School vouchers are a related issue. A voucher system allows parents to use tax dollars to keep their children out of the public schools entirely. Parents receive a voucher from the government that they can give to a private or parochial school to cover part of the cost of their child's tuition. Proponents say that vouchers force failing public schools to improve their instructional programs or face a permanent loss of revenue. Opponents, however, argue that vouchers weaken the public schools by siphoning off revenue and say that vouchers subsidize many families that would have sent their children to private or parochial schools anyway. They note that vouchers are of little use to students from poor families because they lack the additional money required to pay the full tuition costs at a nonpublic school.

Although the courts have upheld the constitutionality of vouchers in some circumstances, polls indicate that Americans are divided over whether they would like to see a universal voucher system.[25] The question gets majority support when it is framed in the context of choice among public schools but is opposed by the majority when private and parochial schools are included among the choices. The issue of vouchers reflects the tensions inherent in the concept of equal opportunity. Vouchers expand opportunity by increasing the number of choices available to students. Yet not all students are able to take advantage of the choices, and not all taxpayers want their tax dollars used to support private and parochial schools. (Another public school issue—uniform testing of all schoolchildren—is discussed in the next section.)

The Federal Role in Education: Political Differences

Education has traditionally been a state and local responsibility. Most school policies—from length of the school year to teachers' qualifications—are set by state legislatures and local school boards. Over 90 percent of the funds spent on schools are provided through state and local tax revenues.

Federal intervention in school policy has often been resisted by states and localities, as exemplified by their response to desegregation and busing directives (see Chapter 5). State and local governments have been less hesitant when it comes to federal education grants, but it is difficult to get congressional support for grant programs targeted at those schools that are most in need. Few members of Congress are willing to support large appropriations for education that do not benefit their constituents, a situation that has reduced Washington's contribution to a goal—quality education for every American child—that nearly every official endorses, at least in principle.

Indeed, not until 1965, with passage of the Higher Education Act and the Elementary and Secondary Education Act (part of President Lyndon Johnson's Great Society initiatives), did the federal government become involved in public education in a comprehensive way.[26] Earlier federal efforts in the area of education had been either one-time or targeted interventions. In 1862, for example, Congress passed the Morrill Act, which provided states with free tracts of land if they used the land to establish colleges—the nation's great "land-grant" universities are the product of that legislation. Another one-time federal program was the G.I. Bill, enacted after World War II, giving financial assistance to enable military veterans to attend college or vocational school.

The Supreme Court has held that American children are entitled to an "adequate" education but do not have a right to an "equal" education. America's public schools differ greatly in quality primarily as a result of differences in the wealth of the communities they serve. Some public schools are overcrowded and have few facilities and little equipment. Others are very well equipped, have spacious facilities, and offer small class sizes.

With passage of the 1965 legislation, the federal government assumed an ongoing role in public education. Federal grants to public schools and colleges became a regular part of their funding, though still a smaller part than that provided by state and local governments (see Chapters 3 and 18). The Higher Education Act became the foundation for Pell Grants, federal loans to college students, and federally subsidized college work-study programs. The Elementary and Secondary Education Act provides funding for items such as school construction, textbooks, special education, and teacher training. Federal funding is split almost evenly between support for colleges and support for elementary and secondary schools.

In recent years, education has increasingly become an issue of national debate, involving Washington officials ever more deeply in the issues.[27] President Bill Clinton rejected the idea of unrestricted school choice, arguing that it would weaken the nation's public schools and make them a repository of America's poorest children. Clinton persuaded Congress instead to appropriate billions in new funding to enable overcrowded schools to hire tens of thousands of new teachers. President George W. Bush brought a different education agenda to the White House, persuading Congress in 2001 to enact the No Child Left Behind Act. The legislation requires national testing in reading, math, and science and ties federal funding to the test results. Schools that show no improvement in students' test scores after two years receive an increased amount of federal aid. If these schools show no improvement by the end of the third year, however, their students become eligible to transfer elsewhere, and their school's federal assistance is reduced.

Few federal education policies have provoked as much controversy as No Child Left Behind.[28] The National Education Association (NEA) claims that the law has forced teachers to teach to the national tests and thus has interfered with real learning in the classroom. Congressional Democrats say that the program has failed to provide struggling schools with enough funds to improve the quality of classroom education and has encouraged the flight of students from public to private schools. For their part, congressional Republicans have applauded the law, saying that it holds teachers and schools accountable for their students' performance. Congressman John Boehner (R-Ohio) said, "Money alone is not the answer to the problems facing our children's schools. High standards and accountability for results—not just spending—are the key to erasing the achievement gap in education."[29]

Some states and localities have embraced No Child Left Behind as an answer to underperforming schools. Some schools have, in fact, improved in terms of their performance on the national tests. Other states and localities have opposed the act, saying that the federal government has not provided the funds necessary to fully implement the testing program. In the 2008 presidential campaign, Barack Obama said he backed full funding of NCLB while John McCain proposed to strengthen NCLB by getting rid of ineffective teachers and allowing students greater choice among schools. Opinion polls show that Americans are split nearly 50-50 on NCLB, with Republicans more supportive of it and Democrats less supportive.[30]

Thus, many of the partisan and philosophical differences that affect federal welfare policy also affect federal education policy. Democrats are more inclined to find the answer to how to improve schools in increased federal spending on education, particularly in less affluent communities, while Republicans are more inclined to look to marketlike mechanisms such as school choice and achievement tests.

THE AMERICAN WAY OF PROMOTING THE GENERAL WELFARE

All democratic societies promote economic security, but they do so in different ways and to different degrees. Economic security has a higher priority in European democracies than in the United States. European democracies have instituted programs such as government-paid health care for all citizens, compensation for all unemployed workers, and retirement benefits for all elderly citizens. As this chapter shows, the United States provides these benefits only to some citizens in each category. On the other hand, the American system of public education dwarfs those in Europe.

The American way of welfare was on display in the 2008 presidential election campaign. More than 40 million Americans do not have health insurance and do not qualify for Medicaid. Although both Barack Obama and John McCain spoke of a need to extend health care insurance to more people, neither candidate proposed anything like a European-style system. They focused instead on expanding employer-provided health care. Even if fully implemented, this approach would leave at least 15 million Americans without health insurance. Anything more substantial would risk the public and congressional rejection that President Bill Clinton encountered when he sought a near-universal health care system in 1993.

The differences between the European and American approaches to welfare stem from historical and cultural differences. Democracy in Europe developed in reaction to centuries of aristocratic rule, which brought the issue of economic privilege to the forefront. When strong labor and socialist parties then emerged as a consequence of industrialization, European democracies initiated sweeping social welfare programs designed to bring about greater economic equality. Social inequality was harder to root out because it was thoroughly embedded in European society, shaping everything from social manners to education. Private schools and university training were the preserve of the elite, a tradition that, though now past, continues to affect how Europeans think about educational opportunity.

The American historical experience is a different one. Democracy in America grew out of a tradition of limited government that emphasized personal liberty, which included a belief in self-reliance. This belief contributed to Americans' strong support for public education and their weak support for public assistance. Unlike political equality, the idea of economic equality never captured Americans' imagination. Try as they might during America's Industrial Age, labor and socialist parties were unable to gain large and loyal followings. Even today, when Americans think of the plight of poorer people, they are as likely to make moral judgments as political ones. Political scientists Stanley Feldman and John Zaller found that Americans' support for public assistance programs rests more on compassion for the poor than on an ideological belief in economic sharing.[31] Or, as the political scientist Robert Lane expressed it, Americans have a preference for market justice, meaning that they prefer that society's material benefits be allocated through the economic marketplace rather than through government policies.[32]

SUMMARY   Self-Test www.mhhe.com/pattersonwtp8e

The United States has a complex social welfare system of multiple programs addressing specific welfare needs. Each program applies only to those individuals who qualify for benefits by meeting the specific eligibility criteria. In general, these criteria are designed to encourage self-reliance or, when help is necessary, to ensure that laziness is not rewarded or fostered. This approach to social welfare reflects Americans' traditional belief in individualism.

Poverty is a large and persistent problem in the United States. About one in nine Americans falls below the government-defined poverty line, including a disproportionate number of children, female-headed families, minority-group members, and rural and inner-city dwellers. The ranks of the poor are increased by economic recessions and are reduced through government assistance programs.

Welfare policy has been a partisan issue, with Democrats taking the lead on government programs to alleviate economic insecurity and Republicans acting to slow down or decentralize these initiatives. Changes in social welfare have usually resulted from presidential leadership in the context of public support for the change. Welfare policy traditionally has involved programs to provide jobs and job training, education programs, income measures, and especially transfer payments through individual-benefit programs.

Individual-benefit programs fall into two broad categories: social insurance and public assistance. The former includes programs such as social security for retired workers and Medicare for the elderly. Social insurance programs are funded by payroll taxes paid by potential recipients, who thus, in a sense, earn the benefits they later receive. Because of this arrangement, social insurance programs have broad public support. Public assistance programs, in contrast, are funded by general tax revenues and are targeted toward needy individuals and families. These programs are not controversial in principle; most Americans believe that government should assist the truly needy. However, because of a widespread belief that most welfare recipients could get along without assistance if they tried, these programs do not have universal public support, are only modestly funded, and are politically vulnerable.

Social welfare is a contentious issue. In one view, social welfare is too costly and assists too many people who could help themselves; another view holds that social welfare is not broad enough and that too many disadvantaged Americans live in poverty. Because of these irreconcilable differences and because of federalism and the widely shared view that welfare programs should target specific problems, the existing system of multiple programs, despite its administrative complexity and inefficiency, has been the only politically feasible solution.

The balance between economic equality and individualism tilts more heavily toward individualism in the United States than in other advanced industrialized democracies. Other democracies, for example, have government-paid health care for all citizens whereas the United States does not. Compared to other democracies, however, the United States attempts to more equally educate its children, a policy consistent with its cultural emphasis on equality of opportunity. Like social welfare, however, education is a contentious issue involving disputes over the federal government's role, school choice, spending levels, and mandatory testing.

KEY TERMS

effective tax rate (*p. 599*)
entitlement programs (*p. 589*)
equality of opportunity (*p. 600*)
in-kind benefit (*p. 596*)
means test (*p. 593*)
negative government (*p. 588*)

positive government (*p. 588*)
poverty line (*p. 584*)
public assistance (*p. 593*)
social insurance (*p. 589*)
transfer payments (*p. 589*)

SUGGESTED READINGS

Alesina, Alberto, and Edward Glaeser. *Fighting Poverty in the U.S. and Europe: A World of Difference.* New York: Oxford University Press, 2006. A comparison of poverty policies in the United States and Europe.

Howard, Christopher. *The Welfare State Nobody Knows: Debunking Myths About U.S. Social Policy*. Princeton, N.J.: Princeton University Press, 2006. A critical assessment of the U.S. social welfare system.

Kornbluh, Felicia Ann. *The Battle for Welfare Rights: Politics and Poverty in Modern America*. Philadelphia: University of Pennsylvania Press, 2007. An analysis of welfare rights and conditions, with particular attention to the feminization of poverty.

Patterson, James T. *America's Struggle Against Poverty in the Twentieth Century*. Cambridge, Mass.: Harvard University Press, 2000. A careful study of poverty and its history.

Quadagno, Jill. *One Nation, Uninsured: Why the United States Has No National Health Insurance*. New York: Oxford University Press, 2005. A look at the politics of U.S. health care policy.

Reed, Douglas S. *On Equal Terms: The Constitutional Politics of Educational Opportunity*. Princeton, N.J.: Princeton University Press, 2003. An insightful analysis of school reform issues.

Spring, Joel H. *The American School 1642–2004: From the Puritans to No Child Left Behind*. New York: McGraw-Hill, 2008. A history of U.S. public schools.

Van Dunk, Emily, and Anneliese M. Dickman, *School Choice and the Question of Accountability*. New Haven, Conn.: Yale University Press, 2003. A careful look at the voucher system as applied in the Milwaukee school system.

LIST OF WEBSITES

http://www.doleta.gov/ The U.S. Department of Labor's website on the status of the welfare-to-work program, including state-by-state assessments.

http://www.nea.org/ The home page of the National Education Association; provides information on the organization's membership and policy goals.

http://www.os.dhhs.gov/ The website of the Department of Health and Human Services—the agency responsible for most federal social welfare programs.

http://www.npc.umich.edu The website of the University of Michigan's National Poverty Center, which seeks to stimulate interest in policy issues and to transmit research findings to policymakers.

POLITICS IN THEORY AND PRACTICE

Thinking: How has U.S. policy on welfare and education been influenced by Americans' belief in individualism? By America's federal system of government?

Participating: When it comes to partisan politics, poverty is a contentious issue. Republicans and Democrats disagree mightily on the question of how far government should go in helping the poor. On the other hand, virtually all

Americans—on the right and on the left—support private efforts to help the poor. Numerous local religious, civic, social, and economic groups run programs for the poor, such as food kitchens and clothing drives. Also, many national organizations work locally to assist the poor. An example is Habitat for Humanity, which builds modest houses with volunteer labor and then makes them available to low-income families, which assist in the construction and receive low-interest or no-interest mortgages to pay for the cost of construction materials. Consider volunteering some of your time to a group that gives a helping hand to those in need—whether a church or a community group or a nonprofit organization like Habitat for Humanity. Habitat for Humanity has a website that makes it easy for you to volunteer.

Extra Credit

For up-to-the-minute *New York Times* articles, interactive simulations, graphics, study tools, and more links and quizzes, visit the text's Online Learning Center at **www.mhhe.com/pattersonwtp8e.**

Welfare Reform

By Bill Clinton

One of the most significant legislative initiatives of the late twentieth century was the Welfare Reform Act of 1996, which ended the decades-long family assistance program and replaced it with Temporary Assistance to Needy Families (TANF). On the tenth anniversary of that legislation, former President Bill Clinton wrote an op-ed piece in the New York Times *on what the passage of the Welfare Reform Act says about politics and policy. He argues that bipartisanship is a critical component of successful efforts to tackle large and controversial issues such as welfare reform.*

Ten years ago today I signed the Personal Responsibility and Work Opportunity Reconciliation Act. By then I had long been committed to welfare reform. As a governor, I oversaw a workfare experiment in Arkansas in 1980 and represented the National Governors Association in working with Congress and the Reagan administration to draft the welfare reform bill enacted in 1988.

Yet when I ran for president in 1992, our system still was not working for the taxpayers or for those it was intended to help. In my first State of the Union address, I promised to "end welfare as we know it," to make welfare a second chance, not a way of life, exactly the change most welfare recipients wanted it to be.

Most Democrats and Republicans wanted to pass welfare legislation shifting the emphasis from dependence to empowerment. Because I had already given 45 states waivers to institute their own reform plans, we had a good idea of what would work. Still, there were philosophical gaps to bridge. The Republicans wanted to require able-bodied people to work, but were opposed to continuing the federal guarantees of food and medical care to their children and to spending enough on education, training, transportation and child care to enable people to go to work in lower-wage jobs without hurting their children.

On Aug. 22, 1996, after vetoing two earlier versions, I signed welfare reform into law. At the time, I was widely criticized by liberals who thought the work requirements too harsh and conservatives who thought the work incentives too generous. Three members of my administration ultimately resigned in protest. Thankfully, a majority of both Democrats and Republicans voted for the bill because they thought we shouldn't be satisfied with a system that had led to intergenerational dependency.

The last 10 years have shown that we did in fact end welfare as we knew it, creating a new beginning for millions of Americans.

In the past decade, welfare rolls have dropped substantially, from 12.2 million in 1996 to 4.5 million today. At the same time, caseloads declined by 54 percent. Sixty percent of mothers who left welfare found work, far surpassing predictions of experts. Through the Welfare to Work Partnership, which my administration started to speed the transition to employment, more than 20,000 businesses hired 1.1 million former welfare recipients. Welfare reform has proved a great success, and I am grateful to the Democrats and Republicans who had the courage to work together to take bold action.

The success of welfare reform was bolstered by other anti-poverty initiatives, including the doubling of the earned-income tax credit in 1993 for lower-income workers; the 1997 Balanced Budget Act, which included $3 billion to move long-term welfare recipients and low-income, noncustodial fathers into jobs; the Access to Jobs initiative, which helped communities create innovative transportation services to enable former welfare recipients and other low-income workers to get to their new jobs; and the welfare-to-work tax credit, which provided tax incentives to encourage businesses to hire long-term welfare recipients.

I also signed into law the toughest child-support enforcement in history, doubling collections; an increase in the minimum wage in 1997; a doubling of federal financing for child care, helping parents look after 1.5 million children in 1998; and a near doubling of financing for Head Start programs.

The results: child poverty dropped to 16.2 percent in 2000, the lowest rate since 1979, and in 2000, the percentage of Americans on welfare reached its lowest level in four decades. Overall, 100 times as many people moved out of poverty and into the middle class during our eight years as in the previous 12. Of course the booming economy helped, but the empowerment policies made a big difference.

Regarding the politics of welfare reform, there is a great lesson to be learned, particularly in today's hyper-partisan environment, where the Republican leadership forces bills through Congress without even a hint of bipartisanship. Simply put, welfare reform worked because we all worked together. The 1996 Welfare Act shows us how much we can achieve when both parties bring their best ideas to the negotiating table and focus on doing what is best for the country.

The recent welfare reform amendments, largely Republican-only initiatives, cut back on states' ability to devise their own programs. They also disallowed hours spent pursuing an education from counting against required weekly work hours. I doubt they will have the positive impact of the original legislation.

We should address the inadequacies of the latest welfare reauthorization in a bipartisan manner, by giving states the flexibility to consider higher education as a category of "work," and by doing more to help people get the education they need and the jobs they deserve. And perhaps even more than additional welfare reform, we need to raise the minimum wage, create more good jobs through a commitment to a clean energy future and enact tax and other policies to support families in work and child-rearing.

Ten years ago, neither side got exactly what it had hoped for. While we compromised to reach an agreement, we never betrayed our principles and we passed a bill that worked and stood the test of time. This style of cooperative governing is anything but a sign of weakness. It is a measure of strength, deeply rooted in our Constitution and history, and essential to the better future that all Americans deserve, Republicans and Democrats alike.

What's Your Opinion?

Do you share former President Clinton's assessment of the 1996 Welfare Reform Act—was it the success he claims it to be? Do you agree or disagree with his claim about the importance of bipartisanship? Why?

CHAPTER 17

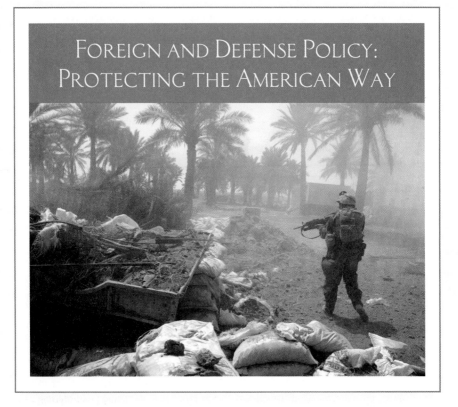

FOREIGN AND DEFENSE POLICY: PROTECTING THE AMERICAN WAY

66 We the people of the United States, in order to . . . provide for the common defense . . . **99**

PREAMBLE, U.S. CONSTITUTION

The leaders of eight of the world's most powerful nations met in Japan in 2008 for their annual G8 summit. The 2008 meeting, which was the final summit for President George W. Bush and the first for British Prime Minister Gordon Brown and Russian President Dmitry Medvedev, addressed a wide range of global issues. Climate change was on the agenda, as was the issue of sustainable energy supplies. A joint policy toward African economic development was also discussed, along with global trade and the protection of intellectual property rights. Iraq received only passing attention, although approaches to international terrorism and nuclear nonproliferation were areas of discussion.

As the G8 summit illustrates, national security is an issue of economic strength as well as of military power. The world's top leaders did not ignore the military threats existing in the world, but they concentrated on economic and related issues. The emphasis reflected a core reality: the goal of foreign policy includes the preservation of a nation's way of life as well as its physical security. In the case of the United States, this goal requires both a level of military readiness that will protect the United States and a level of marketplace vitality that will enable a society of 300 million people to thrive in an increasingly globalized economy.

National security, unlike other areas of government policy, rests on relations with actors outside rather than within the country. As a result, the chief instruments of national security policy differ substantially from those of domestic policy. One of these instruments is diplomacy—the process of negotiation between countries. The lead agency in U.S. diplomatic efforts is the Department of State, which is headed by the secretary of state and coordinates the efforts of U.S. embassies abroad, each of which is directed by a U.S. ambassador. American diplomacy also takes place through international organizations—such as the United Nations—to which the United States belongs. A second instrument of foreign policy is military power. The lead agency in military affairs is the Department of Defense, which is headed by the secretary of defense and oversees the three U.S. military branches—the Army, Navy, and Air Force. Here, too, the United States sometimes works through alliances, the most important of which is the North Atlantic Treaty Organization (NATO). NATO has nearly thirty member nations, including the United States, Canada, and most Western and Eastern European countries. A third instrument of world politics is intelligence gathering, or the process of monitoring other countries' activities. For many reasons, but primarily because all countries pursue their own self-interest, each nation keeps a watchful eye on other nations. In the United States, the task of intelligence gathering falls to specialized federal agencies including the Central Intelligence Agency (CIA) and the National Security Agency (NSA). Economic exchange, the fourth instrument of foreign affairs, involves both international trade and foreign aid. U.S. interests in this area are promoted by a range of U.S. agencies, such as the Agriculture, Commerce, Labor, and Treasury Departments, as well as specialty agencies such as the Federal Trade Commission. The United States also pursues its economic goals through international organizations of which it is a member, including the World Trade Organization (WTO), the World Bank, and the International Monetary Fund (IMF).

The national security policies of the United States include an extraordinary array of activities—so many, in fact, that they could not possibly be addressed adequately in an entire book, much less a single chapter. There are roughly two hundred countries in the world, and the United States has relations of one kind or another—military, diplomatic, economic—with all of them. This chapter narrows the subject by concentrating on a few main ideas:

★ *Since World War II, the United States has acted in the role of world leader, which has substantially affected its military, diplomatic, and economic policies.*

★ *The United States maintains a high degree of defense preparedness, which mandates a substantial level of defense spending and a worldwide deployment of U.S. conventional and strategic forces.*

★ *Changes in the international marketplace have led to increased economic interdependence among nations, which has had a marked influence on the U.S. economy and on America's security planning.*

THE ROOTS OF U.S. FOREIGN AND DEFENSE POLICY

Historical Background

Prior to World War II, the United States was an **isolationist** country, deliberately avoiding a large role in world affairs. A different America emerged from the war. It had more land, sea, and air power than any other country in the world; a huge military-industrial base; and several hundred overseas military bases. The United States had become an **internationalist** country, deeply involved in the affairs of other nations.

It was also a nation not fully at peace. The United States was locked in a sprawling conflict with the Soviet Union, which had aided the takeover of power by communist parties in Eastern Europe. Poland, Hungary, Czechloslovakia, and the other Eastern European nations were forced into the Soviet orbit, leading Britain's Winston Churchill to say that an "iron curtain" had fallen across Europe. Thereafter, U.S. security policy was designed to contain Soviet power. President Harry Truman and other American leaders regarded communist Russia as an implacable foe, a view that led to the formulation of the doctrine of **containment**—the idea that the Soviet Union could be stopped from achieving its global ambitions only by the forceful use of American power.[1]

The Cold War Era

Developments in the late 1940s embroiled the United States in a **cold war** with the Soviet Union.[2] The term refers to the fact that the two countries were not directly engaged in actual combat (a "hot war") but were locked

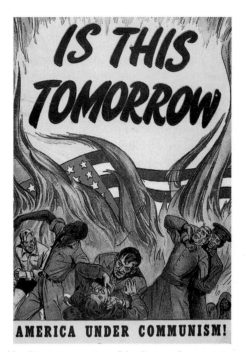

Cold war propaganda, like this poster warning of the danger of communism, contributed to a climate of opinion in the United States that led to public support for efforts to contain Soviet power.

in deep-seated hostilities that lasted forty-five years. The structure of international power was **bipolar:** the United States against the Soviet Union. Each side was supreme in its sphere and was blocked from expanding its influence by the power of the other. For example, when the Soviet-backed North Koreans invaded South Korea in June 1950, President Truman sent troops into the conflict, which ended three years later in stalemate and resulted in the death of 35,000 U.S. soldiers.

A major turning point in U.S. foreign policy was the Vietnam War. Responding to the threat of a communist takeover, the United States became ever more deeply involved in the civil war in Vietnam. By the late 1960s, 550,000 Americans were stationed in South Vietnam. Although U.S. forces were technically superior in combat to the communist fighters, Vietnam was a guerrilla war, with no front lines and few set battles.[3] U.S. public opinion, most visibly among the young, gradually turned against the war, contributing to President Lyndon Johnson's decision not to seek reelection in 1968. Public opinion forced Richard Nixon, who became president in 1969, to aim not for victory but for a gradual disengagement. U.S. combat troops left Vietnam in 1973, and two years later North Vietnamese forces completed their takeover

of the country. Vietnam was the most painful and costly application of the containment doctrine: 58,000 American soldiers lost their lives in the fighting.

America's defeat in Vietnam forced U.S. policymakers to reconsider the
country's international role. The "lesson of Vietnam" was that there were
limits to the country's ability to assert its will in the world. Nixon sought
to reduce tensions with communist countries, asserting that the United
States could no longer be the free world's "Lone Ranger." In 1972, Nixon
visited the People's Republic of China, the first official contact with that
country since the communists seized power in 1949. Nixon also initiated
the Strategic Arms Limitation Talks (SALT), which resulted in reductions
in the nuclear weapon arsenals of the United States and the Soviet Union.
This spirit of cooperation lasted until the Soviet invasion of Afghanistan
in 1979, which convinced U.S. leaders that the USSR was still bent on expansion and was a threat to Western interests in the oil-rich Middle East.
Ronald Reagan, elected president in 1980, called for a renewed hard line
toward the Soviet Union, which he described as the "evil empire."

Although U.S. policymakers did not know it at the time, the Soviet
Union was collapsing under the weight of its heavy defense expenditures,
its isolation from Western technology and markets, and its inefficient centralized economy. In 1985, the Soviet Union's newly chosen leader, Mikhail
Gorbachev, ordered its troops to leave Afghanistan (which had become his
country's Vietnam) and announced a plan to restructure Soviet society, an
initiative known as *perestroika*. However, Gorbachev's reforms came too
late to save the Soviet Union. In 1989, Soviet troops withdrew from Eastern
Europe, freeing Poland, Austria, and other Eastern European countries
from Soviet control and culminating in the dismantling of the Berlin Wall
that separated communist East Germany from democratic West Germany.
In late 1991, the leaders of the Russian, Belarus, and Ukrainian republics
declared that the Soviet Union no longer existed. The bipolar power structure that had dominated world politics since the end of World War II had
collapsed. The new structure was **unipolar**—the United States was now the
world's unchallenged superpower.

A New World Order

The end of the cold war prompted the first President Bush in 1990 to call
for a "new world order." George H. W. Bush advocated **multilateralism**—
the idea that major nations should act together in response to problems
and crises. Included in Bush's plan was a stronger role for multinational
organizations such as the UN and NATO.

Multilateralism defined America's response to the Iraqi invasion of Kuwait
in August 1990. President Bush obtained UN resolutions ordering Iraq to

withdraw from Kuwait and authorizing the use of force if it did not. Five months later, a half million troops, mostly American but including contingents from nearly two dozen nations, attacked Iraq, first with an aerial bombardment and then with ground troops. Four days into the ground fighting, Iraqi units fled the battlefield, ending the war.

The Gulf operation was a military triumph, prompting President Bush to declare that the United States had "kicked the Vietnam syndrome [the legacy of America's defeat in Vietnam] once and for all." The Gulf War, however, was in another way less successful. Believing that an overthrow of Hussein's regime would destabilize Iraq, President Bush ordered a halt to the hostilities after Iraqi forces retreated. Hussein remained in power but was ordered by a UN resolution to dismantle his weapons programs, subject to UN inspections. However, Hussein repeatedly interfered with UN inspectors' attempts to verify the status of his weapons programs, raising concerns about his intentions.

Multilateralism carried over into the Clinton administration. Confronting Serb atrocities in Bosnia—where tens of thousands of Muslims and Croats were murdered, raped, and driven from their homes—President Bill Clinton pursued UN economic sanctions as a means of halting the slaughter. When sanctions failed, the United States and its NATO allies attacked Serb forces with air power. The result was a U.S.-negotiated peace agreement (the Dayton Accords) that included the deployment to Bosnia of nearly 60,000 peacekeeping troops, including 20,000 Americans. War in the Balkans flared again in 1999 when the Serbs undertook a campaign of "ethnic cleansing" in the Serbian province of Kosovo, whose population was 90 percent Albanian. When attempts at a negotiated settlement failed, NATO planes, including U.S. aircraft, attacked Serbia.[4] After weeks of intensive bombing, Yugoslav president Slobodan Milosevic (who died in 2006 while on trial for war crimes) pulled his troops out of Kosovo. Ethnic Albanians moved back in and, despite the presence of UN peacekeeping troops, launched revenge attacks on some of the Serbs who remained. (In 2008, Kosovo became an independent state.)

As these examples indicate, multilateralism was only partly successful as a strategy for resolving international conflicts. With the deployment of enough resources, the world's major powers showed that they could act together with some success. However, these interventions offered no guarantee of long-term success. Regional and internal conflicts typically stem from enduring ethnic, religious, factional, or national hatreds or from chronic problems such as famine, overcrowding, or government corruption. Even if these hatreds or problems can be momentarily eased, they are often too deep-seated to be permanently resolved.

In March 2003, by order of President George W. Bush, U.S. troops attacked Iraq. The intense combat phase was relatively short, ending in the defeat of Iraqi forces. However, the reconstruction phase that followed was marked by continuing violence and destruction. Seen here is a view of U.S. soldiers through a bullet hole in a window.

The War on Terrorism

Upon assuming the presidency in 2001, George W. Bush pointedly said that he would not follow his father's multilateral approach to world affairs. He declared that he would reduce America's military presence abroad, as well as its reliance on the United Nations. He also announced that the United States would not participate in either the Kyoto Accord (a global climate treaty) or the International Criminal Court (the ICC, a permanent tribunal with jurisdiction over war crimes). However, the terrorist attacks of September 11, 2001, on the World Trade Center and the Pentagon forced Bush to change course. Although he continued to oppose the ICC and the Kyoto Accord, Bush urged other nations to join the United States in a global "war on terrorism."

Unlike past wars, the war on terrorism targets not nations but groups engaged in terrorism that is aimed at U.S. interests at home and abroad. A war without sharply defined battlefronts, it is being waged through a wide variety of instruments, including military force, intelligence gathering, law enforcement, foreign aid, international cooperation, and immigration control. The tactics are also unusual. The rooting out of terrorist cells in the United States and Europe, for example, is entrusted to law enforcement agencies rather than to military units.

The war on terrorism resulted in the first major reorganization of the U.S. national security bureaucracy since the Department of Defense was created after World War II to combine the previously separate War and Navy Departments. This time, the new agency was the Department of Homeland Security (DHS), which was created in 2002 to coordinate domestic efforts to protect the United States against terrorist threats. The DHS's responsibilities include securing the nation's borders, enhancing defenses against biological attacks, preparing emergency personnel (police, firefighters, and rescue workers) for their roles in responding to terrorist attacks, and coordinating efforts to stop domestic terrorism.[5]

The first U.S. military action in the war on terrorism was an attack on Afghanistan. Its Taliban-led government had provided training sites and protection to the al Qaeda terrorists who carried out the September 11 attacks. Backed by a UN resolution authorizing the use of force and supported by other NATO member countries, the United States toppled the Taliban government in early 2002; however, al Qaeda leader Osama bin Laden and most of his top lieutenants evaded capture.

In 2002, President Bush labeled Iraq, Iran, and North Korea an "axis of evil," thereby signaling a widening of the war on terrorism. Shortly thereafter, he announced a new national security doctrine: the **preemptive war doctrine.** Speaking at West Point, Bush said that the threat of international terrorism meant that the United States could not afford to wait until it was attacked by hostile nations. Bush declared that America was prepared to take "preemptive action."[6] This concept was not wholly new—U.S. officials had long maintained a right to strike first if faced with a direct and serious threat. What was new about the Bush doctrine was that it extended the option to include military action against less immediate threats.

The Iraq War

In the summer of 2002, Bush targeted the regime of Iraq's Saddam Hussein, claiming that it had weapons of mass destruction (WMDs)—chemical and biological weapons, and possibly nuclear weapons. That October, Congress authorized the use of military force against Iraq if it did not voluntarily disarm. Facing the possibility of an unwanted war in Iraq, America's European allies urged that the disarmament of Iraq occur through the use of UN weapons inspectors. In late 2002, the United Nations passed a resolution requiring Iraq to accept weapons inspections. A two-track policy ensued. UN weapons inspectors entered Iraq in search of WMDs, while at the same time the United States deployed combat units to the Middle East.

POLITICAL CULTURE

Liberty, Equality, and Self-Government

Defense Policy
During the 1950s, when the cold war was at a peak, President Dwight
D. Eisenhower warned against actions that undermined the principles
for which America stands. "The problem in defense," Eisenhower said,
"is how far you can go without destroying from within what you are trying to defend from without." He worried that threats originating abroad
would lead Americans to compromise the nation's ideals. Eisenhower
believed that excessive government secrecy—justified in the name of national security—threatened liberty. He worried that a huge permanent
military and the industrial firms that benefited from it would sap America
of its resources and encourage the country to seek military solutions to
international problems. If America was to remain a beacon of freedom
for the world, it had to remain steadfast in its ideals.

Similar concerns have been raised in the context of the war on terrorism. Nearly all Americans agree that the terrorist threat cannot be met
without making some adjustments in how government operates. However,
disagreement has arisen over specific policies, such as the prolonged detention of noncitizens, the preemptive invasion of Iraq, and the hundreds
of billions being spent on the reconstruction of Iraq and Afghanistan. How
much leeway do you think policymakers should have in their pursuit of the
war on terrorism? If you disagree on what America's leaders have done,
what are the alternatives, and how, if at all, are they more consistent with
America's ideals?

Over strong objections from France, Germany, and Russsia, and despite
the UN's refusal to authorize a military attack, President Bush in March
2003 ordered U.S. forces to invade Iraq. Although British units were also
involved, the assault was essentially an act of **unilateralism**—the situation
in which one nation takes action against another state or states.[7] The Iraqi
regime quickly collapsed—Hussein was deposed after less than a month of
fighting. However, the postcombat phase proved deadlier than the Bush
administration had anticipated. Roadside mines and suicide bombers took
a heavy toll on U.S. soldiers, and the cost of rebuilding Iraq soon exceeded
$100 billion. Moreover, the WMDs that had been the justification for the
war were not to be found. In early 2004, the chief U.S. weapons inspector,

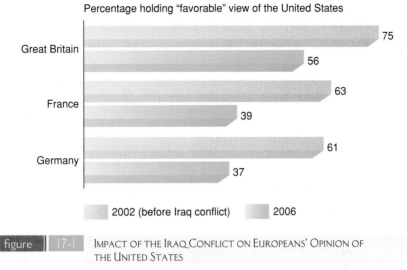

Percentage holding "favorable" view of the United States

- Great Britain: 75 / 56
- France: 63 / 39
- Germany: 61 / 37

2002 (before Iraq conflict)   2006

figure 17-1   IMPACT OF THE IRAQ CONFLICT ON EUROPEANS' OPINION OF THE UNITED STATES

The Iraq conflict led to a sharp decline in Europeans' opinion of the United States.
Source: The Pew Research Center for the People and the Press surveys.

David Kay, testified before Congress that U.S. intelligence agencies had grossly exaggerated the extent of Iraq's weapons program.

The American public, which had backed the invasion of Iraq, came to question the war. Opinions elsewhere were harsher. For the first time since World War II, Western Europeans held that the United States should not be entrusted with world leadership. A year before the war, roughly 65 percent of Western Europeans had expressed a favorable opinion of the United States; fewer than 50 percent held that view after the invasion (see Figure 17-1). This attitude hampered America's ability to get European governments to contribute to the postwar reconstruction of Iraq. Although some assistance was provided, it was limited by public opposition to what was seen as "America's war." Postwar reconstruction was also hampered by instability in Iraq. Age-old animosities between Sunni, Shiite, and Kurdish groups within Iraq blocked political compromise and fueled violence. As the sectarian killings escalated, the animosities deepened. Foreign-born fighters compounded the problem. Iraq's lengthy border with Iran and Syria—countries antagonistic to the United States—allowed Islamic militants from other countries to join the fighting in Iraq.

During White House deliberations before the war, Secretary of State Colin Powell had invoked what he called "the Pottery Barn rule." Powell warned that officials who believed Iraqis would welcome U.S. troops with open arms were engaging in wishful thinking. Foreseeing a difficult postinvasion phase, Powell said, "If you break it, you own it." Indeed, the United States has largely gone it alone in the reconstruction of Iraq, at considerable cost in terms of American lives and dollars. Ninety percent of the casualties and the monetary costs have been borne by the United States.

In 2007, President Bush authorized a "surge" to afford the struggling Iraqi government an opportunity to govern more effectively. Thirty-thousand U.S. soldiers were added to the 130,000 troops already there, and military operations were launched to quell the sectarian violence. The surge contributed to a reduction in the violence, but the Iraqi government continued to have difficulty asserting its authority and resolving contentious issues, such as how the oil revenues would be distributed among Iraq's regions. Against this backdrop, the 2008 presidential candidates differed sharply on the future course of Iraq policy, with Barack Obama promising to withdraw U.S. troops and John McCain promising to stay in Iraq until it had a stable government.

The difficulty of the Iraq reconstruction phase has limited America's ability to respond to other fronts in the war on terrorism. Since the Iraq invasion, North Korea has acquired nuclear weapons, Iran is developing the technology that could lead to the acquisition of such weapons, and Taliban forces in Afghanistan have regrouped and are expanding the fighting there. Thus, as was true of multilateralism, unilateralism has been shown to have limits. Even with the world's most powerful military, the United States has found it difficult to go it alone in Iraq. Wars like those in Iraq and Vietnam do not lend themselves to quick and tidy battlefield solutions. It is one thing to defeat a conventional army in open warfare and quite another to prevail in a conflict in which the fight is not so much a battle for territory as for people's loyalties, especially when the people involved distrust each other, as in the case of Iraq's Sunnis, Shiites, and Kurds.

THE MILITARY DIMENSION OF NATIONAL SECURITY POLICY

The launching of the war on terrorism brought about the first major increase—several hundred billion dollars—in U.S. defense spending since the 1980s. The United States for decades has spent far more on defense than any other country and, with the recent increase, now accounts for roughly half of all military spending worldwide (see "How the United States Compares"). U.S. defense spending is six times that of China and nearly ten times that of Russia.

🌐 HOW THE UNITED STATES COMPARES

Worldwide Military Spending

The United States spends roughly half of all the money spent worldwide on the military. The U.S. military establishment is huge and is deployed all over the world, and American taxpayers spend more than half a trillion dollars each year to support it. China is second in military spending, but its expenditures are only a sixth those of the United States. Russia spends about a tenth of what the United States spends. Even on a per-capita basis, the United States ranks far ahead of other nations in military spending.

The United States has pressured its Western allies to carry a larger share of the defense burden, but some of these countries have resisted, contending that the cost would be too high and that their security would not be substantially improved. Of the Western European countries, Britian spends the most; its military spending on a per-capita basis is about a third that of the United States.

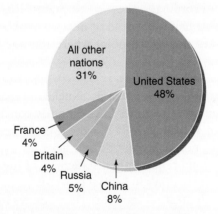

Source: Center for Arms Control and Non-Proliferation, 2008.

Military Power, Uses, and Capabilities

U.S. military forces are trained or called on for different types of military action, ranging from nuclear conflict to guerrilla warfare.

Nuclear War Capability Although the possibility of all-out nuclear war with Russia declined dramatically with the end of the cold war, the

United States retains a nuclear arsenal designed to prevent such a war from ever happening. **Deterrence policy** is based on the notion that any nation would be deterred from launching a full-scale nuclear attack on the United States by the knowledge that, even if it destroyed the country, it too would be obliterated. America's nuclear weapons are deployed in what is called the "nuclear triad." This term refers to the three ways nuclear weapons can be launched: by land-based missiles, by submarine-based missiles, and by bombers. The triad provides a second-strike capability—that is, the ability to absorb a first-strike nuclear attack and survive with enough nuclear punch for a massive retaliation (second strike). Since the end of the cold war, the United States and Russia have negotiated reductions in their nuclear arsenals and have created monitoring systems designed to reduce the possibility that either side could launch an effective surprise attack.

A greater fear today than nuclear war with Russia is the possibility that a terrorist group or rogue nation will smuggle a nuclear device into the United States and detonate it. The technology and materials necessary to build a nuclear weapon (or to buy one clandestinely) are more readily available than ever before. Accordingly, the United States, Russia, and other nations are cooperating to halt the spread of nuclear weapons. This effort has had some success, but not to the point where the nuclear threat has been eliminated.

Conventional and Guerrilla War Capability   Nuclear preparedness is just one part of America's combat readiness. A second is conventional-force preparedness. Not since World War II has the United States fought an all-out conventional war, nor at present does it have the capacity to fight one. That type of war would require a reinstatement of the military draft and full mobilization of the nation's industrial capacity. Instead, the United States today has an all-volunteer military force (see "States in the Nation") that is second to none in its destructive power. When U.S. forces invaded Iraq in 2003, they were outnumbered by three to one yet took only three weeks to seize control of Baghdad, at which point the remaining Iraqi army units quit the field.

The U.S. Navy has a dozen aircraft carriers, scores of attack submarines, and hundreds of fighting and supply ships. The U.S. Air Force has thousands of high-performance aircraft, ranging from fighter jets to jumbo supply planes. The U.S. Army has roughly 500,000 regular troops and more than 300,000 Reserve and National Guard soldiers, who are supplied with tanks, artillery pieces, armored personnel carriers, and attack helicopters. This armament is doubly lethal because it is linked to

★ STATES IN THE NATION

The All-Volunteer Military's Recruits

Until 1973, the United States had an active military draft. Upon reaching the age 18, males were required to register for the draft. Local draft boards would then pick the draftees based on quotas that varied with the size of the local population. Accordingly, each state contributed equally to the military's manpower needs relative to its population size. Today's military is an all-volunteer force, and the states' contributions vary significantly. The map below indicates the degree to which each state is over- and underrepresented in the military as indicated by the ratio of military recruits from a state to the number of males ages 18–34

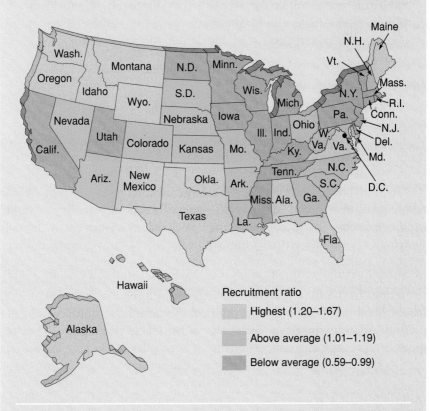

Recruitment ratio

Highest (1.20–1.67)

Above average (1.01–1.19)

Below average (0.59–0.99)

Source: Adapted from Tim Kane, "Who Bears the Burden? Demographic Characteristics of U.S. Military Recruits Before and After 9/11," Heritage Foundation, Center for Data Analysis Report #05-08, November 7, 2005.

(continued)

in that state's population. Montana has the most recruits relative to its population, followed by Alaska, Wyoming, and Maine. Utah, Rhode Island, and Massachusetts rank lowest.

Q: Why might recruits come disproportionately from states like Montana, Alaska, Wyoming, and Maine as well as from the South?

A: According to Department of Defense data, recruits are more likely to come from rural areas, particularly areas where few well-paying jobs are available to young adults. The four states with the highest recruitment ratios have these characteristics. As for the South, it has a strong military tradition and numerous military installations. Individuals from areas near these installations, as well as the sons and daughters of military personnel, are more likely to enlist in the military. (Mississippi and Tennessee, with the South's lowest recruitment rates, have relatively few military installations.)

sophisticated surveillance, targeting, and communication systems. No other nation has anywhere near the advanced weapons systems that the United States possesses.

This capability, however, is not a large advantage in the type of war taking place in Iraq and Afghanistan—guerrilla actions featuring roadside explosive devices and suicide bombings. Such tactics are extremely difficult to defend against and virtually impossible to stop by conventional military means. To defeat such an enemy requires the full support of the local population. Without this backing, the enemy has the capacity to sustain operations over a long period in an attempt to force a withdrawal of U.S. forces. Such situations require a political solution, not a military one, and political solutions are never as decisive as battlefield encounters. They require compromise and concessions from both sides. An occupying power, such as the United States, often is at a disadvantage in these negotiations because its interests include the withdrawal of its forces. If the occupier is dealing with a determined enemy that has the will and the capacity to continue the fight indefinitely, as was the case in Vietnam and could be the situation in Iraq, at some point it can be forced to accept an arrangement that is far less satisfying than the outcome that was anticipated upon entering into war.

The Politics of National Defense

Policy elites, public opinion, and special interests all play significant roles in national defense policy. The U.S. public usually supports the judgments of its political leaders on the use of military force. In nearly all military initiatives of the past half-century, Americans have backed the action. When President Bush spoke of the need for an invasion and then ordered U.S. forces into Iraq in 2003,[8] two-thirds of Americans supported the decision. The other third were split between those who opposed the war and those who were unsure about whether it was the proper course of action. Public support for a war can persist, as was the case during the first six years of the Vietnam conflict. However, if the war seems endless and as the human and financial toll rises, public support erodes. A swing in public opinion against the Vietnam War forced U.S. policymakers to withdraw American troops in 1973. Public opinion on the Iraq war soured more quickly, partly because the official reason for the war—the threat of Iraq's weapons of mass destruction—proved erroneous. Research on the Korean and Vietnam wars indicates that, once Americans turn against a war, it is almost impossible to regain their support for it. If that pattern holds true for Iraq, U.S. policymakers have only limited options in trying to resolve that conflict.

Wars are only one area of national defense policy, however. In other areas, such as the recent decision to expand NATO to include Eastern European countries, public opinion plays only a small role.[9] The general public is not interested or informed enough about most national security issues to contribute to their resolution, particularly during the formative stage when critical first decisions are made. The American people ordinarily trust their leaders to make the right decisions in such cases and will back them unless the decisions turn out badly.

Although citizens may assume that national security policy is decided strictly on the basis of what is necessary to protect U.S. interest, the assumption is unwarranted. In his 1961 farewell address, President Dwight D. Eisenhower, who had commanded U.S. forces in Europe during World War II, warned Americans against "the unwarranted influence" and "misplaced power" of what he termed "the **military-industrial complex.**" Eisenhower was referring to the fact that national defense is big business, involving the annual expenditure of hundreds of billions of dollars.[10] As Eisenhower described it, the military-industrial complex has three components: the military establishment, the arms industry, and the members of Congress from states and districts that depend heavily on the arms industry. All three benefit from a continuously high level of defense

★ ‖ LEADERS

Dwight D. Eisenhower
(1890–1969)

One of four army generals to be elected to the presidency, Dwight D. Eisenhower left his mark on war and peace. Born in Abilene, Texas, Eisenhower was an accomplished athlete and student, and in his senior year of high school, he received an appointment to West Point. During World War II, he commanded the Allied Forces that landed in North Africa and drove the German army back to the European mainland. He was Supreme Commander of the multinational force that on June 6, 1944 (D-Day), landed at Normandy, initiating the drive across Europe that eventually would force Germany to surrender. He declined an opportunity to run for the presidency in 1948 but accepted a Republican draft to run in 1952. Given his stature as the most popular figure in America, Eisenhower won easily.

Though trained in the art of war, Eisenhower sought throughout his presidency to reduce cold war tensions. He signed the truce that led to the end of the Korean conflict. Although he was unsuccessful in negotiating a thaw in the nuclear arms race with Soviet leaders, he convinced them that the United States was not seeking their country's destruction. In 1956, after Egypt nationalized the Suez Canal, a plan by the governments of Britain, France, and Israel to take it back by force was aborted when Eisenhower refused to support it, saying that Egypt had a right to self-determination and that the United Nations, not the force of arms, was the proper avenue for settling the dispute. As he was leaving the presidency, he used his farewell address to warn of the dangers of the military-industrial complex, arguing that sustained high levels of military expenditure and secrecy would only weaken America in the long run.

spending. A considerable proportion of U.S. defense spending reflects the self-interest of the military-industrial complex rather than what is required to keep America safe. The problem is that no one knows exactly what that proportion is.

THE ECONOMIC DIMENSION
OF NATIONAL SECURITY POLICY

Economic considerations are a vital component of national security policy. National security is more than an issue of military might. It is also a question of maintaining a position in the world that will enable the United States to remain an economically prosperous society.

In economic terms, the world today is tripolar—power is concentrated in three centers. One center is the United States, which produces roughly 20 percent of the world's goods and services. Another center is Japan and China, which account for more than 15 percent of the world's economy. The third and largest center, responsible for more than 25 percent of the world's economy, is the twenty-five-country European Union (EU). The EU is dominated by Germany, Britain, and France, which together account for roughly half its economy.

By some indicators, the United States is the weakest of the three economic centers. For example, it has the worst trade imbalance. Although the United States exports roughly $1 trillion annually in goods and services, it imports an even larger amount. The result is a trade deficit that is easily the world's largest. The United States has not had a trade surplus since 1975, and in recent years it has frequently had deficits exceeding $500 billion (see Figure 17-2). In other ways, however, the United States is the strongest of the three economic powers. For one thing, the American economy is the best balanced. Like the other economic powers, the United States has a strong industrial base, but it has a stronger agricultural sector and more abundant natural resources. Its vast fertile plains have made it the world's leading agricultural producer. The United States ranks among the top three countries worldwide in production of wheat, corn, potatoes, peanuts, cotton, eggs, cattle, and pigs. As for natural resources, the United States ranks among the top five nations in deposits of copper, uranium, lead, sulfur, zinc, coal, gold, iron ore, natural gas, silver, and magnesium.[11]

According to the Switzerland-based World Economic Forum, the United States also is more economically competitive than are its major trading rivals (see Chapter 15). The United States owes this position to factors such as its technological know-how.[12] This competitive advantage has been evident since the early 1990s. The slowdown in the U.S. economy that began in 2008 tempered the belief that technological know-how had unleashed unstoppable growth. Nevertheless, other countries have looked to the United States, particularly its technology sector, for policy and market innovations that can drive their own economic growth.

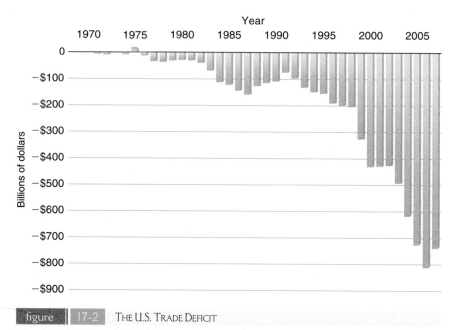

figure 17-2 THE U.S. TRADE DEFICIT

Not since 1975 has the United States had a trade surplus; the deficit reached a record level in 2006. *Source: U.S. Bureau of Economic Analysis, 2008.*

Nevertheless, the United States cannot "go it alone" economically. It depends on other countries for raw materials, finished goods, markets, and capital to meet Americans' production and consumption demands. Meeting this objective requires the United States to exert global economic influence. The broad goals of the United States in the world economy include the following:[13]

- Sustaining a stable and open system of trade that will promote prosperity at home
- Maintaining access to energy and other natural resources vital to the strength of the U.S. economy
- Keeping the widening gap between the rich and poor countries from destabilizing the world economy

Promoting Global Trade

After World War II, the United States helped erect a global trading system centering on itself. The U.S. dollar had become the major currency in international trade, replacing the English pound, which had held that position for more than a century. The war had weakened Britain's economic position in the

Historical Background

world and elevated that of the United States, which moved swiftly to solidify its dominance. A leading initiative was the European Recovery Plan, better known as the Marshall Plan, that provided unprecedented aid (more than $100 billion in today's dollars) for the postwar rebuilding of Europe. Apart from enabling the countries of Western Europe to better confront the perceived Soviet threat, the Marshall Plan served the economic needs of the United States. Wartime production had lifted the country out of the Great Depression, but the end of the war had brought a recession and renewed fears of hard times. A rejuvinated Western Europe furnished a market for American products. In effect, Western Europe became a junior partner within a system of global trade dominated by the United States.

Since then, major changes have taken place in the world economy. Germany is now a trading rival of the United States, as is Japan, which also received substantial postwar reconstruction assistance from the United States. More recently, China and the European Union have taken their place as trading giants, and Russia, propelled by its huge oil and gas reserves, is developing into one.

At the same time, the American economy depends more heavily on international commerce than in any period in the past. The domestic manufacturing sector that once was the source, directly or indirectly, of most U.S. jobs has shrunk, and many of the goods that Americans now buy, from their television sets to their automobiles, are produced by foreign firms. Indeed, nearly all large U.S. firms are themselves **multinational corporations,** with operations in more than one country. From a headquarters in New York City, a firm has no difficulty directing a production facility in Thailand that is filling orders for markets in Europe and South America. Money, goods, and services today flow freely and quickly across national borders, and large firms increasingly think about markets in global rather than national terms.

Economic globalization is a term that describes the increased interdependence of nations' economies. This development is both an opportunity for and a threat to U.S. economic interests. The opportunity rests with the possibility of increased demand abroad for U.S. products and lower prices to U.S. consumers as a result of inexpensive imports. The threat lies in the fact that foreign firms also compete in the global marketplace and may use their competitive advantages, such as cheaper labor, to outposition U.S. firms.

In general, international commerce works best when countries trade freely with one another. This situation keeps the prices of traded items, whether finished goods or raw materials, at their lowest level, resulting in

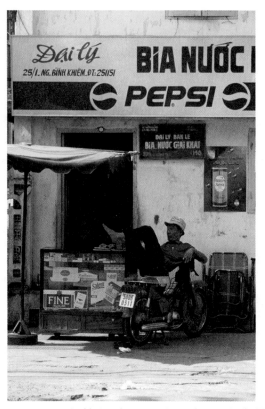

Some U.S. firms are now as recognizable in other countries as they are in the United States. A Pepsi sign adorns the front of this small shop in Vietnam's Ho Chi Minh City (formerly Saigon).

economic efficiency (see Chapter 15). However, global trade is a political issue as well as an economic one, and different countries and interests have different views on how trade among nations should be conducted. **Free trade** describes the situation where barriers to trade between nations are kept to a minimum. Proponents of free trade claim that the long-term economic interests of all countries are advanced when tariffs and other trade barriers are kept to a minimum. Most free-trade advocates couple their advocacy with fair-trade demands, but they are committed, philosophically and practically, to the idea that free trade fuels economic growth, results in a net gain for business, and provides consumers with lower-priced goods.

As opposed to the free-trade argument, **protectionism** emphasizes the immediate interests of domestic producers and includes measures designed to enable them to compete with foreign competitors in the domestic market. For some protectionists, the issue is simply a matter of defending domestic firms against the actions of their foreign competitors. For others, the issue is one of fair trade; they are protectionists in those instances where foreign firms have an unfair competitive advantage—as, for example, when government subsidies allow them to market their goods at an artificially low price. Protectionist sentiment has usually come from Congress rather than the White House. Although most members of Congress say they support free trade and some are unabashed advocates of it, many of them act differently when their state or district is threatened by foreign competition. Then they often try to protect their constituents' interests through measures such as favorable treatment of U.S. goods or tariffs on the goods of foreign competitors.

During the past two decades, the free-trade position has usually prevailed in U.S. policy disputes. In 1993, for example, Congress ratified the North American Free Trade Agreement (NAFTA), which creates a mostly free market among the United States, Canada, and Mexico. Although NAFTA was opposed by most congressional Democrats and by environmental and labor groups that objected to its weak protection of their interests, proponents prevailed due to the backing of President Bill Clinton and most congressional Republicans. The final votes needed for passage were gained by promises of trade protection for Florida citrus and vegetable growers. Another example of support for free trade is U.S. membership in the World Trade Organization (WTO). The WTO, created in 1995, is the formal institution through which most nations negotiate general rules of international trade.[14] The WTO's mission is to promote a global free market through reductions in tariffs, protections for intellectual property (copyrights and patents), and similar policies. WTO members (roughly one hundred thirty in number) are committed to an open trade policy buttressed by regulations designed to ensure fair play among participating nations. Trade disputes among WTO members are settled by arbitration panels, which consist of representatives from the member nations. In 2003, for example, the WTO held that U.S. tariffs on imported steel, which were intended to protect U.S. steelmakers, were illegal under WTO trade rules and had to be rescinded.

Recently, protectionist sentiment has gained strength in the United States. The WTO, for example, has been criticized for placing trade ahead of environmental protection and human rights. Some countries have gained a trade advantage through production processes that degrade the environment and exploit workers, including child laborers. Loss of jobs has also been an issue. Employment in American textile factories, for example, has declined in the face of foreign competition. Even some high-tech jobs have been shipped abroad. Telephone-based technical services, for example, often can be provided at lower cost by hiring educated English-speaking technicians in India instead of their American counterparts.

The jobs issue did not receive much attention during the late 1990s, when the overall U.S. economy was growing at a rapid pace. More recently, as trade deficits mounted and U.S. manufacturing jobs continued to be lost, the question of whether America benefits from free-trade initiatives has become a heated political issue. Free-trade agreements have produced increasingly fierce debate in Congress. Barack Obama and John McCain split sharply on the issue in the 2008 presidential campaign. McCain said that protectionism was no substitute for retraining America's workers to adjust to global trade, while Obama promised protections for America's workers in trade agreements.

Public opinion on global trade has also shifted. Although the American people have not been as supportive of free trade as their leaders, they were about equally divided on its merits in polls taken during the late 1990s. In more recent years, a majority of Americans have come to believe that international trade is hurting the country. Twice as many Americans believe it hurts the nation as believe it serves the country's interest (see Figure 17-3).

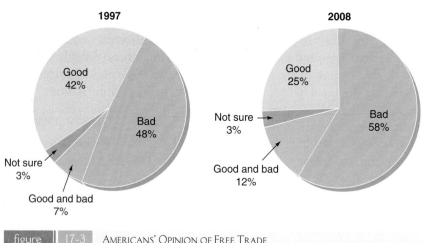

figure 17-3 AMERICANS' OPINION OF FREE TRADE

"Do you think the fact that the American economy has became increasingly global is good because it has opened up new markets for American products and resulted in more jobs, or bad because it has subjected American companies and employees to unfair competition and cheap labor?" *Source: Figure created from NBC/Wall Street Journal polls of June 1997 and March 2008.*

U.S. officials have struggled to find an effective response to this development. Economists argue that the job losses are simply part of the "creative destruction" that occurs naturally in free markets. Firms have no choice but to adapt if they are to survive. Public officials, however, cannot so easily take such a long-range view, because they face immediate pressures from constituents who have lost jobs and from communities that have lost firms. In response to these pressures, U.S. officials have sought to preserve free trade by insisting that foreign governments improve their labor and environmental practices and end their protectionist policies. The stated goal is to make global trade work in ways that will allow U.S. goods to compete on an even playing field. However, other countries are not always convinced that the United States itself plays fair. In 2006, WTO trade talks collapsed in part because the United States refused to reduce its hefty farm subsidies, which enable U.S. agricultural producers to sell their products at a lower price, thereby giving them an advantage over other producers in world commodity markets.

Trade with China in particular is an issue that looms ever larger with U.S. policymakers.[15] In the past decade, America's trade deficit with China has increased more than thirtyfold, surpassing $250 billion annually. The United States has provided China with a marketplace for its goods, which has helped fuel China's economic growth. China in turn has provided the United States with inexpensive goods, which has satisfied America's consumers and helped keep inflation in check. But Congress is increasingly concerned with the trade deficit. Many members of Congress have urged China to increase the value of its currency, which would raise the price of its goods and thereby dampen consumer demand in the United States. Such a step would make U.S. goods more competitive with those produced in China and offer some protection to U.S. firms and workers.

China is also a key to the future of the U.S. dollar as the dominant currency of international trade. As America's trade imbalance has grown, and as the United States has piled up increasing levels of government and consumer debt, the value of the dollar has been declining. Because of trade imbalances, China, Japan, and several other countries have accumulated several trillion dollars in U.S. currency and securities, which decline in value with every drop in the dollar. About 65 percent of all international reserves are in dollars, but the proportion is slowly dropping, with the euro (the European dollar) as the leading alternative. Since 2000, the euro has climbed from less than 20 percent of reserves to 25 percent. Should the trend accelerate, the dollar could conceivably lose the benchmark status it has held since World War II, which would weaken it further.

Maintaining Access to Oil and Other Natural Resources

Although the United States is rich in natural resources, it is not self-sufficient. Oil is the main problem; domestic production provides only about half the nation's needs. Oil has been called "black gold," and even that description understates its significance. Oil is the engine of American society, powering the economy and providing fuel for automobiles and heat for homes and offices. For decades, the United States has used its economic and military power to protect its access to oil.

Outside the United States, most of the world's oil is found in the Middle East, Latin America, Africa, and Russia. Access to oil occurs through world markets. After World War II, the United States acquired a foothold in those markets when its leading oil companies, with their technical expertise and huge amounts of capital, acquired a stake in Middle Eastern oil fields. Since then, U.S. firms have been leaders in worldwide oil exploration and production. Underpinning their activities is the military might of the United States. For example, the U.S. Navy patrols the world's shipping routes to ensure that oil tankers reach their destinations safely.

Oil has a major influence on U.S. foreign policy. The 1991 Gulf War was driven by a concern with oil. Iraq's invasion of Kuwait threatened access not only to Kuwait's oil fields but also to those of its neighbors. Access to oil may also have contributed to President Bush's decision in 2003 to invade Iraq, which has oil reserves of more than 100 billion barrels, second only to those of Saudi Arabia. Oil has also restricted U.S. actions. When Iranian militants in 1979 overthrew their country's pro-Western ruler and seized U.S. embassy personnel as hostages, the United States refrained from a military response in part out of fear of disrupting the flow of Iranian oil. In 2008, when Russia invaded parts of neighboring Georgia, a U.S. ally, the restrained response of the United States and its European allies was a result in part of Europe's dependence on Russian oil and natural gas.

The issue of oil will grow in significance in coming years.[16] Oil production may be nearing peak capacity. New oil fields are still being developed, but the world's major oil reserves are being depleted. Meanwhile, the demand for oil is rising as a result of the rapid economic growth of China, India, and other emerging industrialized countries. Oil topped $140 a barrel for the first time in 2008. If a major disruption in the world's oil supply were to occur, oil prices would skyrocket, possibly causing a global recession.

Assisting Developing Nations

Although political instability in less developed countries can disrupt world markets, less developed countries also offer marketplace opportunities. In order to develop further, they need to acquire the goods and services that more industrialized countries can provide. To foster this demand, the United States and the other industrialized countries provide developmental assistance to poorer countries. Contributions include direct foreign aid and also indirect assistance through international organizations, such as the International Monetary Fund (IMF) and the World Bank. These two organizations were created by the United States and Great Britain at the Bretton Woods Conference near the end of World War II. The IMF makes short-term loans to prevent countries experiencing temporary problems from collapsing economically or resorting to destructive practices such as the unrestricted printing of paper money. The World Bank, on the other hand, makes long-term development loans to poor countries for capital investment projects such as dams, highways, and factories.

Since World War II, the United States has been the leading source of aid to developing countries. Although the United States still contributes the most in terms of total dollars, Canada, Japan, and the European countries spend more on a per-capita basis than does the United States (see Figure 17-4). The United States has narrowed the gap since the events of

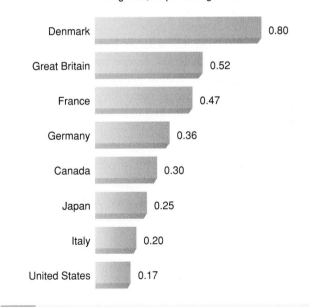

Foreign aid, as percentage of GNI

Denmark	0.80
Great Britain	0.52
France	0.47
Germany	0.36
Canada	0.30
Japan	0.25
Italy	0.20
United States	0.17

figure 17-4 ASSISTANCE TO DEVELOPING COUNTRIES, AS A PERCENTAGE OF GROSS NATIONAL INCOME

The United States ranks highest in terms of total amount spent on foreign aid to developing countries but ranks lower in terms of percentage of gross national income (GNI). Data exclude Iraq reconstruction spending. *Source: OECD (Organization for Economic Cooperation and Development), 2008.*

September 11, 2001, which awakened some policymakers to the fact that global poverty generates resentment of the United States.[17]

Public opinion is an obstacle to higher levels of spending on foreign aid. Polls show that most Americans believe the United States is already spending huge amounts on foreign aid. In a poll that asked Americans to name the largest federal programs, foreign aid topped the list, with 27 percent identifying it as the most expensive program.[18] In fact, foreign aid is far from the top. Nevertheless, Americans' perception makes foreign aid a potent political issue for politicians who would like to decrease it. Jesse Helms (R-N.C.), a past chair of the Senate Foreign Relations Committee, liked to say that foreign aid was nothing more than pouring billions of dollars "down foreign ratholes."[19]

Under President George W. Bush, following a precedent established a quarter-century earlier by President Jimmy Carter, the United States increasingly tied its foreign aid to developing countries' commitment to development, human rights, and democratization. This precondition does not apply to all foreign assistance. For decades, Israel has been at or near the top in terms of the amount of U.S. foreign aid received. After Eygpt made peace with Israel in 1979, it also became a major foreign-aid recipient. More recently, assistance to the Palestinians was increased when their leadership agreed to work toward a peaceful solution to their conflict with the Israelis. These efforts reflect America's long-standing commitment to the preservation of the state of Israel. In the case of the poorer countries, Bush's Millennium Challenge Account program provided proportionately more money to those countries that were making progress in improving the lives of their people. Critics charged that the Bush administration never delivered as much money to these countries as had been promised and that money was not withheld from authoritarian regimes that were instrumental in its war on terrorism. Nevertheless, the program was applied in parts of Africa, South America, and Asia. The largest Millenium Challenge grant was $700 million to Tanzania to reduce poverty in that country through improvements in water, energy, and transportation.

A CHALLENGING WORLD

Seldom has the United States faced as bewildering an array of foreign and defense policy challenges as it faces today. "The world will never again be the same" was a common refrain after September 11, 2001, but few analysts foresaw just how much the world would change in a few short years, let alone the difficulties the United States would have in adjusting to it.

The terrorist threat has expanded beyond all expectations. According to the National Intelligence Estimate that U.S. intelligence agencies compile yearly, global terrorism has worsened in the past few years, partly because the Iraq conflict mobilized and united Islamic extremists around the globe. What analysts disagree about is the duration of America's struggle with radical Islamists. Some analysts predict that the conflict will unwind within a decade or so. Others see it stretching across a far longer period, much like the religiously motivated Thirty Years' War that consumed the first half of the seventeenth century in Europe.

No less daunting is the challenge of the global economy. A decade or so ago, the U.S. economy was the envy of the world, but it is now wobbling as a result of developments at home and abroad. Even the U.S. dollar—long the symbol of America's preeminence in the world—has lost much of its luster. Some analysts predict that the United States will soon recapture its global momentum. Other analysts foresee a long-term decline, fueled by America's financial excesses and oil dependency and by surging economies elsewhere, particularly China's.

SUMMARY   Self-Test www.mhhe.com/pattersonwtp8e

The chief instruments of national security policy are diplomacy, military force, economic exchange, and intelligence gathering. These are exercised through specialized agencies of the U.S. government, such as the Departments of State and Defense, that are largely responsive to presidential leadership. National security policy has also relied on international organizations, such as the United Nations and the World Trade Organization, that are responsive to the global concerns of major nations.

From 1945 to 1990, U.S. foreign and defense policies were dominated by a concern with the Soviet Union. During most of this period, the United States pursued a policy of containment based on the premise that the Soviet Union was an aggressor nation bent on global conquest. Containment policy led the United States to enter into wars in Korea and Vietnam and to maintain a large defense establishment. U.S. military forces are deployed around the globe, and the nation maintains a large nuclear arsenal. The end of the cold war, however, made some of this weaponry and strategic planning less relevant to America's national security.

A first response to the post–cold-war world was multilateralism—the idea that major nations could achieve common goals by working together, including using force as a means of restraining regional conflicts. The interventions in the Persian Gulf and the Balkans during the 1990s are examples. They demonstrated that major nations can intervene with some success in global hot spots but also showed that the ethnic, religious, and national conflicts that fuel these flashes are not easily resolved. The terrorist attacks on the World Trade Center and the Pentagon in

2001 led to broad changes in national security organization and strategy. Increased spending on defense and homeland security has been coupled with a partial reorganization of U.S. intelligence, law enforcement, and immigration agencies, as well as new laws affecting the scope of their activities. However, the defining moment of the post–September 11 period was America's invasion of Iraq in 2003, which was rooted in President George W. Bush's preemptive war doctrine and his willingness to commit the United States to unilateral action.

In recent decades, the United States has increasingly taken economic factors into account in its national security considerations, which has meant, for example, that trade has played a larger part in defining its relationships with other countries. The trading system that the United States helped erect after World War II has given way to one that is more global in scale and more competitive. Changes in communication, transportation, and computing have altered the way large corporations operate, and as businesses have changed their practices, nations have had to adapt. The changes include the emergence of regional and international economic structures, such as the European Union, NAFTA, and the WTO. Nevertheless, nations naturally compete for economic advantage, including access to natural resources; accordingly, trade is a source of conflict as well as a source of cooperation. In the coming years, oil is likely to be at the center of the conflict.

KEY TERMS

bipolar (power structure) (*p. 617*)
cold war (*p. 616*)
containment (*p. 616*)
deterrence policy (*p. 626*)
economic globalization (*p. 633*)
free trade (*p. 634*)
internationalist (*p. 616*)
isolationist (*p. 616*)

military-industrial complex
  (*p. 629*)
multilateralism (*p. 618*)
multinational corporations (*p. 633*)
preemptive war doctrine (*p. 621*)
protectionism (*p. 634*)
unilateralism (*p. 622*)
unipolar (power structure) (*p. 618*)

SUGGESTED READINGS

Clarke, Richard A. *Against All Enemies: Inside America's War on Terror*. New York: Free Press, 2004. A best-selling book by the nation's former top-ranking presidential adviser on terrorism.

Fishman, Ted C. *China, Inc.: How the Rise of the Next Superpower Challenges America and the World*. New York: Scribner, 2005. A look at China's rapid economic growth and its implications.

Hixson, Walter L. *The Myth of American Diplomacy: National Identity and U.S. Foreign Policy*. New Haven, Conn.: Yale University Press, 2008. An analysis of the influence of America's cultural ideals on its foreign policy.

Nye, Joseph S. *Soft Power: The Means to Success in World Politics*. New York: Public Affairs, 2004. An argument for making diplomacy, assistance, and other forms of "soft power" the basis of U.S. foreign policy.

Odom, William E. *Fixing Intelligence*. New Haven, Conn.: Yale University Press, 2003. A detailed critique of U.S. intelligence efforts by a former military intelligence officer.

Stiglitz, Joseph E., and Linda J. Bilmes. *The Three Trillion Dollar War: The True Cost of the Iraq Conflict*. New York: W.W. Norton, 2008. An analysis of the current and future costs associated with the Iraq war, written by a Nobel Prize–winning economist and a former Commerce Department official.

Sobel, Richard. *The Impact of Public Opinion on U.S. Foreign Policy Since Vietnam*. New York: Oxford University Press, 2001. An account of public opinion's impact on foreign policy.

Woodward, Bob. *Plan of Attack*. New York: Simon & Schuster, 2004. An inside look at the Bush administration's decision to go to war in Iraq.

LIST OF WEBSITES

http://www.defenselink.mil/ The U.S. Department of Defense website; provides information on each of the armed services, daily news from the American Forces Information Service, and other material.

http://www.cfr.org/ A website that includes reports and assessments of the Council of Foreign Relations and transcripts of speeches by U.S. and world political leaders on topics of international interest.

http://www.igc.org/igc The website of the Institute for Global Communications (IGC); provides information and services to organizations and activists on a broad range of international issues, including human rights.

http://www.wto.org/ The World Trade Organization (WTO) website; contains information on the organization's activities and has links to related sites.

POLITICS IN THEORY AND PRACTICE

Thinking: What are the major objectives of U.S. foreign and defense policy? What are the mechanisms for pursuing those objectives?

Participating: In his 1961 inaugural address, President John F. Kennedy said, "Ask not what your country can do for you. Ask what you can do for your country." Kennedy called America's young people to service on behalf of their country. His call was not just a call to military service. One of Kennedy's early initiatives, the Peace Corps, offered Americans the opportunity to apply their skills to development projects in other countries. Under Kennedy's successor, President Lyndon Johnson, a domestic version of the Peace Corps—Volunteers in Service to America (VISTA)—was established. Before the military draft ended in 1973, male Americans expected to serve their country. Not all did so, but millions served in the Army, Navy, Air Force, or Marines. Since the end of the draft, Congress has from time to time considered establishing a National Service that would require every young American man and woman to serve the country in one way or another for a set period of time. However, you do not need an act of Congress if you want to serve your country. There are a range of alternatives including the all-volunteer military, the Peace Corps, and AmeriCorps (a network of local, state, and national service programs).

Extra Credit

For up-to-the-minute *New York Times* articles, interactive simulations, graphics, study tools, and more links and quizzes, visit the text's Online Learning Center at www.mhhe.com/pattersonwtp8e.

Iraq Policy

By Barack Obama/John McCain

In 2003, at the order of President George W. Bush, U.S. forces attacked Iraq. Within a few weeks, the regime of Saddam Hussein had been toppled. The reconstruction phase, however, proved far more difficult than the White House had promised. Continuing attacks on U.S. forces and Iraqi civilians slowed the rebuilding of Iraq's infrastructure and the creation of an effective Iraqi government. Two years after the invasion, a majority of Americans had come to believe that the invasion of Iraq was a mistake and the percentage who held this opinion increased as the war continued beyond this point. Polls indicated, however, that Americans were divided on the issue of the next step. Some Americans preferred a rapid withdrawal from Iraq while others held that the United States needed to stay long enough to allow the Iraqi government to gain the strength it would need to pacify the country. These opposing views clashed head-on during the 2008 presidential campaign. Democratic nominee Barack Obama, who had opposed the Iraq invasion, promised a phased withdrawal of U.S. forces. Republican nominee John McCain promised to keep troops in Iraq until U.S. objectives there had been achieved.

Barack Obama, Democratic Presidential Nominee: When I am Commander-in-Chief, I will set a new goal on Day One: I will end this war. Not because politics compels it. Not because our troops cannot bear the burden—as heavy as it is. But because it is the right thing to do for our national security, and it will ultimately make us safer. In order to end this war responsibly, I will immediately begin to remove our troops from Iraq. We can responsibly remove 1 to 2 combat brigades each month. If we start with the number of brigades we have in Iraq today, we can remove all of them 16 months. After this redeployment, we will leave enough troops in Iraq to guard our embassy and diplomats, and a counter-terrorism force to strike al Qaeda if it forms a base that the Iraqis cannot destroy.

What I propose is not—and never has been—a precipitous drawdown. It is instead a detailed and prudent plan that will end a war nearly seven years after it started. My plan to end this war will finally put pressure on Iraq's leaders to take responsibility for their future. Because we've learned that when we tell Iraq's leaders that we'll stay as long as it takes, they take as long as they want.

We need to send a different message. We will help Iraq reach a meaningful accord on national reconciliation. We will engage with every country in the region—and the UN—to support the stability and territorial integrity of Iraq. And we will launch a major humanitarian initiative to support Iraq's refugees and people. But Iraqis must take responsibility for their country. It is precisely this kind of approach—an approach that puts the onus on the Iraqis, and that relies on more than just military power—that is needed to stabilize Iraq.

John McCain, Republican Presidential Nominee: We have the responsibility to finish the job—to place true sovereignty in the hands of the Iraqi people. . . . If we leave, violence will fill the vacuum as groups struggle for political power, and we risk all-out civil war. At the very least, scores will be settled, warlords will reign, and the violence we see today will pale in comparison to the bloodletting. . . .

If we leave, we doom reform in the Arab world. Why should other Arabs embrace democracy and freedom when it cannot take root even after a wholesale regime change in Iraq? If we leave, we risk turning Iraq into a failed state, handing its neighbors—including leading terrorist sponsors Iran and Syria—a prime opportunity to expand their influence in the region, and creating a breeding ground for terrorism.

But if we succeed in stabilizing the country, in building a new government to which we hand sovereignty, in establishing a political system based on freedom and democracy, what will we then have accomplished? . . . If we succeed, we send a message to every despot in the region that their day is done—that no people will tolerate forever leaders who deprive them of liberty. If we succeed, we help create in the center of the Middle East a representative and humane government that provides an example to the region. We help bring an end to the political repression and economic stagnation in which extremist roots grow. People in the region can then express their views within the political system, rather than being forced to its margins. They will have access to economic opportunity that will bring them hope, rather than despair.

What's Your Opinion?

Which argument—Obama's or McCain's—do you find more persuasive? What additional claims might you make to support your position on Iraq?

APPENDIXES

The Declaration of Independence
IN CONGRESS, JULY 4, 1776

The Unanimous Declaration of the Thirteen United States of America

When, in the course of human events, it becomes necessary for one people to dissolve the political bands which have connected them with another, and to assume, among the powers of the earth, the separate and equal station to which the laws of nature and of nature's God entitle them, a decent respect to the opinions of mankind requires that they should declare the causes which impel them to the separation.

We hold these truths to be self-evident, that all men are created equal; that they are endowed by their Creator with certain unalienable rights; that among these, are life, liberty, and the pursuit of happiness. That, to secure these rights, governments are instituted among men, deriving their just powers from the consent of the governed; that, whenever any form of government becomes destructive of these ends, it is the right of the people to alter or to abolish it, and to institute a new government, laying its foundation on such principles, and organizing its powers in such form, as to them shall seem most likely to effect their safety and happiness. Prudence, indeed, will dictate that governments long established, should not be changed for light and transient causes; and, accordingly, all experience hath shown, that mankind are more disposed to suffer, while evils are sufferable, than to right themselves by abolishing the forms to which they are accustomed. But, when a long train of abuses and usurpations, pursuing invariably the same object, evinces a design to reduce them under absolute despotism, it is their right, it is their duty, to throw off such government and to provide new guards for their future security. Such has been the patient sufferance of these colonies, and such is now the necessity which constrains them to alter their former systems of government. The history of the present King of Great Britain is a history of repeated injuries and usurpations, all having, in direct object, the establishment of an absolute tyranny over these States. To prove this, let facts be submitted to a candid world:

He has refused his assent to laws the most wholesome and necessary for the public good.

He has forbidden his governors to pass laws of immediate and pressing importance, unless suspended in their operation till his assent should be obtained; and, when so suspended, he has utterly neglected to attend to them.

He has refused to pass other laws for the accommodation of large districts of people, unless those people would relinquish the right of representation in the legislature; a right inestimable to them, and formidable to tyrants only.

He has called together legislative bodies at places unusual, uncomfortable, and distant from the depository of their public records, for the sole purpose of fatiguing them into compliance with his measures.

He has dissolved representative houses repeatedly for opposing, with manly firmness, his invasions on the rights of the people.

He has refused, for a long time after such dissolutions, to cause others to be elected; whereby the legislative powers, incapable of annihilation, have returned to the people at large for their exercise; the state remaining, in the meantime, exposed to all the danger of invasion from without, and convulsions within.

He has endeavored to prevent the population of these States; for that purpose, obstructing the laws for naturalization of foreigners, refusing to pass others to encourage their migration hither, and raising the conditions of new appropriations of lands.

He has obstructed the administration of justice, by refusing his assent to laws for establishing judiciary powers.

He has made judges dependent on his will alone, for the tenure of their offices, and the amount and payment of their salaries.

He has erected a multitude of new offices, and sent hither swarms of officers to harass our people, and eat out their substance.

He has kept among us, in time of peace, standing armies, without the consent of our legislatures.

He has affected to render the military independent of, and superior to, the civil power.

He has combined, with others, to subject us to a jurisdiction foreign to our Constitution, and unacknowledged by our laws; giving his assent to their acts of pretended legislation:

For quartering large bodies of armed troops among us:

For protecting them by a mock trial, from punishment, for any murders which they should commit on the inhabitants of these States:

For cutting off our trade with all parts of the world:

For imposing taxes on us without our consent:

For depriving us, in many cases, of the benefit of trial by jury:

For transporting us beyond seas to be tried for pretended offences:

For abolishing the free system of English laws in a neighboring province, establishing therein an arbitrary government, and enlarging its boundaries, so as to render it at once an example and fit instrument for introducing the same absolute rule into these colonies:

For taking away our charters, abolishing our most valuable laws, and altering, fundamentally, the powers of our governments:

For suspending our own legislatures, and declaring themselves invested with power to legislate for us in all cases whatsoever.

He has abdicated government here, by declaring us out of his protection, and waging war against us.

He has plundered our seas, ravaged our coasts, burnt our towns, and destroyed the lives of our people.

He is, at this time, transporting large armies of foreign mercenaries to complete the works of death, desolation, and tyranny, already begun, with circumstances of cruelty and perfidy scarcely paralleled in the most barbarous ages, and totally unworthy of the head of a civilized nation.

He has constrained our fellow citizens, taken captive on the high seas, to bear arms against their country, to become the executioners of their friends, and brethren, or to fall themselves by their hands.

He has excited domestic insurrections amongst us, and has endeavored to bring on the inhabitants of our frontiers, the merciless Indian savages, whose known rule of warfare is an undistinguished destruction of all ages, sexes, and conditions.

In every stage of these oppressions, we have petitioned for redress, in the most humble terms; our repeated petitions have been answered only by repeated injury. A prince, whose character is thus marked by every act which may define a tyrant, is unfit to be the ruler of a free people.

Nor have we been wanting in attention to our British brethren. We have warned them, from time to time, of attempts made by their legislature to extend an unwarrantable jurisdiction over us. We have reminded them of the circumstances of our emigration and settlement here. We have appealed to their native justice and magnanimity, and we have conjured them, by the ties of our common kindred, to disavow these usurpations, which would inevitably interrupt our connections and correspondence. They, too, have been deaf to the voice of justice and of consanguinity. We must, therefore, acquiesce in the necessity which denounces our separation, and hold them as we hold the rest of mankind, enemies in war, in peace, friends.

We, therefore, the representatives of the United States of America, in general Congress assembled, appealing to the Supreme Judge of the world for the rectitude of our intentions, do, in the name, and by the authority of the good people of these colonies, solemnly publish and declare, that these united colonies are, and of right ought to be, free and independent states: that they are absolved from all allegiance to the British Crown, and that all political connection between them and the state of Great Britain is, and ought to be, totally dissolved; and that, as free and independent states, they have full power to levy war, conclude peace, contract alliances, establish commerce, and to do all other acts and things which independent states may of right do. And, for the support of this declaration, with a firm reliance on the protection of Divine Providence, we mutually pledge to each other our lives, our fortunes, and our sacred honor.

The foregoing Declaration was, by order of Congress, engrossed, and signed by the following members:

JOHN HANCOCK

New Hampshire
Josiah Bartlett
William Whipple
Matthew Thornton

Massachusetts Bay
Samuel Adams
John Adams
Robert Treat Paine
Elbridge Gerry

Rhode Island
Stephen Hopkins
William Ellery

Connecticut
Roger Sherman
Samuel Huntington
William Williams
Oliver Wolcott

New York
William Floyd
Philip Livingston
Francis Lewis
Lewis Morris

New Jersey
Richard Stockton
John Witherspoon
Francis Hopkinson

John Hart
Abraham Clark

Pennsylvania
Robert Morris
Benjamin Rush
Benjamin Franklin
John Morton
George Clymer
James Smith
George Taylor
James Wilson
George Ross

Delaware
Caesar Rodney
George Reed
Thomas M'Kean

Maryland
Samuel Chase
William Paca
Thomas Stone
Charles Carroll, of
    Carrollton

Virginia
George Wythe
Richard Henry Lee
Thomas Jefferson
Benjamin Harrison
Thomas Nelson, Jr.
Francis Lightfoot Lee
Carter Braxton

North Carolina
William Hooper
Joseph Hewes
John Penn

South Carolina
Edward Rutledge
Thomas Heyward, Jr.
Thomas Lynch, Jr.
Arthur Middleton

Georgia
Button Gwinnett
Lyman Hall
George Walton

Resolved, That copies of the Declaration be sent to the several assemblies, conventions, and committees, or councils of safety, and to the several commanding officers of the continental troops; that it be proclaimed in each of the United States, at the head of the army.

The Constitution of the United States of America[1]

We the People of the United States, in Order to form a more perfect Union, establish Justice, insure domestic Tranquility, provide for the common defence, promote the general Welfare, and secure the Blessings of Liberty to ourselves and our Posterity, do ordain and establish this CONSTITUTION for the United States of America.

ARTICLE I

Section 1

All legislative Powers herein granted shall be vested in a Congress of the United States, which shall consist of a Senate and House of Representatives.

Section 2

The House of Representatives shall be composed of Members chosen every second Year by the People of the several States, and the Electors in each State shall have the Qualifications requisite for Electors of the most numerous Branch of the State Legislature.

No Person shall be a Representative who shall not have attained to the Age of twenty-five Years, and been seven Years a Citizen of the United States, and who shall not, when elected, be an Inhabitant of that State in which he shall be chosen.

[Representatives and direct Taxes[2] shall be apportioned among the several States which may be included within this Union, according to their respective Numbers, which shall be determined by adding to the whole Number of free Persons, including those bound to Service for a Term of Years, and excluding Indians not taxed, three fifths of all other Persons.][3] The actual Enumeration shall be made within three Years after the first Meeting of the Congress of the United States, and within every subsequent Term of ten Years, in such Manner as they shall by Law direct. The Number of Representatives shall not exceed one for every thirty Thousand, but each State shall have at Least one Representative; and until such enumeration shall be made, the State of New Hampshire shall be entitled to chuse three, Massachusetts eight, Rhode-Island and Providence Plantations one, Connecticut five, New York six, New Jersey four, Pennsylvania eight, Delaware one, Maryland six, Virginia ten, North Carolina five, South Carolina five, and Georgia three.

When vacancies happen in the Representation from any State, the Executive Authority thereof shall issue Writs of Election to fill such Vacancies.

---

[1] This version, which follows the original Constitution in capitalization and spelling, was published by the United States Department of the Interior, Office of Education, in 1935.
[2] Altered by the Sixteenth Amendment.
[3] Negated by the Fourteenth Amendment.

The House of Representatives shall chuse their Speaker and other Officers; and shall have the sole Power of Impeachment.

Section 3

The Senate of the United States shall be composed of two Senators from each State, chosen by the Legislature thereof, for six Years; and each Senator shall have one Vote.

Immediately after they shall be assembled in Consequence of the first Election, they shall be divided as equally as may be into three Classes. The Seats of the Senators of the first Class shall be vacated at the Expiration of the second Year, of the second Class at the Expiration of the fourth Year, and of the third Class at the Expiration of the sixth Year, so that one-third may be chosen every second Year; and if Vacancies happen by Resignation, or otherwise, during the Recess of the Legislature of any State, the Executive thereof may make temporary Appointments until the next Meeting of the Legislature, which shall then fill such Vacancies.

No Person shall be a Senator who shall not have attained to the Age of thirty Years, and been nine Years a Citizen of the United States, and who shall not, when elected, be an Inhabitant of that State for which he shall be chosen.

The Vice President of the United States shall be President of the Senate, but shall have no vote, unless they be equally divided.

The Senate shall chuse their other Officers, and also a President pro tempore, in the absence of the Vice President, or when he shall exercise the Office of President of the United States.

The Senate shall have the sole Power to try all Impeachments. When sitting for that purpose they shall be on Oath or Affirmation. When the President of the United States is tried, the Chief Justice shall preside: And no person shall be convicted without the Concurrence of two thirds of the Members present.

Judgment in Cases of Impeachment shall not extend further than to removal from Office, and disqualification to hold and enjoy any Office of honor, Trust, or Profit under the United States: but the Party convicted shall nevertheless be liable and subject to Indictment, Trial, Judgment and Punishment, according to Law.

Section 4

The Times, Place and Manner of holding Elections for Senators and Representatives, shall be prescribed in each State by the Legislature thereof; but the Congress may at any time by Law make or alter such Regulations, except as to the Places of Chusing Senators.

The Congress shall assemble at least once in every Year, and such Meeting shall be on the first Monday in December, unless they shall by Law appoint a different Day.

Section 5

Each House shall be the Judge of the Elections, Returns and Qualifications of its own Members, and a Majority of each shall constitute a Quorum to do Business; but a smaller number may adjourn from day to day, and may be authorized to compel the Attendance of absent Members, in such Manner, and under such Penalties, as each House may provide.

Each House may determine the Rules of its Proceedings, punish its Members for disorderly Behaviour, and, with the Concurrence of two thirds, expel a Member.

Each House shall keep a Journal of its Proceedings, and from time to time publish the same, excepting such Parts as may in their Judgment require Secrecy; and the Yeas and Nays of the Members of either House on any question shall, at the Desire of one fifth of those Present, be entered on the Journal.

Neither House, during the Session of Congress, shall, without the Consent of the other, adjourn for more than three days, nor to any other Place than that in which the two Houses shall be sitting.

Section 6

The Senators and Representatives shall receive a Compensation for their Services, to be ascertained by Law, and paid out of the Treasury of the United States. They shall in all Cases, except Treason, Felony, and Breach of the Peace, be privileged from Arrest during their Attendance at the Session of their respective Houses, and in going to and returning from the same; and for any Speech or Debate in either House, they shall not be questioned in any other Place.

No Senator or Representative shall, during the Time for which he was elected, be appointed to any civil Office under the Authority of the United States, which shall have been created, or the Emoluments whereof shall have been increased, during such time; and no Person holding any Office under the United States shall be a Member of either House during his continuance in Office.

Section 7

All Bills for raising Revenue shall originate in the House of Representatives; but the Senate may propose or concur with Amendments as on other bills.

Every Bill which shall have passed the House of Representatives and the Senate, shall, before it becomes a Law, be presented to the President of the United States; if he approve he shall sign it, but if not he shall return it, with his Objections, to that House in which it shall have originated, who shall enter the Objections at large on their Journal, and proceed to reconsider it. If after such Reconsideration two thirds of that House shall agree to pass the bill, it shall be sent, together with the objections, to the other House, by which it shall likewise be reconsidered, and if approved by two thirds of that House, it shall become a Law. But in all such Cases the Votes of both Houses shall be determined by Yeas and Nays, and the Names of the Persons voting for and against the Bill shall be entered on the Journal of each House respectively. If any Bill shall not be returned by the President within ten Days (Sundays excepted) after it shall have been presented to him, the Same shall be a Law, in like Manner as if he had signed it, unless the Congress by their Adjournment prevent its Return, in which Case it shall not be a Law.

Every Order, Resolution, or Vote to which the Concurrence of the Senate and House of Representatives may be necessary (except on a question of Adjournment) shall be presented to the President of the United States; and before the Same shall take Effect, shall be approved by him, or being disapproved by him, shall be repassed by two thirds of the Senate and House of Representatives, according to the Rules and Limitations prescribed in the Case of a Bill.

Section 8

The Congress shall have Power To lay and collect Taxes, Duties, Imposts and Excises, to pay the Debts and provide for the common Defence and general Welfare of the United States; but all Duties, Imposts and Excises shall be uniform throughout the United States;

To borrow money on the credit of the United States;

To regulate Commerce with foreign Nations, and among the several States, and with the Indian Tribes;

To establish a uniform rule of Naturalization, and uniform Laws on the subject of Bankruptcies throughout the United States;

To coin Money, regulate the Value thereof, and of foreign Coin, and fix the Standard of Weights and Measures;

To provide for the Punishment of counterfeiting the Securities and current Coin of the United States;

To establish Post Offices and post Roads;

To promote the Progress of Science and useful Arts, by securing for limited Times to Authors and Inventors the exclusive Right to their respective Writings and Discoveries;

To constitute Tribunals inferior to the Supreme Court;

To define and punish Piracies and Felonies committed on the high Seas, and Offenses against the Law of Nations;

To declare War, grant Letters of Marque and Reprisal, and make Rules concerning Captures on Land and Water;

To raise and support Armies, but no Appropriation of Money to that Use shall be for a longer Term than two Years;

To provide and maintain a Navy;

To make Rules for the Government and Regulation of the land and naval forces;

To provide for calling forth the Militia to execute the Laws of the Union, suppress Insurrections and repel Invasions;

To provide for organizing, arming, and disciplining the Militia, and for governing such Part of them as may be employed in the Service of the United States, reserving to the States respectively, the Appointment of the Officers, and the Authority of training the Militia according to the discipline prescribed by Congress;

To exercise exclusive Legislation in all Cases whatsoever, over such District (not exceeding ten Miles square) as may, by Cession of particular States, and the acceptance of Congress, become the Seat of the Government of the United States, and to exercise like Authority over all Places purchased by the Consent of the Legislature of the State in which the Same shall be, for the Erection of Forts, Magazines, Arsenals, Dock-yards, and other needful Buildings;—And

To make all Laws which shall be necessary and proper for carrying into Execution the foregoing Powers, and all other Powers vested by this Constitution in the Government of the United States, or in any Department or Officer thereof.

Section 9

The Migration or Importation of such Persons as any of the States now existing shall think proper to admit, shall not be prohibited by the Congress prior to the

Year one thousand eight hundred and eight, but a tax or duty may be imposed on such Importation, not exceeding ten dollars for each Person.

The privilege of the Writ of Habeas Corpus shall not be suspended, unless when in Cases of Rebellion or Invasion the public Safety may require it.

No bill of Attainder or ex post facto Law shall be passed.

No capitation, or other direct, Tax shall be laid unless in Proportion to the Census or Enumeration herein before directed to be taken.

No Tax or Duty shall be laid on Articles exported from any State.

No Preference shall be given by any Regulation of Commerce or Revenue to the Ports of one State over those of another: nor shall Vessels bound to, or from, one State, be obliged to enter, clear, or pay Duties in another.

No Money shall be drawn from the Treasury, but in Consequence of Appropriations made by Law; and a regular Statement and Account of the Receipts and Expenditures of all public Money shall be published from time to time.

No Title of Nobility shall be granted by the United States: And no Person holding any Office of Profit or Trust under them, shall, without the Consent of the Congress, accept of any present, Emolument, Office, or Title, of any kind whatever, from any King, Prince, or foreign State.

Section 10

No State shall enter into any Treaty, Alliance, or Confederation; grant Letters of Marque and Reprisal; coin Money; emit Bills of Credit; make any Thing but gold and silver Coin a Tender in Payment of Debts; pass any Bill of Attainder, ex post facto Law, or Law impairing the Obligation of Contracts, or grant any Title of Nobility.

No State shall, without the Consent of the Congress, lay any Imposts or Duties on Imports or Exports, except what may be absolutely necessary for executing its inspection Laws; and the net Produce of all Duties and Imposts, laid by any State on Imports or Exports, shall be for the use of the Treasury of the United States; and all such Laws shall be subject to the Revision and Control of the Congress.

No state shall, without the Consent of Congress, lay any duty of Tonnage, keep Troops, or Ships of War in time of Peace, enter into any Agreement or Compact with another State, or with a foreign Power, or engage in War, unless actually invaded, or in such imminent Danger as will not admit of delay.

ARTICLE II

Section 1

The executive Power shall be vested in a President of the United States of America. He shall hold his Office during the Term of four years, and, together with the Vice President, chosen for the same Term, be elected, as follows:

Each State shall appoint, in such Manner as the Legislature thereof may direct, a Number of Electors, equal to the whole Number of Senators and Representatives to which the State may be entitled in the Congress: but no Senator or Representative, or Person holding an Office of Trust or Profit under the United States, shall be appointed an Elector.

[The Electors shall meet in their respective States, and vote by Ballot for two persons, of whom one at least shall not be an Inhabitant of the same State with themselves. And they shall make a List of all the Persons voted for, and of the Number of Votes for each; which List they shall sign and certify, and transmit sealed to the Seat of the Government of the United States, directed to the President of the Senate. The President of the Senate shall, in the Presence of the Senate and House of Representatives, open all the Certificates, and the Votes shall then be counted. The Person having the greatest Number of Votes shall be the President, if such Number be a Majority of the whole Number of Electors appointed; and if there be more than one who have such Majority, and have an equal Number of Votes, then the House of Representatives shall immediately chuse by Ballot one of them for President; and if no Person have a Majority, then from the five highest on the List the said House shall in like Manner chuse the President. But in chusing the President, the Votes shall be taken by States, the Representation from each State having one Vote; a quorum for this Purpose shall consist of a Member or Members from two-thirds of the States, and a Majority of all the States shall be necessary to a Choice. In every Case, after the Choice of the President, the Person having the greatest Number of Votes of the Electors shall be the Vice President. But if there should remain two or more who have equal votes, the Senate shall chuse from them by Ballot the Vice President.][4]

The Congress may determine the Time of chusing the Electors, and the Day on which they shall give their Votes; which Day shall be the same throughout the United States.

No person except a natural-born Citizen, or a Citizen of the United States, at the time of the Adoption of this Constitution, shall be eligible to the Office of President; neither shall any Person be eligible to that Office who shall not have attained to the Age of thirty-five years, and been fourteen Years a Resident within the United States.

In Case of the Removal of the President from Office, or of his Death, Resignation, or Inability to discharge the Powers and Duties of the said Office, the same shall devolve on the Vice President, and the Congress may by Law provide for the Case of Removal, Death, Resignation, or Inability, both of the President and Vice President, declaring what Officer shall then act as President, and such Officer shall act accordingly, until the disability be removed, or a President shall be elected.

The President shall, at stated Times, receive for his Services a Compensation, which shall neither be increased nor diminished during the Period for which he shall have been elected, and he shall not receive within that Period any other Emolument from the United States, or any of them.

Before he enter on the execution of his Office, he shall take the following Oath or Affirmation:—"I do solemnly swear (or affirm) that I will faithfully execute the Office of President of the United States, and will, to the best of my Ability, pre-serve, protect, and defend the Constitution of the United States."

Section 2

The President shall be Commander in Chief of the Army and Navy of the United States, and of the Militia of the several States, when called into the actual Service of

[4] Revised by the Twelfth Amendment.

the United States; he may require the Opinion, in writing, of the principal Officer in each of the executive Departments, upon any subject relating to the Duties of their respective Offices, and he shall have Power to Grant Reprieves and Pardons for Offenses against the United States, except in Cases of Impeachment.

He shall have Power, by and with the Advice and Consent of the Senate, to make Treaties, provided two-thirds of the Senators present concur; and he shall nominate, and by and with the Advice and Consent of the Senate, shall appoint Ambassadors, other public Ministers and Consuls, Judges of the supreme Court, and all other Officers of the United States, whose Appointments are not herein otherwise provided for, and which shall be established by Law: but the Congress may by Law vest the Appointment of such inferior Officers, as they think proper, in the President alone, in the Courts of Law, or in the Heads of Departments.

The President shall have Power to fill up all Vacancies that may happen during the Recess of the Senate, by granting Commissions which shall expire at the End of their next Session.

Section 3

He shall from time to time give to the Congress Information of the State of the Union, and recommend to their Consideration such Measures as he shall judge necessary and expedient; he may, on extraordinary occasions, convene both Houses, or either of them, and in Case of Disagreement between them, with respect to the Time of Adjournment, he may adjourn them to such Time as he shall think proper; he shall receive Ambassadors and other public Ministers; he shall take care that the Laws be faithfully executed, and shall Commission all the Officers of the United States.

Section 4

The President, Vice President and all civil Officers of the United States, shall be removed from Office on Impeachment for, and Conviction of, Treason, Bribery, or other high Crimes and Misdemeanors.

ARTICLE III

Section 1

The judicial Power of the United States, shall be vested in one supreme Court, and in such inferior Courts as the Congress may from time to time ordain and establish. The Judges, both of the supreme and inferior Courts, shall hold their Offices during good Behaviour, and shall, at stated Times, receive for their Services, a Compensation, which shall not be diminished during their Continuance in Office.

Section 2

The judicial Power shall extend to all Cases, in Law and Equity, arising under this Constitution, the Laws of the United States, and Treaties made, or which shall be made, under their Authority;—to all Cases affecting ambassadors, other public ministers and consuls;—to all cases of admiralty and maritime Jurisdiction;—to Controversies to which the United States shall be a Party;—to Controversies between two or more states;—between a State and Citizens of another State;[5]—between Citizens of different States—between Citizens of the same State claiming Lands under Grants of different States, and between a State, or the Citizens thereof, and foreign States, Citizens, or Subjects.

In all Cases affecting Ambassadors, other public Ministers and Consuls, and those in which a State shall be Party, the supreme Court shall have original Jurisdiction. In all the other Cases before mentioned, the supreme Court shall have appellate Jurisdiction, both as to Law and Fact, with such Exceptions, and under such Regulations as the Congress shall make.

The trial of all Crimes, except in Cases of Impeachment, shall be by Jury; and such Trial shall be held in the State where the said Crimes shall have been committed; but when not committed within any State, the Trial shall be at such Place or Places as the Congress may by Law have directed.

Section 3

Treason against the United States, shall consist only in levying War against them, or in adhering to their Enemies, giving them Aid and Comfort. No Person shall be convicted of Treason unless on the Testimony of two Witnesses to the same overt Act, or on Confession in open Court.

The Congress shall have power to declare the Punishment of Treason, but no Attainder of Treason shall work Corruption of Blood, or Forfeiture except during the Life of the Person attainted.

ARTICLE IV

Section 1

Full Faith and Credit shall be given in each State to the public Acts, Records, and judicial Proceedings of every other State. And the Congress may by general Laws prescribe the Manner in which such Acts, Records and Proceedings shall be proved, and the Effect thereof.

Section 2

The Citizens of each State shall be entitled to all Privileges and Immunities of Citizens in the several States.

A Person charged in any State with Treason, Felony, or other Crime, who shall flee from Justice, and be found in another State, shall on demand of the executive Authority of the State from which he fled, be delivered up, to be removed to the State having Jurisdiction of the crime.

No Person held to Service or Labour in one State, under the Laws thereof, escaping into another, shall, in Consequence of any Law or Regulation therein, be discharged from such Service or Labour, but shall be delivered up on Claim of the Party to whom such Service or Labour may be due.

---

[5] Qualified by the Eleventh Amendment.

Section 3

New States may be admitted by the Congress into this Union; but no new State shall be formed or erected within the Jurisdiction of any other State; nor any State be formed by the Junction of two or more States, or parts of States, without the Consent of the Legislatures of the States concerned as well as of the Congress.

The Congress shall have Power to dispose of and make all needful Rules and Regulations respecting the Territory or other Property belonging to the United States; and nothing in this Constitution shall be so construed as to Prejudice any Claims of the United States, or of any particular State.

Section 4

The United States shall guarantee to every State in this Union a Republican Form of Government, and shall protect each of them against Invasion; and on Application of the Legislature, or of the Executive (when the Legislature cannot be convened) against domestic Violence.

ARTICLE V

The Congress, whenever two-thirds of both Houses shall deem it necessary, shall propose Amendments to this Constitution, or, on the Application of the Legislatures of two-thirds of the several States, shall call a Convention for proposing Amendments, which, in either Case, shall be valid to all Intents and Purposes, as part of this Constitution, when ratified by the Legislatures of three-fourths of the several States, or by Conventions in three-fourths thereof, as the one or the other Mode of Ratification may be proposed by the Congress; Provided that no Amendment which may be made prior to the Year One thousand eight hundred and eight shall in any Manner affect the first and fourth Clauses in the Ninth Section of the first Article; and that no State, without its Consent, shall be deprived of its equal Suffrage in the Senate.

ARTICLE VI

All Debts contracted and Engagements entered into, before the Adoption of this Constitution, shall be as valid against the United States under this Constitution, as under the Confederation.

This Constitution, and the Laws of the United States which shall be made in Pursuance thereof; and all Treaties made, or which shall be made, under the Authority of the United States, shall be the supreme Law of the Land; and the Judges in every State shall be bound thereby, any Thing in the Constitution or Laws of any State to the Contrary notwithstanding.

The Senators and Representatives before mentioned, and the Members of the several State Legislatures, and all executive and judicial Officers, both of the United States and of the several States, shall be bound by Oath or Affirmation to support this Constitution; but no religious Tests shall ever be required as a qualification to any Office or public Trust under the United States.

ARTICLE VII

The Ratification of the Conventions of nine States shall be sufficient for the Establishment of this Constitution between the States so ratifying the same.

Done in Convention by the Unanimous Consent of the States present the Seventeenth Day of September in the Year of our Lord one thousand seven hundred and Eighty seven, and of the Independence of the United States of America the Twelfth. In Witness whereof We have hereunto subscribed our Names.[6]

George Washington
President and deputy
from Virginia

New Hampshire
John Langdon
Nicholas Gilman

Massachusetts
Nathaniel Gorham
Rufus King

Connecticut
William Samuel Johnson
Roger Sherman

New York
Alexander Hamilton

New Jersey
William Livingston
David Brearley
William Paterson
Jonathan Dayton

Pennsylvania
Benjamin Franklin
Thomas Mifflin
Robert Morris
George Clymer
Thomas FitzSimmons
Jared Ingersoll
James Wilson
Gouverneur Morris

Delaware
George Read
Gunning Bedford, Jr.
John Dickinson
Richard Bassett
Jacob Broom

Maryland
James McHenry
Daniel of St. Thomas
   Jenifer
Daniel Carroll

Virginia
John Blair
James Madison, Jr.

North Carolina
William Blount
Richard Dobbs Spaight
Hugh Williamson

South Carolina
John Rutledge
Charles Cotesworth
   Pinckney
Charles Pinckney
Pierce Butler

Georgia
William Few
Abraham Baldwin

Articles in Addition to, and Amendment of, the Constitution of the United States of America, Proposed by Congress, and Ratified by the Legislatures of the Several States, Pursuant to the Fifth Article of the Original Constitution[7]

AMENDMENT I

Congress shall make no law respecting an establishment of religion, or prohibiting the free exercise thereof; or abridging the freedom of speech, or of the press; or the

---

[6] These are the full names of the signers, which in some cases are not the signatures on the document.

[7] This heading appears only in the joint resolution submitting the first ten amendments, which are collectively known as the Bill of Rights. They were ratified on December 15, 1791.

right of the people peaceably to assemble, and to petition the Government for a redress of grievances.

AMENDMENT II

A well regulated Militia, being necessary to the security of a free State, the right of the people to keep and bear Arms shall not be infringed.

AMENDMENT III

No Soldier shall, in time of peace, be quartered in any house, without the consent of the Owner, nor in time of war, but in a manner to be prescribed by law.

AMENDMENT IV

The right of the people to be secure in their persons, houses, papers, and effects, against unreasonable searches and seizures, shall not be violated, and no Warrants shall issue, but upon probable cause, supported by Oath or affirmation, and particularly describing the place to be searched, and the persons or things to be seized.

AMENDMENT V

No person shall be held to answer for a capital or otherwise infamous crime, unless on a presentment or indictment of a Grand Jury, except in cases arising in the land or naval forces, or in the Militia, when in actual service in time of War or public danger; nor shall any person be subject for the same offence to be twice put in jeopardy of life or limb; nor shall be compelled in any criminal case to be a witness against himself, nor be deprived of life, liberty, or property, without due process of law; nor shall private property be taken for public use, without just compensation.

AMENDMENT VI

In all criminal prosecutions, the accused shall enjoy the right to a speedy and public trial, by an impartial jury of the State and district wherein the crime shall have been committed, which district shall have been previously ascertained by law, and to be informed of the nature and cause of the accusation; to be confronted with the witnesses against him; to have compulsory process for obtaining witnesses in his favour, and to have the Assistance of Counsel for his defence.

AMENDMENT VII

In suits at common law, where the value in controversy shall exceed twenty dollars, the right of trial by jury shall be preserved, and no fact tried by a jury, shall be otherwise reexamined in any Court of the United States, than according to the rules of the common law.

AMENDMENT VIII

Excessive bail shall not be required, nor excessive fines imposed, nor cruel and unusual punishments inflicted.

AMENDMENT IX

The enumeration of the Constitution, of certain rights, shall not be construed to deny or disparage others retained by the people.

AMENDMENT X

The powers not delegated to the United States by the Constitution, nor prohibited by it to the States, are reserved to the States respectively, or to the people.

AMENDMENT XI [1795]

The Judicial power of the United States shall not be construed to extend to any suit in law or equity, commenced or prosecuted against one of the United States by Citizens of another State, or by Citizens or Subjects of any Foreign State.

AMENDMENT XII [1804]

The Electors shall meet in their respective States and vote by ballot for President and Vice-President, one of whom, at least, shall not be an inhabitant of the same State with themselves; they shall name in their ballots the person voted for as President, and in distinct ballots the person voted for as Vice-President, and they shall make distinct lists of all persons voted for as President, and of all persons voted for as Vice-President, and of the number of votes for each, which lists they shall sign and certify, and transmit sealed to the seat of the government of the United States, directed to the President of the Senate;—The President of the Senate shall, in the presence of the Senate and House of Representatives, open all the certificates and the votes shall then be counted;—The person having the greatest number of votes for President, shall be the President, if such number be a majority of the whole number of Electors appointed; and if no person have such majority, then from the persons having the highest numbers not exceeding three on the list of those voted for as President, the House of Representatives shall choose immediately, by ballot, the President. But in choosing the President, the votes shall be taken by states, the representation from each state having one vote; a quorum for this purpose shall consist of a member or members from two-thirds of the states, and a majority of all the states shall be necessary to a choice. And if the House of Representatives shall not choose a President whenever the right of choice shall devolve upon them, before the fourth day of March next following, then the Vice-President shall act as President, as in the case of the death or other constitutional disability of the President.—The person having the greatest number of votes as Vice-President, shall be the Vice-President, if such number be a majority of the whole number of Electors appointed, and if no person have a majority, then from the two highest numbers on the list, the Senate shall choose the Vice-President; a quorum for the purpose shall consist of two-thirds of the whole number of Senators, and majority of the whole number shall be necessary to a choice. But no person constitutionally ineligible to the office of President shall be eligible to that of Vice-President of the United States.

AMENDMENT XIII [1865]

Section 1

Neither slavery nor involuntary servitude, except as a punishment for crime whereof the party shall have been duly convicted, shall exist within the United States, or any place subject to their jurisdiction.

Section 2

Congress shall have power to enforce this article by appropriate legislation.

AMENDMENT XIV [1868]

Section 1

All persons born or naturalized in the United States, and subject to the jurisdiction thereof, are citizens of the United States and of the State wherein they reside. No State shall abridge the privileges or immunities of citizens of the United States; nor shall any State deprive any person of life, liberty, or property, without due process of law; nor deny to any person within its jurisdiction the equal protection of the laws.

Section 2

Representatives shall be apportioned among the several States according to their respective numbers, counting the whole number of persons in each State, excluding Indians not taxed. But when the right to vote at any election for the choice of electors for President and Vice-President of the United States, Representatives in Congress, the Executive and Judicial officers of a State, or the members of the Legislature thereof, is denied to any of the male inhabitants of such State, being twenty-one years of age, and citizens of the United States, or in any way abridged, except for participation in rebellion, or other crime, the basis of representation therein shall be reduced in the proportion which the number of such male citizens shall bear to the whole number of male citizens twenty-one years of age in such State.

Section 3

No person shall be a Senator or Representative in Congress, or elector of President and Vice-President, or hold any office, civil or military, under the United States, or under any State, who, having previously taken an oath, as a member of Congress, or as an officer of the United States, or as a member of any State legislature, or as an executive or judicial officer of any State, to support the Constitution of the United

States, shall have engaged in insurrection or rebellion against the same, or given aid or comfort to the enemies thereof. But Congress may by a vote of two-thirds of each House, remove such disability.

Section 4

The validity of the public debt of the United States, authorized by law, including debts incurred for payment of pensions and bounties for services in suppressing insurrection or rebellion, shall not be questioned. But neither the United States nor any State shall assume or pay any debts or obligation incurred in aid of insurrection or rebellion against the United States, or any claim for the loss or emancipation of any slave; but all such debts, obligations, and claims shall be held illegal and void.

Section 5

The Congress shall have the power to enforce, by appropriate legislation, the provisions of this article.

AMENDMENT XV [1870]

Section 1

The right of citizens of the United States to vote shall not be denied or abridged by the United States or by any State on account of race, color, or previous condition of servitude.

Section 2

The Congress shall have power to enforce this article by appropriate legislation.

AMENDMENT XVI [1913]

The Congress shall have power to lay and collect taxes on incomes, from whatever source derived, without apportionment among the several States, and without regard to any census or enumeration.

AMENDMENT XVII [1913]

The Senate of the United States shall be composed of two Senators from each State, elected by the people thereof, for six years; and each Senator shall have one vote. The electors in each State shall have the qualifications requisite for electors of the most numerous branch of the State legislatures.

When vacancies happen in the representation of any State in the Senate, the executive authority of such State shall issue writs of election to fill such vacancies: Provided, That the legislature of any State may empower the executive thereof to make temporary appointments until the people fill the vacancies by election as the legislature may direct.

This Amendment shall not be so construed as to affect the election or term of any Senator chosen before it becomes valid as part of the Constitution.

AMENDMENT XVIII [1919]

Section 1

After one year from the ratification of this article the manufacture, sale, or transportation of intoxicating liquors within, the importation thereof into, or the exportation thereof from the United States and all territory subject to the jurisdiction thereof for beverage purposes is hereby prohibited.

Section 2

The Congress and the several States shall have concurrent power to enforce this article by appropriate legislation.

Section 3

This article shall be inoperative unless it shall have been ratified as an Amendment to the Constitution by the legislatures of the several States, as provided in the Constitution, within seven years from the date of the submission hereof to the States by the Congress.

AMENDMENT XIX [1920]

The right of citizens of the United States to vote shall not be denied or abridged by the United States or by any State on account of sex.

Congress shall have power to enforce this article by appropriate legislation.

AMENDMENT XX [1933]

Section 1

The terms of the President and Vice-President shall end at noon on the 20th day of January, and the terms of Senators and Representatives at noon on the 3d day of January, of the years in which such terms would have ended if this article had not been ratified; and the terms of their successors shall then begin.

Section 2

The Congress shall assemble at least once in every year, and such meeting shall begin at noon on the 3d day of January, unless they shall by law appoint a different day.

Section 3

If, at the time fixed for the beginning of the term of the President, the President elect shall have died, the Vice-President elect shall become President. If a President shall not have been chosen before the time fixed for the beginning of his term or if the President elect shall have failed to qualify, then the Vice-President elect shall act as President until a President shall have qualified; and the Congress may by law provide for the case wherein neither a President elect nor a Vice-President elect shall have qualified, declaring who shall then act as President, or the manner in which one who is to act shall be selected, and such person shall act accordingly until a President or Vice-President shall have qualified.

Section 4

The Congress may by law provide for the case of the death of any of the persons from whom the House of Representatives may choose a President whenever the right of choice shall have devolved upon them, and for the case of the death of any of the persons from whom the Senate may choose a Vice-President whenever the right of choice shall have devolved upon them.

Section 5

Sections 1 and 2 shall take effect on the 15th day of October following the ratification of this article.

Section 6

This article shall be inoperative unless it shall have been ratified as an amendment to the Constitution by the legislatures of three-fourths of the several States within seven years from the date of its submission.

AMENDMENT XXI [1933]

Section 1

The eighteenth article of amendment to the Constitution of the United States is hereby repealed.

Section 2

The transportation or importation into any State, Territory, or possession of the United States for delivery or use therein of intoxicating liquors, in violation of the laws thereof, is hereby prohibited.

Section 3

This article shall be inoperative unless it shall have been ratified as an amendment to the Constitution by conventions in the several States, as provided in the Constitution, within seven years from the date of the submission hereof to the States by the Congress.

AMENDMENT XXII [1951]

No person shall be elected to the office of the President more than twice, and no person who has held the office of President, or acted as President, for more than two years of a term to which some other person was elected President shall be elected to the office of the President more than once.

But this Article shall not apply to any person holding the office of President when this Article was proposed by the Congress, and shall not prevent any person who may be holding the office of President, or acting as President, during the term within which this Article becomes operative from holding the office of President or acting as President during the remainder of such term.

This article shall be inoperative unless it shall have been ratified as an amendment to the Constitution by the legislatures of three-fourths of the several states within seven years from the date of its submission to the states by the Congress.

AMENDMENT XXIII [1961]

Section 1

The District constituting the seat of Government of the United States shall appoint in such manner as the Congress may direct:

A number of electors of President and Vice-President equal to the whole number of Senators and Representatives in Congress to which the District would be entitled if it were a State, but in no event more than the least populous State; they shall be in addition to those appointed by the States, but they shall be considered, for the purposes of the election of President and Vice-President, to be electors appointed by a State; and they shall meet in the District and perform such duties as provided by the twelfth article of Amendment.

Section 2

The Congress shall have power to enforce this article by appropriate legislation.

AMENDMENT XXIV [1964]

Section 1

The right of citizens of the United States to vote in any primary or other election for President or Vice President, for electors for President or Vice President, or for Senator or Representative in Congress, shall not be denied or abridged by the United States or any state by reason of failure to pay any poll tax or other tax.

Section 2

The Congress shall have the power to enforce this article by appropriate legislation.

AMENDMENT XXV [1967]

Section 1

In case of the removal of the President from office or of his death or resignation, the Vice President shall become President.

Section 2

Whenever there is a vacancy in the office of the Vice President, the President shall nominate a Vice President who shall take office upon confirmation by a majority vote of both Houses of Congress.

Section 3

Whenever the President transmits to the President Pro Tempore of the Senate and the Speaker of the House of Representatives his written declaration that he is unable to discharge the powers and duties of his office, and until he transmits to them a written declaration to the contrary, such powers and duties shall be discharged by the Vice President as Acting President.

Section 4

Whenever the Vice President and a majority of either the principal officers of the executive departments or of such other body as Congress may by law provide, transmit to the President Pro Tempore of the Senate and the Speaker of the House of Representatives their written declaration that the President is unable to discharge the powers and duties of his office, the Vice President shall immediately assume the powers and duties of the office as Acting President.

Thereafter, when the President transmits to the President Pro Tempore of the Senate and the Speaker of the House of Representatives his written declaration that no inability exists, he shall resume the powers and duties of his office unless the Vice President and a majority of either the principal officers of the executive departments or of such other body as Congress may by law provide, transmit within four days to the President Pro Tempore of the Senate and the Speaker of the House of Representatives their written declaration that the President is unable to discharge the powers and duties of his office. Thereupon Congress shall decide the issue, assembling within forty-eight hours for that purpose if not in session. If the Congress, within twenty-one days after receipt of the latter written declaration, or, if Congress is not in session, within twenty-one days after Congress is required to assemble, determines by two-thirds vote of both Houses that the President is unable to discharge the powers and duties of his office, the Vice President shall continue to discharge the same as Acting President; otherwise, the President shall resume the powers and duties of his office.

AMENDMENT XXVI [1971]

Section 1

The right of citizens of the United States, who are eighteen years of age or older, to vote shall not be denied or abridged by the United States or by any State on account of age.

Section 2

The Congress shall have the power to enforce this article by appropriate legislation.

AMENDMENT XXVII [1992]

No law varying the compensation for the service of Senators and Representatives shall take effect until an election of Representatives shall have intervened.

Federalist No. 10
(JAMES MADISON)

Among the numerous advantages promised by a well-constructed union, none deserves to be more accurately developed than its tendency to break and control the violence of faction. The friend of popular governments never finds himself so much alarmed for their character and fate as when he contemplates their propensity to this dangerous vice. He will not fail, therefore, to set a due value on any plan which, without violating the principles to which he is attached, provides a proper cure for it. The instability, injustice, and confusion introduced into the public councils have, in truth, been the mortal diseases under which popular governments have everywhere perished, as they continue to be the favorite and fruitful topics from which the adversaries to liberty derive their most specious declamations. The valuable improvements made by the American constitutions on the popular models, both ancient and modern, cannot certainly be too much admired; but it would be an unwarrantable partiality to contend that they have as effectually obviated the danger on this side, as was wished and expected. Complaints are everywhere heard from our most considerate and virtuous citizens, equally the friends of public and private faith and of public and personal liberty, that our governments are too unstable, that the public good is disregarded in the conflicts of rival parties, and that measures are too often decided, not according to the rules of justice and the rights of the minor party, but by the superior force of an interested and overbearing majority. However anxiously we may wish that these complaints had no foundation, the evidence of known facts will not permit us to deny that they are in some degree true. It will be found, indeed, on a candid review of our situation, that some of the distresses under which we labor have been erroneously charged on the operation of our governments; but it will be found, at the same time, that other causes will not alone account for many of our heaviest misfortunes; and, particularly, for that prevailing and increasing distrust of public engagements and alarm for private rights which are echoed from one end of the continent to the other. These must be chiefly, if not wholly, effects of the unsteadiness and injustice with which a factious spirit has tainted our public administration.

By a faction I understand a number of citizens, whether amounting to a majority or minority of the whole, who are united and actuated by some common impulse of passion, or of interest, adverse to the rights of other citizens, or to the permanent and aggregate interests of the community.

There are two methods of curing the mischiefs of faction: the one, by removing its causes; the other, by controlling its effects.

There are again two methods of removing the causes of faction: the one, by destroying the liberty which is essential to its existence; the other, by giving to every citizen the same opinions, the same passions, and the same interests.

It could never be more truly said than of the first remedy that it was worse than the disease. Liberty is to faction what air is to fire, an aliment without which it instantly expires. But it could not be a less folly to abolish liberty, which is essential to political life, because it nourishes faction than it would be to wish the annihilation of air, which is essential to animal life, because it imparts to fire its destructive agency.

The second expedient is as impracticable as the first would be unwise. As long as the reason of man continues fallible, and he is at liberty to exercise it, different opinions will be formed. As long as the connection subsists between his reason and his self-love, his opinions and his passions will have a reciprocal influence on each other; and the former will be objects to which the latter will attach themselves. The diversity in the faculties of men, from which the rights of property originate, is not less an insuperable obstacle to a uniformity of interest. The protection of these faculties is the first object of government. From the protection of different and unequal faculties of acquiring property, the possession of different degrees and kinds of property immediately results; and from the influence of these on the sentiments and views of the respective proprietors ensues a division of the society into different interests and parties.

The latent causes of faction are thus sown in the nature of man; and we see them everywhere brought into different degrees of activity, according to the different circumstances of civil society. A zeal for different opinions concerning religion, concerning government, and many other points, as well of speculation as of practice; an attachment to different leaders ambitiously contending for pre-eminence and power; or to persons of other descriptions whose fortunes have been interesting to the human passions, have, in turn, divided mankind into parties, inflamed them with mutual animosity, and rendered them much more disposed to vex and oppress each other than to co-operate for their common good. So strong is this propensity of mankind to fall into mutual animosities that where no substantial occasion presents itself the most frivolous and fanciful distinctions have been sufficient to kindle their unfriendly passions and excite their most violent conflicts. But the most common and durable source of factions has been the various and unequal distribution of property. Those who hold and those who are without property have ever formed distinct interests in society. Those who are creditors, and those who are debtors, fall under a like discrimination. A landed interest, a manufacturing interest, a mercantile interest, a moneyed interest, with many lesser interests, grow up of necessity in civilized nations, and divide them into different classes, actuated by different sentiments and views. The regulation of these various and interfering interests forms the principal task of modern legislation and involves the spirit of party and faction in the necessary and ordinary operations of government.

No man is allowed to be a judge in his own cause, because his interest would certainly bias his judgment, and, not improbably, corrupt his integrity. With equal, nay with greater reason, a body of men are unfit to be both judges and parties at the same time; yet what are many of the most important acts of legislation but so many judicial determinations, not indeed concerning the rights of single persons, but concerning the rights of large bodies of citizens? And what are the different classes of legislators but advocates and parties to the causes which they determine? Is a law proposed concerning private debts? It is a question to which the creditors are parties on one side and the debtors on the other. Justice ought to hold the balance between them. Yet the parties are, and must be, themselves the judges; and the most numerous party, or in other words, the most powerful faction must be expected to prevail. Shall domestic manufacturers be encouraged, and in what degree, by restrictions on foreign manufacturers? [These] are questions which would be differently decided by the landed and the manufacturing classes, and probably by neither with a sole regard to justice and the public good. The apportionment of taxes on the various descriptions of property is an act which seems to require the most exact impartiality; yet there is, perhaps, no legislative act in which greater opportunity and temptation are given to a predominant party to trample on the rules of justice. Every shilling with which they overburden the inferior number is a shilling saved to their own pockets.

It is in vain to say that enlightened statesmen will be able to adjust these clashing interests and render them all subservient to the public good. Enlightened statesmen will not always be at the helm. Nor, in many cases, can such an adjustment be made at all without taking into view indirect and remote considerations, which will rarely prevail over the immediate interest which one party may find in disregarding the rights of another or the good of the whole.

The inference to which we are brought is that the *causes* of faction cannot be removed and that relief is only to be sought in the means of controlling its *effects*.

If a faction consists of less than a majority, relief is supplied by the republican principle, which enables the majority to defeat its sinister views by regular vote. It may clog the administration, it may convulse the society; but it will be unable to execute and mask its violence under the forms of the Constitution. When a majority is included in a faction, the form of popular government, on the other hand, enables it to sacrifice to its ruling passion or interest both the public good and the rights of other citizens. To secure the public good and private rights against the danger of such a faction, and at the same time to preserve the spirit and the form of popular government, is then the great object to which our inquiries are directed. Let me add that it is the great desideratum by which alone this form of government can be rescued from the opprobrium under which it has so long labored and be recommended to the esteem and adoption of mankind.

By what means is this object attainable? Evidently by one of two only. Either the existence of the same passion or interest in a majority at the same time must be prevented, or the majority, having such coexistent passion or interest, must be rendered, by their number and local situation, unable to concert and carry into effect schemes of oppression. If the impulse and the opportunity be suffered to coincide, we well know that neither moral nor religious motives can be relied on as an adequate control. They are not found to be such on the injustice and violence of individuals, and lose their efficacy in proportion to the number combined together, that is, in proportion as their efficacy becomes needful.

From this view of the subject it may be concluded that a pure democracy, by which I mean a society consisting of a small number of citizens, who assemble and administer the government in person, can admit of no cure for the mischiefs of faction. A common passion or interest will, in almost every case, be felt by a majority of the whole, a communication and concert result from the form of government itself; and there is nothing to check the inducements to sacrifice the weaker party or an obnoxious individual. Hence it is that such democracies have ever been spectacles of turbulence and contention; have ever been found incompatible with personal security or the rights of property; and have in general been as short in their lives as they have been violent in their deaths. Theoretic politicians, who have patronized this species of government, have erroneously supposed that by reducing mankind to a perfect equality in their political rights, they would at the same time be perfectly equalized and assimilated in their possessions, their opinions, and their passions.

A republic, by which I mean a government in which the scheme of representation takes place, opens a different prospect and promises the cure for which we are seeking. Let us examine the points in which it varies from pure democracy, and we shall comprehend both the nature of the cure and the efficacy which it must derive from the Union.

The two great points of difference between a democracy and a republic are: first, the delegation of the government, in the latter, to a small number of citizens elected by the rest; secondly, the greater number of citizens and greater sphere of country over which the latter may be extended.

The effect of the first difference is, on the one hand, to refine and enlarge the public views by passing them through the medium of a chosen body of citizens, whose wisdom may best discern the true interest of their country and whose patriotism and love of justice will be least likely to sacrifice it to temporary or partial considerations. Under such a regulation it may well happen that the public voice, pronounced by the representatives of the people, will be more consonant to the public good than if pronounced by the people themselves, convened for the purpose. On the other hand, the effect may be inverted. Men of factious tempers, of local prejudices, or of sinister designs, may, by intrigue, by corruption, or by other means, first obtain the suffrages, and then betray the interests of the people. The question resulting is, whether small or extensive republics are most favorable to the election of proper guardians of the public weal; and it is clearly decided in favor of the latter by two obvious considerations.

In the first place it is to be remarked that however small the republic may be the representatives must be raised to a certain number in order to guard against the cabals of a few; and that however large it may be they must be limited to a certain number in order to guard against the confusion of a multitude. Hence, the number of representatives in the two cases not being in proportion to that of the constituents, and being proportionally greatest in the small republic, it follows that if the proportion of fit characters be not less in the large than in the small republic, the former will present a greater option, and consequently a greater probability of a fit choice.

In the next place, as each representative will be chosen by a greater number of citizens in the large than in the small republic, it will be more difficult for unworthy candidates to practice with success the vicious arts by which elections are too often carried; and the suffrages of the people being more free, will be more likely to center on men who possess the most attractive merit and the most diffusive and established characters.

It must be confessed that in this, as in most other cases, there is a mean, on both sides of which inconveniencies will be found to lie. By enlarging too much the number of electors, you render the representative too little acquainted with all their local circumstances and lesser interests; as by reducing it too much, you render him unduly attached to these, and too little fit to comprehend and pursue great and national objects. The federal Constitution forms a happy combination in this respect; the great and aggregate interests being referred to the national, the local and particular to the State legislatures.

The other point of difference is the greater number of citizens and extent of territory which may be brought within the compass of republican than of democratic government; and it is this circumstance principally which renders factious combinations less to be dreaded in the former than in the latter. The smaller the society, the fewer probably will be the distinct parties and interests composing it; the fewer the distinct parties and interests, the more frequently will a majority be found of the same party; and the smaller the number of individuals composing a majority, and the smaller the compass within which they are placed, the more easily will they concert and execute their plans of oppression. Extend the sphere and you take in a greater variety of parties and interests; you make it less probable that a majority of the whole will have a common motive to invade the rights of other citizens; or if such a common motive exists, it will be more difficult for all who feel it to discover their own strength and to act in unison with each other. Besides other impediments, it may be remarked that, where there is a consciousness of unjust or dishonorable purposes, communication is always checked by distrust in proportion to the number whose concurrence is necessary.

Hence, it clearly appears that the same advantage which a republic has over a democracy in controlling the effects of faction is enjoyed by a large over a small republic—is enjoyed by the Union over the States composing it. Does this advantage consist in the substitution of representatives whose enlightened views and virtuous sentiments render them superior to local prejudices and to schemes of injustice? It will not be denied that the representation of the Union will be most likely to possess these requisite endowments. Does it consist in the greater security afforded by a greater variety of parties, against the event of any one party being able to outnumber and oppress the rest? In an equal degree does the increased variety of parties comprised within the Union increase this security. Does it, in fine, consist in the greater obstacles opposed to the concert and accomplishment of the secret wishes of an unjust and interested majority? Here again the extent of the Union gives it the most palpable advantage.

The influence of factious leaders may kindle a flame within their particular States but will be unable to spread a general conflagration through the other States. A religious sect may degenerate into a political faction in a part of the Confederacy; but the variety of sects dispersed over the entire face of it must secure the national councils against any danger from that source. A rage for paper money, for an abolition of debts, for an equal division of property, or for any other improper or wicked project, will be less apt to pervade the whole body of the Union than a particular member of it, in the same proportion as such a malady is more likely to taint a particular county or district than an entire State.

In the extent and proper structure of the Union, therefore, we behold a republican remedy for the diseases most incident to republican government. And according to the degree of pleasure and pride we feel in being republicans ought to be our zeal in cherishing the spirit and supporting the character of Federalists.

Federalist No. 51

(JAMES MADISON)

To what expedient, then, shall we finally resort, for maintaining in practice the necessary partition of power among the several departments as laid down in the Constitution? The only answer that can be given is that as all these exterior provisions are found to be inadequate, the defect must be supplied, by so contriving the interior structure of the government as that its several constituent parts may, by their mutual relations, be the means of keeping each other in their proper places. Without presuming to undertake a full development of this important idea I will hazard a few general observations which may perhaps place it in a clearer light, and enable us to form a more correct judgment of the principles and structure of the government planned by the convention.

In order to lay a due foundation for that separate and distinct exercise of the different powers of government, which to a certain extent is admitted on all hands to be essential to the preservation of liberty, it is evident that each department should have a will of its own; and consequently should be so constituted that the members of each should have as little agency as possible in the appointment of the members of the others. Were this principle rigorously adhered to, it would require that all the appointments for the supreme executive, legislative, and judiciary magistracies should be drawn from the same fountain of authority, the people, through channels having no communication whatever with one another. Perhaps such a plan of constructing the several departments would be less difficult in practice than it may be in contemplation appear. Some difficulties, however, and some additional expense would attend the execution of it. Some deviations, therefore, from the principle must be admitted. In the constitution of the judiciary department in particular, it might be inexpedient to insist rigorously on the principle; first, because peculiar qualifications being essential in the members, the primary consideration ought to be to select that mode of choice which best secures these qualifications; second, because the permanent tenure by which the appointments are held in that department must soon destroy all sense of dependence on the authority conferring them.

It is equally evident that the members of each department should be as little dependent as possible on those of the others for the emoluments annexed to their offices. Were the executive magistrate, or the judges, not independent of the legislature in this particular, their independence in every other would be merely nominal.

But the great security against a gradual concentration of the several powers in the same department consists in giving to those who administer each department the necessary constitutional means and personal motives to resist encroachments of the others. The provision for defense must in this, as in all other cases, be made commensurate to the danger of attack. Ambition must be made to counteract ambition. The interest of the man must be connected with the constitutional rights of the place. It may be a reflection on human nature that such devices should be necessary to control the abuses of government. But what is government itself but the greatest of all reflections on human nature? If men were angels no government would be necessary. If angels were to govern men, neither external nor internal controls on government would be necessary. In framing a government which is to be administered by men over men, the great difficulty lies in this: you must first enable the government to control the governed; and in the next place oblige it to control itself. A dependence on the people is, no doubt, the primary control on the government; but experience has taught mankind the necessity of auxiliary precautions.

This policy of supplying, by opposite and rival interests, the defect of better motives, might be traced through the whole system of human affairs, private as well as public. We see it particularly displayed in all the subordinate distributions of power, where the constant aim is to divide and arrange the several offices in such a manner as that each may be a check on the other—that the private interest of every individual may be a sentinel over the public rights. These inventions of prudence cannot be less requisite in the distribution of the supreme powers of the State.

But it is not possible to give to each department an equal power of self-defense. In republican government, the legislative authority necessarily predominates. The remedy for this inconveniency is to divide the legislature into different branches; and to render them, by different modes of election and different principles of action, as little connected with each other as the nature of their common functions and their common dependence on the society will admit. It may even be necessary to guard against dangerous encroachments by still further precautions. As the weight of the legislative authority requires that it should be thus divided, the weakness of the executive may require, on the other hand, that it should be fortified. An absolute negative on the legislature appears, at first view, to be the natural defense with which the executive magistrate should be armed. But perhaps it would be neither altogether safe nor alone sufficient. On ordinary occasions it might not be exerted with the requisite firmness, and on extraordinary occasions it might be perfidiously abused. May not this defect of an absolute negative be supplied by some qualified connection between this weaker department and the weaker branch of the stronger department, by which the latter may be led to support the constitutional rights of the former, without being too much detached from the rights of its own department?

If the principles on which these observations are founded be just, as I persuade myself they are, and they be applied as a criterion to the several State constitutions, and to the federal Constitution, it will be found that if the latter does not perfectly correspond with them, the former are infinitely less able to bear such a test.

There are, moreover, two considerations particularly applicable to the federal system of America, which place that system in a very interesting point of view.

First. In a single republic, all the power surrendered by the people is submitted to the administration of a single government; and the usurpations are guarded against by a division of the government into distinct and separate departments. In the compound republic of America, the power surrendered by the people is first divided between two distinct governments, and then the portion allotted to each subdivided among distinct and separate departments. Hence a double security arises to the rights of the people. The different governments will control each other, at the same time that each will be controlled by itself.

Second. It is of great importance in a republic not only to guard the society against the oppression of its rulers, but to guard one part of the society against the injustice of the other part. Different interests necessarily exist in different classes of citizens. If a majority be united by a common interest, the rights of the minority will be insecure. There are but two methods of providing against this evil: the one by creating a will in the community independent of the majority—that is, of the society itself; the other, by comprehending in the society so many separate descriptions of citizens as will render an unjust combination of a majority of the whole very improbable, if not impracticable. The first method prevails in all governments possessing an hereditary or self-appointed authority. This, at best, is but a precarious security; because a power independent of the society may as well espouse the unjust views of the major as the rightful interests of the minor party, and may possibly be turned against both parties. The second method will be exemplified in the federal republic of the United States. Whilst all authority in it will be derived from and dependent on the society, the society itself will be broken into so many parts, interests and classes of citizens, that the rights of individuals, or of the minority, will be in little danger from interested combinations of the majority. In a free government the security for civil rights must be the same as that for religious rights. It consists in the one case in the multiplicity of interests, and in the other in the multiplicity of sects. The degree of security in both cases will depend on the number of interests and sects; and this may be presumed to depend on the extent of country and number of people comprehended under the same government. This view of the subject must particularly recommend a proper federal system to all the sincere and considerate friends of republican government, since it shows that in exact proportion as the territory of the Union may be formed into more circumscribed Confederacies, or States, oppressive combinations of a majority will be facilitated; the best security, under the republican forms, for the rights of every class of citizen, will be diminished; and consequently the stability and independence of some member of the government, the only other security, must be proportionately increased. Justice is the end of government. It is the end of civil society. It ever has been and ever will be pursued until it be obtained, or until liberty be lost in the pursuit. In a society under the forms of which the stronger faction can readily unite and oppress the weaker, anarchy may as truly be said to reign as in a state of nature, where the weaker individual is not secured against the violence of the stronger; and as, in the latter state, even the stronger individuals are prompted, by the uncertainty of their condition, to submit to a government which may protect the weak as well as themselves; so, in the former state, will the more powerful factions or parties be gradually induced, by a like motive, to wish for a government which will protect all parties, the weaker as well as the more powerful. It can be little doubted that if the State of Rhode Island was separated from the Confederacy and left to itself, the insecurity of rights under the popular form of government within such narrow limits would be displayed by such reiterated oppressions of factious majorities that some power altogether independent of the people would soon be called for by the voice of the very factions whose misrule had proved the necessity of it. In the extended republic of the United States, and among the great variety of interests, parties, and sects which it embraces, a coalition of a majority of the whole society could seldom take place on any other principles than those of justice and the general good; whilst there being thus less danger to a minor from the will of a major party, there must be less pretext, also, to provide for the security of the former, by introducing into the government a will not dependent on the latter, or, in other words, a will independent of the society itself. It is no less certain than it is important, notwithstanding the contrary opinions which have been entertained, that the larger the society, provided it lie within a practicable sphere, the more duly capable it will be of self-government. And happily for the republican cause, the practicable sphere may be carried to a very great extent by a judicious modification and mixture of the federal principle.

GLOSSARY

affirmative action Programs designed to ensure that women, minorities, and other traditionally disadvantaged groups have full and equal opportunities in employment, education, and other areas of life.

agency point of view The tendency of bureaucrats to place the interests of their agency ahead of other interests and ahead of the priorities sought by the president or Congress.

agenda setting The power of the media through news coverage to focus the public's attention and concern on particular events, problems, issues, personalities, and so on.

agents of socialization Those agents, such as the family and the media, that have a significant influence on citizens' political socialization.

air wars The fact that modern campaigns are often a battle of opposing televised advertising campaigns.

alienation A feeling of personal powerlessness that includes the notion that government does not care about the opinions of people like oneself.

Anti-Federalists Opponents of the Constitution during the debate over ratification.

apathy A feeling of personal noninterest or unconcern with politics.

appellate jurisdiction The authority of a given court to review cases that have already been tried in lower courts and are appealed to it by the losing party; such a court is called an appeals court or appellate court. (See also **original jurisdiction.**)

authoritarian government A form of government in which leaders, though they admit to no limits on their powers, are effectively limited by other centers of power in the society.

authority The recognized right of an individual or institution to exercise power. (See also **power.**)

autocracy A form of government in which absolute control rests with a single person.

balanced budget When the government's tax revenues for the year are roughly equal to its expenditures.

bill A proposed law (legislative act) within Congress or another legislature. (See also **law.**)

Bill of Rights The first ten amendments to the Constitution. They include such rights as freedom of speech and trial by jury.

bipolar (power structure) A power structure dominated by two powers only, as in the case of the United States and the Soviet Union during the cold war.

block grants Federal grants-in-aid that permit state and local officials to decide how the money will be spent within a general area, such as education or health. (See also **categorical grants.**)

brief A written statement by a party in a court case that details its argument.

budget deficit When the government's expenditures exceed its tax revenues.

budget surplus When the government's tax and other revenues exceed its expenditures.

bureaucracy A system of organization and control based on the principles of hierarchical authority, job specialization, and formalized rules. (See also **formalized rules; hierarchical authority; job specialization.**)

bureaucratic accountability The degree to which bureaucrats are held accountable for the power they exercise.

bureaucratic rule The tendency of large-scale organizations to develop into the bureaucratic form, with the effect that administrators make key policy decisions.

cabinet A group consisting of the heads of the (cabinet) executive departments, who are appointed by the president, subject to confirmation by the Senate. The cabinet was once the main advisory body to the president but no longer plays this role. (See also **cabinet departments.**)

cabinet (executive) departments The major administrative organizations within the federal executive bureaucracy, each of which is headed by a secretary (cabinet officer) and has responsibility for a major function of the federal government, such as defense, agriculture, or justice. (See also **cabinet; independent agencies.**)

candidate-centered politics Election campaigns and other political processes in which candidates, not political parties, have most of the initiative and influence. (See also **party-centered politics.**)

capital-gains tax Tax that individuals pay on money gained from the sale of a capital asset, such as property or stocks.

capitalism An economic system based on the idea that government should interfere with economic transactions as little as possible. Free enterprise and self-reliance are the collective and individual principles that underpin capitalism.

categorical grants Federal grants-in-aid to states and localities that can be used only for designated projects. (See also **block grants.**)

checks and balances The elaborate system of divided spheres of authority provided by the U.S. Constitution as a means of controlling the power of government. The separation of powers among the branches of the national government, federalism, and the different methods of selecting national officers are all part of this system.

citizens' (noneconomic) groups Organized interests formed by individuals drawn together by opportunities to promote a cause in which they believe but that does not provide them significant individual economic benefits. (See also **economic groups; interest group.**)

civic duty The belief of an individual that civic and political participation is a responsibility of citizenship.

civil law Laws governing relations with or between private parties where no crimi-

nal act is alleged and where the parties are making conflicting claims or are seeking to establish a legal relationship.

civil liberties The fundamental individual rights of a free society, such as freedom of speech and the right to a jury trial, which in the United States are protected by the Bill of Rights.

civil rights (equal rights) The right of every person to equal protection under the laws and equal access to society's opportunities and public facilities.

civil service system See **merit system.**

clear-and-present-danger test A test devised by the Supreme Court in 1919 to define the limits of free speech in the context of national security. According to the test, government cannot abridge political expression unless it presents a clear and present danger to the nation's security.

clientele groups Special interest groups that benefit directly from the activities of a particular bureaucratic agency and are therefore strong advocates of the agency.

cloture A parliamentary maneuver that, if a three-fifths majority votes for it, limits Senate debate to thirty hours and has the effect of defeating a filibuster. (See also **filibuster.**)

cold war The lengthy period after World War II when the United States and the USSR were not engaged in actual combat (a "hot war") but were nonetheless locked in a state of deep-seated hostility.

collective (public) goods Benefits that are offered by groups (usually citizens' groups) as an incentive for membership but that are nondivisible (e.g., a clean environment) and therefore are available to nonmembers as well as members of the particular group. (See also **free-rider problem; private goods.**)

commerce clause The clause of the Constitution (Article I, Section 8) that empowers the federal government to regulate commerce among the states and with other nations.

common-carrier function The media's function as an open channel through which political leaders can communicate with the public. (See also **partisan**

function; signaling function; watchdog function.)

communism An economic system in which government owns most or all major industries and also takes responsibility for overall management of the economy.

compliance The issue of whether a court's decisions will be respected and obeyed.

concurring opinion A separate opinion written by a Supreme Court justice who votes with the majority in the decision on a case but who disagrees with their reasoning. (See also **dissenting opinion; majority opinion; plurality opinion.**)

confederacy A governmental system in which sovereignty is vested entirely in subnational (state) governments. (See also **federalism; unitary system.**)

conference committees Temporary committees that are formed to bargain over the differences in the House and Senate versions of a bill. The committee's members are usually appointed from the House and Senate standing committees that originally worked on the bill.

constituency The individuals who live within the geographical area represented by an elected official. More narrowly, the body of citizens eligible to vote for a particular representative.

constitution The fundamental law that defines how a government will legitimately operate.

constitutional democracy A government that is democratic in its provisions for majority influence through elections and constitutional in its provisions for minority rights and rule by law.

constitutionalism The idea that there are definable limits on the rightful power of a government over its citizens.

containment A doctrine, developed after World War II, based on the assumptions that the Soviet Union was an aggressor nation and that only a determined United States could block Soviet territorial ambitions.

cooperative federalism The situation in which the national, state, and local levels work together to solve problems.

criminal law Laws governing acts deemed illegal and punishable by government, such as robbery. Government is always

a party to a criminal law case; the other party is the individual accused of breaking the law.

de facto discrimination Discrimination on the basis of race, sex, religion, ethnicity, and the like that results from social, economic, and cultural biases and conditions. (See also **de jure discrimination.**)

de jure discrimination Discrimination on the basis of race, sex, religion, ethnicity, and the like that results from a law. (See also **de facto discrimination.**)

decision A vote of the Supreme Court in a particular case that indicates which party the justices side with and by how large a margin.

deficit spending When the government spends more than it collects in taxes and other revenues.

delegates Elected representatives whose obligation is to act in accordance with the expressed wishes of the people whom they represent. (See also **trustees.**)

demand-side economics A form of fiscal policy that emphasizes "demand" (consumer spending). Government can use increased spending or tax cuts to place more money in consumers' hands and thereby increase demand. (See also **fiscal policy; supply-side economics.**)

democracy A form of government in which the people govern, either directly or through elected representatives.

demographic representativeness The idea that the bureaucracy will be more responsive to the public if its employees at all levels are demographically representative of the population as a whole.

denials of power A constitutional means of limiting governmental action by listing those powers that government is expressly prohibited from using.

deregulation The rescinding of excessive government regulations for the purpose of improving economic efficiency.

détente A French word meaning "a relaxing" and used to refer to an era of improved relations between the United States and the Soviet Union that began in the early 1970s.

deterrence policy The idea that nuclear war can be discouraged if each side in a conflict has the capacity to destroy the other with nuclear weapons.

devolution The passing down of authority from the national government to states and localities.

direct primary See **primary election.**

dissenting opinion The opinion of a justice in a Supreme Court case that explains his or her reasons for disagreeing with the majority's decision. (See also **concurring opinion; majority opinion; plurality opinion.**)

dual federalism A doctrine based on the idea that a precise separation of national power and state power is both possible and desirable.

due process clause (of the Fourteenth Amendment) The clause of the Constitution that has been used by the judiciary to apply the Bill of Rights to the actions of state governments.

economic conservatives Those who believe government tries to do too many things that should be left to firms and economic markets. (See also **economic liberals; libertarians; populists; social conservatives; social liberals.**)

economic depression A very severe and sustained economic downturn. Depressions are rare in the United States: the last one was in the 1930s.

economic globalization The increased interdependence of nations' economies. The change is a result of technological, transportation, and communication advances that have enabled firms to deploy their resources across the globe.

economic groups Interest groups that are organized primarily for economic reasons but that engage in political activity in order to seek favorable policies from government. (See also **citizens' groups; interest group.**)

economic liberals Those who believe government should do more to assist people who have difficulty meeting their economic needs on their own. (See also **economic conservatives; libertarians; populists; social conservatives; social liberals.**)

economic recession A moderate but sustained downturn in the economy. Recessions are part of the economy's normal cycle of ups and downs.

economy A system of production and consumption of goods and services that are allocated through exchange among producers and consumers.

effective tax rate The actual percentage of a person's income that is spent to pay taxes.

efficiency An economic principle that holds that firms should fulfill as many of society's needs as possible while using as few of its resources as possible. The greater the output (production) for a given input (for example, an hour of labor), the more efficient the process.

elastic clause See **"necessary and proper" clause.**

Electoral College An unofficial term that refers to the electors who cast the states' electoral votes.

electoral votes The method of voting that is used to choose the U.S. president. Each state has the same number of electoral votes as it has members in Congress (House and Senate combined). By tradition, electoral voting is tied to a state's popular voting; thus, the presidential candidate with the most popular votes overall usually also has the most electoral votes.

elitism The view that the United States is essentially run by a tiny elite (composed of wealthy or well-connected individuals) who control public policy through both direct and indirect means.

entitlement program Any of a number of individual benefit programs, such as social security, that require government to provide a designated benefit to any person who meets the legally defined criteria for eligibility.

enumerated (expressed) powers The seventeen powers granted to the national government under Article I, Section 8 of the Constitution. These powers include taxation and the regulation of commerce as well as the authority to provide for the national defense.

equal-protection clause A clause of the Fourteenth Amendment that forbids any state to deny equal protection of the laws to any individual within its jurisdiction.

equal rights See **civil rights.**

equality The notion that all individuals are equal in their moral worth and are thereby entitled to equal treatment under the law.

equality of opportunity The idea that all individuals should be given an equal chance to succeed on their own.

equality of result The objective of policies intended to reduce or eliminate the effects of discrimination so that members of traditionally disadvantaged groups will have the same benefits of society as do members of advantaged groups.

equity (in relation to economic policy) The situation in which the outcome of an economic transaction is fair to each party. An outcome can usually be considered fair if each party enters into a transaction freely and is not knowingly at a disadvantage.

establishment clause The First Amendment provision that government may not favor one religion over another or favor religion over no religion, and that prohibits Congress from passing laws respecting the establishment of religion.

exclusionary rule The legal principle that government is prohibited from using in trials evidence that was obtained by unconstitutional means (for example, illegal search and seizure).

executive departments See **cabinet departments.**

executive leadership system An approach to managing the bureaucracy that is based on presidential leadership and presidential management tools, such as the president's annual budget proposal. (See also **merit system; patronage system.**)

expressed powers See **enumerated powers.**

externalities Burdens that society incurs when firms fail to pay the full cost of resources used in production. An example of an externality is the pollution that results when corporations dump industrial wastes into lakes and rivers.

factional (minor) party A minor party created when a faction within one of the

major parties breaks away to form its own party.

facts (of a court case) The relevant circumstances of a legal dispute or offense as determined by a trial court. The facts of a case are crucial because they help determine which law or laws are applicable in the case.

federalism A governmental system in which authority is divided between two sovereign levels of government: national and regional. (See also **confederacy; unitary system.**)

Federalists Supporters of the Constitution during the debate over ratification.

filibuster A procedural tactic in the U.S. Senate whereby a minority of legislators prevents a bill from coming to a vote by holding the floor and talking until the majority gives in and the bill is withdrawn from consideration. (See also **cloture.**)

fiscal federalism Expenditure of federal funds on programs run in part through states and localities.

fiscal policy A tool of economic management by which government attempts to maintain a stable economy through its taxing and spending decisions. (See also **demand-side economics; monetary policy; supply-side economics.**)

formalized rules A basic principle of bureaucracy that refers to the standardized procedures and established regulations by which a bureaucracy conducts its operations. (See also **bureaucracy.**)

framing The process of selecting certain aspects of reality and making them the most salient part of the communication, thereby conveying a particular interpretation of a situation.

free-exercise clause A First Amendment provision that prohibits the government from interfering with the practice of religion or prohibiting the free exercise of religion.

free-rider problem The situation in which the benefits offered by a group to its members are also available to nonmembers. The incentive to join the group and to promote its cause is reduced because nonmembers (free riders) receive the benefits (e.g., a cleaner environment) without having to pay any of the group's costs. (See also **collective goods.**)

free-trade position The view that the long-term economic interests of all countries are advanced when tariffs and other trade barriers are kept to a minimum. (See also **protectionism.**)

freedom of expression Americans' freedom to communicate their views, the foundation of which is the First Amendment rights of freedom of conscience, speech, press, assembly, and petition.

gender gap The tendency of women and men to differ in their political attitudes and voting preferences.

gerrymandering The process by which the party in power draws election district boundaries in a way that advantages its candidates.

government corporations Bodies, such as the U.S. Postal Service and Amtrak, that are similar to private corporations in that they charge for their services, but different in that they receive federal funding to help defray expenses. Their directors are appointed by the president with Senate approval.

graduated personal income tax A tax on personal income in which the tax rate increases as income increases; in other words, the tax rate is higher for higher income levels.

grants-in-aid Federal cash payments to states and localities for programs they administer.

grants of power The method of limiting the U.S. government by confining its scope of authority to those powers expressly granted in the Constitution.

grassroots lobbying A form of lobbying designed to persuade officials that a group's policy position has strong constituent support.

grassroots party A political party organized at the level of the voters and dependent on their support for its strength.

Great Compromise The agreement of the constitutional convention to create a two-chamber Congress with the House apportioned by population and the Senate apportioned equally by state.

hard money Campaign funds given directly to candidates to spend as they choose.

hierarchical authority A basic principle of bureaucracy that refers to the chain of command within an organization whereby officials and units have control over those below them. (See also **bureaucracy.**)

hired guns The professional consultants who run campaigns for high office.

honeymoon period The president's first months in office, a time when Congress, the press, and the public are more inclined than usual to support presidential initiatives.

ideology A consistent pattern of opinion on particular issues that stems from a core belief or set of beliefs.

ideological (minor) party A minor party characterized by its ideological commitment to a broad and noncentrist philosophical position.

imminent lawless action test A legal test that says government cannot lawfully suppress advocacy that promotes lawless action unless such advocacy is aimed at producing, and is likely to produce, imminent lawless action.

implied powers The federal government's constitutional authority (through the "necessary and proper" clause) to take action that is not expressly authorized by the Constitution but that supports actions that are so authorized. (See also **"necessary and proper" clause.**)

in-kind benefit A government benefit that is a cash equivalent, such as food stamps or rent vouchers. This form of benefit ensures that recipients will use public assistance in a specified way.

inalienable (natural) rights Those rights that persons theoretically possessed in the state of nature, prior to the formation of governments. These rights, including those of life, liberty, and property, are considered inherent and as such are inalienable. Since government is established by people, government has the responsibility to preserve these rights.

independent agencies Bureaucratic agencies that are similar to cabinet departments but usually have a narrower area of responsibility. Each such agency is headed by a presidential appointee who is not a cabinet member. An example is the National Aeronautics and Space Administration. (See also **cabinet departments.**)

individual goods See **private goods.**

individualism The idea that people should take the initiative, be self-sufficient, and accumulate the material advantages necessary for their well-being.

inflation A general increase in the average level of prices of goods and services.

initiative The process by which citizens can place legislative measures on the ballot through signature petitions; if the measure receives a majority vote, it becomes law.

inside lobbying Direct communication between organized interests and policymakers, which is based on the assumed value of close ("inside") contacts with policymakers.

interest group A set of individuals who are organized to promote a shared political interest. (See also **citizens' groups; economic groups.**)

interest-group liberalism The tendency of public officials to support the policy demands of self-interested groups (as opposed to judging policy demands according to whether they serve a larger conception of "the public interest").

internationalist A person who holds the view that the country should involve itself deeply in world affairs. (See also **isolationist.**)

iron triangle A small and informal but relatively stable group of well-positioned legislators, executives, and lobbyists who seek to promote policies beneficial to a particular interest. (See also **issue network.**)

isolationist A person who holds the view that the country should deliberately avoid a large role in world affairs and, instead, concentrate on domestic concerns. (See also **internationalist.**)

issue network An informal network of public officials and lobbyists who have a common interest and expertise in a given area and who are brought together

temporarily by a proposed policy in that area. (See also **iron triangle.**)

job specialization A basic principle of bureaucracy that holds that the responsibilities of each job position should be explicitly defined and that a precise division of labor within the organization should be maintained. (See also **bureaucracy.**)

judicial activism The doctrine that the courts should develop new legal principles when judges see a compelling need, even if this action places them in conflict with precedent or the policy decisions of elected officials. (See also **judicial restraint.**)

judicial conference A closed meeting of the justices of the U.S. Supreme Court to discuss and vote on the cases before them; the justices are not supposed to discuss conference proceedings with outsiders.

judicial restraint The doctrine that the judiciary should broadly defer to precedent and the judgment of legislatures. The doctrine claims that the job of judges is to work within the confines of laws set down by tradition and lawmaking majorities. (See also **judicial activism.**)

judicial review The power of courts to decide whether a governmental institution has acted within its constitutional powers and, if not, to declare its action null and void.

jurisdiction (of a congressional committee) The policy area in which a particular congressional committee is authorized to act.

jurisdiction (of a court) A given court's authority to hear cases of a particular kind. Jurisdiction may be original or appellate.

laissez-faire doctrine A classic economic philosophy that holds that owners of businesses should be allowed to make their own production and distribution decisions without government regulation or control.

large-state plan See **Virginia Plan.**

law (as enacted by Congress) A legislative proposal, or bill, that is passed by both the House and Senate and is either signed or not vetoed by the president. (See also **bill.**)

lawmaking function The authority (of a legislature) to make the laws necessary to carry out the government's powers. (See also **oversight function; representation function.**)

laws (of a court case) The constitutional provisions, legislative statutes, or judicial precedents that apply to a court case.

legitimacy (of judicial power) The issue of the proper limits of judicial authority in a political system based in part on the principle of majority rule.

libel Publication of material that falsely damages a person's reputation.

libertarians Those who believe government tries to do too many things that should be left to firms and individuals and who oppose government as an instrument of traditional values. (See also **economic conservatives; social conservatives; economic liberals; social liberals; populists.**)

liberty The principle that individuals should be free to act and think as they choose, provided they do not infringe unreasonably on the rights and freedoms of others.

limited government A government that is subject to strict limits on its lawful uses of powers and hence on its ability to deprive people of their liberty.

living constitution theory A method of interpreting the Constitution that emphasizes the principles it embodies and their application to changing circumstances and needs.

lobbying The process by which interest-group members or lobbyists attempt to influence public policy through contacts with public officials.

logrolling The trading of votes between legislators so that each gets what he or she most wants.

majoritarianism The idea that the majority prevails not only in elections but also in determining policy.

majority opinion A Supreme Court opinion that results when a majority of the justices is in agreement on the legal basis of the decision. (See also **concurring opinion; dissenting opinion; plurality opinion.**)

means test The requirement that applicants for public assistance must demonstrate they are poor in order to be eligible for the assistance. (See also **public assistance.**)

merit (civil service) system An approach to managing the bureaucracy whereby people are appointed to government positions on the basis of either competitive examinations or special qualifications, such as professional training. (See also **executive leadership system; patronage system.**)

military-industrial complex The three components (the military establishment, the industries that manufacture weapons, and the members of Congress from states and districts that depend heavily on the arms industry) that mutually benefit from a high level of defense spending.

momentum (in campaigns) A strong showing by a candidate in early presidential nominating contests, which leads to a buildup of public support for the candidate.

monetary policy A tool of economic management, available to government, based on manipulation of the amount of money in circulation. (See also **fiscal policy.**)

money chase U.S. campaigns are very expensive and candidates must spend a great amount of time raising funds in order to compete successfully.

multilateralism The situation in which nations act together in response to problems and crises.

multinational corporations Business firms with major operations in more than one country.

multiparty system A system in which three or more political parties have the capacity to gain control of government separately or in coalition.

national debt The total cumulative amount that the U.S. government owes to creditors.

natural rights See **inalienable rights.**

"necessary and proper" clause (elastic clause) The authority granted Congress in Article I, Section 8 of the Constitution "to make all laws which shall be necessary and proper" for the implementation of its enumerated powers. (See also **implied powers.**)

negative government The philosophical belief that government governs best by staying out of people's lives, thus giving individuals as much freedom as possible to determine their own pursuits. (See also **positive government.**)

neutral competence The administrative objective of a merit-based bureaucracy. Such a bureaucracy should be "competent" in the sense that its employees are hired and retained on the basis of their expertise and "neutral" in the sense that it operates by objective standards rather than partisan ones.

New Jersey (small-state) Plan A constitutional proposal for a strengthened Congress but one in which each state would have a single vote, thus granting a small state the same legislative power as a larger state.

news The news media's version of reality, usually with an emphasis on timely, dramatic, and compelling events and developments.

news media See **press.**

nomination The designation of a particular individual to run as a political party's candidate (its "nominee") in the general election.

noneconomic groups See **citizens' groups.**

North-South Compromise The agreement over economic and slavery issues that enabled northern and southern states to settle differences that threatened to defeat the effort to draft a new constitution.

objective journalism A model of news reporting that is based on the communication of "facts" rather than opinions and that is "fair" in that it presents all sides of partisan debate. (See also **partisan press.**)

oligarchy Government in which control rests with a few persons.

open party caucuses Meetings at which

a party's candidates for nomination are voted on and that are open to all the party's rank-and-file voters who want to attend.

open-seat election An election in which there is no incumbent in the race.

opinion (of a court) A court's written explanation of its decision, which serves to inform others of the legal basis for the decision. Supreme Court opinions are expected to guide the decisions of other courts. (See also **concurring opinion; dissenting opinion; majority opinion; plurality opinion.**)

original jurisdiction The authority of a given court to be the first court to hear a case. (See also **appellate jurisdiction.**)

originalism theory A method of interpreting the Constitution that emphasizes the meaning of its words at the time they were written.

outside lobbying A form of lobbying in which an interest group seeks to use public pressure as a means of influencing officials.

oversight function A supervisory activity of Congress that centers on its constitutional responsibility to see that the executive carries out the laws faithfully and spends appropriations properly. (See also **lawmaking function; representation function.**)

packaging (of a candidate) In modern campaigning, the process of recasting a candidate's record into an appealing image.

partisan function (of the press) Efforts by media actors to influence public response to a particular party, leader, issue, or viewpoint.

partisan press Newspapers and other communication media that openly support a political party and whose news in significant part follows the party line. (See also **objective journalism.**)

party caucus A group that consists of a party's members in the House or Senate and that serves to elect the party's leadership, set policy goals, and determine party strategy.

party-centered politics Election campaigns and other political processes in which political parties, not individual candidates, hold most of the initiative and influence. (See also **candidate-centered politics.**)

party coalition The groups and interests that support a political party.

party competition A process in which conflict over society's goals is transformed by political parties into electoral competition in which the winner gains the power to govern.

party discipline The willingness of a party's House or Senate members to act together as a cohesive group and thus exert collective control over legislative action.

party identification The personal sense of loyalty that an individual may feel toward a particular political party. (See also **party realignment.**)

party leaders Members of the House and Senate who are chosen by the Democratic or Republican caucus in each chamber to represent the party's interests in that chamber and who give some central direction to the chamber's deliberations.

party organizations The party organizational units at national, state, and local levels; their influence has decreased over time because of many factors. (See also **candidate-centered politics; party-centered politics; primary election.**)

party realignment An election or set of elections in which the electorate responds strongly to an extraordinarily powerful issue that has disrupted the established political order. A realignment has a lasting impact on public policy, popular support for the parties, and the composition of the party coalitions. (See also **party identification.**)

patronage system An approach to managing the bureaucracy whereby people are appointed to important government positions as a reward for political services they have rendered and because of their partisan loyalty. (See also **executive leadership system; merit system; spoils system.**)

pluralism A theory of American politics that holds that society's interests are substantially represented through the activities of groups.

plurality opinion A court opinion that results when a majority of justices agree on a decision in a case but do not agree on the legal basis for the decision. In this instance, the legal position held by most of the justices on the winning side is called a plurality opinion. (See also **concurring opinion; dissenting opinion; majority opinion.**)

policy Generally, any broad course of governmental action; more narrowly, a specific government program or initiative.

policy formation The stage of the policy process where a policy is formulated for dealing with a policy problem.

policy implementation (in reference to bureaucracy) The primary function of the bureaucracy; it refers to the process of carrying out the authoritative decisions of Congress, the president, and the courts.

policy implementation (in reference to policy process) The stage of the policy process where a policy is put into effect and evaluated.

political action committee (PAC) The organization through which an interest group raises and distributes funds for election purposes. By law, the funds must be raised through voluntary contributions.

political culture The characteristic and deep-seated beliefs of a particular people.

political movements See **social movements.**

political participation Involvement in activities intended to influence public policy and leadership, such as voting, joining political parties and interest groups, writing to elected officials, demonstrating for political causes, and giving money to political candidates.

political party An ongoing coalition of interests joined together to try to get their candidates for public office elected under a common label.

political socialization The learning process by which people acquire their political opinions, beliefs, and values.

political system The various components of American government. The parts are separate, but they connect with each other, affecting how each performs.

politics The process through which society settles its conflicts and decides the policies by which it will be governed.

population In a public opinion poll, the people (for example, the citizens of a nation) whose opinions are being estimated through interviews with a sample of these people.

populists Those who believe government should do more to solve the nation's problems and who look to it to uphold traditional values. (See also **economic conservatives; social conservatives; economic liberals; social liberals; libertarians.**)

pork-barrel projects Legislative acts whose tangible benefits are targeted at a particular legislator's constituency.

positive government The philosophical belief that government intervention is necessary in order to enhance personal liberty when individuals are buffeted by economic and social forces beyond their control. (See also **negative government.**)

poverty line As defined by the federal government, the annual cost of a thrifty food budget for an urban family of four, multiplied by three to allow also for the cost of housing, clothes, and other expenses. Families below the poverty line are considered poor and are eligible for certain forms of public assistance.

power The ability of persons or institutions to control policy. (See also **authority.**)

precedent A judicial decision in a given case that serves as a rule of thumb for settling subsequent cases of a similar nature; courts are generally expected to follow precedent.

preemptive war doctrine The idea, espoused by president George W. Bush, that the United States could attack a potentially threatening nation even if the threat had not yet reached a serious and immediate level.

presidential approval ratings A measure of the degree to which the public approves or disapproves of the president's performance in office.

presidential commissions Organizations within the bureaucracy that are headed by commissioners appointed by the president. An example is the Commission on Civil Rights.

press (news media) Those print and broadcast organizations that are in the news-reporting business.

primary election (direct primary) A form of election in which voters choose a party's nominees for public office. In most states, eligibility to vote in a primary election is limited to voters who designated themselves as party members when they registered to vote. A primary is direct when it results directly in the choice of a nominee; it is indirect (as in the case of presidential primaries) when it results in the selection of delegates who then choose the nominee.

prior restraint Government prohibition of speech or publication before the fact, which is presumed by the courts to be unconstitutional unless the justification for it is overwhelming.

private (individual) goods Benefits that a group (most often an economic group) can grant directly and exclusively to the individual members of the group. (See also **collective goods.**)

probability sample A sample for a poll in which each individual in the population has a known probability of being selected randomly for inclusion in the sample. (See also **public opinion poll.**)

problem recognition The stage of the policy process where conditions in society become recognized as a policy problem.

procedural due process The constitutional requirement that government must follow proper legal procedures before a person can be legitimately punished for an alleged offense.

procedural law Laws governing the legal process that define proper courses of action by government or private parties.

proportional representation A form of representation in which seats in the legislature are allocated proportionally according to each political party's share of the popular vote. This system enables smaller parties to compete successfully for seats. (See also **single-member districts.**)

prospective voting A form of electoral judgment in which voters choose the candidate whose policy promises most closely match their own preferences. (See also **retrospective voting.**)

protectionism The view that the immediate interests of domestic producers should have a higher priority (through, for example, protective tariffs) than should free trade between nations. (See also **free-trade position.**)

public assistance Social welfare programs funded through general tax revenues and available only to the financially needy. Eligibility for such a program is established by a means test. (See also **means test; social insurance.**)

public goods See **collective goods.**

public opinion The politically relevant opinions held by ordinary citizens that they express openly.

public opinion poll A device for measuring public opinion whereby a relatively small number of individuals (the sample) is interviewed for the purpose of estimating the opinions of a whole community (the population). (See also **probability sample.**)

public policy A decision of government to pursue a course of action designed to produce an intended outcome.

public policy process The political interactions that lead to the emergence and resolution of public policy issues.

purposive incentive An incentive to group participation based on the cause (purpose) that the group seeks to promote.

realignment See **party realignment.**

reapportionment The reallocation of House seats among states after each census as a result of population changes.

reasonable-basis test A test applied by courts to laws that treat individuals unequally. Such a law may be deemed constitutional if its purpose is held to be "reasonably" related to a legitimate government interest.

recall The process by which citizens can petition for the removal from office of an elected official before the scheduled completion of his or her term.

redistricting The process of altering election districts in order to make them as

nearly equal in population as possible. Redistricting takes place every ten years, after each population census.

referendum The process through which the legislature may submit proposals to the voters for approval or rejection.

reform (minor) party A minor party that bases its appeal on the claim that the major parties are having a corrupting influence on government and policy.

registration The practice of placing citizens' names on an official list of voters before they are eligible to exercise their right to vote.

regulation Government restrictions on the economic practices of private firms.

regulatory agencies Administrative units, such as the Federal Communications Commission and the Environmental Protection Agency, that have responsibility for monitoring and regulating ongoing economic activities.

representation function The responsibility of a legislature to represent various interests in society. (See also **lawmaking function; oversight function.**)

representative democracy A system in which the people participate in the decision-making process of government not directly but indirectly, through the election of officials to represent their interests.

republic Historically, the form of government in which representative officials met to decide on policy issues. These representatives were expected to serve the public interest but were not subject to the people's immediate control. Today, the term *republic* is used interchangeably with *democracy.*

reserved powers The powers granted to the states under the Tenth Amendment to the Constitution.

retrospective voting A form of electoral judgment in which voters support the incumbent candidate or party when their policies are judged to have succeeded and oppose the candidate or party when their policies are judged to have failed. (See also **prospective voting.**)

rider An amendment to a bill that deals with an issue unrelated to the content of the bill. Riders are permitted in the Senate but not in the House.

right of privacy A right implied by the freedoms in the Bill of Rights that grants individuals a degree of personal privacy upon which government cannot lawfully intrude. The right gives individuals a level of free choice in areas such as reproduction and intimate relations.

sample In a public opinion poll, the relatively small number of individuals interviewed for the purpose of estimating the opinions of an entire population. (See also **public opinion poll.**)

sampling error A measure of the accuracy of a public opinion poll. It is mainly a function of sample size and is usually expressed in percentage terms. (See also **probability sample.**)

selective incorporation The process by which certain of the rights (for example, freedom of speech) contained in the Bill of Rights become applicable through the Fourteenth Amendment to actions by the state governments.

self-government The principle that the people are the ultimate source and proper beneficiary of governing authority; in practice, a government based on majority rule.

senatorial courtesy The tradition that a U.S. senator from the state in which a federal judicial vacancy has arisen should have a say in the president's nomination of the new judge if the senator is of the same party as the president.

seniority A member of Congress's consecutive years of service on a particular committee.

separated institutions sharing power The principle that, as a way to limit government, its powers should be divided among separate branches, each of which also shares in the power of the others as a means of checking and balancing them. The result is that no one branch can exercise power decisively without the support or acquiescence of the others.

separation of powers The division of the powers of government among separate institutions or branches.

service relationship The situation in which party organizations assist candidates for office but have no power to require them to accept or campaign on the party's main policy positions.

service strategy Use of personal staff by members of Congress to perform services for constituents in order to gain their support in future elections.

signaling (signaler) function The accepted responsibility of the media to alert the public to important developments as soon as possible after they happen or are discovered. (See also **common-carrier function; partisan function; watchdog function.**)

single-issue (minor) party A minor party formed around a single issue of overriding interest to its followers.

single-issue politics The situation in which separate groups are organized around nearly every conceivable policy issue and press their demands and influence to the utmost.

single-member districts The form of representation in which only the candidate who gets the most votes in a district wins office. (See also **proportional representation.**)

slander Spoken words that falsely damage a person's reputation.

small-state plan See **New Jersey Plan.**

social capital The sum of face-to-face interactions among citizens in a society.

social conservatives Those who believe government power should be used to uphold traditional values. (See also **social liberals; economic conservatives; economic liberals; libertarians; populists.**)

social contract A voluntary agreement by individuals to form a government, which is then obligated to work within the confines of that agreement.

social insurance Social welfare programs based on the "insurance" concept, so that individuals must pay into the program to be eligible to receive funds from it. An example is social security for retired people. (See also **public assistance.**)

social liberals Those who believe it is not government's role to buttress traditional values at the expense of unconventional or new values. (See also **social conservatives; economic conservatives; economic liberals; libertarians; populists.**)

social (political) movements Active and sustained efforts to achieve social and political change by groups of people who feel that government has not been properly responsive to their concerns.

socialism An economic system in which government owns and controls many of the major industries.

soft money Campaign contributions that are not subject to legal limits and are given to parties rather than directly to candidates.

solicitor general The high-ranking Justice Department official who serves as the government's lawyer in Supreme Court cases.

sovereignty The ultimate authority to govern within a certain geographical area.

split ticket The pattern of voting in which the individual voter in a given election casts a ballot for one or more candidates of each major party.

spoils system The practice of granting public office to individuals in return for political favors they have rendered. (See also **patronage system.**)

standing committees Permanent congressional committees with responsibility for a particular area of public policy. An example is the Senate Foreign Relations Committee.

stewardship theory A theory that argues for a strong, assertive presidential role, with presidential authority limited only at points specifically prohibited by law. (See also **Whig theory.**)

strict-scrutiny test A test applied by courts to laws that attempt a racial or ethnic classification. In effect, the strict-scrutiny test eliminates race or ethnicity as legal classification when it places minority group members at a disadvantage. (See also **suspect classifications.**)

suffrage The right to vote.

sunset law A law containing a provision that fixes a date on which a program will end unless the program's life is extended by Congress.

supply-side economics A form of fiscal policy that emphasizes "supply" (production). An example of supply-side economics would be a tax cut for business. (See also **demand-side economics; fiscal policy.**)

supremacy clause Article VI of the Constitution, which makes national law supreme over state law when the national government is acting within its constitutional limits.

suspect classifications Legal classifications, such as race and national origin, that have invidious discrimination as their purpose and are therefore unconstitutional. (See also **strict-scrutiny test.**)

symbolic speech Action (for example, the waving or burning of a flag) for the purpose of expressing a political opinion.

totalitarian government A form of government in which the leaders claim complete dominance of all individuals and institutions.

transfer payment A government benefit that is given directly to an individual, as in the case of social security payments to a retiree.

trustees Elected representatives whose obligation is to act in accordance with their own consciences as to what policies are in the best interests of the public. (See also **delegates.**)

two-party system A system in which only two political parties have a real chance of acquiring control of the government.

tyranny of the majority The potential of a majority to monopolize power for its own gain and to the detriment of minority rights and interests.

unilateralism The situation in which one nation takes action against another state or states.

unipolar (power structure) A power structure dominated by a single powerful actor, as in the case of the United States after the collapse of the Soviet Union.

unitary system A governmental system in which the national government alone has sovereign (ultimate) authority. (See also **confederacy; federalism.**)

unit rule The rule that grants all of a state's electoral votes to the candidate who receives most of the popular votes in the state.

veto The president's rejection of a bill, thereby keeping it from becoming law unless Congress overrides the veto.

Virginia (large-state) Plan A constitutional proposal for a strong Congress with two chambers, both of which would be based on numerical representation, thus granting more power to the larger states.

voter turnout The proportion of persons of voting age who actually vote in a given election.

watchdog function The accepted responsibility of the media to protect the public from deceitful, careless, incompetent, and corrupt officials by standing ready to expose any official who violates accepted legal, ethical, or performance standards. (See also **common-carrier function; partisan function; signaler function.**)

Whig theory A theory that prevailed in the nineteenth century and held that the presidency was a limited or restrained office whose occupant was confined to expressly granted constitutional authority. (See also **stewardship theory.**)

whistle-blowing An internal check on the bureaucracy whereby individual bureaucrats report instances of mismanagement that they observe.

writ of certiorari Permission granted by a higher court to allow a losing party in a legal case to bring the case before it for a ruling; when such a writ is requested of the U.S. Supreme Court, four of the Court's nine justices must agree to accept the case before it is granted certiorari.

NOTES

CHAPTER ONE

[1]Alexis de Tocqueville, *Democracy in America (1835–1840)*, eds. J. P. Mayer and A. P. Kerr (Garden City, N.Y.: Doubleday/ Anchor, 1969), 640.

[2]See John Harmon McElroy, *American Beliefs: What Keeps a Big Country and a Diverse People United* (Chicago: I. R. Dee, 1999); but see Michael B. Katz and Mark J. Stern, *One Nation Divisible: What America Was and What It's Becoming* (New York: Russell Sage Foundation, 2006).

[3]Clinton Rossiter, *Conservativism in America* (New York: Vintage, 1962), 67; see also Robert A. Ferguson, *Reading the Early Republic* (Cambridge, Mass.: Harvard University Press, 2004).

[4]Tocqueville, *Democracy in America*, 310.

[5]James Bryce, *The American Commonwealth*, vol. 2 (New York: Macmillan, 1960), 247–54. First published in 1900.

[6]See Michael Foley, *American Credo: The Place of Ideas in American Politics* (New York: Oxford University Press, 2007).

[7]Paul Gagnon, "Why Study History?" *Atlantic Monthly*, November 1988, 47.

[8]Robert Middlekauff, *The Glorious Cause: The American Revolution, 1763–1789* (New York: Oxford University Press, 2007).

[9]Louis Hartz, *The Liberal Tradition in America* (New York: Harcourt, Brace, 1953), 12; see also Jeffrey Stout, *Democracy and Tradition* (Princeton, N.J.: Princeton University Press, 2004).

[10]James Bryce, *The American Commonwealth*, vol. 2 (Indianapolis, Ind.: Liberty Fund, 1995), 1419.

[11]See Seymour Martin Lipset, *American Exceptionalism: A Double-Edged Sword* (New York: Norton, 1996); Claude Lévi-Strauss, *Structural Anthropology* (Chicago: University of Chicago Press, 1983); Clifford Geertz, *Myth, Symbol, and Culture* (New York: Norton, 1974).

[12]U.S. Census Bureau data, 2006.

[13]Quoted in Ralph Volney Harlow, *The Growth of the United States*, vol. 2 (New York: Henry Holt, 1943), 497.

[14]For a substantial look at Lincoln's positions on slavery, see George M. Fredrickson, *Big Enough to Be Inconsistent: Abraham Lincoln Confronts Slavery and Race* (Cambridge, Mass: Harvard University Press, 2008).

[15]Theodore H. White, *America in Search of Itself: The Making of the President, 1956–1980* (New York: Harper & Row, 1982).

[16]Harold D. Lasswell, *Politics: Who Gets What, When, How* (New York: McGraw-Hill, 1938).

[17]See Charles H. McIlwain, *Constitutionalism: Ancient and Modern* (Ithaca, N.Y.: Cornell University Press, 1983).

[18]Russell Hardin, *Liberalism, Constitutionalism, and Democracy* (New York: Oxford University Press, 1999).

[19]Harold D. Lasswell and Abraham Kaplan, *Power and Society* (New Haven, Conn.: Yale University Press, 1950), 75–77.

[20]Benjamin I. Page and Robert Shapiro, "Effects of Public Opinion on Policy," *American Political Science Review* 77 (March 1983): 178; see also Lawrence R. Jacobs and Robert Shapiro, *Politicians Don't Pander* (Chicago: University of Chicago Press, 2000).

[21]See Robert Dahl, *On Democracy* (New Haven, Conn.: Yale University Press, 2000).

[22]C. Wright Mills, *The Power Elite* (New York: Oxford University Press, 1965).

[23]G. William Domhoff, *Who Rules America? Power and Politics*, 5th ed. (New York, McGraw-Hill, 2005).

[24]See, for example, Dahl, *On Democracy*.

[25]See H. H. Gerth and C. Wright Mills, eds., *From Max Weber: Essays in Sociology* (New York: Oxford University Press, 1958).

[26]Roberto Michels, *Political Parties* (New York: Collier Books, 1962). First published in 1911.

[27]David Easton, *The Political System* (New York: Knopf, 1965), 97.

[28]E. E. Schattschneider, *Two Hundred Million Americans in Search of a Government* (New York: Holt, Rinehart &Winston, 1969), 42.

CHAPTER TWO

[1]Quoted in Charles S. Hyneman, "Republican Government in America," in George J. Graham Jr. and Scarlett G. Graham, eds., *Founding Principles of American Government*, rev. ed. (Chatham, N.J.: Chatham House, 1984), 19.

[2]See Russell Hardin, *Liberalism, Constitutionalism, and Democracy* (New York: Oxford University Press, 1999); A. John Simmons, *The Lockean Theory of Rights* (Princeton, N.J.: Princeton University Press, 1994).

[3]George Bancroft, *History of the Formation of the Constitution of the United States of America*, 3d ed., vol. 1 (New York: D. Appleton, 1883), 166.

[4]Quoted in "The Constitution and Slavery," Digital History Website, December 1, 2003.

[5]Gaillard Hunt, ed., *The Writings of James Madison* (New York: Putnam, 1904), 274; see also Garret Ward Sheldon, *The Political Philosophy of James Madison* (Baltimore: Johns Hopkins University Press, 2000).

[6]See Vincent Ostrom, *The Political Theory of a Compound Republic: Designing the American Experiment* (Lanham, Md.: Lexington Books, 2007).

[7]See *Federalist* Nos. 47 and 48.

[8]Richard Neustadt, *Presidential Power* (New York: Macmillan, 1986), 33.

[9]Henry J. Abraham, *The Judicial Process*, 6th ed. (New York: Oxford University Press, 1993), 320–22.

[10]*Marbury v. Madison*, 1 Cranch 137 (1803).

[11]Martin Diamond, *The Founding of the Democratic Republic* (Itasca, Ill.: Peacock, 1981), 62–71.

[12]*Federalist* No. 10.

[13]Leslie F. Goldstein, "Judicial Review and Democratic Theory: Guardian Democracy vs. Representative Democracy," *Western Political Quarterly* 40 (1987): 391–412.

[14]Benjamin Ginsberg, *The Consequences of Consent* (New York: Random House, 1982), 22.

[15]Robert Dahl, *Pluralist Democracy in the United States* (Chicago: Rand McNally, 1967), 92.

[16]This interpretation is taken from Walter Lippmann, *Public Opinion* (New York: Free Press, 1965), 178–79.

[17]Michael McGeer, *A Fierce Discontent: The Rise and Fall of the Progressive Movement in America, 1870–1920* (New York: Free Press, 2005).

[18]Charles S. Beard, *An Economic Interpretation of the Constitution* (New York: Macmillan, 1941). First published in 1913.

[19]See Randall G. Holcombe, *From Liberty to Democracy* (Ann Arbor: University of Michigan Press, 2002).

CHAPTER THREE

[1]Woodrow Wilson, *Constitutional Government in the United States* (New York: Columbia University Press, 1908), 173.

[2]"NCSL Task Force on No Child Left Behind Report," National Conference of State Legislatures, Denver, Colorado, February 23, 2005; for a broader perspective, see Patrick J. Mcquinn, *No Child Left Behind and the Transformation of Federal Education Policy, 1965–2005* (Lawrence: University Press of Kansas, 2006).

[3]See Samuel Beer, *To Make a Nation: The Rediscovery of American Federalism* (Cambridge, Mass.: Belknap Press of Harvard University, 1993).

[4]*Federalist* No. 2; for the Anti-Federalist view, see Saul Cornell, *The Other Founders* (Chapel Hill: University of North Carolina Press, 1999).

[5]*McCulloch v. Maryland*, 4 Wheaton 316 (1819).

[6]*Gibbons v. Ogden*, 22 Wheaton 1 (1824).

[7]Oliver Wendell Holmes Jr., *Collected Legal Papers* (New York: Harcourt, Brace, 1920), 295–96.

[8]See John C. Calhoun, *The Works of John C. Calhoun* (New York: Russell & Russell, 1968).

[9]*Dred Scott v. Sanford*, 19 Howard 393 (1857).

[10]*U.S. v. Cruikshank*, 92 U.S. 452 (1876).

[11]*Slaughter-House Cases*, 16 Wallace 36 (1873); *Civil Rights Cases*, 109 U.S. 3 (1883).

[12]*Plessy v. Ferguson*, 163 U.S. 537 (1896).

[13]*Santa Clara County v. Southern Pacific Railroad Co.*, 118 U.S. 394 (1886).

[14]*U.S. v. E. C. Knight Co.*, 156 U.S. 1 (1895).

[15]*Hammer v. Dagenhart*, 247 U.S. 251 (1918).

[16]*Lochner v. New York*, 198 U.S. 25 (1905).

[17]Alfred H. Kelly, Winifred A. Harbison, and Herman Belz, *The American Constitution*, 7th ed. (New York: Norton, 1991), 529; but see also Kimberley Johnson, *Governing the American State: Congress and the New Federalism, 1877–1929* (Princeton, N.J.: Princeton University Press, 2006).

[18]James E. Anderson, *The Emergence of the Modern Regulatory State* (Washington, D.C.: Public Affairs Press, 1962), 2–3.

[19]*Schechter Poultry Co. v. United States*, 295 U.S. 495 (1935).

[20]*NLRB v. Jones and Laughlin Steel*, 301 U.S. 1 (1937).

[21]*American Power and Light v. Securities and Exchange Commission*, 329 U.S. 90 (1946).

[22]Louis Fisher, *American Constitutional Law*, 6th ed. (Durham, N.C.: Carolina Academic Press, 2005), 390.

[23]*North American Company v. Securities and Exchange Commission*, 327 U.S. 686 (1946).

[24]*Brown v. Board of Education*, 347 U.S. 483 (1954).

[25]See Thomas Anton, *American Federalism and Public Policy* (Philadelphia: Temple University Press, 1989).

[26]Morton Grodzins, *The American System: A New View of Government in the United States* (Chicago: Rand McNally, 1966).

[27]Rosella Levaggi, *Fiscal Federalism and Grants-in-Aid* (Brookfield, Vt.: Avebury, 1991).

[28]Timothy J. Conlan, *From New Federalism to Devolution* (Washington, D.C.: Brookings Institution, 1998).

[29]*Garcia v. San Antonio Authority*, 469 U.S. 528 (1985).

[30]See Tinsley E. Yarbrough, *The Rehnquist Court and the Constitution* (New York: Oxford University Press, 2000); David L. Hudson, *The Rehnquist Court: Understanding Its Impact and Legacy* (Westport, CT.: onn Praeger, 2006).

[31]*United States v. Lopez*, 514 U.S. 549 (1995).

[32]*Printz v. United States*, 521 U.S. 98 (1997).

[33]*Kimel v. Florida Board of Regents*, 528 U.S. 62 (2000).

[34]*Board of Trustees of the University of Alabama v. Garrett*, 531 U.S. 356 (2002).

[35]*Gonzales v. Raich*, No. 03-1454 (2005).

[36]Patrick M. Garry, *An Entrenched Legacy: How the New Deal Constitutional Revolution Continues to Shape the Role of the Supreme Court* (State College: Pennsylvania State University Press, 2008).

[37]Andrew W. Dobelstein, *Politics, Economics, and Public Welfare* (Englewood Cliffs, N.J.: Prentice-Hall, 1980), 5.

[38]Lloyd A. Free and Hadley Cantril, *The Political Beliefs of Americans* (New York: Simon & Schuster, 1968), 21.

[39]Survey for the Times Mirror Center for the People and the Press by Princeton Survey Research Associates, July 12–27, 1994.

CHAPTER FOUR

[1]Julian P. Boyd, ed., *The Papers of Thomas Jefferson*, vol. 12 (Princeton, N.J.: Princeton University Press, 1955), 440.

[2]*Anderson v. Creighton*, 483 U.S. 635 (1987).

[3]*United States v. Carolene Products Co.*, 304 U.S. 144 (1938).

[4]*Schenck v. United States*, 249 U.S. 47 (1919).

[5]*Dennis v. United States*, 341 U.S. 494 (1951); for a broad look at the relationship between issues of national security and liberty, see Geoffrey Stone, *War and Liberty: An American Dilemma: 1790 to the Present* (New York: W. W. Norton, 2007).

[6]See, for example, *Yates v. United States*, 354 U.S. 298 (1957); *Noto v. United States*, 367 U.S. 290 (1961); *Scales v. United States*, 367 U.S. 203 (1961).

[7]*United States v. O'Brien*, 391 U.S. 367 (1968).

[8]*Texas v. Johnson*, 109 S. Ct. 2544 (1989).

[9]*New York Times Co. v. United States*, 403 U.S. 713 (1971).

[10]*Nebraska Press Assn. v. Stuart*, 427 U.S. 539 (1976).

[11]*Barron v. Baltimore*, 7 Peters 243 (1833).

[12]*Gitlow v. New York*, 268 U.S. 652 (1925).

[13]*Fiske v. Kansas*, 274 U.S. 30 (1927); *Near v. Minnesota*, 283 U.S. 697 (1931); *Hamilton v. Regents, U. of California*, 293 U.S. 245 (1934); *DeJonge v. Oregon*, 299 U.S. 253 (1937).

[14]*Near v. Minnesota*, 283 U.S. 697 (1931).

[15]*Brandenburg v. Ohio*, 395 U.S. 444 (1969).

[16]*R.A.V. v. St. Paul*, No. 90-7675 (1992).

[17]*Wisconsin v. Mitchell*, No. 92-515 (1993).

[18]*National Socialist Party v. Skokie*, 432 U.S. 43 (1977).

[19]*Forsyth County v. Nationalist Movement*, No. 91-538 (1992).

[20]*Milkovich v. Lorain Journal*, 497 U.S. 1 (1990); see also *Masson v. The New Yorker*, No. 89-1799 (1991).

[21]*New York Times Co. v. Sullivan*, 376 U.S. 254 (1964).

[22]*Roth v. United States*, 354 U.S. 476 (1957).

[23]*Miller v. California*, 413 U.S. 15 (1973).

[24]*Barnes v. Glen Theatre*, No. 90-26 (1991).

[25]*Stanley v. Georgia*, 394 U.S. 557 (1969).

[26]*Osborne v. Ohio*, 495 U.S. 103 (1990); see also *Ashcroft v. Free Speech Coalition*, No. 00-795 (2002).

[27]*United States v. Williams*, No. 06-694 (2008).

[28]*Denver Area Consortium v. Federal Communications Commission*, No. 95-124 (1996); *Reno v. American Civil Liberties Union*, No. 96-511 (1997); *Ashcroft v. ACLU*, No. 03-0218 (2004).

[29]*Engel v. Vitale*, 370 U.S. 421 (1962).

[30]*Abington School District v. Schempp*, 374 U.S. 203 (1963).

696   Notes

[31]*Wallace v. Jaffree*, 472 U.S. 38 (1985).
[32]*Santa Fe Independent School District v. Does*, No. 99-62 (2000).
[33]*Van Orden v. Perry*, No. 03-1500 (2005).
[34]*McCreary County v. American Civil Liberties Union*, No. 03-1693 (2005).
[35]*Board of Regents v. Allen*, 392 U.S. 236 (1968).
[36]*Lemon v. Kurtzman*, 403 U.S. 602 (1971).
[37]Ibid.
[38]*Mitchell v. Helms*, No. 98-1648 (2000).
[39]*Zelman v. Simmons-Harris*, No. 00-1751 (2002); see also *Locke v. Davey*, No. 02-1315 (2004).
[40]*Locke v. Davey*, No. 02-1315 (2004).
[41]*Hein v. Freedom from Religion*, No. 06-157 (2007).
[42]*Wisconsin v. Yoder*, 406 U.S. 295 (1972); see also *Church of the Lukumi Babalu Aye v. City of Hialeah*, No. 91-948 (1993).
[43]*Edwards v. Aguillard*, 487 U.S. 578 (1987).
[44]*District of Columbia v. Heller*, No. 07-290 (2008).
[45]*Griswold v. Connecticut*, 381 U.S. 479 (1965); for an assessment of the Ninth Amendment, see Daniel A. Farber, *Retained by the People: The "Silent" Ninth Amendment and the Constitutional Rights Americans Don't Know They Have* (New York: Basic Books, 2007).
[46]*Vacco v. Quill*, 117 S.C. 36 (1996); *Washington v. Glucksberg*, No. 96-110 (1997); *Gonzalez v. Oregon*, No. 04-63 (2006).
[47]*Roe v. Wade*, 401 U.S. 113 (1973).
[48]*Gregg v. United States*, No. 00-939 (2001).
[49]*Webster v. Reproductive Health Services*, 492 U.S. 490 (1989); see also *Rust v. Sullivan*, No. 89-1391 (1991).
[50]*Planned Parenthood v. Casey*, No. 91-744 (1992).
[51]*Ayotte v. Planned Parenthood of Northern New England*, No. 04-1144 (2006).
[52]*Stenberg v. Carhart*, No. 99-830 (2000).
[53]*Gonzalez v. Carhart*, No. 05-380 (2007).
[54]*Bowers v. Hardwick*, 478 U.S. 186 (1986).
[55]*Lawrence v. Texas*, 539 U.S. 558 (2003).
[56]*McNabb v. United States*, 318 U.S. 332 (1943).
[57]*Powell v. Alabama*, 287 U.S. 45 (1932).
[58]*Palko v. Connecticut*, 302 U.S. 319 (1937).
[59]*Mapp v. Ohio*, 367 U.S. 643 (1961).
[60]*Gideon v. Wainwright*, 372 U.S. 335 (1963).
[61]*Malloy v. Hogan*, 378 U.S. 1 (1964).
[62]*Miranda v. Arizona*, 384 U.S. 436 (1966); see also *Escobedo v. Illinois*, 378 U.S. 478 (1964).
[63]*Pointer v. Texas*, 380 U.S. 400 (1965).
[64]*Klopfer v. North Carolina*, 386 U.S. 213 (1967).
[65]*Duncan v. Louisiana*, 391 U.S. 145 (1968).
[66]*Benton v. Maryland*, 395 U.S. 784 (1969).
[67]*Dickerson v. United States*, No. 99-5525 (2000).
[68]*Missouri v. Siebert*, 542 U.S. 600 (2004).
[69]*Michigan v. Sitz*, No. 88-1897 (1990).
[70]*Indianapolis v. Edmund*, No. 99-1030 (2001).
[71]*Kyllo v. United States*, No. 99-8508 (2001).
[72]*Ferguson v. Charleston*, No. 99-936 (2001).
[73]*Board of Education of Independent School District No. 92 of Pottawatomie County v. Earls*, No. 01-332 (2002).
[74]*Weeks v. United States*, 232 U.S. 383 (1914).
[75]*Nix v. Williams*, 467 U.S. 431 (1984); see also *United States v. Leon*, 468 U.S. 897 (1984).
[76]*Whren v. United States*, 517 U.S. 806 (1996).

[77] *Hudson v. Michigan*, No. 04-1360 (2006).

[78] *Townsend v. Sain*, 372 U.S. 293 (1963).

[79] *Keeney v. Tamaya-Reyes*, No. 90-1859 (1992); see also *Coleman v. Thompson*, No. 89-7662 (1991).

[80] *Bowles v. Russell*, No. 06-5306 (2007).

[81] *Felker v. Turpin*, No. 95-8836 (1996); but see *Stewart v. Martinez-Villareal*, No. 97-300 (1998).

[82] *Williams v. Taylor*, No. 99-6615 (2000).

[83] *Miller-El v. Cockrell*, No. 01-7662 (2003); *Wiggins v. Smith*, No. 02-311 (2003).

[84] Kurt Heine, "Philadelphia Cops Beat One of Their Own," *Syracuse Herald-American*, January 15, 1995, A13.

[85] Alejandro Del Carmen, *Racial Profiling in America* (Upper Saddle River, N.J.: Prentice-Hall, 2007).

[86] *Wilson v. Seiter*, No. 89-7376 (1991).

[87] *Harmelin v. Michigan*, No. 89-7272 (1991).

[88] *Lockyer v. Andrade*, No. 01-1127 (2003); see also *Ewing v. California*, No. 01-6978 (2003).

[89] *Atkins v. Virginia*, No. 01-8452 (2002); *Panetti v. Quarterman*, No. 06-6407 (2007).

[90] *Roper v. Simmons*, No. 03-633 (2005); *Kennedy v. Louisiana*, No. 07-343 (2008).

[91] *Baze v. Rees*, No. 07-5439 (2008); see also *Hill v. McDonough*, No. 05-8794 (2006).

[92] *Ring v. Arizona*, No. 01-488 (2002).

[93] *Blakely v. Washington*, No. 02-1632 (2004).

[94] "Justices: Judges Can Slash Crack Sentences," CNN.com, December 10, 2007.

[95] *Kimbrough v. United States*, No. 06-6330 (2007).

[96] *Korematsu v. United States*, 323 U.S. 214 (1944).

[97] Case cited in Charles Lane, "In Terror War, 2nd Track for Suspects," *Washington Post*, December 1, 2001, A1.

[98] *Rasul v. Bush*, No. 03-334 (2004); *al-Odah v. United States*, No. 03-343 (2004).

[99] *Hamdi v. Rumsfeld*, No. 03-6696 (2004); see also, *Rumsfeld v. Padilla*, No. 03-1027 (2004).

[100] *Hamdan v. Rumsfeld*, No. 05-184 (2006).

[101] *Boumediene et al. v. Bush*, No. 06-1195 (2008).

[102] Quoted in "Feds Get Wide Wiretap Authority," CBSNEWS.com, November 18, 2002.

[103] See Alpheus T. Mason, *The Supreme Court: Palladium of Freedom* (Ann Arbor: University of Michigan Press, 1962); see also Jeffrey Rosen, *The Most Democratic Branch: How the Courts Serve America* (New York: Oxford University Press, 2006).

CHAPTER FIVE

[1] Speech of Martin Luther King Jr. in Washington, D.C., August 2, 1963.

[2] *Washington Post* wire story, May 14, 1991.

[3] "African-American Health," amednews.com (online newspaper of the American Medical Association), May 1, 2000.

[4] Robert Nisbet, "Public Opinion Versus Popular Opinion," *Public Interest* 41 (1975): 171.

[5] See, for example, Gloria J. Browne-Marshall, *Race, Law, and American Society: 1607 to Present* (New York: Routledge, 2007).

[6] Douglas A. Blackmon, *Slavery by Another Name: The Re-Enslavement of Black Americans from the Civil War to World War II* (New York: Doubleday, 2008).

[7] *Plessy v. Ferguson*, 163 U.S. 537 (1896).

[8] Ada Lois Sipuel Fisher, Danney Gable, and Robert Henry, *A Matter of Black and White: The Autobiography of Ada Lois Sipuel Fisher* (Norman: University of Oklahoma Press, 1996).

[9] *Brown v. Board of Education of Topeka*, 347 U.S. 483 (1954).

[10] See, for example, Alejandro Del Carmen, *Racial Profiling in America* (Upper Saddle River, N.J.: Prentice-Hall, 2007).

[11]Data from National Office of Drug Control Policy, 1997.

[12]See Keith Reeves, *Voting Hopes or Fears?* (New York: Oxford University Press, 1997); Tali Mendelberg, *The Race Card* (Princeton, N.J.: Princeton University Press, 2001).

[13]See Kathleen S. Sullivan, *Women and Rights Discourse in Nineteenth-Century America* (Baltimore, Md.: Johns Hopkins University Press, 2007).

[14]*Tinker v. Colwell*, 193 U.S. 473 (1904).

[15]See Jane Mansbridge, *Why We Lost the ERA* (Chicago: University of Chicago Press, 1986).

[16]*Pennsylvania State Police v. Suder*, No. 03-95 (2004).

[17]*Burlington Northern and Santa Fe Railroad Company v. White*, No. 05-259 (2006).

[18]Jennifer L. Lawless and Richard L. Fox, *It Takes a Candidate: Why Women Don't Run for Office* (New York: Cambridge University Press, 2005).

[19]Lois Duke Whitaker, ed., *Voting the Gender Gap* (Urbana: University of Illinois Press, 2008).

[20]U.S. Department of Education, 2006.

[21]See Sara M. Evans and Barbara Nelson, *Wage Justice* (Chicago: University of Chicago Press, 1989).

[22]U.S. Census Bureau data, 2008; see also Daniel McCool, Susan M. Olson, and Jennifer L. Robinson, *Native Vote: American Indians, the Voting Rights Act, and the Right to Vote* (New York: Cambridge University Press, 2007).

[23]See David E. Wilkins, *American Indian Politics and the American Political System* (Lanham, Md.: Rowman & Littlefield, 2006).

[24]William Evans and Julie Topoleski, "The Social and Economic Impact of Native American Casinos," National Bureau of Economic Research, Working Paper No. 9198, September 2002, Cambridge, Massachusetts.

[25]Sean Page, "Gambling on the Future: US Native American Casinos," BNET web story, December 22, 1997.

[26]James G. Gimpel, "Latinos and the 2002 Election: Republicans Do Well When Latinos Stay Home," Center for Immigration Studies, University of Maryland, January 2003, web download; see also Jorge Ramos, *The Latino Wave: How Hispanics Are Transforming Politics in America* (New York: Harper Paperbacks, 2005); F. Chris Garcia and Gabriel Sanchez, *Hispanics and the U.S. Political System: Moving into the Mainstream* (Upper Saddle River, N.J.: Prentice-Hall, 2007).

[27]James Truslow Adams, *The March of Democracy*, vol. 4 (New York: Scribner's, 1933), 284–85.

[28]*Lau v. Nichols*, 414 U.S. 563 (1974).

[29]See Gordon Chang, ed., *Asian Americans and Politics* (Stanford, Calif.: Stanford University Press, 2001).

[30]*Kimel v. Florida Board of Regents*, No. 98-791 (2000); but see *CBOCS West, Inc. v. Humphries*, No. 06-1431 (2008).

[31]*Board of Trustees of the University of Alabama v. Garrett*, No. 99-1240 (2002); *Tennessee v. Lane*, No. 02-1667 (2004).

[32]See William N. Eskridge Jr., *Dishonorable Passions: Sodomy Laws in America, 1861–2003* (New York: Viking, 2008); Nancy D. Polikoff, *Beyond (Straight and Gay) Marriage: Valuing All Families Under the Law* (Boston: Beacon Press, 2009); Craig A. Rimmerman and Clyde Wilcox, *The Politics of Same-Sex Marriage* (Chicago: University of Chicago Press, 2007).

[33]*Romer v. Evans*, 517 U.S. 620 (1996).

[34]*Lawrence v. Texas*, 539 U.S. 558 (2003).

[35]*Boy Scouts of America v. Dale*, No. 99-699 (2000).

[36]*Craig v. Boren*, 429 U.S. 190 (1976).

[37]*Rostker v. Goldberg*, 453 U.S. 57 (1980).

[38]*United States v. Virginia*, No. 94-1941 (1996).

[39]U.S. Conference of Mayors Report, 1998; see also Survey by Federal Financial Institutions Examination Council, 1998.

[40]V. O. Key Jr., *Southern Politics* (New York: Knopf, 1949), 495.
[41]*Smith v. Allwright*, 321 U.S. 649 (1944).
[42]*League of United Latin American Voters v. Perry*, No. 05-204 (2006).
[43]*Muller v. Johnson*, No. 94-631 (1995); *Bush v. Verg*, No. 94-805 (1996); *Shaw v. Hunt*, No. 94-923 (1996).
[44]*Easley v. Cromartie*, No. 99-1864 (2001).
[45]Terry H. Anderson, *The Pursuit of Happiness: A History of Affirmative Action* (New York: Oxford University Press, 2005).
[46]*University of California Regents v. Bakke*, 438 U.S. 265 (1978).
[47]*Steelworkers v. Weber*, 443 U.S. 193 (1979); *Fullilove v. Klutnick*, 448 U.S. 448 (1980).
[48]*Local No. 28, Sheet Metal Workers v. Equal Employment Opportunity Commission*, 478 U.S. 421 (1986); see also *Local No. 93, International Association of Firefighters v. Cleveland*, 478 U.S. 501 (1986); *Firefighters v. Stotts*, 459 U.S. 969 (1984); *Wygant v. Jackson*, 476 U.S. 238 (1986).
[49]*Adarand v. Pena*, No. 94-310 (1995).
[50]*Gratz v. Bollinger*, No. 02-516 (2003).
[51]*Grutter v. Bollinger*, No. 02-241 (2003).
[52]See J. Edward Kellough, *Understanding Affirmative Action: Politics, Discrimination, and the Search for Justice* (Washington, D.C.: Georgetown University Press, 2006).
[53]*Swann v. Charlotte-Mecklenburg County Board of Education*, 402 U.S. 1 (1971).
[54]Christopher Jencks and Meredith Phillips, eds., *The Black-White Test Score Gap* (Washington, D.C.: Brookings Institution Press, 1998).
[55]*Milliken v. Bradley*, 418 U.S. 717 (1974).
[56]*Board of Education of Oklahoma City v. Dowell*, 498 U.S. (1991).
[57]*Sheff v. O'Neill*, No. 95-2071 (1996).
[58]*Parents Involved in Community Schools v. Seattle*, No. 05-908 (2007); *Meredith, Custodial Parent and Next Friend of McDonald v. Jefferson County Board of Education*, No. 05-915 (2007).
[59]Gunnar Myrdal, *An American Dilemma: The Negro Problem and Modern Democracy* (New York: Harper, 1944).

CHAPTER SIX

[1]V. O. Key Jr., *Public Opinion and American Democracy* (New York: Knopf, 1961), 8.
[2]See Brandice Canes-Wrone, *Who Leads Whom? Presidents, Policy, and the Public* (Chicago: University of Chicago Press, 2005).
[3]See Jeremy Bentham, *An Introduction to the Principles of Morals and Legislation* (Oxford, England: Clarendon Press, 1996). First published in 1789.
[4]Vincent Hutchings, *Public Opinion and Democratic Accountability: How Citizens Learn About Politics* (Princeton, N.J.: Princeton University Press, 2005).
[5]Elisabeth Noelle-Neumann, *The Spiral of Silence*, 2d ed. (Chicago: University of Chicago Press, 1993), ch. 1.
[6]"Study Finds Widespread Misperceptions on Iraq Highly Related to Support for War," web release of the Program on International Policy Attitudes, School of Public Affairs, University of Maryland, October 2, 2003.
[7]Joshua Buntin III, "Start with Civics 101," *Miami Herald*, January 21, 2008, p. 25A.
[8]Survey of Students of the Eight Ivy League Schools by Luntz & Weber Research and Strategic Services, for the University of Pennsylvania's Ivy League Study, November 13–December 1, 1992.
[9]See R. Michael Alvarez and John Brehm, *Hard Choices, Easy Answers* (Princeton, N.J.: Princeton University Press, 2002); see also Samuel L. Popkin, *The Reasoning Voter* (Chicago: University of Chicago Press, 1991).
[10]See Herbert Asher, *Polling and the Public*, 7th ed. (Washington, D.C.: Congressional Quarterly Press, 2007).

[11]Political Arithmetic, May 31, 2007, web release.

[12]M. Kent Jennings and Richard G. Niemi, *Generations and Politics* (Princeton, N.J.: Princeton University Press, 1981).

[13]See Orit Ichilov, *Political Socialization, Citizenship Education, and Democracy* (New York: Teachers College Press, 1990).

[14]Noelle-Neumann, *The Spiral of Silence.*

[15]Jon Western, *Selling Intervention and War: The Presidency, the Media, and the American Public* (Baltimore, Md.: Johns Hopkins University Press, 2005); see also Wojtek Mackiewicz Wolfe, *Winning the War of Words: Selling the War on Terror from Afghanistan to Iraq* (Westport, Conn.: Praeger, 2008).

[16]See, however, Dietram A. Scheufele, Matthew C. Nisbet, and Dominique Brossard, "Pathways to Political Participation: Religion, Communication Contexts, and Mass Media," *International Journal of Public Opinion Research* 15 (Autumn 2003): 300–24.

[17]The classic study of citizen ideology is Philip Converse, "The Nature of Belief Systems in Mass Publics," in David Apter, ed., *Ideology and Discontent* (New York: Free Press, 1965), 206.

[18]Kenneth D. Wald, *Religion and Politics in the United States* (Lanham, Md.: Rowman & Littlefield, 2003).

[19]CNN/USA Today Poll conducted by the Gallup Organization, 1997.

[20]Lois Duke Whitaker, ed., *Voting the Gender Gap* (Urbana: University of Illinois Press, 2008).

[21]Susan A. MacManus, *Young v. Old: Generational Combat in the Twenty-first Century* (Boulder, Colo.: Westview Press, 1996).

[22]See Angus Campbell, Philip Converse, Warren Miller, and Donald Stokes, *The American Voter* (New York: Wiley, 1960), chs. 3 and 4.

[23]Martin P. Wattenberg, *Where Have All the Voters Gone?* (Cambridge, Mass.: Harvard University Press, 2002).

[24]Donald Green, Bradley Palmquist, and Eric Schickler, *Partisan Hearts and Minds* (New Haven, Conn.: Yale University Press, 2002).

[25]See William Domhoff, *Who Rules America?* 5th ed. (New York: McGraw-Hill, 2005).

[26]Benjamin I. Page and Robert Y. Shapiro, "Effects of Public Opinion on Policy," *American Political Science Review* 77 (March 1983): 178; see also Richard Sobel, *The Impact of Public Opinion on U.S. Foreign Policy* (New York: Oxford University Press, 2001); James Stimson, *Tides of Consent: How Public Opinion Shapes American Politics* (New York: Cambridge University Press, 2004).

[27]Lawrence R. Jacobs and Robert Y. Shapiro, *Politicians Don't Pander* (Chicago: University of Chicago Press, 2000).

[28]Christopher J. Grill, *The Public Side of Representation: A Study of Citizens' View About Representatives and the Representative Process* (Albany: State University of New York Press, 2007).

CHAPTER SEVEN

[1]Walter Lippmann, *Public Opinion* (New York: Free Press, 1965), 36.

[2]Quoted in Ralph Volney Harlow, *The Growth of the United States* (New York: Henry Holt, 1943), 312.

[3]Example from Gus Tyler, "One Cheer for the Democrats," *New Leader*, November 3, 1986, 6.

[4]Thomas E. Patterson, *The Vanishing Voter* (New York: Vintage, 2003), p. 10.

[5]Mark N. Franklin, *Voter Turnout and the Dynamics of Electoral Competition in Established Democracies Since 1945* (New York: Cambridge University Press, 2004).

[6]Patterson, *The Vanishing Voter*, 134.

[7]Russell Dalton, "The Myth of the Disengaged American," web publication of the Comparative Study of Electoral Systems, October 2005, 2.

[8]Patterson, *The Vanishing Voter*, 179–80.

[9]*Crawford et al. v. Marion County Election Board et al.*, No. 07-21 (2008).

[10]Ivor Crewe, "Electoral Participation," in David Butler, Howard R. Penniman, and Austin Ranney, eds., *Democracy at the Polls* (Washington, D.C.: American Enterprise Institute, 1981), 251–53.

[11]Richard Boyd, "Decline of U.S. Voter Turnout," *American Politics Quarterly* 9 (April 1981): 142.

[12]David Hill, *American Voter Turnout: An Institutional Perspective* (Boulder, Colo.: Westview Press, 2006).

[13]David C. Leege, Kenneth D. Wald, Brian S. Krueger, and Paul D. Mueller, *The Politics of Cultural Differences* (Princeton, N.J.: Princeton University Press, 2002).

[14]Larry Bartels, *Unequal Democracy: The Political Economy of the Gilded Age* (Princeton, N.J.: Princeton University Press, 2008).

[15]Patterson, *The Vanishing Voter*, 135.

[16]See Bruce Bimber and Richard Davis, *Campaigning Online* (New York: Oxford University Press, 2003); Bruce Bimber, *Information and American Democracy* (New York: Cambridge University Press, 2003); Joe Trippi, *The Revolution Will Not Be Televised* (New York: HarperCollins, 2004).

[17]Dalton, "The Myth of the Disengaged American," 2.

[18]Robert Putnam, *Bowling Alone* (New York: Simon & Schuster, 2000); but see Cliff Zukin et al., *A New Engagement: Political Participation, Civic Life, and the Changing American Citizen* (New York: Oxford University Press, 2006).

[19]See Benjamin Ginsberg, *The Consequences of Consent* (New York: Random House, 1982), ch. 2.

[20]See, for example, Charles J. Stewart, Craig Allen Smith, and Robert E. Denton Jr., *Persuasion and Social Movements*, 5th ed. (Long Grove, Ill.: Waveland Press, 2007).

[21]ABC News/Washington Post poll, March 23, 2003.

[22]Dalton, *Citizen Politics*, 38.

[23]Gallup poll, January 2003.

[24]William Watts and Lloyd A. Free, eds., *The State of the Nation* (New York: University Books, Potomac Associates, 1967), 97.

[25]Robert E. Lane, "Market Justice, Political Justice," *American Political Science Review* 80 (1986): 383; see also Jennifer Nedelsky, *Private Property and the Limits of American Constitutionalism* (New York: Oxford University Press, 1990).

[26]Sidney Verba and Norman Nie, *Participation in America* (New York: Harper & Row, 1972), 131.

[27]Robert Kaplan, "Was Democracy Just a Moment?" *Atlantic Monthly*, December 1997. Retrieved from Atlantic Monthly website.

[28]Daniel Pope, ed., *American Radicalism* (New York: Blackwell, 2001).

[29]Bartels, *Unequal Democracy*.

CHAPTER EIGHT

[1]E. E. Schattschneider, *Party Government* (New York: Rinehart, 1942), 1.

[2]See John Aldrich, *Why Parties? The Origin and Transformation of Political Parties in America* (Chicago: University of Chicago Press, 1995); L. Sandy Maisel, *American Political Parties and Elections* (New York: Oxford University Press, 2007).

[3]E. E. Schattschneider, *The Semisovereign People: A Realist's View of Democracy in America* (New York: Holt, Rinehart & Winston, 1961), 140.

[4]Thomas E. Patterson, *The Vanishing Voter* (New York: Knopf, 2002), ch. 2.

[5]See Richard P. McCormick, *The Second American Party System: Party Formation in the Jacksonian Era* (Chapel Hill: University of North Carolina Press, 1966).

[6]Alexis de Tocqueville, *Democracy in America (1835–1840)*, eds. J. P. Mayer and A. P. Kerr (Garden City, N.Y.: Doubleday/Anchor, 1969), 60.

[7]Aldrich, *Why Parties?* 151.

[8]See Kristi Andersen, *The Creation of a Democratic Majority, 1928–1936* (Chicago: University of Chicago Press, 1979).

[9]See Kevin Phillips, *The Emerging Republican Majority* (New Rochelle, N.Y.: Arlington House, 1969).

[10]See Arthur C. Paulson, *Electoral Realignment and the Outlook for American Democracy* (Boston: Northeastern University Press, 2006).

[11]Gallup Organization, 2008.

[12]Lewis L. Gould, *Grand Old Party* (New York: Random House, 2003); but see also Jacob S. Hacker and Paul Pierson, *Off-Center: The Republican Revolution and the Erosion of American Democracy* (New Haven, Conn.: Yale University Press, 2006).

[13]See John B. Judis and Ruy Teixeira, *The Emerging Democratic Majority* (New York: Scribner, 2002).

[14]See, for example, Everett Carll Ladd, "The Brittle Mandate: Electoral Dealignment and the 1980 Presidential Election," *Political Science Quarterly* 96, No. 1 (Spring, 1981): 1–25.

[15]Clinton Rossiter, *Parties and Politics in America* (Ithaca, N.Y.: Cornell University Press, 1960), 11; see also James H. Fowler and Oleg Smirnov, *Mandates, Parties, and Voters: How Elections Shape the Future* (Philadelphia: Temple University Press, 2007).

[16]Nancy Gibbs and Michael Duffy, "Fall of the House of Newt," *Time*, November 16, 1998, 47.

[17]Jeffrey M. Stonecash, *Political Parties Matter: Realignment and the Return of Partisan Voting* (Boulder; Colo.: Lynne Reinner, 2005).

[18]John Green, Mark Rozell, and William Clyde Wilcox, eds., *The Christian Right in American Politics* (Washington, D.C.: Georgetown University Press, 2003).

[19]Micah L. Sifrey, *Spoiling for a Fight: Third-Party Politics in America* (New York: Routledge, 2003).

[20]Daniel A. Mazmanian, *Third Parties in Presidential Elections* (Washington, D.C.: Brookings Institution, 1984), 143–44.

[21]See Lawrence Goodwyn, *The Populist Movement* (New York: Oxford University Press, 1978).

[22]Lewis L. Gould, *Four Hats in the Ring: The 1912 Election and the Birth of Modern American Politics* (Lawrence: University Press of Kansas, 2008).

[23]See Anthony King, *Running Scared* (New York: Free Press, 1997); but see James E. Campbell, *The American Campaign: U.S. Presidential Campaigns and the National Vote* (College Station: Texas A&M Press, 2008).

[24]See Paul S. Herrnson and John C. Green, eds., *Responsible Partisanship* (Lawrence: University Press of Kansas, 2003).

[25]See Marjorie Randon Hershey, *Party Politics in America*, 13th ed. (New York: Longman, 2009).

[26]David Adamany, "Political Parties in the 1980s," in Michael J. Malbin, ed., *Money and Politics in the United States* (Chatham, N.J.: Chatham House, 1984), 114.

[27]*Senator Mitch McConnell et al. v. Federal Election Commission et al.*, No. 02-1674 (2003).

[28]Michael J. Malbin, *The Election After Reform: Money, Politics, and the Bipartisan Campaign Reform Act* (Lanham, Md.: Rowman & Littlefield, 2006).

[29]Joseph Napolitan, *The Election Game and How to Win It* (New York: Doubleday, 1972); for a contemporary look at the campaigning process, see D. Sunshine Hillygus and Todd G. Shields, *The Persuadable Voter: Wedge Issues in Presidential Campaigns* (Princeton, N.J.: Princeton University Press, 2008).

[30]Federal Elections Commission data, 2008.

[31]David B. Magelby, J. Quin Monson, and Kelly D. Patterson, eds., *Dancing Without Partners: How Candidates, Parties and Interest Groups Interact in the New Campaign Finance Environment* (Provo, Utah: Brigham Young University Press, 2005).

[32]David Chagall, *The New King-Makers* (New York: Harcourt Brace Jovanovich, 1981).

[33]Lawrence R. Jacobs and Robert Y. Shapiro, *Politicians Don't Pander: Political Manipulation and the Loss of Democratic Responsiveness* (Chicago: University of Chicago Press, 2000).

[34]Emmett H. Buell Jr. and Lee Sigelman, *Attack Politics: Negativity in Presidential Campaigns Since 1960* (Lawrence: University Press of Kansas, 2008). For opposing views on the effect of negative advertising, see Stephen Ansolabehere and Shanto Iyengar, *Going Negative* (New York: Free Press, 1995), and John Geer, *In Defense of Negativity* (Chicago: University of Chicago Press, 2006).

[35]Darrell M. West, *Air Wars: Television Advertising in Election Campaigns,1952–2004*, 4th ed. (Washington, D.C.: Congressional Quarterly Press, 2005), 140–46.

[36]Ibid, 12.

[37]Peter J. Peterson, *Running on Empty: How the Democratic and Republican Parties Are Bankrupting Our Future and What Americans Can Do About It* (New York: Farrar, Straus, and Giroux, 2005).

CHAPTER NINE

[1]E. E. Schattschneider, *The Semisovereign People: A Realist's View of Democracy in America* (New York: Holt, Rinehart & Winston, 1960), 35.

[2]See Matthew J. Burbank, Ronald J. Hrebenar, and Robert C. Benedict, *Parties, Interest Groups, and Political Campaigns* (Boulder, Colo.: Paradigm, 2008).

[3]Alexis de Tocqueville, *Democracy in America, 1835–1840*, eds. J. P. Mayer and A. P. Kerr (Garden City, N.Y.: Doubleday/Anchor, 1969), bk. 2, ch. 4.

[4]Mancur Olson, *The Logic of Collective Action*, rev. ed. (Cambridge, Mass.: Harvard University Press, 1971), 147; see also Theda Skocpol, *Diminished Democracy* (Norman: University of Oklahoma Press, 2003).

[5]See Jack L. Walker, *Mobilizing Interest Groups in America* (Ann Arbor: University of Michigan Press, 1991).

[6]Olson, *The Logic of Collective Action*, 64.

[7]Christopher J. Bosso, "The Color of Money: Environmental Groups and the Pathologies of Fund Raising," in Allan J. Cigler and Burdett Loomis, *Interest Group Politics*, 4th ed. (Washington, D.C.: Congressional Quarterly Press, 1995), 101–3.

[8]Kay Lehman Schlozman and John T. Tierney, *Organized Interests and American Democracy* (New York: Harper & Row, 1986), 54; see also Jeffrey M. Berry and Clyde Wilcox, *The Interest Group Society*, 5th ed. (New York: Longman, 2008).

[9]Norman J. Ornstein and Shirley Elder, *Interest Groups, Lobbying, and Policymaking* (Washington, D.C.: Congressional Quarterly Press, 1978), 82–86.

[10]See John Mark Hansen, *Gaining Access* (Chicago: Chicago University Press, 1991); Bruce Wolpe and Bertram Levine, *Lobbying Congress* (Washington, D.C.: Congressional Quarterly Press, 1996).

[11]See Paul S. Herrnson, Ronald G. Shaiko, and Clyde Wilcox, *The Interest Group Connection: Electioneering, Lobbying, and Policymaking in Washington*, 2d ed. (Washington, D.C.: Congressional Quarterly Press, 2004).

[12]Quoted in Ornstein and Elder, *Interest Groups, Lobbying, and Policymaking*, 77.

[13]Steve Reinberg, "Debate Builds over Drug Companies' Fees to FDA," *Washington Post*, April 13, 2007, electronic version.

[14]Paul J. Quirk, *Industry Influence in Federal Regulatory Agencies* (Princeton, N.J.: Princeton University Press, 1981); John E. Chubb, *Interest Groups and the Bureaucracy: The Politics of Energy* (Stanford, Calif.: Stanford University Press, 1983), 200–1.

[15]Lee Epstein and C. K. Rowland, "Interest Groups in the Courts," *American Political Science Review* 85 (1991): 205–17.

[16]Richard Davis, *Electing Justice: Fixing the Supreme Court Nomination Process* (New York: Oxford University Press, 2005).

[17]Hugh Heclo, "Issue Networks and the Executive Establishment," in Anthony King, ed., *The New American Political System* (Washington, D.C.: American Enterprise Institute, 1978), 87–124.

[18]Ornstein and Elder, *Interest Groups, Lobbying, and Policymaking*, 88–93.

[19]Quoted in Mark Green, "Political PAC-Man," *The New Republic*, December 13, 1982, 20; see also Richard Skinner, *More Than Money: Interest Group Action in Congressional Elections* (Lanham, Md.: Rowman & Littlefield, 2006); Mark J. Rozell, Clyde Wilcox, and David Madland, *Interest Groups in American Campaigns*, 2d ed. (Washington, D.C.: Congressional Quarterly Press, 2005).

[20]Quoted in Larry Sabato, *PAC Power: Inside the World of Political Action Committees* (New York: Norton, 1984), 72.

[21]Federal Elections Commission data, 2008.

[22]See Thomas L. Gatz, *Improper Influence* (Ann Arbor: University of Michigan Press, 1996); Gene M. Grossman and Elhanan Helpman, *Interest Groups and Trade Policy* (Princeton, N.J.: Princeton University Press, 2002); Harry L. Wilson, *Guns, Gun Control, and Elections: The Politics and Policy of Firearms* (Lanham, Md.: Rowman & Littlefield, 2006).

[23]Walker, *Mobilizing Interest Groups in America*, 112.

[24]Theodore J. Lowi, *The End of Liberalism: The Second Republic of the United States* (New York: Norton, 1979).

[25]Larry Bartels, *Unequal Democracy: The Political Economy of the New Gilded Age* (Princeton, N.J.: Princeton University Press, 2008).

CHAPTER TEN

[1]Theodore H. White, *The Making of the President, 1972* (New York: Bantam Books, 1973), 327.

[2]See Bill Kovach and Tom Rosenstiel, *The Elements of Journalism* (New York: Three Rivers Press, 2001).

[3]See Rodger Streitmatter, *Mightier Than the Sword: How the News Media Have Shaped American History* (Westport, Conn.: Praeger, 2008).

[4]Frank Luther Mott, *American Journalism, a History: 1690–1960* (New York: Macmillan, 1962), 114–15; see also Si Sheppard, *The Partisan Press: A History of Media Bias in the United States* (Jefferson, N.C.: McFarland, 2007).

[5]Mott, *American Journalism*, 122–23, 220–27.

[6]Edwin Emery, *The Press and America: An Interpretive History of the Mass Media* (Englewood Cliffs, N.J.: Prentice-Hall, 1977), 350.

[7]Quoted in Mott, *American Journalism*, 529.

[8]Quoted in David Halberstam, *The Powers That Be* (New York: Knopf, 1979), 208–9.

[9]Donald Shaw and Maxwell McCombs, *The Emergence of American Political Issues: The Agenda-Setting Function of the Press* (St. Paul, Minn.: West, 1977).

[10]Bernard C. Cohen, *The Press and Foreign Policy* (Princeton, N.J.: Princeton University Press, 1963), 13.

[11]Thomas E. Patterson, *The American Democracy*, 5th ed. (New York: McGraw-Hill, 2001), 309–10.

[12]Kathleen Hall Jamieson and Karlyn Kohrs Campbell, *The Interplay of Influence*, rev. ed. (Boston: Wadsworth, 2005), 4.

[13]Michael Schudson, *Discovering the News* (New York: Basic Books, 1981).

[14]Michael Schudson, "What Time Means in a News Story." Gannett Center for Media Studies, New York, 1986. Occasional Paper No. 4, 8.

[15]Comment at the annual meeting of the American Association of Political Consultants, Washington, D.C., 1977.

[16]Project for Excellence in Journalism, "Character and the Primaries of 2008," web release, May 29, 2008.

[17]Michael X. Delli Carpini and Scott Keeter, *What Americans Know About Politics and Why It Matters* (New Haven: Conn.: Yale University Press, 1997).

[18]Times Mirror Center for the People and the Press survey, 1994.

[19]W. Lance Bennett, Regina G. Lawrence, and Steven Livingston, *When the Press Fails: Political Power and the News Media from Iraq to Katrina* (Chicago: University of Chicago Press, 2008).

[20]Quoted in David Shaw, "Beyond Skepticism: Have the Media Crossed the Line into Cynicism?" *Los Angeles Times*, April 17, 1996, A1.

[21]Clark Hoyt, "What That McCain Article Didn't Say," *New York Times*, web release, February 24, 2008.

[22]See Scott McClellan, *What Happened: Inside the Bush White House and Washington's Culture of Deception* (New York: Public Affairs, 2008).

[23]Stephen J. Farnsworth and S. Robert Lichter, *The Mediated Presidency: Television News and Presidential Governance* (Lanham, Md.: Rowman & Littlefield, 2006).

[24]Kiku Adatto, "Sound Bite Democracy," Joan Shorenstein Center on the Press, Politics, and Public Policy, Research Paper R-2, Harvard University, Cambridge, Mass., June 1990.

[25]Center for Media and Public Affairs data, 2008

[26]Thomas Patterson, *Out of Order* (New York: Knopf, 1993), ch. 2.

[27]Robert Entman, "Framing: Towards Clarification of a Fractured Paradigm," in Denis McQuail's, ed., *McQuail's Reader in Mass Communication Theory* (London: Sage, 2002); 391–92.

[28]Michael Levy, "Disdaining the News," *Journal of Communication* (1981): 24–31.

[29]Thomas E. Patterson, *The Vanishing Voter* (New York: Knopf, 2002), 59.

[30]Walter Lippmann, *Public Opinion* (New York: Free Press, 1965), 214. First published in 1922.

[31]Greg Mitchell, "E&P/TIPP Poll: Bird in the Hand for Bush?" *Editor & Publisher*, November 6, 2000.

[32]*Editor & Publisher*, online edition, November 1, 2004.

[33]Bernard Goldberg, *Bias: A CBS Insider Exposes How the Media Distort News* (New York: Harper Paperbacks, 2003).

[34]David H. Weaver, Randal A. Beam, Bonnie J. Brownlee, Paul S. Voakes, G. Cleveland Wilhoit, *The American Journalist in the 21st Century* (Mahwah, N.J.: LEA, 2006).

[35]Center for Media and Public Affairs, *Media Monitor*, various dates.

[36]Michael Robinson, "Public Affairs Television and the Growth of Political Malaise," *American Political Science Review* 70 (1976): 409–32.

[37]Center for Media and Public Affairs, *Media Monitor*, various dates.

[38]Ibid.

[39]Mark Rozell, "Press Coverage of Congress," in Thomas Mann and Norman Ornstein, eds., *Congress, the Press, and the Public* (Washington, D.C.: American Enterprise Institute and Brookings Institution, 1994), 109.

[40]Robinson, "Public Affairs Television and the Growth of Political Malaise."

[41]The press's negativity and sensationalism have had another effect as well; they have damaged the press's credibility. According to a 2007 survey conducted by the Center for Public Leadership at Harvard University's John F. Kennedy School of Government, the press has the lowest public confidence rating of any major U.S. institution.

[42]Joseph N. Cappella and Kathleen Hall Jamieson, *Spiral of Cynicism* (New York: Oxford University Press, 1997), 159.

[43]Quoted in Doreen Carvajal, "For News Media, Some Introspection," *New York Times*, April 5, 1998, 28.

[44]Project for Excellence in Journalism, "The Debate Effect," web release, October 27, 2004.

[45]William Cole, ed, *The Most of A. J. Leibling* (New York: Simon, 1963), 7.

[46]See Bruce A. Bimber and Richard Davis, *Campaigning Online: The Internet in U.S. Elections* (New York: Oxford University Press, 2003).

[47]Robinson, "Public Affairs Television and the Growth of Political Malaise."

[48]Donald F. Roberts, Uila G. Foehr, Victoria J. Rideout, and Mollyann Brodie, "Kids and Media at the New Millennium," A Kaiser Family Foundation Report, November 1999, 19.

[49]See David T. Z. Mindich, *Tuned Out: Why Americans Under 40 Don't Follow the News* (New York: Oxford University Press, 2005).

[50]Thomas E. Patterson, "Young People and News," report of the Joan Shorenstein Center on the Press, Politics, and Public Policy, John F. Kennedy School of Government, Harvard University, June, 2007.

[51]Martin P. Wattenberg, *Is Voting for Young People?* (New York: Pearson Longman, 2008), 32.

[52]Ibid. 75–80.

CHAPTER ELEVEN

[1]Roger H. Davidson and Walter J. Oleszek, *Congress and Its Members*, 10th ed. (Washington, D.C.: Congressional Quarterly Press, 2008), 4.

[2]See Paul S. Herrnson, *Congressional Elections: Campaigning at Home and in Washington*, 5th ed. (Washington, D.C.: Congressional Quarterly Press, 2008).

[3]See Gary C. Jacobson, *The Politics of Congressional Elections*, 5th ed. (New York: Longman, 2001).

[4]Bruce Cain, John Ferejohn, and Morris P. Fiorina, *The Personal Vote* (Cambridge, Mass.: Harvard University Press, 1987).

[5]Information provided by Clerk of the House.

[6]U.S. Code Online, 2006.

[7]Edward Sidlow, *Challenging the Incumbent: An Underdog's Undertaking* (Washington, D.C.: Congressional Quarterly Press, 2003); David C. W. Parker, *The Power of Money in Congressional Campaigns, 1880–2006* (Norman: University of Oklahoma Press, 2008).

[8]Quoted in Jennifer Babson and Kelly St. John, "Momentum Helps GOP Collect Record Amounts from PACs," *Congressional Quarterly Weekly Report*, December 3, 1994, 3456.

[9]Quoted in "A Tale of Myths and Measures: Who Is Truly Vulnerable?" *Congressional Quarterly Weekly Report*, December 4, 1993, 7; see also Dennis F. Thompson, *Ethics in Congress* (Washington, D.C.: Brookings Institution Press, 1995).

[10]James E. Campbell, *The Presidential Pulse of Congressional Elections* (Lexington: University Press of Kentucky, 1993).

[11]Robert Erikson, "The Puzzle of Midterm Losses," *Journal of Politics* 50 (November 1988): 1011–29.

[12]Linda L. Fowler and Robert D. McClure, *Political Ambition* (New Haven, Conn.: Yale University Press, 1989).

[13]Keith R. Poole and Howard Rosenthal, "Patterns of Congressional Voting," *American Journal of Political Science* 35 (February 1991): 228.

[14]*Congressional Quarterly Weekly Report*, various dates.

[15]Linda Witt, Karen M. Paget, and Glenna Matthews, *Running as a Woman: Gender and Power in American Politics* (New York: Free Press, 1993); Sue Thomas, *How Women Legislate* (New York: Oxford University Press, 1994); Tali Mendelberg, *The Race Card* (Princeton, N.J.: Princeton University Press, 2001).

[16]Steven Smith, *Party Influence in Congress* (New York: Cambridge University Press, 2007); Barbara Sinclair, *Party Wars: Polarization and the Politics of National Policy Making* (Norman: University of Oklahoma Press 2006).

[17]Randall Strahan, *Leading Representatives: The Agency of Leaders in the Politics of the U.S. House* (Baltimore, Md. Johns Hopkins University Press, 2007); David King, *Turf Wars* (Chicago: University of Chicago Press, 1997).

[18]See Stephen E. Frantzich and Steven E. Schier, *Congress: Games and Strategies* (Dubuque, Iowa: Brown & Benchmark, 1995), 127.

[19]See Gerald S. Strom, *The Logic of Lawmaking* (Baltimore, Md.: Johns Hopkins University Press, 1990).

[20]See Barbara Sinclair, *Unorthodox Lawmaking: New Legislative Processes in the U.S. Congress*, 3d ed. (Washington, D.C.: Congressional Quarterly Press, 2007).

[21]See Jon R. Bond and Richard Fleisher, eds., *Polarized Politics: Congress and the President in a Partisan Era* (Washington, D.C.: Congressional Quarterly Press, 2000).

[22]See Gary Orfield, *Congressional Power: Congress and Social Change* (New York: Harcourt Brace Jovanovich, 1975).

[23]James L. Sundquist, "Congress and the President: Enemies or Partners?" in Lawrence C. Dodd and Bruce I. Oppenheimer, eds., *Congress Reconsidered* (New York: Praeger, 1977), 240.

[24]Barry C. Burden, *Personal Roots of Representation* (Princeton, N.J.: Princeton University Press, 2007).

[25]Keith Krehbiel, "Are Congressional Committees Composed of Preference Outliers?" *American Political Science Review* 84 (1990): 149–64; Richard L. Hall and Bernard Grofman, "The Committee Assignment Process and the Conditional Nature of Committee Bias," *American Political Science Review* 84 (1990): 1149–66.

[26]Jason Mycoff, *Confrontation and Compromise: Presidential and Congressional Leadership, 2001–2006* (Lanham, Md.: Rowman & Littlefield, 2007).

[27]Joel A. Aberbach and Mark A. Peterson, eds., *The Executive Branch* (New York: Oxford University Press, 2005), 534–35.

[28]Davidson and Oleszek, *Congress and Its Members*, 7.

CHAPTER TWELVE

[1]Woodrow Wilson, *Constitutional Government in the United States* (New York: Columbia University Press, 1908), 67.

[2]Sidney Milkis and Michael Nelson, *The American Presidency: Origins and Development, 1790–2007*, 5th ed. (Washington, D.C.: Congressional Quarterly Press, 2007).

[3]James W. Davis, *The American Presidency* (New York: Harper & Row, 1987), 13; see also Bruce Ackerman, *The Failure of the Founding Fathers* (Cambridge, Mass.: Belknap Press of Harvard University Press, 2005).

[4]See Barry M. Blechman and Stephen S. Kaplan, *Force Without War* (Washington, D.C.: Brookings Institution, 1978); Arthur M. Schlesinger Jr., *War and the American Presidency* (New York: W. W. Norton, 2004).

[5]*United States v. Belmont*, 57 U.S. 758 (1937).

[6]Robert DiClerico, *The American President*, 5th ed. (Englewood Cliffs, N.J.: Prentice-Hall, 1999), 47.

[7]Quoted in Wilfred E. Binkley, *President and Congress*, 3d ed. (New York: Vintage, 1962), 142.

[8]Theodore Roosevelt, *An Autobiography* (New York: Scribner's, 1931), 383.

[9]See Richard M. Pious, *The American Presidency* (New York: Basic Books, 1979), 83.

[10]Harry S Truman, *Years of Trial and Hope* (New York: Signet, 1956), 535.

[11]See Thomas S. Langston, *The Cold War Presidency: A Documentary History* (Washington, D.C.: Congressional Quarterly Press, 2006).

[12]James Bryce, *The American Commonwealth* (New York: Commonwealth Edition, 1908), 230.

[13]Erwin C. Hargrove, *The Effective Presidency: Lessons on Leadership from John F. Kennedy to George W. Bush* (Boulder, Colo. Paradigm, 2007).

[14]James W. Ceaser, *Presidential Selection: Theory and Development* (Princeton, N.J.: Princeton University Press, 1979).

[15]John S. Jackson and William J. Crotty, *The Politics of Presidential Selection* (New York: Longman, 2001).

[16]See John G. Geer, *In Defense of Negativity* (Chicago: University of Chicago Press, 2006).

[17]John P. Burke, *The Institutionalized Presidency* (Baltimore: Johns Hopkins University Press, 1992); Charles E. Walcott and Karen M. Hult, *Governing the White House* (Lawrence: University Press of Kansas, 1995).

[18]Quoted in Stephen J. Wayne, *Road to the White House, 1992* (New York: St. Martin's Press, 1992), 143; but see Jody C. Baumgartner, *The American Vice Presidency Reconsidered* (Westport, Conn.: Praeger, 2006).

[19]See Barton Gellman and Jo Becker, "Angler: The Cheney Vice Presidency," *Washington Post*, June 24–27, 2007, a four-part series of articles.

[20]See Jeffrey E. Cohen, *The Politics of the United States Cabinet* (Pittsburgh: University of Pittsburgh Press, 1988); Shirley Anne Warshaw, *Powersharing: White House–Cabinet Relations in the Modern Presidency* (Albany: State University of New York Press, 1995).

[21]James Pfiffner, *The Modern Presidency* (New York: St. Martin's Press, 1994), 123.

[22]Quoted in James MacGregor Burns, "Our Super-Government—Can We Control It?" *New York Times*, April 24, 1949, 32.

[23]See Paul C. Light, *Thickening Government: Federal Hierarchy and the Diffusion of Accountability* (Washington, D.C.: Brookings Institution, 1995).

[24]Erwin Hargrove, *The Power of the Modern Presidency* (New York: Knopf, 1974); see also John H. Kessel, *Presidents, the Presidency, and the Political Environment* (Washington, D.C.: Congressional Quarterly Press, 2001); Stephen Skowronek, *Presidential Leadership in Political Time: Reprise and Reappraisal* (Lawrence: University Press of Kansas, 2008).

[25]James P. Pfiffner, *The Strategic Presidency: Hitting the Ground Running*, 2d ed. (Chicago: Dorsey Press, 1996).

[26]Aaron Wildavsky, "The Two Presidencies," *Trans-Action*, December 1966, 7.

[27]Pfiffner, *The Modern Presidency*, ch. 6.

[28]Thomas P. (Tip) O'Neill, with William Novak, *Man of the House: The Life and Political Memoirs of Speaker Tip O'Neill* (New York: Random House, 1987), 297.

[29]Charles O. Jones, *The Presidency in a Separated System* (Washington, D.C.: Brookings Institution Press, 2005).

[30]Richard E. Neustadt, *Presidential Power and the Modern Presidents* (New York: Free Press, 1990), 71–72.

[31]Ibid., 33.

[32]Charlie Savage, "Senator Considers Suit over Bush Law Challenge," *Boston Globe*, June 28, 2006, electronic version.

[33]John E. Mueller, "Presidential Popularity from Truman to Johnson," *American Political Science Review* 64 (March 1970): 18–34; Kathleen Frankovic, "Public Opinion in the 1992 Campaign," in Gerald M. Pomper, ed., *The Election of 1992* (Chatham, N.J.: Chatham House, 1993); Chris J. Dolan, *The Presidency and Economic Policy* (Lanham, Md.: Rowman & Littlefield, 2007).

[34]Samuel Kernell, *Going Public: New Strategies of Presidential Leadership*, 3d ed. (Washington, D.C.: Congressional Quarterly Press, 1997), 1; see also Robert M. Eisinger, *The Evolution of Presidential Polling* (New York: Cambridge University Press, 2003); Stephen J. Farnsworth and S. Robert Lichter, *Mediated Presidency: Television News & Presidential Governance* (Lanham, Md.: Rowman & Littlefield, 2005).

[35]Hugh Heclo, "Introduction: The Presidential Illusion," in Hugh Heclo and Lester M. Salamon, eds., *The Illusion of Presidential Government* (Boulder, Colo.: Westview Press, 1981), 2.

[36]Theodore J. Lowi, *The "Personal" Presidency: Power Invested, Promise Unfulfilled* (Ithaca, N.Y.: Cornell University Press, 1985).

Chapter Thirteen

[1]Norman Thomas, *Rule 9: Politics, Administration, and Civil Rights* (New York: Random House, 1966), 6.

[2]James P. Pfiffner, "The National Performance Review in Perspective," working paper 94-4, Institute of Public Policy, George Mason University, 1994, 2.

[3]Ibid., 12.

[4]Max Weber, *Economy and Society*, trans. Guenther Roth and Claus Wittich (New York: Bedminster Press, 1968), 23; see also Paul Du Gay, *The Values of Bureaucracy* (New York: Oxford University Press, 2005).

[5]See Cornelius M. Kerwin, *Rulemaking*, 3d ed. (Washington, D.C.: Congressional Quarterly Press, 2003); Daniel E. Hall, *Administrative Law: Bureaucracy in a Democracy* (Upper Saddle River, N.J.: Prentice Hall, 2005).

[6]Michael Lipsky, *Street-Level Bureaucracy* (New York: Russell Sage Foundation, 1980); see also George Serra, "Citizen-Initiated Contact and Satisfaction with Bureaucracy," *Journal of Public Administration* 5 (April 1995): 175–88.

[7]Paul Van Riper, *History of the United States Civil Service* (Evanston, Ill.: Peterson, 1958), 36.

[8]David H. Rosenbloom, *Federal Service and the Constitution* (Ithaca, N.Y.: Cornell University Press, 1971), 83.

[9]Gregory A. Huber, *The Craft of Bureaucratic Neutrality: Interests and Influence in Governmental Regulation of Occupational Safety* (New York: Cambridge University Press, 2007); Herbert Kaufman, "Emerging Conflicts in the Doctrine of Public Administration," *American Political Science Review* 50 (December 1956): 1060.

[10]Kaufman, "Emerging Conflicts in the Doctrine of Public Administration," 1062.

[11]Quoted in Hugh Heclo, *A Government of Strangers* (Washington, D.C.: Brookings Institution, 1977), 225.

[12]Norton E. Long, "Power and Administration," *Public Administration Review* 10 (Autumn 1949): 269; Joel D. Aberbach and Bert A. Rockman, *In the Web of Politics* (Washington, D.C.: Brookings Institution Press, 2000).

[13]See Heclo, *A Government of Strangers*, 117–18.

[14]Quoted in Aaron Wildavsky, *The Politics of the Budgetary Process*, 4th ed. (Boston: Little, Brown, 1984), 19; see also Dennis D. Riley, *Bureaucracy and the Policy Process: Keeping the Promises* (Lanham, Md.: Rowman & Littlefield, 2005).

[15]Joel D. Aberbach and Bert A. Rockman, "Clashing Beliefs Within the Executive Branch," *American Political Science Review* 70 (June 1976): 461.

[16]See B. Dan Wood and Richard W. Waterman, *Bureaucratic Dynamics* (Boulder, Colo.: Westview Press, 1994); Edward C. Page and Bill Jenkins, *Policy Bureaucracy: Government with a Cast of Thousands* (New York: Oxford University Press, 2005).

[17]See John Brehm and Scott Gates, *Working, Shirking, and Sabotage* (Ann Arbor: University of Michigan Press, 1996).

[18]Long, "Power and Administration," 269; see also John Mark Hansen, *Gaining Access* (Chicago: University of Chicago Press, 1991).

[19]Charles T. Goodsell, *The Case for Bureaucracy*, 2d ed. (Chatham, N.J.: Chatham House, 1985), 55–60; see also B. Guy Peters, *The Politics of Bureaucracy*, 5th ed. (New York: Routledge, 2001).

[20]William T. Gormley Jr. and Steven J. Balla, *Bureaucracy and Democracy* (Washington, D.C.: Congressional Quarterly Press, 2003); Kevin B. Smith, *Public Administration: Power and Politics in the Fourth Branch of Government* (New York: Oxford University Press, 2006).

[21]See Paul Light, *Thickening Government* (Washington, D.C.: Brookings Institution, 1995); James G. March and Johan P. Olson, "Organizing Political Life: What Administrative Reorganization Tells Us About Government," *American Political Science Review* 77 (June 1983): 281–96.

²²Donald F. Ketti, *System Under Stress: Homeland Security and American Politics* (Washington, D.C.: Congressional Quarterly Press, 2007).
²³Kenneth J. Meier, *Regulation* (New York: St. Martin's Press, 1985), 110–11.
²⁴See Heclo, *A Government of Strangers.*
²⁵See Donald Kettl, *Deficit Politics* (New York: Macmillan, 1992).
²⁶See Joel D. Aberbach, *Keeping a Watchful Eye* (Washington, D.C.: Brookings Institution, 1990).
²⁷David Rosenbloom, "The Evolution of the Administrative State, and Transformations of Administrative Law," in David Rosenbloom and Richard Schwartz, eds., *Handbook of Regulation and Administrative Law* (New York: Marcel Dekker, 1994), 3–36.
²⁸See *Vermont Yankee Nuclear Power Corp. v. National Resources Defense Council, Inc.,* 435 U.S. 519 (1978); *Chevron v. National Resources Defense Council,* 467 U.S. 837 (1984); *Heckler v. Chaney,* 470 U.S. 821 (1985); but see *FDA v. Brown & Williamson Tobacco Co.* (2000).
²⁹*Pigeford v. Veneman,* U.S. District Court for the District of Columbia, Civil Action No. 97-1978 (1999).
³⁰See Brian J. Cook, *Bureaucracy and Self-Government* (Baltimore, Md.: Johns Hopkins University Press, 1996).
³¹David Osborne and Ted Gaebler, *Reinventing Government: How the Entrepreneurial Spirit Is Transforming the Public Sector* (New York: Addison-Wesley, 1992); see also Elaine Ciulla Kamarck, *End of Government... as We Know It: Making Public Policy Work* (Boulder, Colo.: Lynne Rienner, 2007).
³²Pfiffner, "The National Performance Review in Perspective," 7; see also David G. Frederickson and H. George Frederickson, *Measuring the Performance of the Hollow State* (Washington, D.C.: Georgetown University Press, 2006).
³³Ronald C. Moe, "The 'Reinventing Government' Exercise: Misinterpreting the Problem, Misjudging the Results," *Public Administration Review,* March/April 1994, 125–36.

CHAPTER FOURTEEN

¹*Marbury v. Madison,* 5 U.S. 137 (1803).
²*Swann v. Charlotte-Mecklenburg County Board of Education,* 402 U.S. 1 (1971).
³*Brown v. Board of Education of Topeka,* 347 U.S. 483 (1954).
⁴*Parents Involved in Community Schools v. Seattle,* No. 05-908 (2007); *Meredith, Custodial Parent and Next Friend of McDonald v. Jefferson County Board of Education,* No. 05-915 (2007).
⁵Linda Camp Keith, "The United States Supreme Court and Judicial Review of Congress, 1803–2001," *Judicature* 9(2007): 166.
⁶Rebecca Mae Salokar, *The Solicitor General: The Politics of Law* (Philadelphia: Temple University Press, 1992); see also Cornell W. Clayton, *The Politics of Justice: The Attorney General and the Making of Legal Policy* (Armonk, N.Y.: Sharpe, 1992).
⁷Henry Glick, *Courts, Politics, and Justice,* 3d ed. (New York: McGraw-Hill, 1993), 120.
⁸Timothy R. Johnson, Paul Wahlbeck, and James Spriggs, "The Influence of Oral Arguments on the U.S. Supreme Court," *American Political Science Review* 100 (2006): 99–113.
⁹Lawrence Baum, *The Supreme Court,* 8th ed. (Washington, D.C.: Congressional Quarterly Press, 2003), 120.
¹⁰*Gideon v. Wainwright,* 372 U.S. 335 (1963).
¹¹See Forest Maltzman, Paul Wahlbeck, and James Spriggs, *The Collegial Game: Crafting Law on the U.S. Supreme Court* (New York: Cambridge University Press, 2000.)
¹²From a letter to the author by Frank Schwartz of Beaver College; this section reflects substantially Professor Schwartz's recommendations to the author, as does the later section that addresses the federal court myth.
¹³*Hutto v. Davis,* 370 U.S. 256 (1982).
¹⁴*Lawrence v. Texas,* No. 02-102 (2003).

[15]*Bowers v. Hardwick*, 478 U.S. 186 (1986).

[16]See Richard Davis, *Electing Justices* (New York: Oxford University Press, 2005).

[17]See Lee Epstein and Jeffrey Segal, *Advice and Consent: The Politics of Judicial Appointments* (New York: Oxford University Press, 2005).

[18]Robert Scigliano, *The Supreme Court and the Presidency* (New York: Free Press, 1971), 146; see also Lee Epstein and Jack Knight, *The Choices Justices Make* (Washington, D.C.: Congressional Quarterly Press, 1998).

[19]Quoted in Baum, *The Supreme Court*, 37.

[20]See Virginia A. Hettinger et al., *Judging on a Collegial Court: Influences on Federal Appellate Decision Making* (Charlottesville: University of Virginia Press, 2006).

[21]John Gottschall, "Reagan's Appointments to the U.S. Courts of Appeals," *Judicature* 48 (1986): 54.

[22]See Robert A. Carp and Ronald Stidham, *The Federal Courts*, 4th ed. (Washington, D.C.: Congressional Quarterly Press, 2001).

[23]Joseph B. Harris, *The Advice and Consent of the Senate* (Berkeley: University of California Press, 1953), 313.

[24]Quoted in Louis Fisher, *American Constitutional Law* (New York: McGraw-Hill, 1990), 5.

[25]Quoted in Charles P. Curtis, *Law and Large as Life* (New York: Simon & Schuster, 1959), 156–57.

[26]See Lee Epstein and Jack Knight, *The Choices Justices Make* (New York: Longman, 1995); Thomas G. Hansford and James F. Spriggs II, *The Politics of Precedent on the Supreme Court* (Princeton, N.J.: Princeton University Press, 2006).

[27]*Faragher v. City of Boca Raton*, No. 97-282 (1998).

[28]Stephen L. Wasby, *The Supreme Court in the Federal Judicial System*, 4th ed. (Chicago: Nelson-Hall, 1993), 53.

[29]For a helpful explanation of amicus curiae briefs, see Bradley Best, "Amicus Curiae," in David Schultz and John P. Vile, eds., *The Encyclopedia of Civil Liberties in America, Volume 1* (Armonk, N.Y.: M. E. Sharpe, 2005), 33–35.

[30]John Schmidhauser, *The Supreme Court* (New York: Holt, Rinehart & Winston, 1964), 6.

[31]Linda Greenhouse, "In Steps Big and Small, Supreme Court Moved Right," *New York Times*, July 1, 2007, electronic version.

[32]Jeffrey A. Segal and Harold J. Spaeth, *The Supreme Court and the Attitudinal Model Revisited* (New York: Cambridge University Press, 2002).

[33]Linda Greenhouse, "In a Momentous Term, Justices Remake the Law, and the Court," *New York Times*, July 1, 2003, A1.

[34]*Bush v. Gore*, No. 00-949 (2000).

[35]See, however, James L. Gibson, Gregory A. Caldeira, and Lester Kenyatta Spence, "The Supreme Court and the U.S. Presidential Election of 2000," *British Journal of Political Science* 33 (2003): 535–56.

[36]David M. O'Brien, *Storm Center: The Supreme Court in American Politics*, 7th ed. (New York: Norton, 2005), 14–15.

[37]Ross Sandler and David Schoenbrod, *Democracy by Decree* (New Haven, Conn.: Yale University Press, 2003).

[38]Henry J. Abraham, "The Judicial Function Under the Constitution," *News for Teachers of Political Science* 41 (Spring 1984): 14.

[39]Alexander M. Bickel, *The Supreme Court and the Idea of Progress* (New Haven, Conn.: Yale University Press, 1978), 173–81.

[40]Frederic R. Kellogg, *Oliver Wendell Holmes, Jr.: Legal Theory and Judicial Restraint* (New York: Cambridge University Press, 2006).

[41]*Schenck v. United States*, 249 U.S. 47 (1919).

[42]Frank H. Easterbrook, "Do Liberals and Conservatives Differ in Judicial Activism?" *University of Colorado Law Review* 73 (2002): 1401.

[43]Quoted in Linda Greenhouse, "The Justices Decide Who's in Charge," *New York Times*, June 27, 1999, sect. 4, 1.

[44]See Antonin Scalia, *A Matter of Interpretation: Federal Courts and the Law* (Princeton, N.J.: Princeton University Press, 1997).

[45]Remarks by Antonin Scalia at the University of Delaware, April 30, 2007. Reported on the Web by *University of Delaware Daily*.

[46]Stephen Breyer, "Our Democratic Constitution," James Madison Lecture, New York University Law School, New York, October 22, 2001.

CHAPTER FIFTEEN

[1]E. E. Schattschneider, *The Semisovereign People* (New York: Holt, Rinehart and Winston, 1960).

[2]Aaron Wildausky, *The Politics of the Budgetary Process*, 4th ed. (Glenview, Ill.: Scott Foresman, 1984).

[3]Marc Allen Eisner, Jeffrey Worsham, and Evan J. Rinquist, *Contemporary Regulatory Policy* (Boulder, Colo.: Lynne Rienner, 2006).

[4]The section titled "Efficiency Through Government Intervention" relies substantially on Alan Stone, *Regulation and Its Alternatives* (Washington, D.C.: Congressional Quarterly Press, 1982).

[5]See Marc Allen Eisner, *Regulatory Politics in Transition*, 2d ed. (Baltimore, Md. Johns Hopkins University Press, 1999).

[6]See Richard A. Harris and Sidney M. Milkis, *The Politics of Regulatory Change* (New York: Oxford University Press, 1996).

[7]Lawrence E. Mitchell, *Corporate Irresponsibility* (New Haven, Conn.: Yale University Press, 2003).

[8]H. Peyton Young, *Equity: In Theory and Practice* (Princeton, N.J.: Princeton University Press, 1995).

[9]"Hill Foes of New Clean Air Rules Unite Behind Moratorium Bill," *Congressional Quarterly Weekly Report* (Spring 1998): 61.

[10]Board on Population Health and Public Health Practice, *The Future of Drug Safety: Promoting and Protecting the Health of the Public* (Washington, D.C.: National Academies Press, 2007).

[11]See Thomas Streeter, *Selling the Air* (Chicago: University of Chicago Press, 1996); Robert McChesney, *The Problem of the Media* (New York: Monthly Review Press, 2004); Christopher J. Bosso, *Environment, Inc.: From Grassroots to Beltway* (Lawrence: University Press of Kansas, 2005).

[12]Rachel Carson, *The Silent Spring* (Boston: Houghton Mifflin, 1962); see also Lester R. Brown, *Plan B2.0: Rescuing a Planet Under Stress and a Civilization in Trouble* (New York: W. W. Norton, 2006).

[13]Robert B. Keiter, *Keeping Faith with Nature* (New Haven, Conn.: Yale University Press, 2003).

[14]*U.S. News & World Report*, June 30, 1975, 25.

[15]*Whitman v. American Trucking Association*, No. 99-1257 (2001).

[16]*Massachusetts v. EPA*, No. 05-1120 (2007).

[17]See Walter A. Rosenbaum, *Environmental Politics and Policy*, 6th ed. (Washington, D.C.: Congressional Quarterly Press, 2004); Norman J. Vig and Michael E. Kraft, eds., *Environmental Policy: New Directions for the Twenty-first Century* (Washington, D.C.: Congressional Quarterly Press, 2003).

[18]Elliot A. Rosen, *Roosevelt, the Great Depression, and the Economics of Recovery* (Charlottesville: University of Virginia Press, 2007).

[19]See Robert Lekachman, *The Age of Keynes* (New York: Random House, 1966); see also Richard Kopke, Geoffrey M. B. Tootell, and Robert K. Trist, eds., *The Macroeconomics of Fiscal Policy* (Cambridge, Mass.: MIT Press, 2006).

[20]See Bruce Bartlett, *Reaganomics: Supply-Side Economics* (Westport, Conn.: Arlington House, 1981).

[21]For opposing views on the success of the tax-cutting strategy, see Gene W. Heck, *Building Prosperity: Why Ronald Reagan and the Founding Fathers Were Right on the Economy* (Lanham, Md.: Rowman & Littlefield, 2007); Bryan D. Jones and Walter Williams, *The Politics of Bad Ideas: The Great Tax-Cut Delusion and the Decline of Good Government in America* (New York: Longman, 2008).

[22]See Richard Duncan, *The Dollar Crisis: Causes, Consequences, Cures*, rev. ed. (New York: John Wiley & Sons, 2005).

[23]U.S. Senate clerk, 2002.

[24]See Allen Schick, *The Federal Budget*, 3d ed. (Washington, D.C.: Brookings Institution Press, 2007).

[25]Alan O. Ebenstein, *Milton Friedman: A Biography* (New York: Palgrave Macmillan, 2007).

[26]Martin Mayer, *FED: The Inside Story of How the World's Most Powerful Financial Institution Drives the Markets* (New York: Free Press, 2001).

CHAPTER SIXTEEN

[1]Quoted in E. J. Dionne Jr., "Reflecting on 'Reform,'" *Washington Post*, web download, February 15, 2004.

[2]Press releases of House Committee on Ways and Means and National Conference of State Legislatures, September 19 and June 26, 2002, respectively.

[3]See Felicia Ann Kornbluh, *The Battle for Welfare Rights: Politics and Poverty in Modern America* (Philadelphia: University of Pennsylvania Press, 2007).

[4]Michael Harrington, *The Other America: Poverty in the United States* (New York: Macmillan, 1962); see also James T. Patterson, *America's Struggle Against Poverty in the Twentieth Century* (Cambridge, Mass.: Harvard University Press, 2000).

[5]Charles Murray, *Losing Ground: American Social Policy, 1950–1980* (New York: Basic Books, 1984).

[6]Signe-Mary McKernan and Caroline Ratcliffe, "Events That Trigger Poverty Entries and Exits," *Social Science Quarterly* 86 (2005): 1146–69.

[7]See Katherine S. Newman, *No Shame in My Game* (New York: Alfred A. Knopf and Russell Sage Foundation, 1999), 41.

[8]V. O. Key Jr., *The Responsible Electorate* (Cambridge, Mass.: Belknap Press of Harvard University, 1966), 43.

[9]Everett Carll Ladd, *American Political Parties* (New York: Norton, 1970), 205.

[10]Institute on Taxation and Economic Policy poll, 2002.

[11]For a general overview of 1950s and 1960s policy disputes, see James Sundquist, *Politics and Policy* (Washington, D.C.: Brookings Institution, 1968).

[12]See Jason DeParle, *American Dream: Three Women, Ten Kids, and a Nation's Drive to End Welfare* (New York: Penguin, 2005).

[13]Quoted in Malcolm Gladwell, "The Medicaid Muddle," *The Washington Post National Weekly Edition*, January 16–22, 1995, 31.

[14]Jill Quadagno, *One Nation, Uninsured: Why the United States Has No National Health Insurance* (New York: Oxford University Press, 2005).

[15]See Christopher Howard, *The Welfare State Nobody Knows* (Princeton, N.J.: Princeton University Press, 2006).

[16]Alberto Alesina and Edward Glaeser, *Fighting Poverty in the U.S. and Europe* (New York: Oxford University Press, 2006).

[17]Robert D. Ebel, Tuan Minh Le, and Zicheng Li Swift, "National Tax Levels and the Rich vs. the Poor," publication of the Tax Policy Center, Washington, D.C., June 6, 2005.

[18]Paul Krugman, "Hey, Lucky Duckies," *New York Times*, December 3, 2002, A31.

[19]Said of George H. W. Bush at the 1988 Democratic Convention. The quote is variously attributed to Ann Richards or Jim Hightower.

[20]For a history of public education, see Joel H. Spring, *The American School 1642–2004* (New York: McGraw-Hill, 2008).

[21]Based on Organization for Economic Cooperation and Development (OECD) data, 2006; see Douglas S. Reed, *On Equal Terms: The Constitutional Politics of Educational Opportunity* (Princeton, N.J.: Princeton University Press, 2003).

[22]Kaiser Family Foundation/Washington Post/Kennedy School of Government poll, September 1999.

[23]See John E. Chubb and Terry M. Moe, *Politics, Markets, and America's Schools* (Washington, D.C.: Brookings Institution, 1990); Tony Wagner and Thomas Vander Ark, *Making the Grade* (New York: Routledge, 2001).

[24]See Jeffrey R. Henig, *Rethinking School Choice* (Princeton, N.J.: Princeton University Press, 1995).

[25]Phi Delta Kappa/Gallup poll, 2002.

[26]See Lee Anderson, *Congress in the Classroom* (College Station: Pennsylvania State University Press, 2007).

[27]See Neal McCluskey, *Feds in the Classroom* (Lanham, Md.: Rowman & Littlefield, 2007).

[28]See, for example, David Hursh, *High Stakes Testing and the Decline of Teaching and Learning* (Lanham, Md.: Rowman & Littlefield, 2008.)

[29]Press release, Congressman John Boehner, January 4, 2003.

[30]Phi Delta Kappa/Gallup poll, 2005.

[31]Stanley Feldman and John Zaller, "The Political Culture of Ambivalence: Ideological Responses to the Welfare State," *American Journal of Political Science* 36, no. 1 (1992): 268–307.

[32]Robert E. Lane, "Market Justice, Political Justice," *American Political Science Review* 80 (1986): 383.

CHAPTER SEVENTEEN

[1]See Mr. X. (George Kennan), "The Sources of Soviet Conduct," *Foreign Affairs* 25 (July 1947): 566–82.

[2]See Wilson Miscamble, *From Roosevelt to Truman: Potsdam, Hiroshima, and the Cold War* (New York: Cambridge University Press, 2008).

[3]David M. Barrett, *Uncertain Warriors: Lyndon Johnson and His Vietnam Advisors* (Lawrence: University Press of Kansas, 1993); see also Stanley Karnow, *Vietnam: A History* (New York: Penguin, 1983).

[4]See Dag Henriksen, *NATO's Gamble* (Annapolis, Md.: Naval Institute Press, 2007).

[5]See Mark Sauter and James Carafano, *Homeland Security* (New York: McGraw-Hill, 2005).

[6]West Point speech, June 1, 2002; for an opposing view, see Gary Hart, *The Shield and the Cloak: The Security of the Commons* (New York: Oxford University Press, 2006).

[7]Nick Ritchie, *The Political Road to War with Iraq: Bush, 9/11 and the Drive to Overthrow Saddam* (New York: Routledge, 2007).

[8]See Ofira Seliktar, *The Politics of Intelligence and American Wars with Iraq* (New York: Palgrave Macmillan, 2008).

[9]See Ole Holsti, *Public Opinion and American Foreign Policy* (Ann Arbor: University of Michigan Press, 1996); Richard Sobel, *The Impact of Public Opinion on U.S. Foreign Policy Since Vietnam* (New York: Oxford University Press, 2001).

[10]George C. Wilson, *This War Really Matters: Inside the Fight for Defense Dollars* (Washington, D.C.: Congressional Quarterly Press, 2000).

[11]U.S. government data, various agencies, 2008.

[12] *The World Competitiveness Yearbook* (Lausanne, Switzerland: International Institute for Management Development, 2008).

[13] American Assembly Report (co-sponsored by the Council on Foreign Relations), *Rethinking America's Security* (New York: Harriman, 1991), 9.

[14] Robert Z. Lawrence, *The United States and the WTO Dispute Settlement System* (New York: Council on Foreign Relations, 2007).

[15] Ted C. Fishman, *China, Inc.: How the Rise of the Next Superpower Challenges America and the World* (New York: Scribner, 2005).

[16] John Duffield, *Over a Barrel: The Costs of U.S. Foreign Oil Dependence* (Stanford, Calif.: Stanford Law and Politics, 2007.)

[17] See Joseph S. Nye, *Soft Power: The Means to Success in World Politics* (New York: Public Affairs, 2003); Michael Lind, *The American Way of Strategy* (New York: Oxford University Press, 2006).

[18] Hobart Rowen, "The Budget: Fact and Fiction," *The Washington Post National Weekly Edition*, January 16–22, 1995, 5.

[19] Tom Masland, "Going Down the Aid 'Rathole'?" *Newsweek*, December 5, 1994, 39.

CREDITS

PHOTO CREDITS

Chapter 1 Opener: © Damian Dovarganes/Pool/Reuters/Corbis; p. 3: © Justin Sullivan/Getty Image; p. 4: © Chromosohm Media/Stock Boston; p. 10: © Ernest C. Withers, Courtesy, Panopticon Gallery, Boston, MA; p. 16: © Eric Gay/AP Images; p. 19: © Bob Daemmrich/Image Works; p. 25: Library of Congress, Prints & Photographs Division [LC-USZC4-2474] **Chapter 2** Opener: © The Granger Collection; p. 38: ©Bettmann/ Corbis; p. 42: © Bettmann/Corbis; p. 55: © Archivo Iconografico, S.A./Corbis; p. 56: © The Granger Collection; p. 63: © Bob Daemmrich/Image Works **Chapter 3** Opener: © The Granger Collection; p. 77: © The Granger Collection; p. 82: © The Granger Collection; p. 84: Library of Congress, Prints and Photographs Division [LC-B811-560]; p. 85: © The Granger Collection; p. 88: © Scherl/Sueddeutsche Zeitung Photo/ Image Works; p. 91: © Jonathan Blair/Corbis **Chapter 4** Opener: © Paul Sancya/AP Images; p. 112: © Eric Risberg/AP Images; p. 116: © Paul Conklin/PhotoEdit; p. 120: © AP Images; p. 126: © Greg Gibson/AP Images; p. 132: © Jeff Greenberg/age fotostock; p. 135: Library of Congress, Prints and Photographs Division **Chapter 5** Opener: © Lisa Nipp/AP Images; p. 154: © Charles Moore/Black Star; p. 164: © Adele Starr/AP Images; p. 166: © Nati Harnik/AP Images; p. 169: © The Art Archive/Culver Pictures; p. 175: © Manish Swarup/AP Images; p. 182: © Danny Moloshok/AP Images **Chapter 6** Opener: © Charles Gupton/Corbis; p. 196: © Joel Stettenheim/Corbis; p. 199: © Bettmann/Corbis; p. 210: Library of Congress, Prints and Photographs Division [LC-USA62-117 121]; p. 211: © Charles E. Rotkin/Corbis; p. 217: Courtesy, Obama for America/wwwbarackobama.com **Chapter 7** Opener: © Jonathan Nourok/Getty Images; p. 227: © Culver Pictures; p. 236: © The Granger Collection; p. 237: © The Charlotte Observer/AP Images; p. 241: © Frederic Larson/Corbis; p. 243: © AP Images **Chapter 8** Opener: © Bob Daemmrich/Corbis; p. 259: Library of Congress, Prints and Photographs Division [LC-USZ62-13016]; p. 260: © Bettmann/Corbis; p. 271: Library of Congress, Prints & Photographs Division; p. 278: © Alex Wong/Getty Images; p. 286: © Toby Jorrin/AP Images **Chapter 9** Opener: © AP Images; p. 302: Library of Congress, Prints and Photographs Division [LC-USZ62-62-1304]; p. 304: Library of Congress, Prints & Photographs Division; p. 308: © Noah Berger/AP Images; p. 311: © Chip Somodevilla/Getty Images; p. 317: © Gerald Herbert/AP Images **Chapter 10** Opener: © David Duprey/AP Images; p. 332: © Timothy A. Clary/Getty Images; p. 335: © Stock Montage; p. 337: © Michael Smith/Getty Images; p. 346: © Underwood & Underwood/Corbis; p. 352: © AP Images; p. 357: © Jason DeCrow/AP Images; p. 362: © Patrick Olear/PhotoEdit **Chapter 11** Opener: © Vanessa Vick/Photo Researchers; p. 373: Library of Congress, Prints & Photographs Division [LC-USZ62-37502]; p. 380: © Bettmann/Corbis; p. 394: Courtesy, Office of the Speaker, Washington, DC; p. 404: © Allan Tannenbaum **Chapter 12** Opener: © Punchstock/Brand X Pictures; p. 419: © Doug MillsAP Images; p. 422: © Christie's Images/Corbis; p. 425: © UPI/Bettmann/Corbis; p. 430: © Jan Morten Bjornbakk/SCANPIX/AP Images; p. 434: © Win McNamee/Getty Images; p. 441: © UPI/Bettmann/Corbis; p. 447: © Rene Burri/Magnum Photos **Chapter 13** Opener: © Medioimages/Getty R-F Website; p. 461: © AP Images; p. 468: All Rights Reserved in Photographs © United States Postal Service. Used with Permission; p. 478: © Marc Bryan-Brown/WireImage/Getty Images; p. 482: © Rick Wilking/Reuters/Corbis; p. 486: © White House Historical Association/White House Collection [No. 22] **Chapter 14** Opener: © Collection of the Supreme Court of the United States; p. 501: ©Michael Conroy/AP Images; p. 504: Library of Congress, Prints & Photographs Division [LC-USZ62-54940]; p. 510: © AP Images; p. 512: © Collection, The Supreme Court Historical Society. Photo by Steve Petteway, Supreme Court; p. 521: © Landon Nordeman/Getty Images; p. 527(both): © AP Images **Chapter 15** Opener: © Win McNamee/Getty Images; p. 543: © Najlah Feanny/Corbis; p. 545: © Ryan McVay/Getty Images; p. 552: © Alfred Eisenstaedt/Time Life Pictures//Getty Images; p. 553: © John M. Roberts/Corbis; p. 556: © Lawrence Bender Prods./The Kobal Collection/Lee, Eric **Chapter 16** Opener: © J. Scott Applewhite/AP Images; p. 590: Library of Congress, Prints and Photographs Division [LC-USA62-117 121]; p. 594: © Dana Fineman; p. 602: © Jim West/Image Works; p. 605: © Bob Daemmrich/Image Works **Chapter 17** Opener: © Robert Nickelsberg/Getty Images; p. 617: © The Michael Barson Collection; p. 620: © Nicolas Asfouri/AFP/Getty Images; p. 630: © Ed Clark/Life Magazine/Time & Life Pictures/Getty Images; p. 634: © Wolfgang Kaehler/Corbis.

Credits 717

Text and Line Art Credits

Chapter 1, Table 1-2: From *Survey of American Political Culture, Volume 2* (Institute for Advanced Studies in Culture, University of Virginia). Reprinted with permission. James Carroll, "What We Love About America" from *The Boston Globe* (July 3, 2006): A11. Reprinted with the permission of James Carroll. **Chapter 2,** Map, page 62: From Initiative and Referendum Institute, University of Southern California. Reprinted with permission. **Chapter 3,** Samuel H. Beer, "The National Idea in American Politics" from *To Make a Nation: The Rediscovery of American Federalism.* Copyright © 1993 by the President and Fellows of Harvard College. Reprinted with the permission of The Belknap Press of Harvard University Press. **Chapter 4,** Map, page 137: From Death Penalty Information Center (2008). Reprinted with permission. Graph, Page 139: From National Council on Crime and Delinquency (2006). Reprinted with permission. **Chapter 5,** Map, page 156: National Conference of State Legislatures (2008). Reprinted with permission. Graph, page 159: From Inter-Parliamentary Union (2008). Reprinted with permission. Figure 5-2: Pew Research Center for the People and the Press, Global Attitudes survey (2002). Reprinted with permission. Figure 5-4: Pew Research Center for the People and the Press, Global Attitudes survey (2002). Reprinted with permission. Figure 5-6: Pew Research Center for the People and the Press (March 22, 2007). Reprinted with permission. Martin Luther King, Jr., "Letter from Birmingham Jail" from *Why We Can't Wait* (New York: Harper & Row, 1963). Copyright © 1963, 1964 by Martin Luther King, Jr, renewed 1991, 1992 by Coretta Scott King. Reprinted with the permission of Writer's House, LLC. **Chapter 6,** Figure 6-1: Reprinted with the permission of the National Opinion Research Center, University of Chicago. Graph, page 202: From Thomas Patterson, *The American Democracy, Seventh Edition.* Copyright © 2006 by The McGraw-Hill Companies. Reprinted with permission. Figure 6-4: Pew Research Center for the People and the Press (2002). Reprinted with permission. John Mueller, "The Iraq Syndrome" from *Foreign Affairs* 84, no. 6 (November/December 2005). Copyright © 2005 by the Council on Foreign Relations, Inc. Reprinted by permission of *Foreign Affairs*, www.ForeignAffairs.org. **Chapter 7,** Table 7-1: From Survey of American Political Culture, Institute for Advanced Studies in Culture, University of Virginia (1996). Reprinted with permission. Figure 7-3: From Russell J. Dalton, "The Myth of the Disengaged American," *CSES Report* (October 25, 2005). Reprinted with permission. Figure 7-4: From Russell J. Dalton, "The Myth of the Disengaged American," *CSES Report* (October 25, 2005). Reprinted with permission. **Chapter 8,** Map, page 283: From National Conference of State Legislatures (2008). Reprinted with permission. Ronald Brownstein, "GOP Has Lock on South, and Democrats Can't Find Key" from *Los Angeles Times* (December 15, 2004). Reprinted with permission. **Chapter 9,** Graph, page 300: From World Values Survey Association (2008). Reprinted by permission. Map, page 319] From National Conference of State Legislatures (2008). Reprinted by permission. Jonathan D. Salant, "The Lobbying Game Today" from *Extensions* (Fall 2006). Reprinted with the permission of the Carl Albert Center. **Chapter 10,** Figure 10-1: Adapted from Daniel C. Hallin, "Sound Bite News: Television Coverage of Elections 1968–1988" from *Journal of Communication* 42 (Spring 1992): 6. Reprinted with the permission of Blackwell Publishers, Ltd. The 1992–2008 data are from the Center for Media and Public Affairs. Figure 10-2: Adapted from Project for Excellence in Journalism, "State of the Media 2008." Reprinted with permission. Figure 10-3: From survey by Shorenstein Center on the Press, Politics and Public Policy (Harvard University, 2007). Reprinted with permission. Alex Jones, "To Publish, or Nor to Publish?" Shorenstein Center on the Press, Politics and Public Policy. Reprinted with permission. **Chapter 11,** Paul S. Hernson, "Running for Congress, Staying in Congress" from *Congressional Elections: Campaigning at Home and in Washington.* Copyright © 2003. Reprinted with the permission of Congressional Quarterly Press. **Chapter 13,** Box, page 477] Adapted from B. Guy Peters, *The Politics of Bureaucracy, Fifth Edition.* Copyright © 2001 by Routledge. Reprinted with the permission of International Thomson Publishing Services. **Chapter 14,** Map, page 509: From The Council of State Governments. Reprinted with permission. **Chapter 15,** Figure 15-2: From OECD (2008). Reprinted with permission. Figure 15-3: Pew Research Center for the People and the Press, Global Attitudes survey (2002). Reprinted with permission. Al Gore, "Global Warming" excerpt from speech at Beacon Theater, New York City (January 15, 2004). Reprinted with the permission of the author. **Chapter 16,** Graph, page 587: From OECD (2008). Reprinted with permission. Figure 16-2: Pew Research Center for the People and the Press, Global Attitudes survey (2002). Reprinted with permission. Bill Clinton, "Welfare Reform" [original title "How We Ended Welfare Together"] from *The New York Times* (August 22, 2006): A 19. Copyright © 2006 by The New York Times Company. Reprinted with permission. **Chapter 17,** Figure 17-1: Pew Research Center for the People and the Press, Global Attitudes survey (2002). Reprinted with permission. Graph, page 625: From Center for Arms Control and Non-Proliferation (2008). Reprinted with permission. Map, page 627: Adapted from Tim Kane, "Who Bears the Burden? Characteristics of U.S. Military Recruits Before and After 9/11" (Heritage Foundation, Center for Data Analysis Report #05-08, November 7, 2005). Used by permission of The Heritage Foundation. Figure 17-4: From Organization for Economic Cooperation and Development (2008). Reprinted with permission.

INDEX

718